31387

34

31387

AVIATION IN LEICESTERSHIRE AND RUTLAND

AVIATION IN LEICESTERSHIRE AND RUTLAND

ROY BONSER

Midland Publishing

This book is dedicated to
all who trained in and flew from
the two counties.

Aviation in Leicestershire and Rutland
© Roy Bonser, 2001
ISBN 1 85780 089 3

Edited by Ken Ellis

First published in 2001 by
Midland Publishing
4 Watling Drive, Hinckley, LE10 3EY, England.
Tel: 01455 254 490 Fax: 01455 254 495

Midland Publishing is an imprint of
Ian Allan Publishing Ltd.

Worldwide distribution (except North America):
Midland Counties Publications
4 Watling Drive, Hinckley, LE10 3EY, England
Tel: 01455 233 747 Fax: 01455 233 737
E-mail: midlandbooks@compuserve.com

North America trade distribution:
Specialty Press Publishers & Wholesalers Inc.
11605 Kost Dam Road
North Branch, MN 55056, USA
Tel: 651 583 3239 Fax: 651 583 2023
Toll free telephone: 800 895 4585

Design concept and editorial layout
© Midland Publishing and
Stephen Thompson Associates.

Printed by Ian Allan Printing Ltd
Riverdene Business Park, Molesey Road
Hersham, Surrey, KT12 4RG, England.

Jacket illustration:
A wartime scene representative of several
airfields of Leicestershire and Rutland,
that of a Vickers Wellington-equipped
Operational Training Unit.
Groundcrew prepare 'Wimpeys'
of No.14 OTU for more arduous training flights
at Cottesmore.
From an original painting by Roy Garner.

Half-title page illustration:
A pair of Royal Air Force Argosy C.1s
formate on the rear door of another.
The Argosy was the last
of a famous line of aircraft
to bear the Armstrong Whitworth name.
Seventy-three Argosies were built at Bitteswell
between 1959 and 1966.
AWA via Ken Ellis

Title page illustration:
The very beginnings of British jet engine
development took place in Leicestershire
under the guidance of a young Air Force Officer.
That same individual – the late Sir Frank Whittle
– is here seen standing by an early example
of a Power Jets W.2/700, during his visit
to Lutterworth on 15th June 1987.
Author

Contents

Preface 6
Acknowledgements 6

Chapters
   1 An Outline History 9
   2 Bitteswell 35
   3 Built at Bitteswell 57
   4 Bottesford 83
   5 Braunstone 101
   6 Bruntingthorpe 109
   7 Castle Donington –
      East Midlands Airport 127
   8 Cottesmore 139
   9 Desford 171
  10 Desford's Spitfires and Twins 193
  11 Husbands Bosworth 203
  12 Leicester East - Leicester Airport 211
  13 Loughborough 221
  14 Brush - Built 231
  15 Market Harborough 241
  16 Melton Mowbray 249
  17 North Luffenham 261
  18 Nuneaton 283
  19 Ratcliffe 291
  20 Rearsby 303
  21 Taylorcraft - Auster - Beagle 313
  22 Saltby 333
  23 Woolfox Lodge 341
  24 Wymeswold 351

Appendices
   A Blaby Wharf - No.65 MU 365
   B Airstrips and Landing Grounds 367
   C Major Aircraft Accidents 372
   D Aviation Memorials 380
   E Royal Observer Corps 384
   F USAAF Stations 386
   G The Duke of Rutland 386

Select Bibliography 387
Index 388

Preface

ON LEAVING school in 1943, I began my working life with Reid and Sigrist Ltd at Desford. As a very minor cog in the wheel of the Civilian Repair Organisation I helped with the repair of Boulton Paul Defiants. My association with the aviation industry did not progress beyond a brief wartime experience, but I retained a lifelong interest in all things aeronautical.

Some years ago I thought it might make an interesting exercise to record the history of Desford airfield and so began a protracted period of research. This project was to gradually expand to eventually encompass the whole of Leicestershire and Rutland and culminate in this book.

Although my name appears upon the cover, I could not have achieved the end result without a great deal of help.

Official records have contributed in a substantial way to this narrative. For their help I am grateful to the staffs of the Public Record Office, Kew; the Ministry of Defence Air Historical Branch; the Royal Air Force Museum, Hendon; the County Record Office, Wigston and the Bishop Street Reference Library. All were often able to point me in the right direction. County newspapers, past and present have also been a welcome source of information.

My research has also taken me into many private homes. There, without exception, I met with considerable kindness and interest. Sadly, several people who helped during the formative years of what became this book have now passed away. I record their names as a small memorial.

There are those who gave long periods of their time to answer my endless barrage of questions, others freely gave access to their photographic collections and records. No matter how great or small their contribution to all I owe a debt of gratitude and their names appear below.

On a personal note, it is my hope that this book will add depth to the aviation history of the two counties and also help correct some of the anomalies that have arisen over the course of time. Doubtless there are those who will not fully agree with my writings. Corrective proof will always be welcomed, but, I trust that should errors have occurred that they are not too numerous.

One regret is that I have been unable to provide a more comprehensive photographic coverage of the Second World War period. Despite diligent searches in archives and personal collections, gaps still exist. Maybe the publication of this book will bring more to light? Any additional photographs and information will be gratefully received, via my publisher, please – all items will be acknowledged and returned upon request.

Acknowledgements

MY THANKS go to the following individuals who have made this book possible: Bert Aggas, Bill Baguley, Nigel Bailey-Underwood, Dennis Baker, Ron Bass, Norman Bate, Eric Belcher, Dave Benfield, Malcolm Bills, Mrs Julien Birchall, Ron Blake, Albert Boothaway, Chaz Bowyer, British Midland Airways, D S and M Brookman, C H T Brown, A G Bullmore, Bill Bushell, Phil Butler, Bill Chorley, Jack W Clarke, John H Collier, A E Coltman, Geoff Cooke, Martin Cooke, Cyril Corbett, Tim Crowe, Roy Davis, John Dewis, Victor M and Mary Doree, Neville Doyle, Syd Ellis, Norman Ellison, Reg Emerson, Mike Everton, G Farmer, R A Fathers, Stan Fine, Rob Forbes, Neville Franklin, Roy Garner, Pat Geary, Alastair Goodrum, Rigby Graham, Peter Green, Terry Hancock, Jim Hart, Norman Hayes, Frank H Hayward, Dave Heaney, B V Hewes, Trevor Hickman, A C Hodgkin, Harry Holmes, Vince Holyoak, Graham Hopkin, H A Howes, Colin Huston, Paul A Jackson, Barry James, Tony Jarram, Bob Lavender, Richard R Leader, Fred Lewin, Barry Lewis, Linda Love of East Midlands Airport, Bill Mallord, Peter March, Maurice Marsh, Brian Martin, Derek D Martin, Neville Martin, Sam Meakin, Monty Mendham, J O Muncaster, Roy Nixon, Eddie Norton, Richard Nutt, Jim Oates, Ian O'Neill, Dave Peel, Pat Penny, Jim Pickering, Colin Purvis, Dennis Reynolds, Robin Ridley, Norman Roberson, Bruce Robertson, Chris Salter, Dave Sargent, Colin Smith, David J Smith, Peter Stoddart, W W Storer, John Stubbs, Derek Sturgess, Jonathan Styles, Bill Taylor, Ray Tailby, Goff Tearle, Dick Teasdale, Julian Temple, Andy Thomas, Dr Hugh Thomas, Tony Thorpe, Tony Traylen, Ken F & Bettina Tunnicliffe, Stan Vigor, John Walls, Roy Walters, David Walton, Alan Warnes of *AirForces Monthly*, Doug Watson, Horace A Webster, John P Wells, John Whall, Brandon White, Albert Whitehouse, Ray Williams, Mary Winn, Bill Woodward, Alan J Wright, Gordon Young.

Mary Denton drew the maps. Others are given credit with their photographs.

To anyone not mentioned I offer sincere apologies, it is purely an oversight on my part and not intentional.

A special thank you is due to Jim Morrow and Ken Ellis. Jim for the vast amount of material he made available, Ken for his editorial expertise, additional material and research. Also thanks to both for acting as my personal pilot on occasions during the air-to-ground photo-shoots.

I would also like to record my appreciation to my daughter Alison for her constant battle with the manuscript, coping with many revisions and corrections.

My wife, Sylvia, deserves heartfelt thanks for her infinite patience while suffering endless scattered notes and trial readings.

Roy Bonser
Earl Shilton, Leicestershire   March 2001

A visual taste of the variety of aviation, past and present, in the two counties. Left, top to bottom - *Pioneer days: a Blériot at Melton Mowbray* (via Dave Birch). *Early civil flying: the County Flying Club's Drone in use as a carnival float* (K F Tunnicliff). *Peacetime RAFVR: Hawker Harts and an Audax ready for duty at Desford* (R Emmerson). *Brothers in arms: USAAF CG-4A assault gliders ready for launch from RAF Cottesmore -* (Arthur Pearcy collection). Right, top to bottom: *The bravado of test flying: Vampire F.1 over Meteor F.4 at Bitteswell* (A Boothaway). *The 'living museum' at Bruntingthorpe: from a Leicestershire Aero Club Cessna 152* (Author). *Gateway to the world: East Midlands Airport* (EMA). *Multi-role and multi-national: Tornados at Cottesmore* (Peter R March).

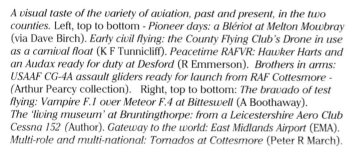

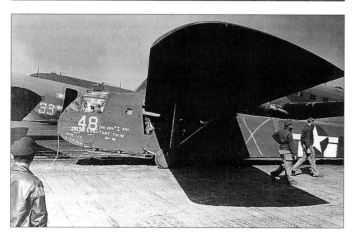

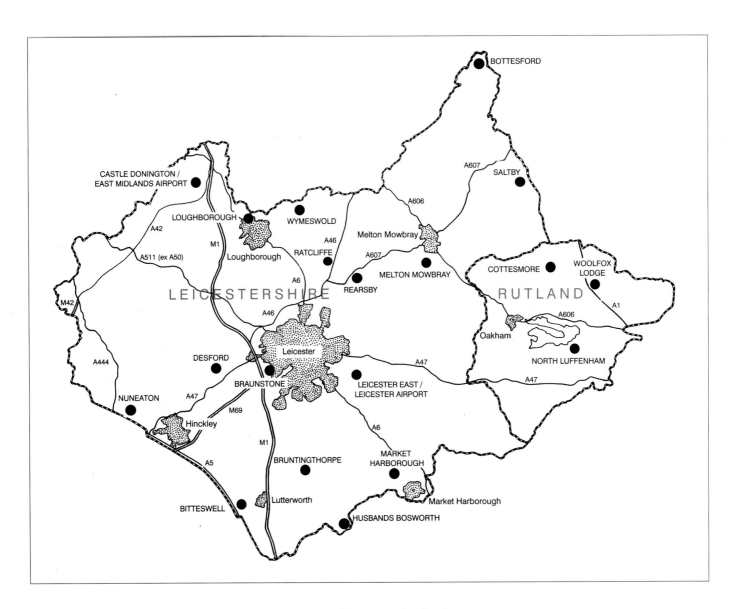

*An outline map of the county showing the
approximate position of the airfields, main
centres of population, and major roads.*

Chapter One

An Outline History

Dignitaries gather around BE.12 6508 for its naming ceremony in Western Park, Leicester, 3rd June 1916. The crowd, estimated at over 40,000 people and the houses on Letchworth Road provide the background.
Leicestershire Museums Collection

Early Days

References to early aviation within the two counties are rather sparse, but the association between Leicestershire and aeronautics can be traced back at least as far as 1824 when a balloon ascent was made in Leicester from a site close to the old gas works, which then stood in Belgrave Gate. Rutland can lay claim to have an even earlier connection for on 1st November 1813 Mr Sadler of Nottingham alighted from his balloon at Dekens Lodge, Pickworth. He had travelled

a distance of some 34 miles, a journey which at times must have been quite unpleasant for on occasions he had flown through dense cloud and drizzle which had frozen and formed icicles upon his person. The balloon, which is said to have cost £900 and to have stood to a height of 30ft when inflated, must have made an imposing sight with its ornate basket, trimmed with leather and velvet, suspended from the crimson and yellow silk envelope. (Research has failed to conclusively prove which of the famed Sadler family, James, John or Wyndham, all of whom were active balloonists at this time, was flying the Pickworth balloon.)

Although these events must have been the chief topic of conversation locally for many days afterwards they can have created nothing like the sensation which followed what was intended to have been a spectacular balloon ascent in 1866.

The occasion was an Ancient Order of Foresters' gathering on Victoria Park, then Leicester Race Course. Henry Tracey Coxwell, a pioneer balloonist, was brought to the meet with his 'great gas balloon, the wonder of the age'. The balloon was inflated and as Coxwell was about to make his ascent, one of the crowd, a Nottingham man named Pegg, seized hold of the basket and insisted on being taken aloft.

Pegg's demand was refused, as the balloon would have been unable to lift the extra weight. The crowd supported the Notts man and, in an ugly mood, surged around the balloon. At this Coxwell then threatened to deflate the balloon, an action which further incensed the crowd. When it was seen that the threat had been carried out they attacked the deflating gas-bag. In a few minutes it had been torn to pieces, the basket was set alight and paraded around the

CORONATION BALLOON.

Under the Patronage of the Worshipful the Mayor.

MR. GREEN

RESPECTFULLY announces to the Inhabitants of Leicester and its vicinity, that he purposes, On MONDAY, July 26th, At Three o'clock in the Afternoon, making his Eighteenth

AERIAL VOYAGE,

From a commodious situation belonging to Mr. BRADLEY, adjoining the GAS WORKS.
Tickets of admission to witness the INFLATION, ATTACHING THE CAR, and LAUNCHING THE BALLOON, at 2s. and 3s. each, may be had of Mr. COMBE, Mr. CHAMBERLAIN, and Mr. COCKSHAW, Booksellers.
Bands of Music will attend, and Seats, with other accommodations will be provided.
ORDER OF SIGNALS.—A Gun will be fired to announce the commencement of Inflation; a second Gun will fired when the process is completed; and the Ascent will be notified by a third Gun and a Pilot Balloon.—To afford the Public as ample an opportunity as possible for inspecting the Balloon, the doors will be opened at Twelve o'clock.

An advert for Mr Green's aerial voyage of 26th July 1824 that appeared in the Illustrated Leicester Chronicle. *via Dr Hugh Thomas*

A faithful replica of the Pilcher Hawk is displayed at Stanford Hall. It was built by apprentices from Armstrong Whitworth in 1958. Ken Ellis

A monument marks the spot where Percy Sinclair Pilcher crashed in his Hawk glider in the grounds of Stanford Hall on 30th September 1899. Pilcher died of his injuries two days later. Author

race course, while the unfortunate Coxwell was set upon and badly hurt. Police were called in to quell the disturbance and damage was assessed at several hundred pounds.

Towards the end of the 19th century aviation pioneers began to explore the problems of manned winged flight. In Germany Otto Lilienthal was one such pioneer and when news of his gliding experiments reached England they caught the imagination of a young man, Percy Sinclair Pilcher.

Born in 1866 Pilcher, from early youth, took an interest in bird flight and in the possibilities of mechanical flight. In 1895 he constructed his first glider, modelling it on pictures of Lilienthal's machine. At first his attempts at Eynsford, Kent, to fly the Bat, as it was called, were unsuccessful but after making modifications he succeeded on 12th September in making the first ever controlled flight in the British Isles.

He continued with his experiments, built other gliders and by 1899 had achieved considerable success; he was even examining the possibility of installing a small engine in one of his designs. In September of 1899 Pilcher came to Leicestershire on a visit to his friend, the Honourable Adrian Verney-Cave, later to be the sixth Lord Braye, at Stanford Hall, near Lutterworth. He brought with him his latest gliders, one a new design of triplane layout and also his most successful one to date, the Hawk.

On 30th September, a day of frequent showers and gusty winds, he prepared to demonstrate the Hawk to members of the Aeronautical Society who had come to see him. At about 4 o'clock in the afternoon, although Pilcher considered the weather was unfavourable, he decided to go ahead. To launch his glider he used a method he had pioneered with a rope and pulley system drawn by a couple of horses. At the first attempt the Hawk rose easily into the air after a short run, but the line broke and Pilcher was forced to descend prematurely.

Although the gliders had been sheltered before the trials Pilcher is said to have remarked that rain had made the machine very heavy and that it was difficult to reach the desired speed. However a second launch was made and as before the Hawk rose easily, but when it was about 30ft up a crack was heard and the tail seemed to collapse. The glider and its pilot fell to the ground just over the county border in Northamptonshire. Pilcher suffered severe concussion, fractures to the left thigh and right shin bone. He never regained consciousness and died from concussion of the brain and spine on the evening of Monday, 2nd October 1899.

His untimely death, at the age of 33, is considered by historians to have been a great loss to aviation. Many have thought it possible that he would have achieved the goal of powered flight before it was attained by the Wright Brothers in 1903. The memory of his association with Stanford Hall is still preserved. A full scale replica of the Hawk, built by Armstrong Whitworth Aircraft apprentices, was presented to Lord Braye by the Royal Aeronautical Society in 1958. It now forms the centrepiece of the museum exhibit, while in parkland nearby a monument erected by the Society at an earlier date marks the spot where he fell.

The advent of powered flight in 1903 seems to have had no immediate impact in county circles and it was not until 1909 that any real interest was shown. In September of that year a meeting was held at the Bell Hotel in Leicester, the outcome of which was the formation of the Leicester Aero Club. At that time though the object appears to have been to stimulate an awareness of aviation matters in general rather than attempt any practical exercise.

Apparently the event which aroused the most interest in aviation around this time was the *Daily Mail* Circuit of Britain air race of 1911. Competitors were required to cover a course of over 1,000 miles divided into several stages, each with compulsory stops *en route*. The prize for the eventual winner was £10,000, a sum which attracted many of the top aviators of the day. Hendon to Edinburgh was the second stage and when it became known that the route would take the aircraft over Leicestershire excitement grew. It was further heightened by the news that several competitors intended to refuel on the Polo Ground at Brentingby, near Melton Mowbray.

The race began on Saturday, 22nd July with a 20 mile first stage from Brooklands to Hendon. Of the 30 entrants 21 came to the starting line; of these, 17 ultimately managed to complete the short trip, two were left at the post and two crashed – not an auspicious beginning.

No flying took place on Sunday, much to the surprise of the foreign pilots, but an early start was planned for Monday, 24th with the first aeroplane scheduled to leave at 4am. It is reported that so great was the interest in the race that nearly half a million people were present to see the start at Hendon. Many had spent the night camped in neighbouring fields.

Though the crowd was not of the same magnitude, a similar situation existed further north. Before daylight people began to leave towns and villages throughout Leicestershire and Rutland, all making their way towards Brentingby. By dawn it seemed that most of the inhabitants of Melton Mowbray were on the move. Early mist dispersed to give way to a beautiful July morning. By 5am a huge crowd occupied the Polo Ground and vantage points around, all waiting for their first sighting.

B C Hucks in his Blériot at Loughborough during the Daily Mail-*sponsored series of events to popularise the art of flying.*
via Derek Sturgess

There were several false alarms when early birds were mistakenly identified, then at just after 5.15am, the first aeroplane was sighted. It was the Morane-Borel monoplane piloted by the Frenchman Jules Vedrines who in turn was closely followed by the Blériot monoplane of 'Beaumont' (Lt de V Conneau). Both aircraft flew directly overhead, the sound of their motors clearly heard and fading into the distance.

Next to come into view, at 5.37am, was Gustav Hamel, a little off course flying close to Melton Mowbray with the engine of his Blériot giving some trouble. After deciding to land he touched down in Freeboroughs Field, near the Isolation Hospital on Scalford Road. At first it was thought that the problem was a broken inlet valve but after he and a friendly chauffeur had almost stripped the engine it was diagnosed as sooted spark plugs. With engine reassembled and plugs replaced he was able to take-off and resume the race once more at just after 10am.

At the Polo Ground officials had roped off a large area and made a charge for admission, hoping to swell club funds. Just after 6am, when an aeroplane was seen to be coming in to land, a large section of the crowd outside the ground were overcome with excitement whereupon they rushed forward, brushed police and officials aside and surged into the enclosure. The aeroplane, a Bristol biplane, flown by C Howard Pixton, made an excellent landing. Almost immediately it was surrounded by enthusiastic spectators, all wanting to congratulate the airman and get as close as possible. Mechanics speedily refuelled the Bristol from a supply of two gallon cans carried on a small dray. While this was being done many of those close to the biplane seized the opportunity to inscribe their signatures

on its covering. Some, for good measure, even added their addresses. Pixton had no trouble in restarting and was away again at 6.20am. Others were not so fortunate.

Collyns Pizey mistook Oakham for Melton, circuited the town twice in his Bristol biplane looking for the landing ground before realising his error then making his way to Brentingby where he landed at 7am. He had been having trouble with his propeller so this was changed. After refuelling he had problems with his engine which was only restarted with considerable difficulty. Finally he managed to take-off at 7.45am, only to hit the polo scoreboard, causing sufficient damage to the aeroplane to put him out of the race.

These unprecedented events so thrilled the crowd that few entertained the idea of leaving for work. Similarly the hundreds of school children present had no intention of missing all the excitement. In Melton Mowbray the numbers actually in attendance were so small that by 9.15am it was decided to close the schools for the day.

Other aviators flew over the field, then, at 11am Olivier de Montalent brought his Breguet biplane in to land. Fuel was soon taken on board but when the moment came to take-off the pilot considered that flying conditions were unfavourable and chose to wait. It proved to be a prolonged delay which gave the crowd ample time to view the Breguet as de Montalent did not depart until almost 4.15pm.

Aircraft continued to pass over at infrequent intervals; those clearly identified were the Cody Biplane flown by its designer S F Cody and a Nieuport monoplane piloted by the American, C T Weymann. It was not until 7.45 in the evening that the last aircraft of the day winged its way northwards and brought to an end a memorable occasion.

Fifteen aeroplanes had left Hendon that morning, but only three completed the journey to Edinburgh that day. Several competitors were eliminated due to accidents, in fact only five managed to make the first

control point at Harrogate. Although four contestants eventually completed the entire course only two, Vedrines and 'Beaumont' were involved in the final stages of the race with the latter being declared the winner.

An intriguing side effect of the race was that it apparently aroused considerable interest amongst members of the Leicester Aero Club. This in turn reputedly led to a great deal of activity within the club. At the general meeting on 8th September 1911 it was stated that several members were engaged in building full-sized machines as well as models. Work was so advanced that it was hoped one locally-built aeroplane would shortly be ready to give exhibition flights. Unfortunately, no report on this latter event has come to light so whether it ever took place is open to doubt.

All over the country exhibitions of flying became novel attractions and several notable aviators of the day made fleeting visits to the two counties to show off their prowess. Displays were not restricted by the lack of proper landing areas; any suitable area of ground was pressed into use to as a temporary flying field. A vintage year for such occasions was 1912, when such famous pilots as R B Slack, B C Hucks and Gustav Hamel all paid visits.

Robert Slack was engaged by International Correspondence Schools to undertake, on their behalf, a 1,000 mile tour of England, starting and finishing at Hendon. It was in these travels that he visited Leicestershire where his first landing was unintentional. On 18th July he left Bedford intending to fly to Leicester. He had however reckoned without the wind which proved to be too strong and he was forced to land at Foxton, near Market Harborough. He was unable to resume his journey until the 26th when he flew as far as Thurmaston. Next day he left for Nottingham and after an overnight stay continued on his way, this time bound for Birmingham. Again he failed to reach his intended destination and made a second involuntary landing in the county. A faulty engine was to blame but a safe touch down was made in a hayfield at Ravenstone where his Blériot was picketed down for the night. At 12 noon on the following day he headed once more for Birmingham but yet again his progress was hampered, this time by thunderstorms *en route*. These made forced landings necessary and it was not until 12 noon on Saturday the 30th that he finally reached Castle Bromwich.

Following the success of the Circuit of Britain the *Daily Mail* sponsored a scheme in 1912 which was to further popularise flying. The paper secured the services of a number of prominent British and Continental aviators who were then commissioned to tour some of the more rural areas of England. These tours accomplished a great deal and gave large numbers of people the opportunity to see some first class flying.

Leicestershire was on the itinerary of Benjamin C Hucks who enjoyed quite a reputation as a sporting pilot. He had arranged to fly at Loughborough on 17th July but for some reason did not arrive until the 24th. A telegram had been sent announcing his departure from Birmingham but he reached his destination before the message so consequently there was no welcoming crowd to greet him.

An amusing story is told of his arrival at Loughborough. In the local court, sentence was about to be passed on a rather unpleasant case of horse cruelty when a shout of 'There's the plane!' was heard. Magistrates, police, witnesses, accused and almost everyone else in the courtroom forgot the matter in hand and rushed out of the building hoping to catch a glimpse of the aircraft. Newspapers of the time fail to record the final outcome of the case.

Hucks proceeded to give five excellent demonstration flights before leaving for Long Eaton, Derbyshire. He returned to Loughborough on Saturday 27th, then carried on to Leicester. There, he loaded letters on board his aeroplane which he then conveyed to Coventry. This must have been the first time that air mail was ever flown out of the county.

Gustav Hamel ground-running the engine of his Blériot at Hinckley in 1912. Those assisting must have reeked of burnt castor oil after the event! Mrs Julien Birchall

Hamel (marked with an 'x' above his head) talking with an excited crowd alongside his aeroplane at Hinckley after his mishap of 20th July 1912. Mrs Julien Birchall

Gustav Hamel and his Blériot, ready to take the special aerial edition of the Leicester Daily Post *aloft from the old County Cricket Ground on Aylestone Road, Leicester, to a field alongside the Ashby Road in Loughborough on 30th November 1912.* Author's collection

Of the aviators on the display circuit by far the most famous to come to Leicestershire and Rutland in 1912 was Gustav Hamel. By the time of his first visit of the year he was already well known due to the considerable amount of publicity his achievements had received. He had won several air races in the south of England, one of which was the 'Aerial Derby', yet another of the *Daily Mail's* enterprises. Also to his credit were four Channel crossings and the first journey to be made by a British pilot (his father was a German doctor, but Gustav was born in London in 1889) between the capitals of London and Paris. In addition he had been the first man to carry aerial mail in England, from London to Windsor in 1911, and had had the distinction of giving a private flying display for His Majesty King George V.

His first engagement in the county was at a fete organised by Hinckley Conservative Party in support of the local candidate in forthcoming parliamentary elections. The event was held at the Outwoods on the outskirts of the town on 20th July and despite the day being rather miserable several thousand people paid an admission fee of one shilling (5p) to enter the ground. Although there was a full programme in support there was no doubt who and what were the chief attractions.

Hamel took off early in the afternoon on what was intended to be the first of several flights then after 15 minutes in the air he brought the Blériot in to land. On the first two attempts, for some reason, he chose to overshoot. The third ended in disaster. Hamel was seen to half jump, half tumble from the cockpit and hang on to the aeroplane trying desperately to prevent it crashing into a hedge. He did not succeed, was knocked over and pinned beneath the tailplane. There was an immediate rush of spectators and officials to the spot, then a cheer of relief was heard as the pilot was extricated and seen to be unhurt. Not so the Blériot; this had sustained damage to the

propeller and port wing which curtailed all further flights for the day. The mishap was doubly unfortunate for he was to have flown, complete with a lady passenger, over the County Cricket Ground in Leicester where a match between Leicestershire and the Australian touring team was in progress.

He returned to both counties towards the end of the year visiting both Market Harborough and Uppingham School but it was at Leicester that he added to his continually growing prestige. There, on 30th November, he became the first aviator in the world to deliver newspapers by air. The occasion was really a publicity stunt arranged by the *Leicester Daily Post*, the city's one and only morning paper (which ceased publication in 1921). Hamel took off from the old County Cricket Ground on Aylestone Road at 11.15 am bound for Loughborough and following the main Leicester to Loughborough road at a height of around 200ft he occasionally dropped copies of the *Daily Post* to crowds along the route. Conditions were far from ideal with banks of fog and a 30mph wind; by the time he reached Loughborough the 'intrepid aviator' was quite numb with cold. By the afternoon however he had recovered sufficiently to be able to give two exhibition flights.

As flying techniques advanced, so more varied exhibitions of the sport began to be offered. Not only was this intended to show off the aviator's skill, but also to entice large numbers of the public to attend. Dependent as they were on the weather not all displays went as planned. An account of the visit of E R Whitehouse to Leicester in June 1913 is a good illustration of these points.

As a preliminary, an advertisement placed in the *Daily Post* read:

'Flying at Borderick's Pastures, Thurmaston, Leicester. The Daring Hendon Airman, Mr E R Whitehouse with his Wonderful Bird-like Aeroplane the Handley-Page Monoplane, will give Exhibitions of Bomb Dropping, High Flying, Passenger Carrying and Flying in Dusk Guided by Rockets and Flares, on Thursday and Saturday June 5th and 7th 1913. Admission 6d, 1/- and 2/6.

'Scientific and Instructive Aviation Co Ltd, St Albans.'

But, contemporary reports on the event paint a different picture:

'On Thursday, 5th, although great crowds were drawn to the venue, owing to gusty conditions no flying was possible until 7pm when Whitehouse was able to take-off and give a demonstration of banking and "volplaning". 'Saturday was no better with the same conditions as Thursday prevailing. However, to avoid disappointing the large numbers of people who were again drawn to Borderick's Pastures free admission was given to view the aeroplane. Once again, towards evening, conditions improved and Whitehouse was able this time to make several flights. During the first of these he flew around the outskirts of the city, while the second was devoted to a demonstration of the art of banking and switchback flying. Then, to round off the evening he took off at dusk, made another fine flight after which he was guided in to land by the light of petrol flares.'

It is probably only a coincidence but shortly after Whitehouse's visit an effort was made to establish aviation in Leicester. On Wednesday, 18th June 1913 an aviation meeting was held at the Grand Hotel with Samuel Faire in the chair. Its purpose was to discuss a proposed aerodrome and factory for Leicester. Evidently though the meeting accomplished little for neither aerodrome nor factory was instituted at this time.

Many enterprises undertook war work in the two counties. Wadkin & Co of Leicester developed several types of machine to assist in the mass production of wooden aeroplane parts, including propellers. Reproduced from an advertisement in Flight *magazine, 14th November 1918. via Author*

First World War

With the outbreak of World War I in 1914 flying gained a new, and eventually grimmer, purpose. The flying services, the Royal Flying Corps (RFC) and the Royal Naval Air Service (RNAS) expanded rapidly. However, for a time, this growth and with it the establishment of aerodromes and landing grounds passed the two counties by. The major factor which was to alter this situation, as far as Leicestershire was concerned, was the setting up of Home Defence Squadrons to combat the threat posed by the incursions of German Zeppelin airships over the British Isles. The menace of these raiders was brought home sharply to the people of Leicestershire and in particular the inhabitants of Loughborough on the night of 31st January 1916.

At 12.06pm on that date Zeppelin LZ-20 with Kapitanleutnant Franz Stabbert in command left its base at Tondern as part of a nine airship force with orders to 'Attack England middle or south, if at all possible Liverpool'. After being airborne for over 7½ hours LZ-20 is believed to have crossed the coast between the Humber and the Wash at 7.45pm. The airship proceeded inland and Stabbert's raid report indicates that an hour later LZ-20 was faintly lit by searchlights through cloud and fired on by a 'battery' which was silenced after six explosive bombs were released. The missiles fell on the town of Loughborough, ten people

were killed, 12 more injured and considerable damage caused to civilian property. Stabbert thought he was in the vicinity of Sheffield and continued westwards for a short time but as the airship was experiencing some engine trouble he elected not to endeavour to reach Liverpool so he made his main attack. By this time LZ-20 had passed over Leicestershire and the 27 bombs dropped fell on Burton-Upon-Trent.

Bombs again fell on county soil on the night of 5th/6th March 1916. This time they came from the Zeppelin LZ-13 which like LZ-20 before was also experiencing loss of engine power and in order to lighten ship, the commander Kapitanleutnant Heinrich Mathy, was forced to jettison a large part of the airship's offensive load. Thirty incendiary and 15 explosive bombs were released which fell on fields between Sproxton and Thistleton causing little damage. It is recorded that the detonations of the high explosive missiles could be heard as far away as Norwich.

The Home Defence unit to be charged with the air defence of the Midlands was 38 Squadron which reformed for this purpose at Castle Bromwich, Warwickshire, in July 1916. By October of that year the unit had moved further eastwards and established its headquarters at Melton Mowbray. Unfortunately this move did not lead to recognised aerodromes being set up within the counties as the unit's three main flight stations were all situated in Lincolnshire. It did however result in nine landing fields of differing dimensions being laid out in Leicestershire. Little is known of their use, but it is possible that detached flights may have operated from them. It is most likely though that their main functions were connected with training exercises and as emergency landing grounds.

Aircraft of 38 Squadron RFC made many attempts to intercept the Zeppelin raiders whenever they entered the unit's area of operation. Unfortunately their efforts met with scant success as the following two incidents serve to illustrate.

On the night of 1st/2nd October 1916 a ten airship raid was launched against London and the Midlands. Seven eventually crossed the English coast and one of these, the LZ-21 commanded by Oberleutnant zur See K Frankenburg, managed to penetrate as far inland as Oakham. Over central England a blanket of cloud and mist covered large areas which made things difficult for airship and aircraft alike. Only one sortie, a weather reconnaissance, was flown by 38 Squadron. This ended in a forced-landing, in the course of which the aircraft was wrecked and the pilot, Captain C T Black, slightly injured.

What was probably the closest contact occurred on the night of 19th/20th October 1917. On this occasion the raid was intended to strike industrial targets in northern England and eleven Zeppelins were involved. At various times during the night eight 38 Squadron aircraft were airborne as part of the defences. One of these, FE.2b B422, piloted by Lieutenant G H Harrison was flying at 13,000ft in the vicinity of Leicester when a Zeppelin, believed to have been LZ-45, was observed some 2,000ft above. Harrison succeeded in narrowing the gap to about 1,000ft and had managed to fire three bursts into the tail end of the airship when his machine gun jammed. He spent some minutes trying to clear the stoppage but was unsuccessful and was forced to break off the engagement. On landing at Stamford it was found that the encounter had not been one-sided, return fire from the airship had damaged the wing fabric of B422 in several places.

—

During the course of the war, many large municipalities were invited by the Imperial Air Fleet Committee (IAFC) to participate in the scheme to raise funds for the purpose of providing aircraft for Colonial units co-operating with British forces. Leicester was one of those which responded to the call. The Chamber of Commerce accepted responsibility for raising a sum of 2,000 guineas and within ten days of members being invited to subscribe the amount had been raised. Presentation of the aircraft, BE.12 6508, was made to the Honourable Sir George Perley KCMG MP, High Commissioner for Canada by Alec Lorrimer, President of the Chamber of Commerce, on Saturday, 3rd June 1916. The ceremony, which was made into quite an event, took place in Western Park before a crowd of over 40,000 people. Many dignitaries, including Lord Desborough, President of the IAFC, were present.

Lady Perley christened the aircraft *Leicester* by breaking the customary bottle of champagne while 2,000 children, specially trained for the occasion, sang the patriotic songs 'The Maple Leaf' and 'Hail Canada'. It was a cloudy, windy day, so as a result little could be heard of the speeches and most of the crowd barely caught a glimpse of the aircraft until it took off to depart. For many it was still a memorable occasion as it was the first time they had had the opportunity to see an aeroplane at fairly close quarters. It was reported that the BE.12 had a very short service life with 21 Squadron on the Western Front.

The next aircraft to bear the name *Leicester* was BE.2e B4404. This served with 9 (Training) Squadron until it was crashed by Sergeant A Lowe at Postwick near Norwich on 4th September 1917. Another BE.2e, B6151, then bore the name while flying with 45 Training Depot Squadron, Rendcombe, Gloucestershire, in 1918. This last BE.2e was replaced by Sopwith Snipe E8213 which, as *Leicester - Canada*, was taken home by the Royal Canadian Air Force.

It was the exigencies of wartime which brought aircraft manufacture, on a large scale, to Leicestershire for the first time. The Brush Electrical Engineering Company of Loughborough obtained contracts to build machines of established designs for both the RFC and the RNAS. In all over 360 aircraft were built by the company. Some of these were erected and flown locally from Loughborough Meadows while others were despatched, by road and rail, unassembled, to be finished elsewhere.

Other companies within the two counties contributed to aircraft production in many different ways. For example, cane aeroplane seats were made by the Willowbrook Company in Loughborough, selected timber and bent timber aeroplane components were supplied by Hopton and Sons, Union Works, Market Harborough while Wadkin and Company of Leicester contributed to mass production of parts with specialised woodworking equipment such as automatic propeller shaping machines and strut copying lathes.

–

Eventually the Zeppelin menace passed and soon after came the end of the war. Then the landing grounds which still remained in Leicestershire fell into disuse and as they had been no more than oversize grass fields with perhaps a canvas hangar and a few huts or tents for living accommodation, they quickly reverted to pastoral uses. In a very short time little remained to show that the fields had ever served another purpose. (See pages 16 and 17.)

Daimler-built BE.12 6508 was named Leicester *in a ceremony at Western Park on 3rd June 1916.*
via Cross & Cockade

The Canadian flag draped over the propeller boss, Sopwith Snipe E8213 during the ceremony to name it Leicester - Canada. *The aircraft was taken to Canada.*
via Bruce Robertson

First World War Landing Grounds

Initially the RFC landing grounds set up in Leicestershire were established for use by 38 (Home Defence) Squadron. This unit was reformed at Castle Bromwich, Warwickshire, on the 14th July 1916 for the purpose of defending the Midlands against the Zeppelin menace. By 1st October 1916 unit headquarters had been moved to Melton Mowbray and the unit's three Flights were deployed at Buckminster ('B'), Leadenham ('C') and Stamford ('A'). Although the first of these Flight stations bears a Leicestershire name, all were in fact in Lincolnshire.

It is interesting to note that the Squadron Commander until mid-1917 was Captain A T Harris, who was destined to become, as an Air Chief Marshal, Commander-in-Chief of Bomber Command 1942 to 1945 and eventually Marshal of the RAF, Sir Arthur Harris.

Although aircraft of the squadron carried out anti-Zeppelin patrols throughout their stay in the area they met with little success. In May 1918 the unit left for France to begin night bombing operations. They left behind a small nucleus to form 90 Squadron which then assumed the Midlands defence role.

By the time this unit had become operational, the threat of Zeppelin raids had passed and so it saw no action before the Armistice. The squadron was disbanded in June 1919 and it is believed that by this time the landing grounds in Leicestershire were no longer used.

Documentary or photographic evidence which would help provide a better picture of this First World War activity within the county has proved elusive and, inevitably, few people remain alive today able to recall events during that era.

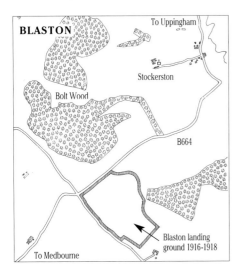

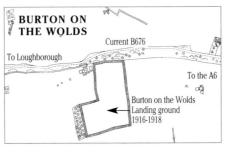

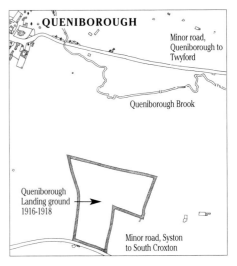

Blaston [SP 830 963]
This Home Defence landing ground which was brought into use late in 1916 replaced a smaller one about three miles to the south west at Welham. The area covered by this new field was about 70 acres making it the largest of 38 Squadron's landing grounds established within Leicestershire's boundaries during the First World War. The landing ground was situated one and a half miles from the village in the north-east south-east quadrant formed by the cross roads on the B664 about one mile to the south-west of Stockerston.

Designated as a night landing ground it remained in the care of the unit until May 1918 when the unit left for France to serve in the night bomber offensive against Germany. Thereafter the newly formed 90 Squadron assumed responsibility for the Blaston site until it was closed down following the end of hostilities.

Brentingby [SP 784 184]
A 30 acre site located between the village and Gravel Hole Spinney was used for a short time in 1916 as a night landing ground. Late in that year it was closed in favour of another site at Scalford. In the early 1930s, the area gained a new lease of life when a landing ground was re-established under the auspices of the Automobile Association.

Buckminster [SK 895 235]
Although an airfield bearing the name of this Leicestershire village existed during the First World War it was situated just over the county

boundary in Lincolnshire and so falls outside the area defined by this book. Details of this airfield are to be found in the book The Airfields of Lincolnshire since 1912 *published in 1984 by Midland Counties Publications.*

Burton on the Wolds [SP 609 213]
Located to the south side of the B676 Six Hills to Burton on the Wolds road and adjacent to Horse Leys Farm, this 27 acre site became a night landing ground in mid-1916. After 38 Squadron departed to France in the summer of 1918 use was transferred to 90 Squadron. While in their charge it was reclassified as a second class landing ground by day and third class by night. Towards the end of 1918 the site was vacated and it reverted to farmland. In recent years it has been noted that the flying of microlight aircraft has taken place from the field.

Castle Donington [SP 449 256]
This was the smallest of 38 Squadron's landing grounds in Leicestershire. Covering approximately 20 acres it was situated to the south east corner of the area which is now the East Midlands Airport. Little is known about the field or its activity there. The only information available indicates that it was established late in 1916, downgraded for day use only in mid-1917 and by 1918 it was not in use. See Chapter Eight for its relationship with the Airport.

Loughborough Meadows [SP 542 212]
Not in the strictest sense an established landing ground but nevertheless an extremely convenient stretch of land suitable for flying. When Brush Electrical Engineering Co Ltd, undertook contracts to build military aircraft during the First World War they used this large expanse of flat ground close to their Falcon Works to great advantage. See Chapter Thirteen.

The land proved excellent for flying and a large number of the aircraft built by the company at this time made their first flights from

Loughborough Meadows. *It is also said that many Brush-built aircraft were delivered direct from the field to service establishments by Teddy Barrs, a pilot in the company's employ.*

Peckleton [SP 479 022]
A landing ground bearing this name was established on J H Cart's farm, near to the village of Desford, in mid-1916. Brought into use as a night landing ground the site is believed to have been little used and by the middle of 1917 it had been downgraded as suitable for day use only. During 1918 the RFC vacated the field and it once again became farm land. This area of land reverted to aviation once more in 1929 when it became a part of Desford Aerodrome.

Queniborough [SP 656 114]
Another of 38 Squadron's night landing grounds was set up near to this village, off Ridgemere Lane, in the mid-1916. It continued to be used for this purpose until some time in 1917 when it became available for day landings only. By 1918 use of the 25 acre site had been discontinued.

Scalford [SP 744 216]
Actually nearer to Melton Mowbray than the village after which it was named and situated off the A606 Nottingham road opposite Sysonby Lodge Farm, this landing ground became one of the largest in Leicestershire during the First World War. The area officially encompassed was 45 acres but measured closer to 60.

Established initially as a night landing ground it replaced a similar type of field which 38

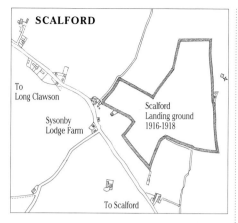

SCALFORD

To Long Clawson

Sysonby Lodge Farm

Scalford Landing ground 1916-1918

To Scalford

Squadron had previously used at Brentingby to the east of Melton Mowbray. One factor which in all probability influenced the change and choice of site was the fact that the squadron's headquarters were moved from Castle Bromwich, Warwickshire, in October 1916 to a new home on Scalford Road, Melton Mowbray. The use of a landing ground in close proximity to unit headquarters would be of great value for communication and liaison purposes, especially as the three Flight Stations of the Squadron were some distance away in Lincolnshire.

The field was used by the unit from late 1916 until it departed for a tour of duty in France in May 1918. To fill the gap left by this move, 90 Squadron formed at Buckminster and assumed responsibility for Scalford until it was closed down following the German capitulation.

Scalford was to be used briefly for flying activities again during the 1930s by Sir Alan Cobham when his National Aviation Day Displays toured the country. When Melton Mowbray was on the itinerary the 'Old Aerodrome, Nottingham Road' became the venue for the air show.

Welham [SP 770 933]
In 1916 a landing ground of some 35 acres was established about half a mile outside this village on the left hand side of the Welham to Slawston road. Occupation of the site was very brief and it can have been little used for by the end of the year it had been vacated in favour of a much larger field at Blaston.

During the Second World War this former landing ground was the scene of quite a different type of air activity when it became part of a parachute drop zone. As such it was used by Allied airborne forces for training exercises in preparation for the invasion of Europe and other operations.

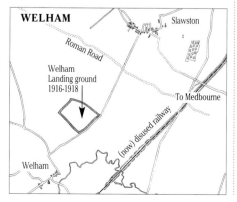

WELHAM

Slawston

Roman Road

Welham Landing ground 1916-1918

To Medbourne

(now) disused railway

Welham

Between the Wars

In 1919 an attempt was made to introduce organised flying into the counties with the formation of the Leicestershire and Rutland Aero Club under the presidency of Sir Samuel Faire. Despite the fact that many trained airmen had returned to civilian life, the club failed to gain favour and was disbanded the following year. So, it was left to an occasional visit by itinerant aviators to keep alive some interest in flying. These small companies or individuals would hire a suitable field for a day or so and offer the thrill of flying to anyone in the vicinity who could afford to pay for the experience. Then, when the customers dwindled, they would move on to ply their trade in another locality.

Members of the Leicestershire Chamber of Commerce were next to try to arouse an active interest in aviation. To this end a lecture was arranged at the De Montfort Hall in 1926 where the principal speakers were Sir Alan Cobham and Sir Sefton Brancker, then the Director of Civil Aviation. Over 2,000 people attended the meeting, the successful outcome of which was to be seen shortly afterwards when a Commercial Aviation Committee was formed. Subsequently a sub-committee was added to explore the possibility of establishing an airport at Leicester.

In the meantime interested members of the Chamber continued to examine other aspects of aviation and it was decided as a first step to form a flying club. Accordingly Leicestershire Aero Club was born on 30th November 1928. After initial difficulty in obtaining land on which to pursue their activities, suitable acreage was located near Desford. This site was quickly developed and formally opened as Desford Aerodrome in September 1929.

During 1929 Sir Alan Cobham undertook a flying tour of the British Isles, the purpose of which was to try to convince local authorities of the need for municipal aerodromes. Between May and October in the de Havilland DH.61 Giant Moth G-AAEV *Youth of Britain* he visited 110 important towns and cities. These included Leicester and Loughborough. It was Sir Alan's opinions and advice which later played a large part in the choice of location of the aerodromes at both these places.

From September of 1930, Leicestershire could boast of a second established airfield when one was opened near Ratcliffe on the Wreake. Its owner was W Lindsay Everard who, throughout his life, was to be a patron of the county aero clubs and a staunch advocate for aviation in all its aspects.

The 1930's were a time when all types of aviation burgeoned within the United Kingdom, which in turn led to many new landing grounds being laid out. A regional planning report of 1932 noted that the site had been acquired at Braunstone Frith for a future Leicester Airport. The report also envisaged a rapid development in air travel and sites to serve communities at Ashby de la Zouch, Coalville, Hinckley, Humberstone, Kibworth, Loughborough, Lutterworth and Melton Mowbray were mentioned. Only one of these, Loughborough, was to be eventually developed.

It was during this period that the Syston-based company of En-Tout-Cas Limited, was extremely active in this field. Then, as now, the firm was held in high regard for its expertise in establishing sports grounds and tennis courts. This reputation was even further enhanced by the excellence of their airfield construction and the company was eventually responsible for fulfilling many major contracts, both civil and military.

Visits by aviators offering joyrides were still commonplace for much of the 1930s but it was the new innovation of the large touring airshow which really attracted the public. Foremost amongst the entrepreneurs who developed this type of entertainment was Sir Alan Cobham. During the first half of the decade the National Aviation Day Displays staged by his company proved very popular and attracted thousands of spectators. Although civil airfields were being developed on an increasing scale, show organisers did not rely on established landing grounds alone. Like the pioneer aviators in the past, a rented field in close proximity to the chosen town often served as a temporary flying ground for the duration of the display. In summer months Cobham's flying circus toured all over the British Isles and visits to Leicestershire were usually included in the itinerary. Coalville, Desford, Loughborough, Market Harborough and Melton Mowbray were all visited on occasion, invariably to the delight of the local people for many of whom the event was an unforgettable experience.

In 1935 the city of Leicester was put on the commercial air map for the first time with the commencement of scheduled airline services from the newly-opened municipal aerodrome at Braunstone. Managing this new project were Leicestershire Aero Club who moved to Braunstone from Desford specifically for that purpose. The latter airfield was then taken over by the firm of Reid & Sigrist, who expanded and further developed the site in order to establish a civilian flying school. There, under government contract, selected pupils were trained as pilots and air observers for the rapidly growing RAF.

It was also in 1935 that the county's second flying club was formed, this was known as the Leicestershire Flying Pou Club. At that time the 'Flying Flea' craze was at its height, members intentions were to build their own aircraft from the designs of Frenchman Henri Mignet as published in his book *The Flying Flea*, and hopefully fly it from a field which they rented near Melton Mowbray. The Flea (its correct designation being the Mignet HM.14 Pou du Ciel), however, was found to be unsafe and also unsuitable for club flying so a new aircraft, a Kronfeld Drone, was acquired. It was realised that this could not be flown with safety from their present field so a more

spacious location was sought. Thanks to their benefactor, Lindsay Everard, this was found at Rearsby. A small airfield was built and the County Flying Club, as it had then become, moved in as tenants in 1938.

–

Undoubtedly in the light of subsequent events, the most significant aviation development of this era in Leicestershire was the decision made by A L Wykes in November 1938 to start aircraft construction on a commercial basis. Already a textile machinery

manufacturer at Thurmaston, he set aside part of his Britannia Works for this purpose. The company which he founded was called Taylorcraft Aeroplanes (England) Ltd. By April 1939 aircraft started to leave the works and as the company possessed no airfield of their own, final assembly and test flights were carried out at Lindsay Everard's airfield at Ratcliffe. Aircraft continued to leave the works until August 1939, production was then suspended owing to the outbreak of war being imminent.

The heady days of joy-riding and visiting flying circuses were witnessed by thousands from the two counties. O P Jones and crew stand with a member of the local constabulary in front of their Berkshire Aviation Tours Avro 504K at The Outwoods, Hinckley. Mrs Julien Birchall

Youth of Britain, Sir Alan Cobham's DH.61 Giant Moth G-AAEV believed to be at Loughborough during his 1929 fact-finding tour of Britain that was to give rise to many municipal aerodrome projects. H Warren

To round off the civil aviation scene for the 1930s the second civic airport in the county of Leicester was in the process of being built at Loughborough. Work commenced in 1938 but war was destined to intervene before the project was complete.

From the mid-1930s military aviation in Britain progressed rapidly. In the main this was due to the impetus given by the initiation, in 1934, of the RAF Expansion Scheme. This was part of the British Government's re-armament programme, the necessity for which was brought about by the ominous signs and rumblings emitting from Hitler's Germany at this time.

Under the scheme the number of RAF squadrons was greatly increased, leading to the need for more airfields to house them. One of these new sites was the only pre-war, purely military, airfield to come within the scope of this history. It was built at Cottesmore in Rutland, opened in March 1938 and soon had elements of Bomber Command in residence.

Another aspect of the Expansion Scheme was the formation of the RAF Volunteer Reserve during 1937. In common with other major cities a unit of this reserve was formed in Leicester and much of the recruit training was carried out in conjunction with the Reid & Sigrist organisation at Desford. The School here then received the service designation 7 Elementary & Reserve Flying Training School.

The small dimensions of Comper Swift G-AAZC allowed it to become the perfect centre-piece for the formal ball of the Leicestershire Aero Club at the Grand Hotel, Leicester, 27th February 1931. via Author

Percival Gull Six. Exhibited at Lewis's. 1936.

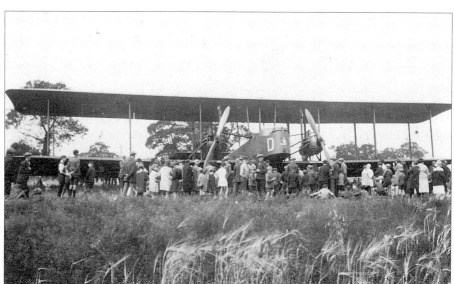

Left: *Syston-based En-Tout-Cas Ltd earned a good reputation for the building of airfields. An advert from* The Aeroplane *for 2nd November 1938 shows some of the company's work at Desford. See Chapter Nine. via Author*

Top: *A souvenir postcard marking the occasion when Amy Mollison's Percival Gull Six G-ADZO was displayed inside Lewis's*

department store in Leicester, June 1936. Amy (née Johnson) had created a record out-and-back time to the Cape in the aircraft the previous month. via Author

Bottom right: *Vickers Virginia IX J7438 'D' of 7 Squadron draws an inquisitive crowd following its forced-landing at Belcher's Bar, near Ibstock, in the late 1920s. via F B Aggas*

Second World War

At the end of the 1930s civil aviation thrived in the counties and the RAF had gained a firm foothold. With the declaration of war against Germany on 3rd September 1939, the whole scene changed.

All private and club flying was banned and civil flying anywhere within the United Kingdom required a special permit for each flight. Within a short time most of the private and public aerodromes were taken over for military purposes and many of the aircraft which had been stored by the clubs and private owners were requisitioned. Thus approximately a further 100 airfields became available for use on a war footing while many former civilian aircraft were able to be utilised for liaison purposes.

As hostilities gained momentum ever increasing air power meant a requirement for many more airfields throughout the country. Sites within Leicestershire and Rutland, many of which had been surveyed before 1939, were developed. In all hundreds of acres of fertile agricultural land was compulsorily requisitioned to disappear beneath thousands of tons of concrete and brick. Between early 1940 and the end of 1944, 13 new airfields were built within the county boundaries. Scattered throughout the area they were located at Bitteswell, Bottesford, Bruntingthorpe, Castle Donington, Husbands Bosworth, Leicester East, Market Harborough, Melton Mowbray, Nuneaton, Saltby and Wymeswold all in Leicestershire, while the remaining two were situated in Rutland at North Luffenham and Woolfox Lodge.

This total could have been increased for sites were surveyed at Croft, Countesthorpe, Foxton Lodge, Kilby, Ragdale and Snarestone in Leicestershire plus Essendine in Rutland. It was envisaged that Ragdale would become a second satellite of Wymeswold but this plan was not proceeded with; instead a bombing range was established there for the use of 28 Operational Training Unit (OTU). An Admiralty minute of 11th August 1942 stated that the proposed Fleet Air Arm airfield to house an Advanced Flying Unit (AFU) at Snarestone would require 600 acres of land, 360 of which were arable, the rest grass. It is hardly surprising that nothing became of the proposals for this project and of the one at Essendine due to overwhelming objections from the agricultural community.

Although the major part of the wartime role of these new airfields and of some of those already established, was predominantly in a training capacity, early in the war several bases made significant contributions to the air offensive against the Third Reich. These were the three airfields in Rutland and at Bottesford. The operational squadrons then occupying these stations participated in many bombing operations against the enemy. Most major targets of the time both in Germany and Occupied Europe were attacked, the units involved often incurring heavy losses.

In their training role the bases within the two counties were responsible for many thousands of airmen receiving tuition at various levels and trades. Located as they are in the heart of England, with large areas of relatively flat countryside, Leicestershire and Rutland were ideally suited for the training scheme. At some time during the war all airfields within Leicestershire and Rutland, with the exception of Ratcliffe, Rearsby and Loughborough, were committed to aircrew training in some form.

Basic flying training was catered for at Desford together with its satellite Braunstone; thousands of embryo pilots received their first insight into flying at these stations. Bitteswell, Bruntingthorpe, Castle Donington, Husbands Bosworth, Market Harborough, Nuneaton and Wymeswold all housed bomber OTUs in due course. After receiving their specific trade training elsewhere, the various classes of aircrew assembled to form the bomber crews which would eventually fly together on operations.

Perhaps it is not strictly true to infer that Rearsby and Loughborough were not involved in training as both were used at some time by Air Training Corps gliding schools. Ratcliffe though, for the duration of the war was a base of the Air Transport Auxiliary, an organisation staffed by civilians of both sexes whose main duties were the ferrying of aircraft from the manufacturers and repair works to RAF Maintenance Units and stations.

The Lord Mayor's Spitfire Fund campaign was advertised widely – Illustrated Leicester Chronicle, August 1940. via Dr Hugh Thomas

Airfield construction involved massive plant and huge workforces. While this illustration is thought not of an airfield in the two counties, it shows the complexity of the operation. via Allan T Condie

As there had been in the First World War so during this second global conflict there were to be presentation aircraft and in this respect it was the Vickers-Supermarine Spitfire which was to predominate. In the late summer of 1940 the fate of the British nation depended on the efforts of the RAF, who, against all odds were fighting the German *Luftwaffe* in the skies over southern England. After the withdrawal of the British forces from France, at Dunkirk in May 1940, all that stood in the way of a German invasion were the RAF squadrons of Hurricanes and Spitfires.

The period from 10th July to 31st October came to be known historically as 'The Battle of Britain'. Day after day the conflict was fought and the British public held its breath as their fate was decided by the heroic actions of a few hundred brave young men.

Inquiries were forthcoming as to what way could the people show their support for these gallant airmen? Lord Beaverbrook, who was then in charge of the Ministry of Aircraft Production suggested 'Buy a Spitfire'. For this privilege a figure of £5,000 was quoted with the donor having the right to name a Spitfire or, should it be chosen, a Hurricane.

This was a considerable amount of money in those days but Sir Harry Oakes, a Canadian mining millionaire started the ball rolling by immediately sending off a cheque for £5,000. His gesture was given a huge amount of publicity and caught the imagination of the British public. Soon it was being said 'Why not have a fund for our own Spitfire?' and so the Spitfire Funds were born.

In the Belgrave area of Leicester one was quickly started at the instigation of Council-

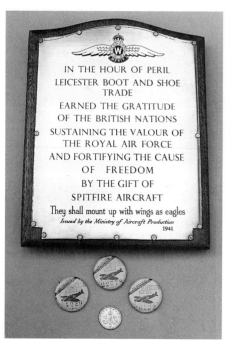

lor Vesty and shortly afterwards the Lord Mayor of Leicester, Alderman George Parbury announced, on 13th August 1940, the formation of the Leicester and County Spitfire Fund. This was launched eight days later and on the same day a cheque for £5,000 was received. It came from a well known local benefactor S H B Livingston who said he wished to give the scheme a good send off.

Another individual donor of the necessary sum was David Burrows, owner of British Waste in Saffron Lane. He also requested that he be allowed to fly the aircraft in action. His wish was not granted but nevertheless his contribution stood.

The thought of contributing to their own Spitfires appealed to the people of Leicester and many ways of raising money were devised. A Messerschmitt Bf 109 which had been shot down over Kent arrived and was erected in Victoria Park. Buckets were placed at strategic points and the public were invited to throw their loose change into them as they viewed the enemy fighter. Headquarters for the fund were provided by Browetts, the car dealers, at 64 Granby Street and here on sale were button badges depicting a Spitfire and each costing sixpence (2½p). All badges had their own individual serial number and purchasers wore them with pride to show they had at least made a small contribution to the fund. Street collections were organised, dances, whist drives and auctions held, these together with many other attractions all helped to increase the total raised.

When the Lord Mayor's fund finally closed enough money had been collected to provide for seven Spitfires. Three of these

Above: *Alderman George Parbury viewing the wreck of a German Messerschmitt Bf109 which was displayed in Victoria Park during the Spitfire Fund campaign.* Illustrated Leicester Chronicle via Dr Hugh Thomas

Bottom left: *The plaque given to Leicester's boot and shoe industry by MAP for their donation towards W3242. Below are three of the numbered badges given out to those donating to the Spitfire Fund. A 5p piece provides scale.* R Nixon

became the *City of Leicester Flight - I, II* and *III*, for another the name *Crispin of Leicester* was chosen by the city's boot and shoe industry while *The George Parbury* was named after the Lord Mayor. When the two individual donors chose the names to be applied to their aircraft one became *The Harry Livingston* and the other *Brenda* the name of David Burrows' dearly loved wife.

Many city industries organised their own collections. Some had passed the results on to the main fund while others were able to reach the £5,000 goal and name their own aircraft. The first of these were the companies which formed the Ernest Lille Group comprising of Faire Brothers, Steels and Busks and John Traverners. Their Spitfire bore the title *St George*; this was Faire Brothers trade mark and a more patriotic name would have been hard to find. It was the first Spitfire to come off the Supermarine production line at Woolston which became a presentation aircraft. Leicester's hosiery trade raised enough money to enable them to present three Spitfires. These were named *Hosiery Flight Leicester*, *NFHMA - Leicester I* and *NFHMA - Leicester Section*.

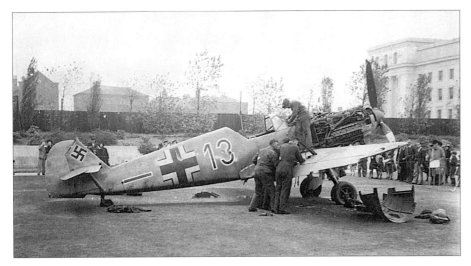

County towns responded magnificently to Lord Beaverbrook's appeal and all had their own funds. Melton Mowbray was spurred into action by the scholars of Ashby Road Primary School who started to collect aluminium pots and pans to 'build Spitfires to beat Hitler'. This in turn encouraged the *Melton Times* to start the Melton Mowbray and District Spitfire Fund. A Junkers Ju 88 bomber was erected at the Kings Head Garage, admission to view was one shilling (5p) for adults, sixpence (2½p) for children and, for those wanting a really close look, five shillings (25p). Over 10,000 people paid to see this attraction and many more bought miniature Spitfires on sale in local shops. Their aircraft, when presented bore the towns coat of arms in addition to the title *Melton Mowbray and District*.

The Hinckley Urban District Council fund got off to a flying start. Within 24 hours the Hinckley Hosiery Manufacturers Association had raised £5,000 and George Ward JP, a Barwell boot and shoe manufacturer donated a similar sum. In all the district raised enough to cover the cost of four Spitfires which were named *Barwell, Burbage, Earl Shilton* and *Hinckley - HHMA*.

Another was donated by a farmer, W H Herbert of Whetstone Pastures; he named the aircraft *The Pastures* after his home.

In Loughborough the Mayor G H Dean organised Loughborough's Fighter Fund and when the necessary sum was raised it was stipulated that it was to be a Hawker Hurricane which bore the name *Loughborough*. Directors of Herbert Morris Cranes in the same town are also believed to have

provided funds for the purchase of three aircraft, the Spitfire Mk.V AA964 *Dirty Girty of Vancouver* and two Fairey Swordfish naval torpedo aircraft, which were named *Wendy Leigh of Hungerton* and *Tangerine of Loughborough*. The serial numbers of these two Swordfish aircraft are not yet known and it is the subject of ongoing research.

There were many local Spitfire Funds in Leicestershire and Rutland which did not reach their target and so were unable to claim a Spitfire, but their efforts were not in vain as over £100,000 was raised in less than six months. This, when added to the massive total raised by the funds nationally, enabled aircraft to be supplied which helped the RAF to turn the tide and eventually take the war to the enemy on an ever increasing scale.

(A brief service history of each of the Leicestershire presentation aircraft can be found on pages 23 to 25.)

Presentation Aircraft

Barwell

Spitfire Mk.Vb W3173   *3.5.41 to 9.12.44*

This Spitfire served with 609 Squadron at Biggin Hill, Gravesend, both Kent, and Duxford, Cambridgeshire, during 1941-42. While with this unit F/O 'Skip' Ogilvie DFC and P/O 'Strope' Seghers each claimed a Messerschmitt Bf 109 and Sub Lt Maurice Choron a 'probable'.

There followed periods with the Air Fighting Development Unit and then to 129 Squadron before being passed to 53 Operational Training Unit at Kirton in Lindsey, Lincolnshire, in 1944. On 27th September when being flown by Lt de Keruerequin, a Free French pilot under training, W3173 crashed immediately after take-off. The pilot suffered serious injuries and the aircraft was damaged beyond repair and written off.

Brenda

Spitfire Mk.Va R7230   *26.3.41 to 14.1.42*

While flying with 611 Squadron at Hornchurch, Essex, R7230 was to destroy one Messerschmitt Bf 109 and damage another. After further service with 602 and 603 Squadrons it was damaged beyond repair in a landing accident while with 81 Squadron at Ouston, Northumberland.

Burbage

Spitfire Mk.Vb X4668   *undated to 27.6.41*

Arrived at 74 Squadron, Gravesend, Kent in May 1941. While flying X4668 P/O Warren Sandeman, a New Zealander, claimed two Messerschmitt Bf 109s destroyed. Others who enjoyed some success in the aircraft were P/O Bob Poulton and a Sergeant York, both of whom were credited with 'probables'.

The end for *Burbage* came on 27th June 1941. Flying on CIRCUS 26, a sweep over occupied France, enemy aircraft were encountered near St Omer. X4668 was shot down and disappeared without trace together with its pilot Squadron Leader John Mungo-Park DFC.

City of Leicester Flight - City of Leicester I

Spitfire Mk.IIa, later Va P8563 26.5.41 to 26.3.42

Flown by 315 (Polish) Squadron from Northolt in the summer of 1941, *Leicester I* flew on many occasions on offensive sweeps. On one patrol

Burbage, Spitfire Vb X4668. The censor has obscured buildings below the nose. Photographs of presentation aircraft were made widely available for publicity purposes and it was vital to make sure that no valuable intelligence 'leaked' from the photographs!

Barwell, Spitfire Vb W3173. There is another Spitfire in the background to the left of the rudder. Close examination of the area above the rear fuselage shows that the censor has clumsily tried to erase another aircraft in the background. Judging by the scribbling, this may well have been a Blackburn Botha twin-engined bomber! Both via Sam Meakin

Crispin of Leicester, Spitfire VB W3242. More censor handiwork, to the left – a Blenheim? via Roy Nixon

while being flown by Sgt Anders Chudek it was instrumental in destroying a Bf 109 and damaging another. After a spell with 308 Squadron it passed to 81 Squadron, Turnhouse, Scotland. On 26th March 1942 a young Canadian, P/O Hal Appel, took off in appalling weather conditions to patrol Seaham Harbour. While flying inland he lost contact with his leader, flew into high ground and was killed.

City of Leicester Flight - City of Leicester II

Spitfire Mk.IIb P8565   *27.5.41 to 21.6.45*

P8565's first unit was 118 Squadron, Ibsley, Hampshire in August 1941 and was soon in action. Within a few days of its arrival and with P/O David Fulford at the controls its guns destroyed a Bf 109 over Cherbourg. Later after moving to Castletown, Caithness, Scotland, it served with 124 and 54 Squadrons. In 1943

P8565 was converted to serve in the air sea rescue role thus changing from Samaritan to Samaritan. It joined 276 (ASR) Squadron, Harrowbeer, Devon, and for 16 months it scoured the English Channel helping locate ditched aircrew. Often this hazardous duty meant flying close to the enemy coastline placing these now obsolete aircraft at the mercy of superior *Luftwaffe* fighters. Many airmen were to owe their lives to these ASR Spitfires. *Leicester II's* final tour of duty was with 5 (Pilot) Advanced Flying Unit, Ternhill, Shropshire where it served in a training role until struck off charge.

City of Leicester Flight - City of Leicester III

Spitfire Mk.IIa P8657   *7.5.41 to 1.4.45*

After short spells with 152 and 130 Squadrons at Portreath, Cornwall, P8657 moved north to join 411 Squadron, Royal Canadian Air Force, at

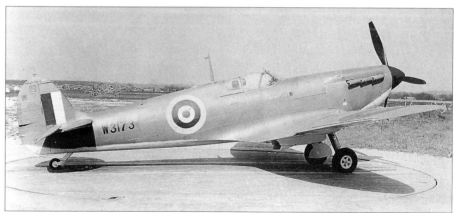

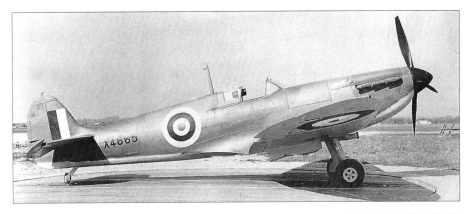

Digby, Lincolnshire. On the move again it was taken on charge by 121 (Eagle) Squadron, the second of these American manned units to form. Many of 121's pilots used *Leicester III* to achieve operational standard.

P8657 moved to Scotland next where it joined 340 Squadron, a Free French unit then stationed at Drem, East Lothian. It was damaged in combat and after repair went on to fly with 58 and 61 OTUs before becoming ground instructional airframe 4431M with 6 Radio School at Bolton, Lancashire.

Crispin of Leicester

Spitfire Mk.Vb W3242   *20.5.41 to 9.12.41*

Used by 611 Squadron at Hornchurch where W3242 became the personal aircraft of P/O W G G Duncan-Smith. This pilot received many letters and gifts from Leicester people including cakes, Leicester City Football Club scarves and even a proposal of marriage!

While flying *Crispin* he destroyed a Bf 109, claimed one as probable and another two damaged. Promoted to Flight Lieutenant and posted to 603 Squadron he took W3242 with him; this was very unusual. While being flown by another squadron member, P/O Percy Lamb, on a convoy patrol off Harwich on 9th December 1941, it developed engine trouble. Lamb was forced to bale out but was quickly rescued.

Earl Shilton

Spitfire Mk.Va X4665   *5.41 to 14.7.41*

Before being delivered to the RAF X4665 became a film star when it was used by the Crown Film Unit in the making of *Ferry Pilot*. Linking up shots were required and these were

Earl Shilton, *Spitfire Va X4665. This aircraft appeared in the film* Ferry Pilot *in early May 1941. Like many presentation aircraft, it had a short life, being shot down in July 1941.*

Hinckley and District Hosiery Manufacturers' Mk.IIa P7916, Hinckley – HHMA. Its career included three operational units and the same number of OTUs. Both via Sam Meakin

performed by *Earl Shilton* flown by Hugh Bergel of the Air Transport Auxiliary, on 9th May 1941 over the Chiltern Hills.

It was delivered to 603 (City of Edinburgh) Squadron, later in the month. With this unit it was flown many times on shipping patrols and sweeps by P/O Hugh Blackall but it was Sgt A C Hunter who was in the cockpit when it was shot down by Bf109s on 14th July 1941. The sergeant survived to become a Prisoner of War.

While with 603 Squadron, X4665 is believed to have been renamed 'Royal Scot'.

The George Parbury

Spitfire Mk.Vb P8538   *2.6.41 to 26.6.41*

This Spitfire had a short life. While being delivered to 92 Squadron, Biggin Hill, on 26th June, its American ATA pilot, First Officer Willard Estes overshot on landing and collided with a building. Estes was killed and P8538 written off.

The Harry Livingston

Spitfire Mk.Vb P8532   *15.5.41 to 26.6.41*

A short but active life was to be the lot of P8532 after it arrived at Biggin Hill, Kent on 23rd June

1941 to serve with 92 Squadron. Sent into action almost immediately it destroyed a Bf 109 while being flown by Sgt Don Kingaby DFM and Bar. Next day P/O Neville Duke was credited with damaging another. Four days later it was shot down over France; the pilot, Sergeant G W Aston was reported missing.

Hinckley - HHMA

Spitfire Mk.IIa P7916   *23.1.41 to 26.1.45*

First delivered to 145 Squadron at Tangmere, Sussex in 1941, it flew with this unit for several months before being transferred to 485 (New Zealand) Squadron at Leconfield, Yorkshire. Later in the year it moved to 130 Squadron, Portreath, Cornwall, with whom it did many sweeps over France. It was then transferred to Eglinton, Northern Ireland, and used by the American 133 (Eagle) Squadron as it worked up to operational standard. No.134 Squadron then arrived and they too used P7916 for training.

By now this Spitfire had been superseded by more updated models and it was passed on for training purposes with Operational Training Units. In turn it served with three of these 52, 57 and 58. After a further stint with the Fighter Leaders School it was finally struck off charge on 26th January 1945 bringing to an end a very useful career.

Hosiery Flight Leicester

Spitfire Mk.Vb W3314   *7.6.41 to 22.7.44*

This Spitfire's first unit was 92 Squadron, Biggin Hill, Kent, with whom it flew on many sweeps over enemy territory. Over the next three years it served with 131, 243, 65, 130, and 349 Squadrons. Its final unit was 26 Squadron and here it met with a tragic end. On 22nd July 1944 while being flown by F/Lt Harold Adams it was involved in a mid-air collision with two other Spitfires from the same unit. All three pilots were killed and W3314 crashed at Old Alresford, Hampshire.

Melton Mowbray & District

Spitfire Mk.IIb P8522   *8.5.41 to 26.1.45*

P8522 first served with 303 (Polish) Squadron, Northolt, Middlesex, and in the hands of one of their pilots, F/O Wojciech Kolaczkowski, it is credited with destroying two Bf 109s one in the air over France, the other on the ground. By September 1941 improved Spitfire variants had become available and it was passed on to be used in turn by 65, 616 and 611 Squadrons as a training aircraft. After a spell with 1 Coastal Artillery Co-operation Unit it went on to train more pilots at 61 OTU until it was eventually struck off charge on 26th January 1945.

NFHMA-Leicester I

Spitfire Mk.Vb AD303   *1.10.41 to 8.11.41*

Delivered to 316 (Polish) Squadron at Church Stanton/Culmhead, Somerset in October 1941 AD303 was flown on many occasions by S/Ldr Waclaw Wilczewski. On 8th November 1941 he took off on CIRCUS 110, a bomber escort mission to Lille. During this sortie the aircraft was hit by flak, the pilot sustaining head and leg injuries. Forced to bale out he became a Prisoner of War and spent many months in hospital recovering from his wounds.

NFHMA - Leicester Section

Spitfire Mk.Vb AD357 *undated to 4.45*

After flying with 412 Squadron, Royal Canadian Air Force at Digby and Wellingore, Lincolnshire, it went on to join the American 309th Fighter Squadron at Westhampnett, Sussex. While with this unit one of its exploits was to take part in the famous Dieppe Raid.

In 1943 it was converted into a Seafire Mk.Ib PA112 and as such it was flown by 759, 790 and 748 Squadrons of the Fleet Air Arm. In April 1945, while being flown by Sub Lt G R Todd, it was damaged beyond repair in an incident at Dale, Pembrokeshire.

Loughborough

Hurricane Mk.IIb Z2815 *29.1.41 to 7.3.42*

Apart from being the only Hurricane, it was the only Leicestershire presentation aircraft to be sent abroad. Z2815 arrived in Malta at the height of the siege of that island in 1941. All aircraft were at a premium and so desperate was the situation that the aircraft had to be shared by 185 and 605 Squadrons at Hal Far. On many occasions only six Hurricanes were available to counter superior odds. On 29th December 1941 Squadron Leader S A D Pike in Z2815 was able to lead nine aircraft to intercept 15 plus Bf 109s and in the ensuing combat he damaged three of their number. *Loughborough's* fighting days came to an end on 7th March 1942 when it was finally struck off charge.

The Pastures

Spitfire Mk.Va R7295 *8.4.41 to 16.6.41*

Delivered to 54 Squadron at Hornchurch in May 1941 this aircraft was on patrol on 16th June when it was attacked and shot down. The pilot, F/O George Grant-Govan, baled out and was later rescued by a passing naval launch.

St George

Spitfire Mk.Ia X4592 *1.10.40 to 18.4.41*

After flying with 41 Squadron at Hornchurch during the Battle of Britain X4592 passed to 611 Squadron and on 25th February 1941 was lost escorting bombers to Dunkirk. Pilot Officer Donald Stanley was the first member of the RAF to lose his life in a Leicester-donated aircraft.

Spitfire Va R7295 The Pastures *had an operational life of less than two months. In the original print, biplanes (DH Hornet Moths?) can be seen above the tail section and under the propeller spinner. The censor has also been busy under the nose, obscuring another aircraft. via Roy Nixon*

Groundcrew working on City of Leicester Flight – City of Leicester II, Spitfire IIb P8565 at Castle Bromwich, May 1941. Roy Nixon via Dr Hugh Thomas

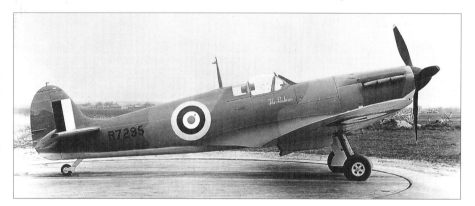

The Spitfire 'Industry'

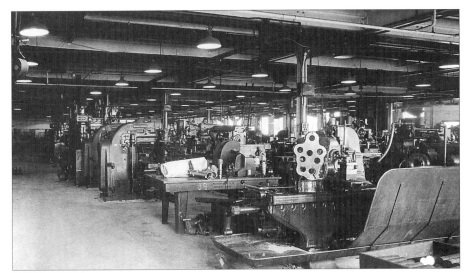

The Spitfire oleo undercarriage shop at No.10 Factory, Cascelloid Ltd, in Owen Street, Coalville.

Capstan lathes churning out Spitfire parts at No.11 Factory, H Flude & Co, Rugby Street, Hinckley.

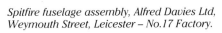

Spitfire fuselage assembly, Alfred Davies Ltd, Weymouth Street, Leicester – No.17 Factory.

The famous elliptical shape of the Spitfire wing in the wing structure assembly shop of No.21 Factory, The Old Skating Rink, Western Boulevard, Leicester.

The hardchrome desposition plant, working on undercarriage components, at A S Yates Ltd, Blackbird Road, Leicester. This was No.23 Factory in the production dispersal scheme.

No.34 Factory, at Searles Elastic Web Manufacturers, Whitwick, making undercarriage oleos. All R R Leader

The War Effort

Throughout the war there were to be many instances of sporadic attacks by enemy aircraft within the two counties. Leicester was to face its greatest ordeal early in the conflict. The city was to experience bombing attacks by the *Luftwaffe* on eight occasions between 21st August 1940 and 13th July 1941. These raids varied greatly in scale and intensity with the worst attacks occurring during November 1940 when Leicester experienced its own Blitz.

The most serious of these series of raids took place on the night of 19th/20th November. It started shortly after 7.30pm when flares began to light the sky over the city and very soon afterwards incendiary bombs were reported to have fallen in many districts. Within the short space of time bombs and parachute land mines were adding to the destruction and chaos. Between 9.30 pm and 10.45pm the raid reached its peak. It was then that the worst single incident of the night occurred. Heavy bombs which exploded in the densely populated Highfield Street and Titchborne Street area killed 41 people with many more injured.

By the time the 'All Clear' sounded just after 4am many areas of the city had suffered appalling damage. Raging fires had destroyed several factories but it was the residential areas which suffered most. When the cost was counted it was found

that 108 people had lost their lives, another 203 were injured while over 5000 homes and factories had received varying degrees of damage. That this was Leicester's worst night of the war is beyond doubt when the overall casualty figures for the eight raids totalled 122 killed and 284 injured.

In 1940 Leicester was not alone in its suffering, far greater loss of life and damage occurred in other Midland cities such as Birmingham and Coventry. It was attacks on these heavily industrialised centres which were to have a direct bearing on certain aspects of Leicestershire's war effort.

To help meet an ever increasing demand for aircraft, a number of civilian firms, some with long established interest in the aviation industry, became associated with several county airfields. As a direct result of the output from these firms thousands of new and repaired aircraft were made available for service. A brief outline of this activity is given in table form on page 30.

Many of the components to serve these assembly lines and repair shops were fabricated within the county. In size they ranged from complete airframes and major subassemblies to small detailed fittings and such were the demands of wartime that many of the firms and factories impressed into this vital work had no previous experience in the manufacture of aircraft parts.

One notable type of aircraft for which major sub-assemblies were made within

the city was the Avro Lancaster bomber. Ailerons, fuselage sections and wing outer trailing edges were built at the Leicester Corporation Bus and Tram Depot on Abbey Park Road, while centre fuselage and nose sections together with outer wings were fabricated in Briton Road at the Leicester Bus Garage. Freeman, Hardy & Willis were responsible for the manufacture of fuselage floor assemblies and main instrument panels, while many components both large and small were finished in machine shops which operated in works on St Saviours Road where D Henderson & Sons had once made shoes.

Perhaps the best illustration is the important contribution which Leicestershire made to the manufacture of Supermarine Spitfires. At Castle Bromwich in Warwickshire just prior to the war, a huge factory was built and it was here that a large proportion of Spitfire production was eventually concentrated. Following enemy air attacks in August 1940 it was realised just how vulnerable these works could be, so moves

During Leicester's 'Wings for Victory' week in 1944, No.10 (Coalville) and No.34 (Whitwick) plants created a splendid float for fund raising. While neither factory made Spitfire wings, this creation generated an impressive image, even though it was probably 'borrowed' from No.21 Factory in Leicester. R R Leader

Extreme nose sections and tailplanes for Avro Lancasters under construction at the Leicester Bus Garage, Briton Road.
via Midland Air Museum

were made to disperse certain specialised machinery and manufactory processes. In the Midlands, away from the heavily industrialised centres, there existed large numbers of buildings which were either empty or housed businesses whose products were not considered essential to the war effort. It was to these that the management of Castle Bromwich turned. Many of these premises were inspected and, if thought suitable, requisitioned to be absorbed into the complex production scheme.

A number of properties situated in Leicester and certain areas of the county were found to be acceptable and, within a short space of time, taken over. These works eventually contributed many different parts towards the finished aircraft, but, two areas of production are outstanding. The first of these was in the manufacture of undercarriage units.

From the autumn of 1940 production of this indispensable component began to be concentrated within Leicestershire. In the south of the county machine shops for auto and capstan lathe operations were set up at Hinckley in parts of the hosiery works belonging to H Flude & Co Ltd, on Rugby

Road, these then became No.11 and 11a Factories. A short distance away, on the edge of the town, No.12 Factory, a specialised tool room, was established at Payne's Garage on the Watling Street. A few miles to the north, in the town of Coalville the premises of Cascelloid Ltd, a firm famous in pre-war days for the manufacture of celluloid dolls, became No.10 Factory, where in addition to certain machining operations, final assembly and testing of the finished product took place. Nearby in Whitwick the elastic web works of Searles Ltd was added as another machine shop, designated No. 34 Factory. Several of the finished parts required to be heavily chrome plated, so a special plant was established solely for this purpose at the Omega Works of A S Yates, Hosiery Manufacturers on Blackbird Road, Leicester: this became No.22 Factory.

Despite the many problems which arose from the transfer of production, completed units were soon leaving the Coalville works. As is only to be expected, output at first was small but this situation did not prevail for long. Although peaks and troughs constantly occurred on the monthly production graph, average figures between September 1940 and 1945 always showed an upward trend. The yearly totals for pairs of main undercarriage legs produced from 1940 to 1944 show the rate at which this was achieved:

1940	1941	1942	1943	1944
450	2,055	3,326	5,408	9,040

In addition to the main units, tail wheel oleos were also manufactured in the Leicestershire group of factories. Although comprehensive figures relating to the output of this component are not available it is known that over 4,580 were completed in 1944 alone.

From April 1945, the month which saw the highest overall output, a staggering total of 1240 pairs, production began to decline rapidly until it was finally run down in December of that year. By then the grand total of pairs of main undercarriage units manufactured in Leicestershire stood at 28,567, a quantity sufficient to have equipped every Spitfire and Seafire built and still have left 5,808 pairs of spares.

Airframe sections were the other major parts of the Spitfire with which the county had an association. Fuselages and wings were the principal sections to be fabricated in quantity and production of these was concentrated at two main centres, both located within the city. An old skating rink on Western Boulevard was impressed into service as No.21 Factory where jigs for the assembly of wing sections were installed. Some distance away in Weymouth Street, fuselages were built at No.17 Factory, formerly the premises where A D Davies Ltd, had manufactured cardboard boxes. Production from these two factories continued until late in 1945 and although the total output from either is not known, figures exist

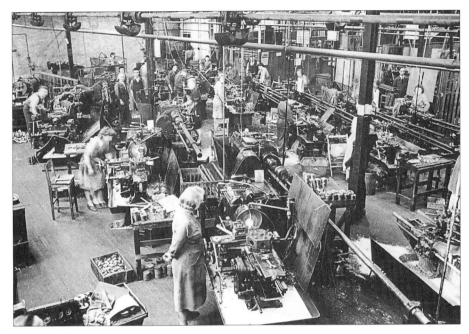

which show that between January 1942 and December 1944 1,223 pairs of wings and 1,167 fuselages were constructed.

Many of these locally-built component parts were fed directly to an assembly line installed in hangars, which had been built just prior to the war, on the south side of the airfield at Desford. Although not primarily intended to serve in this capacity, when dispersal became necessary, these buildings were made available. This was known as No.8 Factory and from late 1940 completed aircraft began to leave these works and continued to do so until September 1945. Again it has proven difficult to arrive at an accurate figure but it is believed that a total well in excess of 1,000 new Spitfires were assembled and flown from Desford.

As the war progressed and the prospect of the Allied invasion of Europe drew nearer several airfields within the two counties became host to American units of the United States Army Air Force IXth Troop Carrier Command. This force was responsible for the delivery of airborne troops, gliders and supplies, eventually carrying out this duty in all major airborne assaults on 'Festung Europa'. Bases housing elements of this force were Cottesmore, Saltby and, for a brief period, Bottesford. Much of their training for these tasks was carried out over the counties, glider towing and paratroop dropping being a daily sight. Leicester East was another station engaged on similar duties, albeit with RAF units in residence.

In the final stages of the war several airfields changed their roles yet again. Some became part of RAF Transport Command where their duties now consisted of converting many former bomber crew members to the more mundane, but safer, task of operating transport aircraft. Bases thus engaged were Castle Donington, Bitteswell, Leicester East, Nuneaton and Wymeswold. Other stations were committed to teaching crews the intricacies of flying multi-engined bombers and Heavy Conversion Units occupied all three of Rutland's airfields, together with Bottesford and Saltby.

Out of all Leicestershire's RAF stations Melton Mowbray was unique in its function. Throughout its active life it was the home of units which prepared aircraft and trained crews in readiness to make the long and often arduous delivery flights to overseas commands.

Leicestershire's Major Aircraft Plants

Airfield	Company	Type	Process
Bitteswell	Armstrong Whitworth	Lancaster	Assembly line
Desford	Reid & Sigrist	Defiant	Repair and modification
		Mitchell	Repair and modification
Desford	Vickers-Armstrong	Spitfire	Assembly line
Loughborough	Airwork	Boston	Repair and modification
		Havoc	Repair and modification
Loughborough	Brush	Dominie	Final assembly
Rearsby	Taylorcraft	Auster	Manufacture
		Hurricane	Repair and modification
		Tiger Moth	Repair and modification
		Typhoon	Repair and modification

Top: *D Henderson & Sons, another Leicester shoe manufacturer, turned its hand to producing Lancaster components.*

Centre: *Lancaster floor assemblies underway at Freeman Hardy & Willis, Leicester.*
Both via the Midland Air Museum

The Jet Age

During the closing months of the war an intriguing sound was often to be heard in the vicinity of RAF Bruntingthorpe. It was the noise created by the then new, and still very secret, turbojet engines which were being flight tested from that airfield by Power Jets (Research & Development) Ltd. The link between the county and this revolutionary type of aero engine was forged at a much earlier date, in 1938. For several years from this date a great deal of the pioneering work carried out by Frank Whittle (later Sir Frank) in connection with this method of propulsion was centred in the south Leicestershire town of Lutterworth.

Early combustion experiments began in October 1936 at the British Thomson-Houston (BT-H) works in Rugby. From a safety aspect some of these tests were often quite frightening and before long it was considered advisable for Power Jets Limited, Whittle's company, to find alternative accommodation. This did not prove too difficult to arrange as BT-H possessed a disused foundry, the Ladywood Works, in Leicester Road, Lutterworth. Part of these were made available for rent.

Whittle, and his one full-time employee, started to prepare a section of the Ladywood Works in early 1938. For some time their activities were viewed with some suspicion by the local police who thought it possible that they had IRA connections. In the interim the experimental engine was rebuilt in its second form by BT-H and testing began at Lutterworth in April. Some progress was made but on 6th May following a turbine failure the engine was almost totally destroyed.

To Power Jets this was a severe setback as insufficient finance was a continual handicap. But, a new Air Ministry contract was obtained which covered most of the cost of engine reconstruction and a further period of experimental running. With the engine in its third form tests resumed on 26th October.

By December the number of company employees had risen to five with the addition of a secretary, an office boy and two night watchmen. As far as other labour was concerned, Power Jets were fortunate in that they were able to borrow fitters and other skilled workmen from BT-H. Conditions at Ladywood Works were still very spartan and could hardly have impressed visitors. In the offices were bare wooden floors, white-washed unplastered walls and a minimum of furniture, mostly bought second hand in Lutterworth.

The third Whittle turbojet on the test bench at the Ladywood Works, Lutterworth.
Author's collection

Progress in the early months of 1939 was very slow. In spite of this though increased interest began to be shown from several quarters. Evidence of this was borne out in July when Power Jets received a contract for a flight engine, the W.1. Also, there were signs that the financial situation would be a little easier after several of the firms backing the company increased their investment.

The outbreak of war in September 1939 brought no immediate sense of urgency to the research programme. Before the end of the year the Air Ministry did sanction the installation of some additional test equipment at the Ladywood Works and two further contracts were received. One covered spares for the experimental engine and the W.1, while the other, by far the more important, was for a more powerful engine - the W.2. In addition a few more staff were engaged and this enabled a drawing office and a small workshop to be started. By the end of January 1940 the total strength of the company was still no more than 25 and this included three directors.

Late in January the experimental engine was demonstrated on separate occasions for the benefit of two important visitors, Sir Henry Tizard, chairman of the Aeronautical Research Committee and Air Vice Marshal Tedder, then Director General of Research and Development. Both went away very impressed with what they had seen.

Although a considerable amount of time was being expended in solving combustion problems other factors played their part in hindering progress. Two main bearing failures caused considerable delays. Foundry sand is believed to have been the culprit. Fine particles of this abrasive medium could often be seen falling from cracks in the ceiling of the test house during engine runs. However, design of the W.1 was well advanced and that of the W.2 was in its early stages.

As staff continued to increase, the limited space at the Ladywood Works began to be filled to overflowing. Working conditions became quite impossible; at times, engineers sat and worked on stairs leading to the offices. To help alleviate the situation a railway coach was hired to serve as a temporary office and rooms were rented in Brownsover Hall, near Rugby for Whittle and the design staff. These measures provided only limited relief so more temporary wooden huts were erected and, at last, two test houses built. Space was still at a premium and Power Jets tried to obtain permission to use the whole of the Ladywood Works. This proved to be quite a battle as BT-H wished to disperse magneto production and for this reason wanted the whole of the premises. Eventually a compromise was reached whereby they shared the works almost equally.

By the end of the year there was at last a second engine at Lutterworth, after the W.1X was delivered from BT-H on 11th December. This was a composite engine which had been built from components rejected for the W.1 and others originally intended for the experimental engine. Its arrival was fortuitous for on 22nd February 1941 the long career of the experimental engine ended when it was damaged beyond repair.

A great deal of valuable work was accomplished with the W.1X and by the end of March over 40 hours running had been completed. The W.1 had arrived from BT-H in February but it was decided to work extensively with the W.1X in order to eliminate snags in this way.

At the beginning of April 1941 the first Gloster-Whittle E28/39, W4041, the aircraft built to air test the W.1 was complete. As this engine had not yet run it was decided to use the W.1X for taxi trials. These took place at Hucclecote, Gloucestershire, on 7th-8th April and on the second date the test pilot P E G Sayer accomplished three short hops of some 200 to 300 yards with an engine not intended for flight. Following the trials the W.1X was removed from the airframe and returned to Lutterworth to continue experimental bench running.

The W.1 ran for the first time three days after the taxi trials. Test running went without a hitch and by early May the engine had been sent to Gloster's for installation. The venue chosen for the first flight was Cranwell, Lincolnshire, and after transport there by road the aircraft was ready for ground runs on 14th May. The first flight was scheduled for the 15th but to begin with conditions were very unfavourable. They had, however, improved by evening and shortly after 7.45pm, W4041, with Sayer at the controls, took off from Cranwell's runway. Just seventeen minutes later he landed safely, bringing the maiden flight to a successful conclusion and in so doing made aviation history.

Within the next three months more development engines joined the W.1X at Lutterworth. These were the W.1A, W.2 and W.2 Mk IV. Bench testing continued apace but accidents involving the W.1X and W.2 both caused delays. Damage in both cases was due to foreign bodies passing through the engine and a similar incident was narrowly averted with the W.1A. Although an inquiry proved nothing conclusive, sabotage was not ruled out. Another type of engine to be put on test during the latter half of the year was the Rover-Whittle W.2B. Production of this engine was eventually taken over from the Rover Motor Company by Rolls-Royce Ltd, and developed into the Welland and Derwent turbojets which powered most of the Gloster Meteor series of aircraft.

Insufficient working space and the unsuitable conditions at the Ladywood Works were still a serious handicap. From early in 1941 representations had been made to see if an alternative site could be found. The company preferred a new purpose-built factory and in October plans were approved by the Directorate of Aircraft Production for a new works to be built at Whetstone, near Leicester. Building work on these new premises was so rapid that by May 1942 parts of the works were in use.

During 1943 the factory was completed and gradually development work was transferred from Lutterworth. The Ladywood Works however still had a part to play for in 1944 the company established there the first School of Gas Turbine Technology.

In April 1944 Power Jets Ltd was nationalised, a course of action which had been advocated in certain quarters for some time. From that date it became clear that the firm would not compete with established engine manufacturers in large scale production. In the future its primary function would be as suggested by the new title – Power Jets (Research & Development) Limited. The company continued to contribute in many ways to the progress of jet engine science and was eventually responsible for a considerable number of valuable technical advances.

From July 1946 the Whetstone works, the school at Lutterworth and flight testing, by then carried out at Bitteswell, all became part of the National Gas Turbine Establishment. As such they continued their work until by the early 1950s all three had left Leicestershire to become established at Pyestock, Hampshire.

The much-developed Power Jets site at Whetstone, now owned by Alsthom Automation. The original Power Jets site is marked. Author

WAAFs of No.14 Operational Training Unit marching past the saluting officer at the Victory Parade in Market Harborough, May 1945. via F B Aggas

Post-War

Following the Allied victory over the Axis powers in 1945 the airfield situation within the two counties altered almost overnight. Bases which were no longer needed were soon closed for flying. In just over a year from the date of Japan's surrender the number of active military airfields had been reduced to four. Many of the inoperative stations were retained for a time on a care and maintenance basis. On some, runways and hangars were utilised as storage areas for vast quantities of redundant equipment. At others the living sites became staging posts for service personnel prior to their demobilisation, while on several the hutted accommodation provided temporary homes for refugees and displaced persons awaiting resettlement or repatriation.

Gradually the people and the impedimenta of war were dispersed; in time the disused airfields were de-requisitioned and sold. On-site auctions disposed of the materials and temporary buildings which still remained, while structures of a more permanent nature were usually either demolished or gutted and the shell left to decay.

In post-war years service aviation in Leicestershire has been confined to very few airfields. For a short time volunteer units of the RAF continued to operate at Desford and Wymeswold but eventually cuts in defence spending led to them being disbanded. After a long period of inactivity Bruntingthorpe was extensively rebuilt in 1954-55 to become a United States Air Force Base. The USAF remained in residence until 1962, then once more this airfield was closed and lapsed into disuse.

Only in Rutland has military aviation continued, almost without interruption, since the end of the Second World War. Of the county's three airfields, Woolfox Lodge has the shortest post-war history. After many years of inaction it was reactivated and between 1960-1963 it became the base for a squadron of Bristol Bloodhound surface-to-air missiles.

North Luffenham has enjoyed a long and eventful life. For many years units of both the Royal and Royal Canadian Air Forces were resident. Then, for a time, it became a base for part of Britain's strategic missile force. Although inactive in the sense that aircraft are no longer based there, the station still played an essential part of the RAF as the home of several ground training centres. It closed as an RAF base in 1998 and was handed over to the Army, although the vital work of bomb disposal training will continue for the foreseeable future.

The last of Rutland's trio, Cottesmore, has from its opening in 1938 been in almost constant use and only for short periods has the station been reduced to inactive status. For many years, aircrew from Germany, Italy and Great Britain were trained to fly the Panavia Tornado, an aircraft that equips the strike forces of the air arms of the three nations, and together form a key element in the North Atlantic Treaty Organisation. This role changed in the spring of 1999 when the base took on a new focus as home of two RAF Harrier squadrons that were previously based in Germany. In July 2000 they were joined by No.1 Squadron from RAF Wittering. From 2003 there are plans for further aircraft to move into Cottesmore when Royal Navy Sea Harriers are due to arrive from Yeovilton, Somerset, in order to establish, along with RAF and RN Harrier training units at RAF Wittering, a true multi-force unit under the 'Joint Force Harrier' banner.

In 1946 the wartime restrictions which had been placed on light aviation were lifted and club and private flying became popular once more. Interest in these pastimes was revived in the early years after the war, activity being centred on the aerodromes at Desford, Loughborough and Ratcliffe. All enjoyed mixed success but at none of these venues was light aviation destined to continue for any great length of time.

In the field of light aviation in Leicestershire it was Rearsby which predominated for many years post-war. Although some club flying took place from this airfield emphasis was on the manufacture of aircraft for both civil and military markets. After Taylorcraft (England) Ltd had suffered several periods of fluctuating fortunes and experienced sundry changes of title, economic pressures finally forced Beagle Aircraft, as the company had then become, into liquidation. This resulted in the closure of the aircraft works in March 1970 and the eventual sale of the airfield.

Bitteswell was another airfield which also enjoyed a long association with the aircraft industry but here the manufacture and repair of military aircraft predominated and once again a changing pattern of requirements led to its closure in 1982.

Although the preceding paragraphs present a rather dismal picture of post-war aviation in Leicestershire, civil aviation still retains a firm foothold. At the present time two airfields are very active. One of these is Leicester East, where Leicestershire Aero Club have now become firmly established

Air displays and air events have always featured heavily in the two counties. A selection of programmes, outer circle from the top, clockwise: Wymeswold 1955; ATA Benevolent Fund Air Display, Ratcliffe, 1945; 6th International Challenge, Leicestershire Aero Club, 1982; Auster Flying Club, Rearsby, Coronation Year Display, 1953; Leicestershire Aero Club International Air Display, 1982; Leicestershire Aero Club Air Display, Ratcliffe, 1949; Battle of Britain 40th Anniversary Air Display, Leicester, 1980; Auster Flying Club, Rearsby, 1948; British Aerospace, Bitteswell, Family Day, 1980; Leicester Gliding Club Air Meeting, Rearsby, 1945. Inner, left to right: Leicestershire Aero Club International Air Festival, 1951; RAF Cottesmore Air Display, 1972; Leicestershire Aero Club Air Display, 1975. Author

and thrives. The other is the former RAF base at Castle Donington. Over the last 20 years this once derelict airfield has undergone a dramatic transformation to become the busy and expanding East Midlands Airport of today. The sport of gliding is also catered for within the county; Saltby and Husbands Bosworth are currently used by Buckminster and Coventry Gliding Clubs respectively. In addition a small amount of air activity still takes place on occasion at Bruntingthorpe, where a thriving aviation museum has been established.

Today, the number of active aviation sites in the two counties almost corresponds to that of roughly 60 years earlier. In some respects it can be said that the wheel has turned full circle, for hot air balloon ascents now prove popular attractions at fetes and galas while the sports of hang gliding and flying microlights have their devotees.

Of the former airfields, many have reverted to agriculture, others have been put to diverse purposes. One is now a maximum security prison, another a motor vehicle research establishment, several are now large industrial estates, while the hangars on others are used for the storage of various commodities and at least one has been used as a centre for police training. It is extremely doubtful if any of these once busy airfields will ever come to life again.

Despite the ravages of time, the old airfield sites remain and some are still easily recognisable for what they once were. With others it proves more difficult but most retain some tangible link with their past, be it derelict buildings, decaying runways or maybe an old hangar now used as a factory.

It is interesting to reflect that whether seen as a windswept waste in winter, a vast cereal crop in summer or as the present day home of a modern industry, the airfields of the two counties made a lasting contribution to British aviation history.

Leicestershire Aero Club's International Air Displays always attracted rare and exciting overseas performers. Lockheed F-104G Starfighter 26+60 of the West German Bundesmarine, trailing vortices from its wingtips during a slow fly-by. Alan Curry

A view from the control tower at Leicester East as the 'Red Arrows' perform at the International Air Display.
Leicester Aero Club via Ken Ellis

Chapter Two

Bitteswell

WHEN AN airfield is built, in the majority of cases it is the farming community which suffers the most when large tracts of agricultural land are taken over and absorbed into the enterprise. In this respect, Bitteswell was no exception. Most of the area encompassed by the airfield was originally farmed by the Stanhope family and the first intimation of its possible use for another purpose came with the arrival during 1938 of the survey party from the Ministry of Public Buildings and Works. A favourable report must have been the outcome of their visit for in due course the land was requisitioned by the Air Ministry.

Construction of a grass airfield on the site began in March 1940 and by the June of the following year work was considered sufficiently advanced to begin the opening up

procedure. The station, by then part of 93 Group, Royal Air Force Bomber Command, was intended to serve as a satellite of 18 (Polish) Operational Training Unit (OTU), based at RAF Bramcote, an airfield in the extreme north-east of Warwickshire. Two officers and 105 men, with Flight Lieutenant L G Blomfield in command, left Bramcote on 3rd June under orders to clear the landing ground at Bitteswell and set up station defence prior to flying commencing.

Judging by contemporary records when they arrived the new airfield must have been in a rather rough state, accommodation and other facilities being very rudimentary. Neither mains water nor electricity were as yet laid on and very few buildings had been finished so, for the time being, personnel were in the main housed under

An impressive assembly of Armstrong Siddeley test aircraft arranged on their 'Old Site' apron, photographed late 1953 or early 1954.
At the rear: Lancastrian C.2 VM733, Sapphire turbojet test-bed. Middle row: English Electric Canberra B.2, WV787, Sapphire test-bed; Blackburn YB-1, WB797, testing the Double Mamba turboprop. Front row: Sapphire test-bed Meteor F.8, WA820; Double Mamba-powered Fairey Gannet, VR557 (2nd prototype); Westland Wyvern S.4, VZ747 testing the Python turboprop. Rolls-Royce, via Dave Sargent

canvas. For the next two months activity by both civilian contractors and the RAF centred on making the airfield operable and improving conditions generally.

By the end of July considerable advances had been made in all directions. Much of the perimeter road and several dispersal

Personnel of 105 Operational Training Unit ceremoniously arranged in front of one of the unit's Wellington Xs, Spring 1945. E Walker

A CG-4 assault glider at Bitteswell on 12th September 1944, having landed during a training flight. With many airfields in the area involved in readying the airborne forces, this was a common occurrence. Maurice Marsh

points had been finished, the runways and many essential buildings had been, or were on the verge of completion. How much progress had been made can be judged by the fact that on 12th August night flying training was able to commence and six days later the airfield housed resident aircraft when 'D' Flight, 18 OTU, was formed, equipped with six Vickers Wellingtons.

August and September were months of consolidation both on the airfield and domestic sites in preparation for the approach of winter. Mains water and electricity were at last provided for the station, technical and administration buildings were sited and well underway. The watch office was completed and in operation, also the Officers Mess was occupied. But in all probability, the two events most appreciated by the 'Erks' were the opening of the cookhouse and being able to vacate their tented accommodation for the luxury of more permanent hutments. September proved memorable in other ways also.

Villagers of Ullesthorpe, to the north, and Bitteswell itself suffered the annoyance and inconvenience of seeing their link with the main A5 to the west severed when the road which ran across the airfield was finally blocked off with Dannert wire barriers. It was never to be re-opened and was eventually replaced by the new section of road which skirts the north western edge of the airfield. Although most of the old road disappeared during further development work two short stretches were allowed to remain to be incorporated into the road system within the site.

September closed on a very sombre note when the only fatal accident recorded by 18 OTU at Bitteswell occurred. On the night of the 29th, Wellington IC R3216 crashed during night flying practice, killing seven of the eight man crew. First to reach the scene was a duty MT driver, S W J Green, who at considerable risk managed to extricate the rear gunner from the blazing wreck. For his heroism in rescuing this sole survivor he was later awarded the George Medal.

As Bitteswell at this time served as a satellite of the Polish OTU it was logical that a large proportion of the air and ground crews associated with the station should originate from Poland. This situation was even more pronounced from early in October when the crews of 'D' Flight aircraft became composed entirely of personnel of Polish origin. Indeed, while the airfield was attached to 18 OTU the influx of airmen of that nationality increased to such a degree on occasion that even now it is sometimes referred to locally as the time of the 'Polish invasion'.

Although great efforts had been made to prepare for winter it was soon evident that Bitteswell's grass runways were inadequate to cope with the deteriorating weather and constant use. Within a short space of time the condition of the airfield was reduced to such a state that it became impossible to operate aircraft with safety. On 18th December 'D' Flight was disbanded; early in 1942 the six Wellingtons were transferred to Moreton-in-Marsh, Gloucestershire, and the airfield was notified as unserviceable.

Over a year was to elapse before it opened for business once more, but in the interim important changes had taken place. To prevent recurrence of the problems that winter could cause three concrete runways, complete with connecting perimeter track and hard standings were laid down.

While the major reconstruction work was in hand on the airfield, contractors were also busy developing a site adjacent to the south west corner. In this area a hangar system was erected for the use of Sir W G Armstrong Whitworth Aircraft Ltd (AWA). The main works of this company were then situated at Baginton and Whitley, both close to Coventry, Warwickshire.

Following the heavy bombing raids on Coventry it was considered advisable to scatter parts of some of the vital industries within its environs. As major aircraft manufacturers with contracts to build Avro Lancasters, AWA fell within this category and Bitteswell was chosen as a dispersed site for the final assembly and flight testing of some of the aircraft. Completed Lancasters began to leave the works during the second half of 1943 and continued to be produced until the assembly line was run down late in 1945. (See Chapter Three, *Built at Bitteswell*, for a detailed run down of production.)

Although the airfield was in no fit state to operate aircraft while work was in progress the station was not entirely devoid of RAF activity. Base facilities were still utilised to enable many ground personnel from the Group to be given 'backers up' training in the art of airfield defence so that in the event of an emergency they could be called upon to play a supporting role to the RAF Regiment detachments.

When the airfield re-opened in May 1943 the station was no longer a part of 93 Group having been transferred to 92 Group in February of that year. No change in status resulted from the reshuffle; Bitteswell was still classed as a satellite station used for training crews for Bomber Command. This time though the station was attached to 29 OTU which moved from North Luffenham to Bruntingthorpe late in May 1943.

During the change of station the OTU took the opportunity to initiate the split system of training whereby type conversion was carried out at the satellite and operational training at the parent station. This situation was to be found at several airfields in the two counties.

By 1st June 1943 movement of the unit was complete and the Wellingtons of 'A' and 'B' Flights were installed at Bitteswell. They soon became acclimatised to their new home and within the space of ten days both day and night flying had begun. As they had just left a grass surfaced airfield, pilots spent quite a few of these early flying hours adjusting to take-off and landing on concrete runways.

RAF Bitteswell – 1st December 1944

Latitude	52° 27' 30" N
Longitude	1° 14' 30" W
Height above Sea Level	420ft
Command	Transport (RAF)
Nearest Railway Station	Lutterworth (LNER) 2 miles
Function	OTU (Satellite)
Affiliated Airfields	Bramcote (Parent)

Landing Area – Runways

QDM	Dimensions	Extensibility	Remarks
358°	1,400 x 50 yards	–	Entails
042°	2,000 x 50 yards	2,600 yards	demolition
108°	1,400 x 50 yards	1,550 yards	of house.
Type of Surface		Concrete and wood chips	

Permanent Landmarks

By Day	W/T masts, Rugby, eight miles
By Night	Nil

Permanent Obstructions Masts at Rugby, 6-8 miles SSE, 27 up to 820ft.

Facilities

Airfield Lighting	Mk.II
Flying Control	Yes

Accommodation   All temporary buildings

Technical	Hangars		Hardstandings	
	Type	No	Type	No
	T.2	1	Spectacle	16
	B.1	1	Dispersed	11
Domestic	Officers	SNCOs	ORs	Total
RAF	90	353	732	1,175
WAAF	3	16	84	103

The station's complement of aircraft received a further boost when, after a short stay at Bruntingthorpe, the OTU's Avro Anson Flight flew into Bitteswell on 9th June. At this time these aircraft were on strength mainly to enable bomb aimers to receive tuition in the technique of aerial map reading. Ground defence training also continued to be carried out at the station; 92 Group Defence School being established for this purpose, making full use of the firing range situated in the NW corner of the airfield.

Control of Bitteswell remained in the hands of 29 OTU until the end of October 1944. Flying by the unit ceased on the night of 28th/29th and the station closed as a satellite of Bruntingthorpe one day later.

Within less than a month the airfield was active again, this time as an additional satellite to Bramcote which was by now part of Transport Command and the parent station of 105 OTU. On 22nd November 'B' Flight of this unit moved in from the OTU's other satellite, RAF Nuneaton, located to the north of the town, to be followed three days later by 'D' Flight from the same source. These two flights were responsible for unit conversion training and as they were equipped with Wellingtons little change was noted at Bitteswell, the pattern of operations from the station continuing much as it had under 29 OTU.

As with all RAF stations, occasionally the daily routine was enlivened by incidents which were of a very diverse nature as illustrated by the following examples recorded in the unit Operational Record Book (ORB) during 1945.

'*January 21st* - On this date Corporal W Little observed a man acting in rather a suspicious manner in the vicinity of Wellington Mk.X NC709 of 'D' Flight. He notified his Flight Sergeant who took action by detailing two men to assist Corporal Little in apprehending the individual. Meanwhile the man, realising that he was under observation, walked round to the rear of the aircraft and broke into a run in an attempt to escape. Corporal Little gave chase, caught the man and escorted him to 'D' Flight dispersal hut where he was found to be an escaped *Luftwaffe* pilot, Leutnant Kurt Ibing (No.774188), who had absconded from a Prisoner of War camp near Crewe. He was later handed over to the civilian police at Lutterworth to await return.' One cannot help but reflect on the possible outcome of Ibing's visit to the airfield had it not been for the Corporal's vigilance.

'*February 2nd* - When engaged in a glider towing exercise the tow rope connecting USAAF Douglas C-47 Skytrain to its charge, a WACO Hadrian, parted while they were passing over Bitteswell. The glider landed safely, to be followed almost immediately by its tug which then embarked the glider

Representative Serials of Bitteswell-based units

No.18 Operational Training Unit
From 30.6.41 to 7.2.43.   Code 'LD-'.

Vickers Wellington IC	R3216
Vickers Wellington IV	Z1414

No.29 Operational Training Unit
From 1.6.43 to 1.11.44.   Codes 'NT-' and 'TF-'.

See parent station - Bruntingthorpe, Chapter Six

No.105 Operational Training Unit
From 22.11.44 to 17.7.45.   Code '8F-'.

Vickers Wellington X	HE908, LP679, LP822, NA733, NC665, NC667, NC709, NC713, NC857
Douglas Dakota III	FD940, FL517, FL518. KG731, KG744

crew and within minutes was airborne on the return journey to their base in Saltby. Next day a relief crew was brought in by another C-47 of the 314th TCG to retrieve the Hadrian.'

Tow failure was a fairly common occurrence in the skies over the county during the latter half of 1944 and the early months of 1945, but few of the gliders inadvertently released were fortunate enough to find an airfield almost beneath them to land on. (The WACO CG-4 troop-carrying assault glider was known as the Haig by the Americans, but seems to have been universally called by its RAF name, the Hadrian, when deployed in Europe.)

'*May 11th* - An unusually severe hailstorm passed over the airfield and the stones which fell were so large that considerable damage was caused to many of the aircraft parked in the open. After an assessment of the damage had been made it was found that it included over 40 complete penetrations of wing fabric on 19 different aircraft, necessitating 383 man hours being spent on repairs.' Weather often figures in official station documents mainly when fog or other inclement conditions hamper flying operations, but rarely are incidents such as this recorded.

'*June 23rd* – In the early hours of the morning at 03:37 Wellington X LP822 overshot on landing and crashed on the A5 road that borders a side of the airfield. Although the aircraft was seriously damaged it did not catch fire nor were any casualties sustained. After the accident the pilot stated that the brakes had failed, but these were found to be in perfect condition when inspected later. As a result the incident was classified as an error of judgement on his part.'

On 1st June, following re-organisation, the station became a part of 4 Group, Transport Command, and later in the month 105

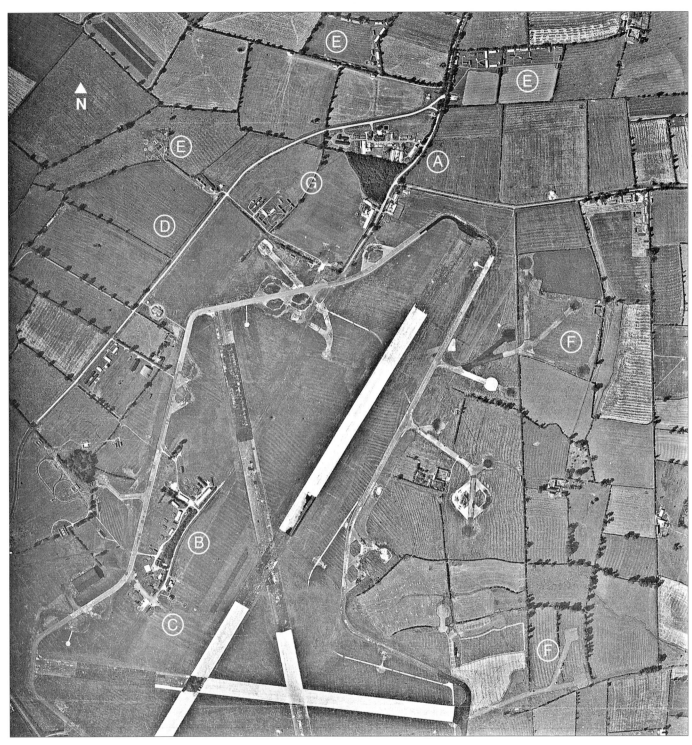

OTU began to re-equip with the Douglas Dakota, conversion training of unit instructors onto this type of aircraft starting at Bitteswell on 8th June. Most instructors had a high regard for their old 'Wimpeys' but the Dakota was welcomed as a replacement. Eric Walker, a former staff pilot explained the difference:

'In June 1945 conversion to Dakota IIIs began. After about four hours flying we were considered fit to carry out instruction, the syllabus remained the same. As for the Dakota that was quite a revelation, there was an automatic pilot which actually worked and also an excellent radio compass for getting you back to base easily. As if this wasn't enough, you could smoke during flight, something quite impossible in a Wellington which always smelt of petrol because the fabric covering was usually soaked in spillage.'

Dakotas operated from Bitteswell for about five weeks, then on 17th July 105 OTU's association with the station came to an end and the three flights departed, leaving only a care and maintenance party to look after the RAF facilities. 'B' and 'D' Flights travelled the relatively short distance back up the A5 to their former home at Nuneaton while 'C' Flight moved much further north to take up residence at Crosby-on-Eden, Cumberland.

For a time Bramcote retained an interest in the airfield as occasional visits were made by Ansons of 1513 Radar Approach Training Flight which was part of that station's complement. As the name implies, the flight undertook the training of instrument and radar-directed approaches in poor visibility or at night. After 266 Maintenance Unit, an equipment disposal depot, was formed at Bramcote in January 1946, some facilities at Bitteswell were used as a sub-site until January 1947.

The RAF eventually relinquished command of Bitteswell and control of the airfield passed into the hands of the Ministry of Supply. Within a short time the former RAF station became one of the main centres in the country for aircraft engaged in jet engine development. Principally involved in this field were the National Gas Turbine Establishment (NGTE), Armstrong Siddeley Motors Limited (ASM), and AWA. The successors of AWA were to have an increasing interest in the site and under their management the airfield and its facilities were destined for many years to be a significant part of the British aircraft manufacturing industry.

First signs of this new role for Bitteswell began to appear in April 1946. Early in the month Power Jets (Research and Development) Limited began to consider the airfield as an alternative base for their trials and communications aircraft. Power Jets was the company established around Frank Whittle's pioneering of the turbojet engine, much of the early bench testing of which had been undertaken in rudimentary facilities in Lutterworth. Operations at Bruntingthorpe were duly wound up and by the end of May all the fleet had been flown to Bitteswell where part of the hangar complex previously used by AWA for Lancaster assembly had been taken over. From 1st July, Power Jets lost its separate identity entirely when it was absorbed into the newly-created National Gas Turbine Establishment (NGTE).

It was also in April that AWA began to renew their interests in Bitteswell when they began to use the airfield for the purpose of test flying the AW.52G. This small-scale experimental glider of unconventional all-wing design was built by AWA in order to study the flight characteristics of this type of aircraft in preparation for a larger scale development, the jet powered AW.52J. The unusual combination of the AW.52G and its tug, the last airworthy Armstrong Whitworth Whitley (Mk.V LA951), became a familiar sight in the area for quite a period of time.

Much of the work carried out by the NGTE was of a very sensitive nature and notice boards soon informed would-be spectators of the dire penalties which could be incurred if one was caught in breach of the Official Secrets Act. Far from acting as a deterrent, these notices only seemed to act as a spur to aviation enthusiasts who could regularly be seen waiting for a glimpse of, or even indulging in a little surreptitious photography of, the test fleet aircraft as they crossed the A427 road (as was) to get to or from the airfield. Although in later years this road crossing was to be used to a lesser degree it was to remain a feature of the airfield throughout its active life.

In many instances the external appearance of the aircraft engaged on NGTE research projects remained unaltered, while in others the installation of an experimental engine meant a drastic redesign of some section of the airframe. One of the more visual projects carried out at Bitteswell concerned a series of experiments to examine the feasibility of using gas turbine engines to lay smoke screens from ships and aircraft. The airfield was used for the 'sea' trials of what were referred to as 'fog oil tests' and within a few minutes of a test engine beginning its run a dense cloud of acrid smoke began to develop. The noise of the turbojet coupled with the sudden appearance of the smoke cloud doubtless had the effect of generating a great deal of rumour and speculation in the locality. All the airborne trials were carried out with Gloster Meteor I EE221 and at least one public demonstration of 'fog oil' in action was given. The occasion was the Auster Flying Club rally at Rearsby on 29th June 1947.

Although it had now passed into the hands of the Ministry of Supply (MoS), the airfield still retained some contact with RAF training. Between July 1946 and May 1947, it became a Relief Landing Ground for 20 Service Flying Training School, Church Lawford, Warwickshire. During this period, the North American Harvard advanced trainers of this unit were to be seen in the vicinity engaged in circuit training.

ASM of Parkside, Coventry, who were in the process of developing a range of turboprop and turbojet aero engines, started to use Bitteswell as a base for flight testing in October 1947. Initially they made use of the hangar nearest to the A5 (No.1), eventually acquiring No.2 also.

ASM's first test-bed aircraft, the Lancaster III ND784, arrived at the airfield on the 21st from Hamble, Hampshire, where it had been extensively modified by Air Service Training. This aircraft was no stranger to ASM products as it had previously been used at Bruntingthorpe to air test the ASX (Armstrong Siddeley Experimental) turbojet. That engine had been carried in the bomb bay but a complete redesign of the forward fuselage made it possible to install an ASM Mamba turboprop in the nose. ND784 was to be employed on development work with this type of engine for several years until it was withdrawn from service and finally scrapped in 1951.

Converted bomber and transport aircraft proved to be very suitable as flight test vehicles and were widely used for this purpose by all the major companies involved in exploring the new jet engine technology. In addition to ND784 two more Lancasters, two Lincolns and a Lancastrian were to be used by ASM for engine evaluation, while another pair of Lancasters and a Lincoln were similarly employed by the NGTE. Unfortunately one of their Lancasters, LL735, a Mk II built by AWA, was written off following a landing accident on the airfield on 2nd February 1950.

On numerous occasions during the late 1940s and early 1950s aircraft belonging to firms engaged in various research projects paid visits to the NGTE facility at Bitteswell. Frequently to be seen were the engine test-bed aircraft of Rolls-Royce Limited which flew in from Rolls' airfield at Hucknall, north of Nottingham. Quite often these visits were only of brief duration but sometimes they were more prolonged and on occasion extended over several weeks.

An event eagerly awaited by AWA employees at Bitteswell took place on 1st December 1947 when the first AW.52J, TS363, was flown in from Boscombe Down, Wiltshire, where preliminary flight trials had taken place. Just over a fortnight later on the 16th the first public demonstration of this Rolls-Royce Nene powered flying wing was staged at the airfield for the benefit of a large gathering of representatives from the government, industry and press.

Although less than five hours flying had been completed prior to the 16th, Squadron Leader Eric Franklin, AWA's chief test pilot, gave an excellent demonstration of the aircraft. Published reports were quite enthusiastic and a great deal was expected of the aircraft in the future. However, from the first, test results were very disappointing.

The second AW.52J, TS368, first flew at Bitteswell on 1st September 1948. It differed from TS363 only in that it was powered by less powerful Rolls-Royce Derwent engines. Both aircraft then became involved in the test programme but the trials continued to

The NGTE hybrid Wellington II/VI W5518 taxying from the 'Old Site' for a test flight from the airfield. From this angle, apart from the Rolls-Royce Merlin 62s and the faired off nose, the aircraft looks unremarkable. Note the Gloster Meteor in the background. H Bachelor

Wellington W5518 again, crossing the A427 (now the A4303) Lutterworth road from the 'Old Site' onto the airfield. The extended tail housing a Whittle turbojet is well evident while the 'Prototype P' marking is just visible behind the roundel. Jim Morrow

produce poor results. A further setback occurred on 30th May 1949 when TS363 was lost. During the course of a test flight asymmetric flutter developed which became so violent that the AWA pilot, J O Lancaster, was forced to abandon the aircraft and in so doing became the first man to make an emergency escape by means of a Martin Baker ejector seat. Strange to relate, after the ejection the flutter stopped and TS363 glided down to crash land with relatively little damage in open countryside near Long Itchington, Warwickshire.

This incident, combined with the poor test results served to curtail further development of the AW.52. The surviving aircraft, TS368, saw little further use at Bitteswell until it finally left on 25th October 1950 on delivery to the RAE at Farnborough, where it was scrapped in 1953 after limited use.

Around this time AWA were also heavily involved in another project, the AW.55 Apollo. This was a short/medium haul airliner, in direct competition to the Vickers Viscount, with which the company hoped to break into the civil market. The Apollo had arisen from the deliberations of the Brabazon Committee, named after its chairman, Lord Brabazon of Tara, to predict the civil aircraft that would need to be built to meet the market after the Second World war finished. Both the Apollo and Viscount were pitched at the Type 2 requirement, for a short range turboprop. Although the Viscount went on to become a major triumph the Apollo was unsuccessful in its bid to find customers and only two were built, both of which made transient visits to Bitteswell during their respective test programmes.

Although AWA must have had high hopes of success with AW.52 and the Apollo, in the post war years the company became more and more involved with aircraft designed by other organisations. When the war ended contracts were held for a large number of Avro Lincolns and despite these orders being severely cut back enough remained to keep the Baginton production line going, albeit on a reduced scale. Contracts for the modification and conversion of a number of Lancasters and Lincolns also helped to keep a nucleus of the skilled workforce

Bitteswell-based Unit or Operator Accidents

29.9.41 Wellington IC R3216 18 OTU
Crashed at Bitteswell while engaged on night flying practise. Of the eight crew, there was only one survivor, the rear gunner.

17.4.45 Wellington X NC667 105 OTU
Force-landed due to loss of power in port engine shortly after take-off. Crew suffered minor injuries, aircraft destroyed by fire before crash tender arrived. Two sources give differing locations for this crash, in field adjoining airfield and 2½ miles distant.

16.5.45 Wellington X NC713 105 OTU
While on night circuit training, aircraft reported engine trouble at 0440 hours. When coming in to land at about 200ft, the starboard wing suddenly burst into flames. All crew killed.

23.6.45 Wellington X LP822 105 OTU
Overshot landing at Bitteswell, damaged beyond repair.

7.7.45 Wellington X HE908 105 OTU
Belly-landed at Bitteswell after colliding with Oxford I NM795 of 1513 Beam Approach Training Flight, Bramcote. No injuries.

30.5.49 AW.52J TS363 AWA
Became uncontrollable during high speed tests. The pilot, J O Lancaster, ejected from the aircraft, becoming the first man to use a Martin Baker seat in an emergency. The aircraft later crashed and was destroyed.

2.2.50 Lancaster II LL735 NGTE
Undercarriage collapsed and structural damage caused during heavy landing in poor visibility. Aircraft not repaired.

18.5.54 Wyvern S.4 VZ747 ASM
Crashed near Pailton, south west of the airfield at 1634 hours. Test pilot 'Eddie' Griffiths killed.

14.8.54 Hunter F.2 WN905 AWA
Lost part of undercarriage on high speed run and abandoned near East Langton, north of Market Harborough. Test pilot Martin Walton survived.

10.11.54 Canberra B.2 WD933 ASM
Written off in a spectacular crash-landing on the airfield at 16;26 hours, during which the aircraft overturned. Both crew survived.

For 29 Operational Training Unit, see parent station – Bruntingthorpe, Chapter Six.

intact. Bitteswell benefited slightly from these orders; aircraft were often placed in temporary storage there until required at Baginton. Also a small amount of work on both types was carried out at the airfield.

Another aircraft with which AWA was to have a notable association was the Gloster Meteor. The building of complete aircraft of this type commenced at Baginton in 1949 after AWA received a sub-contract order for 45 of the Mk.4 single-seat fighter. Further direct contracts for single-seat Mk.8s followed and between 1950 and 1953 the company produced 450 of this model. While the Mk.8s were still on the production line AWA were given the task of developing a two-seat night fighter version, a decision which was to have considerable impact on the future use of Bitteswell. Flight testing of the Mk.4s and the majority of the Mk.8s took place at Baginton and they revealed the

RG324, the AW.52G flying-wing experimental glider, with Eric Franklin in the front cockpit.. It first flew on 2nd March 1945 from Baginton. Note the airspeed indicator probes and wool tufts on the upper port wing to aid in the monitoring of air flow. via Author

shortcomings of that grass airfield for the operation of fast jet aircraft. So, from 1951 AWA began to make increasing use of Bitteswell with its concrete runways.

The escalation of war in Korea during 1950 made Britain look to the state of its armed forces. It was evident that the RAF and Fleet Air Arm (FAA) were in dire need of modernisation as many aircraft of Second World War vintage were still in service. A 'Super Priority' programme for the rapid re-equipment of the services was initiated by the government in 1951 which resulted in large contracts for up-to-date equipment being placed with major aircraft manufacturers. Although AWA had designed none of the aircraft concerned, the company had capacity available, so was to benefit from the orders placed for the products of other members of the Hawker Siddeley Group of which it was part.

Two of the aircraft ordered in quantity were the Hawker Aircraft Company's Sea Hawk single-seat naval fighter and Hunter single-seat day fighter. Hawkers found it impossible to meet their commitments for both types and after 35 Sea Hawks had been completed at Kingston/Dunsfold, all future

National Gas Turbine Establishment Aircraft at Bitteswell

Type	Serial	Dates on Charge
Avro Anson C.19	VM360	28.5.47 to 1.9.47
Avro Lancaster II	LL735	5.7.46 to 2.2.50
Avro Lancaster III	RE137	6.10.48 to 12.10.49
Avro Lincoln B.2	SX971	28.9.50 to 10.7.52
De Havilland Dominie I	X7413	? to 4.1.50
De Havilland Dominie I *	NR698	2.9.47 to 13.10.47
De Havilland Tiger Moth I	T5901	14.5.46 to 15.1.47
De Havilland Vampire F.1	TG421	4.6.48 to 25.6.52
De Havilland Vampire F.3	VT818	22.5.50 to 15.9.50
Fairey Firefly I	DT932	1.8.46 to 12.11.46
Handley Page Hastings prot.	TE583	30.5.51 to 16.5.52
Gloster Meteor F.1	EE215	14.5.46 to ?
Gloster Meteor F.1	EE221	25.5.46 to 23.3.48
Gloster Meteor F.4	EE480	9.5.46 to 19.12.49
Gloster Meteor F.4	EE522	28.5.48 to 27.10.50
Gloster Meteor F.4	RA490	11.1.49 to 16.7.52
Gloster Meteor F.4	RA491	20.5.49 to 12.7.49
Gloster Meteor T.7	VW443	6.5.49 to 8.7.52
Gloster Meteor PR.10	WB164	8.1.52 to 26.6.52
Miles Magister I	L8051	14.5.46 to 15.1.47
Percival Proctor IV	NP308	20.12.48 to 13.5.49
Supermarine Spitfire IX	NH403	3.9.49 to ?
Vickers VA.486 Wellington II/VI	W5518	14.5.46 to 25.11.48

* Built by Brush at Loughborough, see Chapter Fourteen.

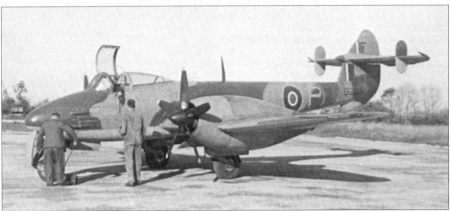

production and design/development responsibility was transferred to AWA. Thereafter Bitteswell became responsible for all Sea Hawk contracts and development work.

Use of Bitteswell increased accordingly and during 1952 AWA were able to acquire further accommodation on the airfield. This was made possible by the closing down of the NGTE facility. By July only two of the establishment's aircraft remained at the airfield, Meteor T.7 VW443 and Lincoln I SX971. These flew out on the 8th and 10th respectively to the Royal Aircraft Establishment (RAE) at Farnborough and so brought to an end an interesting part of Bitteswell's history.

After the departure of the NGTE, ASM's test unit remained in operation at Bitteswell and they took over No.2 hangar to house their expanding fleet of flying test-beds. Throughout the 1950s continual development work was carried out on the company's expanding range of engines. The Mamba, Double Mamba and Python turboprops together with the Adder, Viper and Sapphire turbojets were subjected to extensive test programmes at the airfield. All were eventually used for military applications and a very varied fleet of aircraft was employed to carry out trials.

In addition to jet engines, ASM also experimented with two liquid fuel rocket motors, the Snarler and the Screamer. Although both were installed in test aircraft only one, the Snarler, was flown at Bitteswell. Flights were made in the Hawker P.1072, VP401, which had been modified to carry the motor in addition to its Rolls-Royce Nene. Although there were few occasions when rocket power was used, some measure of success was achieved. After the Air Ministry began to show an interest in augmented turbojet thrust (re-heat or afterburning) the Screamer project was cancelled in December 1955, even though Meteor F.8 VZ517 had been converted to accept the rocket and systems under the fuselage and flight testing at Bitteswell was imminent.

The AW.52G under tow, probably on a test flight out of Bitteswell. Tug for most flights was the last airworthy AW Whitley. The small propellers above the main wheels are wind-powered generators developing power for the boundary layer control system. via Author

Readying the Trent Meteor EE227/G for a test flight. The Trent was effectively a turboprop version of the Derwent II turbojet.
Albert Boothaway

Lancaster III ND784 proved to be an adaptable test-bed for ASM. It first acted as a test-bed for the ASX turbojet with the engine mounted in the bomb bay (illustrated). Later it flew with a Mamba turboprop in the nose.
Peter Green collection

Flight testing has always had its risks, particularly during the transition from piston to gas turbine powerplants and the introduction in changes to the geometric shape of wings, fuselages and other aerodynamic improvements, in the late 1940s and early 1950s. For ASM 1954 was a particularly bad year, as on 18th May Westland Wyvern S.4 VZ747, powered by a Python turboprop, was conducting re-light tests when it crashed near Pailton church some three miles from Bitteswell with the loss of their experienced chief test pilot 'Eddie' Griffiths. Later in the year on 10th November, Sapphire-powered English Electric Canberra B.2 WD933 crashed on the airfield, after one of the engines had 'flamed out' and the other was accidentally shut down. Re-light attempts had failed, so coupled with no hydraulics, a gliding landing on the grass parallel to the main runway 04/22 was attempted. Unfortunately a wingtip caught the concrete of an intersecting runway and flipped the Canberra onto its back, skidding across the main runway. Eventually, the aircraft came to a halt on the grass, having come off the runway. The two crew members, ASM pilot Jim Starkey and observer Peter Taylor were rescued unhurt but naturally shaken, having been saved by their ejector seat headrests.

Another accident during 1954 occurred to the Hunter F.2 WN905 during a production test flight on 14th August. AWA test pilot Peter Martin R Walton, experienced undercarriage problems after take-off from Bitteswell and ejected successfully from the aircraft. The Hunter came down near East Langton, north of Market Harborough, close to a cricket match in progress. Accidents also happened on the ground, one in particular in November 1955, cost the life of Dr Quentin Reeves, sound suppression specialist and detuner patent holder. This tragedy occurred while a Hunter was being run up into the detuner in the ASM operating area.

Another major incident was the successful belly-landing on foam by Fairey Gannet AS.1 WN345 during a late afternoon in October 1958. The accident to this aircraft was made more 'hair raising' to witnesses, who watched chief test pilot Tom Frost, attempt, several times, to nudge the jammed nosewheel of the Gannet with the cockpit canopy of Hunting Jet Provost T.2 XD694. As a precaution Harry Rayner flying the Gannet, had shut down the rear driven prop of the contra-rotating Double Mamba. Frost's efforts were to no avail and the nosewheel remained partially retracted. Eventually, Rayner brought the Gannet in for a perfect landing on the foam. Within a few weeks the aircraft was back in the air continuing its test programme.

As AWA production gained momentum following the influx of new orders, existing workspace at Bitteswell began to prove inadequate. To solve the problem, work began in the north-east corner of the airfield on what was to become known as the 'New Site'. Three type B1 hangars complete with the necessary office accommodation were erected during July and August 1953, primarily to support production and development flight testing. Close to these hangars was the former RAF communal area which still contained many serviceable and useful buildings. These were also refurbished and impressed into use by AWA to serve various auxiliary purposes.

A good view of the control tower and ancillary buildings as NGTE Lancaster II (powered by Bristol Hercules VI radials) LL735, makes a low run, circa 1945. Albert Boothaway

Fine study of Lancaster II LL735, probably from one of the NGTE Dominie biplanes, ready for a photo session with the famed aviation photographer Charles E Brown. A Metrovick F2/4 Beryl turbojet is mounted in the tail, with a huge air scoop mounted atop the rear fuselage. Albert Boothaway

A further hangar was added to the existing three a year later and during June-July 1960 a fifth and final example, a former type B1, built for wartime use by the RAF alongside the old A427 road to Lutterworth, was dismantled, resurrected and reclad, alongside the other four. The base left vacant by this resiting was later taken over by Bitteswell Cropdryers, a firm who were contracted by AWA to mow the airfield. Years later a purpose-built single-storey building was erected on the same former hangar base, for Semelab, the company which still occupies the site today.

AWA re-introduced the method they had successfully adopted during wartime in which Baginton-built sub-assemblies were transported by road to Bitteswell. Following completion of the 'New Site' this system was expanded and eventually the final assembly and testing of all aircraft built by the company took place at the airfield.

In addition to production of Sea Hawks and Meteors, some of which were destined for overseas markets, lines for the assembly of Hunters and Gloster Javelin all weather fighters were also established.

National Gas Turbine Establishment test pilot Squadron Leader John Fifield demonstrates how to conduct a very low beat-up of Bitteswell in an early Meteor. Jim Morrow

Meteor F.1 EE221 of the NGTE fleet, in front of the flight sheds on the 'Old Site'. It was in this aircraft that Frank Whittle made his memorable solo flight at Bruntingthorpe (see Chapter Six) in October 1945. Albert Boothaway

Classic portrait of the Nene-powered AW.52J over a snow-covered Leicestershire, on a test flight out of Bitteswell. The aircraft crashed on 30th May 1949. via Author

Opposite page:

Top: *The AW Apollo airliner was powered by four Mamba turboprops. The prototype (illustrated) first flew as VX220 on 10th April 1949 and carried out much of its test flying from Bitteswell.* Rolls-Royce, via Ken Ellis

Bottom: *A close-up of the four hangars on the 'Old Site', circa 1952, with the A5 road in the foreground. On the apron is the YB-1 and a Meteor test-bed – probably F.8 WA820 which had distinctively large nacelles to house its Sapphire engines. The brick-built first floor room above the side offices at the apron end of No.1 Hangar was used by ASM as the test pilots' office until 1959.* Dick Teasdale

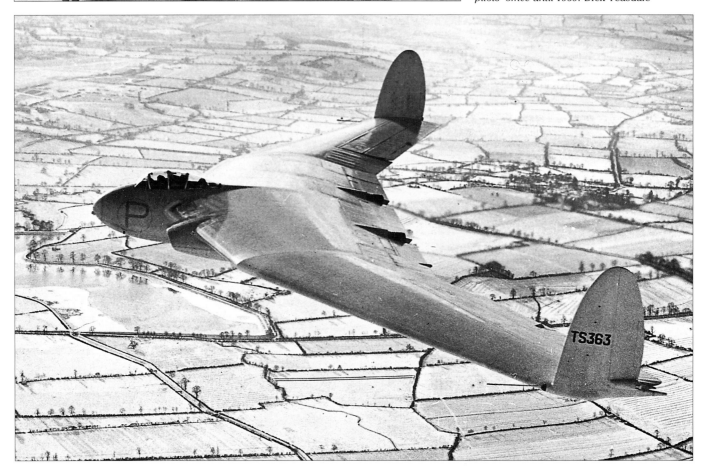

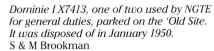

Dominie I X7413, one of two used by NGTE for general duties, parked on the 'Old Site'. It was disposed of in January 1950.
S & M Brookman

The Hawker P.1040 1st prototype, VP401, (later named Sea Hawk) was re-designated P.1072 when fitted with an ASM Snarler liquid fuel rocket motor. As the first British mixed-power prototype it made its maiden flight in November 1950, and although successful, the realisation that the future lay with re-heat and not rocket boost, led to the trials programme being halted. via Author

A vertical view of the southern part of Bitteswell, taken on 29th January 1952. Suitable landmarks are the control tower (A) complete with signal square and airfield identifier letters 'BT'; the A5 (B) and the Lutterworth road (C). South of that road and to the right of the photograph is the single hangar (D) moved in 1960 to the 'New Site'. Among the aircraft to be seen on the 'Old Site' (E) are a turboprop Dakota, three Lincolns and seven Meteors. DoE

Ground-running the Mamba turboprop test-bed, Dakota IV KJ839, on the 'Old Site' circa 1949-50. via Dave Sargent

The last production AWA-built Lancaster I, TW911, which was fitted with two ASM Python turbo-props in the outer positions. It completed its test work around May 1952 and was then scrapped. Officially it was struck off charge on 17th January 1953. via Neville Franklin

The last engine tested in the rear fuselage of Lancaster III SW342 was the ASM Viper with reheat. The Viper went on to become one of the most successful turbojets produced. Behind ASM's Lancaster can be seen a Meteor T.7 (NGTE's VW443 ?) and Armstong Whitworth's communication 'hack', Proctor V, G-AHBD. via Dick Teasdale

This rise in activity naturally led in turn to a considerable increase in noise emanating from the airfield. As was to be expected, this brought forth complaints from all quarters but especially from nearby Lutterworth. A great deal of the trouble was caused by the ground running of engines from two parts of the airfield, firstly by ASM test-beds being given sometimes lengthy testing, in the area of the 'Old Site' and by new production aircraft undergoing initial pre-flight engine tests. As well as routine departing and arriving air traffic in the area of Bitteswell, sonic booms from Hunters on air test were an added source of annoyance, particularly with local greenhouse owners. However, the building of an efficient sound suppression pen and detuner in the 'New Site' area, went some way towards curing the first problem, while a government ban on overland supersonic flying, eliminated another.

Although 1956 was the year in which AWA bought the Bitteswell facility outright from the Ministry of Supply, it was also a time when the long term prospects for the aviation industry looked dismal. Despite this, AWA initiated an airfield refurbishment programme and during a four-week period straddling July-August the main 04/22 runway was resurfaced. While this occurred, AWA's Hunter and Javelin flight-testing was curtailed and ASM moved some of their fleet over to Honiley in Warwickshire, to enable vital engine testing to continue.

Not widely known is the fact that ASM fitted a Sapphire 7 engine to the second production Hunter F.5, WN955, as early as 1955. This is believed to have been a private venture initiative by AWA to compare it with the Avon 200-powered Hunter F.6, which AWA were about to assemble and which was seen to have tremendous potential.

Although ASM and AWA test pilots undertook nine flights in G-1-2, a Sapphire 7 powered Hunter, between 2nd February and 8th March 1956, this line of development does not appear to have been proceeded with.

The precise identity of the aircraft marked G-1-2 has still to be confirmed.

In March 1956 the last Sea Hawk, FGA.6 XE490, was delivered to the FAA but, fortunately the production jigs were retained intact at Baginton. As re-equipment programmes began to tail off, the UK's 'infamous' Defence White Paper of March 1957, seemed only to confirm the prospect of an end to large-scale military aircraft orders.

Fortunately, AWA still had a fair proportion of their Javelin contract to complete, and even though many of these were obliged to depart for a spell of temporary storage due to lack of components, prior to delivery to the RAF, the last of the FAW.7s to be completed at Bitteswell flew out in February 1959. A dozen or so, having already been converted to FAW.9 standard elsewhere, returned in 1962-63 to be further modified with refuelling probes, becoming FAW.9Rs in the process. A further eleven, which had been converted to 9R standard 'in the field' at RAF Horsham St Faith, Norfolk, returned to Bitteswell for repainting during 1963-64.

Concurrent with the Javelin production, ASM developed a more powerful re-heated version of the Sapphire for the FAW.8 and '9. FAW.1 XA560 was the first to be so fitted and was tested extensively along with FAW.7s XH707 and XH746 which were also converted with an interim re-heat system by ASM. They were later joined by FAW.7 XH753 which arrived from Gloster's with a definitive system already fitted.

Meanwhile AWA had assumed responsibility for the integration of the DH Firestreak air-to-air-missile with the Javelin's fire control system. Firestreaks were fitted as standard on the later marks of Javelin, notably the FAW.7, '8, '9/'9R. Initially, in mid-1956, AWA were using modified FAW.4 XA632 with dummy missiles for aerodynamic simulation. Later, further Mk.4s were utilised, XA724 and XA725, plus FAW.2 XA771 and FAW.7 XH705. This work was completed by the end of 1958.

Hunter F.6 production, which started with the test-flying of XF373 in July 1955, finished in April 1957 with the delivery of XG168, the 124th example: a fine achievement. Despite the needs of the production programme at this time, repair work for Meteor F.8s, NF.11s, '12s, '13s and '14s, Sea Hawks and Hunters had been simultaneously carried out. During the second half of 1957, the Bitteswell Javelin production was supplemented by a programme to convert several recently retired Meteor NF.11s to a target towing version. This followed a successful series of flight tests by the prototype, WD767, which had begun in December 1956. Designated TT.20s, they were initially converted for Fleet Air Arm use, but a small contract for six of these aircraft was also undertaken for the Danish Air Force.

The US-funded Mutual Defense Assistance Program (MDAP) placed 'offshore orders' for Sea Hawks required by the Dutch naval air arm, Marine Luchtvaart Dienst, and the new West German naval air arm, the Marineflieger. Having retained the production jigs, the Dutch order for 22 F.50s commenced delivery in July 1957 with serial number 6-50 and was completed with the delivery on 22nd February 1958 with 6-71. The German order for a total of 68, equally divided between F.100 and F.101s (fighter and fighter-reconnaissance respectively), commenced with the first flight of VA+220 in November 1957 and was completed with the delivery of Mk.101 RB+376 in April 1959.

This was not the end of the Bitteswell Sea Hawk saga, for the Indian Navy had placed an order. The first nine were refurbished former Royal Navy FB.3 airframes brought up to FGA.6 standard and serialled IN151 to IN159. The next 14 (IN160 to IN173) were new production FGA.6s, and a further seven were refurbished former Royal Navy FB.5s, again to FGA.6 standard. India took delivery of a further 16 former Royal Navy aircraft and several airframes for spares, though these were all refurbished and test-flown by Shorts at Sydenham, in Northern Ireland. The first Indian Sea Hawk, IN151, was flying in December 1959 and the last of the deliveries from Bitteswell went in February 1963.

In August 1956, with little prospect of future large scale military orders, AWA with the support of the Hawker Siddeley Group as a whole decided to attempt to once more break into the civil market. An extensive survey had revealed possible sales for a civil freighter and the design conceived to exploit this situation was the four-engined AW.650 Argosy. Progress on the project was swift and only 28 months elapsed from the initial designs to first flight of the prototype, G-AOZZ, on 8th January 1959.

AWA became the sole occupants of the Bitteswell site in 1959 after a merger had taken place between Bristol Aero Engines and ASM. News that the two companies were to combine was first announced in April 1958, one year later the amalgamation was complete and a new organisation, Bristol Siddeley Engines, had been created. In the months that followed the Bitteswell-based part of the enterprise was gradually run down in order to concentrate test flying at Filton, near Bristol.

Operations were finally wound up in August 1959 when between the 18th and 30th the four remaining aircraft of the former ASM test fleet were flown out to their new base. During their 12 years at Bitteswell the various flying test-beds which ASM employed became a very familiar sight for their appearances had not been restricted to Bitteswell alone; they were often a welcome and popular addition to the pro-

gramme of numerous airshows throughout the country.

By the end of 1959 production of the Argosy had gained momentum and five more aircraft had made their first flights at Bitteswell. The company took every opportunity to further interest in the Argosy. The second aircraft, G-APRL, which had flown during February, was shown off to the Prime Minister Harold Macmillan at Cottesmore during April 1959. The fourth aircraft, G-APRN, resplendent in Riddle Airlines livery, was displayed at the Paris Air Show in May 1959. The same aircraft and the fifth to fly, G-APVH, both appeared at the Farnborough airshow in September. The sixth aircraft, G-APWW, appeared during October 1959. In spite of company predictions apart for an order for seven from Riddle Airlines of Miami, USA, and three others being refurbished for use by British European Airlines (BEA) there was little other airline interest.

By the time G-ATTC, BEA's last aircraft was delivered in November 1966, a total of 73 Argosies had been built but only 17 were for the civil market. The remainder was made up of three contracts for an RAF version, the AW.660 or Argosy C.1. These were placed following successful trials from May 1960 with the converted second production Argosy 100, G-APRL, fitted with a 'beaver tail' opening rear fuselage. The Argosy was designed initially to replace the ageing Vickers Valetta and later the Handley Page Hastings tactical transports with the RAF. The Valetta was directly descended from the Wellingtons that used to fly from Bitteswell. The first production Argosy C.1, XN814, made its first flight at Bitteswell on 4th March 1961 and the last of the 56 aircraft, XR143, was delivered during April 1964.

In the hope of making the Argosy attractive to a wider market, several variations of the AW.650 and AW.660 were studied and modelled during 1957-58, including Rolls-Royce twin-Tyne engine versions (known as the AW.651 and '661 respectively) and the AW.670, a 126-seat Airbus version with a double-bubble fuselage and uprated Rolls-Royce Dart powerplants. None progressed beyond this stage and were shelved due to lack of customer interest and/or finance. Lack of orders for the Argosy was very disappointing and it is reported that in the end a substantial loss was sustained by AWA.

At the beginning of the 1960s the company was still optimistic about the future and a great deal of time and effort was devoted to the AW.681 jet, a vertical/short take-off and landing (V/STOL) tactical transport aircraft for which the RAF then had a requirement as a replacement for the Blackburn Beverley and Handley Page Hastings transports.

Government policies were to determine not only the future of AWA but also that of Bitteswell. It was another White Paper in the early 1960s which led to the structure of the British aircraft industry undergoing a drastic change. Within the space of a few years the reorganisation which took place throughout the Hawker Siddeley Group of companies was considerable and eventually this was to have a marked effect on the type of work carried out at Bitteswell. The first phase was entered into on 2nd October 1961 when Sir W G Armstrong Whitworth Aircraft Company Limited and Gloster Aircraft Company Ltd were combined to form Whitworth Gloster Ltd.

Further amalgamation took place in 1963 with the result that on 1st July Bitteswell became part of the Avro Whitworth Division of Hawker Siddeley Aviation. A final round of consolidation was to follow during 1965 which saw the names of the pioneer aircraft manufacturers totally erased leaving the title Hawker Siddeley Aviation, Bitteswell.

While this rationalisation and integration was going on, Argosy production reached its peak in 1962, but a lack of further orders resulted in large scale redundancies at both Baginton and Bitteswell in the first half of 1963. The company still retained high hopes that the promise shown by the AW/HS.681 would eventually provide a return to full employment in the long term. This prospect came a step closer to reality in March 1963 when a contract for a full design study was received and a further boost to morale followed in September with the award of a contract to build the aircraft.

This situation was destined to be rather short lived for in February 1965 during yet another onslaught on the aircraft industry, the Labour government of the day cancelled all further work related to the project. The outcome of this decision was quite catastrophic for not only were massive redundancies inevitable but, by December the Baginton plant had been closed completely leaving the works at Bitteswell and the Hawker Siddeley Dynamics facility at Whitley as the sole survivors of the 'Pioneers of Progress' as AWA were proudly known in their heyday.

In addition to their manufacturing capabilities AWA had, for many years, enjoyed an excellent reputation for the quality of their overhaul, repair, modification and conversion service. From 1959 there was an increase in this type of work at Bitteswell and after the demise of the HS.681 it was this which enabled the plant to continue to operate. It soon became a main centre providing support for many of the aircraft produced by Hawker Siddeley (HS) Group companies. Over the years the greater proportion of this work was to be provided by such types as the Folland Gnat advanced trainer, Hawker Hunter, Avro Shackleton maritime patrol aircraft and the Avro Vulcan bomber, with the HS Buccaneer naval

Above: *Sapphire test-bed Canberra B.2 WD933 overturned during an emergency wheels-up unpowered crash-landing at Bitteswell on 10th November 1954. Fortunately, both pilot and observer were saved by their ejection seat headrests.* via Dave Sargent

Below: *The prototype Jet Provost T.1, XD674, was employed by ASM as a Viper engine test-bed at Bitteswell from May 1955 to June 1957.*

Javelin FAW.4, XA721, Bitteswell's second production aircraft, went to Gloster Aircraft Co. for flight trials. Both via Ray Williams

strike aircraft and HS Trident airliner contributing to a lesser degree.

The association between the Vulcan and Bitteswell began in January 1959 and was to last for over 20 years. During this time most of the aircraft built passed through the works on occasion, some received attention several times with the result that totals of six or seven visits eventually became quite common and for one, XM599, eight were recorded.

Although not so prolific in numbers, the Avro Shackleton too accounted for considerable work and between 1959 and 1981 MR.2 and MR.3 maritime versions and T.4 crew trainers were all dealt with. While in the works, several MR.2s underwent protracted programmes of conversion and modification enabling them to have an extended life in the airborne early warning role as AEW.2s.

Experience in building Hunters meant that a good proportion of Bitteswell's workforce had attained great knowledge of the aircraft. This was an attribute which was of great advantage to the company as they continued to overhaul and modify aircraft for both the RAF and FAA.

Additional work was generated by early Hunter variants which had been phased out of service with the RAF and certain foreign air forces. Considerable numbers of these still excellent airframes were repurchased by HS for possible resale. For several years a steady market existed overseas for these Hunters, many of which were to receive attention at Bitteswell. Although some arrived from other HS plants for finishing touches to be applied, many were extensively refurbished and up-graded at the airfield. All eventually emerged in 'as new' condition and these Hunters from Bitteswell helped to equip the air arms of Chile, India, Jordan, Lebanon, Qatar, Singapore and Switzerland.

Out of a total of 105 Gnat T.1s built for the RAF at least 72 individual aircraft passed through Bitteswell on overhaul or repair. Although most of this work took place between September 1968 and May 1972, small numbers of this diminutive trainer continued to visit the airfield for attention until the type was finally phased out of service with the advent of the Hawk.

During August and September 1972 two very different Gnats made a brief appearance at Bitteswell. These were single-seat fighter versions of the aircraft which had been built in India by Hindustan Aeronautics Limited (HAL) and known as the Ajeet. This pair, together with a HAL HJT-16 Kiran, a trainer indigenous to India, were brought to the UK to appear at the Society of British Aircraft Constructors Show at Farnborough. Assembly of the three aircraft took place in the workshops during August and all gave short demonstrations at the airfield prior to their departure for Farnborough. After participating in the show they made return flights to Bitteswell where they were dismantled once more, packed and flown out to India via London Airport.

Of all the Gnats worked on at Bitteswell it is probably those of the Royal Air Force's premier aerobatics team, the 'Red Arrows', which are best remembered. Beginning in 1968 selected aircraft belonging to the team arrived at the airfield at the close of the display season. During the winter they were subjected to a thorough refurbishing in readiness for the rigours of another season on the display circuit. As a mark of their appreciation for the excellent way in which the aircraft were prepared it became the custom for the team to give a display at Bitteswell, usually in the spring. This became an event eagerly awaited by the workforce and a practice which was to continue until the airfield ceased to operate. (Perhaps with this in mind, the public house on the Bitteswell road out of Lutterworth, is now called the 'Red Arrow'.)

Another contract concerned the Handley Page Victor. Following retirement from first line service some two dozen of these aircraft were selected for conversion to the K.2 tanker version. Although the major part of the work was carried out at Woodford, south of Manchester, the forward fuselage section and cockpit area were detached and transported to Bitteswell for complete refurbishment, modification and rewiring.

Decreasing output from the works meant that the airfield, together with its excellent radar and radio aids, was quite often under used. During the late 1960s and for most of the 1970s this was partly compensated for by a considerable amount of movements by RAF units and civilian organisations which used the airfield facilities for training. Hunting Jet Provosts from No.2 Flying Training School (FTS) at Syerston, Nottinghamshire, and the Royal Air Force College, Cranwell, Lincolnshire, Vickers Varsity and HS Dominie navigation trainers from various flying training schools were often to be seen carrying out circuits and approach exercises. On the civilian side, major flying schools such as CSE, Oxford, and the College of Air Training, Hamble, Hampshire, contributed many of the aircraft engaged in similar activities.

For the latter half of 1967 Saturday afternoons and all day Sunday were given over to gliding with the blessing of the management and under the auspices of the Upward Bound Trust. Using a Slingsby T.31 Tandem Tutor, a former wartime barrage balloon winch and the free services of former Glider Pilot Regiment Staff Sergeants as instructors, young people between the ages of 16 and 21 were given a gliding course for the sum of £7. This was considerably less than for similar tuition offered by other gliding clubs at that time. Gliding at Bitteswell was terminated due to a different standard of instructor being required although the Trust carried on the scheme at its other base at Thame, Buckinghamshire.

1967 was also the year when the first 'Families Day' was held at Bitteswell and on Sunday 21st May many thousands of people had the opportunity to judge how, in the two years since the huge upheaval, the site had been transformed into a very efficient Group overhaul and repair centre. Apart from the yearly 'Red Arrows' workers' benefits from 1969 onwards, it was a further 13 years before the site held its next and last, 'Families Day', in June 1980.

Radical alterations to the structure of the aviation industry which were initiated during 1977-78 by the Labour government were to involve Bitteswell and create yet another new title for the works. On 24th May 1977 the issued share capital of the British Aircraft Corporation, Hawker Siddeley Aircraft, Hawker Siddeley Dynamics and Scottish Aviation was assigned to a new corporation, British Aerospace (BAe) and nationalisation was completed on 1st January 1978 when the assets of these various companies were acquired. The life of the conglomerate in this form was however brief. The election of the Conservative government with its differing attitudes towards public ownership led to de-nationalisation of the industry and to British Aerospace Plc being established on 1st January 1981.

By this time, other factors were beginning to appear which would have a bearing on the future of Bitteswell. Aircraft which had long been part of the airfield scene were now, by aviation standards, old. The Vulcan was nearing the end of its active service life, few Shackletons remained flying, and the Gnat had already been superseded in its training role by the HS Hawk T.1. The Buccaneer was still being worked on in small numbers but on 2nd February 1980 a tragic low-level accident occurred to XV345, a 15 Squadron S.2B aircraft involved in a 'Red Flag' exercise over the Nellis ranges in Arizona, USA, when a wing detached during a tight turn. This effectively stopped the existing work programme but after a review and intense inspections several of the Buccaneers on overhaul at the time of the accident were eventually completed, although some of the former Fleet Air Arm S.2As that had arrived for eventual conversion to RAF S.2Bs were transported away by road, possibly to BAe Woodford, for use as spares in the later defined repair programme.

Hawks provided a fair proportion of the work at Bitteswell between October 1979 and February 1982. During this time around 40 new Hawks were assembled in the works, while modification work was carried out on a number of others. The Hawk was also selected as the aircraft to replace the 'Red Arrows' Gnats. Carrying on the established pattern, the team's new mounts were modified and prepared for their aerobatic role within the works. These Hawks in their striking red, white and blue livery were officially handed over with due ceremony on 15th November 1979. They returned for a winter overhaul several times thereafter.

Among the last overhaul contracts to be carried out at the airfield was one for the overhaul of the outer folding wing sections of the RAF's McDonnell Douglas Phantom FGR.2 fighters. The major work on the aircraft was undertaken at Holme-on-Spalding Moor in Yorkshire, and a complete airframe was never to arrive at Bitteswell, although one example was seen flying circuits.

Although it had been suspected for some time that job losses were in the offing few of the 1,000 strong workforce were prepared for the announcement of 22nd March 1982, that the entire Bitteswell plant was to close. A combination of defence cuts and slumps in the international aircraft markets was blamed for the decision. Although representations were made in various quarters in an attempt to gain a stay of execution, there was no reprieve.

Ironically, in the weeks leading up to final closure, Britain once again went to war. It was the Vulcan, in the twilight of its prolonged operational life and on the verge of being replaced by the Panavia Tornado, that went into action, and it can be argued that it was the care and attention devoted to these elderly aircraft by the Bitteswell workforce that ensured sufficient were still available to mount Operation 'Corporate', the bombing of Stanley airfield on East Falkland Island, in May 1982.

On 30th June 1982 the airfield was closed to operations. To mark the occasion a small flying display was staged. Several favourites such as the Vulcan and Shackleton made farewell flypasts and the 'Red Arrows' gave their final display at Bitteswell.

The Avro Ashton was developed as a purpose-built test-bed. Mk.4 WB494 had a Sapphire turbojet slung under the centre section and was tested extensively from Bitteswell. The circular rig in front of the Sapphire's air intake is for icing trials. Rolls-Royce via Dave Sargent

Fairey Gannet AS.1 WN345 in an undignified position on the runway, October 1958. It was repaired and continued trials of the Double Mamba coupled turboprop. Rolls-Royce via John Dewis *and* Dave Sargent

The wartime control was retained and given a Visual Control Room (VCR) top. Within the VCR an air traffic controller is using a signals lamp. Jim Morrow

The prototype Argosy is towed across the Lutterworth road from the 'Old Site' to the airfield ready for fitting out and flight trials. It made its first flight on 8th January 1959.
HSA via Harry Holmes

An Argosy fuselage on a special trailer negotiates a sharp bend coming off the old A46 Coventry-Leicester road beyond Wolvey to turn towards the A5 and Bitteswell.
via Neville Martin

The general run-down of the works continued until the final closure took place in March 1983.

The next stage of the complex history of Bitteswell began in February 1984 when BAe put the whole site up for sale. In all 567 acres, together with a half million square feet of industrial buildings were on offer, to be sold as a whole or in three lots.

Rumours soon began to circulate regarding future use of the airfield including one which intimated that it would become an operational base with the 'Stars and Stripes' flying from the flagpole. It was also reliably reported that US Air Force, Europe, had looked over the Bitteswell facilities, with respect to placing overhaul contracts, ini-

tially for Fairchild A-10A Thunderbolt II 'tank busters' of the 81st Tactical Fighter Wing based in Suffolk. Apparently, they were not too impressed by the security of the airfield. Whether this was the real reason may never be known, for eventually the A-10 contract was to be carried out at RAF Kemble in Gloucestershire.

At one stage the site received some consideration as the possible location for an inland freight port providing safe parking for lorries and estimated 1,600 jobs. Metroplex, the consortium behind the scheme, found that motorway access from Bitteswell did not meet their requirements.

Speculation ended on 28th November 1984 when BAe released the news that the entire site had been bought by Mr Douglas Arnold for a sum in excess of £3 million. Already a well known figure in aviation circles, the new owner disclosed through the press that it was his intention to house his large collection of Second World War vintage aircraft at Bitteswell Airport, as it had been renamed. In addition it was hoped to create jobs at the airfield by bringing back aircraft repair and overhaul work. Negotiations were said to be in progress concern-

ing the reconditioning of Boeing 707 jetliners for an American company. Approaches had also been made by companies interested in using hangars for grain storage but Mr Arnold said he was not in favour of this, owing to the small number of employees required to run this type of operation.

Apart from the erection of name boards proclaiming it to be Bitteswell Airport there were few outward signs of change in 1985. Internally, it was a different story. Despite earlier statements to the contrary much of the hangar space was given over to the storage of grain. Vast quantities of this commodity were transported to the site which became one of the largest of several EEC intervention stores in the country, eventually housing over 58,000 tonnes of surplus grain. To limit the possibility of fire, all the hangar electrical services, including the roof lighting system, was removed.

From the late spring of 1985 Arnold began to move his vintage aircraft to his new base. Most of these arrived by road in a dismantled state but a number of airworthy veterans, including a North American P-51D Mustang, Boeing B-17G Flying Fortress and several Supermarine Spitfires, were flown in at irregular intervals.

Apart from these infrequent arrivals and visits by the company's Britten Norman Islander, the only flying to take place at the airfield was carried out by Midland Ultralights Ltd who set up workshop facilities in one of the larger buildings on the 'New Site' with offices nearby in North Kilworth. From 1984 the company built the French-designed Sirocco 377GB single-seat microlight under licence and were offered at a 'fly-away' price of £5,600 in 1985. The testing of these microlight aircraft, together with some flying training, brought forth the inevitable complaints from local residents whose main concern appeared to be that aircraft noise would increase to previous levels. Midland Ultralights built around a dozen Siroccos and two or three of another type, the Firefly, at Bitteswell.

Opposite page:

A good view of the whole airfield, 8th May 1962 with the A5/Lutterworth road junction in the foreground. Much of the hardstandings on the 'Old Site' are devoted to car parking. In the top distance, the 'New Site' has three Argosies outside and a Vulcan in white anti-flash colours.

An aerial view of the 'New Site', close to the threshold of the north-eastern Runway 22, on the northern edge of the airfield. In the foreground is the diverted Ullesthorpe to A5 Pailton road and to the centre left one of the wartime communal sites. A camouflaged Vulcan and a Hunter are parked out.
Both via Neville Martin

Another event which gave rise to their concern was when the National Drag Racing Club staged a rather noisy race meeting on the airfield on 19th May. As it later transpired they need not have worried.

By the autumn the greater part of the Arnold collection, known as Warbirds of Great Britain, had arrived at Bitteswell and the prospect of being able to see many aircraft belonging to the Second World War era made the airfield attractive to enthusiasts. Most of those who hoped to see the collection were destined to be disappointed. Aircraft were rarely to be seen outside while visitors who asked to see inside the hangar were not made welcome and discouraged from returning.

Towards the end of the year it began to be rumoured that the airfield was again on the market. This time speculation was soon over for on 22nd January 1986 the news was released that the entire site had been acquired by the MFI group of companies. It was immediately announced that it was hoped to develop a distribution complex which would serve the group's future needs. The planned development was to be in three phases spread over a period of ten years. On completion four million square feet of warehousing will have been built.

Following the sale of the airfield, aeronautical activity soon became practically non-existent. Microlight flying, which had been a bone of contention, ceased early in May when Midland Ultralights vacated their 'New Site' premises.

The airfield's previous owner soon began to disperse his collection. In most cases dismantled aircraft were consigned to a series of shipping containers for transport to other locations, principally Biggin Hill, Kent, and Bournemouth, Dorset. Several aircraft were sold to British buyers. The Imperial War Museum at Duxford and Aces High at North Weald became the respective owners of a Lancaster and Lincoln while the Royal Air Force Museum received a Republic P-47D Thunderbolt. Systematic packing of containers continued well into the autumn and

Vulcan B.2 XL426 in the markings of the famous 'Dam Busters', 617 Squadron, makes an approach to Runway 04, over the 'new' roundabout at the A5, 30th July 1973. Brandon White

Midland Ultralights made use of the old RAF site at the rear of the 'New Site' for their operations. To the left is the prototype Midland Ultralight Sirocco 377GB G-MMLL with another Sirocco fuselage centre. Author

North American P-51D Mustang G-PSID taxies across the Lutterworth road from the 'Old Site' to the airfield, following a route taken by many different types before it. Roy Garner

A view from the air in 1998, this time looking south. The 'New Site' buildings are in the foreground, while a portion of runway ends abruptly in the warehouse complex.

Hangars on the 'Old Site' during demolition in March 1990. A huge book distribution and warehouse complex now occupies the area.
Both Author

by the close of the 1986 the largest item to remain was the Flying Fortress G-FORT. When this airworthy veteran was finally flown out on 9th May 1987 it became the last aircraft to use Bitteswell's A427 road crossing as it was towed across from the 'Old Site' onto the airfield.

The distinction of being the last fixed wing aircraft to fly out from the airfield must go to Spitfire IX G-MKIX (NH238). By the time of its departure on 28th November 1987 the old road crossing had been closed so it was towed along the A427 to enter the airfield by a newly-formed entrance. As it took off and the nostalgic sound of its Merlin engine faded into the distance it signified that it really was the end of the road for Bitteswell.

Between the two preceding dates, the 'Old Site' was the venue for part of a unique aeronautical event. Civic celebrations were held in nearby Lutterworth on the morning of 15th June 1987 to commemorate the 50th anniversary of the first running of a British jet engine, to honour its inventor and to mark the town's subsequent association with jet engine development.

Following these events, the most distinguished guest, Sir Frank Whittle, together with many other invited guests, journeyed out to No.6 Hangar to partake of a buffet lunch surrounded by an exhibition of early jet engines and memorabilia. Early in the afternoon as a finale to the day a short air display was staged. Four Hunting Jet Provosts from the RAF College, Cranwell, performed formation flypast followed by two HS Harriers of 233 Operational Conversion Unit, Wittering, which rounded off their display by bowing to Sir Frank who in turn returned the compliment.

MFI's vast enterprise with its promise of employment in a locality hard hit by recession found almost unanimous favour and a great deal was soon done to further its progress. During 1987 restructuring of the MFI/ASDA group took place, leading to an alliance between Gazely Properties (ASDA – Associated Dairies) and the Church Commissioners, to form the Lutterworth Partnership. Under this new management work has proceeded apace and as it progressed many of the former airfield buildings, which formed no part of the overall plan, soon became victims of the demolition teams.

At one time the owners entertained the possibility of preserving the control tower but this was not to be and, from an historical viewpoint, it became the first important building to be demolished. Over the weekend of 19th-20th March 1988 it was reduced to a heap of rubble with other buildings in that area soon following suit.

Next in line were the 'Old Site' hangars bordering the A427 (since renumbered the A4303 and further heavily modified during 1998 as part of the Lutterworth bypass). Destruction of the line of four T2s together with ancillary buildings, began on 9th January 1990 and continued for several weeks. The remaining pair of hangars, Nos.5 and 6, survived until June 1991, then they too suffered the same fate. On the airfield the lone T2 hung on until the next year then it also disappeared in the name of progress.

The one-time airfield has changed out of all recognition, much of it vanishing as vast warehouses are erected. Just one corner of the land that once formed the airfield remains virtually untouched. All the hangars built post-war on the 'New Site' are still intact and close to these is a small 'time capsule' of Second World War airfield architecture. Buildings from the RAF era which are still structurally intact at the end of 2000 include the former sick quarters, decontamination centre, institute and dining halls.

When Stage 3 of the development reaches this area doubtless everything that is left will succumb to the bulldozer and the last link between this former airfield and its wartime past will vanish. Only memories and roads such as Hunter Boulevard and Argosy Drive within the Magna Park site will then remain to remind visitors of an aeronautical past. These will represent only a scant memorial to an airfield that contributed in no small way, during war and peace, to 42 years of British aviation history.

Armstrong Siddeley Motors Test and Communication Aircraft at Bitteswell

Type	Identity	From / to	Engine on Test or Role
Avro Anson C.19 srs 1	G-AGUH	11.12.50 to 4.59	Communications
Avro Lancaster III	ND784	2.5.46 to 24.7.46	ASX
		21.10.47 to 4.51	Mamba. A/c scrapped
Avro Lancaster III	SW342	19.1.49 to 8.56	Mamba, Adder, Viper. Aircraft scrapped
Avro Lancaster 1	TW911	30.12.48 to 5.52	Python. A/c scrapped
Avro Lancastrian C.2	VM733	7.3.50 to 8.57	Sapphire. A/c scrapped
Avro Lincoln B.2	RE418	12.12.51 to 29.2.52	Python
Avro Ashton Mk.4	WB494	6.2.58 to 2.8.59	Sapphire
Avro Athena (prototype)	VM132	29.6.50 to 1.52	Mamba. A/c scrapped
Blackburn YB.1	WB797	10.4.51 to 7.55	Double Mamba
Boulton Paul Balliol (proto)	VL892	7.7.50 to 6.7.50	Mamba
Boulton Paul Balliol (proto)	VL935	10.48 to 6.7.51	Mamba
Douglas Dakota IV	KJ839	1.6.49 to 4.58	Mamba. To G-APML 1958.
English Electric Canberra B.2	WD933	13.4.51 to 10.11.54	Sapphire. Written off in crash-landing on airfield
English Electric Canberra B.2	WK141	14.1.55 to 18.9.59	Sapphire, Viper (from 10.58)
English Electric Canberra B.2	WK163	1.55 to 2.12.55	Viper (under stbd wing)
English Electric Canberra B.2	WV787	1.9.52 to 5.6.58	Sapphire
Fairey Gannet (2nd prototype)	VR557	11.12.52 to 5.8.55	Double Mamba
Fairey Gannet AS.1	WN340	14.4.54 to 8.58	Double Mamba. A/c scrapped
Fairey Gannet AS.1	WN345	11.55 to 25.9.59	Double Mamba
Fairey Gannet AS.1	WN395	6.10.54 to 11.8.59	Double Mamba
Fairey Gannet AS.1	WN404	1.3.56 to 25.4.56	Double Mamba
Fairey Gannet AS.1	XA396	3.6.58 to 2.7.58	Double Mamba
Gloster Meteor F.8	VZ517	17.9.53 to 12.55	Screamer rocket motor
Gloster Meteor F.8	WA820	22.3.51 to 4.54	Sapphire
Gloster Javelin FAW.1	XA557	30.6.55 to 28.9.59	Sapphire
Gloster Javelin FAW.1	XA560	9.2.56 to 20.9.59	Sapphire (re-heat)
Gloster Javelin FAW.5	XA711	16.5.57 to 5.3. 58	Sapphire
Gloster Javelin FAW.7	XH707	28.8.57 to 13.2.58	Sapphire (re-heat)
Gloster Javelin FAW.7	XH746	20.12.57 to 15.7.59	Sapphire (re-heat)
Gloster Javelin FAW.9	XH753	12.12.58 to 18.3.59	Sapphire (definitive re-heat)
Gloster Javelin FAW.7	XH713	21.4.59 to 8.7.59	Sapphire
Gloster Javelin FAW.8	XJ125	24.4.59 to 20.8.59	Sapphire
Hawker Hunter F.2	WN889	28.1.54 to 2.58	Sapphire
Hawker Hunter F.5	WP113	20.4.55 to 15.9.55	Sapphire
Hawker Hunter F.5	WP114	30.4.55 to 15.2.58	Sapphire
Hawker P.1072	VP401	29.7.50 to 16.4.52	Snarler liquid fuel rocket
Hunting Jet Provost 1	G-AOBU*	26.10.56 to 20.11.56	Viper. (*G-26-1 from 10.56)
Hunting Jet Provost 1	G-AOUS	5.12.58 to 27.5.59	Viper
Hunting Jet Provost T.1	XD674	19.5.55 to 4.6.57	Viper
Hunting Jet Provost T.2	XD694	7.6.57 to 15.9.59	Viper
Hunting Jet Provost T.3	XM353	18.2.59 to 15.9.59	Viper
Miles Marathon	VX231	5.6.58 to 10.59	P.182 installation not proceeded with. Scrapped
Short Seamew AS.1	XA209	12.4.56 to 12.7.56	Mamba
Westland Wyvern TF.2	VW868	22.1.51 to 16.2.54	Python
Westland Wyvern S.4	VW882	19.11.51 to 12.9.52	Python
Westland Wyvern S.4	VZ747	26.10.53 to 18.5.54	Python. Crashed nr Pailton
Westland Wyvern S.4	VZ777	12.54 to 4.55	Python
Westland Wyvern S.4	WL881	23.10.54 to 10.12.56	Python

Armstrong Whitworth Test and Communications Aircraft at Bitteswell

Type	Identity	From / to	Role
Avro 19 Series 1	G-AHYN	17.1.52 to ?	Communications
Avro Lancaster I	PA366	? to 30.8.50	Tug for AW.52G
Avro Lincoln B.1	RE253	? to 5.5.53	
AW.52G	RG324	4.46 to 1.6.50	Research glider
AW.52J	TS363	1.12.47 to 3.5.49	Flight test. Crashed at Long Itchington
AW.52J	TS368	1.9.48 to 25.10.50	Flight test
AW.55 Apollo	VX220	12.8.49 to ?	(Dual identity - G-AIYN)
AW.55 Apollo	VX224	17.9.53 to 15.10.53	Flight test
AW Whitley VII	LA951	4.46 to 1.10.47	Tug for AW.52G
De Havilland Rapide	G-AEML	3.46 to .62	Communications
Percival Proctor 5	G-AHBD	48 to ?	Communications
Gloster Meteor F.4	VW303	6.2.53 to 28.12.53	
Gloster Meteor T.7	VW413	22.12.48 to ?	Conv to aerodynamic NF.11
Vickers Valetta C.1	VL264	10.5.50 to 8.2.55	BT-H navigation systems tests

Warbirds of Great Britain - Aircraft at Bitteswell

Type	Identity	Arrived	Departed	Note
Avro Lancaster X	KB889	3.85	14.5.86	R
Avro Lincoln 2	G-29-1	3.85	10.9.86	R
Bell RP-63A Kingcobra	N52113	?	88	R
Boeing B-17G Fortress	G-FORT	2.85	9.5.87	F
Boeing Stearman A75N	G-AWLO	10.85	5.86	F
Folland Gnat T.1	?	12.87		1
Folland Gnat T.1	?	12.87		1
Folland Gnat T.1	?	12.87		1
Hawker Tempest II	?	?		2
Messerschmitt Bf 109G-6	610824	mid 85	88	R
Messerschmitt Bf 109G-14	G-SMIT	mid 85	88	R
North American P-51D Mustang	G-PSID	9.85	3.3.87	F
Percival Provost T.1	WV483	9.85	2.86	R
Republic P-47D Thunderbolt	13021	mid 85	?	R
Republic P-47D Thunderbolt	13064	mid 85	86	R
Vickers-Supermarine Spitfire IX	G-MKIX	late 85	28.11.87	F
Vickers-Supermarine Spitfire IX	BR601	11.86	?	R
Vickers-Supermarine Spitfire IX	NH799	?	9.86	R
Vickers-Supermarine Spitfire XIV	G-WWII	?	9.86	R
Vickers-Supermarine Spitfire XIV	MV262	?	7.8.86	R
Vickers-Supermarine Spitfire XIV	RM694	late 85	?	R
Vickers-Supermarine Spitfire XVI	G-BXVI	?	?	R
Vickers-Supermarine Spitfire XVI	G-SXVI	4.86	?	R
Vickers-Supermarine Spitfire XVIII	G-BRAF	late 85	?	R

Notes:

During Warbirds of Great Britain's tenure at Bitteswell, keeping a record of the aircraft within was probably more difficult than in the AWA days at the height of the so-called 'Cold War'!
The listing above is as accurate as can be achieved at present. In the list -

F: Indicates aircraft that were flown in and out.

R: Indicates those aircraft that arrived and left by road are marked 'R'.

1: Three unidentified aircraft in dismantled state.

2: Probably 6 airframes, all ex-Indian Air Force and in varying states of completeness.

Other Companies' Aircraft at Bitteswell

Rolls-Royce: *Avro Lancaster:* Mk.VI JB675, Mk.III ND340, Mk.VI NG465 icing test, Mk.I PP779. *Avro Lancastrian:* C.3 VH742, C.2 VM728, C.2 VM729, C.2 VM732.

De Havilland Hornet: F.1 PX288. *De Havilland Vampire:* F.1/F.2 TG280. *Gloster Meteor:* F.1 EE227/G Trent turbo-props, F.3 EE339, F.4 prototype EE360/G, F.4 EE517, F.4 RA435, F.4 VT196, F.4 VT279. *Miles Monarch:* G-AFLW. *Miles Whitney Straight:* G-AEUZ. *Percival Proctor:* Mk.IV G-AHFR, II G-AHVG, V G-AKIU.

Martin-Baker *Gloster Meteor:* F.3 EE415, F.3 EE416.

Dunlop *De Havilland Dove:* Srs 1 WJ310. Gloster Meteor: F.4 VW303, NF.11 prototype WA547.

Chapter Three

Built at Bitteswell

The fourth Argosy, G-APRN, flying over the 'Old Site' at Bitteswell. Despite wearing the colours of US customer Riddle Airlines, it entered service with BEA. HSA

IT IS POSSIBLE to describe Bitteswell as one of Leicestershire's best kept aviation secrets. Locals and enthusiasts know that 'some' aircraft construction was undertaken there and that many aircraft were rebuilt, refurbished or converted to new roles at the airfield. Armstrong Whitworth Aircraft (AWA – later Whitworth Gloster, Hawker Siddeley and British Aerospace) undertook a considerable amount of work from Bitteswell and up until now this has not been adequately documented, with many sources quoting

almost all of the AWA-built aircraft as coming from the 'parent' factories at Coventry with Bitteswell reduced to the status of a flight test station.

As will be seen from the extensive tables and notes appearing in this chapter, Bitteswell was responsible for the assembly and flight test of a surprising number of aircraft. Chapter Two has provided an examination of the activities of AWA from the point of view of where they fit into the overall history of the airfield. This chapter serves to examine in greater depth Bitteswell's production record. Necessarily, this means that much tabular presentation is required, but this is by far and away the best manner of getting over the extensive and at times complex nature of Bitteswell's output.

Additionally, mention is made of the many aircraft overhauled, modified or refurbished at Bitteswell. While much of the data exists to furnish even more information, it is felt that for the purposes of this book, the mention of such aircraft and programmes be given a less detailed approach.

It is important to point out that with the increasing complexity of aircraft from the Second World War onwards airframes (ie fuselages, wings, control and tail surfaces and sub-assemblies that go to make up these items) were built in a wide series of locations. This was due to the dispersal operation to make the entire production of a type difficult, if not impossible, to 'take out' in one saturation bombing raid by the enemy and also to utilise to the full 'spare'

Summary of Aircraft Assembled, Overhauled and Converted at Bitteswell

Year	Lancaster	Meteor	Sea Hawk	Hunter	Javelin	Argosy	Hawk	Overhauls / Conversions
1943	see p.59/60	–	–	–	–	–	–	–
1944	see p.59/60	–	–	–	–	–	–	–
1945	see p.59/60	–	–	–	–	–	–	–
1950	–	NF.11	–	–	–	–	–	–
1951	–	NF.11	–	–	–	–	–	–
1952	–	F.8	–	–	–	–	–	–
	–	NF.11	–	–	–	–	–	–
	–	NF.13	–	–	–	–	–	–
1953	–	F.8	F.1	F.2	–	–	–	–
	–	NF.11	F.2					
	–	NF.12	–	–	–	–	–	–
	–	NF.13	–	–	–	–	–	–
	–	NF.14	–	–	–	–	–	–
1954	–	F.8 prone	F.2	F.2	–	–	–	–
	–	NF.14	FB.3	F.5	–	–	–	–
	–	–	FGA.4	–	–	–	–	–
1955	–	–	FGA.4	F.5	–	–	–	–
	–	–	FGA.6	F.6	–	–	–	–
1956	–	–	–	F.6	FAW.4	–	–	Meteor F.8
	–	–	–	–	FAW.5	–	–	–
1957	–	–	Mk.50 (N)	F.6	FAW.4/5	–	–	Javelin
	–	–	–	–	FAW.7	–	–	Meteor
1958	–	–	Mk.50 (N)	–	FAW.7	–	–	Meteor, Shackleton
	–	–	Mk.100	–	–	–	–	
1959	–	–	FGA.6 (I)	–	–	–	–	Hunter (T.7/T.8), Lincoln, Shackleton
	–	–	Mk.101	–	–	Srs 100	–	Vulcan
1960	–	–	FGA.6 (I)	–	–	Srs 100	–	Anson T.21/22, Shackleton, Vulcan
1961	–	–	FGA.6 (I)	–	–	Srs 100	–	Meteor T.7, Vulcan
	–	–	–	–	–	C.1	–	
1962	–	–	FGA.6 (I)	–	–	C.1	–	Javelin, Vulcan
1963	–	–	FGA.6 (I)	–	–	C.1	–	Javelin, Trident, Vulcan
1964	–	–	–	–	–	C.1	–	Meteor T.7, Beverley, Javelin
	–	–	–	–	–	Srs 200	–	Trident, Vulcan
1965	–	–	–	–	–	Srs 200	–	Beverley, Trident, Vulcan
1966	–	–	–	–	–	Srs 200	–	Hunter (India), Hunter (Iraq), Hunter (Jordan), Trident, Vulcan
1967	–	–	–	–	–	–	–	Hunter, Hunter (Jordan), Trident, Vulcan
1968	–	–	–	–	–	–	–	Hunter, Hunter (Jordan), Shackleton, Argosy C.1/E.1, Vulcan
1969	–	–	–	–	–	–	–	Gnat, Hunter (India), Hunter (Jordan), Shackleton, Vulcan, Argosy (civil)
1970	–	–	–	–	–	–	–	Gnat, HS.748, Hunter, Hunter (Qatar, Switzerland), Nimrod, Shackleton, Vulcan
1971	–	–	–	–	–	–	–	Gnat, Hunter, Hunter (Chile, Jordan, Qatar, Singapore, Switzerland), Nimrod, Shackleton, Vulcan
1972	–	–	–	–	–	–	–	Gnat, Hunter (Chile, Singapore), Shackleton, Vulcan
1973	–	–	–	–	–	–	–	Gnat, Hunter, Hunter (Chile, India, Singapore), Shackleton, Vulcan
1974	–	–	–	–	–	–	–	Buccaneer, Gnat, Vulcan Argosy C.1 to T.2 (cancelled 1975)
1975	–	–	–	–	–	–	–	Buccaneer, Gnat, Hunter, Vulcan
1976	–	–	–	–	–	–	–	Buccaneer, Gnat, Hunter, Shackleton, Vulcan
1977	–	–	–	–	–	–	–	Bucanneer, Gnat, Hunter (Lebanon) Shackleton, Vulcan
1978	–	–	–	–	–	–	–	Buccaneer, Gnat, Harrier, Hawk Shackleton, Vulcan
1979	–	–	–	–	–	–	T.1	Buccaneer, Harrier, Hawk, Shackleton Vulcan
1980	–	–	–	–	–	–	T.1	Buccaneer, Harrier, Hawk, Hunter, Shackleton, Vulcan
1981	–	–	–	–	–	–	T.1	Buccaneer, Harrier, Hunter, Shackleton, Vulcan
1982	–	–	–	–	–	–	T.1	Buccaneer

Notes:
See the individual type summaries for details. In the Sea Hawk column (N) indicates aircraft for the Netherlands, (I) for India.

or 'latent' capacity in associated industries. (The Avro Lancaster programme is a classic example of this industrial technique, see Chapter One for Leicester's contribution, and see also Chapter Ten, *Desford's Spitfires and 'Twins'*.)

Final assembly and flight testing (what many people associate with the term 'built') could take place equally at several sites and it is this element in which Bitteswell fitted into the AWA production 'chain'. Sub-assemblies or airframe sections were not made at Bitteswell; that would have required a far more extensive and complex infrastructure than the buildings that made up the areas known as the 'Old Site' and the 'New Site'.

Bitteswell's role was to take sub-assemblies from other sites (principally the extensive AWA plants in and around Coventry, including the huge factories at Baginton and Whitley, but also from other sources), to assemble and fit these sections out, to carry out flight test, rectification if need be and then to effect despatch to the customer. (This is well illustrated by the Argosy fuselage negotiating a turn in Chapter Two.)

In the case of the RAF or the Royal Navy, despatch to the customer more often than not involved 'signing off' the aircraft at Bitteswell as a service ferry pilot arrived to fly it to its destination. In the RAF's case this was frequently to a Maintenance Unit (MU) where inspection, pre-service installations or modifications, or storage awaiting allocation to a unit, was carried out. For overseas customers despatch was undertaken by a mixture of AWA test pilots, customer pilots and contract ferry pilots from civilian organisations.

Mention has already been made of the confusion existing in many previously published books and articles relating to what-was-built-where by AWA. This has not been helped by some official records quoting the delivery point as 'Baginton' when in many cases it was fairly certainly Bitteswell. In all probablility the confusion has arisen from the use of parent company headed paperwork by those at the latter airfield.

The basis of this chapter is the logbooks from the control tower at Bitteswell, which provide a unique and precious insight into the achievements of this Leicestershire assembly and test flight centre. Every effort has been made not to add to this primary source and the dates etc given in the tables are (with very few exceptions, which are annotated) taken directly from the logbooks. Further notes in the narratives that follow the tables help to explain the situation further and to highlight anomalies.

Prior to 1953-54 some of the information presented might well relate to *both* Baginton and Bitteswell. Baginton airfield witnessed many first flights, often with the landing being made at Bitteswell for flight

BARTER BOOKS
Alnwick Station, NE66 2NP
Tel. 01665 604888
www.barterbooks.co.uk

HC #02

REG SB   20-05-2012 11:19

SB

1	HARDBACKS		48.00
	BARTER		-41.00
	TOTAL		7.00
	CASH		7.00

One of the largest
secondhand bookshops
in Britain

test to continue. Wherever it has been possible to discern if a movement in the Bitteswell tower logbooks relates to a 'hop' from Baginton or a maiden flight from Bitteswell, this has been noted. In many pre-1953 instances the exact venue of the 'first flight' remains unconfirmed.

From 1953-54 when the 'New Site' was fully operational, following an arrangement with the Ministry of Supply, Baginton then ceased to be a site for final assembly and test flight, with Bitteswell taking over that mantle. The advent of the Gloster Meteor F.8 and other heavier and more powerful jets made the flying ground at Baginton (it had no hard runways at this stage) increasingly unsuitable, especially for 'circuits and bumps'. However, in spite of a notable lack of company records, it is now thought fairly certain that all Meteor night-fighters prior to the NF.14, made their first flights from Baginton, landing at Bitteswell – the inference being that the NF.14s and all aircraft produced thereafter first flew from Bitteswell.

The bulk of the assembly and flight test work carried out concerned the designs of other companies (eg the Hawker Hunter), reflecting AWA's proven role as a major sub-contractor and programme manager. Design and development of the Meteor night-fighter series was made entirely AWA's and,

Avro Lancaster Is under final assembly at Bitteswell. The example in the foreground, LM296, served with 50 Squadron and survived the war to be struck off charge in April 1946.
via Midland Air Museum

following prototype testing and a small production batch built at Kingston, all Hawker Sea Hawk production was vested in AWA, allowing the parent company to concentrate on the 'super-priority' Hunter. Only the Argosy freighter and tactical airlifter originated from AWA's own drawing boards during this period. Had it been allowed to come to fruition, the advanced HS.681 tactical jet transport would surely have undergone assembly and flight test at Bitteswell.

Contrary to many published sources, the Argosy was *not* the last aircraft to be assembled and flight tested from Bitteswell. From 1979 until 1982, Hawker Siddeley Hawks for the RAF were assembled and test flown over a decade after the last Argosy had taken to the skies. (The final aircraft to be assembled and test flown from Bitteswell were the microlights of Midland Ultralights; their story is related in Chapter Two.)

An examination of the table summarising the aircraft flown from Bitteswell will show that increasing reliance was placed on overhaul, modification, conversion or refurbishment work. This began with RAF Meteor F.8s in 1956 and Gloster-built Javelin FAW.5s the following year, ending in 1982 with the Hawker Siddeley Buccaneer S.2. Major overhauls and other work carried out on the RAF's Avro Vulcan 'V-Bomber' fleet constituted a long and lucrative undertaking for AWA and its corporate successors.

Aircraft are dealt with in the narrative in approximate chronological order of type. Data tables further expand the subject, where appropriate.

Avro Lancaster

AWA produced 1,328 Avro Lancaster four-engined bombers as part of the massive programme that evolved to build Bomber Command's most successful 'heavy'. The vast majority of these were assembled at Baginton, with the first example flying in 1943. The type went on to supplant the AW Whitley twin-engined medium bomber on the huge assembly line.

Overall, production of the Avro Lancaster amounted to 7,374 units, with production being undertaken by Avro, AWA, Austin Motors, Metropolitan-Vickers and Vickers-Armstrong in the UK and, to a more limited extent, Victory Aircraft in Canada.

As was shown in Chapter One, a whole host of industries and workshops were brought into the production scheme, producing sub-asemblies.

An unknown number of Lancasters were assembled and test flown from the new dispersed site on the southern boundary of Bitteswell during 1944 and 1945. No records have been found to denote exactly which Lancasters originated at Bitteswell.

No AWA-built Lancaster survives intact today.

AWA also received a contract to build the Lancaster's successor, the Lincoln. AWA's later production of the Avro Lincoln was only carried out at Baginton and some 281 were complete with large numbers being cancelled following the end of hostilities.

Serial batches for the AWA Lancasters are given overleaf.

AWA-built Avro Lancasters

(Contract 5/Acft/239/C.4(c))

Mk.I and Mk. B.1(FE)
The Mk. B.1(FE) being Far East-modified examples for the projected 'Tiger Force'). Rolls-Royce Merlin engines: LL740–758, LL771–813, LL826–867, LL880–923, LL935–977, LM100–142, LM156–192, LM205–243, LM257–296; NF906–939, NF952–999, NG113–149, NG162–206, NG218–259, NG263–308, NG321–367, NG379–421, NG434–469, NG482–503, RF120–161, RF175–197, SW296 316, TW647 671, TW858–873, TW878–911. *911 units.*

Mk.II
Bristol Hercules radial engines;
DS601–635, DS647–692, DS704–741, DS757–797, DS813–852, LL617–653, LL666–704, LL716–739. *300 units.*

Mk.III
US-built Packard Merlin engines:
RF198–216, RF229–273, RF286–326, SW283–295. *118 units.*

Gloster Meteor

In 1949 AWA were given a contract to build a batch of Gloster Meteor F.4 and the later F.8 twin-jet day-fighters. Assembly and flight test of Meteors from Bitteswell started with a batch of F.8s from 1952. The F.8 was a single-seat day-fighter, the prototype first flying on 12th October 1948 from Gloster's airfield at Moreton Valence, Gloucestershire. In all 1,183 Mk.8s were built out of the total production of 3,545 Meteors.

Meteors appear in the Bitteswell tower logbook from WK906, which was the first of the final AWA batch, ordered in 1951. It is possible that all of these aircraft made their first flights at Baginton and that the date given in the accompanying table represents either their first appearance 'in the circuit' at Bitteswell, or a landing following first flight out of Baginton.

A good example of this is WK935, the last AWA-produced Meteor F.8. It first flew over a year after the others in the batch. This was because it was extensively modified at Baginton with a radically extended new nose section to take a pilot in the prone position. (This was pioneered by the Reid & Sigrist Desford trainer when converted to Bobsleigh form – see Chapter Ten.) In the hands of AWA's Chief Test Pilot, Eric Franklin, WK935 made its first flight at Baginton on 10th February 1954, landing at Bitteswell.

As already outlined, development of the two-seat night-fighter versions of the Meteor was handed over entirely to AWA in 1949 and their drawing office was totally responsible for the considerable modifications required to turn the Meteor from a single-seat day fighter into a two-seater with increasing night and all-weather intercept capability.

The parent design company, Gloster, was heavily committed to developing the ultimate day fighter version, the Mk.8 and further down the line was preparing the way for the delta-winged Javelin, the first purpose-built all-weather UK jet fighter. (Both the Meteor F.8 and the Javelin were also to be built under sub-contract by AWA.) It was this huge workload that predicated the transfer of the night-fighter requirement to Bitteswell and AWA.

First variant was the NF.11, based largely upon the two-seat trainer variant, the T.7, with an F.8 tail unit, a Mk.10 air interception radar in an extended nose and four 20mm cannon in the outer wings. The first prototype, WA546, was first flown on 31st May 1950 and was followed by two more prototypes (WA547 and WB543), all from Baginton. WB543 had its undercarriage collapse due to a heavy landing at Bitteswell on 1st December 1950 and it was not flown out to Baginton again until 29th January 1952.

Following these came WD585, the first of 352 production NF.11s for the RAF. It made its debut in the Bitteswell tower log on 14th November 1950, a remarkably short time after the prototype. Production was completed in early 1953 – see the table. As the NF.11 represented a considerable leap in night-fighter potential many visited Bitteswell on one, two or more occasions for modifications and 'tweaks'.

The Royal Danish Air Force (Kongelige Danske Flyvevåbnet) ordered 20 NF.11s, and these featured in the Bitteswell logbooks. They were despatched briefly to one of three RAF Maintenance Units, presumably for a special fit, and then returned to Bitteswell for onward delivery. (See table.)

The French Air Force (L'Armée de l'Air) received 41 NF.11s, mostly from RAF stocks from 1952 through to 1954 (serial numbers NF11-1 to NF11-41) and some refurbished examples later again. All of these were dealt with in one form or another at Bitteswell. A total of 25 were given RAF serial numbers (WM296 to '307, 368 to '371 and 375 to '383) but issued direct to the French. Although these were considered as 'new-build', these machines cannot be separated from the examples taken from RAF charge, and it is not possible to discern them as being in French guise in the Bitteswell tower log.

NF11-1 is preserved today at Brienne le Château in France. This machine provides a good 'snapshot' of French NF.11 activity at Bitteswell. It arrived from Baginton on 3rd December 1952, despatched to Wroughton on the 11th, returning on the 18th. It was delivered to Le Bourget, near Paris, on 7th January 1953.

Twenty NF.11s were later converted to TT.20 target tug status by AWA for the Royal Navy. Six Royal Danish Air Force examples were similarly adapted.

The NF.12 differed from the NF.11 in having a longer nose to house the US-built APS.21 radar and a larger fin area. The aerodynamic prototype was a converted NF.11 WD687 (often referred to as the NF.11½); the first prototype, WS590 was first flown on 21st April 1953. The RAF ordered 100, production being completed in late 1953 – see the table. Many of the NF.12s returned to Bitteswell on one, two or more occasions for modifications and 'tweaks'.

Essentially a development of the NF.11, the NF.13 featured tropicalised equipment for operation in the Middle East. The first prototype was WM308, first flown on 21st December 1952 and arriving at Bitteswell two days later. The RAF ordered 40, all despatched in 1953 – see table. Of these, six each were later supplied to the air forces of Egypt (1955), Israel (1956 and 1958) and Syria (1954) and two to France (1956); all went through Bitteswell. (See table.)

The final two-seat night-fighter version was the NF.14, a much-refined variant of the NF.12. The most obvious feature was the two-piece 'blown' canopy, first tested on NF.11 WM261, instead of the multi-framed 'glasshouse' previously used and dating from the Meteor T.7.

The NF.14 was also longer and offered better flying characteristics. Many aircraft made return trips to Bitteswell for attention or modification. The RAF ordered 100 – see table. In later life some airframes were converted to navigator trainers with the unofficial designation NF(T).14.

During 1956 and 1957, Bitteswell carried out unspecified work on a series of Meteors from the Belgian Air Force (Force Aérienne Belge). These aircraft comprised three T.7 two-seaters (ED1, '7 and '34), ten F.8 day fighters (EG6, '17, '30, '57, '58, '73, '228, '235, '245 and '255) and six former RAF NF.11s (EN2, '5, '6, '10, '11 and '12).

At the same time as the Belgian contract was in process, a total of 25 RAF F.8s were processed, coming in for modifications or repair work. Another Meteor type commonly seen at Bitteswell was the T.7 two-seat advanced trainer. During 1956-58, '60-61 and '64, 23 were modified and/or repaired. One of these was VZ649, which arrived from Worksop on 24th January 1957, departing to Kirkbride on 2nd August 1957. This T.7 was fitted with the camera nose of a PR.10 high altitude reconnaissance version. During March 1956, two production PR.10s (VS976 and VW376) arrived for modification work.

AWA-produced Gloster Meteors

Meteor F.8 (Contract 6/Acft/6066/CB.7(a) 6.12.50)

Serial	First Flight	Despatched	To
WK906 to WK910			see notes
WK911	29.8.52	15.9.52	Wattisham
WK912	1.9.52	15.9.52	Little Rissington
WK913	3.9.52	17.9.52	Lyneham
WK914	4.9.52	22.9.52	Church Fenton
WK915	8.9.52	7.10.52	Leconfield
WK916	12.9.52	2.10.52	Tangmere
WK917	16.9.52	2.10.52	Tangmere
WK918	19.9.52	7.10.52	Leuchars
WK919	22.9.52	9.10.52	St Athan
WK920	24.9.52	24.10.52	Worksop
WK921	26.9.52	29.10.52	Leuchars
WK922	2.10.52	29.10.52	Worksop
WK923	2.10.52	30.10.52	Stradishall
WK924	8.10.52	30.10.52	Worksop
WK925	9.10.52	30.10.52	Worksop
WK926	16.10.52	5.11.52	Defford
WK927	17.10.52	25.11.52	see notes
WK928	28.10.52	11.11.52	Lyneham
WK929	17.11.52	11.12.52	Worksop
WK930	19.12.52	29.1.53	Leconfield
WK931	17.12.52	22.1.53	Little Rissington
WK932	23.12.52	29.1.53	Hawarden
WK933	2.2.53	24.2.53	Lyneham
WK934	23.2.53	10.3.53	Little Rissington
WK935	10.2.54	31.8.54	

Notes: WK906, believed to have first flown 31.7.52, but no documented despatch date. WK907 to WK910 have no documented first flight or despatch dates. *(RAF records indicate that WK906 to '910 were accepted for service during August and September 1952. It is possible that they were test-flown and delivered direct from Baginton).* WK927 was delivered by AVM Atcherley, ferrying it to Newton. He brought it back on 3.12.52, taking it out again to Newton 23.1.53. It came in from Linton-on-Ouse on 17.6.53, with Atcherley flying it out again to Newton on 19.6.53. WK935 was delivered to Farnborough, having made its first flight from Baginton. This was the prone-pilot Meteor and is preserved at the RAF Museum Cosford, Shropshire.

Meteor NF.11 (Contract 6/Acft/3437/CB.5(b) 31.5.49)

Serial	First Flight	Despatched	To
WD585	14.11.50	18.11.50	West Raynham
WD586	15.3.51		see notes
WD587	15.3.51		see notes
WD588	21.8.51	6.9.51	West Raynham
WD589	17.2.51	28.5.53	Wroughton
WD590	15.3.51	11.3.53	Aston Down
WD591	16.2.51	23.3.54	Boscombe Down
WD592	15.3.51	16.1.53	Baginton
WD593			see notes
WD594	28.3.51	13.4.51	West Raynham
WD595	14.4.51	11.5.51	West Raynham
WD596	14.4.51	23.2.54	High Ercall
WD597	10.5.51	23.8.51	Tangmere
WD598	10.5.51	28.8.51	Aston Down
WD599	31.5.51	20.8.51	Tangmere
WD600	21.5.51	27.8.51	Tangmere
WD601	1.6.51	27.8.51	Tangmere
WD602	5.6.51	27.8.51	Tangmere
WD603	4.6.51	29.8.51	Tangmere
WD604	17.7.51	20.2.53	Wroughton
WD605	21.6.51	29.8.51	Tangmere
WD606	20.6.51	6.9.51	Coltishall
WD607	25.6.51	31.8.51	Coltishall
WD608	26.6.51	31.8.51	Coltishall
WD609	4.7.51	6.9.51	Coltishall
WD610	9.7.51	6.9.51	Coltishall
WD611	10.7.51	6.9.51	Coltishall
WD612	17.7.51	6.9.51	Coltishall
WD613	18.7.51	12.9.51	Coltishall
WD614	19.7.51	17.9.51	West Malling
WD615	24.7.51	17.9.51	West Malling
WD616	25.7.51	17.9.51	West Malling
WD617	27.7.51	21.9.51	West Malling
WD618	26.7.51	21.9.51	West Malling
WD619	13.8.51	21.9.51	West Malling
WD620	14.8.51	21.9.51	West Malling
WD621	16.8.51	26.9.51	High Ercall
WD622	21.8.51	26.9.51	High Ercall
WD623	4.9.51	28.9.51	High Ercall
WD624	27.8.51	28.9.51	High Ercall
WD625	4.9.51	12.10.51	West Malling
WD626	31.8.51		see notes

Serial	First Flight	Despatched	To
WD627	5.9.51	27.11.51	High Ercall
WD628	13.9.51	1.11.51	High Ercall
WD629	8.9.51	28.9.51	Hawarden
WD630	12.9.51	17.10.51	High Ercall
WD631	14.9.51	24.10.51	High Ercall
WD632	20.9.51	1.11.51	High Ercall
WD633	24.9.51	23.10.51	High Ercall
WD634	25.9.51	6.11.51	High Ercall
WD640	28.9.51	17.10.51	High Ercall
WD641	26.9.51	17.10.51	High Ercall
WD642	9.10.51	28.11.51	High Ercall
WD643	12.10.51	6.11.51	High Ercall
WD644	17.10.51	22.11.51	Coltishall
WD645	11.10.51	1.11.51	High Ercall
WD646	12.10.51	15.11.51	Watton
WD647	30.10.51	16.11.51	Coltishall
WD648	17.10.51	10.12.51	West Raynham
WD649	19.10.51		see notes
WD650	24.10.51	27.11.51	Linton-on-Ouse
WD651	29.10.51	17.12.51	High Ercall
WD652	23.10.51	30.11.51	Linton-on-Ouse
WD653	27.10.51	30.11.51	Linton-on-Ouse
WD654	1.11.51	30.11.51	Linton-on-Ouse
WD655	3.11.51	27.11.51	Linton-on-Ouse
WD656	9.11.51	17.12.51	High Ercall
WD657	9.11.51	30.11.51	Linton-on-Ouse
WD658	14.11.51	15.1.52	High Ercall
WD659	14.11.51	31.12.51	High Ercall
WD660	14.11.51	20.12.51	Linton-on-Ouse
WD661	17.11.51	20.12.51	Linton-on-Ouse
WD662	21.11.51	31.12.51	High Ercall
WD663	27.11.51	28.12.51	High Ercall
WD664	27.11.51	28.12.51	High Ercall
WD665	27.11.51	7.2.52	Linton-on-Ouse
WD666	29.11.51	18.1.52	High Ercall
WD667	28.11.51	17.12.51	High Ercall
WD668	30.11.51	31.12.51	High Ercall
WD669	15.11.51	22.1.52	Llandow
WD670	6.3.52	6.7.53	see notes
WD671	5.12.51	11.1.52	High Ercall
WD672	27.12.51	14.1.52	High Ercall
WD673	15.12.51	8.1.52	High Ercall

Serial	First Flight	Despatched	To
WD674	18.12.51	11.1.52	High Ercall
WD675	27.12.51	8.1.52	High Ercall
WD676	15.1.52	5.2.52	Llandow
WD677	11.1.52	5.2.52	Wroughton
WD678	4.1.52	5.2.52	Llandow
WD679	3.1.52	5.2.52	Wroughton
WD680	11.1.52	12.2.52	Wroughton
WD681	7.1.52	5.2.52	Wroughton
WD682	10.1.52	5.2.52	Llandow
WD683	4.1.52	5.2.52	Llandow
WD684	7.1.52	5.2.52	Llandow
WD685	7.1.52	7.2.52	Llandow
WD686	22.4.52	27.2.53	Defford
WD687	16.6.52	28.1.53	Boscombe Down
WD688	7.1.52	5.2.52	Wroughton
WD696	9.1.52	8.2.52	Aston Down
WD697	10.1.52	22.2.52	Llandow
WD698	10.1.52	20.2.52	Llandow
WD699	14.1.52	20.2.52	Llandow
WD700	16.1.52	12.2.52	Aston Down
WD701	16.1.52	13.2.52	Wroughton
WD702	21.1.52	20.2.52	St Athan
WD703	21.1.52	21.2.52	Leeming
WD704	21.1.52		see notes
WD705	26.1.52	26.2.52	Wroughton
WD706	29.1.52	21.2.52	Leeming
WD707	26.1.52	13.3.52	Aston Down
WD708	29.1.52	18.3.52	Coltishall
WD709	30.1.52	21.3.52	Coltishall
WD710	1.2.52	22.2.52	Leuchars
WD711	4.2.52	1.4.52	Coltishall
WD712	7.2.52	1.4.52	Tangmere
WD713	6.2.52	18.3.52	Coltishall
WD714	7.2.52	21.3.52	Coltishall
WD715	11.2.52	1.4.52	Tangmere
WD716	11.2.52	18.3.52	Coltishall
WD717	13.2.52	18.3.52	Coltishall
WD718	13.2.52	22.4.52	Coltishall
WD719	19.2.52	21.3.52	Coltishall
WD720	19.2.52	21.3.52	Coltishall
WD721	7.5.52	18.7.52	Boscombe Down
WD722	20.2.52	26.3.52	Tangmere
WD723	21.2.52	1.4.52	Coltishall
WD724	22.2.52	21.3.52	Hawarden
WD725	26.2.52	26.3.52	Tangmere
WD726	26.2.52	3.4.52	Llandow
WD727	28.2.52	31.3.52	Llandow
WD728	3.3.52	9.4.52	Llandow
WD729	4.3.52	7.4.52	Llandow
WD730	6.3.52	7.4.52	Llandow
WD731	6.3.52	4.4.52	Llandow
WD732	10.3.52	4.4.52	Llandow
WD733	10.3.52	4.4.52	Llandow
WD734	17.3.52	9.4.52	Llandow
WD735	18.3.52	4.4.52	Llandow
WD736	19.3.52	10.7.52	see notes
WD737	19.3.52	23.4.52	Llandow
WD738	21.3.52	18.4.52	Llandow
WD739	22.3.52	22.4.52	Coltishall
WD740	26.3.52	24.4.52	Coltishall
WD741	28.3.52	23.4.52	Coltishall
WD742	31.3.52	25.4.52	Coltishall
WD743	27.6.52	2.10.52	Defford
WD744	22.7.52	6.11.52	Defford
WD745	21.8.52	2.10.52	Defford
WD751	3.4.52	8.5.52	Coltishall
WD752	3.4.52	25.4.52	Coltishall
WD753	7.4.52	8.5.52	Coltishall
WD754	9.4.52	8.5.52	Coltishall
WD755	9.4.52	8.5.52	Coltishall
WD756	9.4.52	8.5.52	Coltishall
WD757	9.4.52	8.5.52	Coltishall
WD758	17.4.52	12.5.52	Coltishall
WD759	21.4.52	22.5.52	Coltishall
WD760	23.4.52	12.5.52	Coltishall
WD761	22.4.52	15.5.52	Coltishall
WD762	24.4.52	14.5.52	Tangmere
WD763	25.4.52	22.5.52	West Malling
WD764	28.4.52	22.5.52	Coltishall
WD765	30.4.52	22.5.52	Martlesham Heath
WD766	30.4.52	26.5.52	Coltishall
WD767	6.5.52	26.5.52	Coltishall
WD768	6.5.52	4.6.52	Coltishall
WD769	6.5.52	4.6.52	Martlesham Heath
WD770	7.5.52	26.5.52	Coltishall
WD771	12.5.52	10.6.52	Coltishall
WD772	12.5.52		see notes
WD773	12.5.52	10.6.52	Llandow
WD774	13.5.52	10.6.52	Wroughton
WD775	14.5.52	9.6.52	High Ercall
WD776	15.5.52	12.6.52	Llandow
WD777	16.5.52	9.6.52	High Ercall
WD778	26.5.52	18.6.52	Llandow
WD779	19.5.52	12.6.52	Llandow
WD780	21.5.52	20.6.52	Coltishall
WD781	22.5.52	16.6.52	Llandow
WD782	23.5.52	16.6.52	Martlesham Heath
WD783	26.5.52	18.6.52	Llandow
WD784	28.5.52	20.6.52	Llandow
WD785	24.7.52	9.10.52	Lyneham
WD786	2.9.52	17.9.52	Leeming
WD787	28.5.52	23.6.52	Llandow
WD788	30.5.52	19.6.52	Llandow
WD789	9.6.52	26.6.52	Wroughton
WD790	9.6.52	25.6.52	Defford
WD791	12.11.52	20.1.53	West Raynham
WD792	10.6.52	24.6.52	Tangmere
WD793	16.6.52	1.7.52	Boscombe Down
WD794	16.6.52	30.6.52	High Ercall
WD795	18.6.52	30.6.52	High Ercall
WD796	18.6.52	7.7.52	Wroughton
WD797	11.8.52	2.10.52	Boscombe Down
WD798	20.6.52	10.7.52	West Raynham
WD799	25.6.52	11.7.52	West Raynham
WD800	26.6.52	14.7.52	Wroughton
(Contract 6/Acft/6141/CB.7(b) 22.12.50, part)			
WM143	26.6.52	11.7.52	Wroughton
WM144	27.6.52	21.7.52	Wroughton
WM145	1.7.52	21.7.52	Lyneham
WM146	2.7.52	17.7.52	High Ercall
WM147	2.7.52	23.7.52	Wroughton
WM148	3.7.52	25.7.52	High Ercall
WM149	4.7.52	23.7.52	Llandow
WM150	7.7.52	23.7.52	Llandow
WM151	8.7.52	25.7.52	Leeming
WM152	11.7.52	28.7.52	High Ercall
WM153	11.7.52	29.7.52	Lyneham
WM154	11.7.52	21.10.52	Little Rissington
WM155	15.7.52	24.2.53	Llandow
WM156	15.7.52	29.7.52	Bassingbourn
WM157	17.7.52	10.10.52	Aston Down
WM158	17.7.52	14.10.52	Wroughton
WM159	18.7.52	9.10.52	Lyneham
WM160	18.7.52	19.8.52	Coltishall
WM161	21.7.52	15.10.52	Aston Down
WM162	23.7.52	20.8.52	Coltishall
WM163	24.7.52	28.8.52	Lyneham
WM164	25.7.52	20.8.52	Coltishall
WM165	25.7.52	28.8.52	Aston Down
WM166	25.7.52	16.9.52	Hawarden
WM167	31.7.52	29.8.52	Hawarden
WM168	30.7.52	28.8.52	Lyneham
WM169	15.8.52	29.9.52	Wroughton
WM170	14.8.52	27.10.52	Llandow
WM171	18.8.52	21.10.52	Little Rissington
WM172	19.8.52	15.10.52	Wroughton
WM173	20.8.52	1.9.52	Leeming
WM174	21.8.52	15.9.52	West Malling
WM175	21.8.52	8.9.52	Aston Down
WM176	22.8.52	15.9.52	West Mallling
WM177	25.8.52	11.9.52	West Malling
WM178	26.8.52	17.9.52	Leeming
WM179	28.8.52	14.10.52	Lyneham
WM180	28.8.52	24.9.52	Wroughton
WM181	29.8.52	23.9.52	Lyneham
WM182	2.9.52	24.9.52	Wroughton
WM183	3.9.52	23.9.52	Wroughton
WM184	3.9.52	22.9.52	Lyneham
WM185	4.9.52	14.10.52	Lyneham
WM186	5.9.52	29.9.52	Lyneham
WM187	5.9.52	9.2.53	Aston Down
WM188	8.9.52	23.3.53	Little Rissington
WM189	8.9.52	24.10.52	Manby
WM190	12.9.52	2.10.52	Lyneham
WM191	12.9.52	10.10.52	Lyneham
WM192	16.9.52	10.10.52	Lyneham
WM221	19.9.52	21.10.52	Lyneham
WM222	18.9.52	15.10.52	Wroughton
WM223	18.9.52	14.10.52	Lyneham
WM224	26.9.52	15.10.52	Aston Down
WM225	25.9.52	23.10.52	Coltishall
WM226	26.9.52	27.10.52	Llandow
WM227	26.9.52	21.10.52	Little Rissington
WM228	30.9.52	23.10.52	see notes
WM229	2.10.52	21.10.52	Little Rissington
WM230	7.10.52	6.11.52	Leeming
WM231	16.10.52	6.11.52	High Ercall
WM232	22.10.52	11.11.52	Wroughton
WM233	24.10.52	28.1.53	Lyneham
WM234	29.10.52	17.11.52	Little Rissington
WM235	30.10.52	17.11.52	Wroughton
WM236	7.11.52	11.12.52	Lyneham
WM237	10.11.52	12.12.52	Little Rissington
WM238	3.11.52	17.11.52	Little Rissington
WM239	5.11.52	11.12.52	Wroughton
WM240	10.11.52	11.12.52	Wroughton
WM241	7.11.52	11.12.52	Wroughton
WM242	11.11.52	12.12.52	High Ercall
WM243	17.11.52	11.12.52	Wroughton
WM244	11.11.52	18.12.52	Llandow
WM245	11.11.52	11.12.52	Wroughton
WM246	17.11.52	27.1.53	Little Rissington
WM247	18.11.52	22.1.53	Little Rissington
WM248	19.11.52	15.12.52	Aston Down
WM249	19.11.52	18.12.52	Leeming
WM250	1.12.52	18.12.52	Leeming
WM251	19.11.52	12.12.52	High Ercall
WM252	20.11.52	18.12.52	Merryfield
WM253	20.11.52	12.12.52	High Ercall
WM254	24.11.52	18.12.52	Leeming
WM255	10.12.52	22.1.53	Wroughton
WM256	26.11.52	18.12.52	Leeming
WM257	28.11.52	31.12.52	Little Rissington
WM258	27.11.52	31.12.52	Little Rissington
WM259	12.12.52	22.1.53	Wroughton
WM260	12.12.52	22.1.53	Wroughton
WM261	15.7.53	27.7.53	see notes
WM262	10.12.52	16.3.53	Wisley
WM263	17.12.52	27.1.53	Lyneham
WM264	16.12.52	22.1.53	Wroughton
WM265	16.1.53	28.1.53	Wroughton
WM266		8.4.53	see notes
WM267		31.3.53	see notes
WM268		8.4.53	see notes
WM269		1.4.53	see notes
WM270		31.3.53	see notes
WM292		1.4.53	see notes
WM293	18.3.53	31.3.53	Wroughton
WM294	19.3.53	13.4.53	Wroughton
WM295	30.3.53	25.8.53	Wisley
WM296 to WM307			To France

Originally built at Bitteswell as an NF.11, WD767 was the prototype AWA Meteor TT.20 target-towing conversion, making its first flight in the new configuration on 6th December 1956. Note the large winch installation over the starboard inner wing, the cable guides under the fuselage and the sleeve target. For real air gunnery work, the target would be streamed a long, long way behind the aircraft! AWA

Serial(s)	First Flight	Despatched	To
WM368 to WM371			To France
WM372		29.1.54	Cranfield
WM373	3.2.54	24.2.54	Cranfield
WM374	22.2.54	12.3.54	Cranfield
WM375 to WM383			To France
WM384 to WM403			To Denmark

Notes: The first tower log entry for WD585 is 14.11.50. Other sources quote 19.10.50 as the first flight date, so possibly flown and air tested at Baginton before 'hopping' to Bitteswell for pre-delivery preparation. WD586 and WD587 no documented despatch details. WD593 no documented first flight or despatch date. (These and others lacking documentation were also possibly test flown and delivered from Baginton). WD604 was retained by AWA for tip-tank trials before delivery to Wroughton, sans tanks. WD626 and WD649 no documented despatch details. WD670 was in and out from Boscombe Down (for radar trials) on at least two occasions in between first flight and the last documented despatch (a mis-scribe for 1953?) to Defford. WD686 believed tested NF.12 radar hence delayed first flight. WD687 converted on line to prototype NF.12. WD704 no documented despatch details. WD736 in from Baginton at 1134 hours; it force-landed at Hatfield Broadoak at 1616 hours same day while on a test flight; despatched to Wroughton. WD772 no documented despatch details. WD791 modified radar nose (possibly NF.12 second prototype) hence delayed first flight. WM228, while on test 2.10.52 landed at Edge Hill when short of fuel. It returned to Bitteswell the following day and was later despatched to Little Rissington. WM261 was test-fitted with the NF.14 blown canopy; despatched out to Boscombe Down. WM262 and

WM295 to Wisley for 'Blue Boar' trials (Vickers-Armstrong TV-guided nuclear stand-off missile) later cancelled. WM266 and WM267, there are two dates noted as deliveries from Baginton in the logbook, 23.1.53 and 13.3.53 for both of these aircraft; delivery outbound to Wroughton and Lyneham respectively. WM268 and WM269, again two dates given for both aircraft, 23.1.53 and 16.3.53 for WM268 and 27.1.53 and 16.3.53 for WM269; both delivered onwards to Wroughton. WM270 has two dates annotated, 26.1.53 and 17.3.53, it went outbound to Lyneham. WM292 as before, 27.1.53 and 18.3.53, outbound to Lyneham. WM372, WM373, WM374 all to Fairey's at Cranfield for 'Blue Sky' (Fireflash) trial installations; WM372 to Sealand 21.10.54 to ship to Australia.

Several are still extant: WD592 privately owned in the USA; WD646 at North Weald, Essex (as TT.20); WD686 at the Muckleburgh Collection, Weybourne, Norfolk; WM167 kept airworthy at Bournemouth, Dorset, by Jet Heritage; WM261 (in the guise of an NF.14) at the Museum of Flight, East Fortune, Scotland as G-ARCX.

Danish Meteor NF.11

Serial	First Flight	Despatched	To	Delivered
501	22.10.52	27.10.52	WR*	28.11.52
502	24.10.52	28.10.52	WR	28.11.52
503	28.10.52	30.10.52	HE	28.11.52
504	31.10.52	5.11.52	LL	12.12.52
505	27.10.52	30.10.52	HE	28.11.52
506	31.10.52	5.11.52	LL	12.12.52
507	3.11.52	28.11.52	HE	31.12.52
508	7.11.52	4.12.52	HE	31.12.52
509	5.12.52	11.12.52	WR	23.1.53
510	3.12.52	10.12.52	HE	23.1.53
511	10.12.52	12.12.52	WR	23.1.53
512	12.12.52	19.12.52	WR	23.1.53
513	7.1.53	21.1.53	WR	24.2.53
514	12.1.53	21.1.53	WR	24.2.53
515	21.1.53	26.1.53	WR	24.2.53
516	21.1.53	26.1.53	WR	24.2.53
517	25.2.53	9.3.53	WR	28.3.53
518	27.2.53	12.3.53	LL	28.3.53
519	27.2.53	9.3.53	LL	28.3.53
520	7.3.53	9.3.53	LL	28.3.53

Notes: The RAF serials WM384 to WM403 were allocated for these Danish aircraft. After work at Bitteswell, each aircraft was sent on to an RAF MU, for special fitment. * The RAF Maintenance Units are given the following abbreviations: HE: High Ercall; LL: Llandow; WR: Wroughton. The 'Delivered' date is the date the aircraft were finally despatched from Bitteswell, following return from the MU in question. All were delivered to Ålborg in Denmark, apart from 501, 502, 503 and 505; they took off from Bitteswell destined for Ålborg, but landed at Karup due to bad visibility. Six returned to Bitteswell for conversion to TT.20 target tugs in 1958: 504, 508, 512, 517, 518, 519. No.504 is preserved today at Ålborg.

Meteor NF.12 (Contract 6/Acft/6412/CB.7(b) 28.2.51)

Serial	First Flight	Despatched	To
WS590	21.4.53	6.5.53	Wroughton
WS591	21.4.53	4.5.53	Wroughton
WS592	23.4.53	4.5.53	Wroughton
WS593	23.4.53	11.5.53	Wroughton
WS594	28.4.53	11.5.53	Wroughton
WS595	28.4.53	11.5.53	Wroughton
WS596	28.4.53	11.5.53	Wroughton
WS597	29.4.53	11.5.53	Wroughton
WS598	30.4.53	13.5.53	Llandow
WS599	4.5.53	13.5.53	Llandow
WS600	4.5.53	15.5.53	Llandow
WS601	4.5.53	15.5.53	Llandow
WS602	6.5.53	19.5.53	Lyneham
WS603	7.5.53	19.5.53	Lyneham
WS604	8.5.53	19.5.53	Lyneham
WS605	11.5.53	26.5.53	Lyneham
WS606	11.5.53	28.5.53	Llandow
WS607	11.5.53	28.5.53	Llandow
WS608	13.5.53	26.5.53	Lyneham
WS609	13.5.53	28.5.53	Llandow
WS610	15.5.53	28.5.53	Lyneham
WS611	15.5.53	29.5.53	Lyneham
WS612	18.5.53	28.5.53	Wroughton
WS613	19.5.53	4.6.53	Wroughton
WS614	18.5.53	29.5.53	Llandow
WS615	19.5.53	28.5.53	Llandow
WS616	20.5.53	28.5.53	Llandow

Serial	First Flight	Despatched	To
WS617	20.5.53	4.6.53	Wroughton
WS618	22.5.53	10.6.53	Wroughton
WS619	22.5.53	10.6.53	Lyneham
WS620	25.5.53	10.6.53	Lyneham
WS621	25.5.53	10.6.53	Wroughton
WS622	28.5.53	18.6.53	Wroughton
WS623	28.5.53	18.6.53	Lyneham
WS624	29.5.53	18.6.53	Aston Down
WS625	30.5.53	18.6.53	Lyneham
WS626	8.6.53	26.6.53	Lyneham
WS627	8.6.53	18.6.53	Aston Down
WS628	9.6.53	22.6.53	Lyneham
WS629	10.6.53	22.6.53	Lyneham
WS630	15.6.53	6.7.53	Aston Down
WS631	16.6.53	6.7.53	Wroughton
WS632	16.6.53	9.7.53	Llandow
WS633	18.6.53	10.7.53	Llandow
WS634	19.6.53	6.7.53	Wroughton
WS635	20.6.53	20.10.54	Watton
WS636	22.6.53	9.7.53	Llandow
WS637	25.6.53	9.7.53	Lyneham
WS638	26.6.53	10.7.53	Llandow
WS639	26.6.53	10.7.53	Llandow
WS658	30.6.53	10.7.53	Aston Down
WS659	30.6.53	14.7.53	Wroughton
WS660	1.7.53	14.7.53	Wroughton
WS661	1.7.53	12.7.53	Lyneham
WS662	3.7.53	21.7.53	Aston Down
WS663	3.7.53	14.7.53	Lyneham
WS664	6.7.53	20.7.53	Wroughton
WS665	6.7.53	20.7.53	Wroughton
WS666	8.7.53	21.7.53	Wroughton
WS667	9.7.53	23.7.53	Llandow
WS668	9.7.53	23.7.53	Llandow
WS669	13.7.53	23.7.53	Lyneham
WS670	13.7.53	23.7.53	Lyneham
WS671	13.7.53	24.7.53	Lyneham
WS672	13.7.53	24.7.53	Wroughton
WS673	15.7.53	24.7.53	Wroughton
WS674	16.7.53	19.8.53	Llandow
WS675	17.7.53	19.8.53	Llandow
WS676	18.7.53	10.8.53	Wroughton
WS677	20.7.53	30.7.53	Wroughton
WS678	20.7.53	10.8.53	Lyneham
WS679	22.7.53	14.8.53	Llandow
WS680	24.7.53	19.8.53	Lyneham
WS681	24.7.53	14.8.53	Llandow
WS682	30.7.53	21.8.53	Wroughton
WS683	11.8.53	21.8.53	see notes
WS684	13.8.53	7.9.53	Llandow
WS685	14.8.53	11.9.53	Llandow
WS686	17.8.53	1.9.53	Lyneham
WS687	18.8.53	2.9.53	Wroughton
WS688	18.8.53	1.9.53	Lyneham
WS689	20.8.53	1.9.53	Wroughton
WS690	20.8.53	7.9.53	Wroughton
WS691	21.8.53	7.9.53	Lyneham
WS692	25.8.53	7.9.53	Lyneham
WS693	26.8.53	14.9.53	Little Rissington
WS694	28.8.53	14.9.53	Little Rissington
WS695	31.8.53	14.9.53	Little Rissington
WS696	1.9.53	14.9.53	Little Rissington
WS697	2.9.53	22.9.53	Little Rissington
WS698	3.9.53	22.9.53	Little Rissington
WS699	7.9.53	22.9.53	Little Rissington
WS700	8.9.53	22.9.53	Little Rissington
WS715	9.9.53	28.9.53	Little Rissington
WS716	11.9.53	28.9.53	Little Rissington
WS717	14.9.53	28.9.53	Little Rissington
WS718	16.9.53	14.10.53	Langar
WS719	17.9.53	14.10.53	Burtonwood
WS720	18.9.53	14.10.53	Burtonwood
WS721	22.9.53	14.10.53	Langar

Notes: WS635 *was released by C(A) – Controller (Air), an MoS (Ministry of Supply) department, on 24.6.53 for trial installations.* WS683 scheduled to be delivered to Aston Down, but diverted to Wroughton instead. The Newark Air Museum at Winthorpe, Notts, displays NF.12 WS692.

Meteor NF.13 (Contract 6/Acft/6141/CB.7(b) 22.12.50, part)

Serial	First Flight	Despatched	To
WM308	23.12.52	30.1.53	Little Rissington
WM309	30.12.52	2.2.53	Wroughton
WM310	31.12.52	30.1.53	Little Rissington
WM311	1.1.53	4.2.53	Little Rissington
WM312	7.1.53	4.2.53	Aston Down
WM313	12.1.53	2.2.53	Wroughton
WM314	15.1.53	2.2.53	Wroughton
WM315	16.1.53	9.2.53	Aston Down
WM316	16.1.53	9.2.53	Aston Down
WM317	16.1.53	4.2.53	Wroughton
WM318	17.1.53	20.2.53	Wroughton
WM319	26.1.53	23.2.53	Little Rissington
WM320	29.1.53	20.2.53	Wroughton
WM321	30.1.53	23.2.53	Little Rissington
WM322	6.2.53	20.2.53	Wroughton
WM323	9.2.53	24.2.53	Wroughton
WM324	12.2.53	25.2.53	Wroughton
WM325	12.2.53	25.2.53	Little Rissington
WM326	13.2.53	25.2.53	Little Rissington
WM327	12.2.53	23.2.53	Little Rissington
WM328	12.2.53	25.2.53	Little Rissington
WM329	13.2.53	27.2.53	Wroughton
WM330	18.2.53	18.3.53	High Ercall
WM331	16.2.53	27.2.53	Wroughton
WM332	16.2.53	11.3.53	High Ercall
WM333	18.2.53	27.2.53	High Ercall
WM334	19.2.53	10.3.53	Little Rissington
WM335	19.2.53	11.3.53	Wroughton
WM336	20.2.53	18.3.53	High Ercall
WM337	23.2.53	11.3.53	High Ercall
WM338	24.2.53	10.3.53	Little Rissington
WM339	24.2.53	13.3.53	Wroughton
WM340	25.2.53	11.3.53	Wroughton
WM341	7.3.53	27.3.53	High Ercall
WM362	7.3.53	1.4.53	Little Rissington
WM363	7.3.53	27.3.53	High Ercall
WM364	7.3.53	27.3.53	High Ercall
WM365	12.3.53	8.4.53	High Ercall
WM366	20.3.53	10.4.53	Llandow
WM367	20.3.53		see notes

Notes: WM367 *was released by C(A) 17.4.53 to be* retained by AWA for trials. It was flown out to Boscombe Down 19.10.54. No whole former RAF NF.13 exists today.

Export Meteor NF.13s

Egypt: Serials 1427, 1428 and 1429 *(former RAF serials reported elsewhere as WM325, '326 and '328)* in from No.8 Maintenance Unit, Little Rissington in 6.55 and despatched on 25.6.55 via an unrecorded venue. Serials 1430, 1431 and 1432 *(ex-RAF serials reported as WM338, '340 and '362)* in from No.8 Maintenance Unit, Little Rissington, between 12-15.8.55 and despatched on 24.8.55 via Le Bourget, France.

France: WM364 and WM365 flown in from Baginton on 18.5.56 and 28.5.56 respectively. Both despatched to Bretigny 20.6.56. *(Reputedly reserialled NF-F364 and NF-F365 in France)*

Israel: Call-signs 4X-FNA to 'F. The first two were flown in from Baginton in 8.56, the others test flown at Bitteswell 8.56 to 10.56. Despatched as follows: 'A 'B and 'D via Le Bourget 5.9.56; 'C, 'E and 'F via Dijon, *21st March 1958. (Former RAF serials reported as WM366, '334, '312, '309, '320, '335 respectively).*

Syria: Serial numbers 471 to 476, previously WM332, WM336, WM330, WM337, WM341 and WM333 respectively. All flown in from No.29 Maintenance Unit, High Ercall 5.54. Test flights undertaken 5-6.54 and delivered via Le Bourget in two batches as follows: 10.6.54 471, 472 and 473; 1.7.54 474, 475 and 476.

Meteor NF.14 (Contract 6/Acft/6412/CB.7(b) 28.2.51)

Serial	First Flight	Despatched	To
WS722	23.10.53	6.11.53	Langar
WS723	27.10.53	10.11.53	Langar
WS724	2.11.53	13.11.53	Langar
WS725	2.11.53	19.11.53	Langar
WS726	4.11.53	19.11.53	Langar
WS727	4.11.53	19.11.53	Langar
WS728	5.11.53	3.12.53	Langar
WS729	9.11.53	27.11.53	Langar
WS730	9.11.53	27.11.53	Langar
WS731	10.11.53	29.12.53	Defford
WS732	16.11.53	1.12.53	Langar
WS733	14.11.53	1.12.53	Langar
WS734	14.11.53	1.12.53	Langar
WS735	19.11.53	29.12.53	Aston Down
WS736	19.11.53	1.12.54	see notes

Meteor WS788 was first flown at Bitteswell in February 1954. Note the clear-view canopy in place of the 'glasshouse' of the NF.11 to NF.13s. WS788 is seen here in 1960 in the colours of 2 Air Navigation School, while employed as an NF(T).14 navigation trainer.
MAP

Serial	First Flight	Despatched	To
WS737	19.11.53	22.12.53	Langar
WS738	19.11.53	22.12.53	Langar
WS739	25.11.53	11.1.54	Langar
WS740	25.11.53	11.1.54	Langar
WS741	25.11.53	11.1.54	Langar
WS742	25.11.53	14.1.54	see notes
WS743	25.11.53	14.1.54	Langar
WS744	22.12.53	14.1.54	Langar
WS745	22.12.53	25.1.54	Langar
WS746	19.12.53	11.1.54	Langar
WS747	7.1.54	27.1.54	Langar
WS748	19.12.53	19.1.54	Langar
WS749	23.12.53	19.1.54	see notes
WS750	19.12.53	18.1.54	Aston Down
WS751	4.1.54	18.1.54	Aston Down
WS752	8.1.54	19.1.54	Langar
WS753	12.1.54	25.1.54	Langar
WS754	12.1.54	27.1.54	Langar
WS755	16.1.54	27.1.54	Langar
WS756	16.1.54	5.2.54	Langar
WS757	16.1.54	27.1.54	Langar
WS758	16.1.54	5.2.54	Langar
WS759	19.1.54	5.2.54	Langar
WS760	22.1.54	22.2.54	Langar
WS774	26.1.54	22.2.54	Langar
WS775	22.1.54	22.2.54	Little Rissington
WS776	27.1.54	22.2.54	Little Rissington
WS777	27.1.54	22.2.54	Little Rissington
WS778	29.1.54	22.2.54	Wroughton
WS779	1.2.54	24.2.54	Aston Down
WS780	29.1.54	22.2.54	Wroughton
WS781	1.2.54	24.2.54	Aston Down
WS782	1.2.54	23.2.54	Little Rissington
WS783	3.2.54	3.3.54	Little Rissington
WS784	3.2.54	23.2.54	Little Rissington
WS785	4.2.54	24.2.54	Aston Down
WS786	4.2.54	3.3.54	Little Rissington
WS787	10.2.54	28.3.54	Little Rissington
WS788	13.2.54	3.3.54	Little Rissington
WS789	12.2.54	8.3.54	Little Rissington
WS790	12.2.54	11.3.54	Wroughton
WS791	13.2.54	3.3.54	Wroughton
WS792	16.2.54	11.3.54	Little Rissington
WS793	20.2.54	22.3.54	Little Rissington
WS794	20.2.54	22.3.54	Aston Down
WS795	20.2.54	26.3.54	Wroughton
WS796	20.2.54	22.3.54	Little Rissington
WS797	24.2.54	22.3.54	Little Rissington
WS798	24.2.54	25.3.54	Little Rissington
WS799	13.2.54	3.3.54	Wroughton
WS800	13.2.54	3.3.54	Wroughton
WS801	16.2.54	8.3.54	Aston Down
WS802	16.2.54	8.3.54	Little Rissington
WS803	20.2.54	11.3.54	Wroughton
WS804	25.2.54	30.3.54	Little Rissington
WS805	25.2.54	22.3.54	Aston Down
WS806	27.2.54	26.3.54	Little Rissington
WS807	2.3.54	30.3.54	Little Rissington
WS808	4.3.54	31.3.54	Aston Down
WS809	6.3.54	26.3.54	Little Rissington
WS810	10.3.54	26.3.54	Wroughton
WS811	10.3.54	26.3.54	Wroughton
WS812	11.3.54	1.4.54	Aston Down
WS827	16.3.54	31.3.54	Aston Down
WS828	16.3.54	31.3.54	Aston Down
WS829	19.3.54	5.4.54	Little Rissington
WS830	21.3.54	8.4.54	Wroughton
WS831	22.3.54	1.4.54	Aston Down
WS832	25.3.54	14.4.54	Little Rissington
WS833	31.3.54	28.4.54	Wroughton
WS834	31.3.54	21.4.54	Hawarden
WS835	31.3.54	21.4.54	Wroughton
WS836	6.4.54	27.4.54	Little Rissington

The first production Sea Hawk F.2, WF240, made its first flight at Bitteswell on 24th March 1954. The rear fuselage has been supplied ready-painted by Flight Refuelling Limited. Note the test instrumentation cabling from the cockpit to the rear fuselage.
AWA via Dave Sargent

Serial	First Flight	Despatched	To
WS837	6.4.54	23.4.54	Little Rissington
WS838	9.4.54	30.4.54	Wroughton
WS839	11.4.54	26.4.54	Little Rissington
WS840	14.4.54	3.5.54	Wroughton
WS841	23.4.54	7.5.54	Little Rissington
WS842	23.4.54	7.5.54	Wroughton
WS843	27.4.54	12.5.54	Little Rissington
WS844	30.4.54	18.5.54	Wroughton
WS845	5.5.54	25.5.54	Aston Down
WS846	10.5.54	27.5.54	Little Rissington
WS847	16.5.54	27.5.54	Wroughton
WS848	18.5.54	4.9.54	Farnborough

Notes: WS736 despatch date as given in tower log, *but Ministry record card states 'Bitteswell to Langar (Avro) 27.11.53; Langar to 15MU (Wroughton) 1.54'.* WS742 made a precautionary landing at Saltby (Chapter Twenty-Two) and returned to Bitteswell the following day; it left for Aston Down 18.1.54. WS747 Ministry record card states 'Bitteswell to Avro (Langar) 20.1.54 for mods; to 264 Sqn 25.3.54; sold to AWA 24.8.55'. It has been reported as going to French CEV, Bretigny 28.8.55 as NF14-747 but record card does not mention this. WS749 diverted to Baginton on its first test flight, due to fog; flew back to Bitteswell on 29.12.53; it was despatched to Langar. WS796 record card confirms to 8MU Little Rissington and 'sold to France 20.11.55'. Another source suggests it went to the French CEV at Bretigny as NF14-796. The MoD(PE) record card for WS845 states 'AWA to R-R Hucknall 25.5.54 for engine surge investigation until 28.5.55'. WS848 was delivered direct to static aircraft park at Farnborough Air Show; it returned to Bitteswell afterwards and Ministry record card indicates that it was transferred to the Central Fighter Establishment at West Raynham, (Norfolk), on 26.3.55.

A large number of NF.14s survive, including: WS776 once guarding the gate at RAF North Luffenham (Chapter Seventeen) stored at Sandtoft, Lincolnshire; WS788 at the Yorkshire Air Museum, Elvington, Yorkshire; WS832 at the Solway Aviation Museum, Carlisle, Cumbria; and WS843 at the RAF Museum, Cosford, Shropshire.

Hawker Sea Hawk

The attractive-looking Sea Hawk single-seat carrier-borne jet fighter and fighter-bomber was handed over to AWA as a production programme because Hawker faced many demands in the development and production of the Hunter, which had been declared a 'super-priority' by the Ministry of Supply. The first prototype Sea Hawk (then known as the P.1040, serial number VP401) made its maiden flight at Boscombe Down, Wiltshire, on 2nd September 1947.

The first production version, the F.1, had a Rolls-Royce Nene turbojet, armament was four 20mm cannon and there was provision for two underwing fuel drop tanks for extra range. Only 35 Mk.1 production aircraft were to be assembled by Hawker at Langley and Dunsfold before production transferred to AWA at Coventry and Bitteswell. Chief Test Pilot Eric Franklin reportedly flew AWA's first Sea Hawk, WF162, on 18th December 1952, probably from Baginton, as its first Bitteswell tower log entry was recorded on 16th January 1953. Sixty F.1s were assembled and flown by AWA in just 13 months, the final example going out on 18th January 1954. The assembly line rolled straight from the F.1 to the slightly more developed F.2 with 40 joining the Royal Navy's Fleet Air Arm in the first three months of 1954.

As well as the day-fighter role, the Royal Navy also saw the Sea Hawk as a useful strike aircraft and the first fighter-bomber version was the FB.3 which was essentially an F.2 with the provision to carry two 500lb bombs in place of the drop tanks that the F.1 and F.2 could carry. The Navy received 116 examples (see table) and later undertook conversions to FB.5 status with the more powerful Nene engine.

Further development of the FB.3 brought about the first of two dual-purpose fighter and ground attack versions, powered by a

Nene Mk.101 and featuring extra weapons stations. Ninety-seven FGA.4s were delivered between September 1954 and March 1955. Many were later converted to FGA.6 status with the more powerful Nene Mk.103.

The FGA.6, the definitive all-purpose fighter and ground attack version, was to follow; Bitteswell built 87 from new with the last deliveries being made to the FAA in December 1955. As noted above, FGA.4s were also upgraded to this specification. To help speed up Sea Hawk production, all rear fuselage sections were sub-contracted to Flight Refuelling Limited, who delivered them fully painted, to Bitteswell by road, from their Tarrant Rushton facility.

AWA had always hoped the Sea Hawk would appeal to the export market and had high hopes that the Royal Australian Navy would place an order. Other than a few former Fleet Air Arm examples taken for trials, this interest did not translate into an order.

The Sea Hawk production line had closed when the export goal was finally achieved, albeit two orders under US Mutual Defence Assistance Pact funding. Thankfully, all of the jigs and tooling had been retained.

In 1956 the Marine Luchtvaart Dienst (air arm of Koninklijke Luchtmacht, the Royal Netherlands Navy), ordered 22 F.50s (to FGA.6 standard), these being despatched to Valkenburg between July 1957 and January 1958. The second example, 6-51, experienced a red warning light for the starboard main undercarriage during its first flight on 28th May 1957; the leg collapsed on landing but 6-51 was flying again by 19th June.

The Bundesmarine (West German Navy) ordered two versions based on the FGA.6 on 20th February 1957. The Mk.100, was essentially a 'straight' Mk.6 with the major distinguishing feature being the larger fin and rudder fitted to all the German aircraft. The first eleven machines were despatched to Lossiemouth for conversion training under the aegis of the Fleet Air Arm, staging through Bitteswell to Schleswig-Jägel in July 1958. The balance of 34 aircraft were delivered either to Bremen or Schleswig.

The Mk.101 involved more development, being an all-weather fighter with a Ekco Mk.34 radar housed in a pod hung on the inner pylon of the starboard wing. Trials for the various fits for the Mk.101 were carried out on FGA.6 XE456. All the Mk.101s were despatched to Bremen from September 1958 with deliveries complete in April 1959.

The Indian Navy then ordered 14 new-build Sea Hawk FGA.6s (previously misreported as F.50s) plus two batches of former Fleet Air Arm FB.3 and FB.5s refurbished to FGA.6 standard. The new build machines were delivered during 1961; the last of 16 refurbished machines was despatched via Southend on 19th February 1963. Initial deliveries were to various Fleet

Air Arm bases in the UK, where Indian pilots were training, while the final seven were delivered by a private ferry contractor. Later in 1963-64, the Indian Navy acquired a further 16 refurbished machines from Fleet Air Arm stocks (not via AWA) plus additional spare airframes, and in 1966 they boosted their inventory of the type further with 28 redundant Mk.100s and '101s supplied from Germany. (See pages 48 and 68 for details.)

Sea Hawk F.1 (Contract 6/Acft/3142/CB.7(b) 4.11.49, part)

Serial	First Flight	Despatched	To
WF162	16.1.53 ?	27.2.53	Abbotsinch
WF163	28.1.53	7.3.53	Abbotsinch
WF164	25.2.53	24.3.53	Abbotsinch
WF165	12.3.53	24.3.53	Abbotsinch
WF166	27.3.53	16.4.53	Stretton
WF178	17.4.53	28.4.53	Stretton
WF179	29.4.53	13.5.53	Stretton
WF180	7.5.53	20.5.53	Boscombe Down
WF181	15.5.53	27.5.53	Abbotsinch
WF182	28.5.53	18.6.53	Stretton
WF183	11.6.53	21.7.53	Abbotsinch
WF184	16.6.53	7.7.53	Stretton
WF185	25.6.53	7.7.53	Abbotsinch
WF186	2.7.53	15.7.53	Abbotsinch
WF187	11.7.53	14.8.53	Stretton
WF188	15.7.53	14.8.53	Abbotsinch
WF189	20.7.53	19.8.53	Abbotsinch
WF190	27.7.53	28.8.53	Abbotsinch
WF191	31.7.53	24.8.53	Abbotsinch
WF192	20.8.53	31.8.53	Stretton
WF196	24.8.53		see notes
WF197	27.8.53	29.9.53	Stretton
WF198	2.9.53	8.10.53	Abbotsinch
WF199	7.9.53	30.9.53	Stretton
WF200	10.9.53	29.9.53	Stretton
WF201	11.9.53	28.9.53	Abbotsinch
WF202	16.9.53	28.9.53	Abbotsinch
WF203	16.9.53	28.9.53	Stretton
WF204	21.9.53	29.9.53	Stretton
WF205	28.9.53	14.10.53	Abbotsinch
WF206	29.9.53	26.10.53	Abbotsinch
WF207	30.9.53	15.10.53	Stretton
WF208	8.10.53	26.10.53	Abbotsinch
WF209	6.10.53	23.10.53	Stretton
WF210	14.10.53	30.10.53	Stretton
WF211	17.10.53	2.11.53	Stretton
WF212	20.10.53	4.11.53	Abbotsinch
WF213	22.10.53	3.11.53	Stretton
WF214	22.10.53	3.11.53	Stretton
WF215	24.10.53	11.11.53	Abbotsinch
WF216	29.10.53	13.11.53	Abbotsinch
WF217	4.11.53	19.11.53	Stretton
WF218	20.11.53		see notes
WF219	10.11.53	25.11.53	Abbotsinch
WF220	6.11.53	4.3.54	Abbotsinch
WF221	10.11.53	19.11.53	Stretton
WF222	11.11.53	30.11.53	Stretton
WF223	14.11.53	14.12.53	Abbotsinch
WF224	20.11.53	3.12.53	Stretton
WF225	25.11.53	14.12.53	Abbotsinch
WF226	21.11.53	11.1.54	Stretton
WF227	27.11.53	14.12.53	Stretton
WF228	27.11.53	11.1.54	Stretton
WF229	27.11.53	19.12.53	Abbotsinch
WF230	27.11.53	19.12.53	Abbotsinch
WF231	15.12.53	11.1.54	Stretton
WF232	2.12.53	11.1.54	Stretton
WF233	19.12.53	18.1.54	Abbotsinch
WF234	19.12.53	18.1.54	Stretton
WF235	19.12.53	18.1.54	Abbotsinch

Notes: WF196 *retained by AWA as a Trials Installation and development aircraft at Bitteswell;* believed despatched to Farnborough 28.10.54 *for use by Empire Test Pilot School.* WF215 intended for Abbotsinch, but landed at Stretton. WF216 returned that day and did not leave for Abbotsinch until 25.11.53. WF218 believed despatched to Boscombe Down 27.7.54 *en route for tropical trials.* WF225 is today displayed on the main gate at RNAS Culdrose, Cornwall.

Sea Hawk F.2 (Contract 6/Acft/3142/CB.7(b) 4.11.49, part)

Serial	First Flight	Despatched	To
WF240			see notes
WF241	31.12.53	20.1.54	Manby
WF242	29.12.53	2.2.54	Stretton
WF243	5.1.54		see notes
WF244	5.1.54	28.1.54	Stretton
WF245	7.1.54	2.2.54	Stretton
WF246	11.1.54	29.2.54	Stretton
WF247	7.1.54	1.3.54	Abbotsinch
WF248	12.1.54	3.3.54	Abbotsinch
WF249	12.1.54	4.3.54	Abbotsinch
WF250	13.1.54	29.1.54	Stretton
WF251	18.1.54	17.3.54	Boscombe Down
WF252	18.1.54	1.3.54	Abbotsinch
WF253	19.1.54	3.3.54	Stretton
WF254	20.1.54	3.2.54	Stretton
WF255	23.1.54	3.3.54	Stretton
WF256	22.1.54	4.2.54	Stretton
WF257	22.1.54	4.3.54	Abbotsinch
WF258	2.2.54	4.3.54	Abbotsinch
WF259	1.2.54	11.3.54	Stretton
WF260	29.1.54	11.3.54	Abbotsinch
WB261	2.2.54	3.3.54	Stretton
WF262	3.2.54	24.3.54	Abbotsinch
WF263	4.2.54	26.3.54	see notes
WF264	14.2.54	22.3.54	Stretton
WF265	16.2.54	22.3.54	Stretton
WF266	25.2.54	23.3.54	Stretton
WF267	16.2.54	8.3.54	Stretton
WF268	4.3.54	26.3.54	Abbotsinch
WF269	1.3.54	31.3.54	Abbotsinch
WF270	24.2.54	2.4.54	Stretton
WF271	23.2.54	31.3.54	Abbotsinch
WF272	6.3.54	2.4.54	Stretton
WF273	5.4.54	17.5.54	Abbotsinch
WF274	5.3.54	4.5.54	Abbotsinch
WF275	8.3.54	31.3.54	Abbotsinch
WF276	6.3.54	2.4.54	Stretton
WF277	8.3.54	2.4.54	Stretton
WF278	19.3.54	29.4.54	Stretton
WF279	11.3.54	31.3.54	see notes

Notes: WF240 first flown 24.2.54, *used for extensive fuselage resonance and vibration testing, hence laid-up while this was carried out;* first recorded 3.6.55; C(A) release to AWA 17.3.54 *for TI (trial installation and development) prior to despatch to Boscombe Down 20.4.56;* WF243 *C(A) release 7.1.54;* believed despatched to Hucknall 7.5.54. WF263 despatched to Abbotsinch but returned that day, eventually left 30.3.54. WF279 despatched to Abbotsinch, but diverted to Stretton. WF259 is preserved at the Museum of Flight, East Fortune, Scotland.

Sea Hawk FB.3 (Contract 6/Acft/3142/CB.7(b) 4.11.49, part)

Serial	First Flight	Despatched	To
WF280	19.3.54	31.3.54	Boscombe Down
WF281	17.3.54	17.8.55	Abbotsinch
WF282	30.3.54	4.5.54	Abbotsinch
WF283	19.3.54	7.4.54	Abbotsinch
WF284	31.3.54		see notes
WF285	29.3.54	4.5.54	Abbotsinch
WF286	26.3.54	30.4.54	Stretton
WF287	25.3.54	29.4.54	Stretton
WF288	1.4.54	30.4.54	Stretton
WF289	1.4.54	4.5.54	Abbotsinch

Serial	First Flight	Despatched	To
WF293	1.4.54	6.5.54	Abbotsinch
WF294	5.4.54	30.4.54	Stretton
WF295	5.4.54	30.4.54	Stretton
WF296	6.4.54	30.4.54	Stretton
WF297	6.4.54	4.5.54	Stretton
WF298	8.4.54	10.5.54	Stretton
WF299	9.4.54	5.5.54	Stretton
WF300	8.4.54	11.5.54	Abbotsinch
WF301	11.4.54	10.5.54	Abbotsinch
WF302	13.4.54	6.5.54	Abbotsinch
WF303	13.4.54		see notes

(Contract 6/Acft/6244/CB.9(b) 18.1.51)

Serial	First Flight	Despatched	To
WM906	14.4.54	17.5.54	Abbotsinch
WM907	13.4.54	6.5.54	Abbotsinch
WM908	14.4.54	12.5.54	Abbotsinch
WM909	22.4.54	17.5.54	Abbotsinch
WM910	23.4.54	12.5.54	Abbotsinch
WM911	23.4.54	12.5.54	Abbotsinch
WM912	27.4.54	12.5.54	Abbotsinch
WM913	27.4.54	13.5.54	Abbotsinch
WM914	27.4.54		see notes
WM915	30.4.54	19.5.54	Stretton
WM916	30.4.54	19.5.54	Abbotsinch
WM917	3.5.54	20.5.54	Abbotsinch
WM918	5.5.54	26.5.54	Stretton
WM919	4.5.54	19.5.54	Stretton
WM920	5.5.54	20.5.54	Stretton
WM921	7.5.54	20.5.54	Stretton
WM922	5.5.54	25.5.54	Abbotsinch
WM923	7.5.54	26.5.54	Abbotsinch
WM924	14.5.54	27.5.54	Abbotsinch
WM925	12.5.54	16.6.54	Abbotsinch
WM926	13.5.54	31.5.54	Stretton
WM927	11.5.54	25.5.54	Stretton
WM928	14.5.54	1.6.54	Abbotsinch
WM929	14.5.54	31.5.54	Abbotsinch
WM930	16.5.54	31.5.54	Abbotsinch
WM931	17.5.54	9.6.54	Abbotsinch
WM932	18.5.54	17.6.54	Stretton
WM933	19.5.54	11.6.54	Stretton
WM934	20.5.54	9.6.54	Abbotsinch
WM935	21.5.54	14.6.54	Abbotsinch
WM936	21.5.54	16.6.54	Abbotsinch
WM937	25.5.54	11.6.54	Stretton
WM938	26.5.54	16.6.54	Stretton
WM939	26.5.54	17.6.54	Abbotsinch
WM940	26.5.54	17.6.54	Abbotsinch
WM941	28.5.54	16.6.54	Abbotsinch
WM942	27.5.54	17.6.54	Abbotsinch
WM943	31.5.54	22.6.54	Abbotsinch
WM944	1.6.54	23.6.54	Abbotsinch
WM945	2.6.54	22.6.54	Stretton
WM960	4.6.54	22.6.54	Stretton
WM961	10.6.54	29.6.54	Abbotsinch
WM962	3.6.54	28.6.54	Abbotsinch
WM963	4.6.54	29.6.54	Abbotsinch
WM964	11.6.54	6.7.54	Abbotsinch
WM965	11.6.54	29.6.54	Abbotsinch
WM966	12.6.54	6.7.54	Abbotsinch
WM967	14.6.54	7.7.54	Stretton
WM968	15.6.54	29.7.54	Stretton
WM969	16.6.54	5.7.54	Stretton
WM970	17.6.54	13.7.54	Stretton
WM971	21.6.54	7.7.54	Stretton
WM972	21.6.54	7.7.54	Abbotsinch
WM973	22.6.54	7.7.54	Abbotsinch
WM974	22.6.54	13.7.54	Abbotsinch
WM975	23.6.54	14.7.54	Abbotsinch
WM976	23.6.54	14.7.54	Abbotsinch
WM977	24.6.54	15.7.54	Abbotsinch
WM978	25.6.54	19.7.54	Abbotsinch
WM979	28.6.54	19.7.54	Abbotsinch
WM980	30.6.54	16.8.54	Abbotsinch
WM981	2.7.54	13.8.54	Abbotsinch

Serial	First Flight	Despatched	To
WM982	30.6.54	13.8.54	Abbotsinch
WM983	1.7.54	15.7.54	Boscombe Down
WM984	1.7.54	13.8.54	Stretton
WM985	5.7.54	23.7.54	Stretton
WM986	6.7.54	30.8.54	Stretton
WM987	9.7.54	17.8.54	Stretton
WM988	9.7.54	18.8.54	Abbotsinch
WM989	9.7.54	16.8.54	Abbotsinch
WM990	9.7.54	18.8.54	Abbotsinch
WM991	12.7.54	18.8.54	Abbotsinch
WM992	14.7.54	16.9.54	Boscombe Down
WM993	16.7.54	23.8.54	Abbotsinch
WM994	16.7.54	25.8.54	Abbotsinch
WM995	16.7.54	26.8.54	Abbotsinch
WM996	20.7.54	25.8.54	Abbotsinch
WM997	19.7.54	26.8.54	Abbotsinch
WM998	21.7.54	7.9.54	Abbotsinch
WM999	27.7.54	30.8.54	Stretton
WN105	27.7.54	30.8.54	Stretton
WN106	27.7.54	13.9.54	Stretton
WN107	30.7.54	20.9.54	Stretton
WN108	29.7.54	30.8.54	Stretton
WN109	13.8.54	13.9.54	Abbotsinch
WN110	18.8.54	7.9.54	Abbotsinch
WN111	16.8.54	13.9.54	Abbotsinch
WN112	18.8.54	13.9.54	Abbotsinch
WN113	23.8.54	15.9.54	Stretton
WN114	25.8.54	15.9.54	Stretton
WN115	25.8.54	14.9.54	Stretton
WN116	27.8.54	7.10.54	Stretton
WN117	28.8.54	22.9.54	Stretton
WN118	26.8.54	20.10.54	Stretton
WN119	1.9.54	6.10.54	Stretton

Notes: WF284 *retained by AWA for TI and development;* believed despatched 14.9.54 to Boscombe Down *for Rocket Projectile firing trials.* WF303 no documented despatch details. WM914 thought despatched to Boscombe Down 9.11.54; used for F.94 *(and F.24 ?)* camera pod trials, returning 12.11.54 and despatched to Lee-on-Solent 1.2.56. WM928 returned that day and did not leave for Abbotsinch until the following day.

Several still extant, including: WM913 at the Newark Air Museum, Notts; WM961 at Caernarfon Air World, Wales; WM969 at the Imperial War Museum, Duxford, Cambs; WN108 with the Ulster Aviation Society collection at Langford Lodge, Northern Ireland (all in FB.5 guise).

Sea Hawk FGA.4   (Contract 6/Acft/6244/CB.9(b) 1.6.51)

Serial	First Flight	Despatched	To
WV792	31.8.54	27.9.54	Abbotsinch
WV793	10.9.54	27.9.54	Abbotsinch
WV794	1.9.54	4.10.54	Abbotsinch
WV795	8.9.54	27.9.54	Abbotsinch
WV796	9.9.54	4.10.54	Abbotsinch
WV797	13.9.54	6.10.54	Abbotsinch
WV798	14.9.54	7.10.54	Abbotsinch
WV799	14.9.54	6.10.54	Stretton
WV800	15.9.54	6.10.54	Stretton
WV801	20.9.54	12.10.54	Stretton
WV802	20.9.54	6.10.54	Stretton
WV803	21.9.54	20.10.54	Stretton
WV804	23.9.54	14.10.54	Abbotsinch
WV805	23.9.54	28.10.54	Abbotsinch
WV806	24.9.54	19.10.54	Abbotsinch
WV807	27.9.54	14.10.54	Abbotsinch
WV824	28.9.54	20.10.54	Abbotsinch
WV825	1.10.54		see notes
WV826	5.10.54	21.10.54	Stretton
WV827	11.10.54	25.10.54	Stretton
WV828	7.10.54	4.11.54	Stretton
WV829	11.10.54	25.10.54	Stretton
WV830	11.10.54	25.10.54	Stretton
WV831	12.10.54	25.10.54	Stretton

Serial	First Flight	Despatched	To
WV832	15.10.54	3.11.54	Stretton
WV833	12.10.54	28.10.54	Stretton
WV834	15.10.54	9.11.54	Abbotsinch
WV835	18.10.54	3.11.54	Abbotsinch
WV836	19.10.54	24.11.54	Abbotsinch
WV837	19.10.54	9.11.54	Abbotsinch
WV838	22.10.54	24.11.54	Abbotsinch
WV839	22.10.54	9.11.54	Stretton
WV840	25.10.54	9.11.54	Abbotsinch
WV841	29.10.54	22.11.54	Stretton
WV842	3.11.54	23.11.54	Sydenham
WV843	26.10.54	23.11.54	Sydenham
WV844	29.10.54	23.11.54	Sydenham
WV845	2.11.54	17.11.54	Sydenham
WV846	4.11.54	7.12.54	Sydenham
WV847	4.11.54	1.12.54	Sydenham
WV848	8.11.54	3.12.54	Sydenham
WV849	8.11.54	3.12.54	Sydenham
WV850	12.11.54	3.12.54	Sydenham
WV851	9.11.54	7.12.54	Sydenham
WV852	11.11.54	7.12.54	Sydenham
WV853	17.11.54	7.12.54	Sydenham
WV854	17.11.54	7.12.54	Sydenham
WV855	22.11.54	14.12.54	Abbotsinch
WV856	22.11.54	15.12.54	Sydenham
WV857	24.11.54	15.12.54	Sydenham
WV858	24.11.54	15.12.54	Sydenham
WV859	27.11.54	14.1.55	Abbotsinch
WV860	27.11.54	15.12.54	Sydenham
WV861	30.11.54	14.1.55	Abbotsinch
WV862	3.12.54	10.1.55	Stretton
WV863	30.11.54	10.1.55	Stretton
WV864	29.11.54	19.1.55	Abbotsinch
WV865	9.12.54	14.1.55	Abbotsinch
WV866	9.12.54	14.1.55	Abbotsinch
WV867	9.12.54	7.1.55	Stretton
WV868	9.12.54	7.1.55	Stretton
WV869	15.12.54	7.1.55	Stretton
WV870	15.12.54	7.1.55	Stretton
WV871	17.12.54	11.1.55	Stretton
WV902	20.12.54	14.1.55	Abbotsinch
WV903	21.12.54	18.1.55	Abbotsinch
WV904	24.12.54	18.1.55	Abbotsinch
WV905	29.12.54	31.1.55	Abbotsinch
WV906	29.12.54	8.2.55	Abbotsinch
WV907	11.1.55	10.2.55	Abbotsinch
WV908	31.12.54	10.2.55	Abbotsinch
WV909	11.1.55	28.1.55	Stretton
WV910	7.1.55	31.1.55	Stretton
WV911	12.1.55	31.1.55	Stretton
WV912	11.1.55	1.2.55	Stretton
WV913	14.1.55	10.2.55	Abbotsinch
WV914	17.1.55	10.2.55	Abbotsinch
WV915	19.1.55	16.2.55	Abbotsinch
WV916	18.1.55	18.2.55	Abbotsinch
WV917	24.1.55	23.2.55	Abbotsinch
WV918	21.1.55	10.2.55	Abbotsinch
WV919	27.1.55	1.3.55	see notes
WV920	28.1.55	9.3.55	Abbotsinch
WV921	29.1.55	3.3.55	Abbotsinch
WV922	30.1.55	9.3.55	Abbotsinch

(Contract 6/Acft/9601/CB.5(b) 5.6.53)

Serial	First Flight	Despatched	To
XE327	5.2.55	3.3.55	see notes
XE328	7.2.55	29.3.55	Stretton
XE329	8.2.55	28.2.55	Abbotsinch
XE330	10.2.55	17.3.55	Abbotsinch
XE331	10.2.55	9.3.55	Abbotsinch
XE332	15.2.55	16.3.55	Abbotsinch
XE333	11.2.55	9.3.55	Abbotsinch
XE334	18.2.55	15.3.55	Abbotsinch
XE335	18.2.55	16.3.55	Abbotsinch
XE336	19.2.55	21.3.55	Abbotsinch
XE337	21.2.55	16.3.55	Abbotsinch
XE338	28.2.55	21.3.55	Abbotsinch

Notes: WV825 no documented despatch details. *It was retained by AWA for TI of Vortex generators on tailplane and rear fuselage, also powered ailerons; MoD(PE) card indicates received Fleetlands 14.8.57.* WV905 returned same day and did not leave for Abbotsinch until 8.2.55. WV919 despatched to Abbotsinch but diverted to Stretton with u/s radio. XE327 despatched to Boscombe Down *for gunnery trials* but returned and made emergency landing, sent on the following day.

Several extant, including: WV797 at Midland Air Museum, Coventry, Warks; WV828 at De Kooy air base, Netherlands, WV856 with the Fleet Air Arm Museum, Yeovilton, Somerset; WV908 with the Royal Navy Historic Flight, recently airworthy but currently grounded (all in FGA.6 guise).

Sea Hawk FGA.6

Serial	First Flight	Despatched	To
XE339	28.2.55	31.3.55	Abbotsinch
XE340	3.3.55	31.3.55	Abbotsinch
XE341	3.3.55	21.4.55	Abbotsinch
XE342	3.3.55	21.4.55	Abbotsinch
XE343	3.3.55	29.3.55	Abbotsinch
XE344	16.3.55	21.4.55	Abbotsinch
XE362	8.3.55	29.3.55	Abbotsinch
XE363	9.3.55	22.4.55	Abbotsinch
XE364			see notes
XE365	11.3.55	22.4.55	Abbotsinch
XE366	11.3.55	26.4.55	Abbotsinch
XE367	11.3.55	31.3.55	Stretton
XE368	17.3.55	25.4.55	Stretton
XE369	17.3.55	19.4.55	Boscombe Down
XE370	18.3.55	4.5.55	Stretton
XE371	24.3.55	3.5.55	see notes
XE372	21.3.55	28.4.55	Abbotsinch
XE373	28.3.55	11.5.55	Abbotsinch
XE374	28.3.55	12.5.55	Abbotsinch
XE375	28.3.55	2.5.55	Abbotsinch
XE376	1.4.55	2.5.55	Abbotsinch
XE377	1.4.55	5.5.55	Abbotsinch
XE378	5.4.55	11.5.55	Abbotsinch
XE379	6.4.55	12.5.55	Abbotsinch
XE380	6.4.55	11.5.55	Abbotsinch
XE381	6.4.55	25..5.55	Abbotsinch
XE382	13.4.55	11.5.55	Abbotsinch
XE383	14.4.55	12.5.55	Abbotsinch
XE384	19.4.55	11.5.55	Abbotsinch
XE385	19.4.55	11.5.55	Abbotsinch
XE386	22.4.55	23.5.55	Abbotsinch
XE387	25.4.55	16.5.55	Abbotsinch
XE388	22.4.55	16.5.55	Abbotsinch
XE389	25.4.55	1.6.55	Abbotsinch
XE390	28.4.55	20.5.55	Abbotsinch
XE391	30.4.55	23.5.55	Abbotsinch
XE392	4.5.55	1.6.55	Abbotsinch
XE393	4.5.55	25.5.55	Abbotsinch
XE394	10.5.55	9.6.55	Abbotsinch
XE395	11.5.55	1.6.55	Abbotsinch
XE396	13.5.55	9.6.55	Abbotsinch
XE397	13.5.55	9.6.55	Abbotsinch
XE398	16.5.55	13.6.55	Abbotsinch
XE399	16.5.55	13.6.55	Abbotsinch
XE400	24.5.55	15.6.55	Abbotsinch
XE401	2.6.55	21.6.55	Abbotsinch
XE402	27.5.55	21.6.55	Abbotsinch
XE403	6.6.55	30.6.55	Abbotsinch
XE404	10.6.55	30.6.55	Abbotsinch
XE405	9.6.55	30.6.55	Abbotsinch
XE406	13.6.55	5.7.55	Abbotsinch
XE407	14.6.55	30.6.55	Abbotsinch
XE408	16.6.55	5.7.55	Abbotsinch
XE409	17.6.55	11.7.55	Abbotsinch
XE410	20.6.55	19.7.55	Abbotsinch
XE411	21.6.55	21.7.55	Abbotsinch
XE435	27.6.55	13.7.55	Abbotsinch
XE436	27.6.55	17.8.55	Abbotsinch

Serial	First Flight	Despatched	To
XE437	28.6.55	19.7.55	Abbotsinch
XE438	1.7.55	19.7.55	Abbotsinch
XE439	6.7.55	17.8.55	Abbotsinch
XF440	6.7.55	17.8.55	Abbotsinch
XE441	7.7.55	22.8.55	Abbotsinch
XE442	14.7.55	22.8.55	Abbotsinch
XE443	12.7.55	2.9.55	see notes
XE444	16.7.55	23.8.55	Abbotsinch
XE445	19.7.55	9.9.55	Boscombe Down
XE446	27.7.55	23.8.55	Abbotsinch
XE447	3.8.55	25.8.55	Abbotsinch
XE448	8.8.55	25.8.55	Abbotsinch
XE449	9.8.55	26.9.55	Abbotsinch
XE450	10.8.55	29.9.55	Abbotsinch
XE451	17.8.55	28.9.55	Abbotsinch
XE452	25.8.55	29.9.55	Abbotsinch
XE453	6.9.55	14.10.55	Abbotsinch
XE454	5.9.55	14.10.55	Abbotsinch
XE455	12.9.55	17.10.55	Abbotsinch
XE456			see notes
XE457	15.9.55	24.10.55	Abbotsinch
XE458	20.9.55	24.10.55	Abbotsinch
XE459	27.9.55	24.10.55	Abbotsinch
XE460	14.10.55	15.11.55	Abbotsinch
XE461	20.10.55	28.11.55	Abbotsinch
XE462	27.10.55	21.11.55	Anthorn
XE463	8.11.55	5.12.55	Abbotsinch
XE489			see notes
XE490	7.12.55		see notes

Notes: XE364, first flight believed 26.5.55. No documented despatch details. XE371 despatched for Abbotsinch 2.5.55 but returned, delivered the following day. XE443 delivered to Farnborough, *for static display at SBAC show,* returned 12.9.55, going on to Anthorn 21.11.55, only to return. XE456 believed first flown 4.1.56. Exhibited at the SBAC display at Farnborough 1.9 to 11.9.56, returned to Bitteswell; despatched to Boscombe Down 12.12.56, returned 3.1.57. *Used for private venture trials and as TI airframe for the German order. Sold to AWA 10.1.58.* XE489 believed flown 22.11.55, but no documented despatch details. XE490 no record of despatch details; *crashed on delivery 10.1.56 near Abbotsinch; airframe used for ground instruction; not replaced on contract. A further eight FGA.6s, XE491 to '498, were cancelled off the contract and not built.*

Several extant, including: XE340 at the Montrose Air Station Museum, Scotland; XE368 at the Cornwall Aero Park, Helston, Cornwall, XE489 part of the Vallance By-ways collection at Charlwood, Surrey.

The first nine Sea Hawks for the Indian Navy, serialled in the IN15x range, were all former Royal Navy FB.3s that had been refurbished and converted to FGA.6 standard.
Chris Salter collection

Dutch Sea Hawk F.50s

Serial	First Flight	Despatched	To
6-50	13.5.57	18.7.57	Valkenburg
6-51	28.5.57	20.8.57	Valkenburg
6-52	13.6.57	29.7.57	Valkenburg
6-53	28.6.57	5.9.57	Valkenburg
6-54	17.7.57	5.9.57	Valkenburg
6-55	23.7.57	20.8.57	Valkenburg
6-56	12.8.57	17.9.57	Valkenburg
6-57	16.8.57	17.9.57	Valkenburg
6-58	17.9.57	23.10.57	Valkenburg
6-59	2.9.57	1.10.57	Valkenburg
6-60	23.9.57	23.10.57	Valkenburg
6-61	27.9.57	6.11.57	Valkenburg
6-62	2.10.57	23.10.57	Valkenburg
6-63	15.10.57	13.11.57	Valkenburg
6-64	21.10.57	13.11.57	Valkenburg
6-65	25.10.57	26.11.57	Valkenburg
6-66	1.11.57	3.12.57	Valkenburg
6-67	3.12.57	17.1.58	Valkenburg
6-68	13.11.57	17.12.57	Valkenburg
6-69	14.11.57	17.12.57	Valkenburg
6-70	26.11.57	8.1.58	Valkenburg
6-71	2.1.58	29.1.58	Valkenburg

Indian Sea Hawk FGA.6s

Serial	First Flight	Despatched	To
IN151	21.12.59	22.1.60	Lossiemouth
IN152	27.1.60	26.2.60	Lossiemouth
IN153	3.2.60	26.2.60	Lossiemouth
IN154	16.2.60	4.3.60	Lossiemouth
IN155	1.3.60	21.3.60	Lossiemouth
IN156	14.3.60	30.3.60	Lossiemouth
IN157	26.3.60	12.4.60	Lossiemouth
IN158	11.4.60	5.5.60	Lossiemouth
IN159	20.5.60	20.6.60	Brawdy
IN160	2.1.61	30.1.61	Brawdy
IN161	10.1.61	30.1.61	Brawdy
IN162	20.1.61	13.2.61	Brawdy
IN163	31.1.61	27.2.61	Brawdy
IN164	7.2.61	14.3.61	Brawdy
IN165	2.3.61	20.3.61	Brawdy
IN166	9.3.61	27.3.61	Brawdy
IN167	21.3.61	27.4.61	Yeovilton
IN168	28.3.61	27.4.61	Yeovilton
IN169	19.4.61	13.6.61	Yeovilton
IN170	8.5.61	13.6.61	Yeovilton
IN171	15.5.61	7.7.61	Brawdy
IN172	15.6.61	16.8.61	Yeovilton
IN173	20.7.61	16.8.61	Yeovilton
IN174	8.6.62	25.10.62	Cognac
IN175	2.7.62	25.10.62	Cognac
IN176	27.7.62	25.10.62	Cognac
IN177	28.8.62	25.10.62	Cognac

A flight of three West German Bundesmarine Sea Hawk Mk.100s on a sortie out of Bitteswell for a publicity photograph. AWA

Serial	First Flight	Despatched	To
IN178	13.9.62	19.2.63	Southend
IN179	27.9.62	19.2.63	Southend
IN180	31.10.62	19.2.63	Southend

German Sea Hawk Mk.100s

Code	First Flight	Despatched	To
VA+220	26.11.57	13.2.58	Lossiemouth
VA+221	17.12.57	13.2.58	Lossiemouth
VA+222	17.12..57	13.2.58	Lossiemouth
VA+223	20.12.57	18.2.58	Lossiemouth
VA+224	30.12.57	18.2.58	Lossiemouth
VA+225	13.1.58	3.3.58	Lossiemouth
VA+226	16.1.58	18.3.58	Lossiemouth
VA+227	21.1.58	3.3.58	Lossiemouth
VA+228	27.1.58	18.3.58	Lossiemouth
VA+229	3.2.58	12.5.58	Lossiemouth
VA+230	5.2.58	12.5.58	Lossiemouth
VA+231	11.2.58	12.5.58	Lossiemouth
VA+232	18.2.58	2.6.58	Bremen
VA+233	28.2.58	2.6.58	Bremen
VA+234	28.2.58	2.6.58	Bremen
VA+235	4.3.58	8.7.58	Bremen
VA+236	13.3.58	12.6.58	Bremen
VB+120	14.3.58	8.7.58	Bremen
VB+121	20.3.58	12.6.58	Bremen

Code	First Flight	Despatched	To
VB+122	3.4.58	24.6.58	Bremen
VB+123	28.4.58	12.6.58	Bremen
VB+124	15.5.58	24.6.58	Bremen
VB+125	20.5.58	24.6.58	Bremen
VB+126	23.5.58	16.7.58	Bremen
VB+127	30.5.58	16.7.58	Bremen
VB+128	30.5.58	8.7.58	Bremen
VB+129	6.6.58	25.8.58	Bremen
VB+130	10.6.58	17.9.58	Schleswig
VB+131	11.6.58	9.9.58	Bremen
VB+132	12.6.58	16.7.58	Bremen
VB+133	13.6.58	17.9.58	Schleswig
VB+134	13.6.58	14.8.58	Bremen
VB+135	23.6.58	14.8.58	Bremen
VB+136	24.6.58	14.8.58	Bremen

Notes: VA+220 to VA+231 all despatched to Lossiemouth for conversion training. *Another source suggests VA229 to 231 possibly delivered 28.3.58.* All but VA+229 staged back through Bitteswell during July 1958 for delivery to Schleswig-Jägel. VA+234 is preserved at Nordholz air base, Germany.

German Sea Hawk Mk.101s

Code	First Flight	Despatched	To
RB+240	5.6.58	30.9.58	Bremen
RB+241	8.7.58	23.9.58	Bremen
RB+242	9.7.58	9.9.58	Bremen
RB+243	14.7.58	26.8.58	Bremen
RB+244	14.7.58	26.8.58	Bremen
RB+245	22.7.58	9.9.58	Bremen
RB+246	13.8.58	15.10.58	Bremen

Code	First Flight	Despatched	To
RB+247	4.8.58	23.9.58	Bremen
RB+248	5.8.58	17.9.58	Bremen
RB+249	8.8.58	30.9.58	Bremen
RB+250	22.8.58	30.9.58	Bremen
RB+251	28.8.58	15.10.58	Bremen
RB+252	9.9.58	21.10.58	Bremen
RB+253	17.9.58	21.10.58	Bremen
RB+254	22.9.58	21.10.58	Bremen
RB+255	30.9.58	10.11.58	Bremen
RB+256	6.10.58	10.11.58	Bremen
RB+360	10.10.58	10.11.58	Bremen
RB+361	17.10.58	29.12.58	Bremen
RB+362	24.10.58	29.12.58	Bremen
RB+363	31.10.58	29.12.58	Bremen
RB+364	11.11.58	19.1.59	Bremen
RB+365	19.11.58	19.1.59	Bremen
RB+366	24.11.58	19.1.59	Bremen
RB+367	9.12.58	28.1.59	Bremen
RB+368	11.12.58	28.1.59	Bremen
RB+369	22.12.58	28.1.59	Bremen
RB+370	1.1.59	26.2.59	Bremen
RB+371	9.1.59	26.2.59	Bremen
RB+372	26.1.59	1.4.59	Bremen
RB+373	2.2.59	1.4.59	Bremen
RB+374	16.2.59	1.4.59	Bremen
RB+375	25.2.59	21.4.59	Bremen
RB+376	16.3.59	21.4.59	Bremen

Notes: RB+370 ran off the end of Runway 22 while undertaking taxi tests on 9.1.59.

RB+363 is preserved on the main gate at Eggebek air base, Germany.

Hawker Hunter

Due to the outbreak of the Korean conflict, the swept-wing Hawker Hunter became a 'super-priority' programme and it was not surprising that AWA, with their increasing experience in the production of jet fighters, should build the type under sub-contract from Hawkers. Work on the Hunter started in parallel with that of the Sea Hawk and between the two programme this era was a 'golden' one for AWA.

The prototype Hunter, then known as the P.1067, was first flown from Boscombe Down by Neville Duke on 20th July 1951. The importance of the type was apparent and the first production example flew from Dunsfold on 16th May 1953 and the brisk pace was maintained throughout the programme. The Hunter went on to become a legend, both in manufacturing terms and as a superb and adaptable warplane. Total production came to 1,972. As well as the UK production lines at Kingston and Dunsfold, Coventry and Bitteswell and Blackpool (Squires Gate), Hunters were built under licence in Belgium and the Netherlands. Hunters served with at least 18 different air arms the world over.

After the production lines had closed, demand for the type was such that Hawker Siddeley undertook an 'old-for-new' refurbishment programme, taking in retired aircraft and regenerating them for new export markets – nearly 400 airframes were so treated. Bitteswell had a large part to play in that programme as well. Hunter production, modification, product support and the refurbishment programme provided work for the Hawker Siddeley Group and BAe for nearly 40 years.

AWA's first contract for Hunters was for 45 of the F.2 day fighter version for the RAF. AWA were entrusted with the Armstrong Siddeley Sapphire-powered Hunters (the F.2 and the more developed F.5) which were formulated as 'insurance' following the problems faced with the Rolls-Royce Avon-powered F.1s. Ultimately, the Avon Hunter was to reign supreme and the Sapphire machines were in the minority.

The first example was WN888, flown for the first time from Bitteswell on 14th October 1953 and used mostly for manufacturer's trials by the 'parent' company from the airfield at Dunsfold, Surrey. The 18th F.2, WN905, took off from Bitteswell for its first test flight at 3pm on 14th August 1954. Test pilot Martin Walton encountered difficulties and successfully baled out 37 minutes later. The stricken aircraft went on to crash at East Langton, near Market Harborough. The MoS (Ministry of Supply) declined a replacement aircraft and the contract was reduced to 44 units. The last F.2, WN953, was despatched to the RAF on 4th November 1954.

The F.5 was an F.2 with upgraded capabilities, including increased fuel tankage and the ability to carry air-to-ground weapons on additional wing strong points, mirroring the improvements of the F.1 in the Dunsfold-assembled F.4. Indeed, when it first flew from Bitteswell on 19th October 1954, the first F.5 (WN954) beat the first production F.4 (WT701) into the air by a day. The F.2s and F.5s had comparatively short service lives. AWA produced 105 F.5s, with the last, WP193, being despatched on 18th August 1955.

The definitive Hunter day fighter variant was the F.6 and AWA was awarded two contracts to build this Avon-powered version. With a more powerful Avon and all the modifications thrown up from the earlier marks, the prototype F.6 first flew on 22nd January 1954. The improvements included extensions to leading edge of the wing, providing the distinctive 'dog-tooth' format; gun blast deflectors; streamlined fairings to collect spent ammunition links; and modified inboard stores pylons. Some of the modifications were instigated later during the production programme; others were retrospectively fitted.

A batch of 100 units, XF373 to '389, XF414 to '463 and XF495 to '527 was assembled under sub-contract. The first AWA-assembled F.6, XF373, made its initial test flight on 25th May 1955 and the last was despatched in November 1956. A further 28 F.6s, in three batches, XE581 to '583, XE609 to '614 and XG150 to '168, were assembled at Bitteswell under a Hawker Kingston contract. Although interspersed with those of the AWA contract, the final few were completed after the last of the AWA examples, with XG168 the last one to leave in April 1957. All revisited at least once, either for leading edge extension and/or other modifications.

In-service conversions were carried out to AWA-assembled F.6s, but not at Bitteswell. These comprised the interim and the full RAF Middle East standard FGA.9 dedicated ground-attack fighter along with the FR.10 fighter-reconnaissance variant. A later upgrade programme turned F.6s into the improved F.6A. Many Bitteswell Hunter F.6s were involved in the refurbishment programme, going on to serve in other air arms.

An impressive line-up of AWA-built Hunter F.5s of 1 Squadron, at Tangmere, newly-delivered in 1955, and before the 30mm ammunition collector bulges were added. MAP

A major modification programme was carried out at Bitteswell during 1959. This involved the conversion of 18 Hawker-Kingston and Blackpool-built single-seat Hunter F.4s to the two-seat side-by-side advanced trainers: 16 as T.8s for the Royal Navy and two as T.7s* for the RAF. The first aircraft (WV363) arrived at Bitteswell on 16th February and it re-flew in its new guise on 9th April. The conversion involved the severing of the single-seater nose and 'bolting on' a new side-by-side trainer nose. The two-seater nose being much wider, the spine of the aircraft also required work to install a much larger streamlined fairing. The entire programme was completed in late July and involved the following former F.4s: WT701, '702, '722, '745, '755, '772, WV318, '319, '322, '363, '372*, '383, XE665, XF289, '321*, '322, '357, and '358.

On 21st April 1966 a single Hunter Mk.6 flew in from HSA Dunsfold. This signalled the start of what was to become a major 'industry' at Bitteswell, the refurbishing and converting of 'used' Hunters for the export market. The Mk.6 in question was carrying the 'B Condition' marking G-9-169 (a sort of 'trade plate' for aircraft when being tested or ferried by manufacturers or contractors) and had previously served with the Royal Netherlands Air Force as N-221. This was part of a batch of 24 former Belgian and Dutch F.6s being prepared for the Iraqi Air Force by HSA at Dunsfold. The conversion took the aircraft to FGA.9 ground-attack status and the airframes were refurbished to 'as new' standard. It is possible that this one airframe, which was delivered back to Dunsfold 13 days later, was not worked on at Bitteswell but used to familiarise technicians for what was to be an almost continuous work programme until December 1977.

The programme (summarised on page 74) eventually took in 82 complete aircraft plus the major components of many others that were refurbished and returned to Dunsfold.

The 82 included one two-seater and the conversion of a single-seater to a two-seater. Eight countries received Hunters worked on at Bitteswell: Chile, India, Iraq, Jordan, Lebanon, Qatar, Singapore and Switzerland. Other than the two-seats, the bulk of the work involved refurbishing Mk.4 and Mk.6s airframes to the full FGA.9 specification although the Singapore programme also required 26 Mk.4s and Mk.6s to be converted to the equivalent of the RAF's FR.10 fighter-reconnaissance standard.

In general the conversion work averaged about three months and ran remarkably smoothly. One aircraft, however, did insist on standing out from the 'crowd'. This was G-9-425, former RAF F.6 XJ640 under conversion to a F.70A for Lebanon as L-285. This arrived from Dunsfold on 20th May 1977. During test flying G-9-285 made a precautionary landing at RAF Wittering, near Stamford, Lincolnshire, on 22nd November 1977. During subsequent test flights, the Bitteswell tower log notes that the engine fire warning light came on on 2nd, 9th and 14th December! Despite this uncharacteristic attention-seeking, the Hunter, now in Lebanese colours as L-285 was despatched on contract with the other two in the batch via Nice on 21st December.

During the years 1967 to 1981 a total of 11 RAF or Royal Navy Hunters re-attended Bitteswell for unspecified work. Included among these was one of two Hunters that bucked the export 'trend' by returning to RAF service. The aircraft involved had been built in 1958 as XL605, a two-seat advanced T.7 trainer for the RAF. In 1966 it was refurbished at Dunsfold and delivered, with another example, to the Royal Saudi Air Force with the unofficial designation 'T.70'. The Saudis presented the two in 1968 to the Royal Jordanian Air Force, where they were known under the equally spurious designation of 'T.73'. In 1974 the pair were returned to a grateful RAF who could put them to good use. One was given the RAF serial XX467 and this arrived at Bitteswell from RAF St Athan on an unspecified date. It was delivered to the Royal Aircraft Establishment at Farnborough on 11th September 1973 and went on to serve with the Tactical Weapons Unit. This aircraft is now being restored to flying condition for civilian operation.

Hunter F.5 WP133 in the colours of 34 Squadron at Tangmere in 1957. This aircraft was despatched to RAF service from Bitteswell on 2nd May 1955.

Hunter F.6 XF446 flew out on Bitteswell on 9th February 1956 to 5 MU at Kemble. It went on to join the famed 111 Squadron's 'Black Arrows' aerobatic team. Both MAP

Bitteswell-produced Hawker Hunters

Hunter F.2

Serial	First Flight	Despatched	To
WN888	14.10.53		see notes
WN889	19.12.53		see notes
WN890	18.1.54	10.2.54	Boscombe Down
WN891	26.1.54		see notes
WN892	13.2.54	15.7.54	Boscombe Down
WN893	5.3.54	25.8.54	Farnborough
WN894	5.3.54	26.7.54	Boscombe Down
WN895	12.3.54	16.9.54	Kinloss
WN896	16.3.54	16.9.54	Kinloss
WN897	23.3.54	16.9.54	Kinloss
WN898	26.3.54	2.9.54	Kemble
WN899	1.4.54	2.9.54	Kemble
WN900	8.4.54	2.9.54	Kemble
WN901	15.4.54	3.9.54	Kemble
WN902	23.4.54	3.9.54	Kemble
WN903	19.7.54	3.9.54	Kemble
WN904	19.7.54	13.9.54	Kemble
WN905	19.7.54		see notes
WN906	21.7.54	23.9.54	Kemble
WN907	20.7.54	7.9.54	Kemble
WN908	27.7.54	7.9.54	Kemble
WN909	27.7.54	27.9.54	Kinloss
WN910	1.9.54		see notes
WN911	5.8.54	13.9.54	Kemble
WN912	6.8.54	23.9.54	Kemble
WN913	26.8.54		see notes
WN914	25.8.54	28.9.54	Kemble
WN915	25.8.54	20.9.54	Kemble
WN916	1.9.54	14.10.54	Kinloss
WN917	26.8.54	6.10.54	Kinloss
WN918	27.8.54	23.9.54	Kemble
WN919	27.8.54	27.9.54	Kinloss
WN920	28.8.54	28.9.54	Kemble
WN921	8.9.54	1.10.54	Kemble
WN943	13.9.54	21.10.54	Kemble
WN944	14.9.54	7.10.54	Kinloss
WN945	17.9.54	21.10.54	Kinloss
WN946	5.10.54	28.10.54	Kemble
WN947	21.9.54	9.11.54	Kemble
WN948	8.9.54	27.9.54	Kinloss
WN949	15.9.54	14.10.54	Kemble
WN950	14.9.54	1.10.54	Kemble
WN951	17.9.54	21.10.54	Kemble
WN952	23.9.54	14.10.54	Kemble
WN953	5.10.54	4.11.54	Leuchars

Notes: WN888 used by AWA for trials, despatched to Dunsfold 23.12.53, returning from there 20.11.55 and staying until 17.4.56 when it was despatched to Kemble. WN889 used for engine trials; transferred (across the airfield?) to Armstrong Siddeley Motors 26 or 28.1.54. WN891 no documented despatch details, released to AWA for trials by Controller (Air) 23.2.54; to CEPE (Canada) 29.7.54. *WN893 MoD(PE) record card indicates allocation to RAE 30.8.54 for investigation into tightening in turns, then to Bedford 29.11.55.* WN905 took off 14.8.54 at 1500, pilot baled out at 1537, crashed at East Langton, near Market Harborough; contract reduced to take this loss into account. WN910 no documented despatch details, C(A) release to AWA for TI of mods 6.10.54; believed to Kemble 2.3.56. WN913 left for delivery on 27.9.54 but returned to Bitteswell, eventually despatched to Kemble 7.10.54. WN904 is displayed within the camp of No.39 Engineers Regiment at Waterbeach, Cambs (it was previously a famed Hunter base with the RAF).

Hunter F.5

Serial	First Flight	Despatched	To
WN954	19.10.54	4.11.54	Dunsfold
WN955	26.10.54		see notes
WN956	26.10.54	24.11.54	Boscombe Down
WN957	27.10.54	24.11.54	Farnborough
WN958	29.10.54	1.2.55	Kemble
WN959	3.11.54	1.2.55	Kemble
WN960	9.11.54	4.2.55	Kemble
WN961	12.11.54	4.2.55	Kemble
WN962	11.11.54	8.2.55	Kemble
WN963	19.11.54	8.2.55	Kemble
WN964	23.11.54	10.2.55	Kemble
WN965	25.11.54	10.2.55	Kemble
WN966	29.11.54	11.2.55	Kemble
WN967	27.11.54	11.2.55	Kemble
WN968	29.11.54	1.3.55	Kemble
WN969	15.12.54	14.2.55	Kemble
WN970		14.2.55	see notes

Serial	First Flight	Despatched	To
WN971	17.12.54	3.3.55	Kemble
WN972	24.1.55	28.3.55	Kinloss
WN973	17.12.54	18.4.55	Kinloss
WN974	17.12.54	16.2.55	Kemble
WN975	17.12.54	16.2.55	Kemble
WN976	17.12.54	28.3.55	Kinloss
WN977	25.1.55	17.2.55	Kemble
WN978	24.1.55	17.2.55	Kemble
WN979	1.2.55	28.3.55	Kemble
WN980	30.1.55	31.3.55	Kinloss
WN981	30.1.55	16.3.55	Kinloss
WN982	4.2.55	30.3.55	Kemble
WN983	2.2.55	16.3.55	Kinloss
WN984	22.2.55	30.3.55	Kemble
WN985	21.2.55	16.3.55	Kinloss
WN986	22.2.55	22.4.55	Kinloss
WN987	22.2.55	25.4.55	Kinloss
WN988	16.2.55	13.4.55	Kinloss
WN989	21.2.55	6.4.55	Kinloss
WN990	2.3.55	6.4.55	Kinloss
WN991	22.2.55	28.3.55	Kinloss
WN992	22.3.55	25.4.55	Kinloss
WP101	2.3.55	14.4.55	Kinloss
WP102	3.3.55	28.4.55	Kinloss
WP103	4.3.55	25.4.55	Kinloss
WP104	28.3.55	28.4.55	Kemble
WP105	3.3.55	6.4.55	Kinloss
WP106	28.3.55	26.4.55	Kinloss
WP107	4.2.55	3.3.55	Kemble
WP108	5.2.55	2.3.55	Kemble
WP109	7.2.55	1.3.55	Kemble
WP110	8.2.55	2.3.55	Kemble
WP111	4.3.55	14.4.55	Kinloss
WP112	30.3.55	28.4.55	Kinloss
WP113	30.3.55		see notes
WP114	22.3.55		see notes
WP115	29.3.55	22.4.55	Kinloss
WP116	2.3.55	28.4.55	Kinloss
WP117	29.3.55	22.4.55	Kinloss
WP118	31.3.55	18.5.55	Kemble
WP119	28.3.55	25.4.55	Kinloss
WP120	6.4.55	2.5.55	Kemble
WP121	5.4.55	2.5.55	Kinloss
WP122	16.4.55	10.6.55	Kinloss
WP123	6.4.55	9.5.55	Kemble
WP124	8.4.55	26.5.55	Kinloss
WP125	7.4.55	12.5.55	Kemble
WP126	14.4.55	16.5.55	Kemble
WP127	7.4.55	9.5.55	Kemble
WP128	16.4.55	13.6.55	Kinloss
WP129	22.4.55	10.6.55	Kinloss
WP130	26.4.55	6.6.55	Kemble
WP131	13.4.55	12.5.55	Kemble
WP132	19.4.55	19.5.55	Kemble
WP133	29.3.55	2.5.55	Kinloss
WP134	15.4.55	23.5.55	Kemble
WP135	5.4.55	1.6.55	Kinloss
WP136	26.4.55	29.6.55	see notes
WP137	19.4.55	25.5.55	Kemble
WP138	30.4.55	23.5.55	Kemble
WP139	20.4.55	26.5.55	Kinloss
WP140	28.4.55	22.6.55	Kinloss
WP141	22.4.55	19.5.55	Kinloss
WP142	25.4.55	18.5.55	Kemble
WP143	5.5.55	23.6.55	Farnborough
WP144	30.4.55	27.5.55	Kinloss
WP145	25.4.55	10.6.55	Kinloss
WP146	27.4.55	19.5.55	Kinloss
WP147	9.5.55	13.6.55	Kinloss
WP148	11.5.55	13.6.55	Kinloss
WP149	13.5.55	22.6.55	Kinloss
WP150	25.5.55	4.7.55	Kemble
WP179	18.5.55	15.6.55	Kinloss
WP180	18.5.55	16.6.55	Kinloss
WP181	1.6.55	30.6.55	Kemble
WP182	25.5.55	23.6.55	Kinloss
WP183	2.6.55	30.6.55	Kemble
WP184	8.6.55	28.6.55	Kinloss
WP185	8.6.55	28.6.55	see notes
WP186	19.5.55	19.7.55	Kemble
WP187	14.6.55	7.7.55	Kemble
WP188	14.6.55	14.7.55	Kemble
WP189	21.6.55	19.7.55	Kemble
WP190	27.6.55	21.7.55	Kemble
WP191	28.6.55	3.8.55	Kemble
WP192	4.7.55	3.8.55	Kemble
WP193	13.7.55	18.8.55	Kinloss
WP194	7.7.55	29.7.55	Kemble

Notes: WN954 MoD(PE) card indicates C(A) release to AWA 4.11.54. Bitteswell to Dunsfold 4.11.55 for target-towing drogue development (also to Boscombe Down 7.1.57 and Tangmere); returned to Bitteswell 29.1.58, roaded out to St Athan 29.4.58. WN955 no documented despatch details; MoD(PE) card states C(A) release to AWA 4.11.54. Fitted with Sapphire 7 in Private Venture development with Armstrong Siddeley Motors (see page 47); to Boscombe Down 7.1.57 for TI of drogue development. WN970 first flight date not clearly documented, either 30.11.54 or 15.12.54, despatched to Kemble. WP113 released by C(A) 18.4.55 to ASM, used by them between 20.4.55 and 15.9.55, believed despatched finally to Kemble 14.10.55. WP114 C(A) released to ASM 18.4.55; in use from 30.4.55 and finally despatched to Kemble 12.2.58. WP136 for despatch to Kinloss but diverted to Leuchars due to weather. WP185 made an emergency landing at Dishforth en route to Kinloss 28.6.55. Two Bitteswell F.5s survive intact, WP185 with private collectors at Great Dunmow in Essex and WP190 with the Hunter Restoration Flight at Quedgeley, Glos.

Hunter F.6

Serial	First Flight	Despatched	To	Later
XE581	2.12.55	13.1.56	Kemble	FGA.9
XE582	16.12.55	13.1.56	Kemble	FGA.9
XE583	10.1.56	14.2.56	Kemble	–
XE609	9.2.56	5.3.56	Kemble	FGA.9
XE610	10.2.56	8.3.56	Kemble	FGA.9
XE611	28.2.56	26.3.56	Kemble	FGA.9, F.58A
XE612	1.3.56	26.3.56	Kemble	–
XE613	6.3.56	7.5.56	Kemble	FGA.9
XE614	15.3.56	26.4.56	Kemble	FR.10, FR.74B
XF373	25.5.55	13.6.55	Wymeswold	Jordan
XF374	29.6.55		see notes	FGA.9 (R)
XF375	14.7.55		see notes	–
XF376	19.7.55	30.8.55	Boscombe D'	FGA.9
XF377	29.7.55		see notes	Lebanon
XF378	3.8.55	26.9.55	Dunsfold	–
XF379	10.8.55	25.11.55	Dunsfold	Jordan
XF380	16.8.55	25.11.55	Dunsfold	Jordan
XF381	23.8.55	23.9.55	Boscombe D'	Jordan
XF382	2.9.55	28.8.56	see notes	–
XF383	5.9.55	15.2.56	Kemble	–
XF384	6.9.55	25.1.56	Kemble	–
XF385	9.9.55	30.1.56	Kemble	–
XF386	12.9.55	30.1.56	Kemble	–
XF387	15.9.55	15.2.56	Kemble	–
XF388	26.9.55	23.12.55	see notes	FGA.9
XF389	20.9.55	19.12.55	Kemble	FGA.73A
XF414	26.9.55	19.12.55	Kemble	FGA.9
XF415	27.9.55	21.12.55	Kemble	Jordan
XF416	30.9.55	3.1.56	Kemble	FGA.9
XF417	7.10.55	29.12.55	Kemble	Jordan
XF418	7.10.55	29.12.55	Kemble	–
XF419	7.10.55	30.12.55	Kemble	FGA.9
XF420	13.10.55	3.1.56	Kemble	–
XF421	13.10.55	3.1.56	Kemble	FGA.9
XF422	20.10.55	3.1.56	Kemble	FR.10, FR.74B
XF423	17.10.55	3.1.56	Kemble	Jordan FGA.9
XF424	20.10.55	5.1.56	Kemble	FGA.9
XF425	24.10.55	5.1.56	Kemble	–
XF426	28.10.55	9.1.56	Kemble	FR.10, Jordan
XF427	7.11.55	11.1.56	Kemble	–
XF428	4.11.55	9.1.56	Kemble	FR.10, FR.74B
XF429	4.11.55	11.1.56	Kemble	FR.10, F.58A
XF430	4.11.55	11.1.56	Kemble	FGA.9, FGA.70A
XF431	11.11.55	21.1.56	Kemble	FGA.9
XF432	14.11.55	29.12.55	Kemble	FR.74B
XF433	18.11.55	5.1.56	Kemble	–
XF434	21.11.55	29.12.55	Kemble	–
XF435	23.11.55	30.12.55	Kemble	–
XF436	24.11.55	29.12.55	Kemble	FR.10, F.58A
XF437	28.11.55	29.12.55	Kemble	FGA.9, FR.74A
XF438	2.12.55	30.12.55	Kemble	FR.10, F.58A
XF439	6.12.55	3.1.56	Kemble	–
XF440	7.12.55	9.1.56	Kemble	FGA.9
XF441	6.12.55	5.1.56	Kemble	FR.10, FR.74B
XF442	12.12.55	25.1.56	Kemble	FGA.9
XF443	21.12.55	25.1.56	Kemble	–
XF444	2.1.56	30.1.56	Kemble	Jordan
XF445	2.1.56	9.2.56	Kemble	FGA.9
XF446	4.1.56	9.2.56	Kemble	FGA.9, F.56A
XF447	9.1.56	9.2.56	Kemble	FGA.71
XF448	9.1.56	14.2.56	Kemble	–
XF449	17.1.56	14.2.56	Kemble	–
XF450	16.1.56	15.2.56	Kemble	F.60
XF451	30.1.56	8.3.56	Kemble	–
XF452	17.1.56	12.3.56	Dunsfold	Jordan
XF453	30.1.56	8.3.56	Kemble	FR.71A
XF454	20.1.56	1.3.56	Kemble	FGA.9, Jordan
XF455	26.1.56	1.3.56	Kemble	FGA.9
XF456	30.1.56	5.3.56	Kemble	FGA.9, FGA.74
XF457	30.1.56	5.3.56	Kemble	FR.10, FGA.70A
XF458	9.2.56	17.4.56	Kemble	FR.74B
XF459	14.2.56	15.3.56	Kemble	FR.10, T.66E
XF460	9.2.56	1.3.56	Kemble	FR.10, FR.74B
XF461	15.2.56	15.3.56	Kemble	Lebanon
XF462	15.2.56	21.3.56	Kemble	FGA.9, F.58A
XF463	15.2.56	21.3.56	Kemble	F.56
XF495	28.2.56	10.4.56	Kemble	Lebanon
XF496	28.2.56	16.4.56	Kemble	Jordan
XF497	28.2.56	10.4.56	Kemble	F.56
XF498	29.2.56	18.4.56	Kemble	Jordan
XF499	2.3.56	18.4.56	Kemble	F.56
XF500	5.3.56	16.4.56	Kemble	F.56
XF501	12.3.56	17.4.56	Kemble	F.56
XF502	9.3.56	26.4.56	Kemble	–
XF503	14.3.56	26.4.56	Kemble	F.56
XF504	20.3.56	3.5.56	Kemble	FGA.9 (R)
XF505	23.3.56	3.5.56	Kemble	F.56
XF506	26.3.56	7.5.56	Kemble	FGA.9 (R)
XF507	4.4.56	14.5.56	Kemble	–

Serial	First Flight	Despatched	To	Later
XF508	10.4.56	14.5.56	Kemble	FGA.9
XF509	10.4.56	23.5.56	Kemble	–
XF510	19.4.56	31.5.56	Kemble	–
XF511	24.4.56	23.5.56	Kemble	FGA.9
XF512	26.4.56	23.5.56	Kemble	FGA.71
XF513	8.5.56	31.5.56	Kemble	–
XF514	11.5.56	7.6.56	Kemble	Jordan
XF515	23.5.56	13.6.56	Kemble	–
XF516	5.6.56	22.10.56	St Athan	–
XF517	6.6.56	16.10.56	St Athan	FGA.9
XF518	11.6.56	7.11.56	Lyneham	Jordan
XF519	19.6.56	17.10.56	St Athan	FGA.9
XF520	21.6.56	12.10.56	Kemble	FGA.73A
XF521	26.6.56	1.11.56	Kemble	F.56
XF522	4.7.56	23.10.56	Kemble	–
XF523	10.7.56	15.11.56	Kemble	–
XF524	12.7.56	26.11.56	Kemble	–
XF525	15.8.56	28.9.56	Kemble	–
XF526	15.8.56	7.9.56	St Athan	–
XF527	3.9.56	28.9.56	Lyneham	–
XG150	28.3.56	8.5.56	Kemble	F.56
XG151	16.4.56	14.5.56	Kemble	FGA.9
XG152	30.4.56	7.6.56	Kemble	–
XG153	28.5.56	10.10.56	Kemble	FGA.9, FR.74B
XG154	13.6.56	26.10.56	St Athan	FGA.9
XG155	2.7.56	16.11.56	Kemble	FGA.9
XG156	15.8.56	26.11.56	Kemble	FGA.9
XG157	29.8.56	4.10.56	Lyneham	–
XG158	3.9.56	4.10.56	St Athan	–
XG159	15.8.56	27.9.56	Kemble	FGA.73A
XG160	5.9.56	12.10.56	Kemble	–
XG161	17.9.56	4.10.56	Lyneham	–
XG162	12.9.56	16.10.56	Kemble	–
XG163	19.9.56	12.10.56	Kemble	F.56
XG164	27.9.56	9.11.56	Kemble	–
XG165	12.10.56	12.11.56	Kemble	–
XG166	22.10.56	3.12.56	Hawarden	–
XG167	10.1.57	18.2.57	Kemble	Lebanon
XG168	21.2.57	2.4.57	Kemble	FR.10

Notes: XF373 despatched to 'Rolls-Royce Hucknall' who were operating from Wymeswold at that time. XF374, XF375 and XF377, no documented despatch details *but Ministry record cards indicate that XF374 to Dunsfold 3.8.55 for Blue Jay trials;*

XF375 to R-R Hucknall at Wymeswold 31.8.55; XF377 to Dunsfold for armament trials. XF382, no record of despatch destination. XF388 initial test intended for 22.9.55, but take-off abandoned; despatched to R-R at Hucknall. Large numbers survive with private owners, museums, instructional airframes etc.

*Later: Aircraft later converted to other marks for the RAF or refurbished for export, not necessarily at Bitteswell - see narrative for 'home spun' conversions. Decode: FGA.9, converted to ground attack version for the RAF; FGA.9 (R) converted to ground attack version for Rhodesia, NB unofficial designation; FR.10 fighter reconnaissance conversion for RAF; F.56 refurbished day fighter for India, 1957; F.58A refurbished day fighter for Switzerland 1971-1973; F.60 refurbished day fighter for Saudi Arabia, 1966; T.66E refurbished and converted two-seater trainer for India, 1973; FGA.70A refurbished ground attack version for Lebanon, 1966; FGA.71 refurbished ground attack version for Chile, 1966-1968; FR.71A refurbished fighter reconnaissance version for Chile, 1968; FGA.73A refurbished ground attack version for Jordan, 1969; FGA.74 refurbished ground attack version for Singapore, 1970-1971; FR.74A refurbished fighter reconnaissance version for Singapore, 1971 and FR.74B 1972-1973; Jordan, straight supply of 12 F.6s via US MDAP funding, 1958 and some short term FGA.9 loans in 1967; Lebanon, straight supply of 6 F.6s via US MDAP funding, 1958.

Hunter F.6 XF520, largely in primer finish, runs up its engine in the silencer bay during a rare publicity session in June 1956. At a much later date this aircraft became '814/F', an FGA.73 for Jordan. Brandon White

Hunter FGA.74, 501, routing through Luqa, Malta, in November 1970, on delivery to the Singapore Air Defence Command. It had begun life in 1956 as XG260, a Hawker Aircraft (Kingston) built F.6, but was later modified at Dunsfold to FGA.9 standard for the RAF. Finally it was refurbished for export at Bitteswell. MAP

Hunters Refurbished for Export at Bitteswell

Nation	Export Mk	Using	Total	Serials	Programme Dates
Chile	FGA.71	RAF F.6s	6	J-722 to J-727	1970-1971
	FGA.71	RAF F.6	1	J 733	1973
India	F.56A	Belgian F.6s	3	A459, A471, A476	1966
	F.56A	RAF F.6s	3	A967 to A969	1969
	T.66E	RAF F.6	1	S1392	1973
Iraq	F.59B	Dutch F.6	1	662	1966
Jordan	F.73	Jordan F.6s	6	see notes	1966-1968
	F.73A	RAF.6s	2	829, 830	1969
	F.73A	RAF FGA.9s	2	828, 831	1969
	F.73B	RAF F.6s	3	847, 848, 849	1971
Lebanon	F.70A	RAF F.6s	3	L-283 to L 285	1977
Qatar	FGA.78	Dutch F.6s	3	QA-10 to QA-12	1970-1971
	T.79	Dutch T.7	1	QA-13	1971
Singapore	FGA.74	RAF F.6s	12	see notes	1970-1971
	FR.74A	RAF F.6s	4	see notes	1971
	FR.74B	RAF F.4s	8	see notes	1972-1973
	FR.74B	RAF F.6s	14	see notes	1972-1973
Switzerland	F.58A	RN GA.11s	9	J-4118 to J-4126	1970

Notes: All aircraft were allocated G-9-xxx numbers for test in what is 'B Condition' (or best described as 'trade plate') flying. Example, former Royal Netherlands Air Force F.6 N-268 was tested as G-9-286 and first flew as an FGA.78 for Qatar on 12.6.70, becoming QA-10. Singapore FRA.74B 532 was converted from AWA-built F.6 XF432 and first flew as G-9-363 on 29.8.72. It was displayed at the 9.72 SBAC display at Farnborough with the 'full' civilian registration G-BABM.

Jordanian F.73s were refurbished F.6s operated by the Royal Jordanian Air Force, built for the RAF but delivered direct to Jordan in 1958 and were the result of a 1965 repair contract for those F.6s delivered in 1958. Initially 12 aircraft were planned to be refurbished, but this was reduced to 10. Of those known to have been processed at Bitteswell, ie. 702, 704, 705, 708, 709 and 711, only 704 and 711 survived air attacks on their base at Matraq during the 'Six-Day War' of June 1967, because they were on overhaul in the UK at the time.

Singapore Hunters were serialled from 500 onwards. Bitteswell conversions were as follows: FGA.74: 501, 502, 505, 507 to 511, 513, 515, 518, 519. FR.74: 503, 506, 512, 517. FR.74B 520 to 527, 529, 530, 531, 533, 534, 535, 537, 538, 539, 541, 542, 543, 545, 546. (The missing numbers apply to T.75s and T.75A two-seaters converted at Dunsfold.

The 9 ex-Royal Navy Hunter GA.11s for Switzerland were flown into Bitteswell and joined other early marks on the refurbishing line. Unlike the other air arms, Switzerland requested that their two batches totalling 52 F.58Aa and 8 T.68s (ordered in 1970 and 1972) be transported by road and ferry in sections, to be assembled and test flown by the Federal Aircraft Factory on the airfield at Emmen. The following Bitteswell-refurbished export Hunters were originally built for the RAF at Bitteswell: Chile J-723 (XF447), J-725 (XF512). Jordan 704 (XF498), 708 (XF452), 709 (XF444), 829 (XF389). Lebanon: L-283 (XF430). Singapore: 503 (XF437), 509 (XF456), 520 (XG153), 524 (XF422), 525 (XF428), 527 (XF458), 533 (XE614), 545 (XF441), 526 (XF460).

Seen here taxying out for a post-conversion test flight on 2nd April 1959, is one of the 18 Hunter F.4s converted by AWA during 1958-59 into two-seat trainers, complete with its new forward fuselage and tail parachute housing etc. WV372 was the 7th conversion (note the small '7' above the serial number) and one of only two T.7s for the RAF – the others being T.8s (with an arrestor hook) for the Royal Navy. Records indicate that WV372 served with 222 Squadron prior to conversion, which raises the question why the marks on the rear fuselage look like 247 Squadron's. Chris Salter

A pair of FGA.78 single-seaters and T.79 two-seater QA-13 (centre) for Qatar, nearing completion at Bitteswell, in 1971. Brandon White

Gloster Javelin

AWA's links with fellow Hawker Siddeley Group company Gloster and the expertise it had developed in the Meteor night-fighter programme meant that Bitteswell was well placed to build this new delta-winged, twin-engined, transonic all-weather fighter. The intention with the Javelin was that ultimately it would be armed only with guided air-to-air missiles, but early production versions, FAWs 1- 6, were only fitted with four 30mm cannon. The Javelin represented a major technological leap and the early variants were involved in 'shaking down' the many design and operational problems.

The prototype Javelin made its first flight from Gloster's flight test airfield at Moreton Valence on 26th November 1951 but it was December 1955 before any were delivered to an operational unit – a far cry from the speed of the Hunter's entry to service.

The first Javelins built by AWA were 32 FAW.4s, these following 18 examples completed by Gloster's themselves. The FAW.5, with greater range from increased fuel tankage in the wing, was introduced onto the Bitteswell assembly line almost in parallel with the Mk.4 and 44 were constructed. As with the Meteor night-fighters, many of the AWA-produced Javelins revisited for on-going modifications and programme upgrades.

The largest batch built at Bitteswell was the FAW.7, which was the first to be fully operationally equipped with the Firestreak air-to-air missile, two being carried under each wing. It also featured the more powerful AS Sapphire 7 engines (without re-heat) as first tested on FAW.1 XA560 by ASM at Bitteswell in early 1956. Extensive flight testing in 1956 revealed aerothermal problems with the standard 'pen-knib' exhaust outlets and with production of the FAW.7 already into its stride at both AWA and GAC in late 1956, a design solution was found too late.

As a result of this and other equipment shortages, 49 of Bitteswell's 57 FAW.7s were despatched to Kemble on their first flights, for short term storage. From September 1957 to February 1958, 23 of them returned to Bitteswell for the new rear fuselage sections and other modifications, prior to test-flying, painting and final delivery. Most went to the RAF but a few went straight to GAC for upgrading to the re-heated FAW.9 standard, as did the balance of those stored at Kemble.

With the advent of in-flight refuelling, conversion of a dozen or so FAW.9s to FAW.9R status was undertaken in 1962-3, a process that included fixing a huge refuelling probe to the starboard upper fuselage that projected beyond the radar nose. The final Javelin work, in 1963-4, saw 11 FAW.9Rs that had been converted elsewhere, in for painting.

In all, AWA assembled 133 Javelins from a total production run of 435 units.

Bitteswell-produced Gloster Javelins

Javelin FAW.4 (Contract 6/Acft/8336/CB.7(b) 18.6.52)

Serial	First Flight	Despatched	To
XA720	23.2.56		*see notes*
XA721	6.4.56		*see notes*
XA722		23.4.56	Moreton Valence
XA723		2.5.56	*see notes*
XA724	27.4.56	10.2.58	Hatfield
XA725	4.5.56	2.1.58	Boscombe Down
XA726	7.5.56	26.6.56	Lyneham
XA727	14.5.56	29.6.56	Lyneham
XA728	11.5.56	28.6.56	Lyneham
XA729	18.5.56	9.7.56	Lyneham
XA730	28.5.56	2.7.56	Lyneham
XA731	31.5.56	13.7.56	Lyneham
XA732	5.6.56	17.8.56	Lyneham
XA733	11.6.56	12.9.56	Lyneham
XA734	19.6.56	23.8.56	Lyneham
XA735	28.6.56	24.9.56	Moreton Valence
XA736	28.6.56	17.8.56	Lyneham
XA737	10.7.56	26.9.56	Kemble
XA749	10.7.56	24.9.56	Moreton Valence
XA750	15.8.56	1.10.56	Kemble
XA751	15.8.56	11.10.56	Kemble
XA752	17.8.56	5.10.56	Kemble
XA753	15.8.56	1.10.56	Kemble
XA754	20.8.56	19.10.56	Kemble
XA755	4.9.56	23.10.56	Kemble
XA756	13.9.56	8.2.57	St Athan
XA757	6.9.56	6.2.57	St Athan
XA758	21.9.56	6.2.57	St Athan
XA759	26.9.56	20.2.57	St Athan
XA760	28.9.56	20.2.57	St Athan
XA761	11.10.56	20.2.57	St Athan
XA762	17.10.56	25.2.57	St Athan

Notes: The first six aircraft were all loaned back by Controller (Air) for various flight trials. MoD(PE) records give awaiting collection dates for XA720-721 and '723-725 as 29.3, 30.4, 18.5, 16.5 and 16.5.56; XA720-721 possibly to GAC Moreton Valence on first or early flights. XA722 and XA723 no test flight details recorded, despatched to Moreton Valence. XA723 to the CEPE (Central Experimental & Proving Establishment, Namao, Alberta, Canada) for climatic evaluation; XA724-'725 loan to AWA for Blue Jay trials (probably pylon development), then elsewhere.

Javelin FAW.5 (Contract 6/Acft/8336/CB.7(b) 18.6.52)

Serial	First Flight	Despatched	To
XA662	11.10.56	10.1.57	Kemble
XA663	16.10.56	28.11.56	Kemble
XA664	23.10.56	3.1.57	Kemble
XA665	22.10.56	6.12.56	Kemble
XA666	27.10.56	3.1.57	Kemble
XA667	27.10.56		*see notes*
XA688	27.10.56	13.12.56	Kemble
XA689	6.11.56	9.1.57	Kemble
XA690	6.11.56	3.1.57	Kemble
XA691	7.11.56	10.1.57	Kemble
XA692	,14.11.56	6.2.57	Kemble
XA693	15.11.56	22.1.57	Kemble
XA694	27.11.56	15.1.57	Kemble
XA695	29.11.56	22.1.57	Kemble
XA696	28.11.56	11.2.57	Kemble
XA697	27.11.56	30.7.57	St Athan
XA698	16.1.57	6.2.57	Kemble
XA699	7.1.57	17.4.57	St Athan
XA700	24.1.57	31.1.57	Kemble
XA701	10.1.57	1.2.57	Kemble
XA702	22.1.57	6.2.57	Kemble
XA703	15.1.57		*see notes*
XA704			*see notes*
XA705	19.1.57	1.2.57	Kemble
XA706	25.4.57	23.5.57	Benson
XA707			see notes
XA708	13.2.57	3.5.57	St Athan
XA709	15.4.57	13.5.57	Moreton Valence
XA710	17.4.57	16.5.57	St Athan
XA711	13.2.57		*see notes*
XA712	26.3.57	24.4.57	Kemble
XA713	18.4.57	16.5.57	St Athan
XA714	4.4.57	21.5.57	St Athan
XA715	1.4.57	30.4.57	St Athan
XA716	8.5.57	20.6.57	St Athan
XA717	10.4.57	17.5.57	St Athan
XA718	26.4.57	19.6.57	St Athan

Gloster Javelin production under way in No.5 'Old Site' Hangar at Bitteswell, 1957-1958. Note the production/planning sequence number sheet applied to the upper fin leading edge.
David Sargent collection

Serial	First Flight	Despatched	To
XA719	2.5.57	19.6.57	St Athan
XH687	26.3.57	26.4.57	St Athan
XH688	27.3.57	8.5.57	St Athan
XH689	1.4.57	1.5.57	St Athan
XH690	4.4.57	8.5.57	St Athan
XH691	26.4.57	28.5.57	Benson
XH692	15.5.57	30.8.57	St Athan

Notes: Many of the FAW.4s and 5s saw periods of short-term storage at RAF MUs prior to acceptance for service. XA667 despatched to Kemble 9.1.57, returning on 4.4.57; landed with the nosewheel in the 'up' position 17.5.57; after repair and modifications it was despatched to St Athan on 10.7.57. XA703 took off for despatch to Kemble 5.2.57 but returned to Bitteswell, finally despatched on 11.2.57. XA704 no air test prior to delivery, test flight and delivery to Kemble as one flight 31.1.57. XA707 intended to conduct air test and delivery to Kemble as one flight, 5.2.57, but returned to Bitteswell, despatched the following day. Returned 2.5.57, being despatched to St Athan 30.7.57. XA711 issued to Armstrong Siddeley Motors for test purposes at Bitteswell, first noted in their charge 16.5.57. *RAF records suggest XH692 was accepted at St Athan 30.6.57.*

Only one aircraft from this batch survives intact, XA699 is displayed appropriately at the Midland Air Museum at Coventry Airport (or Baginton) where its major components were fabricated.

Javelin FAW.7 (Contract 6/Acft/11329/CB.7(b) 28.9.54)

Serial	First Flight/ Despatched*	To
XH785	25.4.57	Kemble
XH786	16.5.57	Kemble
XH787	16.5.57	Kemble
XH788	22.5.57	Kemble
XH789	30.5.57	Kemble
XH790	7.6.57	Kemble
XH791	14.6.57	Kemble
XH792	4.7.57	Kemble
XH793	4.7.57	Kemble
XH794	4.7.57	Kemble
XH795	11.7.57	Kemble
XH833	25.7.57	Kemble
XH834	13.8.57	Kemble
XH835*	13.6.57	Aldergrove
XH836*	3.6.57	Benson
XH837*	18.7.57	Aldergrove
XH838*	22.7.57	Benson
XH839*	18.7.57	Aldergrove
XH840	27.9.57	Kemble
XH841	4.10.57	Kemble
XH842	16.10.57	Kemble
XH843	21.10.57	Kemble
XH844	23.10.57	Kemble
XH845	1.11.57	Kemble
XH846	1.11.57	Kemble
XH847	13.11.57	Kemble

Serial	First Flight	Despatched	To
XH848	13.11.57		Kemble
XH849	22.11.57		Kemble
XH871	22.11.57		Kemble
XH872	6.12.57		Kemble
XH873	6.12.57		Kemble
XH874			*see notes*
XH875	18.12.57		Kemble
XH876	19.12.57		Kemble
XH877	3.1.58		Kemble
XH878	8.1.58		Kemble
XH879	9.1.58		Kemble
XH880	28.2.58		Kemble
XH881	12.2.58		Kemble
XH882	4.2.58		Kemble
XH883	7.3.58		Kemble
XH884			*see notes*
XH885	4.3.58		Kemble
XH886	14.3.58		Kemble
XH887	17.3.58		Kemble
XH888	3.4.58		Kemble
XH889	1.4.58		Kemble
XH890	14.4.58		Kemble
XH891	15.4.58		Kemble
XH892	23.4.58		Kemble
XH893	29.4.58		Kemble
XH894	6.5.58		Kemble
XH895	16.5.58		Kemble
XH896	5.6.58		Kemble
XH897	16.6.58		Moreton Valence
XH898	11.7.58		Moreton Valence
XH899	24.7.58		Moreton Valence

Notes: With production of the FAW.7s well under way, a shortage of essential components (including the redesigned rear fuselage sections) and lack of storage space at Bitteswell deemed it necessary to despatch the majority (XH785-795, XH833-834, XH840-849, and XH871-896) into temporary storage at RAF Kemble until they could be recalled or sent elsewhere for completion. The great majority of these flights into storage were conducted on the aircraft's maiden flight, exceptions being: XH874 which took off for despatch to Kemble 11.12.57, but returned to Bitteswell; re-despatched to Kemble 17.12.57. XH884 took off for despatch to Kemble 11.3.58, but returned only to be re-despatched to Kemble the following day. Further exceptions were XH835-839, which were first flown on the following respective dates: 8.5.57, 8.5.57, 23.5.57, 30.5.57 and 2.6.57. These and XH897-899 were not recorded as returning to Bitteswell for completion, though they did enter RAF service as FAW.7s. XH871-896 are not recorded as having returned to Bitteswell either and were probably completed (and at the same time converted to FAW.9s) at Gloster's Moreton Valence factory. Of the above the following were converted to FAW.9R status at Bitteswell during 1962-1963: XH873, XH877, XH879, XH886, XH887, XH888, XH893, XH894, XH895, XH896, XH899.

Two survive, both as FAW.9s: XH892 at the Norfolk & Suffolk Aviation Museum, Flixton, Suffolk and XH897 at the Imperial War Museum, Duxford, Cambs.

Avro Shackleton

On 3rd February 1958, AWA accepted the first of what was to be a long and successful programme of deep overhaul and modifications to the RAF's multifarious fleet of Avro Shackleton four-engined maritime patrol aircraft. The first to arrive was MR.3 WR973 which was used by AWA to develop the fuel jettison systems for the forthcoming Argosy programme, after which WR973 departed on 4th March 1959. Later that year, after ASM had left Bitteswell, AWA were able to convert No.2 hangar into a Shackleton wing overhaul shop. Carried out in conjunction with Avro at Langar, (where Shackleton majors had been undertaken for several years) wings were roaded into Bitteswell and then returned to Langar for reassembly and test flying. The Hawker-Siddeley Group decided to close Langar in 1968 and Bitteswell took over their role. Of interest, WR973, which had meanwhile become the first six-engined MR.3 Phase 3 variant, after the fitting of two Bristol Siddeley Viper turbojets in specially modified outboard Griffon nacelles, at Langar in 1966, was to visit Bitteswell three more times, in 1968, 1969-70 and again in late 1970.

A total of 50 individual Shackletons are recorded as being worked on at Bitteswell until the contracts ceased in 1981. During that time, as well as the MR.3, MR.2 maritime patrol, AEW.2 airborne early warning and T.4 crew trainer variants were also modified and overhauled at Bitteswell.

Avro Vulcan

Another large programme was the overhaul and modification work on the mighty Avro Vulcan four-jet delta-winged strategic bomber. From 1959 to 1981 Vulcans were in almost constant attendance at Bitteswell, providing considerable work and financial benefits for AWA and its corporate successors.

Work encompassed most Vulcan variants, the B.1, B.1A and B.2 strategic bombers, B.2MRR specialist maritime reconnaissance variant and lastly, in 1982, support for the K.2 single-point tanker work then being undertaken at HSA's Woodford facility.

The first Vulcans to arrive, for fairly minor modification updates, were the eleven B.1s between January and the end of June 1959.

Vulcan B.1 XH483 of 617 Squadron, taxying out from Bitteswell's 'new site' to the end of runway 22, in March 1959. It is in the early anti-flash white scheme with the unit badge aft of the fuselage roundel.   Chris Salter

They were followed by a further 27 B.1s to be fitted with an extensive ECM suite, work which led to them being redesignated as B.1As and appearing externally not unlike the production B.2s. XH500 was the first of these to arrive, in July 1959, followed, in order of conversion, by XH505, '506, XA904, '912, XH481, '477, '483, '501, XA913, XH479, '478, '504, '498, XA907, XH476, '497, XA909, '906, XH482, '475, '499, '532, '480, XA911, XH502 and '503. It was 14 months before XH500 was returned to 617 Squadron (30th September 1960) but the turnround time had been reduced to about six months by the time the last B.1A, XH503, was returned to the Waddington Wing (44/50/101 Squadrons) on 6th March 1963. In October 1968, one other B.1, the all-white XA903, made trial flights over the airfield in connection with noise tests on the under-slung Olympus 593 (Concorde powerplant).

In 1964, several Vulcan B.2s went through the surface finish and painting facility that was situated in one half of No.6 hangar, 'old site', initially to have their overall white finish replaced with a camouflage scheme. Later that year the first of many B.2s began arriving for deep servicing. It is believed that later this included the fitting of an extra fuel tank in the bomb bay on some aircraft. In 1968, XH539, the Blue Steel test-bed and one of the few remaining white Vulcan B.2s, came to Bitteswell for removal of the inert stand-off bomb and its associated equipment.

By the end of the programme, 113 of the 45 B.1s and 89 B.2s built by Avro, had been through Bitteswell. Many of the Mk.2s visited up to five times; XM612 (now preserved at Norwich Airport) made seven visits, in 1964, '65, '67, '69, '72, '77 and '80-81, while XM599 (see page 48) visited on a record eight occasions. Vulcan B.2 XL426 (illustrated in Chapter Two and today maintained in 'live' condition by the Vulcan Restoration Trust at Southend Airport) serves as a typical example, visiting in 1966, '69, '73-74 and '77-78. The final Vulcan departure from Bitteswell was made by B.2 XJ824 on 4th June 1981, having arrived 17th September 1980. Prior to this, XJ824 (now preserved at the Imperial War Museum, Duxford) had made visits in 1970 and '75-76.

Avro Shackleton AEW.2 WL790 undergoing extensive overhaul and modification.
via Neville Martin

The prototype Argosy, G-AOZZ, on its maiden flight, 8th January 1959. AWA via Ken Ellis

Taken in the new site hangars during a routine inspection or mod-update on the prototype Argosy G-AOZZ, in the foreground. In the rear is an example bound for Riddle Airlines. AWA via Harry Holmes

Armstrong Whitworth Argosy

The background and development of the last AWA-designed aircraft to be built, the Argosy civilian freighter and military airlifter (respectively AW.650 and AW.660), has been detailed in Chapter Two. Work on the prototype, G-AOZZ, began in 1957 and powered by four Rolls-Royce Dart turboprops, it was rolled out on 21st December 1958 and made its first flight from a snow-covered Bitteswell on 8th January 1959. With its 'pod and boom' layout and wide-opening doors at the front and rear of the pressurised fuselage, it offered great promise.

Another five Series 100 examples followed in quick succession during 1959 as the flight trials gained pace. Extensive overseas sales tours were also staged and in 1959 the Argosy made its public debut at both the Paris and Farnborough trade shows. During the latter, the price of a civil freight version was quoted at £460,000.

The use of the wing structure of the Avro Shackleton four-engined maritime patrol aircraft contributed to the relatively swift gestation of the design. With suitable modifications, it met the Argosy's wing needs and accordingly Shackleton tooling could be used – Avro also being a part of the Hawker Siddeley group. The timing of the Argosy design was extremely fortunate for both concerns, Avro delivered the last Shackleton (an MR.3) in June 1959 and therefore could 'roll on' the jigs to meet the needs of AWA.

First order was placed by Riddle Airlines of Miami, USA, for use on LOGAIR contract freight flying for the US Air Force's MATS. Eventually, Riddle took seven series 101s, although in 1962 they were all returned to AWA when Riddle lost the contract. AWA eventually resold the aircraft to other US operators, five going to Capitol Airlines of Nashville and two to Calhoun of Wilmington, who in turn leased them to Zantop Air Transport of Detroit, both of whom had now been awarded the 'Logair' contract. By 1966 the Capitol machines had also passed to Zantop and later that year the latter concern changed its name to Universal Airlines.

The other civilian airline order came from British European Airways (BEA) for use on regular freight routes within Europe. In 1961 BEA took three series 100s (including the prototype). BEA was to prove unhappy with the profit margins on the operation of their series 102s, but could see the potential of the type in its services.

In an effort to find further orders, AWA undertook a complete redesign of the wing to provide a substantial weight reduction, allowing for greater payload. Many other modifications, including a slightly increased width freight floor, were also initiated. All of this brought about further heavy development and production costs.

Ten of the modified airframes were laid down against an order in 1964 from BEA for six series 222 freighters. The prototype series 200, G-ASKZ, made its first flight on 11th March 1964, immediately encountering

The first Argosy C.1, XN814 on a flight from Bitteswell, 1961. Note the clam-shell doors of the 'beaver tail' in the open position and the test air speed indicator pitot tube on the starboard wingtip. AWA via Ken Ellis

problems with low speed flight – something unheard of on the series 100s which were regarded as delightful to fly in all regimes. It was the new fail-safe wing, despite having the same aerodynamics, that imparted undesirable characteristics. Many trials eventually resulted in a 'fix'; this adding further to the spiralling costs of the programme.

Only seven of the series 200 airframes were completed, though beyond their original customers, series 100 and 200 Argosies enjoyed a long and varied life in a variety of countries as freighters and examples served on into the late 1980s in Australia, New Zealand and Alaska.

The military potential of the Argosy was always considered in the design and it was to be the tactical airlifter version that achieved the greatest production figures when the RAF placed a first order for 20 aircraft in January 1959. This was followed by two further orders for 20 and 16 respectively, bringing the total acquisition to 56. The RAF requirement included the need to be able to air drop bulky loads. Accordingly the rear fuselage was redesigned to 'beaver tail' format, with the lower door acting as a drop and loading ramp. To enable parachutists to be dropped, two doors were installed, one on each side of the rear fuselage.

Armstrong-Whitworth Argosy Production at Bitteswell

Identity	Series	Con No	First Flight	Despatched	Customer
G-AOZZ	100	6651	8.1.59	–	Prototype. Later to BEA
G-APRL	101	6652	14.3.59	17.8.61	Riddle, Miami, USA, N6507R
G-APRM	102	6653	26.4.59	23.11.61	BEA, Heathrow
G-APRN	102	6654	13.5.59	6.11.61	BEA, Heathrow
G-APVH	101	6655	20.7.59	22.6.61	Riddle, Miami, USA, N6504R
G-APWW	101	6656	23.9.59	24.1.61	Riddle, Miami, USA, N6503R
G-1-4	101	6657	25.2.61	11.6.61	Riddle, Miami, USA, N6505R
G-1-5	101	6658	26.6.61	18.7.61	Riddle, Miami, USA, N6506R
G-1-6	101	6659	18.11.60	18.12.60	Riddle, Miami, USA, N6501R
G-1-7	101	6660	16.12.60	7.1.61	Riddle, Miami, USA, N6502R
XN814	C.1	6743	4.3.61		see notes
XN815	C.1	6744	22.4.61	6.6.61	A&AEE, Boscombe Down
XN816	C.1	6745	5.6.61	8.9.61	A&AEE, Boscombe Down
XN817	C.1	6746	8.5.61	24.7.61	A&AEE, Boscombe Down
XN818	C.1	6747	5.7.61	28.8.61	A&AEE, Boscombe Down
XN819	C.1	6748	28.7.61	11.10.61	A&AEE, Boscombe Down
XN820	C.1	6749	28.7.61	6.9.61	A&AEE, Boscombe Down
XN821	C.1	6750	22.8.61	13.10.61	RAF, Benson
XN847	C.1	6751	12.9.61	23.11.61	RAF, Benson
XN848	C.1	6752	29.9.61	15.11.61	RAF, Benson
XN849	C.1	6753	12.10.61	11.12.61	RAF, Benson
XN850	C.1	6754	31.10.61	12.1.62	RAF, Benson
XN851	C.1	6755	20.11.61	12.1.62	RAF, Benson
XN852	C.1	6756	5.12.61	23.1.62	RAF, Benson
XN853	C.1	6757	12.12.61	14.2.62	RAF, Benson
XN854	C.1	6758	9.1.62	23.2.62	RAF, Benson
XN855	C.1	6759	17.1.62	14.3.62	RAF, Benson
XN856	C.1	6760	25.1.62	16.3.62	RAF, Benson
XN857	C.1	6761	8.2.62	26.3.62	RAF, Benson
XN858	C.1	6762	19.2.62		see notes
XP408	C.1	6763	2.3.62	2.5.62	RAF, Benson
XP409	C.1	6764	15.3.62	9.5.62	RAF, Benson
XP410	C.1	6765	27.3.62	21.5.62	RAF, Benson
XP411	C.1	6766	6.4.62	30.5.62	RAF, Benson
XP412	C.1	6767	19.4.62	22.6.62	RAF, Benson
XP413	C.1	6768	8.5.62	29.6.62	RAF, Benson
XP437	C.1	6769	23.5.62	24.7.62	RAF, Benson
XP438	C.1	6770	4.6.62	14.8.62	RAF, Benson
XP439	C.1	6771	18.6.62	3.9.62	RAF, Valley
XP440	C.1	6772	28.6.62	19.9.62	RAF, Benson
XP441	C.1	6773	16.7.62	28.9.62	RAF, Benson
XP442	C.1	6774	2.8.62	15.10.62	RAF, Benson
XP443	C.1	6775	27.8.62	22.11.62	RAF, Benson
XP444	C.1	6776	6.9.62	27.11.62	RAF, Benson
XP445	C.1	6777	25.9.62	10.12.62	RAF, Benson

Identity	Series	Con No	First Flight	Despatched	Customer
XP446	C.1	6778	4.10.62	6.3.63	RAF, Benson
XP447	C.1	6779	18.10.62	6.3.63	RAF, Benson
XP448	C.1	6780	29.10.62	11.3.63	RAF, Benson
XP449	C.1	6781	13.11.62	11.3.63	RAF, Benson
XP450	C.1	6782	28.11.62	11.3.63	RAF, Benson
XR105	C.1	6783	7.12..62		see notes
XR106	C.1	6784	9.1.63	5.4.63	RAF, Benson
XR107	C.1	6785	13.2.63	30.4.63	RAF, Benson
XR108	C.1	6786	1.2.63	27.6.63	RAF, Benson
XR109	C.1	6787	20.2.63	9.5.63	RAF, Benson
XR133	C.1	6788	26.2.63	14.5.63	RAF, Benson
XR134	C.1	6789	7.3.63	18.6.63	RAF, Benson
XR135	C.1	6790	20.3.63	9.7.63	RAF, Benson
XR136	C.1	6791	5.4.63	18.7.63	RAF, Benson
XR137	C.1	6792	30.4.63	16.8.63	RAF, Benson
XR138	C.1	6793	20.5.63	29.8.63	RAF, Benson
XR139	C.1	6794	21.6.63	27.9.63	RAF, Benson
XR140	C.1	6795	19.8.63	5.11.63	RAF, Benson
XR141	C.1	6796	13.9.63	20.12.63	RAF, Benson
XR142	C.1	6797	4.11.63	2.1.64	RAF, Benson
XR143	C.1	6798	26.2.64	27.3.64	RAF, Benson
G-ASKZ	200	6799	11.3.64		Series prototype
G-ASXL	222	6800	17.12.64	28.1.65	BEA, Heathrow
G-ASXM	222	6801	24.2.65	2.3.65	BEA, Heathrow
G-ASXN	222	6802	10.3.65	23.3.65	BEA, Heathrow
G-ASXO	222	6803	27.4.65	28.4.65	BEA, Heathrow
G-ASXP	222	6804	14.6.65	16.6.65	BEA, Heathrow
G-ATTC	222	6805	11.11.66	12.11.66	BEA, Heathrow

Notes:

Additionally, two whole airframes built for structural testing and a Series 222 broken up in 1967, construction not completed. Despatch dates given in italics are not recorded in the Bitteswell tower logbook. XN814 retained for manufacturer's trials, despatched to Boscombe Down 29.6.64. XN858 was despatched to Benson 30.3.62, but returned to Bitteswell unserviceable; it was redespatched to Benson on 2.4.62. XR105 retained for manufacturer's trials, despatched to Boscombe Down 26.6.63. Some RAF examples converted to E.1 status as approach aid calibration aircraft and at least one to the abortive T.2 navigator and systems trainer.

The following Argosies are believed extant: N896U (G-AOZZ, the prototype) was stored in Alaska, but since reported with the Yankee Air Force, Michigan, USA; G-APRL with the Midland Air Museum, Coventry Airport, UK; G-BEOZ (G-1-7) stored at East Midlands Airport (part of the former Aeropark collection); XP411 at the Royal Air Force Museum, Cosford, UK; N1430Z (XP447) stored engineless at Lancaster Fox Field, California, though destined for the Museum of Flying at Santa Monica, USA; ZK-SAE (G-ASXN) stored at Blenheim, New Zealand; E.1 XR143 (G-BFVT) was heli-lifted on 15/16th May 1999 from Duncan Aviation's facility at Lincoln, Nebraska, to the Mid-America Air Museum at Sioux City, Iowa, USA.

Argosy C.1, XR134, in the camouflage colour scheme typical of that worn by the RAF Middle East and Far East squadrons but here with Royal Air Force Air Support Command titling, which would have been applied post-August 1967. XR134 served with 114 Squadron at RAF Benson between 1st January 1966 and 20th October 1971, at which point it went into storage at 27 MU, RAF Shawbury. Here, it prepares to depart from a rain-sodden Battle of Britain 'At Home' event.
Chris Salter

With no requirement for the fore-and-aft loading as on the civil aircraft, the nose remained fixed and carried a 'thimble' weather radar. To test the new rear fuselage, the second prototype Argosy, series 101 G-APRL was rebuilt and made its first flight in the new guise on 28th July 1960.

The first example of the AW.660 (XN814), designated Argosy C.1 by the RAF, first flew on 4th March 1961. RAF Argosies had hardworking and extensive lives, including use in Aden and the Far East. The final example (XR143) was delivered out of Bitteswell on 27th March 1964. (See table.) The RAF withdrew the transport Argosy fleet in 1971. Several were converted to E.1 navigation aid calibration aircraft and these served from 1968 until withdrawn in 1978 and placed in storage, mainly at the MUs at Kemble and Shawbury. Fifteen of the surplus C.1s were expected to be converted to T.2 navigation trainers but the 1975 Defence Review negated this requirement and the project was cancelled while work on the first aircraft was underway at Bitteswell. Like the civilian examples, Several ex-RAF aircraft went on to new lives with civilian freight operators.

Folland Gnat T.1

From 1969 to 1978, Bitteswell was involved in the heavy overhaul of the diminutive Folland Gnat T.1 advanced jet trainer. During that time 72 different aircraft arrived at Bitteswell, with 19 of these visiting twice

and XR540 attending for three sessions, in 1968-69, '72 and 1973-74. Among the aircraft worked on were the famous all-red Gnats of the RAF Aerobatic Team, the 'Red Arrows'. The association with the 'Red Arrows' was to be continued when the team re-equipped with the HS Hawk – see below.

Miscellaneous Contracts

During the 1960s and '70s, Bitteswell undertook a variety of work on a diversity of types. In the years 1963-67 the company gleaned some civilian work including repainting of 13 of British European Airways' HS Trident 1 medium haul tri-jets. The year 1970 saw some further civilian work, but this time of an 'in-house' nature on three HS.748 Series 2 twin-turboprop airliners, preparing them for service with customers, one of these was for Zambia Airways.

Two RAF 'one-offs' around this time were Blackburn Beverley C.1 transport XB285 which was in for unspecified work from September 1964 to June 1965 and HS Nimrod MR.1 maritime patrol aircraft XV227 present from April 1970 to January 1971. For much of the time it was engaged on developing systems associated with long overwater 'Tapestry' patrols, and in this respect was frequently seen flying over Bitteswell in quieter periods, more often than not with the two outboard Spey engines shut down.

From 1971, HSA Bitteswell (as it was now known) undertook the overhaul and reconfiguring of the cockpit sections of Handley

Page Victor Mk.2s that were being converted by Hawker Siddeley at Woodford to K.2 tanker configuration.

The former Dan-Air Comet 4C, G-BDIU, made its final flight into Bitteswell on 9th July 1981. It had been acquired by the Ministry of Defence for use in support of the Nimrod programme. Bitteswell dismantled the Comet, part was disposed of as scrap, but the nose section went to RAF Kinloss, in Scotland, for use as a Nimrod cabin procedures trainer, a fuselage section went to Woodford for use as a mock-up in the Nimrod AEW programme and other sections were used for battle damage repair training.

HS (Blackburn) Buccaneer

AWA's contract to overhaul and modify the RAF's fleet of HS (née Blackburn) Buccaneer twin-jet strike aircraft was not without incident. The first aircraft to arrive, XT283, did so on 20th August 1974. Although it burst two tyres on landing during an air test on 3rd December 1975, it was despatched back into service 13 days later. XT275 also burst a tyre in October 1975 and XT286 burst two in December 1979. In May 1976 XV155 had an engine catch fire on landing and in December 1981, XT272 suffered an engine failure while in the Bitteswell circuit.

In all, 32 separate Buccaneers were processed at Bitteswell, with two aircraft visiting twice. The last aircraft to receive attention was XV361 which arrived on 28th November 1978, suffered an undercarriage malfunction during an air test on 27th November 1981 and departed back to service on 5th December 1981.

HS Harrier

The famed 'jump-jet', the HS Harrier vertical/short take-off and landing single-seat strike fighter also featured in the Bitteswell circuit. During 1980 and 1981 the plant worked on at least nine GR.3s for the RAF and two Sea Harrier FRS.1s for the Royal Navy's Fleet Air Arm.

Additionally, Harrier GR.3s XZ965, XZ967, XZ968 and XZ970, fresh from first flight and air test at Dunsfold, were flown to Bitteswell still in primer finish for completion of tactical installations and painting, during July to December 1980.

Gnats galore under overhaul at Bitteswell, 1970. In the background are Hunters under refurbishment and destined for Singapore.
via Neville Martin

HS Hawk T.1

As noted earlier, the Argosy was not the last aircraft to be assembled and test flown at Bitteswell by AWA/HSA. This honour fell to the world-beating Hawker Siddeley (later BAe) Hawk advanced jet trainer.

The Hawk was designed to meet an RAF requirement to replace the Folland Gnat. The prototype first flew on 21st August 1974 from Dunsfold. Since then the Hawk has become a major success story, serving with a wide number of air forces, the world over. A much modified version is in production in the USA by Boeing (McDonnell Douglas as was) as the T-45A Goshawk for the US Navy. The Hawk continues to be built in the UK today, with assembly and flight test taking place at Warton in Lancashire. It is planned to be assembled in Australia with India as another possibility. The two-seat Hawk now has a 'glass cockpit' and is being sold as a 'Lead-in' trainer for more sophisticated types. A single-seat strike attack version, the Hawk 200 is also still in production.

Bitteswell was involved in the post-first flight work and overhaul of at least 25 RAF Hawk T.1s, with XX194, arriving off its first flight at Dunsfold on 3rd February 1978, in all probability the first of those. Another probable was XX258 which allegedly arrived on 2nd May 1979 and departed to Brawdy on 5th June. The 25th has been reported as XX307, and although the arrival date is not known, it departed to Kemble on 29th February 1980. Another source has suggested the last aircraft departed in July 1980. Quite which contract Hawk XX160 was part of is uncertain, but it came to Bitteswell for a total rebuild, flying again on 21st May 1982 and delivery out to Abingdon on the 25th.

Pressures on the HS facility at Dunsfold, where both the Hawk and Harrier (see earlier) 'jump-jet' were assembled and test flown meant that Hawker Siddeley were looking for an additional location for Hawk assembly and testing, and Bitteswell was chosen.

Information abstracted from the tower logs account for at least 39 Hawks being assembled, test flown and delivered from Bitteswell. It is believed that XX291 was the first, making its maiden flight from there on 7th November 1979. Included in this contract (which has been reported as being for 40 aircraft) were examples destined for the RAF Aerobatic Team, the 'Red Arrows'.

With the departure on 9th February 1982 of XX353, the last fully assembled Hawk to be completed, also the last of the 176 Hawk T.1s ordered for the RAF, an incredible era, which had begun with Avro Lancasters in 1944, and gone on to successively embrace Meteors, Sea Hawks, Hunters, Javelins, Shackletons, Vulcans, Argosies, Gnats, Buccaneers and Harriers, finally came to a close at Bitteswell.

Line-up of HP Victor Mk.2 noses undergoing rework at Bitteswell for the Woodford-based K.2 tanker programme. via Neville Martin

RAE West Freugh's yellow and black Buccaneer S.2 XW986 at the Families Day, 15th June 1980. It was extant with Delta Jets at Kemble, Glos, early in 2000. Brandon White

Still in primer finish, Harrier GR.3 XZ968 first flew at Dunsfold on 31st October 1980 and arrived at Bitteswell on 10th December for preparation and fitting out. It is seen crossing the Lutterworth Road into the 'old site' from the airfield . It survived its service career and was at Muckleborough College, Weybourne, early in 2000. Brandon White

HS Hawk T.1 Production at Bitteswell

Serial	First Flight	Despatched	To	Serial	First Flight	Despatched	To	Serial	First Flight	Despatched	To
XX291	7.11.79	29.11.79	Kemble	XX316	28.7.80	27.8.80	Brawdy	XX330	5.12.80	5.1.81	Chivenor
XX293	19.11.79	18.12.79	Valley	XX317	21.8.80	29.9.80	Brawdy	XX331	9.12.80	18.12.80	Chivenor
XX296	29.11.79	20.12.79	Valley	XX318	3.9.80	24.9.80	Brawdy	XX332	12.12.80	5.1.81	Chivenor
XX297	10.12.79	2.1.80	Valley	XX319	19.9.80	15.10.80	Brawdy	XX333	12.12.80	5.1.81	Chivenor
XX299	12.12.79	4.1.80	Valley	XX320	8.10.80	24.11.80	Brawdy	XX345	21.8.81	30.9.81	Chivenor
XX300	12.12.79	22.1.80	Brawdy	XX321	4.11.80	24.11.80	Brawdy	XX346	4.9.81	13.10.81	Chivenor
XX301	25.1.80	13.2.80	Brawdy	XX322	31.10.80	24.11.80	Brawdy	XX347	15.9.81	6.11.81	Abingdon
XX304	13.2.80	7.3.80	Kemble	XX323	3.11.80	1.12.80	Brawdy	XX348	24.9.81	27.10.81	Chivenor
XX306	19.2.80	13.3.80	Valley	XX324	25.11.80	1.12.80	Brawdy	XX349	16.10.81	16.11.81	Abingdon
XX308	26.3.80	23.4.80	Valley	XX325	25.11.80	4.12.80	Brawdy	XX350	27.10.81	19.11.81	Brawdy
XX310	10.4.80	30.4.80	Valley	XX326	4.12.80	16.12.80	Chivenor	XX351	17.11.81	18.1.82	Brawdy
XX312	9.5.80	2.6.80	Valley	XX327	26.11.80	4.12.80	Chivenor	XX352	1.12.81	20.1.82	Chivenor
XX314	11.7.80	31.7.80	Valley	XX329	3.12.80	18.12.80	Chivenor	XX353	21.1.82	9.2.82	Chivenor

A retirement celebration is held with Hawk T.1 XX352, in primer finish, as a backdrop. This aircraft was the penultimate Hawk to be assembled and test flown at Bitteswell, being despatched to the RAF on 20th January 1982. via F Timmins

Included in the Bitteswell-assembled Hawk T.1s were aircraft destined for the Royal Air Force Aerobatic Team, the 'Red Arrows'. RAF PR via Ken Ellis

Chapter Four

Bottesford

WHILE aircrew training predominated as the wartime role of RAF stations in Leicestershire, Bottesford was the one major exception to the rule. For much of its early life operational bomber squadrons flew from the base on many far ranging bombing sorties against the Axis powers in Europe.

Group Captain W G Cheshire became the station's first Commanding Officer (CO) when it was opened on 10th September 1941 and, as was common in countless similar situations which occurred during the Second World War, he found that the base facilities were very incomplete. Shortly after opening up had taken place the Air Officer Commanding, 5 Group Bomber Command, expressed a wish that he hoped operations would commence with one squadron from

Bottesford on 14th October, so building priorities were rearranged in an effort to bring this about. It transpired that the AOC's proposed starting date was over optimistic by almost six weeks. This intervening period was one of constant activity by service personnel and civilian contractors alike, many of the camp sites taking on an ant-like appearance as both sides strove to meet commitments.

When the runways were considered fit for use, a Vickers Wellington made the initial test on 22nd September. This was followed three days later by a lightly-loaded Avro Manchester; both attempts proved successful. The final seal of approval was applied on 3rd October when Wing Commander K P Lewis, OC 207 Squadron at

Flight Lieutenant Jack Sullivan talks to Flight Sergeant 'Freddie' Wilmot of 467 Squadron Royal Australian Air Force on return from a raid in the spring of 1943. Both were later lost, along with their crews, Wilmot on a raid to Düsseldorf in June and Sullivan to Milan in August. M Claridge via V M Holyoak

Waddington, Lincolnshire, brought in one of his unit's Manchesters and made an uneventful landing and take-off at an all up weight of 45,000lbs. This squadron was, when the base was eventually ready, due to become Bottesford's first resident unit.

Progress was being made in many directions but the station was still not quite ready to receive an operational unit so permission

was given, on 11th October, for 12 Service Flying Training School (SFTS), Spitalgate, Lincolnshire, to use the new runways for a time for training purposes. Towards the end of the month evidence that the time was fast approaching for operations to finally commence came when daily lorry convoys began to deliver lethal cargoes, from Norton Disney, Nottinghamshire, to stock the station bomb dump.

On 29th October a call for assistance gave the station crash crew their first serious problem and a foretaste of what the future could hold in store. Supermarine Spitfire V AD178 of 266 Squadron, from Kings Cliffe, Northamptonshire, crashed on the Nottingham to Grantham road close to Sedgebrook. Although the tender was despatched with all speed, on arrival at the scene of the incident the crew could offer little help in the way of aid, as the pilot, Sergeant Gain, had been killed and his aircraft burnt out.

November was the month which saw the culmination of all the efforts which had been expended towards equipping the base to serve as an integral part of Bomber Command. Events began on the 15th with the arrival of the advance party of 207 Squadron together with 14 of their Manchesters. The same day the station acquired a new CO when Wing Commander Swain OBE AFC, reported for duty. Two days later the main party of the squadron arrived from Waddington. Few unit personnel can have realised it but 207 were, for the first time, stationed within the borders of the county of their adoption, having been affiliated to the City of Leicester since June 1939 under the Municipal Liaison Scheme. By the time of their formal adoption on 20th May 1943 they had again left the county.

Dock installations at Lorient in France were the objective on the 23rd November when 207 flew its first 'op' from Bottesford. In contrast to later raids it was a very subdued affair; only two aircraft were involved but they duly delivered 20 x 500lb bombs to the target with the unit's compliments.

Continuing problems which affected the Rolls-Royce Vulture engines fitted to the Manchesters, plus a spell of foul weather restricted operational flying for the remainder of 1941. Few bombing sorties were staged but the targets which did receive the squadron's attentions included Düsseldorf, the Nazi Party HQ at Aachen and docks at Ostend and Calais.

A classic image, a 207 Squadron Manchester at a snow-covered Bottesford during the winter of 1941-1942. V M Holyoak

Squadron Leader K H P Beauchamp and crew at Bottesford, May 1942. Left to right: unknown, Chiasson, Paul, Beauchamp, Oliver, Barnes, Whiteman. via V M Holyoak

In addition to operations, many training flights were carried out and not all of these proved to be entirely uneventful. It was during one of these sorties that the squadron became involved in a rather unusual, but not entirely unique, incident. Six aircraft had been despatched on 23rd December, with instructions to carry out a formation flight over the North Sea and were engaged in this task when, at 16:09 hours two of their number were attacked by Spitfires. Obviously the fighter pilots needed further lessons in aircraft recognition and, thankfully, gunnery as only one of the aircraft sustained slight damage.

The new year brought a change in fortune for 207, at least the Vultures seemed to behave themselves and the weather was not too unkind. Throughout January the squadron participated in several successful raids including both day and night attacks against the German battleships *Scharnhorst* and *Gneisenau* as they lay in Brest harbour. But by far the best news of the month was that the unit was to be re-equipped with Avro Lancasters.

To enable crews to become conversant with handling the four-engined aircraft and to help speed the transition onto Lancasters, 207 Conversion Flight was formed. The arrival of L7530, on 25th January caused quite a stir, not only because it was their first aircraft but also by reason of its rather unusual colour scheme of very light shades of green and fawn. While type conversion was in progress the squadron stood down from operations except when a maximum effort was called for, then, both squadron and Conversion Flight aircraft and crews were required to participate. A series of 'circuits and bumps' with the Conversion Flight initiated crews into flying the Lancaster and later, as they became more proficient, squadron aircraft were used for cross-country flights.

Before they were considered suitable for operational flying replacement crews from twin-engined medium bomber units were required to amass 40 hours flying on Manchesters and Lancasters. Final proof of their competence was the successful completion of an eight hour trip, half in daylight and half in darkness, at altitudes of up to 20,000ft carrying a full war load.

After the many problems they had experienced while operating the Manchester, 207 Squadron considered that when they began to receive Lancasters this unfortunate period in their history was now at an end, but even with these new aircraft fate still contrived to deal them a bitter blow. One such occasion was 28th March.

While carrying out familiarisation flying locally, R5501 'EM-G' was sighted by a pupil from Cranwell, Lincolnshire, in Miles Master II DK973. The advanced trainer must have decided to have some sport with the bomber and the pupil dived in to make a mock attack, misjudged his approach and collided with the Lancaster. The Master spun in and burnt on impact while R5501 dived straight ahead and crashed at Canwick Hill near Bracebridge Heath, Lincolnshire, where it too burst into flames and four of the crew died.

There were few breaks to release the constant pressure that training and re-equipping brought to Bottesford and anyone in the vicinity of the airfield on 6th April might have thought they were suffering from hallucinations when several German aircraft appeared in the circuit. Whatever fears they may have had though were groundless as they belonged to 1426 Enemy Aircraft Flight, a specialist unit which operated captured enemy aircraft and toured airfields throughout the UK giving demonstrations to show personnel just what the opposition looked and performed like.

No.207 Squadron recommenced operations from Bottesford on 24th April when four aircraft were part of a force of some 60 bombers sent to attack the Heinkel works at Rostock. Photo-reconnaissance later revealed considerable damage to the target.

By the end of May the number of Lancasters on strength had increased considerably and the squadron was able to meet with the demand for a maximum effort in support of Operation 'Millenium', the first thousand bomber raid. For this raid on Cologne on 30th May, No.207 were able to despatch 12 aircraft and all returned safely to base after attacking the primary target. Crew debriefing reports contained lurid accounts of huge fires in and around the target area which could be seen by returning aircraft as far away as the Dutch coast.

Two nights later 14 aircraft left Bottesford as part of the raid on Essen, but unfortunately four of these had to return early due to engine trouble. The remainder, on arrival at the target, were hampered by bad visibility which made observation difficult and as a result the raid was not too successful with bombs being scattered over a large area of the Ruhr Valley. Bremen and in particular the Focke-Wulf factory were the objectives for the third thousand bomber raid on 25th June. The 15 Lancasters from 207 Squadron which joined in this attack were again handicapped, this time by almost 10/10ths cloud cover in the target area. Nevertheless

A Manchester being redied for a sea mining ('Gardening') sortie. W A Baguley

Ground crew posing by a 207 Squadron Manchester L7523 'EM-M' during the winter of 1941-1942. This particular aircraft crashed on 14th January 1942, killing all of the crew. V M Holyoak

Personnel of 207 Conversion Flight, Spring 1942. P Ward-Hunt via V M Holyoak

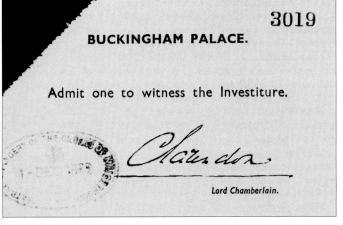

The LUCKY 13 bombed Danzig
One DSO; 6 DFCs; 6 DFMs

One D.S.O., six D.F.C.s and six D.F.M.s have been won by men who took part in the long-distance bombing raid on Danzig submarine works on July 11.

Squadron-Leader K. H. P. Beaumont, who won the D.F.C.' two years ago after raiding Hamburg, gets the D.S.O. The other medal-winners are:—

D.F.C.: Squadron-Leader E. Coton; Flight-Lieut. S. E. Pattinson, of Ealing, W.; Flight-Lieut. R. A. Boddington, of Ilford, Essex; Flying-Officer I. M. Huntley-Wood, of Maidstone, Kent; Flying-Officer M. E. Doble, R.A.F.V.R., of Guildford, Surrey; Pilot-Officer J. E. Partridge, of Northampton. D.F.M.: Flight-Sergt. G. Appleyard, of Leeds; Flight-Sergt. D. G. Barnes, of Hounslow, Middlesex; Flight-Sergt. C. D. Calvert, of Burford, Oxford; Flight-Sergt. R. N. Williams, of Islington, N.; Sergeant M. J. Darvill, of Reading, Berks; Sergeant G. F. McMahon, of Newcastle-on-Tyne.

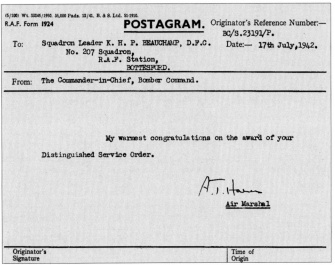

A trio of documents, including a telegram from Air Marshal Harris informing Squadron Leader Beauchamp of the award of the Distinguished Service Order. V M Holyoak

bombs were dropped using GEE fixes resulting in the glare of extensive fires being seen through the clouds. Serious damage was done to the Focke-Wulf works and almost 27 acres were completely destroyed.

During the early 1940s, accidents which resulted from delayed touchdowns and consequent overruns, especially during night operations, became a matter of concern for Bomber Command. A decision was made that some form of airfield arrester gear was required and the Royal Aircraft Establishment (RAE), Farnborough, was given the task of designing a practical apparatus. The outcome was an improved version of the system in use on aircraft carriers.

Following tests at the RAE which proved that a Manchester could be brought to a halt from 72mph within a distance of 460 yards

20 airfields, of which Bottesford was one, were selected to be equipped with these unusual installations. Six sets of equipment were needed for each airfield, one for each end of the three runways. Although 120 sets were manufactured by Mather and Platt of Manchester, it seems doubtful whether all the installations were completed. Bottesford's certainly was and on 15th June 1942 the airfield was closed to flying while the installation was carried out.

The airfield's arrester gear was never used operationally and a year after its completion use of the system was discontinued throughout Bomber Command. In common with other airfields which had been similarly equipped, Bottesford's arrester units were never removed. Together with many associated items, they lie rusted and

forgotten to this day. (The advent of fast jets meant that arrester systems again came in vogue from the mid-1960s and Cottesmore has a sophisticated system in use today.)

Villages in the vicinity were always under the threat of accidents happening to aircraft from the neighbouring airfield. This fear became reality for the villagers of Normanton, immediately west of the airfield, on 19th August. While on night flying training R5863 of the Conversion Flight crashed into the village. All six of the crew perished and the Lancaster was completely destroyed by fire, but no civilians were hurt. Earlier in the month, on the 6th, the airfield itself had been the scene of quite a conflagration when a collision on the flarepath between Manchester L7385 and Lancaster R5550 resulted in both aircraft being destroyed.

Unable to withstand the rigours of the weather and the constant pounding of heavy bombers, the conditions of Bottesford's runways began to deteriorate to such a degree that during August they were declared unserviceable while repairs were carried out. To enable training and operations to continue, on the 23rd, the Conversion Flight was detached to Syerston, Nottinghamshire, and 207 to Swinderby, Lincolnshire. Almost a month elapsed and as repairs were still incomplete it was decided that 207 should be moved to Langar, Nottinghamshire, where it duly established a base from 21st September.

This left Bottesford without a resident unit to return, so when the runways were once more serviceable, 3 Group were permitted the use of the base on a lodger basis for the purpose of reforming 90 Squadron. From 1st November men and equipment started to arrive at the station for the new unit and by the middle of the month its aircraft in the form of Short Stirlings began to be delivered.

On 1st December, the arrival of one of these machines involved the unit in its first accident. An Air Transport Auxiliary pilot delivering BK644 'T' had landed and taxied onto the perimeter track close to a civilian driving a road roller. This workman, when confronted by the Stirling, was scared out of his wits and baled out of his moving vehicle which then proceeded on its way and in the process collided with the tailplane, causing considerable damage.

Stirlings continued to be delivered and by 8th December the squadron was able to carry out a 'Bullseye' exercise which was not entirely without incident. The eight aircraft involved all took off safely, but within a short time one had returned with an engine shut down. Then the Meteorological Officer declared that his predictions were way out and severe icing conditions would prevail. Frantic efforts were made to recall the remaining aircraft and eventually three returned to base, the other four were finally located at other airfields where they had been forced to land.

The unit carried out a considerable amount of local flying entirely without incident until 16th December when Pilot Officer Bryden ran his aircraft off the runway and bogged it down so efficiently that it was not recovered until late next day. Two days later the squadron suffered its first fatality when Flight Sergeant McGavin lost his life

while working on one of the Stirlings. He was endeavouring to secure a tow rope to the knuckle joint of the undercarriage leg when the aircraft collapsed on him, killing him instantly.

In mid-December Headquarters 3 Group intimated that 90 Squadron would move, in the near future, to a new base at Ridgewell in Essex. The main part of this operation was eventually scheduled for 29th December when squadron personnel, with the exception of aircrew, marched to Bottesford railway station and entrained for Ridgewell. The aircraft were also to be flown to their new base that day and with this objective in mind eleven Stirlings took off. Flight Sergeant Freeman in BK625' D' was the first to land whereupon he went off the runway, bounced in a ditch and wrecked his machine, effectively preventing the rest of the squadron from landing, so they were diverted back to Bottesford. They did however manage to fly in successfully the next day.

Towards the end of November 90 Squadron had been joined at Bottesford by another heavy bomber unit which was destined to stay and operate from the station for almost a year. It was the third Royal Australian Air Force (RAAF) bomber squadron, No.467, which had formed at Scampton, Lincolnshire, earlier in the month from where the main party of the unit travelled by road and arrived at Bottesford on 24th November.

Wing Commander Gomm and his 467 Squadron crew enjoying a 'cuppa' from the mobile canteen, with Lancaster III ED539 in the background. V M Holyoak

Their aircraft, 17 Lancaster Is also flew in the same day. In command was Wing Commander C L Gomm DSO DFC, a regular RAF officer who proved to be an excellent choice as CO. Both popular and energetic he spared no effort in welding his new squadron into an efficient fighting force.

No.467 entered into the air war against the Third Reich in January 1943 with a 'Gardening' or sea mining operation on the night of 2nd/3rd when four Lancasters (W4384, W4798, W4825 and W4826) planted 'Vegetables' (mines) in the sea areas with the code names 'Elderberry' and 'Furze'. Action against major targets in Germany soon followed with emphasis on heavy industrial centres in the Ruhr. During January crews were briefed to take part in ten full scale raids, half of which were against Essen and from all operations during the month only two Lancasters were reported missing.

Throughout the next two months the squadron continued to operate on a similar scale with 14 raids during February and 12 in March and although attacks on German targets still predominated the U-boat pens at Lorient and St Nazaire received quite a bit of attention. Long range sorties were also made against Milan and Turin.

Not all the raids achieved their objective and the one against Milan, which took place on 14th/15th February, is one which the squadron would probably rather forget. Ten aircraft were detailed to take part but after the first three had taken off successfully Sergeant Ball ran his Lancaster off the perimeter track and bogged it down in such a position that it prevented the remaining six from getting past. The crash crew worked like Trojans but by the time the obstacle was cleared it was too late and the

rest were forced to abandon all thought of taking part.

All through the first quarter of 1943, 467 Squadron had operated as a two-flight unit but when strength in crews and aircraft eventually became sufficient, a third, 'C', was formed on 30th March. The unit record for these first three months reads:

Aircraft despatched on ops.	258
Successful sorties	236
Missing	6
Tonnage high explosive dropped	346.12
Tonnage Incendiary	402.15
Mines Laid	103

Severe outbreaks of infectious diseases which affected some RAF stations during the war are seldom mentioned. Although such occurrences were rare they did happen. For instance, early in May personnel at Bottesford began to contract diphtheria which spread fairly rapidly so that by the 9th it had reached almost epidemic proportions leaving Headquarters 5 Group with no alternative but to declare the station a

confined camp. For a time life on the base became rather difficult, the situation being further aggravated by the serious water shortages which plagued the camp through the early part of 1943.

While the directive inhibited outside contact it was not allowed to restrict operations. During their isolation 467 Squadron carried out six major raids and some mine laying sorties. Aircrew taking part in these operations were instructed that should they be forced to land away from the base then they must report immediately to the station Medical Officer so that precautions could be taken to prevent any possible spread of the disease. The outbreak finally ran its course and after almost a fortnight quarantine restrictions were lifted on 26th April.

Throughout the late spring and summer Bomber Command took every opportunity to pound cities the length and breadth of Germany. The 'Battle of the Ruhr' continued unabated and many attacks were made upon this strategic area by heavy concentrations of bombers. No.467 Squadron took

part in many of these raids and achieved considerable success, the number of Lancasters despatched was often in the high teens but against Dortmund on 23rd/24th May a unit record, for Bottesford, was achieved with 24 aircraft taking off, attacking the target and returning without loss.

The squadron also ranged further afield, one notable occasion was when eight aircraft of the unit joined a special force in an attack on Friedrichshafen on the night of 19th June. Radio and radar workshops housed in the Zeppelin sheds were the target and the unit CO, Wing Commander Gomm was instrumental in ensuring the success of the raid when he took over as 'Master of Ceremonies', a role introduced by Guy Gibson earlier in the month during the Dams raid.

After encountering severe electrical storms during the outward journey, the 60 bombers taking part arrived over the target in bright moonlight. Gomm noted that the Pathfinder Force (PFF) target indicators were scattered and had fallen a ¼ to 1½ miles east of the workshops. He then proceeded to re-mark the target from low level before ordering the main force to attack. When PFF backing up flares also fell wide he again came to the rescue by computing a 'false' wind which bomb aimers then used to correct the ground error. Target defence was heavier than expected and 24 heavy flak guns plus light anti-aircraft pieces were observed firing into the searchlight cones. Smoke from the target made accurate assessment of results difficult but many buildings were seen to be hit and fires started, considerable damage was caused to the radio and radar workshops.

When the attack was over the force then completely fooled the enemy night fighters, which were undoubtedly waiting for them on the return journey, by continuing southwards and setting course for North Africa – a destination they all reached safely. Wing Commander Gomm landed at Maison Blanche, the rest at Blida in Algeria.

Lancaster I R5509 of 207 Squadron. With F/Sgt N J Sutherland in command, this aircraft failed to return from a 'Gardening' sortie on 16th/17th August 1942. Note that the rear fuselage looks as though it has been grafted on from another aircraft. V M Holyoak

Lancaster III R5868 had carried out 68 'ops' by the time it came to 467 Squadron at Bottesford. The next ten bomb sortie symbols were added while flying from the station. R5868 'S-Sugar' is today preserved in the RAF Museum at Hendon, London.
via Steve Milnthorpe

Debriefing Flying Officer J M Desmond and crew of 467 Squadron after a raid in early 1943. All of this crew were killed while raiding Essen on 27th/28th May 1943.

Crews from 467 Squadron finishing off an operational breakfast on return from a raid, April 1943. Both V M Holyoak

Seven aircraft from 467 Squadron were part of the force which returned to England on 23rd June after having bombed the Italian naval base at Spezia *en route*. Haze and a very effective smoke screen hampered the attackers who found target defences very weak with ineffective anti-aircraft fire and no fighter contacts. All the Bottesford aircraft participating returned safely to base after helping to prove that the concept of shuttle bombing was quite feasible. After landing the crews also proved that they had not been idle during their stay in North Africa when they proceeded to unload fruit, vegetables and quantities of wine from the aircraft.

A summary of operations during the month of June, when compared to the figures for the first three months of the year, gives some indication of how much the squadron had improved its capacity to wage war. The unit operated on eleven nights of the month and carried out 143 sorties in the course of which 800 operational hours were flown. Total tonnage of bombs dropped was 522, divided in the following categories: 123 x 4,000lb, 578 x 500lb, 6,272 x 30lb incendiary and 6,784 x 4lb incendiary. Nine of the eleven operations were against targets in the Ruhr Valley the other two being the Friedrichshafen/Spezia missions. From all operations a total of four aircraft were missing.

In terms of loss to the squadron in machines and experienced crew, the 11th June raid on Düsseldorf proved to be the most costly. Two Lancasters failed to return and crew members of one, W4983, included the Commander of 'B' Flight, Squadron Leader D C Mackenzie, the new leader of 'C' Flight, Squadron Leader B S Ambrose, and Flight Lieutenant L R Betts, the unit's gunnery officer. Since early in the year the squadron had been progressively changing its Mk.I Lancasters for the Mk.III version and by the end of June, with the exception of just one, all 27 aircraft on strength were of the latter type.

Mixture as before was the pattern of the raids carried out by 467 Squadron during July and August, long distance sorties to Italy interspersed with missions to Germany. With Turin as the objective 18 aircraft were despatched from Bottesford on 12th/13th July and as if severe icing conditions and electrical storms were not enough to

contend with two of them made most of the journey on three engines having to cross the Alps twice in this condition. For their perseverance they, and all the crews, found the weather over Turin clear with the result that the target, the Fiat steel, aero engine and automobile factories were hard hit. All unit aircraft returned home safely but disaster overtook LM311 when in sight of base. Executing a banked turn while on approach to land the tail unit appeared to break off and the Lancaster crashed a short distance from the airfield. All on board were killed.

No.467 also participated in Operation 'Gomorrah', the devastating series of raids on Hamburg which began on 24th/25th July and ended on 2nd/3rd August. Firestorms which raged through the city reduced over 6,000 acres to smouldering ruins. In the

course of the four raids in which the unit took part 64 sorties were flown from these three Lancasters failed to return.

In the middle of August, 467 Squadron paid three visits to Milan the last of these, on the 15th/16th, proved to be a sombre event for the unit. Out of ten aircraft taking part two were lost, one was captained by Wing Commander Gomm and the other by Flight Lieutenant J McD Sullivan, a deputy flight Commander on his 22nd operation. The loss of the Wing Commander was very deeply felt by all ranks of the squadron. As a CO he had been an efficient and understanding leader who had nursed his squadron through the formative stages to see it emerge as a very competent and proficient unit. He needed only one more trip to complete his second tour of operations.

SPEZIA
18|19 APRIL 1943

SGT CLAXTON,   SGT WILSON,   SGT EVANS,
SGT FITT,   SGT WILLIAMS,   SGT CLARK,
SGT DISHINGTON.

An aiming point certificate awarded to the crew of Sergeant D B Claxton for the Spezia raid of 18th/19th April 1944. V M Holyoak

A Lancaster of 467 Squadron banks over the bomb dump area around Moss Plantation during the autumn of 1943. Several Lancasters are parked out on dispersal while a host of Horsa gliders are stored on the airfield. Note also the fake 'hedges' painted across the landing ground. H Watson via V M Holyoak

Bright moonlight over the target undoubtedly aided enemy night fighters and many aircraft lost fell to their guns. Two of those which failed to return belonged to 467 Squadron and once again the unit was deprived of seasoned crew members and key personnel. Piloting ED764 was Pilot Officer F W Dixon, a veteran of 21 operations, while members of the crew of LM342 included the acting squadron commander, Squadron Leader A S Raphael DFC, and Flight Lieutenant Parry the squadron bombing leader.

Another of the unit's aircraft, ED545, only managed to return to base thanks to superlative airmanship. While over Peenemünde, cannon fire from a Messerschmitt Bf109, in addition to wounding the rear gunner, Sergeant G W Oliver, shot away turret and hydraulic lines and set ammunition on fire. Despite his injuries and other severe handicaps, Oliver still managed to bring his guns to bear and shoot the fighter down before helping other crew members to extinguish the fires. Elevator and rudder controls had also been damaged in the attack and the pilot, Warrant Officer W L Wilson, displayed expert skills in successfully evading the attentions of several other enemy fighters before returning safely to Bottesford. For their parts in this action Wilson was awarded the Distinguished Flying Cross and Oliver the Conspicuous Gallantry Medal.

Entertainment, in one of its many varied forms, frequently provided a welcome relief from the conditions of stress which were often the outcome of the continued demands and uncertainties of wartime flying. ENSA (the Entertainments National Service Association), with its touring shows and concert parties, was one organisation which did much to provide an entertaining diversion from the exacting routine by regularly bringing a little glamour and gaiety into the lives of many servicemen and women. To be fortunate enough to see one of ENSA's top shows was a rare treat and the opportunity for Bottesford to play host to one of these came on 31st August. Several distinguished guests, including the AOC 5 Group, Air Vice-Marshal the Hon Ralph A Cochrane, joined a packed audience and were treated to an evening of first class

Mid-August was indeed a black period for the squadron as events three nights later proved even further. German propaganda had increasingly forecast the advent of 'secret weapons' of such devastating force that the Allies would have little option but to sue for peace. It was believed that experiments concerned with these devices were taking place at Peenemünde on the Baltic coast and the research centre there had been under surveillance for some time. Recent photographic reconnaissance had confirmed these suspicions and also shown that rocket weapon development was now at such a critical stage as to warrant an all out offensive to destroy the site.

Bomber Command was called upon to mount a maximum effort and on the night of 17th/18th August a force of 597 heavy bombers set out for Peenemünde on Operation 'Hydra'. Pathfinder crews marked the target very accurately and the consecutive waves of bombers which followed dropped 1,937 tons of high explosive and incendiaries on the sprawling complex of buildings which made up the research centre. Damage caused throughout the site was substantial, several areas of the camp being almost totally obliterated.

Forty aircraft were lost during the course of the attack. Even after sustaining these heavy casualties, the raid was deemed to have been an outstanding success and to have achieved its primary objective in delaying the use of the rocket weapons for a measurable time.

entertainment with the popular star of stage and screen, Gracie Fields, topping the bill.

During late August and early September a type of aircraft new to Bottesford began to appear on the airfield. These were Airspeed Horsa troop-carrying gliders which arrived for storage pending their use in forthcoming airborne operations against the enemy. Eventually 32 of these large gliders were present in the care of 30 Heavy Glider Maintenance Section, one of 24 similar units parented by 2 Heavy Glider Maintenance Unit, Snailwell, Cambridgeshire. Control of these gliders was relinquished by the RAF in January 1944 when they were handed over to the United States Army Air Force (USAAF).

Mess parties were another favourite way of letting off steam, regularly starting at the

Work being carried out on the Rolls-Royce Merlins of a 207 Squadron Lancaster. Note the tents in the background.
Author's collection

slightest excuse. A memorable celebration was held on 8th September after a night operation for 14 crews had been scrubbed following the announcement of Italy's unconditional surrender. Perhaps the thought of no more long distance trips over the Alps helped.

The 'Aussies' must have loved Bottesford's weather in all its varied forms, but to some even this could be a source of amusement as shown by entries from 467's Operational Record Book (ORB):

11.09.43 Another stand down with more wet weather. No flying.
12.09.43 Yet again very bad weather with poor visibility and also another stand down.
13.09.43 What a climate – a stand down with very heavy rain. The crews just threw their dinghies out of the windows and paddled away for a practice. Several personnel were noticed to be at least six inches taller by the afternoon but they hadn't given up smoking, it was mud on their feet.

Imagine all that soggy countryside, just the day to hold Exercise 'Bale out' to give the aircrews a chance to brush up on their evasion skills. Forty luckless individuals were taken to the Boothby Pagnell – Birchfield area of Lincolnshire at night in covered vehicles, and dropped off in pairs with instructions to make their way across country and reach Harlaxton, near Grantham, undetected. Quite a few succeeded in this objective but others were not so fortunate, like Flying Officer Martin for instance. He came to a swollen stream, tried to cross by using a vaulting pole, unfortunately the branch he chose proved to be too weak. Result, a very wet and bedraggled officer returned to Bottesford.

Then there was Pilot Officer White whose attempt took the prize for ingenuity. He gained entry to RAF Newton, just east of Nottingham – goodness knows how he got there – informed a Polish airman in charge of an Airspeed Oxford that he was going to take it up on air test and had actually got the engines running before suspicions were

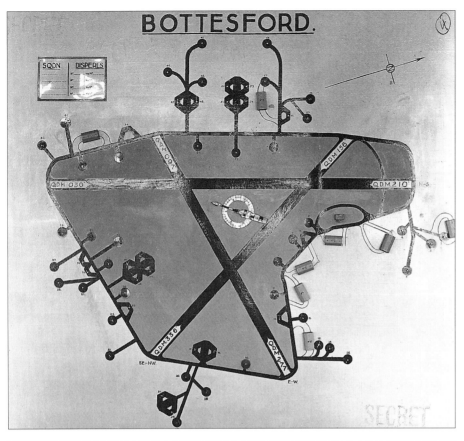

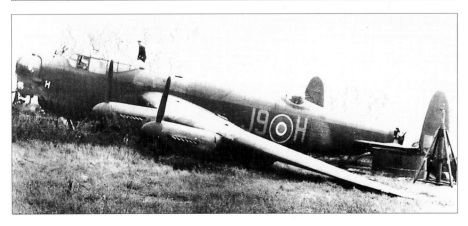

aroused. Not relishing the thought of arrest, he broke out of camp again and returned to base by more conventional means. Security at Newton was in all probability tightened up after this incident.

Operations were often cancelled at a late stage even after aircraft had been made ready and crews briefed; the weather was regularly to blame for these decisions. During October 467 Squadron were able to operate on only nine occasions but for the first four nights of the months the unit could not have been more active, taking part on consecutive nights in raids on Hagen, Munich, Kassel and Frankfurt.

For their contribution to this sustained effort ground crews at Bottesford received a well deserved official commendation. This recognition also served to show the excellent teamwork which existed between the British and Australian personnel servicing the bombers. From the outset it was intended that eventually the unit would be wholly Australian but this object was not achieved while 467 Squadron was at Bottesford.

October was the last full month of operations by the squadron from the station as preparations were in hand for the unit to move to Waddington, Lincolnshire. On 8th November the advance party left to prepare the way but one more op was to take place before the squadron joined them.

Eighteen aircraft were detailed, on 10th November, for an attack on Modane, a railway centre at the French end of the Mont Cenis Tunnel through the Alps. Afterwards it came to be regarded as one of the easiest missions for a long time. As one pilot described it, 'It was a trip of no's - no searchlights, no flak, no fighters'. Overall the raid was an unqualified success, not one of the 311 bombers taking part was lost, the international station was reduced to a complete shambles and the railway line was still inoperable a month later. No.467 Squadron alone must have contributed to a great deal of the destruction as no less than 14 of the returning bombers brought back aiming point photographs.

Next day was moving day and confusion reigned! Was the squadron required for ops or not? At first they were on and panic ensued trying to recover equipment already

A model of Bottesford dated 1st February 1944. Note the numbers given to the dispersals and hangars. via V M Holyoak

Ground crew of 'A' Flight 1668 Heavy Conversion Unit in front of a Lancaster, spring 1945. S G Marsh via V M Holyoak

'J9-H', one of 1668 Heavy Conversion Unit's Lancasters following an accident in January 1945. N Franklin via Andy Thomas

A C-47 Skytrain of the 82nd Troop Carrier Squadron, 436th Troop Carrier Wing, USAAF at Bottesford. W A Baguley

Personnel of Headquarters 50th Troop Carrier Wing at Bottesford, 1944. F Ehrman via V M Holyoak

Major Hugh J Nevins in the cockpit of C-47 'War Weary'. The nose-art shows a dejected-looking Donald Duck towing a pair of CG-4 gliders. W A Baguley

on its way to Waddington. Then, at 14:00 hours the detail was cancelled so the move was on again. It was however now too late for the main party to leave, so the aircrew flew the Lancasters up to their new base leaving the rest of the squadron to follow on the 12th so bringing to a close an eventful chapter in Bottesford's history.

The next phase of the stations's active life proved to be of a rather unsettled nature but in spite of this events which took place at Bottesford during the next seven and a half months give an insight into another facet of Second World War operations.

As part of the build up of Allied forces being assembled in readiness for the eventual invasion of Europe, a new Command, the IX Troop Carrier, was activated in October 1943 within the United States Ninth Air Force. This Command was to be responsible for delivering troops and supplies during forthcoming airborne operations and as it was at first assumed that all such US missions of this type would be carried out from bases in north east England, Headquarters were set up at Grantham, Lincolnshire.

Accordingly most of the stations allocated for the use of IX Troop Carrier Command (TCC) units were at this time grouped fairly close to this town. In November 1943 Bottesford was one of the airfields which passed onto the USAAF inventory becoming Station No.481.

The Headquarters of the 50th Troop Carrier Wing (TCW) was the first American unit to move in and it began to occupy the base on 18th November after vacating Cottesmore where previously it had been housed since 17th October. Four Troop Carrier Groups (TCGs), the 434th, 435th, 436th and 437th were assigned to the Wing. Three were quartered to the north west of Grantham: the 434th at Fulbeck, Lincolnshire, the 435th at Langar and the 437th at Balderton, both in Nottinghamshire, and finally the 436th joined HQ at Station 481 between the end of January and the start of February 1944.

It was also at this time that Bottesford's longest resident unit severed its ties with the station. This was 1524 Blind Approach Training Flight which since its formation in October 1941 had engaged in instructing

Aerial view of Bottesford, dated 11th May 1950. The runways, dispersals and taxi tracks all show signs of the extensive storage of munitions undertaken by 90 Maintenance Unit. The Bottesford to Long Bennington road (A) runs alongside the western perimeter track.

As part of 90 MU's storage activities many small buildings have been erected, particularly around the southern dispersals (B). The unit's work involved a major dispersal operation, so that any safety hazards would not generate a 'knock-on' effect with potentially catastrophic results. DoE

A continuation of the western perimeter of Bottesford. The bomb dump from the station's operational days is located to the east (C) and it is from this aspect that the view of the 467 Squadron Lancaster banking over the airfield was taken. DoE

pilots in the technique of landing with the aid of radio beams. Equipped with Airspeed Oxford crew trainers, 1524 was one of many such units carrying out this essential duty which it was to continue at Tollerton, Nottinghamshire, from March 1944.

Very early in the year it had been realised that any future glider operations stood a greater chance of success if they were carried out from bases further south so these were soon allocated. Two of the 50th's Groups had already made considerable progress in glider towing so all four were reassigned to the 53rd TCW, which was due to specialise in glider operations. Following this reshuffle the four Groups flew south, the 436th taking over the station at Membury, Berkshire, from 3rd March. As can be imagined, given so little time to settle down, the 436th was unable to carry out a full programme of training while at Bottesford. The unit did very little glider towing practice concentrating instead on exercises which would enable them to gain experience in delivering paratroops efficiently.

Another formation which had connections with the station at this time was the IX TCC Pathfinder School. Although this unit officially came into being at Cottesmore on 28th February 1944, its origins can be traced to Bottesford in late January of that year. The purpose of the school was to provide training for pathfinder aircraft navigators and also the jump teams responsible for setting up drop and landing zone guide beacons. Personnel in these specialised categories were taught to use various radar / radio aids, namely the British 'Gee' and 'Rebecca'/'Eureka' systems and the American SCR-717 and BUPS equipment.

At first instruction concentrated on training navigators in the use of 'Gee' and by the end of January school staff and equipment consisted of one radar officer, four instructors, two aircraft with 'Gee' installations, one ground trainer and three ground sets. This situation changed fairly quickly and tuition in the use of SCR-717 was able to be given after five Douglas C-47 Skytrains equipped with this instrument arrived from the Mediterranean Theatre of Operations early in February. Later in the month, in the hope of finding more space and better facilities the unit moved to Cottesmore where in due course it received an official title.

To fill the gaps left by the re-organisation the 50th TCW received as replacements the 439th, 440th, 441st and 442nd TCGs and it was the second of these, the 440th, which came to Bottesford on 11th March. Despite wintry weather daytime formation flying began almost immediately but a full training programme was not embarked upon until April. During this month the Group flew a successful glider exercise and carried out four paratroop drops of which three were

considered very good. Most of these exercises involved units of the 82nd Airborne Division then encamped at various locations throughout Leicestershire.

Up to the end of February the IX TCC thought no more southern bases would be required but a change in plan for the assault phase of Operation 'Overlord' altered this situation. Within a very short space of time the RAF agreed to provide the extra fields needed and allocated four in the south west, Exeter and Upottery in Devon, Merryfield and Weston Zoyland in Somerset. The 50th TCW was designated to occupy these new bases and the attached Groups began to leave the Grantham area during the middle of April. The first to move was the 440th which departed from Bottesford on 18th April bound for Exeter. Two more Groups followed in quick succession, the 441st left Langar for Merryfield on 25th April and next day the 439th went from Balderton to Upottery. The 26th April also saw the 50th TCW Headquarters depart from Bottesford to join the 440th at Exeter. Only one Group was left, the 442nd at Fulbeck where they stayed until June attached to the 52nd TCW.

The USAAF retained control of the base for a further three months after the 50th TCW left and during this time it is possible that the airfield was used on a day to day basis by other IX TCC units still in the area. It was however still used as a storage area for gliders for a detachment of the 33rd Mobile Repair and Reclamation Squadron arrived from Snailwell early in June to inspect and effect any repairs needed.

Bottesford finally reverted to RAF care in July 1944 and it was noted in the station ORB that it was found to be in a serious state of dilapidation with all major buildings in need of repair and redecoration. While some of the defects were more than likely due to the transitory nature of its former occupants, it also tends to support the belief that the airfield was infrequently used and neglected.

On 28th July the station once again became a part of Bomber Command under the control of 5 Group. Little time was lost in setting about refurbishing the base as it was required for another unit to reform there from the end of the month. No.1668 Heavy Conversion Unit (HCU) was the formation resurrected; previously it had enjoyed a brief existence at Balderton from August to November 1942. As an establishment the HCU was allocated 36 Lancasters so, once again, with their arrival, heavy bombers returned to Bottesford's circuit but this time not for operational purposes. Initially the composition of the unit was rather unusual in that it was equipped with a mixture of differently powered Lancasters, the quite rare Hercules radial-engined Mk.II version (built by Armstrong-Whitworth) serving alongside

Semi-submerged braking control unit still in its pit at the end of one of Bottesford's runways. (See page 86). W A Baguley

the more common Mk.I and III variants with in-line Merlin engines.

The HCU began its training programme on 1st September and on the same day 1321 Bomber Defence Training Flight (BDTF) became a part of the station complement. With eight Hawker Hurricane IIcs on strength it was responsible for fighter affiliation training with both 1668 and 1669 HCUs the latter unit occupying the station at Langar, Nottinghamshire.

During this stage of Bottesford's existence very little time went by without some change occurring which affected either station organisation or unit status. In an attempt to rationalise servicing and other procedures it was, at this time, RAF policy to group together bomber stations into formations of three or four which then became officially termed a Base.

On 7th October Bottesford passed into the hands of 7 Group which was formed expressly to control and administer all HCUs. With effect from 7th October 1944 the station became part of 72 Base. This new organisation comprised of a group of three stations, Bottesford, Saltby and Langar, Nottinghamshire, all with compatible training units in residence.

Next to be affected by the reorganisation was 1321 BDTF. On 1st November, after only two months in existence, the unit was disbanded and thereafter the HCUs it served became responsible for their own affiliation flights.

Bottesford also became the home of 7 Group Communications Flight after this unit was reformed there on 11th November

1944. As its title indicates, liaison flights were its main occupation and to carry out these duties it operated a miscellany of aircraft types. The unit's association with Bottesford was destined to be rather short as it left for Spitalgate, Lincolnshire, on 24th March 1945.

March proved to be a month when several alterations took place on the station. The most obvious visual change concerned 1668's aircraft. During the month the HCU finally disposed of its remaining Lancaster IIs and became wholly equipped with 32 of the Merlin-engined variety. In addition the tired old Hurricanes were withdrawn from the Affiliation Flight and replaced by Supermarine Spitfire Vs and Bristol Beaufighter VIs, this latter type being added to the inventory for the purpose of night fighter affiliation.

On the 15th of the month 1669 HCU at Langar was disbanded which meant that 72 Base virtually ceased to exist from that date though officially this came about on 1st April when Bottesford was incorporated into 73 Base, North Luffenham.

March was also the month when the *Luftwaffe* paid a brief visit to the station. On the night of the 20th warning was received of enemy intruder activity in the area and a Tannoy message was broadcast which cautioned camp personnel to pay particular attention to blackout regulations. In some cases this warning went unheeded and

exposed lights were still to be seen when, at 22:20 hours a twin-engined aircraft, identified as a Junkers Ju 188 by the local Royal Observer Corps post, attacked the station. The intruder made its approach from the north west at an estimated height of less than 1,000ft and when over the camp it dropped two clusters of 17x10kg SD 10 anti-personnel bombs about 30 yards from the NAAFI. Clearly visible in the bright moonlight the enemy aircraft then turned to port and at a much lower altitude flew south west across the airfield firing a burst from its cannons into one of the hangars as it did so.

On reaching the south west corner of the airfield the aircraft again turned to port, made a circuit along the eastern perimeter, then, in a shallow dive it made a further attack in the same direction as before. The Junkers then continued on to Bottesford village where it fired on the Bottesford to Nottingham train which was standing at the station. No hits were made on the train but windows in a nearby farmhouse were shattered. The intruder made a final turn to port and disappeared in the direction of Grantham, possibly in pursuit of a Lancaster which had passed over the airfield with recognition lights on.

At RAF Bottesford no casualties resulted from the attack but several station buildings received slight damage, in addition on one of the dispersals Lancaster I SW252 was shot through the main spar. Not a raid calculated to have a marked effect on the war but it did prove that the *Luftwaffe* still possessed a sting, even at this late stage.

Damage to based unit aircraft was rarely enemy inflicted, more often it was attributable to error on the part of trainee crews or structural failure in war-weary machines. Causes of accidents were diverse as is illustrated by the following selected incidents:

12.12.44 Lancaster III JA908
Experienced difficulty in attempting to land at Bottesford after losing an engine. It was diverted to East Kirkby, Lincolnshire, where it crashed and was written off.

15.1.45 Lancaster III LM619
Piloted by Pilot Officer Thompson, crashed on aerodrome circuit at Westborough, Lincs. Cause unknown, aircraft burnt out and all crew killed with the exception of the rear gunner.

26.2.45 Lancaster II LL666
Flying Officer Petfield, when taking off, hit a flock of birds shortly before becoming airborne. The Perspex nose cone was broken in two places and a propeller damaged but he managed to complete the circuit and land safely.

26.2.45 Lancaster II DS838
While taxiing for take-off, Flying Officer Mackenzie over-heated the brakes and ran 15ft off the perimeter track. There the ground collapsed sufficiently to damage the propellers, starboard side and rear fuselage.

25.3.45 Hurricane IIc   PZ745
Suffered a collapsed undercarriage on landing due to failure of the operating pillar bracing strut.

31.3.45 Lancaster III   JA962
Damaged by enemy flak over the Channel Islands.

26.5.45 Lancaster III   LM340
Landed with a large hole in the mid-upper turret and the gunner slightly injured. A 'smoke-puff' had been fired which blew straight back down the aircraft and entered the turret.

In mid-July a new element was added to crew training with the arrival of six Lancasters from Lindholme, Yorkshire, fitted with 'Gee-H', the blind bombing radar system. The intended programme was inhibited somewhat as the HCU had been informed of an impending move to Cottesmore and the intake for the month was restricted to one course of eleven crews. Previously the unit had a planned output of 28 crews in the winter months and 44 during the summer though actual output tended to fluctuate due to weather and other variable factors. Most of the crews under training anticipated being sent to the Far East to continue the war against the Japanese so doubtless the surrender of their forces and VJ-Day on 15th August gave many a great sense of relief.

On the great day all station personnel paraded at 10:00 hours in the Recreational Hangar where they were addressed by the Station Commander. Then followed a short Service of Thanksgiving after which everyone, apart from those concerned with essential services, were free to celebrate the occasion in any way they wished. As a precautionary measure, to prevent anyone overcome with high spirits, liquid or otherwise, being tempted to indulge in a joy ride, all of the aircraft were immobilised on the evening of the 14th by removing the contact breakers. These were only replaced after the exuberance had subsided and the station began to return to normality on the 17th. No.1668 HCU continued training at Bottesford for a short time after VJ Day before finally moving out to Cottesmore on 9th September.

As far as flying was concerned this was the end of the airfield's active life but it was soon in use for an entirely different purpose. On 1st October the station became a Storage Sub-Site of 256 Maintenance Unit (MU), Barkston Heath, Lincolnshire, an Equipment Disposal Depot until December 1948.

Although Bottesford had officially closed it still had a duty to perform and an RAF presence was maintained when 93 MU took it over from January 1949 as one of its many sub-sites. With its headquarters based first at Wickenby, Lincolnshire, and later Newton, Nottinghamshire, this unit was responsible for the storage and disposal of many types of redundant munitions.

Over the course of the next decade, thousands of tons of ammunition, bombs and explosive devices found a temporary home in Bottesford's many buildings and in open storage on its disused runways. In January 1959, 92 MU, an Ammunition Supply Depot at Faldingworth, Lincolnshire, took over the storage areas and continued to run the site until it was finally closed on 4th March 1960.

Despite Bottesford having been used for storage purposes, during the post-war years much of the airfield had reverted to agriculture and had been farmed by John Rose (Senior) of Kilvington, Nottinghamshire. In 1954 the Air Ministry divided the airfield into lots and it was sold by auction. Over a period of eight years John Rose acquired the area encompassing the landing ground and technical site enabling him to set up the Newark Storage Company, now part of the Roseland Group.

Many of the airfield's important wartime buildings remain in a good state of preservation. The control tower was extensively refurbished and now serves as corporate offices. Much of the runway system still

exists although the need for hard-core in the 1970s meant the loss of the northern end of the main runway, the dispersals and a reduction in width of the perimeter track. Runway surfaces deteriorated over the years but in the early part of 1982 their condition was good enough to allow the ill-fated Vickers Varsity T.1 WJ897 (G-BDFT) of the Leicestershire Aircraft Preservation Group to be flown in and spend some time at the airfield while undergoing maintenance.

On the domestic and other sites away from the airfield, many buildings have been demolished. Where the station sick quarters once stood, Schlumberger Dowell UK now train engineers in oil drilling techniques. Buildings of interest do still exist on the Wireless Telegraphy site while on 2 Site most buildings are still there; many are only shells but they are good examples of wartime airfield architecture.

Fallen comrades were remembered in April 1993 when, after a short service, the 467/463 and 207 Squadron Associations each placed a commemorative plaque in the control tower. On the 50th Anniversary of VE Day in 1995 the Australians returned once more and in a further act of remembrance planted a eucalyptus tree in the former signals square in front of the control tower.

Although time has now passed the airfield by, it is not forgotten by many and is still capable of evoking poignant memories.

Bottesford's control tower before it was converted into offices. Author

Aerial view of Bottesford, 1996, from the north looking south-west. Author

RAF Bottesford – 1st December 1944

Latitude	52° 58' 00" N
Longitude	00° 46' 45" W
Height above Sea Level	110ft
Command	Bomber (RAF)
Nearest Railway Station	Bottesford (LNER) 2 miles
Function	Operational Base
Affiliated Airfields	Langar (Sub-Station), Saltby (Sub-Station)

Landing Area – Runways

QDM	Dimensions	Extensibility	Remarks
210°	1,900 x 50 yards	1,930 yards	Road closure
77°	1,400 x 50 yards	1,825 yards	fr Bottesford to
336°	1,491 x 50 yards	2,000 yards	Gt North Road
Type of Surface	Concrete		

Permanent Landmarks

By Day	Belvoir Castle
By Night	Red Light on Church south of Airfield

Permanent Obstructions Bottesford Church, 314ft

Facilities

Airfield Lighting	Mk.II
Flying Control	Yes

Accommodation   All temporary buildings

Technical	Hangars		Hardstandings	
	Type	No	Type	No
	T.2	10	Hvy Bmbr	50

Domestic	Officers	SNCOs	ORs	Total
RAF	120	340	1,600	2,060
WAAF	10	8	403	421

Representative Serials of Bottesford-based units

No.1524 Beam Approach Training Flight
From   .10.41 to 3.1.44
Airspeed Oxford I   V4171, V4172, V4173, V4192, V4193, V4194, V4195, V4196

No.207 Squadron
From 17.11.41 to 20.9.42   Code 'EM-'
Avro Manchester I/IA   L7300, L7309, L7317, L7322, L7378, L7389, L7391, L7419, L7425, L7454, L7455, L7468, L7476, L7480, L7483, L7484, L7485, L7486, L7488, L7515, L7523, R5778, R5782, R5790, R5791, R5796, R5833, R5835
Avro Lancaster I   R5498, R5499, R5501, R5509, R5550 'B', R5570 'F', R5616, R5617, R5628, R5632, R5633, R5635, R5693, R5755, R5760, R5761, R5847, R5852, R5860, R5863, R5867, R5908, W4120, W4121, W4129, W4130, W4134 'U'.

No.207 Squadron Conversion Flight
From 16.1.42 to 22.8.42
Avro Lancaster I   L7530, L7540, R5499
Avro Manchester I/IA   L7297, L7385, L7397, L7484, L7491, R5791

No.90 Squadron
From 7.11.42 to 29.12.42   Codes 'WP-' and 'XY-'
Short Stirling I   R9256 'G', W7570 'O', W7627 'A', BF 324 'H', BF409 'R', BF410 'E', BF414 'F', BF415 'S', BK598 'N', BK625 'D', BK626 'C', BK627 'F', BK628 'G', BK644 'T'.

No.467 (RAAF) Squadron
From 24.11.42 to 13.11.43   Code 'PO-'
Avro Lancaster I   W4378, W4381, W4382, W4795, W4798, W4822, W4825, W4826, W4893, W4946, DV338, DV378, ED303, ED304, ED360, ED363, ED367, ED525, ED780, LM310
Avro Lancaster III   R5868, W5003, DV226, DV233, DV237, DV240, ED500, ED504, ED523, ED524, ED525, ED526, ED529, ED530, ED531, ED532, ED534, ED535, ED538, ED539, ED541, ED533, ED535, ED536, ED537, ED606, ED621, ED651, ED657, ED695, ED737, ED764, ED768, ED771, ED772, ED803, ED867,

ED949, ED994, ED998, EE135, EE143, EE194, JA675, JA901, JA902, JA906, JA981, JB121, JB124, JB130, JB140, LM311, LM338, LM340, LM342, LM372, LM376.

No.30 Heavy Glider Maintenance Section
Airspeed Horsa I   DP506, DP527, DP534, HG756, HG874, HG934, HG981, LF910, LF950, LF959, LF960, LF963, LG676, LG724, LG732, LG817, LG881, LG888, LG967, LG969, LG975, LJ120, LJ122, LJ127, LJ141, LJ157, LJ159, LJ163, LJ164, LJ179, LJ188, LJ191
From the latter half of 1943 these gliders were placed in storage under the care of 30 Glider Maintenance Section. All transferred to USAAF on 27th January 1944.

436th Troop Carrier Group, USAAF   From 1.44 to 3.3.44
Douglas C-47 Skytrain
79th Troop Carrier Squadron	Code 'S6-'
80th Troop Carrier Squadron	Code '7D-'
81st Troop Carrier Squadron	Code 'U5-'
82nd Troop Carrier Squadron	Code '3D-'

440th Troop Carrier Group, USAAF   From 11.3.44 to 18.4.44
Douglas C-47 Skytrain
95th Troop Carrier Squadron	Code '9X-'
96th Troop Carrier Squadron	Code '6Z-'
97th Troop Carrier Squadron	Code 'W6-'
98th Troop Carrier Squadron	Code '8Y-'

1668 Heavy Conversion Unit
From 28.7.44 to 17.9.45   Codes '9J-', '2K-', 'QY-'
Avro Lancaster I   L7541, L7566, W4193, HK705, HK731, HK732, HK739, HK741, LL742, LL786, LM170, LM188, ME756, NG274, NG295 '2K-N', NG383 '2K-G'
Avro Lancaster II   DS601, DS612, DS613, DS614, DS620, DS622, DS626, DS654, DS707, DS727, DS730, DS763, DS826, DS830, DS838, DS841, DS842, DS848, LL621, LL634, LL636, LL642, LL666, LL700, LL722

Avro Lancaster III   JA684, JA908, JA962, JB130, JB309,
    JB683, LM340, LM368, LM438, LM590, LM619, LM627, LM717,
    LM724, LM744, ME329, ND335, ND383, ND384, ND619,
    ND747, ND787, ND909, ND980, PB487, PB506, PB508, PB577,
    PB596
Avro Lancaster X   FM196 '2K-J'
Hawker Hurricane IIC   LF180, PZ745
Supermarine Spitfire V   EP766
Bristol Beaufighter VI   V8615, ND234

No.1321 Bomber Defence Training Flight
From 1.9.44 to 1.11.44
Hawker Hurricane IIC   LF180, PG601, PG605, PG610,
    PZ735, PZ742, PZ745, PZ747

No.7 Group Communications Flight
From 11.11.44 to 24.3.45
Airspeed Oxford II   V3580
De Havilland Dominie I   X7392
Percival Proctor III   HM323
Miles Magister I   N5408

Bottesford Station Flight
Airspeed Oxford II   V3560   (from 18.8.44 to 8.3.46)
Tiger Moth I   BB808   (from 13.7.42 to 8.7.44)
Tiger Moth II   DE147   (from 31.12.42 to ?)

Serious Accidents to Bottesford-based Aircraft

23.11.41   Manchester I   L7300 'F'   207 Squadron
While on a local flight to Waddington experienced engine problems and crashed into Fiskerton Lake, east of Lincoln. No serious injuries.

27.12.41   Manchester I   L7483 'O'   207 Squadron
Engine problems en route Düsseldorf. Bombs jettisoned into the sea. Undercarriage collapsed in emergency landing at Martlesham Heath, Suffolk. Became instructional airframe 3749M.

9.1.42   Manchester I   L7322 'Q'   207 Squadron
Ops to Brest. Hit by flak and believed crashed in sea off Finisterre. No survivors.

14.1.42   Manchester I   L7309 'O'   207 Squadron
Ops to Hamburg. Attacked by night fighter, crew abandoned aircraft which then crashed near Jever, Germany. One crew killed, five PoWs.

14.1.42   Manchester I   L7523 'M'   207 Squadron
All crew killed when aircraft crashed and burnt out at Cliff House Farm, near Holmpton, Yorks.

28.3.42   Lancaster I   R5501 'G'   207 Squadron
Collided with Master II DK973 of RAF College, Cranwell, and crashed at Canwick Hill, ½ mile east of Bracebridge Heath, Lincs. Four crew in Lancaster and Master pilot killed.

8.4.42   Lancaster I   R5498 'Z'   207 Squadron
Force-landed after both starboard engines cut due to lack of fuel. Crashed and caught fire near Bottesford airfield boundary. Crew escaped with minor injuries, aircraft burnt out.

24.5.42   Lancaster I   R5617   207 Squadron
Flew into slope of Standon Hill near Tavistock, Devon, in bad visibility. Four crew killed, two injured.

4.6.42   Lancaster I   R5847 'Y'   207 Squadron
Ops to Bremen. Shot down by Major Gunter Radusch of II/NJG2 south of Assen, Netherlands. All seven crew killed.

21.6.42   Lancaster I   R5860 'Y'   207 Squadron
Ops to Emden. Starboard engines both caught fire when aircraft on return journey. Fire became uncontrollable and Lancaster was ditched 90 miles out from the Humber estuary. Crew later rescued.

11.7.42   Lancaster I   L7543 'Z'   207 Squadron
Ops to Danzig. No details as to reason for loss. All crew buried at Malbork, Poland.

24.7.42   Lancaster I   R5632 'M'   207 Squadron
Ops to Duisburg. Crashed in North Sea. No survivors.

24.7.42   Lancaster I   R5867 'T'   207 Squadron
Ops to Duisburg. Crashed near Krefeld, no survivors.

6.8.42   Lancaster I   R5761 'T'   207 Squadron
Ops to Essen. Shot down by Oblt Gerhard Loos of I/NJG1 and crashed west of Nijmegen. All crew killed.

6.8.42   Manchester I   L7385 'U'   207 Squadron
         Lancaster I   R5550 'B'   207 Squadron
Manchester was coming in to land at Bottesford when it collided with Lancaster which had taxied on to the active runway without permission. Both aircraft burst into flames and were burnt out. Two in Manchester and three in the Lancaster killed, remainder of both crews injured.

11.8.42   Lancaster I   R5499 'O'   207 Squadron
'Ops Gardening'. Tasked to lay mines in the Kattegat but lost without trace.

Continued overleaf

Aircrew gather outside the 'B' Flight office prior to a raid, March 1943. Note the pigeon containers on the path, to the right. These were for use in an air-sea rescue.
G E Fitt, via V M Holyoak

The derelict 'B' Flight office as it appears today, from a similar angle. The chimney for the 'pot-bellied' stove has gone, but the fixture in the roof to support it remains. V M Holyoak

13.8.42 Lancaster I R5633 'R' 207 Squadron
Ops to Mainz. Reason not known for loss. All crew buried at Durnbach.

13.8.42 Lancaster I R5760 'Y' 207 Squadron
Ops to Mainz. Lost without trace.

17.8.42 Lancaster I R5509 'N' 207 Squadron
Ops, 'Gardening'. Mines to be laid in 'Willow' area (Arcona to the River Dievenow) but aircraft lost without trace.

17.8.42 Lancaster I R5616 'J' 207 Squadron
'Ops Gardening'. Due to lay mines in Swinemunde area. Crashed into sea SSW of Mano Island. Six crew killed, one PoW.

19.8.42 Lancaster I R5863 207 Squadron
While practising overshoot procedure on three engines, crashed in Normanton village at 0115 hours. Aircraft destroyed by fire and six crew killed.

28.8.42 Lancaster I W4129 207 Squadron
Ops to Kassel. Reason for loss not known. Four crew killed, three PoW.

5.9.42 Lancaster I R5755 'N' 207 Squadron
Ops to Bremen. Shot down by Uffz Heinz Vinke of II/NJG2 and crashed into the Ijsselmeer east of Medemblik. No survivors.

7.9.42 Manchester I L7571 'QR-S' 207 Squadron
Ops to Essen. This was a 61 Squadron aircraft borrowed by 207. No further details regarding its loss, but all crew became PoWs.

10.9.42 Lancaster I R5628 'Q' 207 Squadron
Ops, 'Gardening'. Due to lay mines in Kattegat area. Believed shot down by night fighter and crashed into North Sea south west of Thyboron, Denmark.

17.9.42 Lancaster I L7571 'S' 207 Squadron
Ops to Essen. This aircraft had been borrowed by 61 Squadron and was flown from Bottesford by a crew from that unit on this occasion. Reason for loss unknown. All crew PoWs.

9.1.43 Lancaster I ED367 'H' 467 Squadron
Ops to Duisburg. Lost without trace.

18.1.43 Lancaster I W4378 'N' 467 Squadron
Ops to Berlin. Lost without trace.

20.2.43 Lancaster I ED525 467 Squadron
Ops to Wilhelmshaven. Lost without trace.

26.2.43 Lancaster III ED526 'J' 467 Squadron
Ops to Nürnburg. Shot down NW of target city. No survivors.

12.3.43 Lancaster III ED523 467 Squadron
Ops to Stuttgart. No details regarding reason for loss. Two killed, five PoWs.

4.4.43 Lancaster I ED524 'T' 467 Squadron
Ops to Essen. Crashed in target area, no survivors.

17.4.43 Lancaster I ED780 467 Squadron
Ops to Pilsen. Crashed in France, all crew buried in Poix de la Somme churchyard.

17.4.43 Lancaster III ED651 'Y' 467 Squadron
Ops to Pilsen. Reason for loss not known. Three crew PoWs, four killed.

1.5.43 Lancaster III ED771 'E' 467 Squadron
Ops to Essen. Hit by flak and crashed at Harderwijk, Netherlands. Four killed, three PoWs.

14.5.43 Lancaster III ED543 'H' 467 Squadron
Ops to Pilsen. Reason for loss not known. No survivors.

26.5.43 Lancaster III ED695 'J' 467 Squadron
Ops Düsseldorf. Shot down by Oblt Hermann Greiner, IV/NJG1. Crashed at Burgerbrug, Netherlands. Two killed, five PoWs.

26.5.43 Lancaster III ED768 'N' 467 Squadron
Ops to Düsseldorf. Hit by flak and crashed at Gravenwezel, Netherlands. Three died, four PoWs.

28.5.43 Lancaster I ED504 'K' 467 Squadron
Ops to Essen. Crashed near Barlo, near Bocholt. No survivors.

12.6.43 Lancaster I ED304 'C' 467 Squadron
Ops to Düsseldorf. Lost without trace.

12.6.43 Lancaster I W4983 'Z' 467 Squadron
Ops to Düsseldorf. Hit by flak and crashed at Frenz near Eschweiler. No survivors.

17.6.43 Lancaster III ED737 'F' 467 Squadron
Ops to Cologne. Shot down by night fighter. Five killed, three PoWs.

29.6.43 Lancaster I ED363 'E' 467 Squadron
Ops to Cologne. Shot down by Hptm Wilhelm Herget of I/NJG1. Crashed SW of Roermond, Netherlands. Five killed, two PoWs.

13.7.43 Lancaster III ED531 'N' 467 Squadron
Ops to Turin. Crashed after flying into high tension cables near Thyon. No survivors.

13.7.43 Lancaster IIII JA676 'B' 467 Squadron
Ops to Turin. Lost without trace.

13.7.43 Lancaster III LM311 'L' 467 Squadron
Ops to Turin. Suffered severe damage and when preparing to land at Bottesford, fuselage broke into two sections. All crew killed in crash.

17.7.43 Lancaster III ED538 'O' 467 Squadron
Ops to Cislago. Crashed-landed and caught fire when landing in North Africa. No injuries reported.

28.7.43 Lancaster I W4946 'U' 467 Squadron
Ops to Hamburg. Believed shot down by Hptm Hans Joachim Jabs of IV/NJG1. Crashed into the sea off Terschelling. No survivors.

28.7.43 Lancaster III LM311 'H' 467 Squadron
Ops to Hamburg. Shot down by night fighter. Five killed, two PoWs.

30.7.43 Lancaster III ED534 'R' 467 Squadron
Ops to Hamburg. Lost without trace.

3.8.43 Lancaster III ED500 467 Squadron
On night training exercise when power was lost on three engines. Crew baled out with the exception
of the pilot who crash-landed the aircraft at Park Farm three miles south of Audlem, Cheshire.

16.8.43 Lancaster III ED998 'Y' 467 Squadron
Ops to Milan. Attacked by night fighter on outward leg and exploded in mid-air near Chartres. One survivor, became PoW.

16.8.43 Lancaster III JA675 'F' 467 Squadron
Ops to Milan. Shot down by night fighter near Chartres. Five killed, two PoWs.

18.8.43 Lancaster III LM342 467 Squadron
Ops to Peenemünde. Crashed in the Baltic on approach to target. No survivors.

18.8.43 Lancaster III ED764 'N' 467 Squadron
Ops to Peenemünde. Shot down by Lt Peter Erhardt of II/NJG5. Crashed near Greifswald. Five PoWs, two killed.

24.8.43 Lancaster III JB124 467 Squadron
Ops to Berlin. Lost without trace.

28.8.43 Lancaster III EE194 'E' 467 Squadron
Ops to Nurnberg. Crashed at Mansdorf, north of Langenzenn. No survivors.

4.9.43 Lancaster III DV237 467 Squadron
Ops to Berlin. Crashed near Doberitz. No survivors.

4.9.43 Lancaster III ED541 467 Squadron
Ops to Berlin. Crashed near Doberitz. No survivors.

24.9.43 Lancaster III DV233 467 Squadron
Ops to Mannheim. Caught fire and crashed west of Darmstadt after being hit by fire from a Messerschmitt Bf 110. Two killed, five PoWs.

24.9.43 Lancaster III EE135 'Y' 467 Squadron
Ops to Mannheim. Believed crashed near Altertheim. No survivors.

3.10.43 Lancaster III ED530 'O' 467 Squadron
Ops to Munich. Came down in the sea 25 miles off Beachy Head after running out of fuel. No survivors.

3.10.43 Lancaster III ED621 'L' 467 Squadron
Ops to Munich. Reason for loss not known. No survivors.

4.10.43 Lancaster III JA906 'K' 467 Squadron
Ops to Kassel. Crashed into sea off Dutch coast north of Vlissingen while taking evasive action from flak. Four killed, three PoWs.

15.10.43 Lancaster III ED546 467 Squadron
On training exercise, attempted to land at Wittering, Northants, with flaps unserviceable. No casualties.

18.10.43 Lancaster I W4240 'A' 467 Squadron
Ops to Hanover. Crashed north west of Rixforde. Six killed, one PoW.

23.10.43 Lancaster III DV226 467 Squadron
Ops to Kassel. Lost without trace.

3.11.43 Lancaster III JB121 'U' 467 Squadron
Ops to Düsseldorf. Shot down by night fighter near Antwerp when outward bound. Four killed, two PoWs and two evaded capture.

10.10.44 Lancaster II DS763 1668 HCU
Crashed. No further details.

9.11.44 Lancaster II DS614 1668 HCU
Wrecked upon belly-landing at Carnaby, Yorks.

14.11.44 Lancaster II DS620 1668 HCU
Wrecked. No further details.

28.11.44 Lancaster II DS622 1668 HCU
Wrecked. No further details.

12.12.44 Lancaster III JA908 1668 HCU
Lost an engine and after experiencing difficulty in landing at Bottesford was diverted to East Kirkby, Lincolnshire, where the aircraft crashed and was written off.

6.1.45 Lancaster II LL636 1668 HCU
Engine caught fire while taxying at Bottesford.

15.1.45 Lancaster III LM619 1668 HCU
Aircraft crashed in airfield circuit at Westborough, Lincs. Cause not known but aircraft burnt out and all crew, except for the rear gunner, were killed.

23.1.45 Lancaster II LL621 1668 HCU
Wrecked. No further details.

8.2.45 Lancaster III JA684 1668 HCU
Practising three-engined overshoots, hit straw stacks just outside threshold and crashed. Three crew injured.

26.2.45 Lancaster II DS838 1668 HCU
Taxied into soft ground. Damaged but not repaired.

10.3.45 Lancaster III JB228 1668 HCU
Port outer failed, aircraft got into difficulties when landing at Fiskerton, Lincolnshire, crashed and burnt out. Crew safe.

26.3.45 Lancaster II DS620 1668 HCU
Wrecked. No further details.

18.5.45 Lancaster I HK739 1668 HCU
Failed to become airborne and overshot, Bottesford.

Chapter Five

Braunstone

THE QUESTION of a municipal airport to serve the City of Leicester was first raised in council during 1927. A sub-committee was formed to investigate the possibilities and, over a period of time, it considered and examined a number of locations, often calling in expert advisers such as Sir Alan Cobham. Finally, in January 1930 a site was chosen close to the eastern outskirts of the city on land known as Braunstone Frith. A large proportion of this land already belonged to the corporation having been acquired prior to and during 1928; eventually 534 acres were earmarked for the building of the airport and possible extensions.

By existing standards it was an admirable choice of site meeting Air Ministry requirements adequately. Located approximately three miles from the city centre the land was situated on a plateau 326ft above sea level. The prevailing winds being south westerly meant there was little likelihood of smoke from the city obscuring the aerodrome. No major obstructions, such as church steeples and high chimneys, were to be found in the vicinity. Additionally, the land was in close proximity to a London,

Midland and Scottish railway branch line and was also served by an excellent 'A' class road, the A47.

With the location of the airport site established, council deliberations on the project continued for a considerable time, finally coming to a head in August 1932 when tenders were invited for the construction of the landing ground. During this period the council also considered future management of the airport and to this end approached the Leicestershire Aero Club (LAC), then occupying Desford Aerodrome, inviting them to move their base and run the airport with their existing staff when it was ready for occupation. After negotiating certain conditions which included the provision of a clubhouse and hangar, use of the landing ground plus the lease of an area of land for club use and the grant of £200 per annum towards management expenses, the club accepted responsibility for the running of the Municipal Airport.

The successful applicants for the landing ground contract were En-Tout-Cas Limited of Syston, Leicester, and work on the project started on 10th April 1933. By September of that year the whole of the 72½ acres

A pleasant garden party under way in and around the Braunstone clubhouse, during the opening day celebrations, 13th July 1935.
R A Fathers

required for the landing ground had been broken up and levelled, the latter operation entailing almost 28,000 cubic yards of filling being used. Throughout the levelling operations the weather was exceptionally dry and as this was expected to lead to a certain amount of shrinkage of the filled spots during the winter wet period, grass sowing was held over until the spring of 1934.

During the winter of 1933-34 work was commenced on the site at the western side of the aerodrome which was eventually to be occupied by LAC. It was also decided to develop a further area of land on the eastern side in accordance with a plan already submitted to, and approved by, the Air Ministry. This development, when completed, was to embody a waiting room, booking offices, accommodation for HM Customs and Excise, offices for airline companies, a large restaurant on the first floor and a control tower on the second floor. Other facilities included in the plan were a separate

View of the lounge area of the clubhouse in 1935. Author's collection

Air Ministry map showing the main features of Braunstone. The flying area is marked with a thick dotted line. Author's collection

building housing a central heating plant, a garage for a fire tender and a first aid room. Large hangars and workshops were also to be built.

By the summer of 1934 buildings for the use of the Leicestershire Aero Club had been or were in the course of being built. They included a clubhouse, flight office and a hangar 60ft by 60ft, fronted by a concrete parking apron, fuel facilities had been laid on and a compass swinging base established. It had been hoped to have the aerodrome licensed for operation by the summer – an opening date of 7th July had been optimistically quoted in certain aviation magazines. On 28th June a licensing inspection was carried out by Wing Commander Allen of the Air Ministry. A prolonged drought had, however, had an adverse effect on grass growth throughout the landing area, so it was therefore considered unsuitable for aircraft operation and no license was granted at that time.

In the months that followed work contin-

ued on the airfield and by the time of the next inspection, early in 1935, the condition of the landing ground had greatly improved resulting in a licence being issued permitting the airport to be operated from 27th March. LAC had already been using the clubhouse for various social purposes since November 1934, so they immediately set about moving all their flying equipment in from Desford. By Sunday 31st March they were well established in their new home and able to entertain the crews of 20 visiting aircraft. Two commercial airlines, Provincial Airways Limited and Crilly Airways Limited also began to use the aerodrome, the latter company making it a base for its operations.

Using a fleet of de Havilland Dragon twin-engined biplanes and later the General Aircraft Monospar ST-25 Jubilee twin-engined monoplanes, Crilly Airways ran scheduled services which connected Leicester with Bristol and Norwich. Services to these destinations were inaugurated from Braunstone on 2nd April 1935.

Within a few weeks further routes had been added to include Nottingham and Northampton and with the approach of summer seasonal holiday flights to Skegness began on 5th June. Fares for these journeys make interesting reading when compared to today's charges, a return ticket to Bristol or Norwich cost £3, to Nottingham or Northampton it was a mere 15/- (75p), while a Skegness flight could be had for either £1 single or £1/10/- (£1.50) return.

Provincial Airways began their services to the county early in March 1935 using Desford aerodrome on a number of occasions because Braunstone was not yet licensed, but on 2nd April they too transferred their operations to the airport. At first the route flown by the company was Hull, Nottingham, Leicester, Southampton, but after Croydon was substituted for Southampton on 1st July they were able to offer connecting services to Le Touquet and Paris for a return fare of £7 and ten guineas (£10.50) respectively.

Enquiries were received in June from several organisations including the Herts and Essex Aero Club and Marshall's Flying Club, Cambridge, regarding the use of the aerodrome for the training of pilots for the RAF Reserve and also from Leicestershire Air Sports Club who applied to use it for their gliding activities. Unfortunately negative replies had to be sent to these prospective users owing to the terms of the LAC lease.

Preparations for the official opening of the airport on Saturday 13th July 1935 and the accompanying air display occupied a great deal of time during the latter half of June and early July. Day and night working became necessary to finish improvements to access roads to cope with the large crowds expected. Vandalism also reared its ugly head when many wires to the public address system were found cut late on the Friday night making frantic last minute repairs necessary.

July 13th dawned fine and sunny and visiting aircraft began landing as early as 9.45 am. An arrival competition was the first item on the programme and this was won by the Duchess of Bedford who arrived flying solo in her de Havilland Puss Moth G-ABXR. Following this were demonstrations by new aircraft which included an Airspeed Envoy, Avro Cadet, BA Eagle and Swallow, de Havilland Hornet Moth and Miles Falcon. An example of the Falcon, G-ADIU, had been

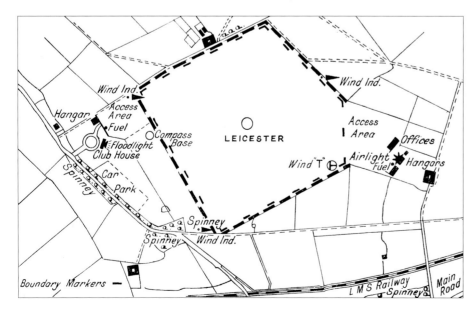

delivered to LAC the previous afternoon. These demonstrations took the programme through to 2.30pm, the time set for the official opening.

Initially it had been hoped that His Royal Highness the Prince of Wales would officiate but the invitation was declined and so the honour fell to Sir Phillip Cunliffe-Lister, Secretary of State for Air, who was ably supported on this auspicious occasion by many local dignitaries including the Lord Mayor of Leicester, Alderman W E Wilford and LAC's Chairman W Lindsay Everard M P .

The official part of the proceedings over, it became the turn of the RAF to entertain the crowd. Items in their display included a 'battle' between Hawker Fury fighters of 1 Squadron and a Boulton Paul Overstrand bomber of 101 Squadron, the latter giving quite an aerobatic performance in its efforts to escape the attentions of the three biplane fighters. Flying Officer I V Hue-Williams demonstrated how *not* to fly an Avro Tutor trainer while Gloster Gauntlet fighters of 19 Squadron led by Squadron Leader J R Cassidy gave an exhibition of formation flying which ended in a pass over the aerodrome depicting the letter 'L'.

Another highlight of the day was the Grosvenor Cup Air Race which consisted of two laps of a 42 mile course. After take-off, competing aircraft flew to a turning point on Lindsay Everard's private aerodrome at Ratcliffe, then onto that well known Leicestershire landmark, Old John in Bradgate Park, before returning to Braunstone. Eleven aircraft completed the race, the eventual winner being Lieutenant Commander C W Phillips flying Mr Lindsay Everard's de Havilland Gipsy Moth G-ACBX, while second and third respectively were Luis Fontes in Miles Hawk Speed Six G-ADGP and C S Napier in his Hendy 302 G-AAVT.

An air-to-ground of Braunstone, probably during the opening ceremonies, and looking north east. Note the prominent landing ground marker and the legend 'LEICESTER'.
Leicestershire Museums Collection

Advertisement for Crilly Airways and their services out of Leicester Airport that appeared in Popular Flying, August 1935. via Author

Hawker Fury Is of the RAF's 1 Squadron performing at the official opening ceremony, 13th July 1935. via C H T Brown

A view of the Leicestershire Aero Club hangar in 1936, before it was extended to double length. Parked at the fuel pumps is the Miles Hawk Major G-ADCF while to the right is DH Dragon G-ACDN of Crilly Airways. In the hangar, left to right: DH Puss Moth G-AAZV Jason II; DH.60M Moth G-ABRF; a British Klemm L.25; a Comper Swift and DH Fox Moth G-ACEY of Crilly Airways.
Leicestershire Museums Collection

After the race two further items remained to bring the programme to a close. The first was a fine display by the record breaking Percival Gull Six G-ADEP, in the hands of its designer Edgar Percival and finally Hawker Harts belonging to 605 Squadron, Royal Auxiliary Air Force, Castle Bromwich, Warwickshire, flew in to give a superb exhibition of formation flying. Rounding off a memorable day, the de Havilland Dragons of Crilly Airways flew joy rides, giving many of the spectators their first taste of air travel. By the time dusk fell and called a halt to the proceedings over 700 passengers had been carried.

With the official celebrations over routine operation of the airport was soon resumed with increases in club flying hours, visiting aircraft and scheduled airline traffic. From 1st August Crilly were able to offer a twice daily service to Liverpool, the first of their Monospars was delivered in September and from 8th October Croydon joined the company's routes. By the autumn of 1935,

with a resident airline established and other aspects of aviation activity flourishing, a bright future appeared to be in prospect for the airport.

Winter, however, reduced the amount of traffic and Crilly's services were modified to meet the decrease in demand. In a bid to expand further the company planned to route from Croydon to Lisbon and for the purpose purchased four Fokker F.XII trimotors from KLM, the Royal Dutch Airline. The service was inaugurated on 1st February 1936 with great publicity, commemorative air mail letters and a special Portuguese stamp. Unfortunately the venture was not a success and after a couple of trips was allowed to peter out. It was referred to in the aviation press at that time as a 'fiasco'. On at least four different occasions one of the Fokker F.XIIs was due to visit Braunstone but no record has been found to show that one ever arrived.

Spring and summer saw a customary increase in flying once more and as if to

shake off winter doldrums two airshows were held during May. C W A Scott brought his National Aviation Day Display on the 2nd while on the 23rd Empire Air Day, a show which became an annual feature in the Braunstone calendar, was held. According to contemporary accounts, both events attracted large attendances, offered good entertainment and were well organised.

Royalty in the person of the former King of Siam, Prajadipok, Prince of Sukhodaya, visited Braunstone on 4th July. After arriving in de Havilland Leopard Moth G-ACSH he was taken on a tour of airport facilities and on completion remarked that it was one of the best laid out that he had so far visited in the country.

Crilly Airways continued to operate from the airfield but early in the autumn a crisis arose when the company ran into financial difficulties and an official receiver was appointed to dispose of the assets. This meant that the airport was without a resident airline operator, with the resulting loss of revenue and empty hangar space. In March 1937 the General Motor and Tyre Company of London applied to take over Crilly Airways lease; they indicated that should their application be successful they intended to transfer aircraft to Leicester and engage staff to operate and service them. However, the company was unsuccessful in its bid and the lease was allowed to lapse.

In spite of these setbacks improvements continued to be made at Braunstone and by early 1937 full night flying equipment had been installed at a cost of £2,000. This facility proved to be much in demand for army co-operation flying and also by many club members.

During the summer of 1937 an advertising campaign was mounted in an effort to attract tenants for the finished first stage of the commercial development on the eastern side of the airport, but as far as can be ascertained no airline companies appeared interested in making Braunstone a permanent base. The comprehensive range of buildings awaiting occupants at this time comprised a hangar 120ft wide and 60ft deep, a combined hangar workshop of slightly larger dimensions, terminal buildings in the form of three large offices and two store rooms in one block, all complete with full central heating.

Part of the Crilly fleet outside the LAC hangar, Monospar ST-25 G-ADPL to the left and a pair of DH Dragons to the right, with G-ACDN in the foreground. Leicestershire Museums Collection

With a price tag of £195 on the rudder, the Broughton-Blayney Brawney visiting Braunstone during a sales tour in 1936. J Whall

As a result of the advertising, enquiries were received from two companies, A A McEvoy Limited, Derby, and A R Williams of Lincoln, who were interested in sites near the airport to manufacture aero engines and from Reid & Sigrist Limited (R&S), the aircraft instrument manufacturers. Nothing came of the first two enquiries, but the latter company offered to lease the hangars and repair shop and were eventually successful in their bid, being offered a lease of five years from December 1937 at £400 per annum with an option of a further five years at £450 per annum. The negotiation of this lease, unfortunately brought no further resident aircraft to Braunstone as R&S ultimately converted the buildings to enable them to produce aircraft instruments.

Flying at the airport was therefore limited to visiting airlines, on a reduced scale, club activities and occasional airshows. Club flying did receive a boost during the latter half of 1938 when the Civil Air Guard was formed. Shortly after the scheme was announced by the Air Ministry in July, the club was invited to participate and in a very short space of time over 250 applications had been received from prospective candidates. From these, 50 members were selected and started their training on 1st October.

In a further effort to obtain greater usage of the aerodrome approaches were made to the Air Ministry early in 1939 enquiring after the possibility of a Royal Auxiliary Air Force unit being stationed there. In reply the Air Ministry stated that, after due consideration, they could not suggest any Royal Air Force purpose for which the aerodrome could be utilised at that time, or in the future. The reasons for their decision were that Braunstone was outside the strategic line, was in too close proximity to the flying school at Desford, and that the Municipal Airport possessed the smallest licensed landing ground in Britain, apart from Barton near Manchester.

Maximum runways at this time were unchanged from the airport's opening and were, north-south 667 yards, east-west 783 yards, north east-south west 633 yards and south east-north west 700 yards. Land amounting to 126 acres was immediately available to suitably extend them to 1,200 yards, 830 yards, 1,430 yards and 960-1,000 yards respectively, but in June 1939 after reviewing the government and general position the Aerodrome Committee decid-

ed to spend no more money on the airport at that time.

With the prospect of war looming, flying at Braunstone increased slightly during the summer of 1939, the chief contribution to this being the use of the aerodrome by several operators engaged in the training of anti-aircraft and searchlight units of the Territorial Army. Foremost amongst the companies participating in this duty were Air Despatch, Yorkshire Airways and North Eastern Airways. Also during 1939 it was proposed that several more Elementary & Reserve Flying Training Schools (E&RFTS) be established. One of these, No.58, was to have been formed at Braunstone but plans were cancelled following the outbreak of war on 3rd September.

In late June another enquiry from R&S, who already ran a flying school nearby at Desford (Chapter Nine), gave hope of further revenue from the airport, they proposed to train military pilots there using a minimum of 12 aircraft. LAC, when advised of this proposal, agreed to facilitate arrangements with R&S but while talks were still taking place war intervened obviating the need for further negotiations.

Britain's entry into the war with Germany meant the curtailment of all civil flying in the British Isles from 3rd September 1939, with the consequent closure of the airport, but even at this time a communication was received on the 15th of the month from D Napier & Son Limited of Acton, London, which brought new hope for the future.

They requested that the council consider the sale of approximately 50 acres near the aerodrome to enable them to build a factory to manufacture aero engines. In addition they wished to erect a hangar on the airport and to test engines there. For this purpose they considered it necessary for the aerodrome to be extended and a new road and railway bridge to be constructed for site access. Cost of these alterations was estimated at £15,000 for airfield extensions and £30,000 for the rest. Urgent meetings resulted in a rapid decision by the Aerodrome Committee who approved in principle the sale of the land and all necessary extensions and construction work.

In spite of this optimistic outlook the proposed project came to nothing when on 29th September, Alderman Wilford, the committee chairman, reported the results of an interview with representatives of the Air and Labour Ministries. These government departments indicated they were not in favour of Napier's choice of site owing to the satisfactory state of employment within the City of Leicester at that time. They asked the company therefore to investigate two other locations before they would even consider allowing Braunstone to be used. Although Napier's indicated that they much preferred their original choice, such were the regulations in force at that time that they were bound to comply with the official request. Eventually, they became established early in 1940 at Luton, Bedfordshire, an airport which is still thriving and very active today.

Almost a month after this setback, on 27th October, the landing ground was requisitioned for military purposes. Shortly afterwards it was allotted to the rapidly expanding 7 Elementary Flying Training School (EFTS) at Desford and throughout the war it was used by them as a satellite field. Many prospective pilots received some of their early training at the airfield,

the de Havilland Tiger Moths of the unit becoming an all too familiar sight in the vicinity. For EFTS use some temporary hutting was erected in the clubhouse area and eventually three Blister hangars were added in one of the fields on the northern border of the aerodrome to enable servicing to be carried out.

While the airfield was adequate for the EFTS aircraft it is obvious that its small size presented problems to some of the more powerful machines which were coming into service. Evidence of this is to be seen in many of the reports on accidents at Braunstone, taken from the Operations Record Book:

8.1.42 Hawker Hurricane II Z3262.
Mistook Braunstone for Rearsby. After touching down pilot found it impossible to pull up and attempted to take-off again over high trees. Aircraft stalled and crashed.

31.1.42 Hawker Hurricane II Z5324.
Skidded and overshot on small aerodrome.

2.7.43 Boulton Paul Defiant.
10 Air Gunnery School, Barrow-in-Furness.
Crashed at 1715 hours. No injuries to personnel.

20.3.44 Miles Master II DL844
7 (Pilot) Advanced Flying Unit, Peterborough.
Crashed on approach to land. Aircraft written off and pilot taken to Leicester Royal Infirmary.

4.5.44 Supermarine Spitfire . . . . . ?
Flying Officer Phillips, Vickers Armstrongs test pilot at Desford experienced engine failure and crashed while attempting to make a belly landing. He was uninjured.

15.1.45 Airspeed Oxford R6025
12 Ferry Unit, Melton Mowbray.
Overshot and went through hedge.

1.2.45 Vickers Wellington X LP300
29 Operational Training Unit. After suffering engine failure the pilot, Flying Officer Stevens, attempted an emergency landing but overshot and crashed through the boundary hedge. One crew member was injured.

21.1.45 Noorduyn Norseman UC-64A 44-70258.
The pilot, 2nd Lieutenant J B Temple, USAAF, in attempting to land, overshot and crashed through the boundary hedge. He was unhurt.

The EFTS aircraft also suffered from the usual crop of training accidents. One incident, because of its bizarre and tragic nature, is worth recording.

On 3rd March 1942 Tiger Moth II N7089 piloted by Flight Lieutenant Newberry, with Leading Aircraftman Allen as pupil, landed on top of a soldier, Private Sykes, who was seriously injured. He was taken to Leicester Royal Infirmary where he later died on 16th March. Consequently a court martial was held at Desford on 28th May to investigate the tragedy and its findings resulted in the Flight Lieutenant being completely exonerated from all blame.

With the ending of the war in 1945 and the subsequent decline in the need for trained aircrew, Braunstone no longer became necessary to the operations of 7 EFTS. Personnel and aircraft were soon withdrawn and the airfield fell into disuse although still retained by the government. Even though no longer in use the landing ground served as the Leicestershire War Agricultural Committee were able to harvest the seasonal hay crops.

Early in 1947 the first intimation that perhaps the airport might function once more occurred when E H G Brookes, who had been an RAF officer in charge of the aerodrome, announced that he would like to carry out charter flying using it as his base. LAC were also keen to return to their old home but as requisitioning was still in force nothing came of Brookes' proposal and the Aero Club were advised to continue to use Ratcliffe for their activities.

Late in August 1947 the aerodrome was finally de-requisitioned but by now it was realised that the encroaching housing estates would severely restrict any aviation development. This, coupled with advances made in multi-engined airliners, ensured that Braunstone would never re-open as Leicester's airport again – it was just too small to be an airport.

It was felt that it could possibly be put to use as a club or light training airfield and Reid & Sigrist, who at this time were still operating a flying training school at Desford in addition to occupying the Braunstone hangars, were offered the tenancy of the aerodrome at £450 per annum with the proviso that they sub-let the clubhouse to Leicestershire Aero Club. Finding Desford more than adequate for their post-war needs the company declined the offer but they did extend their lease period of the hangars.

Vertical view of Braunstone, on 8th December 1948. Clearly visible are the clubhouse and hangar (A) and the EFTS blister hangars (B). The southern boundary comprised the LMS railway line (C) and below that, the A47 Leicester to Hinckley road (D). The pre-war civil hangars are at (E). via Author

The commercial side of Braunstone, occupied by Reid & Sigrist, summer 1946. J Hart

Opposite page:

Desford-based Tiger Moths performing at a pre-Second World War Empire Air Day Display at Braunstone. via Dr Hugh Thomas

Braunstone – 1st December 1944

Latitude	52° 38' 0" N
Longitude	01° 12' 15" W
Height above Sea Level	315ft
Command	Flying Training (RAF)
Nearest Railway Station	Kirby Muxloe (LMS) 2 miles
Function	Elementary Flying Training School (Relief Landing Ground)
Affiliated Airfields	Desford (Parent)

Landing Area – Grass

Hdg	Dimensions	Extensibility
E–W	800 yards	1,400 yards
N–S	600 yards	1,200 yards
Remarks:		Entails heavy demolition of housing estate if extended to NE.

Permanent Landmarks

By Day	Thornton Lake, 3½ miles NW; Groby Pool 2½ miles WNW.
By Night	Nil

Permanent Obstructions Factory E side; Hangar and Club House W side of airfield.

Facilities

Airfield Lighting	Nil
Flying Control	Nil

Accommodation	All temporary buildings except club sheds

Technical	Hangars		Hardstandings	
	Type	No	Type	No
	Civil	3		Nil
	Over Blisters	2		

Domestic	Officers	SNCOs	ORs	Total
RAF	2	4	120	126
WAAF	–	–	–	–

As far as can be ascertained after the withdrawal of the RAF, Braunstone was never again used for organised flying and for many years served as playing fields and a golf course before eventually succumbing to progress and becoming an industrial estate. This change in role has over the past years altered the whole face of the area to such an extent that people find it hard to believe that it was once the site of Leicestershire's Municipal Airport.

Today nothing of significance remains of the former commercial development on the eastern side. Modern structures now replace the hangars and other buildings which at one time stood in this area. On the western side in the corner which was once the preserve of the Aero Club, their purpose built clubhouse has long been demolished. The hangar once used by them and Crilly Airways still stands but that too has been modified for commercial purposes.

The only other tangible evidence of the past is 'The Airmans' inn which is also on the eastern side and stands on Kirby Lane

The club hangar in use by light industry, 1990. Note the refuelling pump stanchion still in place and the anti-collision light on the hangar's gable end. Author

A 1998 air-to-ground of the Braunstone site, looking north east. The flying ground has been consumed in a vast industrial and retail development, while the M1 has changed the perspective considerably. The club hangar (A) remains, while the coppice is a good reference point (B). The 'Airmans Rest' public house lies between the former aerodrome and the M1 (C). Author

almost opposite the now overgrown entrance to what was the Aero Club site. Built in the mid 1930s as a place of refreshment and relaxation for locals and travellers alike it was then called 'The Airmans Rest' a name which until changed in recent years still evoked memories of pre-war flying. For some time also it still retained a last tenuous link with the airport and aviation by possessing its own helicopter landing area, complete with miniature windsock.

Braunstone-based Operators and Aircraft

Crilly Airways
De Havilland: DH.83 Fox Moth G-ACEY.
DH.84 Dragon: G-ACCZ, G-ACDN, G-ACLE.
General Aircraft Monospar ST-22 Jubilee: G-ADPK, G-ADPL and G-ADPM

Leicestershire Aero Club
B A Swallow II: G-ADXH, G-AEKB, G-AESI (crashed 6.38).
De Havilland DH.60G III Moth Major: G-ACBX.
DH.60M Moth: G-ABTF. *DH.82A Tiger Moth:* G-AETO.
DH.85 Leopard Moth: G-ACSF. *DH.94 Moth Minor:* G-AFOP.
Hawker Tomtit: G-AFIB, G-AFKB (crashed near Braunstone 13.7.39), G-AFTA, G-AFVV.
Miles M.3A Falcon Major G-ADIU.

Miscellaneous private owners
B A Eagle G-AENE, L T Lillington.
B A C Drone, G-ADMU, A E Coltman, crashed at Braunstone 15.1.39.
Comper Swift G-ACGL, P G Leeson.
Miles Whitney Straight: G-AEVF, L T Lillington.

No.7 Elementary Flying Training School
See parent station Desford – Chapter Nine.

Chapter Six

Bruntingthorpe

CONSTRUCTED between 1941 and 1943 on approximately 700 acres of agricultural land requisitioned in 1940, the airfield was originally intended for occupation by operational bomber squadrons. When well on the way to completion a reappraisal of the situation, plus an inspection of the site in July 1942, resulted in the airfield being reallocated.

On 7th August 1942 it was allotted to 92 Group, Bomber Command, for use as an Operational Training Unit (OTU) and in September Headquarters Bomber Command proposed to transfer 29 OTU, then occupying the airfields of North Luffenham and Woolfox Lodge in Rutland, and bring the unit to Bruntingthorpe.

Following the arrival of an opening up detachment in late October 1942 the station began to be used initially as a satellite of 29 OTU and by November 6th 'A' Flight was carrying out training sorties from the airfield. On 1st February 1943 Bruntingthorpe became an independent station but it was

not until June that it was fully occupied by 29 OTU with Bitteswell serving as satellite.

During the transition to its new bases the unit took the opportunity to change over to the split system of training whereby both Conversion Flights were located at the satellite while the two Operational Training Flights were housed on the parent station. After first experiencing difficulties, due mainly to workmen still being engaged in installing the runway lighting system, the flying programme finally got under way on 6th June and from that date until 29 OTU was disbanded, the Vickers Wellingtons with which the unit was equipped were seldom absent from the vicinity.

As an old established unit it did not take the OTU long to get into its stride in other aspects of crew training. By the 10th night flying was in progress and practice bombing sorties were being carried out using ranges at Wardley, near Uppingham, Rutland, and Grandborough, near Dunchurch, Warwickshire.

Strategic Air Command Boeing B-47E Stratojet 53-6193 of the 96th Bomb Wing, Dyess AFB, Texas, on its way back to the continental USA in early July 1959, after rotational deployment to Bruntingthorpe as part of the 'Reflex Action' ground alert operation. via Brandon White

To enable another aspect of training to be carried out at Bruntingthorpe, 1683 Bomber Defence Training Flight (BDTF) came into being. Equipped with Miles Martinets and Curtiss Tomahawks, the purpose of this unit was to carry out target towing and fighter affiliation exercises for the benefit of the aircrew training with 29 OTU and those of the neighbouring stations including Market Harborough (Chapter Fifteen), Husbands Bosworth (Chapter Eleven), and Desborough, Northamptonshire.

Personnel to form the Flight were present at Bruntingthorpe by 25th June 1943, but the first of the Tomahawks (AH775) did not arrive until 1st July. From the receipt of this

One of 29 Operational Training Unit's crews pause for a photograph with Wellington III BK181 'TF-V' as a backdrop, July to October 1943. Left to right: 'Taffy' Bull, bomb aimer; Peter Honywood, wireless operator; Bob Phillips, rear gunner; 'Jock' Hamilton, mid-upper gunner; Australian Ernest 'Bill' Berry, pilot; Lenny 'Ginger' Howarth, navigator.
via Brandon White

R1082 receivers and T1083 transmitters, along with their respective headphones and Morse keys, await their trainee wireless operators in a section of the Signals Training Hut at 29 OTU, circa 1944. via Vince Holyoak

On the night of 30th/31st August, four Wellingtons were despatched on a special exercise and for the first time Bruntingthorpe-based aircraft dropped bombs on enemy held targets. Each aircraft carried six 500lb General Purpose bombs and three of these loads were successfully delivered. The operation was marred by the loss of the fourth aircraft, BJ967 'F', which failed to return. Later it was learned that the pilot, Sergeant Wilder, had been rescued from the sea by a Supermarine Walrus amphibian from 11 Group and that the navigator's body had also been recovered. Unfortunately the rest of the crew were reported missing.

In training, accidents cropped up with monotonous frequency, but in most cases resulting in only minor structural damage to the aircraft involved. Many of these incidents occurred during practice landings and to some extent were due to the relative inexperience of the pilots under training, but the constant strain to which airframes were subjected during their OTU lives was a considerable contributory factor. Crashes of a more serious nature involving the loss of not only the aircraft but also of crew members were thankfully not so numerous but one of the worst incidents of this nature to affect 29 OTU occurred on 29th August 1943 when Wellington III BK431 'J' crashed near Oakham, Rutland. The port wing was seen to fold up over the starboard wing and the aircraft then disintegrated in mid-air. Wreckage was scattered over a large area, much being burnt. Six crew members and one Air Training Corps cadet lost their lives.

Throughout September and October considerable time was spent on various projects connected with the airfield. During October the bad weather which occurred seriously curtailed both day and night flying. But full advantage was taken of this situation and by the end of the month the Drem Mk.II lighting system had been completed and the runways, perimeter track and dispersals had all been resurfaced.

With continuous flying and frequent accidental damage, keeping a maximum number of aircraft serviceable became of prime importance with all training units.

aircraft and for the first month of its existence the unit was plagued with faults occurring which rendered machines unserviceable. These troubles culminated on 23rd July when AH864 burst into flames in mid-air. The pilot, Flight Sergeant Merrett, baled out at low altitude and suffered serious injuries while the aircraft dived into the ground near Arnesby to the north and disintegrated. Despite the various problems which beset the unit, it was soon carrying out its allotted task.

As a prelude to their posting to operational squadrons, aircrew in their final phases of training often carried out special exercises in the form of diversionary raids on targets in occupied Europe. On most of these trips the cargo to be delivered consisted of propaganda leaflets though on occasion more lethal loads were carried. The first of these leaflet raids, or 'Nickels' as they were code-named, to be carried out from Bruntingthorpe, was made on 16th June 1943, with Paris as the designated target area. Whether the mission was successful is open to debate; of the four aircraft despatched one returned early while the other three were forced to dispose of their

leaflets blind after encountering extensive cloud cover. Not all sorties of this nature passed without incident and on later occasions aircraft returned with battle damage due to flak or the attentions of enemy night fighters.

Although the station was in full operation, contractors were still very much in evidence during July putting finishing touches to the runway and perimeter track system. Late in the month their help was required further due to rather unusual circumstances. Adverse weather often played havoc with flying programmes, but it was rather rare for exceptionally fine conditions to hinder operations. Towards the end of July and into early August a heat wave had just this effect at Bruntingthorpe. The heat caused some sections of the concrete on the runway to expand to such an extent as to raise them as much as six inches above adjoining sections. Subsequent contractions during the night caused the concrete to crack and turn to rubble, rendering the runways unserviceable. Repairs were executed rapidly and by juggling with the various serviceable sections of runway a training programme was maintained.

RAF Bruntingthorpe – 1st December 1944

Latitude	52° 29' 30" N
Longitude	01° 07' 15" W
Height above Sea Level	450ft
Command	Bomber (RAF)
Nearest Railway Station	Lutterworth (LNER)
Function	Operational Training Unit (Parent)
Affiliated Airfields	Nil

Landing Area – Runways

QDM	Dimensions	Extensibility	Remarks
246°	2,000 x 50 yards	4,000 yards	Entails diversion
185°	1,400 x 50 yards	1,600 yards	of minor roads
132°	1,400 x 50 yards	2,700 yards	

Type of Surface – Concrete and Wood Chips

Permanent Landmarks

By Day	Nil
By Night	Nil

Permanent Obstructions Nil

Facilities

Airfield Lighting	Mk.II
Flying Control	Yes

Accommodation All temporary buildings

Technical	Hangars		Hardstandings	
	Type	No	Type	No
	T.2	4	Frying Pan	30
	B.1	1		

Domestic	Officers	SNCOs	ORs	Total
RAF	214	656	894	1,764
WAAF	10	10	420	440

At 29 OTU the average unit strength at this time was 55 aircraft and some indication of the amount of work required of the Maintenance Wing at Bruntingthorpe is given in the October monthly summary. In all, work was carried out on 32 different aircraft and included eleven major inspections, eight of which were completed. Ten engine changes were carried out, 11 aircraft were received for acceptance checks and a further two were fully modified and fitted with dual Identification, Friend or Foe (IFF) and 'Gee' equipment before being transferred to the newly formed 84 OTU at Desborough.

Over the next few months the only really significant change in the operating routine at Bruntingthorpe occurred early in February 1944, when 1683 BDTF moved out to take up residence at Market Harborough. For a time the unit was still responsible for exercises involving 29 OTU aircraft, but from mid-May the OTU was able to fend for itself in the fighter affiliation field after a flight had been established on unit strength equipped with Hawker Hurricanes.

No.29 Operational Training Unit's turret room, complete with extensive teaching aids.

During the course of the station's active life fire crews had many opportunities to put their training into practice at incidents involving station buildings or aircraft. The majority of the fires they were called out to were soon under control but occasionally a very serious outbreak would really put them to the test.

One such conflagration happened on the morning of 14th June. While undergoing inspection in No.1 Hangar, Wellington X MS480 caught fire. Flames quickly spread and engulfed another Wellington X, LN860, which was on trestles with its undercarriage removed. Preventative measures were to no avail; both aircraft were burnt out, becoming only fit for scrap. Prompt action in pushing a third aircraft from the hangar prevented that too from being caught up in the inferno. Investigation later revealed that the most probable cause of the fire was that a spark from a broken light bulb ignited petrol fumes in the vicinity of MS480.

On 17th October 1944, 29 OTU was informed that with effect from 1st November the unit would become a 'three-quarter' OTU and the Bitteswell satellite transferred to 44 Group Transport Command.

It was proposed to re-open Little Horwood, Buckinghamshire, and 'A' Flight 29 OTU was to be posted in entirety to form the nucleus of a new unit there. As it later transpired 'A' Flight was not severed from the parent unit but Bitteswell was vacated after the termination of night flying on 28th/29th October. Thereafter all aircraft of 29 OTU were established at Bruntingthorpe: 'A' and 'B' Flights – Basic; 'C' Flight – Applied; and 'D' Flight – Hurricanes. Average aircraft and personnel strengths at this time were 47 and 697 respectively.

Late in November 1944 information was received that Bruntingthorpe was to close as a bomber OTU base from 6th February 1945. With this in view the station was visited on 7th December 1944 by a delegation of 44 Group Transport Command to assess if it was suitable to house 105 (T)OTU, the parent station of which was at nearby Bramcote, Warwickshire, or as an alternative field for 1332 (HT) Conversion Unit, Nutts Corner, Northern Ireland. Unfortunately it was found to be unsatisfactory for use by either of the units due mainly to the lack of technical accommodation.

Also during this period, possibly due to the change in training role envisaged for the station, the Bombing Analysis School ended its brief association with Bruntingthorpe. It had been formed there on 5th July 1944 to ensure that instructors received tuition in bombing theory and the latest techniques. After six months the unit departed the station on 5th December bound for Finningley, Yorkshire, where it combined with the Night Bomber Tactical School previously based at Hemswell, Lincolnshire, to form the Bomber Command Instructors' School.

Following Transport Command's findings, further instructions were received on 5th January 1945 to the effect that 29 OTU would not after all be closing down and so training continued from the airfield for several months. On 15th April another signal arrived which stated that no further pupil intakes would be sent to 29 OTU and it would disband after completing the training of crews then with the unit. From this time on there was a progressive reduction in the strength of the OTU with aircraft being flown away to other stations as the number of crews under training decreased. Ten Wellingtons remained when the final training sorties were flown on the night of 26th/27th May 1945 and by early July 29 OTU ceased to exist.

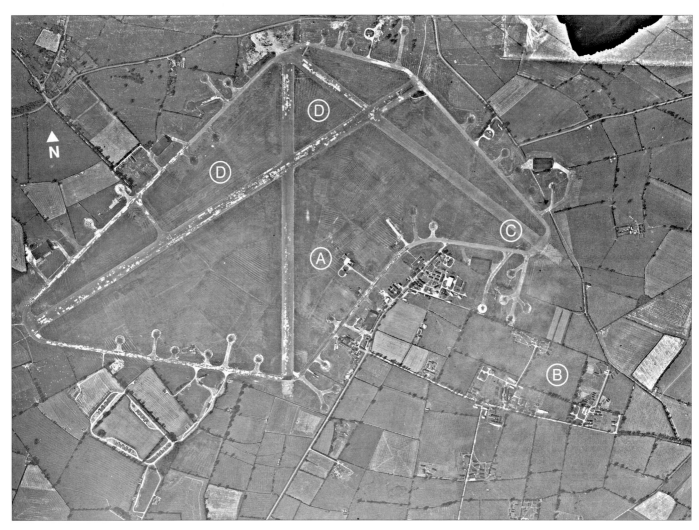

Though the RAF had ceased to operate the airfield for a time they still maintained a strong presence and continued to use the camp facilities which became the home of 11 Aircrew Holding Unit. This was one of several units formed for the purpose of dealing with redundant aircrew while they were awaiting demobilisation or transfer to other trades.

A small amount of flying still took place from Bruntingthorpe after the demise of the OTU in 1945 and also during 1946. Two companies, Power Jets (Research and Development) Limited whose works were then situated at Whetstone, near Leicester, and Armstrong Siddeley Motors of Parkside, Coventry, used the base in connection with development flying of early jet engines.

On 11th September 1944, Power Jets established a flight on the airfield under the auspices of the Controller of Research and Development (CRD Flight). The first aircraft to be allotted was Avro Lancaster II LL735, which was delivered to Bruntingthorpe the very next day. A special hybrid Vickers-Armstrong Wellington II/VI, W5518, followed on 22nd November 1944.

Vertical view of Bruntingthorpe, dated 10th August 1945. The control tower and the 'BP' airfield identifier are at (A). Three sites still in the future when this view was taken are: the 'new' settlement of Upper Bruntingthorpe on what was part of the communal site (B); the 'Butler' hangar of USAF days (C); and the huge area for the storage of cars on the north west edge (D). DoE

Idyllic days with M44 Gliding School at Bruntingthorpe. The vehicle in front of the Kirby Cadet TX.1 is a Beaverette, a very light armoured car, previously used by the airfield defence units and employed by many of the post-war gliding schools for glider retrieval purposes. In all probablility this photograph was taken in the summer of 1947. J Collier

The Power Jets Flight Trials Unit carried out a whole series of tests at Bruntingthorpe connected with early jet engines, using the Lancaster, Wellington and Gloster Meteors. Handley Page Halifax B.VI RG817 was allocated for the unit's use at Bruntingthorpe on 18th June 1945, but apparently it was little used and after a short time with the unit it was flown out to Hawarden, near Chester, to be eventually reduced to scrap. A Fairey Firefly was also issued to the unit, primarily to do air-to-air photography.

Air Commodore Frank Whittle (later Sir Frank) the jet engine pioneer and founder of Power Jets kept a close liaison with the Trials Unit and it was from Bruntingthorpe that he made his first flight in a jet-powered aircraft (Meteor F.1 EE221, see Bitteswell, Chapter Two).

For an aero engine designer to fly solo in an aircraft powered by his own creations is an extremely rare event and the interesting account which follows is an extract from Whittle's autobiography *Jet - The Story of a Pioneer*, which was published by Frederick Muller in 1953:

'During October 1945 I flew a jet aeroplane for the first time myself – this was a Meteor powered by two Power Jets W.2/ 700 engines. Strictly speaking, I should not have done so without CRD's permission and, in fact I did not intend to do so when I climbed into the cockpit – or at least I don't think I did. On the morning of October 19th I went to our airfield at Bruntingthorpe to make one of my periodic visits of inspection. I felt a sudden urge to do some taxying tests in the Meteor. After some 20 minutes of this I returned to Whetstone, but returned to Bruntingthorpe again after lunch. After two flights in a Tiger Moth, I decided to do some more taxying tests. By this time I had acquired a familiarity with the cockpit layout and with the feel of the aircraft up to take-off speed, and so yielded to an irresistible impulse to take off. I landed after a few minutes at very modest speeds – three days later I flew the Meteor again. This time the duration of the flight was 45 minutes and I attained much greater speeds and height than on the first occasion.'

Armstrong Siddeley's test programme, which began in June 1945 was instituted to evaluate progressive development of their ASX (Armstrong Siddeley Experimental) series of turbojets. For the purpose of air testing examples of these engines an Avro Lancaster III ND784/G was used as a testbed, the bomb bay of the aircraft having been specially modified for the purpose.

The ASX 5 and 7 were flown in this manner and by completion of the tests in June 1946 they had amassed 48 hours of flight time.

In the spring of 1946 the Flight Trials Unit, along with other Power Jets (R&D) Ltd's assets, was taken over by the National Gas Turbine Establishment and following this the unit ended its association with Bruntingthorpe. With one exception all aircraft still with the unit had flown the short distance to their new base at Bitteswell by 14th May. For Wellington W5518 the flight was its 70th with the unit. Last to leave was the Meteor EE221 on 25th May and with its departure it was to be over a decade before jet aircraft operated from the station once more.

From October 1946 the airfield was placed on a Care and Maintenance footing and in May 1947 the Air Ministry instructed that it was to be retained for the time being as an unmanned satellite of Bomber Command under the parentage of Cottesmore. Eventually it was intended to transfer the base to Flying Training Command and with this in mind bi-weekly inspections of the camp facilities were carried out by 23 Group, Church Lawford, Warwickshire.

Flying returned to Bruntingthorpe during the summer of 1947 when M44 Gliding School moved in from Rearsby. This was the unit's third home but it was destined to spend less than a year on the airfield and by April 1948 it had moved once more this time to Desford.

In common with many other disused airfields several of the camps domestic sites were used post-war to house displaced persons from Europe. A large proportion of Bruntingthorpe's refugee community was of Lithuanian or Estonian origin and many hut interiors were decorated with crude wall murals depicting scenes which served to remind their inhabitants of home. When eventually they were resettled elsewhere much of the hutted accommodation was allowed to fall into disrepair before being finally sold and cleared.

After several years of inactivity the first intimation of a new lease of life for the airfield came about in 1953. At that time the United States Air Force (USAF) was seeking bases in the UK to enhance the mobility and dispersal of its Strategic Air Command (SAC) bomber wings. Various sites were surveyed and Bruntingthorpe was one of those found suitable for development; a major rebuild of the airfield began in late 1954. More land was acquired to enable the existing 07/25 runway to be extended to 10,000ft and relaid to a greater load-bearing specification, both these requirements being essential to the operation of large jet aircraft.

Most of the remaining wartime runway system, taxiways and dispersals were removed and the spoil incorporated as hard-core for taxiways and the many dispersals sited on both sides of the new runway. The dispersals were complete with underground fuel storage tanks and pressure refuelling points. Up-to-date lighting systems were installed which covered every aspect of this extensive redevelopment. As the Second World War control tower was found to be unsuitable for that purpose it was converted into a weather briefing block and a new tower of modern design was built on the north western side of the airfield. The former RAF hangars which remained, together with many buildings on the technical site, were refurbished for use once more and to these was added a large new 'Butler' hangar.

Initially priority was given to building work directly connected with the operation of SAC aircraft; this inevitably delayed work on the living accommodation and associated facilities for some time. When the first detachment of USAF personnel moved on to the base conditions there can only be described as primitive, such essentials as electricity and sanitary arrangements being most inadequate. So, as the influx of personnel continued to increase, many found

The control tower, before refurbishing.
R Walters

billets in surrounding villages while others were temporarily accommodated in a trailer camp set up on the base.

Although the runway was not completed until July 1957, the airfield was officially handed over to the 3912th Air Base Squadron (later Combat Support Group [SAC] 7th Air Division) USAF, on 15th February 1957. It is possible that the party of USAF officials for the hand-over were aboard Douglas C-54D Skymaster, 42-72489, that visited the nearby airfield at Bitteswell at this time.

By early 1958 the base was fully occupied and the first major trial of the new installations took place over the period 10th-16th March when 30-plus six-engined swept-wing Boeing B-47E Stratojets from the 308th Bomb Wing, at Hunter AFB, Georgia, flew in as part of a mobility exercise code-named Operation 'Snow Flurry'. Towards the end of the exercise, high ranking SAC officers arrived in a Douglas VC-118A Liftmaster to review and inspect the facilities. At this time Bruntingthorpe was termed a post-strike recovery and maintenance base. It could be presumed that arriving bombers would be 'unarmed' and survivors of an initial or subsequent strike. 'Snow Flurry' was the only exercise of this type carried out at Bruntingthorpe. The mass departure of the B-47s during the early morning of Sunday 16th March, woke everyone in the neighbourhood but calmed the fears of many people.

Only one aircraft would be based at Bruntingthorpe for the next eight months – a former 47th Tactical Bomb Wing (TBW) North American B-45C Tornado, 47-0027, which had arrived during late 1958 for fire and rescue practice. During the remainder of 1958, B-47s would, from time to time, carry out approaches along with other types from the Tactical Fighter Wings based in East Anglia, thus keeping the air traffic control facilities active.

Amongst the visitors at this time were Douglas B-66B Destroyers from the 47th TBW, Sculthorpe, in Norfolk plus pairs of North American F-100D and 'F Super Sabres from the 20th Tactical Fighter Wing (TFW) at Wethersfield, Essex. Most frequent were the Douglas AC-47Ds of the 1858th Airways and Air Communications Service Flight from Burtonwood, Cheshire (later at Bovingdon, Hertfordshire), checking and calibrating the airfield's various navigation aids.

During the ensuing months since 'Snow Flurry', SAC had introduced throughout the command, major changes to its deterrent mission policy. Briefly, instead of large quantities of its predominant B-47 fleet being based at UK, Spanish or North African bases for 90-day temporary deployments (TDY), smaller numbers of aircraft for shorter duration detachments, were to be introduced during the latter part of 1958.

This new mission philosophy was known as 'Reflex Alert' and from the beginning of January 1959, SAC 7th Air Division bases, including Bruntingthorpe introduced and shook down these new battle orders. Over a period of a few days nine B-47s Stratojets arrived at Bruntingthorpe and by late January they had been joined by three more.

It was during the arrival of the latter three aircraft, on 31st January, a cold and misty Saturday, that the rarest aircraft type to visit Bruntingthorpe during the 1950s USAF era put in a surprise appearance in the circuit. Only recently has it been revealed that three Martin RB-57D (long span USAF Canberras), operated by Det(achment) 7 of the 4080th Strategic Reconnaissance Wing (SRW) from Laughlin Air Force Base (AFB), Texas, were deployed to RAF Brize Norton, Oxfordshire, on a special Temporary Duty (TDY) code-named 'Border Town'. Arriving on the 26th, they were tasked with a series of clandestine night Electronic Intelligence (ELINT) gathering missions, along the sensitive 'Iron Curtain' border, but had been grounded since their arrival by severe mist and fog. The conditions eased a little on the 31st and the visit to Bruntingthorpe was made during vital orientation and system check flights. Whether one aircraft made three Ground-Controlled Approaches (GCAs) or three RB-57s one each, is still a matter of conjecture, but these visits certainly caused a stir among local enthusiasts. The RB-57s allegedly completed several missions and left Brize Norton for home on 5th April.

From January 1959 until the end of the following June, the 100th Bomb Wing from Pease AFB, New Hampshire, provided the rotational B-47s and from this point on a routine developed, whereby three B-47Es would arrive on a Tuesday and three depart during the following afternoon, usually for the Continental United States (CONUS). By the end of four weeks a complete change of aircraft had taken place. Apart from the two active days very little flying by the based B-47s took place. However, to keep all base personnel in 'trim' and in particular ground servicing and aircrew, frequent 'high profile alert' exercises were held. These ranged from scrambling the crews to the aircraft and just starting the General Electric J47 turbojets, to a mass start of aircraft along the taxiways, and simulated take-offs before returning to dispersals and shutting down. Unlike, 'Snow Flurry', it could be presumed that the aircraft were 'cocked' and ready to go if the warning went red.

To the interested observer, a B-47 taking off from the runway, with its pronounced central hump, was always a dramatic sight. The summer of 1959 was good and hot; this meant that even with the Jet Assisted Take-off (JATO) bottles fitted, the aircraft only just seemed to clear the boundary fence before gaining any height. The powers that be must have been aware of this limitation for the 4ft wooden boundary posts at each end of the runway were deliberately partly sawn through at ground level, so that in the event of a B-47 touching the fence it would give way and not impede the aircraft's take-off. At this time, when flying was taking place, lights and security boxes controlled traffic on the roads at each end of the runway.

At the beginning of July 1959 it fell to the 96th Bomb Wing, from Dyess AFB, Texas, to continue the rotational flights, but this was to be very short-lived, for on 23rd of the month Bruntingthorpe's last deployment of B-47E Stratojets returned to the US.

Activity on the base during this period was not solely confined to B-47s and there were many interesting visitors. These included Boeing WB-50D Superfortresses from the 53rd Weather Reconnaissance Squadron, which were engaged in training sorties from their base at Alconbury, Huntingdonshire. There were also occasional visits by Boeing KC-97G Stratofreighters and RAF aircraft such as English Electric Canberras and de Havilland Vampire T.11s – the latter frequently belonging to the RAF College, at Cranwell in Lincolnshire.

While Strategic Air Command controlled Bruntingthorpe, none of their operational, in other words nuclear-armed, aircraft are said to have used the base. On this issue doubts were sometimes expressed by local residents. In particular, speculation centred around the arrival, when a night practice Base Alert was in progress, of aircraft which were immediately marshalled onto one of the remote, brilliantly floodlit, maximum security dispersals and placed under heavy armed guard...

On 1st September 1959, SAC's tenure of the base came to an end when control officially passed into the hands of Headquarters USAF in Europe (USAFE). From this date also the 3912th Combat Support Group ceased to exist, the base support unit role being taken over by the 7542nd Air Base Squadron.

As a mark of appreciation the following tribute was received at Bruntingthorpe:

'To all personnel I wish to express my appreciation for your past support of the Strategic Air Command, and my regret that USAF commitments necessitates your transfer to another Command.

'That the 7th Air Division has successfully carried out its alert force mission and met the additional responsibilities of assisting the Royal Air Force in its Thor Missile program, is due in large to your outstanding individual and group effort.

'On behalf of all members of the 7th Air Division and SAC I wish you the best of luck in your new assignment.

W H Blanchard
Major General USAF, Commander.'

'Reflex Action' B-47E 53-2336 of the 96th Bomb Wing, piles on the coals during an exercise at Bruntingthorpe in July 1959.
Brandon White

Boeing WB-50D Superfortress 48-0077 of the 53rd Weather Reconnaissance Squadron from Alconbury, visiting Bruntingthorpe, June 1959.
Brandon White

The reasons for the change in the role of the base have their origins in France in early 1959 when the French President, General Charles de Gaulle, became increasingly disturbed at the use of North Atlantic Treaty Organisation (NATO) bases in his country by nuclear-armed aircraft of the USAF. After he had voiced his opinions in no uncertain manner the United States, under Project 'Red Richard' began to withdraw its nuclear capable units from France.

One of the units affected by these moves was the non-nucleur capable 10th Tactical Reconnaissance Wing (TRW) and although the four constituent Tactical Reconnaissance Squadrons (TRS) were based equally in France and Germany, the need to move the nucleur-capable 49th Tactical Fighter Wing (TFW) to Spangdahlem in Germany prompted the entire relocation of the 10th TRW to the UK. The 1st TRS and 30th TRS exchanged their base at Toul-Rosières, France, for Alconbury in Huntingdonshire, while the 19th TRS and 42nd TRS vacated Spangdahlem, Germany, to be housed at Bruntingthorpe and Chelveston, Northants, respectively. Alconbury would also house the 10th TRW's Headquarters of Operations for all three bases.

The first of the 19th TRS' Douglas RB-66 Destroyers flew into Bruntingthorpe on 25th August 1959, with Squadron Commander, Lieutenant Colonel L J Partridge at the controls. Prior to this date much of the unit's stores and equipment had been airlifted to Bruntingthorpe by Douglas C-124C Globemaster IIs and C-133A Cargomasters of the USAF's Military Air Transport Service and Air Materiel Command.

From the changeover date, unit strength built up rapidly and by 12th September the unit establishment of 18 RB-66Bs had been achieved, but due to servicing or deployment, it was rare to see more than 14 of the unit's aircraft at any one time.

While the 19th TRS was resident, a base flight was soon established comprising C-47 transports and Lockheed T-33A jet trainers. The 19th TRS sported a green stripe on the outward facing sides of the engine nacelle, while all the 10th TRW aircraft carried the four squadron colours emanating from a star at the fin tip. When the RB-66s arrived there were two distinguishable variants; several already had their rear-mounted twin radar controlled guns removed and replaced by electronic counter-measures (ECM) fairings. This modification was eventually to extend to the complete squadron, although the aircraft were still known as RB-66s. It would be several years before dedicated ECM EB-66s officially entered service.

During their three-year tenure at Bruntingthorpe, the 19th TRS lost two machines due to accident. One of these tragedies occurred within Leicestershire when RB-66 54-0421 crashed on 12th December 1959 at Welsh Myres Farm, near Skeffington on the A47. All three crew members lost their lives.

Lockheed T-33A 51-8754 of the Bruntingthorpe Base Flight, photographed during the 28th May 1960 Open Day. Ian W O'Neill

Probably taken from on board the Douglas C-124C Globemaster transport in the static display of 28th May 1960, an unusual view of the resident 19th Tactical Reconnaissance Squadron Commanding Officer's RB-66B, 54-0440, which has had the original remotely controlled twin 20mm cannon barbette replaced with the rear fuselage ECM fit. N Franklin

Between April and July 1960, an outside working party from Field Aircraft Services of Wymeswold undertook internal modifications on several 10th TRW aircraft, requiring the use of the 'Butler' hangar. Usually two or three RB-66s would be worked on at a time. As well as RB-66Bs of the 19th TRS (green stripe), 1st TRS (blue stripe) and 30th TRS (yellow stripe), RB-66Cs of the 42nd TRS (red stripe) – distinguishable by their wingtip radar pods – were also to be noted.

On 28th May 1960 the general public in the area were able to sample American hospitality first hand when the base held its one and only Armed Forces Day and Open House. Approximately 20,000 people took advantage of the opportunity and were able to view the base facilities at close quarters. Attractions laid on to entertain the visitors included a comprehensive exhibit of static aircraft and ancillary equipment, baseball games, guard dog demonstrations and helicopter joy-rides. In addition a short flying display was staged during the afternoon.

As well as the large amount of base activity which sometimes took place at weekends, visiting aircraft were still frequent. The occasional Vickers Valiants or Handley Page Victors from 232 Operational Conversion Unit at Gaydon, Warwickshire, would grace the circuit, along with regular visits from USAFE North American F-100Ds and 'Fs, McDonnell F-101A and 'C Voodoos, as well as Boeing KB-50Js from the 420th Air Refuelling Squadron at Sculthorpe, Norfolk.

Not everyone was in accord with the USAF occupation of Bruntingthorpe, the greatest bone of contention being the amount of noise generated by the jet aircraft, especially when on night flying exercises. Complaints were often raised via parish councils and on at least one occasion the Member of Parliament for the area was approached to see if it was possible to have some form of silencing erected to eliminate ground running noise or alternatively if steps could be taken to have the base closed altogether.

Historically, before becoming part of the 10th TRW, the 19th TRS was the original recipient of the first RB-66Bs in Europe, at Sculthorpe in February 1957. At that time the 19th TRS was part of the 66th TRW and was replacing the RB-45C Tornado. The squadron prided itself on its night photography ability, hence the name 'Night Photo Jet' appended at that time. On arriving at Bruntingthorpe, the 19th made the locality aware of its around-the-clock capability, particularly when returning from missions or practising with long GCAs.

During the 19th's stay at Bruntingthorpe several political crises heightened the unit's activity, one of the most notable being the erection of the Berlin Wall in August 1961. NATO air recce units were called upon to maintain coverage along the borders with East Germany, monitoring Soviet and Warsaw Pact intentions. In the event, the local population were lucky that the base was not called upon to house any of the 200 extra Air National Guard and Air Force Reserve aircraft that were mobilised and sent to France and Germany for a two year period.

Eventually the advocates for the closure of the base had their wish, not due to their efforts, but to proposed reductions within USAFE in the UK combined with temporary amendments to earlier decisions by the French government. These amendments meant that for a further four years, certain non-nuclear equipped aircraft could be based on French soil. In August 1962 the last RB-66B left Bruntingthorpe to take up residence at one of the 10th TRW's former bases, Toul-Rosières.

The 'Stars and Stripes' was hauled down for the last time at Bruntingthorpe on 28th September 1962 and the flag placed into the hands of Lieutenant Colonel G D Rawlings, Base Commander at Alconbury, for safe keeping.

While for many the departure was a blessing, for others it meant the loss of revenue from off base billeting or working on base as a civilian employee. Many local businesses, including public houses, also suffered.

A welcome participant in the static aircraft park at the RAF Bruntingthorpe Armed Forces Day air show on 28th May 1960 was this Gloster Javelin FAW.9, from 25 Squadron based at RAF Waterbeach, Cambridgeshire. XH882 'L' was one of those assembled as an FAW.7 by AWA at Bitteswell, during 1958, but, like a number of others, was converted to FAW.9 standard at Gloster's Moreton Valence factory, prior to its service career. XH882 was eventually accepted for RAF service on 29th January 1960. Chris Salter

Douglas RB-66B Destroyer 54-507 tucks up the gear on take-off from Bruntingthorpe, 28th May 1960 during the Open Day. N Franklin

RB-66B Destroyer 54-0521 of the USAF's 1st Tactical Reconnaissance Squadron, based at Alconbury, but under maintenance inside the 'Butler' hangar at Bruntingthorpe, May 1960. N Franklin

Back under RAF control, the airfield was retained as an unmanned satellite of RAF Wittering, Huntingdonshire (later Cambridgeshire), to be used as a possible dispersal airfield for the V-Bomber force. While on this status, although no aircraft were resident, it was visited on several occasions during 1963-64 by Handley Page Victors of both 100 and 139 Squadrons which practised 'roller' landings and take-offs. After the visits by the Victors the airfield is believed to have been used on only one other occasion by service aircraft. This was during May 1970, when six Hawker Siddeley Harrier GR.1s from the newly-reformed 1 Squadron based at Wittering, supported by RAF Regiment and Army units, refuelling tankers, mobile radar installations etc., took part in one of the first Forward Operating Locations (FOL) exercises in the field, for this revolutionary aircraft.

From 1964 the airfield was largely disused and on 16th November 1965 the part which had once been the technical site with its many buildings and the two remaining wartime hangars was split into eight lots and sold by auction. The new permanent housing built during USAF occupation was also eventually sold to private owners to become a new village called Upper Bruntingthorpe. Hangars and other buildings on the site were rented for storage purposes and at times as winter quarters for circus and fairground folk. During the early 1970s the Second World War control tower was used as a centre for research projects carried out under the sponsorship of Loughborough University Physics Department.

Suggestions considered for a more permanent use of the airfield included making it a civil airport, establishing light industrial estates and turning the land into a recreational centre for South Leicestershire. None of these schemes gained approval.

Finally the death knell for Bruntingthorpe as a military airfield was sounded when it was declared surplus to Ministry of Defence requirements. On 23rd March 1973 an auction sale was held to dispose of surplus equipment including airfield lighting fittings, pressure refuelling installations and the 60,000 gallon high level water tank. Many of the airfield's buildings were up for disposal by demolition and clearance, the new control tower disappearing in this way.

Prior to the sale over 600 acres of the airfield had been acquired by Chrysler (UK) Limited for the purpose of establishing a vehicle proving ground. Objections were raised to the proposal but following a five day public enquiry, which began at Husbands Bosworth on 12th December 1972, the company received planning permission to develop the site. Chrysler announced that their initial investment in the project would run into seven figures and the first phase was to include a high speed straight along the two mile runway, the line of the perimeter track was to be converted into a five lane 4.2 mile endurance track, while the 'Butler' hangar would be remodelled as a giant workshop and stores.

The first measure taken by the company was to ensure the security of the area and for this purpose a 7½ft high anti-intruder fence was erected round the greater proportion of their site. A sectional concrete wall completed the enclosure and also effectively parted the former technical site from the airfield. Additionally an earth bank, over 800 yards long and up to 12ft high was thrown up between the perimeter track and Bruntingthorpe village. This was to act as a noise baffle and also to shield head light beams when night running was in progress. To add further to the seclusion many saplings were planted on the outer side of the bank; it was said that eventually 140,000

trees of 15 different varieties would grace the surroundings of the proving ground.

Little more was done towards carrying out the plan which had been formulated. Later financial difficulties followed by the take-over of the company by Peugeot-Talbot led to a change in policy and further development of the proving ground project was shelved.

Following this decision the airfield saw little use. For several seasons the crop of mowing grass was sold by tender while on occasion, under Home Office auspices, police utilised the 'Butler' hangar to practice techniques of riot control and used the airfield for training in dog handling.

In 1983 the site was sold and from that time it has rarely been out of the local news. The new owners were C Walton Limited of Sulby, near Husbands Bosworth, a family concern with interests in farming and land drainage. The company were no strangers to the possession of this type of property as they had long owned a substantial part of the former RAF airfield at Husbands Bosworth. Some of the land returned, within a short space of time, to agriculture but the company still retained the right to run a vehicle proving ground.

Late in 1983 Loughborough and Leicestershire Aircraft Museum (LLAM) then based at East Midlands Airport were faced with finding a new home. The Waltons – keen aircraft enthusiasts themselves – were approached and a verbal agreement was reached whereby a small section of the airfield was made available to house, initially, certain elements of the aircraft collection. To enable a museum to be established, the owners sought planning permission which was duly granted by the local authorities. Over the weekend of 19th-20th November LLAM mounted a massive removal operation and the collection, with the exception of Avro Vulcan XM575 was transferred to Bruntingthorpe.

During the early part of 1984 the group made some progress. Most of the aircraft were reassembled and several new acquisitions joined the collection. Plans were made to fly the Vulcan in and also to open the collection to the public but neither of these events materialised.

In the summer another museum-type operation, British Aviation Heritage (BAH), founded by aircraft owner and restorer Nick Grace also received the Walton's permission to base themselves at Bruntingthorpe.

Angus McVitie demonstrating Spitfire XIV NH749 (G-MXIV) before an invited audience of local dignitaries and Lutterworth school children prior to the British Aviation Heritage event of 24th June 1984. Author

Dedicated to preserving wartime aircraft in flying condition BAH proposed to erect a new hangar for their home. To enable funds to be raised for this venture an airshow was staged on 24th June which featured attractions such as a Supermarine Spitfire, de Havilland Mosquito and rock star Gary Numan flying his Canadian-built North American Harvard plus many stalls and side-shows. The event did not attract a large crowd, only about 3,500 people attending.

There was an unexpected sequel to the show. LLAM, or Bruntingthorpe Aviation Collection as it had become, were given notice to quit the airfield. A radical reorganisation of the group followed, together with a change of title to Phoenix Aviation Museum, later Phoenix Aviation. It was unfortunately to no avail, no new base could be found and eventually most of the aircraft were sold or found new homes elsewhere.

Undeterred by the low turn out in June British Aviation Heritage tried again over the weekend of 15th-16th September. Billed as the Bruntingthorpe Gala, the event featured a whole range of attractions aimed at drawing in family support. Although moderately priced at £1 for adults, 50p for children and free parking it did not achieve its objective with a reported gate only in the region of 2,000 over the two days. This lack of support must have been most disappointing and have had a detrimental effect on BAH plans, for no more events were staged at Bruntingthorpe under their auspices.

These two BAH shows did however have an adverse effect on relations between the airfield owners and the surrounding rural community. Objections were raised at parish level and representations made to local authorities over the noise and traffic levels generated by these and other events held at the airfield. This was the beginning of a series of recriminations which were to become sadly more acrimonious and embittered with the passing of time.

Over the ensuing months the spread of rumour and counter-rumour did not help. There was consternation in surrounding villages at the use of explosives by men of the Royal Marines during a night exercise on the airfield and complaints followed the weekend of 4-5th July 1987 when Nick Grace flew his Spitfire Tr.IX from Bruntingthorpe on several occasions. An announcement that the site could possibly be used for large scale housing was also viewed with concern. These events and more all served to further exacerbate the situation.

On 24th June 1988 the aircraft preservation element on the airfield received a boost when the English Electric Lightning F.6, XR728, flew in from Binbrook, Lincolnshire to be warmly welcomed by its new owners, the Lightning Preservation Group (LPG). A consortium of enthusiasts, they had bought the Mach 2 fighter when it was phased out of service with the RAF. Having received their aircraft in full working order the group made it clear that it was their intention to

Helicopter's eye view of English Electric Lightning F.6, XR728, of the Lightning Preservation Group, on the day of its arrival, 24th June 1988. Author

keep it in that state, news that did not go down well in some quarters.

More speculation, rumour, half truths and lack of firm information continued to add fuel to the ongoing 'battle of the airfield'. Reports of its possible use by Boeing 747 'Jumbo' jets as an international air freight terminal, with Federal Express, UPS and TNT all mentioned as interested parties, led to much media interest and local comment.

Even an exercise in counter terrorism on 23rd-25th June 1989 had its critics. The object of the operation, which involved over 300 police and members of the Special Air Service, was to contain and apprehend terrorist elements who had taken over the control tower and were expecting to be airlifted out. But the area was successfully sealed off before their transport arrived. With the tower under siege and the occupants refusing to surrender it was left to the SAS to storm the building and neutralise the 'terrorists'. The use of firearms, explosives, the minor inconvenience of road blocks and no prior knowledge of the event brought forth a crop of complaints. What would have been the reaction had it been for real?

When plans were proposed for the erection of buildings covering 377,000 sq ft in which to house fire service equipment, stockpiled in case of national emergency, protests erupted again. The main items to be stored were 1,058 'Green Goddess' fire engines and 141 Land Rovers. Thoughts of the constant noise and road testing of these vehicles served to infuriate many in the locality. Both air freight terminal and fire service store schemes were rejected when planning permission was sought.

Yet another tentative plan for the future of Bruntingthorpe was unveiled in February 1991. David Wilson Estates of Leicester proposed a European Business Village development which would occupy all 650 acres of the airfield. It was envisaged that the main business area would flank a shortened runway, with 750 houses, a school, golf course, shops and other amenities occupying the rest of the site. The planting of thousands more trees would further enhance the area. This scheme also appears to have been stillborn.

That the airfield be returned entirely to agriculture is a wish often expressed in the locality. Few of the advocates of this scheme can have realised the magnitude of the task involved in the removal of the two mile runway and its ancillary areas of concrete. Were this operation to take place it is estimated over 1,500,000 tonnes of hard core would be generated. Imagine the noise and dust created, the fleet of heavy lorries needed to remove this spoil. If farming was to return to the site where would the massive quantities of soil needed to fill the huge gash be obtained?

Apart from being used for vehicle testing and the now occasional use by aircraft the runway has seen a variety of uses. It has featured on many occasions in TV commercials. One memorable presentation was for Royal Mail Parcelforce in which 45 British Leyland Roadtrains, Ford Cargos and DAF

400 vans were filmed from a helicopter as they cruised down the two mile stretch alternately creating rocket, aeroplane and arrow shapes. It has also been the scene of many charity pulls in which a variety of the vintage aircraft have featured. In November 1992 it was the venue for an unusual land speed record for tri-cars when a souped-up Sinclair C5 achieved a speed of 60.77mph.

One of the airfield's most popular preservationists, Neville Martin, has fond memories of 1992 for it was on 19th January that he took delivery of two Folland Gnat T.1s for Phoenix Aviation. Both had been bought by tender from the Ministry of Defence but one of them was really special; it was a 65th birthday present from his wife Dawn. Neville was delighted with his Gnats for he had spent many years of his life working on them at Bitteswell.

In July 1992, after 18 months of waiting, Sandy Topen's Vintage Aircraft Team (VAT) received Harborough District Council's blessing to set up a new base at Bruntingthorpe. The move, made necessary due to development at their previous base Cranfield, Bedfordshire, began later in the year. It was not however until mid-1993 that several vintage jets which the group operated were at their new location. The VAT operated at Bruntingthorpe until it ceased to function in 1996 and its varied fleet of aircraft was sold off.

For many concerned with the aircraft preservation movement, aviation enthusiasts in general, the local pressure groups and councils, 1993 was a year to be remembered at the airfield. The occasions which were to make the year so memorable began on 21st January with the arrival of a second Lightning F.6, XS904, for the LPG. Although the type had long been phased out of service, several had been seconded to British Aerospace (BAe) for use in further developing the Panavia Tornado radar systems. When XS904 left Warton, Lancashire, bound for Bruntingthorpe it marked the end

of an era for it was the last flight by a Lightning under UK military aegis.

Some aircraft have, in the past, achieved what might be called cult status, none more so than the Avro Vulcan. When the RAF's last flying example was put up for sale the successful bidders were C Walton (Aviation Division) Limited. A farewell flight over former Vulcan bases was made before heading for Leicestershire and a final circuit before landing at Bruntingthorpe on 23rd March 1993. There about 5,000 of the Vulcan's most avid fans had assembled to greet the arrival of XH558 with a welcome that was both rapturous and emotional. A truly unforgettable experience.

The next event of 1993 which was guaranteed to bring forth howls of protest was the 'Big Thunder' air display. From the first announcement in October 1992 a spate of complaints began to appear in the local press. However, Harborough District Council gave the go ahead and the display took place on 18th July.

Held under the revived BAH logo which had now been adopted by the Waltons – in honour of the pioneering of Nick Grace, who was killed in a motor car accident on 14th October 1988 – the event rivalled many of the UKs established airshows. It contained all the elements to make it popular with the public. Firm favourites such as the 'Red Arrows' and Battle of Britain Memorial Flight performed; there were team and individual aerobatic displays, participating aircraft from the RAF and foreign air arms. All this, allied to extensive side shows and other entertainments made it a very enjoyable day for the large crowd in attendance. In the weeks that followed complaints with regard to various aspects of the show were many but then so were comments and letters making favourable views known.

But there was still one more notable aviation event to take place to round off the year and it was yet another preservation coup for the Walton Aviation Division. On November 19th, a glorious late autumn day, the former 55 Squadron Handley Page Victor K.2, XM715, flew in to join the Vulcan. A veteran of the Gulf War, it too had been bought by tender when no longer required for service by the RAF. Although not on the scale of the Vulcan's reception, the Victor too had its devotees and was warmly welcomed. As an added bonus on the day an English Electric Canberra B2/6, XH568, flew in as the first aircraft for Classic Aircraft Projects. Previously on the strength of the Defence Research Establishment, Thurleigh, Bedfordshire, it made a fine sight resplendent in its red white and dark blue colour scheme.

Neville Martin with his Folland Gnat birthday present, 1992. Leicester Mercury via Neville Martin

During 1994 the storage and valeting of cars continued to play a major part at Bruntingthorpe. The transport of these vehicles to and from the site once again came in for complaint and scrutiny. Yet another plan to develop the airfield was mooted. This time it was for a hi-tech centre with research facilities for the motor and possibly aviation industries. It was estimated 1,400 jobs could be created over the next decade were the project to proceed.

Problems at the airfield even reached national level when it was featured by the Council for the Protection of Rural England (CPRE) in its report 'Leisure Landscapes'. Bruntingthorpe was highlighted because of continual planning clashes over its use for various aviation activities and other events.

'Big Thunder' was held again on 17th July and was said to have been a huge success. Local hotels reported full bookings as tens of thousands of spectators from home and abroad flocked to the show which reputedly cost the organisers almost £500,000 to stage. Its content was much the same mixture as before. Fast taxi runs by the resident Victor, Vulcan and Lightnings delighted the crowd. Nostalgic displays by a Spitfire, Boeing B-17 Flying Fortress, Mosquito and other vintage aircraft brought a lump to many a throat while more modern aircraft thrilled more onlookers.

There were two major aircraft acquisitions by BAH during the year. The first which arrived on 23rd September was the largest aircraft to date to land at Bruntingthorpe, an ex-Air France Boeing 747 'Jumbo' jet. It was to remain firmly grounded after vital parts were removed for spares. In the future it was hoped to put the aircraft to use possibly as a conference centre, museum clubhouse or in TV commercials. None of these plans reached fruition and the aircraft was ultimately destroyed on 17th May 1997 in a much-publicised event staged by the Civil Aviation Authority in conjunction with the

US Federal Aviation Administration. Several controlled explosions served to test and demonstrate the effectiveness of various safety features which had been installed in the airliner's lower deck freight and baggage bays to foil terrorist bomb attacks while one device served to illustrate the result of an absence of any protection. All of this came in the wake of the horrific destruction of the Pan American Boeing 747 over Lockerbie, Scotland, with the loss of all on board.

Disposal of the remaining HS Buccaneers by the Ministry of Defence led to BAH acquiring two examples of this rugged former naval aircraft in the November of 1994. Brought by road from storage at St Athan, South Wales, they were soon reassembled to join the growing collection.

For a change, Bruntingthorpe hosted an event which received no adverse publicity. As part of their VE Day celebrations Lutterworth Rotary Club took over the 'Butler' hangar on 5th May 1995 to stage an evening of nostalgia, dancing to sounds of the 1940s, with Glenn Miller style music played by the 'Memphis Belle' Orchestra. Almost 2,000 people enjoyed the festivities, enlivened by many in period dress who fully entered into the spirit of the occasion, and the arrival of a P-51D Mustang in USAAF colours provided a fitting backdrop. Several major charities were to benefit from this occasion.

Now regarded by many as a firm annual attraction 'Big Thunder' again took to the air on 16th July 1995. This time as well as the usual ingredients the crowd had the added fillip of seeing examples of the Russian Sukhoi Su-27 *Flanker* supersonic fighter perform a series of stunning aerobatics.

November saw the departure from the site of Walon Ltd, the car testing and maintenance firm which had used the airfield for its activities for a number of years. For most of this time it had been the centre of much controversy and restrictions placed on its

The 'Big Thunder' brass plaque was once the winning entry in a competition to design an emblem for the 7542nd Air Base Squadron. At one time a central fixture on the Officers' Mess fireplace, it was 'liberated' after the base closed. Author

operations by Harborough District Council were blamed for the company leaving.

In 1996 'Big Thunder' was replaced by a more limited event, under the heading of 'Rolling Thunder' in which the 'heavy metal' exhibits were run-up and taxied in front of an appreciative audience, and this type of event has been repeated on a fairly regular twice a year basis ever since.

British Aviation Heritage and its more recently launched sister organisation World Aviation Heritage have continued to expand their collections. On 1st July 1996 the incredibly shaped Aerospacelines Super Guppy 201 four-engined freighter touched down on Bruntingthorpe's runway. This aircraft had been passed on by British Aerospace who had inherited it from their partnership with the multi-national Airbus Industrie consortium. The capacious Guppy had been used to fly wing and fuselage sections for Airbus types to the assembly centres at Toulouse in France and Hamburg in Germany. Replaced by a twin-jet SATIC-Airbus A300 Beluga, F-BTGV needed a home and BAH was an ideal location.

Following hard on the heels of the Guppy was the last flying example of the de Havilland Comet four-jet airliner, XS235 *Canopus*. A deal with a UK museum to take on the aircraft foundered, and a responsible home was needed for the aircraft. BAH obliged and the Comet arrived at Bruntingthorpe on 30th October 1997. It has been maintained in taxable condition, as demonstrated as recently as the open day on 7th May 2000.

Moment of detonation in the underfloor cargo holds of the former Air France Boeing 747 on 17th May 1997. The little huts are temporary protection for cameras. BAH

In August 2000 plans were announced to restore *Canopus* to flying condition in a bid to recreate the first passenger-carrying jet airliner flight from England to Johannesburg, which originally took place in May 1952. Initially, the aim was to prepare the Comet for a ferry flight to Lasham, Hampshire, for which the registration G-CPDA was reserved.

Hard work to get another of Bruntingthorpe's residents, Vulcan B.2 XH558 (G-VLCN), back into the air geared up considerably in 2000 with the creation of the Vulcan Operating Company (VOC), in a project to raise around £3 million. By mid-2000 XH558 had passed its pre-Service Technical Survey, with flying colours, although it was reported in November that as yet no commercial organisation had come forward with financial support. However, the Southend-based Vulcan Restoration Trust has now pooled its resources with the VOC. In addition, to raise further funds, a 'Sign-Up' campaign has been launched, inviting members of the public to donate £40 and in return have their names printed on the bomb-bay doors. It was also reported in November that should funding not reach the required targets then a distinct possibility exists of the Vulcan emigrating to fly in the USA. Only time will tell!

Another recent development concerns the Lightning Preservation Group. They received planning permission in the summer of 2000 to erect a pair of 1960s-style Quick Reaction Alert (QRA) shelters to house their two Lightning F.6s. Fund raising for this project is also now in progress.

One cannot deny that over the past few years Bruntingthorpe has become a major force in the field of aircraft preservation and as such a distinct asset not only to the county but also the country as a whole. One would hope that in the future it is permitted to go from strength to strength.

With her bomb bay open and a poignant message within, Avro Vulcan B.2 XH558 makes a pass over Bruntingthorpe, prior to landing, 23rd March 1993. Author

A view of Bruntingthorpe, 1997, looking south west. Compare this with the vertical view taken in 1945. Author

Close-up view of the 'Butler' hangar and its hard standings, looking north west. On the dispersals can be seen, among a host of smaller jets, the Victor, Vulcan, TriStar and Super Guppy. Beyond the threshold of runway 24 can be seen the huge area used for the storage of production motor cars. In between the car storage park and the 'Butler' hangar can be discerned the track of the former cross runway and it is just traceable again in the immediate foreground. Author

Bruntingthorpe-based Units and Aircraft

No.29 Operational Training Unit
From 24.5.43 to 27.5.45   Codes 'NT-' and 'TF-'
Vickers Wellington III X3306, X3307, X3337, X3368, X3421, X3543, X3549, X3553, X3562, X3659, X3765, X3784, X3801, X3812, X3818, X3871, X3872, X3879, X3886, X3887 'E', X3928, X3962, Z1604 'T', Z1664, Z1668, Z1677, Z1734, BJ586, BJ721, BJ757, BJ759, BJ781, BJ782, BJ791, BJ832, BJ838, BJ847, BJ882, BJ905, BJ909, BJ914, BJ922, BJ960, BJ967 'F', BJ978, BK135, BK181, BK191, BK195, BK197, BK204, BK212, BK260, BK334, BK337, BK388, BK393, BK407, BK431 'J', BK437, BK438, BK442, BK444, BK452, BK465, BK469, BK497 'O', BK500, BK545, BK548, BK549, BK550, BK552, BK555, BK563 'G', DF543, DF625, DF669, DF674.
Vickers Wellington X HE156, HE209, HE275, HE282, HE286, HE372, HE473, HE785, HE788, HE847, HE848, HZ412, HZ477, HZ483, JA448, JA449, JA456, JA457, JA466, LN159, LN160, LN175, LN176, LN177, LN178, LN179, LN452, LN455, LN534, LN551, LN569, LN589, LN621, LN646, LN822, LN860, LP300, LP302, LP328, LP332, LP342, LP402, LP413, LP432, LP433, LP434, LP647, LR128, LR129, ME978, MF313, MF314, MF315, MF527, MF528, MF565, MF588, MS474, MS480, NA799, NA856, NA858, NA917, NA918, NA919, NA923, NC648, NC706, NC733, PE915, PE927, PE960, PE961, PE963, PE964, PG175, PG176, PG324, PG346, PG347.

Avro Anson I	N5064, R9606
Airspeed Oxford I	NM592
Airspeed Oxford II	N4760
Boulton Paul Defiant I	AA327
Supermarine Spitfire V	EP244
De Havilland Tiger Moth II	DE431
Hawker Hurricane IIC	BW973, LF741, LF744, LF762, MW352, MW353, MW356
Miles Martinet TT.1	HP434, HP435, JN427, JN506, MS643, MS871
Miles Master II	DK889, DL460, EM328
Westland Lysander IIIA	V9800, V9899, V9901

No.1683 Bomber Defence Training Flight
From 5.6.43 to 3.2.44   Code 'FP-'

Curtiss Tomahawk I	AH775, AH775, AH836, AH842, AH853, AH864
Curtiss Tomahawk IIA	AH882, AH884, AH899 'F', AH929, AH941

Power Jets (Research & Development) Limited

Avro Lancaster II	LL735
Gloster Meteor F.1	EE215, EE221
Gloster Meteor F.3	EE249, EE291
Vickers Wellington II	W5389, W5518
Handley Page Halifax VII	RG817
De Havilland Dominie I	X7489
De Havilland Tiger Moth I	T5901
Miles Magister I	L8051

Armstrong Siddeley Motors Limited
Avro Lancaster III	ND784/G

M44 Gliding School
Slingsby Cadet TX.1	VF191
Slingsby Tutor TX.2	VW535

308th Bomb Wing, SAC, USAF
Operation 'Snow Flurry'   From 10.3.58 to 16.3.58
Boeing B-47E Stratojet   30+ deployed; confirmed a/c: 53-1870, 53-1874, 53-1883, 53-1888, 53-1899, 53-2114, 53-2123, 53-2382, 53-2383, 53-2385, 53-2387, 53-2390, 53-2414

Rare view of a 29 Operational Training Unit Wellington (coded 'TF-O' or 'TF-Q') out on a Bruntingthorpe dispersal. via Brandon White

100th Bomb Wing, SAC, USAF
'Reflex Action' Alert Rotated Aircraft   From 1.1.59 to 30.6.59
Boeing B-47E Stratojet   51-5224, 51-5240, 51-7064, 52-0048, 52-0072, 52-0073, 52-0104, 52-0210, 52-0270, 52-0278, 52-0300, 52-0487, 53-0678, 53-1844, 53-1862, 53-1875, 53-1879, 53-1907, 53-1908, 53-1924, 53-1972, 53-1977, 53-2113, 53-2117, 53-2136, 53-2144, 53-2158, 53-2373, 53-4231, 53-4237, 53-4244, 53-6194, 53-6233.

96th Bomb Wing, SAC, USAF
'Reflex Action' Alert Rotated Aircraft   From 1.7.59 to 23.7.59
Boeing B-47E Stratojet   51-2441, 51-5218, 52-0068, 52-0226, 53-1849, 53-1852, 53-2038, 53-2295, 53-2336, 53-6193

19th Tactical Reconnaissance Squadron, USAFE
From 25.8.59 to 14.8.62
Douglas RB-66B Destroyer   53-0416, 53-0430, 53-0443, 54-0420, 54-0421, 54-0426, 54-0429, 54-0430, 54-0434, 54-0435, 54-0438, 54-0439, 54-0440, 54-0441, 54-0442, 54-0445, 54-0446, 54-0447, 54-0506, 54-0507, 54-0510, 54-0511, 54-0524, 54-0545

Base Flight
Douglas C-47 Skytrain	43-30678
Douglas C-47B Skytrain	43-48673
Lockheed T-33A	51-8754
de Havilland Canada	52-6132 (frequently detached from
L-20A Beaver	HQ 10th TRW, Alconbury)

No.1 Squadron, RAF   From 20.5.70 to 22.5.70
Forward Operating Location evaluation exercise
Hawker Siddeley Harrier GR.1   XV744, XV754, XV776, XV777, XV788 (all from RAF Wittering).

Serious Accidents to Bruntingthorpe-based Acft

9.6.43 Lysander IIIA V9901 29 OTU
While on a target towing exercise the pilot overshot the narrowest part of the landing ground at Holbeach Range and crashed into the seabank. No injuries.

26.6.43 Wellington X HE372 29 OTU
One mile NW of Gilmorton village. Unable to maintain height due to runaway airscrew on one engine. Aircraft Cat.E, all crew slight injuries.

29.6.43 Wellington III Z1668 29 OTU
Glebe Farm, Lutterworth. Crashed in field due to engine failure.

2.7.43 Wellington III BK437 29 OTU
Flew into high ground two miles south of Mountford Farm near Wellesbourne Mountford at 0245 after having been diverted from base following a night cross country exercise. Aircraft caught fire on striking ground. Cat.E.

4.7.43 Wellington III X3871 29 OTU
Crashed on landing at Bruntingthorpe.

7.7.43 Wellington III BK179 29 OTU
Cawston, three miles SW of Rugby. Also reported as near Dunchurch, Warwicks. Wheels up forced-landing after engines failed. Aircraft Cat.E, crew uninjured.

23.7.43 Tomahawk I AH864 1683 BDTF
After experiencing an engine fire in mid-air pilot baled out at low altitude and suffered severe injuries. AH864 crashed near Arnesby and was burnt out.

15.8.43 Wellington III X3786 29 OTU
Aircraft diverted to Wittering, Northants, to make a flapless approach on long runway. Hydraulics suspected unserviceable. Crashed while on approach due to fuel starvation from mishandled supply.

17.8.43 Wellington III BK550 29 OTU
Made a downwind landing at Bitteswell, overshot and crashed. No casualties. Cat.E.

29.8.43 Wellington III BK431 'J' 29 OTU
Near Oakham, Rutland. Port wing folded up over the starboard, aircraft disintegrated in mid-air. Six crew and one ATC Cadet killed.

29.8.43 Wellington III BJ967 29 OTU
Tasked with bombing ammo dump in the Forêt d'Eper-lecques, North of St Omer. Returning when fire in starboard engine forced ditching off Newhaven. One survivor.

6.9.43 Wellington III BK442 29 OTU
Engine caught fire and belly-landed in field near Bitteswell. No casualties but aircraft destroyed by fire.

7.9.43 Wellington III BK497 'O' 29 OTU
Ditched off Pembroke coast on navigational exercise.

25.9.43 Wellington X JA448 29 OTU
Near Walton. Crashed soon after take off at 0130 hours. All crew killed.

1.10.43 Tomahawk IIA AH941 1683 BDTF
Crashed in forced-landing at Grandborough, Warks.

20.10.43 Wellington III BK549 29 OTU
Caught fire in air when on 'Bullseye' exercise. Crashed at Basingstoke, Hampshire. All crew killed.

6.11.43 Wellington X LN551 29 OTU
Engine cut and forced-landed in bad weather at Naseby, crew all injured. Aircraft a write off.

10.11.43 Wellington . . . . 29 OTU
Overshot runway at Desborough while on cross country exercise. Cat.E.

18.12.43 Tomahawk IIA AH884 1683 BDTF
Crashed in forced-landing at Doncaster, short of fuel.

22.12.43 Wellington III LN160 29 OTU
Wigsley. Crashed while attempting to land on one engine. Aircraft Cat.E. Crew uninjured.

5.1.44 Tomahawk I AH842 1683 BDTF
Collided with tractor while taxying at Desborough.

28.1.44 Wellington III X3962 29 OTU
Hit tree in emergency landing near Bruntingthorpe. Cat.E. Crew uninjured.

24.3.44 Wellignton III X3337 29 OTU
Chipping Warden. Forced landing after port engine failure. Aircraft burst into flames on landing and burnt out. Crew status not recorded.

11.4.44 Martinet TT.I JN427 29 OTU
Overturned and written off when engine cut on approach to Bitteswell. Two injured.

8.5.44 Wellington X LN646 29 OTU
Overshot landing at Bruntingthorpe. Damaged beyond repair.

17.5.11 Wellington X MF314 29 OTU
While on navigation exercise dived into ground out of cloud near USAAF airfield at Metfield. Aircraft Cat.E. All crew killed.

14.6.44 Wellington X MS480 and LN 860 29 OTU
Both aircraft destroyed in hangar fire at Bruntingthorpe.

26.6.44 Wellington X MF528 29 OTU
Unable to maintain height after port engine caught fire. Pilot ordered crew to bale out all landed safely with no injuries. Crashed four miles north of Thorney, Lincs.

11.7.44 Wellington III X3306 29 OTU
Bitteswell. Port undercarriage collapsed, aircraft burnt out and was written off.

8.9.44 Wellington III BK552 29 OTU
Near Oswestry, Shropshire. Dived into ground from 1,500ft. Aircraft destroyed, crew all killed.

28.9.44 Wellington X LP342 29 OTU
Branton, near Finningley. Broke up in mid-air and completely disintegrated. Crew status not recorded.

15.10.44 Wellington III BK555 29 OTU
Near Bruntingthorpe village. Fuel starvation caused both engines to fail. Aircraft Cat.E, crew status not recorded.

17.10.44 Wellington III X3879 29 OTU
Near Bitteswell. Starboard engine failure while on approach, due to faulty magneto. Aircraft Cat.E. Crew status not recorded.

19.10.44 Wellington X LP332 29 OTU
Near Castle Donington airfield. Aircraft iced up, became uncontrollable and broke up in inverted dive. One survivor.

19.10.44 Wellington X MF527 29 OTU
Upper Heyford, Oxfordshire. Crashed attempting single engine overshoot. Aircraft Cat.E. Crew status not recorded.

5.1.45 Wellington III BJ909 29 OTU
Flew into ground near Kimcote village while on approach. Aircraft burnt out, one survivor.

17.1.45 Wellington X NC706 29 OTU
Walton Village. Aircraft burnt out, all crew killed.

1.2.45 Wellington X LP300 29 OTU
Braunstone. After suffering engine failure the pilot attempted an emergency landing but overshot and crashed through boundary hedge. One crew member was injured.

7.2.45 Wellington X HE286 29 OTU
Engine cut on overshoot, crashlanded at Gilmorton.

11.2.45 Wellington X JA457 29 OTU
Shearsby. Pilot unable to maintain height on one engine. Aircraft Cat E. Crew status not recorded.

19.2.45 Hurricane IIC LF741 29 OTU
Overshot landing into ditch at Bruntingthorpe. Damaged beyond repair.

4.3.45 Wellington X LN178 29 OTU
Near Shearsby. Aircraft written off. Crew status not recorded. Crashed supposedly due to engine fire but no trace of this on investigation.

13.3.45 Wellington X LP402 29 OTU
Conflicting reports as to cause and place of loss. Official source gives cause as loss of oil pressure, crashed near North Killingholme airfield. Other source gives cause as overshot landing and undercarriage raised to stop, Bruntingthorpe.

22.3.45 Wellington X NA917 29 OTU
Lost height while carrying out single-engined flying practice and crashed within outer circle at Bruntingthorpe. Aircraft Cat.E.

2.4.45 Wellington X LN159 29 OTU
Hit trees while low flying four miles SSW Bruntingthorpe airfield. Aircraft Cat.E. Six crew killed, one died later, one seriously injured.

21.7.45 Meteor F.3 EE291 Power Jets
While engaged in a flying display during an employees Gala Day at Whetstone, the aircraft crashed at very high speed and disintegrated off Hospital Lane, Blaby. The company's chief test pilot, Squadron Leader A O Moffatt was killed in the accident.

14.12.59 RB-66B Destroyer 54-0421 19th TRS, USAF
Returning from Alconbury, Huntingdonshire, when it crashed in a valley on Welsh Myres Farm, about ½ mile from Skeffington. All three crew killed.

16.3.61 RB-66B Destroyer 54-0430 19th TRS, USAF
On a training flight when it disappeared. Believed to have crashed in the sea off Terschelling Island, Netherlands. No survivors.

Bruntingthorpe Armed Forces Open Day, 28th May 1960

Aircraft in the Static Display

Avro Vulcan B.1 *	XH501		RAF, 617 Squadron, Scampton
Convair F-102A Delta Dagger	56-1247	'FC-247'	USAF, 525th TFS, 86th Air Division
De Havilland Vampire T.11 *	XE876	'VT'	RAF, Central Flying School
De Havilland Vampire T.11 *	XH322	'VK'	RAF, CFS, Little Rissington
Douglas C-47D	0-330678		Bruntingthorpe Base Flight 10th TRW
Douglas C-124C Globemaster II	52-0956		USAF, Military Air Transport Service
Douglas RB-66B Destroyer	54-0440	'BB-440'	USAF, 19th TRS, 10th TRW
Fairchild C-119G Flying Boxcar	53-3220		USAF, 322nd Air Division, Evreux
Gloster Javelin FAW.9	XH882	'L'	RAF, 25 Squadron, Waterbeach
Handley Page Hastings C.1A *	TG581	'MOGC-F'	RAF, 242 OCU, Thorney Island
Hunting Jet Provost T.3 *	XM411	'R-G'	RAF, CFS, Little Rissington
Lockheed C-130A Hercules *	56-0545		USAF, 322nd Air Division
Lockheed T-33A	51-8754	'TR-754'	USAF, Bruntingthorpe Base Flight
McDonnell F-101A Voodoo	54-1483	'FB-483'	USAF, 91st TFS, 81TFW
North American F-86D Sabre	52-3946	'FU-946'	USAF, 513th FIS, 86th Air Division
NAF-100D Super Sabre	55-3694	'FW-694'	USAF, 55th Tactical Fighter Squadron
Percival Provost T.1	WV681	'P-F'	RAF, CFS, Little Rissington
Bristol Sycamore 3A	G-AMWH		BEA, Pleasure flying

Flying Display

In above list, * also took part in the flying display.

Avro Shackleton T.4	WB844	'MOTU-L'	RAF, Maritime OTU, Kinloss
Boeing KB-50J Superfortress	49-0368		USAF, 420th ARS,
Bristol Britannia C.1	XL637	'637'	RAF, 99 Squadron, Lyneham
De Havilland Comet C.2	XK699	'699'	RAF, 216 Squadron, Lyneham
Douglas B-66B Destroyer †	54-0503	'BB-503'	USAF, 86th TBS, 47th TBW
Douglas RB-66B	54-0438	'BB-438'	USAF, 19th TRS (with 54-0507)
Hawker Hunter F.6	XE532	'L'	RAF, 92 Squadron aerobatic team, (with XF520 'K', XF522 'D', XG238 'F' or 'P')
McDonnell F-101C Voodoo †	56-0005	'FB-005'	USAF, 81st Tactical Fighter Wing
NA F-100D Super Sabre †	55-2892	'FW-892'	USAF, 48th Tactical Fighter Wing

† Flew in air refuelling demonstration with the KB-50J. Four RB-66s, four F-100s, four F-101s and 12 F-100s all USAFE, took part in a stream flypast, in that order.

Aircraft parked on the northern dispersals of the Airfield, for the day. *
Douglas RB-66B Destroyer   53-416   USAF, 19th Tactical Reconnaissance Sqn with 53-0430, 53-0443, 54-0420, 54-0430, 54-0434, 54-0439, 54-0441, 54-0442, 54-0506, 54-0510, 54-0511, and 54-0543. * Other than for the 'Snow Flurry' exercise, this was the only time these dispersals were known to have been used by the USAF.

Aircraft in the 'Butler' Hangar
(undergoing modifications by Field Aircraft Services working party from Wymeswold)

Douglas RB-66B Destroyer	54-521	USAF, 1st TRS, Alconbury, with 54-0522
Douglas RB-66B Destroyer	54-530	USAF, 30th TRS, Alconbury, with 54-0588

C Walton (Aviation Division) Ltd
British Aviation Heritage
World Aviation Heritage

Aircraft type	Identity		Arrived	Notes
Aerospacelines Super Guppy 201	F-BTGV		1.7.96	–
Avro Vulcan B.2	XH558		23.3.93	–
Avro Vulcan B.2MRR	XH537	nose	2.6.97	on loan
Blackburn Buccaneer S.2B	XX900		27.10.94	–
Boeing 747-100	F-BPVE		23.9.94	see below
Boeing 747-100	G-AWNA		14.11.98	see below
De Havilland Comet 4C 'Canopus'	XS235		3.10.97	–
Handley Page Victor K.2	XM715		19.11.93	–
Lockheed TriStar 1	TF-ABP		4.6.96	see below
SEPECAT Jaguar GR.1	XZ382		22.2.99	on loan
TS-11 Iskra	1018		5.7.96	–
Vickers-Supermarine Spitfire Tr IX	G-BMSB		.95	Left 6.8.97
Vickers Valiant BK.1	XD875	nose	12.93	on loan

The 747 F-BPVE was used for explosive testing on 17th May 1997 and the final sections were removed by April 1998. TriStar 1 TF-ABP and 747 G-AWNA are being used as a source of spares for flying examples.

Loughborough-Leicestershire Aircraft Museum
Phœnix Aviation Museum

Aircraft type	Identity	Arrived	Departed
Avro XIX	G-AGWE	.1.84	.86
Blackburn Buccaneer S.1	XN964	20.11.83	.3.88
Dassault Mystère IVA	No.85	20.11.83	see below
Hawker Hunter F.51	E-407	20.11.83	.10.85
NA F-100D Super Sabre	54-2239	20.11.83	1.11.88

The Mystère remains on site in the care of British Aviation Heritage.

Vintage Aircraft Team

Aircraft type	Identity		Arrived	Departed
Auster AOP.9	G-AYUA	(ex-XK416)	.10.94	see below
De Havilland Tiger Moth	?	frame		see below
De Havilland Vampire FB.6	G-MKVI	(ex-VZ304)	.1.95	3.11.96
De Havilland Vampire FB.9	WL505		.1.95	.2.96
De Havilland Vampire T.11	G-VTII	(ex-WZ507)	mid-93	3.11.96
De Havilland Vampire T.11	G-DHYY	(ex-WZ553)	?	3.10.96
De Havilland Venom FB.50	G-VNOM	(ex-J-1632)	?	?
De Havilland Venom FB.54	G-BLKA	(ex-WR410)	.10.94	5.11.96
De Havilland Canada Chipmunk T.10	WP845		mid 93	4.11.96
Hawker Hunter T.7	XL578		1.2.93	96
Hunting Jet Provost T.3A	G-TORE	(ex-XM405)	?	.7.95
Lockheed T-33A	G-NASA		.10.93	.11.96
Miles Student 2	G-APLK		.1.95	.10.96
Morane Saulnier Alcyon	G-SHOW		.8.95	.8.96

Note: At least one Auster AOP.9 frame and two, perhaps more, Tiger Moth frames were present.

Miscellaneous Aircraft

Aircraft type	Identity		Arrived	Departed	Owner
BAC Jet Provost T.5	XW352		?	.5.96	–
BAC Jet Provost T.5A	XW355		16.8.95	.5.96	–
Beech D.18S	G-BKRN		23.3.96	–	BR
Beech C-45G	G-BKRG		10.3.98	–	BR
De Havilland Chipmunk T.10	WP845	ex-VAT	4.11.96	–	DT
De Havilland Sea Devon C.20	G-SDEV		.9.95	13.10.96	CAP
De Havilland Vampire T.11	XD459	nose	16.8.91	.4.99	–
English Electric Canberra B.2/6	G-BVWC	(WK163)	21.1.95	26.3.00	CAP
English Electric Canberra B.2/6	G-BVIC	(XH568)	19.11.93	–	CAP
English Electric Canberra B(I).8	G-BVXC	(WT333)	28.1.95	–	WP
English Electric Lightning F.3	XP703	nose	.8.89	.97	LPG
English Electric Lightning T.5	ZF595	nose	28.4.97	–	AB
English Electric Lightning T.5	ZF596	nose	?	–	AB
English Electric Lightning F.6	XR728		24.6.88	–	LPG
English Electric Lightning F.6	XS904		21.1.93	–	LPG
English Electric Lightning F.6	XS932	nose	.11.91	9.11.96	LPG
Hawker Hunter F.6A	XK149		.9.94	–	CF
Hawker Hunter T.8M	XL603		.1.95	7.3.00	CF
Hawker Siddeley Buccaneer S.2B	XX894		27.10.94	12.11.96	BPS
Hawker Siddeley Harrier GR.3	XV759	nose	.9.99	–	GS
Hawker Siddeley Harrier GR.3	XV763	nose	4.8.96	–	GS
Hawker Siddeley Harrier GR.3	XV810	nose	?	–	GS
Hunting Jet Provost T.3A	XN584		27.3.95	–	MSB
Luscombe Silvaire 8E	D-EFYR		.88	4.98	–
McDonnell Douglas Phantom FGR.2	XV489	nose	4.93	.97	PRG
McDonnell Douglas Phantom FGR.2	XV490	nose	4.93	10.11.99	–
Piper Aztec 250D	G-BBGE		1.93	5.96	–
Saab Safir 91D	PH-RLR		3.95	.97	–
SBLim-2 (MiG-15bis)	09008		7.10.95	6.96	–
Vickers Viscount 838	XT575	nose	2.94	14.1.96	CFH

Key to Owners:
AB - Andrew Brodie; BPS - Buccaneer Preservation Society; BR - Beech Restorations; CAP - Classic Aviation Projects; CF - Clive Forshaw; CFH - Cockpits For Hire; DT - Dave Thomas; GS - Graham Smith; LPG - Lightning Preservation Group; MSB - M & S Bent; PRG - Phantom Restoration Group; WP - Wintle & Perks.

Phœnix Aviation

Aircraft type	Identity		Arrived	Departed
Blackburn Buccaneer S.1	XN928	nose	24.2.96	.4.99
Boeing 707-436	G-APFG	nose	4.00	–
De Havilland Sea Vixen FAW.2	XJ494		22.6.99	–
De Havilland Sea Vixen FAW.2	XN650	nose	?	8.10.96
De Havilland Sea Vixen D.3	XS577		4.3.97	.4.99
English Electric Canberra PR.7	WH775		.4.93	8.10.95
English Electric Canberra PR.7	WT536	nose	31.8.91	12.5.96
English Electric Canberra PR.9	XH136	nose	.10.93	–
English Electric Canberra B.15	WH960	nose	.3.92	?
English Electric Canberra B.15	WH984	nose	.3.92	1.3.97
English Electric Canberra E.15	WH957	nose	.3.92	.12.93
English Electric Canberra E.15	WH964	nose	31.8.91	25.11.96
English Electric Canberra T.17	WJ565	nose	.3.92	1.2.97
English Electric Canberra T.17	WJ576	nose	.3.96	9.11.99
English Electric Canberra T.17	WK102	nose	.3.92	11.93
English Electric Lighting T.5	XV328	nose	.12.94	–
English Electric Lighting F.6	XS899	nose	.12.94	20.3.96
English Electric Lighting F.6	XS923	nose	.12.94	?
Fairey Gannet AS. . .	?		.11.91	.93
Folland Gnat T.1	XP503		.1.92	24.1.00
Folland Gnat T.1	XP540		.1.92	.8.95
Folland Gnat T.1	XR569		?	–
Gloster Meteor TT.20	WM292		.6.96	23.3.99
Handley Page Victor B.1A	XH592	nose	.10.94	–
Hawker Hunter F.6	N-202	nose	6.99	?
Hawker Hunter F.6	XE656		12.8.98	25.10.98
Hawker Hunter F.6	XG290		.11.91	18.1.92
Hawker Hunter T.7	ET-272	nose	?	.3.98
Hawker Hunter F.51	E-427		.11.90	–
Hawker Hunter F.58	J-4091		.96	–
Hawker Sea Hawk FGA.6	WV795		.8.95	–
Hawker Sea Hawk FGA.6	WV826		2.2.96	11.8.99
Hawker Sea Hawk FGA.6	WV838		?	–
Hawker Sea Hawk FGA.6	XE327		30.3.99	–
Hawker Siddeley Andover CC.2	XS791		.3.95	22.7.00
Hawker Siddeley Buccaneer S.2	?	nose	?	.4.99
Hawker Siddeley Buccaneer S.2A	XT277		.8.93	10.93
Hawker Siddeley Buccaneer S.2B	XV163	nose	.9.93	11.3.97
Hawker Siddeley Harrier GR.3	XV738		14.6.95	10.7.98
Hawker Siddeley Harrier GR.3	XV747		.91	.93
Hawker Siddeley Harrier GR.3	XZ967		14.6.95	10.4.96
Hawker Siddeley Harrier GR.3	ZD668		11.7.95	–
Hawker Siddeley Harrier GR.3	ZD670		11.7.95	mid 96
Hawker Siddeley Harrier T.4	XW270		7.6.96	–
Hunting Jet Provost T.3	XM355		.1.92	?
Hunting Jet Provost T.3	XM376		.5.93	.4.95
Hunting Jet Provost T.3	XM408		.1.92	spring 95
Hunting Jet Provost T.3	XN512		19.12.95	mid-97
Hunting Jet Provost T.3A	XM425		.3.95	13.9.95
Hunting Jet Provost T.3A	XN494		8.6.98	.6.99
Hunting Jet Provost T.4	XP556		?	14.2.96
Hunting Jet Provost T.4	XP563		.3.95	8.1.96
Hunting Jet Provost T.4	XP557		.3.92	12.9.94
Hunting Jet Provost T.4	XP642		2.9.95	.6.97
Hunting Jet Provost T.4	XP688		27.3.95	13.2.97
Hunting Jet Provost T.4	XS176		16.7.99	.8.99
Hunting Jet Provost T.4	XS181		31.3.95	1.12.96
Hunting Jet Provost T.4	XS217		23.3.95	–
Hunting Jet Provost T.5	XS231		.11.90	.6.99
McDonnell Douglas Phantom FG.1	XT874		?	.2.94
Percival Provost T.1	XF844		31.3.95	–
Scottish Aviation Bulldog T.1	XX669		.11.91	30.6.98
Shorts 360	G-ROOM		.93	.10.93
Westland Wasp HAS.1	XT439		.12.95	17.1.96
Westland Wasp HAS.1	XT793		?	.4.94
Westland Wessex HU.5	XT770		25.11.92	.93
Westland Wessex HU.5	XT755		?	.1.96
Westland Wessex HU.5	XT766		?	–
Westland Whirlwind HAS.7	XN385		6.8.95	15.2.97
Westland Whirlwind HAR.10	XN126		1.12.97	14.1.99
Westland Whirlwind HAR.10	XP361		20.3.96	2.7.97

Classic Aviation Project's Canberra B.2/6 XH568 (G-BVIC) arrives with panache from Bedford, 19th November 1993. Author

The Phœnix Air Museum's F-100D Super Sabre during removal by a USAF crew for a new life at Hahn, West Germany, November 1988. Brandon White

A view of part of Neville Martin's Phœnix Aviation area at the height of his acquisitions. In the foreground are four Canberra nose sections, with a mixture of Jet Provosts and Gnats at the rear. Be it an entire airframe, a cockpit section or a much-needed component for a restoration project, Neville has developed a reputation for being able to track it down. Author

Chapter Seven

Castle Donington – East Midlands Airport

FROM BEING a standard RAF satellite station which was allowed to fall into disrepair after the end of the Second World War, to become a successful major airport, is something of a Cinderella story. In all probability very few of the travellers using the East Midlands Airport today are aware of this and fewer still that associations between the site and aviation can be traced back to the First World War.

Late in 1916 a small landing ground covering approximately 20 acres was set up to help serve the needs of 38 Squadron in the Home Defence role. (The unit was flying a mixture of Royal Aircraft Factory BE.2s, BE.12s and FE.2s at this time.) The field was situated close to the south west corner of the present airport in the section currently occupied by the hangars and ancillary buildings of the maintenance area. Owing to a lack of documentary or other evidence it has proved impossible to deduce what, if any, use 38 Squadron made of the field. However, it is known that it was down graded to a day landing ground in mid-1917 and by 1918 its use had been dispensed with

entirely. It took 25 years and another war to bring flying back to the area.

To support the bomber offensive against the Third Reich during the Second World War a massive programme of airfield construction was commenced which reached its peak in the early 1940s. RAF Castle Donington was one of these new air bases.

In 1941 the as yet unbuilt station was selected as a satellite for Wymeswold, under construction a few miles to the east. Although Castle Donington was officially opened on New Year's Day 1943 the occasion was something of an anti-climax for on the eve of the occupation all the runways were condemned. It took six weeks before resurfacing was complete.

For the first ten days of 1943 no flying training was possible although the Vickers Wellingtons of 'C' Flight, 28 Operational Training Unit (OTU) had been able to fly in from Wymeswold on 2nd January. To bring the station up to strength, 'D' Flight was formed on 7th January mainly from personnel drafted in for the purpose from Finningley, Yorkshire. From the 11th limited flying

Tracing its roots back to 1938, British Midland celebrated its 60th anniversary in 1998. During that year, the airline introduced the Airbus A320 and A321 into service, underlining its '60 Years of Excellence' and 'The Airline for Europe' banners. A321-231 G-MIDF illustrated.
British Midland

began to take place continuing to increase as more sections of runway were passed as serviceable until by the end of the month almost the full programme of conversion flying was in progress.

Special exercises formed a part of every crew's training; the aim of some, such as anti-aircraft, searchlight or fighter affiliation, is fairly obvious but the object of others with intriguing code names like 'Bullseye', 'Eric', 'Grand National' and 'Nickelling' is much less apparent. 'Nickelling', or in plain language, propaganda leaflet dropping operations, were consistently carried out by crews from Castle Donington. So much paper was stocked ready to be deposited over enemy-held territory that a special store was needed to house it.

Two of Castle Donington's Wellingtons are known to have been lost during the course of this type of operation. The first aircraft which failed to return had been to 'Nickel' in the Paris area on 3rd June 1943. On the return journey it developed engine trouble which forced it to be ditched 35 miles south south east of St Catherine's Point, Isle of Wight. Five of the crew were later rescued after spending eight hours in their dinghy but the sixth member was missing, presumed to have gone down with the aircraft. Enemy action was responsible for the loss of the second Wellington on 11th August. It too had been on a paper round over France when it was hit by anti-aircraft fire. Severely damaged, it was unable to reach England and came down in the Channel off Shoreham, Sussex. Only two of the crew survived to be picked up by air sea rescue launches.

The other exercises, so necessary for assessing crew progress and proficiency, were also not without danger and many

casualties were sustained in the execution of these tasks. Records show that at least four aircraft and 13 crew members were lost while carrying out specific exercises from Castle Donington during the 20 months that 28 OTU operated there.

In the autumn of 1944 the organisation at the airfield underwent a drastic change; although the station continued to function in a training role, crews were no longer turned out for Bomber Command. Following the satisfactory progress of the Allied advance through Europe and a successful outcome of the war in sight aircrew requirements changed. With this in mind Castle Donington, still a satellite of Wymeswold, was transferred to 44 Group, RAF Transport Command, in October 1944. On the 18th of the month 28 OTU was disbanded and in its place 108 (Transport) OTU was formed.

To enable the new unit to carry out its duties a re-equipment programme was instituted, with the result that the once ever-

present 'Wimpys' disappeared from the airfield circuit to be replaced by Douglas Dakotas. It took some weeks for the unit to re-equip, but by 13th December the first course of conversion flying had been concluded.

Whether it was due to the constant round of circuits and bumps, faulty materials, the elements or a combination of several factors unit records do not state, but whatever the cause, early in 1945, the runways began to present problems once more. Difficulties began in March when 500 yards of the main runway became unserviceable. Throughout April and May the trouble persisted and by June it was even worse; the unsound area had extended to 800 yards. Urgent measures to prevent further deterioration were at last put in hand and by the end of July the major faults had been rectified.

As a unit, 108 (T)OTU had a relatively short life for after ten months it was disbanded and redesignated 1382 (Transport)

Opposite page and below:
Vertical survey photographs of Castle Donington dated 11th August 1945. Lined up on the western edge are seven Dakotas.

Area (A) denotes approximately the 20 acres used by the Royal Flying Corps' landing ground, 1916-17. The tower and its designator 'CD' were located on the western boundary (B).

The south western dispersals cut through the original Kegworth to Melbourne road (C). The current airport road, the A453, uses the section of road marked at (D) while the line (E) shows the approximate location of the A453 coming off the roundabout west of Junction 23A of the M1. The minor road south to Diseworth is at (F). The extension of Runway 27/09 ends approximately at (G). In recent months there has been a radical alteration to the western end of the airfield and its road system. DoE

Early equipment for British Midland at East Midlands Airport was the venerable Douglas Dakota. Dakota IV G-AOGZ, named Darleydale, is illustrated. B Lewis

British Midland Airways operated Vickers Viscount turboprop-powered airliners for 20 years. Illustrated are Series 813s G-AZLR and G-AZNC, part of the cache acquired from South African Airways. Mike Everton

Conversion Unit on 10th August 1945. At the same time control of Castle Donington passed into the hands of 4 Group, Transport Command. Neither of these changes had any great effect on the type of training carried out at the station but later on, in November a straight through system was adopted whereby crews undergoing type conversion received the full course at either Castle Donington or Wymeswold.

When the cessation of hostilities in the Far East brought an end to the Second World War the RAF was left with many airfields it no longer needed. Some had already been phased out following the Allied victory in Europe but now many more were closed, never to be used again. As there was still a requirement for transport crews, Castle Donington remained active but as the months went by the RAF continued to contract in size and in due course it was the turn of Castle Donington to become redundant. No.1382 (T)CU withdrew from the airfield during September 1946 to be centred at Wymeswold (Chapter Twenty-Four), all service equipment was then removed and the station closed down. Little further interest was shown in the site for a number of years and buildings and runways were allowed to fall into disrepair.

The disused airfield almost received a visitor on 22nd July 1952 when Gloster Meteor F.4 VT264 of 215 Advanced Flying School, based at Finningley, Yorkshire, ran out of fuel and attempted to make an emergency landing. Unfortunately the aircraft hit a tree while on the approach to the runway and crashed, killing the pilot.

RAF Castle Donington – 1st December 1944

Latitude	52° 49' 45" N
Longitude	1° 19' 30" W
Height above Sea Level	290ft
Command	Transport (RAF)
Nearest Railway Station	Kegworth (LMS) 3½ miles
Function	Operational Training Unit (Satellite)

Affiliated Airfields   Wymeswold (Parent)

Landing Area – Runways

QDM	Dimensions	Extensibility	Remarks
281°	2,000 x 50 yards	2,400 yards	Extension entails
235°	1,400 x 50 yards	1,700 yards	demolition of
336°	1,100 x 50 yards	1,100 yards	farm buildings
Type of Surface	Concrete		

Permanent Landmarks

By Day	Nil
By Night	Nil

Permanent Obstructions Nil

Facilities

Airfield Lighting	Mk.II
Flying Control	Yes

Accommodation   All temporary buildings

Technical	Hangars		Hardstandings	
	Type	No	Type	No
	T.2	1	Hvy Bmbr	27
	B.1	1		

Domestic	Officers	SNCOs	ORs	Total
RAF	60	212	644	916
WAAF	2	8	180	190

RAF Castle Donington-based Units and Aircraft

No.28 Operational Training Unit
From 1.1.43 to 15.10.44   Codes: 'LB-', 'QN-', 'WY-'

No.108 (Transport) Operational Training Unit
From 10.10.44 to 10.8.45

No.1382 (Transport) Conversion Unit
From 10.8.45 to 31.5.46   Code: 'NU-'

For individual aircraft details, including accidents, see parent unit at Wymeswold, Chapter Twenty-Four.

In the late 1950s the only airfield in the East Midlands catering for civilian passenger traffic was Derby Corporation's airport at Burnaston, south west of the city. It was realised that this small grass airfield would be quite inadequate to cope with future trends in air transport so Nottingham Corporation suggested that a consortium of local authorities in the area be formed to investigate the possibility of financing and building a joint airport. Derby Borough Council, Derbyshire and Leicestershire County Councils, Nottingham City and Nottinghamshire County Councils all indicated an interest in the plan and following a series of meetings a Joint Committee was formed.

Faced with the task of assessing the commercial viability of an airport and the prospect of selecting a suitable site, the five authorities engaged a firm of consultant engineers to study the situation. When their report was submitted it contained the conclusion that for a civil airport capable of dealing with modern aircraft of medium haul size the former RAF airfield at Castle Donington was in an ideal location. They recommended that a single runway be laid initially of 6,000 feet in length with provision to extend to 9,500 to 10,000 feet.

The Joint Committee deliberated on the matter and decided to go ahead with the project. The five authorities agreed to share the capital cost, estimated at £1,375,000 and the running costs. Expenditure was apportioned at two ninths each with Leicestershire the odd man out and responsible for one ninth only. As a first step, the derelict airfield was acquired in June 1963 for the sum of £37,500. Then, following a public inquiry, planning permission was granted by the Minister of Housing and Local Government in February 1964. A contract worth over £82,000 was awarded to Richard Costain (Civil Engineering) Limited and on 9th March the site was handed over to the company for work to begin.

Costain's contract involved the clearance of the site, bulk earth moving of some 63,000 cubic yards and the breaking up and removal of the rotten runway system which had once been the source of so much trouble to the RAF. A new concrete runway, 5,850ft long by 150ft wide was to be laid together with taxiways 60ft wide and a terminal area 722ft long by 364ft wide. About 1½ miles of internal roads and parking areas for 850 cars were also to be provided.

Terminal buildings, an administration block, transmitter station, hangar, workshops and sundry other buildings were required and the Sutton in Ashfield firm of J Searson Limited were made responsible for the erection of these.

Also in 1964 an Airport Director was appointed. Eric C Dyer was the man chosen to fill the post. A former Second World War pilot with service in Fighter, Bomber and Transport Commands of the RAF, he had already gained considerable experience in airfield management while running Leavesden Aerodrome in Hertfordshire for the de Havilland organisation between 1947 and 1961 and then as Commandant of Southampton Airport, Hampshire. At the time of his appointment the administration buildings were not yet ready so in order that he and his staff could begin to shape up the organisation of the airport temporary office accommodation was found in Castle Donington. Eric Dyer was to be the airport's general manager until his retirement in July 1986. Eric was replaced by Terry Lovett who was the airport's managing director until 1997 when John Spooner took over.

After 13 months of intensive activity on the part of the contractors the airport was ready to begin to operate on 1st April 1965. There was a slight delay in the issue of a full Ministry of Civil Aviation Licence after a bulldozer engaged on last minute tidying up inadvertently cut through lighting cables feeding the lead-in lights. Repairs were soon made, next afternoon a licence was issued and East Midlands Airport (EMA) was in business. Almost four months later, on 21st July, the official opening took place when at a more formal ceremony a commemorative plaque was unveiled by His Royal Highness Prince Philip, Duke of Edinburgh.

From the outset EMA could boast of a resident airline. Long before the airport was built Derby Aviation, who then operated from the pre-war grass airfield at Burnaston, indicated their interest in the project. Facilities for their use were included in the planning and coincidental with the opening of the airport British Midland Airways (BMA), as they became in October 1964, moved their operations from Burnaston to EMA.

The company's inaugural flight into the airport was scheduled for the evening of 1st April but the mishap to the approach lighting caused the event to be postponed until next day when BMA's Handley Page Herald 203 G-ASKK landed after a flight from Glasgow. Increases in scheduled flights followed and in 1982 the airline became even more firmly established in the area when nearby Donington Hall was taken over as its headquarters. Over the years, BMA, under the guidance of Sir Michael Bishop, has constantly upgraded the aircraft it operates and continues to expand and prosper.

As part of this growth of the airline, the Airlines of Great Britain Group was established to administer all of the assets, including Manx Airlines, created by a combination of BMA and Air UK in 1982 and the Scottish regional carrier Loganair, that had been acquired in 1983. Some of these operations were later restructured again under the British Regional Airlines banner, but none of these really come into the EMA part of the story. The current logo is a stylish 'BM' and diamond and the airline is currently known as British Midland, having dropped the 'Airways'. All the portents are that aircraft in the airline's livery will be a firm fixture at EMA for the foreseeable future.

Over the years numerous airlines have operated from the airport. Some have since gone but others have taken their place. (See page 138). Much of EMA's traffic, both past and present has been generated by inclusive tour operators carrying holidaymakers to and from their various destinations.

Busy apron scene at EMA on 28th May 1973. In the foreground is Handley Page Herald Series 200 G-ATIG, of the type that opened operations at the airport. In the background is BMA Viscount G-AZNC and Air Bridge Carriers Merchantman G-APES and an AW Argosy. Mike Everton

With the advent of the Boeing 707 into the fleet, British Midland could conduct transatlantic group charters. Originally serving with the Australian airline QANTAS, G-BFLE spent most of its time with BMA flying on lease to other carriers. Alan J Wright

This has resulted in numerous colourful and interesting aircraft being seen on the airport's apron, including Lockheed TriStar, Airbus A330, Boeing 747, 757 and 777, but no visit has been more memorable than that of the supersonic airliner Concorde in 1979. On this the first of many visits, an estimated 60,000 spectators converged upon the airport causing traffic chaos for several miles around.

Increases in traffic have meant, in most years, a steady rise of passengers using the airport. During the first year of operation the number was approximately 96,000 but by 1995 the annual total had risen to 1.9 million and in May the following year, after 31 years of operation, the airport welcomed its 25 millionth passenger.

From the earliest days aircraft maintenance and overhaul has been catered for at EMA. The facilities associated with this industry are situated at the western end of the airfield in an area once occupied by the RAF technical site. Several companies are engaged in this work, chief among them being another long term airport resident Field Aviation Services who moved their activities from Wymeswold in 1968. Latterly known as Hunting Aviation Aircraft Engineering Division, the company was responsible for major contracts involving both civilian and service aircraft. Included in this work was a major contract for British Aerospace for the fitting out to customer requirements of the Jetstream family of twin-turboprop commuter airliners.

In 1984-85 there were high hopes that the company would be able to expand their operations at EMA in order to build the Hunting Firecracker turboprop trainer. This was a contender in a competition for an aircraft to replace the RAF's ageing Hunting Jet Provost trainers. Despite intense Parliamentary lobbying and partisan support, the contract, when announced, favoured the EMBRAER Tucano, a Brazilian aircraft, which was eventually license-built by Shorts in Belfast, Northern Ireland.

One of the more unusual tasks in which Fields were involved between October 1993 and October 1996 was the calibration of navigation and landing aids on RAF and RN bases. A small fleet of Hawker Siddeley Andover E.3s and E.3As were used by the Contract Services Division to carry out this duty and while they retained RAF markings civilian crews were employed.

In 1972 the freight haulier Sagittair closed down and Field Aircraft Services decided to take on their Hawker Siddeley Argosy freighters (see Chapter Three, *Production at Bitteswell*) and Air Bridge Carriers was born. A further change to the title was adopted in 1992 when the company became Hunting Cargo Airlines (HCA) to reflect its place within the Hunting group of companies. Following a rethink of business operations in 1997, the Hunting Group announced that the Aircraft Engineering Division would be put up for sale. Just prior to that HCA had moved from EMA to operate from Dublin, Ireland, and by June 1998

A surplus of Beagle 206s from the production line at Rearsby resulted in several seeking temporary storage at EMA. On Sunday 2nd April 1967, 206s G-AVAL and G-ATYW, both in white primer, were present, as were five other incomplete fuselages. Other inmates visible are Beagle E.3 G-ASCC, Piper PA-28 Cherokee 160 G-ARVW, De Havilland Dragon Rapide G-ALAX and Chipmunks G-AORW and G-APPM. Note the R-R Merlin engines, which are probably spares for British Midland's fleet of Canadair C-4 Argonauts.   Chris Salter

that was also up for sale. Unable to find a buyer for the maintenance business at EMA, the huge hangar complex was closed down by mid-1998. Currently, British Midland and other operators have been looking at the viability of taking over the site, in part or in whole, for airline maintenance work.

From the beginning flying tuition has also been a part of EMA life and this type of flying currently accounts for over 20,000 of the airport's movements annually. East Midlands and Donair Flying Clubs are presently engaged in this type of activity.

In the past there have been other businesses of this type one of which was the Nipper Flying School. This was an offshoot of Nipper Aircraft Limited, a small company set up to market a small single-seater of Belgian design, the Tipsy Nipper III. Nipper acquired a licence to build the diminutive aircraft in 1966 and sub-contracted the construction to Slingsby Aircraft of Kirbymoorside, Yorkshire under their designation of T.66. A total of 29 Nippers were produced, with an unknown number being assembled and test flown at the airport, while others made their first flights in Yorkshire. Nipper Aircraft ceased trading in May 1971.

In recent years, EMA has revelled in the sound of at least one Spitfire in residence or being air tested. Following the closure of their Hucknall site as a viable flying airfield, Rolls-Royce centred their communications flight at EMA and alongside this operated their Spitfire XIV RM689 (G-ALGT) which was a very popular performer at air displays and company events. Sadly, RM689 was lost in a fatal accident at Woodford, near Manchester, on 27th June 1992. Rolls were without a Spitfire for a while, but in late 1997 EMA again boasted a Spitfire in residence with the arrival of Mk.XIX PS853 (G-RRGN).

The Rolls-Royce presence at EMA has also attracted a variety of new airliner types – R-R powered of course – to the airport to show off to employees. One of the first such visits saw the third production Lockheed TriStar, N301EA, of America's Eastern Airlines, stop over from 3rd-7th June 1971, while on its way back to the USA from the Paris Air Show. The visit attracted over 20,000 people, and proved a huge morale booster for the many thousands of R-R employees and their dependents, who three months earlier had seen their company go into receivership and have to be baled out by the UK Government, following unforseen development problems with a fixed-price contract for the then new, but ultimately highly successful, RB.211 engine. The latest such visitation was by a Boeing 777 twin-jet, powered by Trent turbofans, in 1998.

Other Spitfires have also been associated with EMA. Nestled within the industrial area on the southern edge of the airport complex is Trent Aero, a company that for a long while specialised in the restoration to flying condition of Spitfires and other 'warbirds'. Two Spitfires that were restored by Trent Aero made their first flights from EMA's runway, Mk.XI PL983 (G-PRXI) on 17th July 1984 and Mk.IX MJ730 (G-HFIX) on 12th November 1988. Many other projects went through the EMA workshop, including detail parts for other restoration projects. Work in the 'warbird' world has always been subject to its 'ups' and 'downs' and in 1997 Trent Aero ceased such work, specialising instead on contract engineering development projects for the aerospace industry.

In order to cater for increasing numbers of larger aircraft wishing to use the airport and also keep pace with passenger growth decisions to expand the airport's resources were taken in April 1969. Almost £500,000 was expended on a runway extension to 7,500 feet, a parallel taxiway to its eastern end and the widening of existing taxiways to 75 feet. The contract, which was awarded to A Monk & Company, presented some problems for local inhabitants as it led to the closure of a road between Diseworth and Castle Donington while that from Diseworth to Kegworth was re-routed.

Approval for the use of the new runway was given by the Board of Trade on 23rd March 1970. Additional improvements were also carried out to the passenger concourse and these were finished in time to accommodate the Easter influx of passengers.

Another development of the taxiway system in 1981 added a further parallel section to the western end of the runway so obviating the need for aircraft to backtrack. In a later improvement scheme the passenger terminal received a £3.5 million facelift. Extensively refurbished and expanded, the building was officially opened by Her Royal Highness the Princess Anne on 5th December 1986, 21 years after her father had opened the original terminal.

The handling of air freight has also been a major factor in EMA's growth. From the very first, almost every year has seen an upward growth in this aspect of the airport's operations. A significant contributor to EMA's expansion in this field has been the Royal Mail. In May 1979 long distance mail distribution was switched from British Rail to airlines and EMA became one of the main centres in the postal network. Activity associated with this enterprise peaks between 11pm and 1am each night with eight aircraft arriving and departing at intervals. To deal with this expanding trade a purpose-built mail handling centre and associated apron extension was opened in 1985.

Spectator facilities have been in evidence at the airport from the beginning and in May 1979 a small collection of aircraft were put on view in a compound adjacent to the spectator enclosure. Set up by the Loughborough and Leicestershire Aircraft Museum these aircraft were present on the site until November 1983 when their compound and spectator area began to be overrun by encroaching airport development.

Most of the aircraft were dispersed with some going to Bruntingthorpe. One exception was the Avro Vulcan B.2, XM575, which was to be the subject of much wrangling between the airport authorities and its owner, Neville Martin. Arrears in parking fees was the cause, but eventually the aircraft became a prominent feature in a new project, the East Midlands Aero Park.

A view of the huge Fields (later Hunting) maintenance hangar. In the left foreground is former RAF Argosy C.1 XP412, now G-BDCV, which was acquired for spares by Fields in 1975. To the right is A&AEE Argosy C.1 XN817, under contract maintenance. Mike Everton

An example of some of the military exotica handled by Fields at East Midlands: a Short Skyvan 3M of the Singapore Air Defence Force, present on 7th June 1973. Chris Salter

A view inside the Fields hangar in 1987 with British Midland Viscount 813 G-AZNA undergoing a major overhaul. Author

Established at a cost of £300,000 and situated in a compound near the eastern end of the airport, this new enterprise provided an excellent, newly-built visitor centre surrounded by an area of land suitable for the display of preserved aircraft. For those wishing to watch aircraft operations, there was a raised spectator viewing mound and picnic area. Opened in May 1984 the park proved a popular attraction due in no small measure to the collection of aircraft on display which were cared for by the East Midlands Airport Volunteers Association.

Demand for extra land to further increase the number of airport buildings meant the closure of this amenity in 1996. A new site on the north-west side of the airport was allocated and exhibits began to be moved in late 1999 but it has yet to re-open

As with the majority of UK airports EMA has those who oppose its future expansion not least being many residents in the immediate vicinity of the airport. Larger aircraft, higher noise levels, increasing traffic and aircraft accidents all serve to provoke antagonism. Due to approach and take-off patterns the threat of an aircraft accident in a built up area has frequently been foremost in the minds of those opposing development. Unfortunately in the past there have been several incidents which have served to exacerbate the situation.

The most serious of these involved Boeing 737-400 G-OBME of British Midland on 8th January 1989. The twin-jet, on a flight from London-Heathrow to Belfast, suffered engine problems *en route* and attempted an emergency landing at EMA. Sadly, this was not successful and the aircraft crashed short of the runway onto an embankment of the M1 motorway. Forty-seven people lost their lives as a result.

Undoubtedly the most significant event at EMA in recent years has been the privatisation of the airport. That this might happen had been mooted for some time but during 1992 proposals were put forward which saw this possibility become reality.

A BAe Jetstream 31 being fitted out for US airline Piedmont Commuter at EMA, 1987. Author

One of the diminutive Nipper IIIs built by Slingsby on behalf of the EMA-based Nipper Aircraft. Powered by a converted Volkswagen motor car engine, G-AWDD made its first flight in 1968. Ken Ellis collection

When the Hunting-operated HS Andover calibration aircraft were retired in October 1996, E.3 XS603 was used for a publicity shot. Here it is flying over the south shore of Rutland Water, with some of the houses in one of RAF North Luffenham's domestic blocks, in the background. RAF PR

The names of several interested parties were announced and these included Lockheed Air Terminals, a US-owned company, Regional Airports Limited based in Hampshire and Air Centre UK a new company to be formed should a buy out by 400 management and staff be successful. When the sale was eventually finalised and the buyer revealed in August 1993 all were unlucky and the new owners, for the sum of £27.1 million, were the National Express Group.

Since its adoption the airport's name has often been the subject of heated debate. Pressure for a closer identity with Nottingham has on occasion resulted in furious argument and proposals to rename it Nottingham International Airport led to £10,000 being spent on research into a new identity. The net result of this was that in 1983 the airport became East Midlands *International* Airport. During 1994 the ongoing saga came to a head again when the new owners were in the process of reviewing the airport's corporate identity and the 'Nottingham' label was again apparently under consideration. This time the controversy was settled on 20th December when 'International' was dropped and EMIA reverted to EMA. It was intimated that this decision would enable the cities of Derby, Leicester and Nottingham to promote their own identities by adding their respective names as a subtitle.

Since the take-over a number of important developments have been completed while other projects are presently under way or at the planning stage. In April 1996 a new departures building was opened. Built at a cost of £10 million it is capable of handling three million passengers per year which should enable the airport to cope with increases in this type of traffic envisaged for the future. A further £4.5 million investment followed which resulted in the complete refurbishment and an extension to the terminal building together with a further £5.5 million to increase the aircraft parking area.

Local airline Alidair used several Viscounts for charter work in the 1970s, including Series 814 G-AZNH, seen here at Manchester.

ABC-Hunting operated several aircraft for Elan, the parcel delivery service. Agamemnon, Merchantman 953C G-APEM loading freight pallets at EMA. Both Alan J Wright

Constant improvements to the runways and infra-structure at EMA have allowed the airport to handle a wide range of airliners. Laker Skytrain McDonnell Douglas DC-10-30 G-BGXF and BMA Shorts 330 G-BJFK on a snow-filled apron, 15th December 1981. Mike Everton

Preparing Spitfire PR.XI PL983 (G-PRXI) for engine runs during 1987, with North American AT-6A Harvard G-TSIX behind. Author

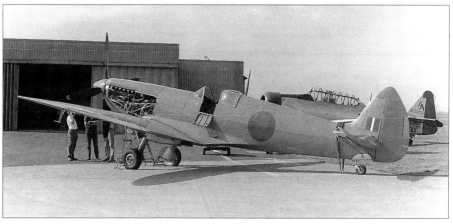

Britannia Airways have long been associated with EMA, their Boeing 737s being frequent visitors from the late 1960s onwards.

Orion Airways was another EMA-based airline, operating from 1980 until 1989 when it merged with Britannia Airways. The airline began operating with a fleet of Boeing 737-200s, including G-BGTY.

For some years the Boeing 737 has been the mainstay of the British Midland fleet. Series 400 G-OBMF on approach to land.

EMA-based Excalibur Airways became the first UK carrier to select the Airbus A320 for charter operations. G-SCSR was one of the four original fleet members in 1992.
All Alan J Wright

EMA became the UK's top airport for freight handling during 1995 and the importance of these operations to the airport is shown by the figures for 1997, during which 126,824 tonnes of cargo and 12,747 tonnes of mail were handled, while passengers carried totalled 1,881,322. Permission was granted for three further freight terminals of 220,000 square feet and planning permission sought for a further cargo terminal. A 600 metre extension to the runway was sanctioned and came into operation in 1999 but a request for an additional 230ft met with a setback in February 1997 when a decision was deferred by North West Leicestershire Council pending further consultations at local level. At 2,890 metres, the runway is now the sixth longest in the country. In June 1998 work began on a new £3.5 million control tower for airport operations, and at 52 metres, is now the second highest in the UK.

Adding further to EMAs diversity, a new air ambulance service was launched on 8th November 1999. Operating an MBB Bö105D helicopter, G-BATC, it is intended to cover most of Derbyshire and Leicestershire from its base at EMA. That a service of this type has long been required is evident when within 24 hours of inception, the helicopter was called upon to attend four incidents and by October 2000 over 350 missions had been carried out.

During 1999 and into 2000, passenger figures continued to increase, breaking previous records. In addition, projects such as the Pegasus Business Park and a £70 million development for DHL were in progress. British Midland announced their intention to resume long distance services in April 2001, and with that in mind placed an order for four Airbus A330s. On 1st February 2001 BMA announced a change of name to 'bmi british midland' and at the same time revealed a new colour scheme for its aircraft.

In September 2000 EMA was put up for sale by its owners, National Express. On the 19th February 2001 it was bought by Manchester Airport plc for £241 million. Future prospects for the UK's 12th largest airport and its 90 tenant companies appear to be assured.

Accidents to East Midlands Airport-based Aircraft

4.4.67 G-ALHG Canadair C-4 Argonaut
British Midland. Crashed in Stockport on approach to
Manchester Airport.

20.2.69 G-AODG Vickers Viscount 736
British Midland Airlines. Damaged beyond repair in landing
accident at EMA.

2.1.76 G-AVCC Cessna 172H
Badly damaged by severe gale at EMA.

28.5.85 G-AXEX Beagle Pup
Donair Crashed one mile west of Donington Hall.

18.1.87 G-BMAU Fokker F.27 Friendship 200
British Midland Airlines. Crashed on edge of Donington Park
motor racing circuit.
Ice on wings and tail believed to be the cause.

8.1.89 G-OBME Boeing 737-400
British Midland Airlines. Crashed on M1 motorway, adjacent
to Kegworth, while attempting to land at EMA, following engine
problems. Forty-seven passengers
lost their lives.

1.9.95 G-AZJKN Jodel HR.100/200B
Extensive damage in forced landing near Long Watton.

For accidents and details of aircraft operated by the RAF
units that flew from Castle Donington, i.e.
  No 28 Operational Training Unit,
  No 108 (Transport)Operational Training Unit,
  No 1382 (Transport) Conversion Unit
– See parent unit, Wymeswold (Chapter Twenty-Four).

*Concordes have visited EMA on several
occasions, often attracting large crowds.
via Dr Hugh Thomas*

*An aerial view of EMA in 1997 looking roughly
north. The size of the apron areas are readily
apparent. In the foreground is the A453
Melbourne to M1 road, in front of the office
complex in the left foreground can be seen
the remains of one of the wartime dispersals.
Above the office complex is the area originally
occupied by the First World War landing
ground. East Midlands Airport*

Aircraft Fleets of Airlines based at East Midlands Airport since 1964

Aircraft on short term leases are *not* included.

Air Bridge Carriers

Type	Duration	Registration(s)
AW.650 Argosy	1972-86	G-APRL*, G-APRN, G-APWW, G-AZHN, G-BEOZ*
HP Herald 401	1984-86	G-BEYF*
Lockheed L.188CF Electra	1989-92	N355WS, N360WS, N667F, N669F, G-FIJR, G-FIJV.
Vickers Viscount 800	1974-80	G-BBDK.
Vickers Merchantman	1978-96	G-APEG, G-APEJ, G-APEK, G-APEM†,G-APEP, G-APES, G-APET.

* Flown for Elan Air from 1984 to 1986. † Flown for Elan Air/DHL from 1987 to 1993.
Renamed in 1992 as Hunting Cargo Airlines - see below.

Alidair

Vickers Viscount 700	1975-81	G-ARBY, G-ARGR, G-ARIR, G-BDIK, G-BFMW
Vickers Viscount 800	1972-75	G-AVIW, G-AVJL, G-ASED, G-AZNH

Later Inter City Airlines, see below.

British Midland Airways (Fleet from late 1964)

Airbus A320-232	1998-	G-MIDW, G-MIDX, G-MIDY, G-MIDZ; G-MIDO to G-MIDV on order
Airbus A321-231	1998-	G-MIDA, G-MIDC, G-MIDE, G-MIDF, G-MIDH, G-MIDI, G-MIDJ, G-MIDK, G-MIDL, G-MIDM. G-MIDN on order.
BAe ATP	1988-	G-BMYK (later G-MANL), G-BMYL, G-BMYM (later G-MAUD)
BAC One-Eleven 500	1970-74	G-AXLL, G-AXLM, G-AXLN
Boeing 707-300	1970-85	G-AYBJ, G-AYVE, G-AYVG, G-AYXR, G-AZWA, G-BAEL, G-BFLD, G-BFLE, G-BMAZ
Boeing 737-300	1987-	G-ECAS, G-OBMA, G-OBMB, G-OBMC, G-OBMD, G-OBMH, G-OBMJ, G-OBML, G-OBMP, G-ODSK, G-OJTW, G-SMDB
Boeing 737-400	1988-	G-OBME, G-OBMF, G-OBMG, G-OBMK, G-OBMM, G-OBMN, G-OBMO, G-SFBH
Boeing 737-500	1994-	G-BVKA, G-BVKB, G-BVKC, G-BVKD, G-BVZE, G-BVZF, G-BVZG, G-BVZH, G-BVZI, G-OBMR, G-OBMX, G-OBMY, G-OBMZ
Canadair C4 Argonaut	1968-	G-ALHG, G-ALHS, G-ALHY
DHC-7-110 Dash Seven	1990-95	G-BOAW, G-BOAY
Douglas DC-3 Dakota	To 1969	G-AGJV, G-AMSX, G-ANTD, G-AOFZ, G-AOGZ, G-APBC.
Douglas DC-9-10	1978-95	G-BFIH (later G-BMAA), G-BMAB, G-BMAC, G-BMAG, G-BMAH, G-BMAI.
Douglas DC-9-30	1984-95	G-BMAK, G-BMAM, G-ELDG, G-ELDH, G-ELDI, G-PKBD, G-PKBE, G-PKBM
Embraer ERJ.145EU ‡	2000-	G-RJXA, G-RJXB, G-RJXC, G-RJXD, G-RJXE, G-RJXF. G-RJXG, G-RJXH, G-RJXI, G-RJXJ on order.
Fokker Friendship 200	1982-1988	G-BAUR, G-BDDH, G-BLGW, G-BHMW, G-BMAP, G-BMAS, G-BMAU, G-BMAW, PH-KFK (later G-BMAE).
Fokker 70	1995-	G-BVTE, G-BVTF, G-BVTG
Fokker 100	1994-	G-BVJA, G-BVJB, G-BVJC, G-BVJD, G-BXWE, G-AXWF.
HP Herald 200	1965-66	G-ASKK
	1973-77	G-ASVO, G-ATIG, G-BAVX.
SAAB 340A/B ‡	1996-	G-GNTA, G-GNTB, G-GNTC, G-GNTD, G-GNTF, G-GNTG, G-GNTH, G-GNTI, G-GNTJ, G-RUNG.
Shorts 330-200	1981–84	G-BJFK
Shorts 360-100	1983-88	G-BMAJ, G-BMAR, G-BMHX, G-BMHY
Vickers Viscount 700	1967-70	G-AOCB, G-AOCC, G-AODG, G-APPX, G-AWCV, G-AWGV
Vickers Viscount 800	1967-87	G-APND, G-APNE, G-APTD, G-ASED, G-AVJA, G-AVJB, G-AWXI, G-AYOX, G-AZLP. G-AZLR, G-AZLS, G-AZLT (later G-BMAT), G-AZNA, G-AZNB, G-AZNC, G-BAPD, G-BAPE, G-BAPF, G-BAPG, G-BCZR, G-BFZL.

‡ Operated by Business Air on behalf of BMA / British Midland Commuter.
  Some of the Business Air fleet may not actually be based at EMA.

Excalibur Airways

Type	Duration	Registration(s)
Airbus A320-212	1992-96	G-HAGT, G-KMAM, G-OEXC, G-SCSR, G-BWCP, G-BWKN, G-BWKO

From April 1992 until liquidated on 26th May 1996.

Genesis Airways

BAe Jetstream 31	1994-95	G-ENIS
Piper Turbo Navajo	1994-95	G-EEAC, G-OPRA

Hunting Cargo Airlines   Formerly Air Bridge Carriers.

Boeing 727-200	1994-97	EI-HCA, EI-HCB, EI-HCC, EI-HCD, EI-HCI, EI-LCH
Lockheed L.188CF Electra	1992-97	EI-CET, EI-CHX, EI-CHZ, G-FIJR, G-FIJV (later EI-CHF), G-FIZU (later EI-CHY), N360Q

All transferred to Dublin-based Hunting Cargo Airlines (Ireland) Ltd in 1997.

Inter City Airlines   Formerly Alidair to March 1981.

Shorts 330-200	1981-83	G-BITV, G-BITX, G-BJFK
Vickers Viscount 700	1981-83	G-ARGR, G-ARIR, G-BFMW

Operations ceased August 1983.

Orion Airways   Fleet from 12th February 1980

Boeing 737-200	1980-88	G-BGTV, G-BGTW, G-BGTY, G-BHCL, G-BHVG, G-BHVH, G-BHVI, G-BJBJ, G-BKHO, G-BKMS, G-BKAP
Boeing 737-300	1985-89	G-BLKB, G-BLKC, G-BLKD, G-BLKE, G-BNRT
Airbus A300B4-203	1987-89	G-BMZK, G-BMZL

The company merged with Britannia Airways in January 1989.

Sagittair

Beech D.18S	1970-72	G-AXWL, G-AYAH
AW.650 Argosy	1971-72	G-APRN, G-APWW, G-AZHN

Loughborough-Leicestershire Aircraft Museum

Aircraft type	Identity	Arrived	Departed
Avro XIX	G-AGWE	.5.83	1.84
Avro Vulcan B.2	XM575	21.8.83	Aeropark
Benson B.8M	G-AXCI	?	20.11.83
Blackburn Buccaneer S.1	XN964	27.10.82	20.11.83
Dassault Mystère IVA	No.85	.7.80	20.11.83
De Havilland Vampire T.11	WZ553	10.3.79	20.11.83
De Havilland Chipmunk T.10	WB624	.80	20.11.83
Hawker Hunter F.51	E-407	.12.79	20.11.83
North American F-100D Super Sabre	54-2239	21.4.78	20.11.83
Percival Provost T.1	XF914	24.10.79	20.11.83
Vickers Varsity T.1	WL626	8.11.79	Aeropark
Westland Whirlwind HAR.3	XG577	21.5.80	.12.83

East Midlands Aeropark
East Midlands Airport Volunteers Association

Aircraft type	Identity		Arrived	Departed
Avro Vulcan B.2	XM575		On site	–
Armstrong Whitworth Argosy 101	G-BEOZ		.6.87	–
Britten SA.1 Sheriff	G-FRJB		1.7.86	–
English Electric Canberra T.17	WH740		8.12.91	–
English Electric Lightning F.53	ZF588		8.1.89	–
Hawker Hunter T.7	XL569		20.2.93	–
Hawker Siddeley Buccaneer S.2B	XV350		11.12.93	–
Vickers Varsity T.1	WL626		On site	–
Vickers Merchantman	G-APES	(nose)	.5.97	–
Westland Whirlwind Srs.3	VR-BEP		.5.86	–

Chapter Eight

Cottesmore

STATION 'B' was the first title applied to Cottesmore when it was initially planned in Scheme 'C' during the RAF's 'Expansion' period of the early 1930s. Construction of the airfield began in mid-1936 and by 11th March 1938 it was sufficiently complete to enable Air Ministry Order No.9 to be executed. This called for the formation of a station headquarters within No.2 Group, Bomber Command, under Wing Commander H V Drew OBE AFC. The order further stated that in addition to the Station Headquarters (SHQ), RAF Cottesmore was to consist of two light bomber squadrons, each equipped with 12 aircraft plus a further 4 held in immediate reserve. Personnel manning each unit consisted of 11 officers, 2 warrant officers, 18 senior non-commissioned officers (SNCOs), including 6 airmen pilots and 115 airmen.

The two squadrons duly arrived on 20th April 1938; 35 and 207 from Worthy Down,

Hampshire, both then equipped with Vickers Wellesley single-engined long range bombers. No.35 was in the process of re-equipping and brought their first Fairey Battle I, a type which was eventually to replace the Wellesley with both squadrons. No.207 received orders to re-equip on 25th April.

Following the arrival of their new aircraft both squadrons spent many hours working up to operational standard, the need for this was emphasised in September when the Munich crisis arose and war with Germany seemed imminent. All leave was cancelled and key personnel recalled; on the 16th of the month Cottesmore prepared to mobilise and plans were in hand to form, using the nucleus of station personnel, 201 (B) Wing. Under Wing Commander Drew and consisting of a Headquarters, the resident units and 98 Squadron from Hucknall, Nottinghamshire, the Wing was to be ready to move and operate on the third day of

TTTE Panavia Tornado GR.1 ZA362 'B-09' of the Royal Air Force captured in a dramatic air-to-air pose while on a sortie from its base at RAF Cottesmore, in January 1984. Klaus Kropf

mobilisation from airfields in Kent. Cottesmore would then house two non-mobilising Bristol Blenheim twin-engined bomber units. This emergency passed when the Prime Minister Neville Chamberlain returned from Germany and, having been lulled by Hitler's promises, felt able to declare 'Peace in Our Time'.

In spite of such assurances the resident squadrons returned to their intensive training and in November, both received a new and increased establishment of 16 aircraft with 16 reserves for No.35 and five for No.207. Extremely harsh conditions during the winter of 1938-1939 made life difficult on the airfield. Large snowfalls hampered

Vickers Wellesley K8530 of 35 Squadron. This view, believed to have been taken at Worthy Down, Hampshire, was prior to the unit's move to Cottesmore. via Author

Formation of 207 Squadron Fairey Buttle Is over Rutland in 1938. Nearest the camera is K9194 which served with the unit from new in May 1938 until October that year. It ended its career in Canada in 1942. via Andy Thomas

Opposite page:

An ill-fated pair from 14 OTU. Handley Page Hampden I, P1316, was set on fire by a heater lamp at Saltby in February 1941, while Hereford I, L6065, from the same stable, crashed in May 1940. via Author

movement considerably but served to provide station personnel with an insight into cold weather operations and in spite of the climate, whenever possible, the tempo of training increased.

During the spring of 1939 steps were taken to camouflage the station. Buildings were painted in a scheme intended to break up their outlines and merge them with the surrounding countryside. Large areas of net were draped over the hangars in an effort to reduce the shadow effect. Roads within the station also received camouflage treatment and hedge lines were drawn across the airfield to give the impression of a network of small fields when seen from the air.

On 1st May 1939 Wing Commander E B Grenfell AFC assumed command of the station and also on this date the unit establishments were revised yet again. This time both units were allocated 24 aircraft with eight in reserve. Both squadrons took part in regional air exercises during the summer and acquitted themselves well. On 28th July 207 Squadron left Cottesmore for annual weapon training at the Armament Training School, Evanton, Scotland, returning on 20th August. Their stay on return was rather brief as both squadrons vacated the station a few days later, 207 on the 24th and 35 the following day, both bound for Cranfield, Bedfordshire. The airfield did not stay empty for on the 25th, 185 Squadron flew in followed by 106 Squadron on 1st September, from Thornaby, Yorkshire, to take up residence. Both units were equipped with Handley Page Hampdens, a twin-engined medium bomber which was to have a lengthy association with Cottesmore.

Following the declaration of war on Germany on 3rd September 1939, Cottesmore was transferred from 2 Group to 5 Group, and the station was brought to an immediate state of readiness in anticipation of large scale air attacks by the *Luftwaffe*. Thankfully, these did not materialise but the sound of air raid warnings was not long delayed, the sirens being heard for the first time at 0250 hours on the 4th. As a precaution against surprise air attacks on the airfield, a 'scatter' scheme was initiated and 106 Squadron left for a very brief stay at Kidlington, Oxfordshire, on 6th September.

Between September and the end of the year, several different army units assisted with airfield defence, the first of these being a detachment of the 1st/5th Leicestershire Regiment Territorial Army commanded by Captain Symington which arrived on 7th September. They were replaced on the 25th by a company of the 5th Battalion Sherwood Foresters. Other units associated with the airfield's defence during this period were a detachment from the 28th Light Anti-aircraft Regiment and 107 and 112 Batteries of the Light Anti-aircraft Brigade.

On 6th October, the station establishment was reduced by one squadron and No.106 was transferred to Finningley, Yorkshire. This situation altered for a time from 9th December when, due to the unserviceability of Cranfield, 207 Squadron returned on temporary attachment. To bring the year to a close, the status of Cottesmore once again changed when both the station and 185 Squadron became part of 6 (Training) Group with effect from 20th December.

Towards the end of January 1940 winter yet again played havoc with station routine, all activities being hampered by unusually heavy snowfalls and extremely bitter conditions. Such severe conditions had not been experienced in the country for over 50 years, and almost a month was to elapse before the airfield was finally declared free from snow and fully serviceable again on 22nd February. March brought a great improvement in weather conditions, so much so that 207 Squadron was able to record a total of 1,365 flying hours for the month.

What was to be the last major re-organisation at Cottesmore for some time took place on 5th April. No.207 Squadron departed to be absorbed into 12 Operational Training Unit (OTU) at Benson, Oxfordshire, while 185 Squadron and SHQ were combined to form 14 OTU. Aircraft establishment for this new unit was 32 Hampdens, 16 Herefords and 24 Avro Anson twin-engined general duties and crew trainer aircraft. The Hereford was a version of the Hampden, powered by Napier Dagger H-format 16-cylinder in-line piston engines in place of the former's Bristol Pegasus radials. The morale of the OTU's WAAF contingent received a boost on the 24th when Her

Royal Highness the Duchess of Gloucester paid a visit in order to inspect them and their quarters.

After France and the Low Countries had succumbed to the German onslaught during the early summer months of 1940, invasion of the United Kingdom by the enemy appeared imminent. Cottesmore was then very occupied with preparing defence measures against this threat. Extensive wiring of the perimeter was carried out, pillboxes and strong points built and trenches dug. Equipment shortages led to improvisation, for example several lorries were converted into armoured cars. The firing range was seldom idle as intensive practice with both rifles and Lewis guns took place. Help with defence came from Local Defence Volunteers and 50 riflemen from a local searchlight unit provided further reinforcements. Armed cycle patrols and practice alarms, held by day and night, helped to keep per-

sonnel in a state of readiness. If the worst had happened and capture of the station appeared inevitable, detailed orders for its destruction were issued.

Before this last drastic action took place, Cottesmore was to be given a definite role to play. Initially, it was to provide replacement crews and aircraft to offset casualties in bomber squadrons equipped with Hampdens and Herefords. In addition, it was to be responsible for two squadrons to operate, under orders from 2 Group, on counter invasion measures.

These two units, designated 'X' and 'Y' Squadrons, were to be equipped with 24 Hawker Audax two-seat army co-operation biplanes and 18 Ansons respectively. While the latter aircraft would be taken from those on the strength of 14 OTU, the Audaxes were to be drawn from 12 Flying Training School (FTS) Grantham, Lincolnshire (6), 11 FTS Shawbury, Shropshire (6) and the rest from 3 FTS Peterborough, Cambridgeshire.

On receipt of the code-word 'Banquet', X' and 'Y' were to be required to stand by on one hour's notice. If sent into action, it was intended that they attack enemy convoys at sea or wherever the enemy was to be found in strength. Pilots were exhorted to employ tactics which ensured maximum damage to their targets. They were to aim at hitting one barge with each attack of one bomb, backed up with machine gun fire on all possible occasions. Every attack was to be pressed home regardless of cost. One shudders to think how Audax biplanes and Ansons might have fared had they encountered *Luftwaffe* fighters. Thankfully they never received an invitation to the 'Feast'.

It was also in the summer of 1940 that the *Luftwaffe* began to show an interest in the station. Their first attack came shortly after midnight on 26th June when a single enemy aircraft released a stick of seven high explosive bombs. Although these missiles were on target, falling across the officers' married quarters, they caused no casualties and only minor structural damage. By mid-September enemy bombers had paid a further four visits to Cottesmore, but on each occasion they failed to inflict either serious damage or casualties.

In an attempt to direct enemy attention away from the established airfields, many decoys known as 'Q' or 'K' sites, were laid out. Cottesmore's decoy was situated in open country to the north-east of the station near Swayfield, Lincolnshire. Several times this 'Q' site proved its worth when the lights displayed attracted bombs intended for Cottesmore.

No.14 OTU had already began to make a form of retaliation during July. On the 25th three Hampdens carried out the first of the unit's many leaflet raids from the station. Code-named 'Nickels' these sorties were mainly against the larger towns and cities in occupied France. Later a more belligerent attitude was adopted when some aircraft

One of 14 OTU's Hampdens overflies one of the same unit's Herefords. The Napier Daggers of the Hereford gave the engine nacelles a very different configuration.
via Author

flew on armed 'Nickels'. On these sorties, in addition to the 'bumph', two 250lb bombs were carried which were intended to be dropped on a military target. Unfortunately, on many occasions, positive identification proved impossible and aircraft returned home with their bomb load intact.

At times the OTU must have been hard pressed to meet flying commitments as the monthly returns of serviceable aircraft illustrate. For example, the figures for October 1940 show that of the 32 Hampdens the average number available was 17. Ansons fared slightly better with 12 from 23, but from 16 Herefords the number was only three. While routine maintenance, modifications, the unreliable Dagger engines of the Herefords and various other factors accounted for a fair proportion of unserviceable aircraft, no doubt the high accident rate helped to boost the figures. During November, for instance, in addition to minor mishaps, at least eight unit aircraft sustained major structural damage while one was completely destroyed.

Due to the constant round of training sorties, the Cottesmore circuit at times was a little congested and also wear and tear on the airfield surface was considerable. Some relief for this situation came during December when the new satellite airfield at Woolfox Lodge, Rutland, was brought into use for night flying training from the 13th. (See Chapter Twenty-Three.)

Although by early 1941 the threat of invasion had receded, it was still considered prudent to test plans laid earlier and a full scale trial of Operation 'Banquet' was held over 29th/30th January. For this exercise though the previous scheme was changed so that 'X' Squadron, equipped with 18 fully armed Hampdens operated from Cottesmore, while the 18 Ansons of 'Y' Squadron used Woolfox Lodge. Then, on 14th February, an exercise of quite a different type was held. On this occasion the station was subjected to a gas attack and to ensure that the exercise took on an air of reality, aircraft were used to spray gas over the airfield. All the defences were manned and several machine gun posts recorded hits on the attackers via camera guns.

After a lull of some months, the *Luftwaffe* renewed interest in the area with both Cottesmore and Woolfox Lodge receiving its attention. On 8th April, Hampden I P2092 was lost to enemy intruder action, shot down by a Junkers Ju 88 of 1/NJG 2 flown by Feldwebel Hans Hahn. P2092 crashed on the main railway line at Little Bytham, north of Stamford, Lincolnshire, with the loss of all three crew members. The Hampden was Hahn's fifth victory and during his brief career as a night fighter pilot, he was to be credited with the destruction of a further seven aircraft. His luck ran out on 11th October when once more intruding in the area. On this occasion he found Airspeed Oxford

II AB767 of 12 FTS, Harlaxton, Lincolnshire, but misjudged his attack and collided with his target. The two aircraft fell near Grantham with the loss of all five on board both.

On the night of 9th April, incendiary bombs fell on Cottesmore, one of these penetrating the roof of 'A' hangar causing slight damage to an instructional airframe. Two days later, in the early hours of 11th April, the station came in for a more prolonged raid which lasted for almost an hour. An estimated 10 to 15 aircraft were involved, dropping flares and various types of bombs from around 10,000ft. Again the station escaped relatively unscathed even though one missile fell on the bomb stores. After this, it was the turn of Woolfox Lodge with four attacks taking place there between 17th April and 18th May, while the 'Q' site attracted bombs on two occasions during the same period.

Those concerned with aircraft serviceability probably heaved a sigh of relief during July when the last Herefords were phased out of service with the OTU. Accidents involving Hampdens still occurred. In

July alone, at least nine incidents were recorded which resulted in aircraft sustaining various degrees of damage and injury to their crews. In addition, two Hampdens were completely written-off in accidents, one of which also involved the loss of an Anson while the two crew members in the Hampden were killed.

Early in August flying began from a new satellite at Saltby, Leicestershire (Chapter Twenty-Two). This activity had not gone unnoticed by the enemy, who attacked the station with a single aircraft on three occasions between 13th and 23rd August. In all, 18 high explosive bombs were dropped, but no damage was caused and casualties were limited to two of a minor nature.

In the autumn a new type of aircraft, the Airspeed Oxford twin-engined crew trainer, began to appear in unit records. By the end of September there were four of these on strength together with 15 Ansons, 45 Hampdens and one de Havilland Tiger Moth two-seater biplane. Later a pair of Westland Lysanders were allocated to the OTU for target towing purposes. Practice bombing and gunnery ranges used by the unit at this time were Grimsthorpe Park, Bourne, Lincolnshire, Whittlesey near Peterborough and Holbeach, Lincolnshire.

Returning to the subject of flying accidents, as far as 14 OTU is concerned, the overall record was not good. Further examples are the series of major incidents affecting the unit at the end of 1941. Between the 8th and 29th December seven aircraft, six Hampdens and an Oxford, were destroyed. Six aircrew lost their lives and several were hospitalised with serious injuries. While the cause of many of these accidents appears to have been attributed to pilot error, a broken throttle lever was responsible for one and failure to clear hoarfrost on the mainplanes another.

Wintry conditions in the first two months of 1942 disrupted the training programme considerably. Ploughs were needed to help clear the first appreciable amounts of snow which fell late in January, but on 2nd February further heavy falls began. These were followed by severe frosts and, for a time, flying became impossible. To enable limited training to continue, personnel of 'A' Flight were transferred to Saltby where, thanks to an efficient snow clearance scheme, conditions were much better. The detachment

lasted from 7th to 20th February, by which time Cottesmore was able to resume a normal routine.

Staff and trainees alike usually welcomed anything which broke the repetitive round of training. An inkling that something out of the ordinary was in store came on 22nd May when orders were received to prepare 27 Hampdens for a flight of approximately 1,000 miles with a full war load. Before long rumours began to circulate on the station that 14 OTU was to take part in a big raid. Although a considerable amount of work was required to bring some of the aircraft up to operational standard, the Maintenance Wing, by strenuous efforts, excelled and eventually succeeded in providing 30 Hampdens plus three in reserve. Speculation as to the purpose came to an end on 30th May when selected crews from the unit were briefed to take part in Operation 'Millennium', the first 1,000 bomber raid on Germany.

The 30 Hampdens detailed for 'Millennium' began to take-off at 22.43 hours on 30th May carrying mixed loads of general purpose and incendiary bombs, their destination Cologne. Only one, P5312, was forced to return early due to the pilot's compass being faulty. Of the remainder, 27 reported bombing their primary target. Overall, the

raid was considered a great success, but it was not accomplished without loss to 14 OTU. On return, Squadron Leader Falconer's aircraft had the misfortune to collide with a Handley Page Halifax four-engined heavy bomber of 78 Squadron near March, Cambridgeshire. He was the only survivor from the Hampden. Another crashed at Horsham St Faith, Norfolk, with the loss of all on board while a third aircraft failed to return from the operation.

Next night, 1st June, it was operations again for the OTU when another 1,000 bomber raid was ordered. This time the target was Essen and the unit made 27 Hampdens available. Two of these took little or no part in the proceedings, an unserviceable engine prevented one from taking off, while P5312 aborted yet again for the same reason as the previous night. Although a thin layer of cloud intervened, the remaining 25 aircraft dropped 52 x 250lb general purpose and 9,640 x 4lb incendiary bombs over the target. All returned home relatively unscathed and only one serious casualty, a Sergeant Weir, was reported. This unfortunate airman died on his return to base from injuries received following an accident in the target area, when he was struck by a 4lb incendiary bomb released by an aircraft overhead.

Anson I N9833 of 185 Squadron taxies out on a snowy Cottesmore during the winter of 1939-1940. A G Griffin via R C Ashworth

Another 185 Squadron Anson, taken in close formation with a fellow over the wintry countryside. E Taylor/MAP

For a third massive raid on 26th June, in which 1,006 aircraft were involved, all 24 Hampdens promised by 14 OTU took-off, their objective, Bremen. Ten-tenths cloud made target identification virtually impossible; nevertheless 19 crews reported their bomb loads dropped in the target area. Of the remaining five aircraft one failed to locate Bremen or any other target, so returned to Cottesmore with its bomb load intact. Another bombed Emden as an alternative target, while a third was forced to jettison its warload over the North Sea after the artificial horizon had failed. The explosion of the Identification Friend or Foe (IFF) destructor caused the early return of one of the remaining two and, lastly, the ill-fated P5312 failed to return from the operation.

Throughout this period of operations, the required quota of aircraft to meet training commitments was also maintained. This was not achieved without some difficulty; servicing presented quite a problem for in a three week period over 100 fitters were posted from the unit. Late in July notification was received that a major change in equipment was soon to affect 14 OTU. All Hampdens were to be phased out of service and in their place the unit would receive Vickers Wellingtons.

In the interim, the Hampdens were still required to soldier on with 30 unit aircraft joining in another 1,000 bomber raid on 31st July, when the target was Düsseldorf. All bomb loads on this occasion were of the high explosive nature, most aircraft carrying 4 x 500lb though five did manage an extra 2 x 250lb. As it turned out, it was not a good night for the OTU.

Various faults caused four aircraft to return early, one of these was minus a navigator, who had baled out over the North Sea. The night also proved very eventful for some of those who reached Düsseldorf, a number returned with flak damage and others came under attack from night-fighters.

One Hampden flown by a pupil pilot, an American, Pilot Officer Curtin, suffered severe damage from both flak and fighters. Despite having his three crew members wounded, one so severely that he later died in hospital, Curtin flew his crippled bomber back to England where he made a crash-landing in a field near Loddiswell, Devon. For his actions, on this his first operational sortie, Pilot Officer Curtin received the immediate award of the Distinguished Flying Cross.

By far the most serious blow to the OTU was the fact that three Hampdens failed to return from the operation. (See the listing of losses, starting on page 165.)

At 1810 hours on 3rd August the *Luftwaffe* made a brief reappearance at Cottesmore when a Dornier Do 217E came out of low cloud and made an attack from about 500ft.

Four bombs were dropped and the station strafed with machine gun fire, but damage was only slight and there were no casualties. Four gunposts opened fire and claimed hits on the intruder. On 15th August, 15 of the unit's Hampdens took part in a new type of exercise called 'Command Bullseye'. Intended as a test of London's defences, the returning crews were most enthusiastic about the whole experience.

The promised Wellingtons began to arrive during August and by the end of the month seven were on strength. When the OTU was required to supply aircraft for operations again in September, it was still the Hampdens that bore the brunt. These operations during the month were very concentrated, the unit participating in three raids within a week. On the night of 10/11th 20 Hampdens took part in a raid on Düsseldorf, 17 were available for a raid on Bremen on the 13/14th, but the number dispatched to Essen on the 16/17th was only 12.

Throughout the OTU suffered mixed fortunes. Each time, for a variety of reasons, a number of aircraft failed to complete their missions. Engine malfunctions were the cause of many early returns, invariably with their bomb loads jettisoned to enable them to stagger home. Losses in aircraft over the three raid period amounted to two missing, and one destroyed in a crash landing made after it ran short of fuel.

In the midst of this period of high activity, an incident also took place at Cottesmore which, with the benefit of hindsight, could be said to have been a portent of things to come. It took the form of an exercise in which paratroops were dropped on the airfield from some of the first United States Army Air Force (USAAF) Douglas C-47 Skytrain twin-engined transports to reach the UK. Intended to ascertain the ability of the station to resist an invading force, it provided an opportunity for various defence measures to be put to the test. They proved to be adequate and the defenders acquitted themselves well. Afterwards, the umpires declared that the attack had been successfully repulsed.

With the changeover to Wellingtons, the Oxfords became surplus to training requirements. These were soon disposed of, the last departing the station on 10th October. It was November though which marked the end of the era for 14 OTU. The number of Wellingtons continued to increase and during the month sufficient had arrived for the changeover to type to be completed – all Hampden training ceased.

Re-equipment was not without its problems. Continual circuit training by two flights, now flying heavier aircraft, began to have an adverse effect on Cottesmore's grass runways. In order to conserve the surface of the airfield 'C' Flight was recalled

from the satellite at Saltby, with 'A' and 'B' Flights transferred there in its place. The move was apparently accomplished quite smoothly with no noticeable interference to the flying programme.

At the end of November 14 OTU was equipped with 45 Wellingtons, 8 Ansons, 2 Lysanders and 1 Boulton Paul Defiant. A number of redundant Hampdens remained on the station, but not for long, the last of these departing during December.

The year 1943 was to be a momentous one for Cottesmore. The opening months were mainly routine with few outstanding incidents recorded. Early in January the station experienced a shortage of water, so severe that strict limitations were imposed as to its use. One can imagine that under such restrictions some rather odorous situations developed, and when an adequate supply was restored after almost three weeks, it was greeted with some relief.

Even with new equipment the OTU was still plagued with a fairly high accident rate. War-weary aircraft, engine failures and pilot error all took their toll on both aircraft and aircrew. Each month had its share, but of those which took place in March, one was unusual and the other a most serious incident. The first of these accidents took place on 10th March when the pilot of Wellington Ic DV864 evidently mistook North Luffenham's 'Q' site for his home base. In attempting to land, the aircraft crashed and burst into flames. Two crew, together with the pilot were killed, while two more received injuries.

The other incident happened on the evening of 31st March when Mk.Ic AD628 'M' landed in poor visibility. The aircraft swung to avoid colliding with the control tower, but in doing so crashed into Mk.Ic X9944 which was standing on the tarmac in front of 'C' Hangar. Both Wellingtons burst into flames, which quickly began to spread and threatened to engulf the hangar with four more Wellingtons inside. Fire crews from Cottesmore helped by brigades from the surrounding areas, fought the blaze and station personnel were able to manhandle the four aircraft clear. Wing Commander Graham, the Commanding Officer, was leading a rescue party to extricate three trapped crew members when a bomb aboard AD628 exploded, wrecking the offices of the maintenance wing. Though only eight feet from the bomb, the Wing Commander received only minor injuries and after receiving treatment he was able to return to render further assistance. For his bravery, Graham was awarded the George Medal. All ranks received praise for their actions which were of the highest order. Regardless of the danger they were instrumental in saving both valuable records and equipment.

A vertical view of Cottesmore, mid-1942. The flying ground can be seen clearly and some of the 'hedges' that were painted on still stand out. The village at the bottom of the picture is Greetham. DofE

Maintenance Section, a detachment of No. 2 Heavy Glider Maintenance Unit, headquartered at Snailwell, Cambridgeshire, assumed responsibility for the gliders and the civil engineering company Wimpeys had moved onto the station to begin major reconstruction. In the ensuing months, the project on which they had embarked transformed the airfield, entailing the laying of a concrete three runway system, together with a perimeter track and hardstandings.

On 1st September, control of the station passed from 92 Group to 5 Group, Bomber Command, then nine days later it was allocated for use by the USAAF. The Americans were not long in arriving, personnel of the Air Support Division Substitution Unit (ASDSU) reaching Cottesmore on the 22nd. By the 27th, the base had been transferred to them becoming USAAF Station 489. They were able to see that satisfactory progress was being made by the contractors, with over a third of the runways and a fifth of the perimeter track completed.

Next to arrive was the Headquarters and HQ Squadron of the IXth Troop Carrier Command (TCC). Activated on 16th October, the HQ was to stay at Cottesmore until 1st December when together with the ASDSU it moved to occupy St Vincents in the town of Grantham, Lincolnshire.

The build up of the IXth TCC in the winter months of 1943 led to several USAAF ground units making transient visits to Cottesmore. Amongst these were the HQs of the 50th Troop Carrier Wing (TCW) and the 434th Troop Carrier Group (TCG). Both departed after a brief stay, the 50th TCW to Bottesford, Leicestershire (Chapter Four), and the 434th TCG to Fulbeck, Lincolnshire.

By February 1944 the new runways were ready for use and on the 16th the first 26 aircraft of the 316th TCG flew in. One of the four Groups allocated to the 52nd TCW, the 316th had already seen nine months service in the Middle East and its aircraft had flown to the UK from Sicily in several stages. Next day, they were joined by 52nd TCW HQ, which was also to be based at Cottesmore. The three remaining TCGs soon occupied bases in the vicinity, the 61st at Barkston Heath, the 313rd at Folkingham (both in Lincolnshire) and the 314th at Saltby.

Further arrivals brought the 316th's C-47 Skytrains and C-53 Skytroopers up to 50 by the 20th, while personnel swelled to almost 3,700. (The C-47 Skytrain, known in the RAF as the Dakota, was the freight and para-

Although the event was still some way off, evidence that preparations were in hand for the invasion of Europe began to appear at Cottesmore and its satellite during May when Airspeed Horsa assault gliders were delivered for external storage on the airfields. Eventually to be used extensively in future airborne assaults, these gliders came in by air with Armstrong Whitworth Whitleys and Albemarles serving as tugs. By the end of the month, nine Horsas were present at Cottesmore and they continued to be flown in at intervals until, by July, the number in store on the two stations was 55.

In August, 14 OTU's tenancy of the station came to an end. On the 1st the unit began to move to a new base at Market Harborough, Leicestershire (see Chapter Fifteen), while the Saltby element was rehoused at Husbands Bosworth, Leicestershire (Chapter Eleven). Transporting the bulk of various impedimenta associated with the unit took almost a fortnight. It was not until the 28th that the final tie was severed when the last four Wellingtons, which had been under maintenance, were flown out.

By this time the airfield had been relegated to Care and Maintenance; 34 Heavy Glider

Above left: *Men of the US 82nd Airborne march past one of the 'C' Type hangars at Cottesmore, containing C-47s of the 37th TCS. Note also the Cletrac tractor outside.* A P Publications

Above right: *This Skytrain of the 36th TCS was involved in a ground collision at Cottesmore just prior to D-Day. The pilot was killed.* A P Publications

Left: *Massed C-47s of the 45th TCS ready for the order to take off.* via Norman Roberson

Below: *Man-handling Waco CG-4A assault gliders alongside their C-47 tugs on the runway at Cottesmore. C-47A-90-DL Skytrain 43-15292 'W7-B' of the 37th TCS survived the war and flew on until August 1956.* A P Publications

troop version of the famed Douglas DC-3; the C-53 was a paratroop-only version.) The station was hard put to house this rapid rise in numbers, with the result that tented accommodation was resorted to and requisition of some local properties became necessary. The latter included Exton Hall, home of the Earl of Gainsborough, eventually becoming a stately billet for Wing HQ.

Another unit to arrive during February was at first without a title. Although it had been in existence, in a formative stage, at Bottesford, Leicestershire, for some weeks. It was only after coming to Cottesmore that it became the IXth Air Force Troop Carrier Command Pathfinder School. It was officially opened as such on 28th February. Using 'Gee-' and SCR-717-equipped C-47s, the school's purpose was to train navigators and others in the use of these radio/radar aids which were to be installed in lead aircraft of the airborne invasion force. The need for more space and better facilities had brought the unit to Cottesmore but, with the 316th's four Troop Carrier Squadrons (TCS) Nos. 36, 37, 44 and 45 in intensive training the base was found to be too congested. On 22nd March the school moved to North Witham, Lincolnshire.

As the 52nd Wing bases were considered, at first, to be too far north for glider missions, the emphasis was on paratroop operations. Much of the training involved the US 82nd Airborne Division, quartered at many locations within the two counties. These were the troops that very shortly the Wing would transport into action as part of the invading force of Operation 'Overlord'.

The 316th's experience overseas paid dividends and, as early as 18th March, they were able to make drops of battalion strength. Some hours were spent, however, in glider towing. These proved that the Wing was quite capable of participating in this type of operation if need be.

Training culminated on the night of 11th/12th May when the 50th, 52nd and 53rd TCWs took part in 'Eagle', a command exercise which has been described as the nearest thing to a true rehearsal held for any American airborne operation in the Second World War. The 52nd Wing contributed 369 aircraft, and for the 316th TCG, all went well until the final stages of the exercise. Returning formations – or serials as they were referred to in airborne parlance – were circling in the vicinity of March, Cambridgeshire, prior to dispersing to return to base when two C-47s of the 316th collided in mid-air. It was a tragic occasion for the unit, for amongst the dead was Lieutenant Colonel Burton R Fleet, the 316th's Commander. To his successor, Lt Colonel Harvey Berger, fell the difficult task of taking over command of the Group with the invasion of Europe so close.

For the 316th, D-Day began early; in the hour before midnight on 5th June, when 72 aircraft took off from Cottesmore to form part of the armada carrying the 82nd Airborne Division on Operation 'Neptune', the airborne assault phase of 'Overlord'.

From the Wing assembly point, to the East of Birmingham, the serials set course, following a chain of flashing light and Eureka radio beacons spaced at 30 mile intervals. After they had crossed the coast at Portland Bill, more navigation aids on board ships were in position to guide them across the Channel. Leading the force were two 36th TCS serials from Cottesmore. The first carried the 2nd Battalion, 505th Parachute Infantry Regiment, the second the 3rd Battalion plus two 75mm Howitzers and 20 artillerymen of the 456th Parachute Field Artillery Battalion. Their objective was Drop Zone (DZ) 'O', an oval of fields just to the north-west of St Mère Église in Normandy.

On the run in to the DZ, the lead serials were forced to climb to clear a cloudbank in their path, consequently many drops were made from a higher altitude than was briefed. Late sighting of the DZ lights, also due to clouds, caused others to overshoot. Nevertheless, the 316th's drops were later

Cottesmore – 1st December 1944

Latitude	52° 43' 45" N
Longitude	00° 39' 15" W
Height above Sea Level	425ft
Command	IXth Troop Carrier Command
	316th Troop Carrier Group
Affiliated Airfields	Nil
Nearest Railway Station	Oakham?
Function	OTU (Satellite)

Landing Area – Runways

QDM	Dimensions	Extensibility	Remarks
230°	2,000 x 50 yards	2,200 yards	Entails
280°	1,600 x 50 yards	–	diversion of a
190°	1,500 x 50 yards	1,700 yards	minor road.
Type of Surface	Tarmac		

Permanent Landmarks

By Day	Nil
By Night	Nil

Permanent Obstructions Nil

Facilities

Airfield Lighting	Mk.II
Flying Control	Yes

Accommodation

Permanent technical and domestic

Technical	Hangars		Hardstandings	
	Type	No	Type	No
	C	4	Concrete	37
	T2	1	Tarmac	17
Domestic	Officers	Enlisted men		Total
USAF	512	2,253		2,765

evaluated as being amongst the best of the whole operation. Of the 1,276 troops carried by the Group, all but two jumped, while only 12 aircraft received slight damage, mainly from rifle and machine gun fire.

The return of the 316th to Cottesmore was a most impressive sight. When the first serial arrived at around 0400 hours, it was still flying in excellent formation. This was an achievement unequalled by any other group engaged in 'Neptune'.

Unfortunately, the same cannot be said of 'Freeport', a re-supply mission flown on D+1. Equally drawn from the four groups of the 52nd, 208 aircraft were scheduled to lift much-needed supplies to the embattled 82nd Airborne. For the 316th, the mission began badly. While taxying into position for take-off, two aircraft of the 36th TCS collided. Both aircraft received substantial damage, one pilot being killed, and the take-off was delayed by 15 minutes.

The remaining 50 aircraft began to leave Cottesmore around 03:30 hours and soon began to encounter thick cloud as they tried to assemble. In spite of the route beacons, many pilots became lost and some of the 316th's rear flights turned back on orders. About 150 aircraft in all reached the DZs, after facing the further hazard of increased enemy ground fire, which was responsible for the loss of several aircraft. A number of 316th aircraft sustained battle damage and two were flown back on one engine. The return to Cottesmore, in contrast to the previous day, was made singly or in small groups.

Another airborne operation planned at this time which would have involved the 316th, was 'Wildoats'. In this enterprise, the British 1st Airborne Division was to be dropped on 14th June in support of a breakthrough by Allied troops. However, the previous day, while some crews were being briefed, an enemy offensive in the landing area caused the operation to be postponed and eventually cancelled.

Although other airborne landings were planned during the campaign in France, none were carried out, due mainly to the eventual speed of the Allied advance and therefore training exercises and supply flights to the Continent occupied the 316th, until the next opportunity to return to action. This came in September 1944 when they took part in Operation 'Market', the airborne assault aimed at the capture of bridges in the Arnhem, Nijmegen and Grave areas of Holland.

On Sunday 17th September, two serials of 45 aircraft loaded with men of the 82nd Airborne, left Cottesmore between 10:35 and 10:50 hours. The first carried paratroops of the 1st Battalion, 505th Parachute Infantry Regiment and Divisional HQ. They were bound for DZ 'N', just south of the town of

Groesbeek. An error in navigation caused the serial to stray far south of its course, but fortunately, correction was made in time and a near perfect drop resulted. A DZ near the village of Overasselt was the target for the second serial, with men of the 1st Battalion, 504th Parachute Infantry aboard. Again, a good drop was made with 32 C-47 loads or sticks of paratroopers landing on the zone, the rest within a mile.

Next day the 52nd Wing mounted another massive operation, with Cottesmore again the scene of great activity, as 82 C-47s marshalled to take re-inforcements to the beleaguered 82nd Airborne. This time the mission was to be quite different from those previously undertaken by the 316th, for each C-47 had in tow a Waco CG-4A assault glider. An additional preparation needed for this type of operation had been completed earlier. Pierced Steel Planking (PSP) had been laid on the areas required for glider marshalling, to prevent loaded machines from sinking into the muddy ground.

Fog and low cloud hindered take-off, and the mission started 50 minutes late, but the 316th's two serials with their badly-needed men and guns of the 319th and 456th Field Artillery Battalions (FAB), had little trouble reaching Holland. The landing zone was in the same area, near Groesbeek, as on the previous day but one of the 316th's serials was guilty of some very inaccurate releases. The first occurred when over half of the gliders were released prematurely over the wrong DZ. Then, after six gliders had been released over the correct DZ, another eight delayed their release and landed some miles to the north east. This was a costly error, for the gliders, together with their contents, fell into enemy hands and the 319th FAB lost 45 men, dead or captured.

Weather conditions over the 52nd Wing bases forced a glider mission planned for the 19th to be postponed. For the next three days, the weather deteriorated even further, thick fog, heavy rain and extensive low cloud, all conspired to keep the massive array of 406 gliders, assembled on Wing bases, grounded. On 23rd September, the weather eventually relented, the operation finally getting under way and 89 C-47/Waco glider combinations left Cottesmore for their destination, a DZ in the vicinity of Overasselt. In the first serial were three companies of the 325th Glider Infantry Regiment, the second carried two batteries of the 80th Airborne Anti-aircraft Battalion, the 508th Command Vehicles and a divisional reconnaissance platoon.

The two formations of C-47s began to release their loads at 16:24 and 16:59 hours respectively, and most of the gliders landed on or close to their designated DZ. Figures released after the event show that this mission by the 52nd Wing was a great success.

Out of over 2,900 troops landed, only ten were unfit for duty and of 24 guns, 82 Jeeps and 47 trailers, only one Jeep could not be used. On the 316th's debit side, two aircraft were shot down and many others received varying degrees of damage, from flak.

The 316th was to fly one more mission in support of 'Market', and again it was of a totally different nature. A newly discovered grass fighter airstrip at Oud Keent, 2¼ miles west of Grave was found to be in good condition and its possibilities were quickly realised. Plans were quickly made to land a British air supply unit called an Airborne Forward Delivery Airfield Group (AFDAG) and an anti-aircraft battery on the strip. The mission was flown on the 26th by six serials of aircraft from the 52nd Wing Cottesmore contributed two of 36 aircraft each, and aboard them were 105 men of the AFDAG, five war correspondents and over 148 tons of combat equipment.

On the whole, the operation went smoothly though there was a moment of concern when the strip was full of aircraft and over 40 enemy fighters were reported approaching. Thanks to excellent fighter patrols, none got through intact, the enemy suffering heavy losses with 32 claimed shot down. The 316th's squadrons returned to Cottesmore without loss, having taken part in what was considered to be the nearest thing to air-landing an airhead, carried out by the Allies in the Second World War.

After the 'Market' missions, the Group once more became involved in transport operations. Although winter began to have a restrictive effect, frequent flights were made to the Continent with supplies, often evacuating casualties on return. An indication as to the scale of these operations is shown in the summary for November 1944:

Combat Equipment	1,481,444lbs
Mail	140,800lbs
Freight	483,938lbs
Ammunition	362,008lbs
Gasoline	397,215lbs
Oil	307,181lbs
Troops	901
Stretcher Cases	810
Walking Wounded	200
Passengers	232

To achieve this, 5,098:35 hours were flown in 691 sorties for the loss of one aircraft.

During December 1944 the 316th TCG began to receive a number of Consolidated C-109s. These were former B-24 Liberator bombers converted into fuel tankers. By removing armour and interior fittings an additional 2,415 gallons of fuel could be carried internally, in auxiliary fuel tanks. Although several crews were trained to fly these aircraft little use was made of them by Cottesmore-based units and by early April 1945 all had been transferred to the 349th TCG at Barkston Heath.

Winter also served to add to the tedium of off duty hours on the base. Dances, film shows, football matches and other entertainments were all forms of diversion. The 316th was fortunate in having an excellent dance band, which was in great demand both on and off base. The Group's American football team, known as 'Berger's Bouncers' was also very popular. On one occasion, 30th December 1944, the team played the 'Bearcats' of the 9th Service Command at Headingley, Yorkshire, before a crowd estimated at 40,000.

Late in February 1945, the 52nd Wing came under orders to move out and occupy bases in France. Rumour also spread that the 316th was to return home to America. Before this could become fact the Group was to play its part in yet one more large scale airborne operation. This was Operation 'Varsity', the assault over the Rhine.

A constant source of concern was the possibility that the *Luftwaffe* might inflict serious damage on troop carrier units, especially during marshalling periods, by making night attacks on the airfields. Their ability to mount this type of raid, even at this stage of the war, was amply demonstrated on the night of 3rd/4th March, when the Germans staged Operation 'Gisela'. During the course of this attack, *Luftwaffe* intruders in the vicinity of British airfields inflicted heavy losses. In the course of the raid, Cottesmore was also on the receiving end.

An air raid warning 'Red' was sounded at 01:00 hours and about 30 minutes later 17 anti-personnel bombs fell on the station. No one was injured, but two C-47s, a Waco, part of the perimeter-track and a nearby farm building were damaged. Enemy intruders intercepted Avro Lancasters flying from nearby Woolfox Lodge, two of these being shot down, one crashing half a mile north east of Cottesmore. The other, Mk.III JB699, was attacked when over the airfield. It went into a vertical dive, which ended with the total destruction of the aircraft less than 500 yards from the control tower. There were no survivors.

For 'Varsity' the three 52nd Wing Groups, the 61st, 315th and 316th, still remaining in England, were given the task of delivering the paratroop echelon of the British 6th Airborne Division. To carry this out, they moved temporarily to forward bases in Essex at Boreham, Chipping Ongar and Wethersfield. The 316th was allocated the latter and aircraft departed Cottesmore on 20th/21st March, to position ready for the operation.

'Varsity' took place on 24th March, with the English-based American serials first away. Blessed with almost perfect weather, they had little trouble on the way out. In the lead formation were 80 aircraft of the 61st and 40 from the 316th, carrying the 3rd Parachute

Douglas C-47A Skytrain 42-100973 Michael *of the 44th TCS basks in the sun at Cottesmore. Note the Horsa assault gliders in the background.*
D Wills

Men of the US Army's 3rd Battalion, 505th Parachute Infantry Regiment preparing for their D-Day sortie from Cottesmore. Captain Robert Kirkwood is smoking the cigar, Lieutenant Pat Ward is wearing the helmet. W Woodward

Paratroops of the 82nd Airborne board a C-47 of the 36th TCS .
The late Arthur Pearcy collection

heavy bombers and Bristol Beaufighters. These started to fly in on 15th September, and by the end of the month the unit had a complement of 31 aircraft.

Conversion training followed pretty much the same pattern evolved in wartime, but crew output was on a much reduced scale. There were some differences, one being Exercise 'Spasm', which would have been impossible during the war. Practiced on many occasions, it entailed a single aircraft flying to Gatow, near Berlin, and returning after an overnight stay.

Another change of control occurred on 21st December, when Cottesmore was passed from 7 Group to 91 Group, Bomber Command. In the same month, Group Captain H McC White assumed command of the station.

VIP visits have always been a fact of life at Cottesmore, and the early months after the end of the war were no exception. On 9th January 1946, the station played host to a Uruguayan Combined Services Mission, led by Colonel Gestido, Director General of Military Aviation. The visit was to acquaint Uruguay with the operation of a HCU and to provide details of the training programme.

With the future requirements for heavy bomber crews on the decline, the continued existence of 1668 HCU was in doubt. It was soon to suffer the fate of many similar units. Operations were wound down during February and on 7th March the unit was formally disbanded. Despite the problems posed by large fluctuations in numbers of staff and inclement weather, in the short time it was at Cottesmore, the HCU had flown 4,285 hours and trained 57 crews.

The sound of Merlins was not to be absent for long though, as the Lancasters were replaced by de Havilland Mosquitos of 16 OTU, on 22nd March, from Upper Heyford, Oxfordshire. Equipped with 15 T.III trainers and B.XVI bombers, together with four Oxfords, the main function of the unit was to train crews for Bomber Command. In addition, it was called upon to give tuition to personnel of the French Air Force, the Armée de l'Air. By August 1946, 48 pilots and 30 navigators of that air arm had completed the requisite courses at Cottesmore.

Brigade. A further 40 from the 316th led the next formation of 122 aircraft, with the 5th Parachute Brigade aboard.

As the two formations ran in and made their drops towards the northern end of the Diersfordter Wald, they met little opposition. But, as they swung on to their homeward course, flak guns began to open up. Worst hit was the second wave of serials, which came under intense and accurate fire. Ten aircraft went down in enemy territory, seven force-landed behind Allied lines and 70 received varying degrees of damage. Initial figures showed 12 aircraft of the 316th missing, but personnel losses released later amounted to less than three complete crews. It was hoped that the 316th would be able to land in France on the return journey. However, the airfield they were to occupy had not been repaired in time, so they faced the long flight home. By 13:00 hours, most of the surviving aircraft had returned direct to Cottesmore at the end of a successful, if costly operation.

After 'Varsity' a return was made to the freighting of supplies, but the Group's days at Cottesmore were numbered, and rumour at last became fact. The 316th were to return to the USA. During April, much of the unit's equipment was disposed of to other groups stationed in the UK and on the Continent, although some aircraft did fly out bound for Pope Field, North Carolina, on 14th May. By 11th June, the 316th had gone.

On 1st July Station 489 became history, as control was transferred from the USAAF back to the RAF and it became part of 7 Group in the process. Cottesmore was then held in temporary establishment, pending the arrival of 1668 Heavy Conversion Unit (HCU) from Bottesford. Group Captain J H T Simpson, the Officer Commanding Bottesford, carried out an inspection of the station on 29th July, but it was not until 1st September that advance parties from the HCU began to take over. One of the last remaining units of its type in the RAF, the HCU was equipped in the main with Avro Lancaster

Two Mosquitos of 204 AFS in front of Cottesmore's tower, with the airfield denominator 'CT' in the foreground.

A line-up of Percival Prentices, with VR268 'U' nearest the camera, in front of Cottesmore's trio of 'C' Type hangars. An Oxford is parked at right. On the extreme right is the station's original Fort Type 207/36 watch office and tower. Both via Chaz Bowyer

On many previous occasions, seasonal weather had disrupted station life, but the winter of 1946/1947 was so severe that Cottesmore and much of the surrounding area ground to a halt. During February 1947, no flying was possible due to heavy snowfalls and blizzard conditions. Roads were impassable and German Prisoners of War still in the vicinity, were put to work helping with clearance operations. The situation became so desperate, that on 6th March, an air drop of bread and medical supplies was made on the airfield by a Lancaster from Lindholme in Yorkshire.

By the time conditions had improved, a change in training procedure had taken place. Aircrew, on reaching 'wings' standard, were now to be sent to Advanced Flying Schools (AFS), before progressing to operational units. Cottesmore was transferred to 21 Group, Flying Training Command (FTC) on 15th March 1947, then 16 OTU was redesignated 204 AFS on 1st May. The unit also exchanged its Mosquito B.XVIs for the FB.VI fighter-bomber version.

No.204 AFS continued to train crews at Cottesmore unit 1st March 1948, when it moved north to Driffield, Yorkshire. Another training unit, 7 Service Flying Training School (SFTS) was soon to be transferred from Kirton in Lindsey, Lincolnshire, on 16th March,

and at the same time the station came under the control of 23 Group, FTC. After arrival, the unit reverted to a former title, to become 7 Flying Training School (FTS). Equipped with de Havilland Tiger Moth biplanes for basic training and North American Harvards for advanced training, the school offered tuition to trainee pilots from both the RAF and Royal Navy. In addition, it also conducted instrument rating and pilot refresher courses.

For many years, it has been customary for units and establishments within the RAF to possess an individual badge. Officially approved by the reigning monarch, these distinctive emblems are unique in respect of their central device and the motto they carry. On 9th June 1949, the graduation day for 9 Pilots Course, Cottesmore received its own badge which was presented with due ceremony by the Earl of Ancaster, the then Lord Lieutenant of Rutland. Its central design consists of an inverted horseshoe, taken from the county arms, upon this are

superimposed first a five pointed star recalling the station's wartime use by the USAAF and second by a hunting horn as a reminder of the county's hunting associations. This is also echoed by the motto, contained in a scroll at the base – *We Rise To Our Obstacles*. When the impressive pillars, which flank the station's main gates, were built during 1950, facsimiles of the badge were incorporated in the brickwork.

Following the outbreak of the Korean war in September 1950, the need arose for more aircrew. To meet this requirement, increasing numbers of national servicemen were offered aircrew training. Replacement of the Tiger Moth with the Percival Prentice T.1 monoplane, had taken place in June 1950 and the Flying Wing at Cottesmore was re-organised into one squadron of these aircraft, two squadrons of the older Harvards and a Headquarters Squadron. This latter element was established to provide continuation training for instructors and to conduct instrument rating tests.

Last minute briefing for a student pilot prior to a sortie in a 7 FTS Balliol in early 1953.
RAF Cottesmore

The increase in circuit training was to cause problems, but by first using Spitalgate, near Grantham, Lincolnshire, as a relief landing ground (RLG) for the Prentices, and later Woolfox Lodge (Chapter Twenty-Three) for Harvards, the difficulty was overcome.

By 1952, after over a decade of service, the Harvard was beginning to be finally phased out of flying training duties with the RAF. Its replacement was the Boulton Paul Balliol T.2, which was gradually introduced until, by March 1953, 7 FTS had received its full complement. One of the first opportunities for the unit to show off these new aircraft publicly came on 15th July 1953, on the occasion of the Coronation Review of the RAF, held at Odiham, Hampshire. Twelve Balliols, led by Wing Commander G MacKenzie DFC, were one of the numerous formations taking part in the flypast in honour of Her Majesty Queen Elizabeth II.

After the war in Korea had ended, in July 1953, reductions in flying training units were made. By the end of the year, it was known that 7 FTS was one of those about to be disbanded, and the unit's long association with Cottesmore came to an end with the graduation of the last courses on 24th March 1954.

Over the six years that 7 FTS had been on the station, many students had successfully completed their various courses. However, their training had not been completed without loss, for over the years 23 aircraft had been written off and at least seven lives lost.

No.7 FTS was reformed at Valley, Anglesey, on 24th March 1954, by redesignating 202 AFS, while Cottesmore entered a brief period of inactivity. This was soon to alter, as the station prepared for a change in role. In May 1954, it once again became part of Bomber Command and returned to 3

Group. Between the 19th and 22nd of the month, the jet age came to Cottesmore with the arrival, from Coningsby, Lincolnshire, of four squadrons, 15, 44/55 (Rhodesia), 57 and 149, all equipped with English Electric Canberra B.2 twin-engined bombers.

Frequent training sorties were soon being flown. They also participated in Command exercises to test not only their skills as an attacking force, but also the preparedness of both UK and North Atlantic Treaty Organisation (NATO) defence systems. The stay of 149 Squadron was rather brief, for on 24th August it left for Ahlhorn, Germany, where it became the first Canberra unit to join the 2nd Allied Tactical Air Force.

As a new aircraft, the Canberra was in demand for overseas tours during the 1950s. Not only were these trips excellent mobility exercises, they were also a method of enhancing British prestige abroad and at the same time generating interest which could lead to future sales. Early in November 1954 six Canberras from 57 Squadron, led by Squadron Leader I G Broom, left Cottesmore for a tour of the Middle East. Iraq was one of the countries visited, and the British Trade Fair there proved an ideal opportunity for showing the flag. Good relations were further enhanced in Amman, Jordan, where His Majesty King Hussein sampled a Canberra flight with a trip in Squadron Leader Broome's aircraft. When the goodwill tour came to an end, the six aircraft had each covered some 8,000 miles by the time they returned home.

Venezuela was one of the countries which purchased the Canberra. Prior to their delivery, 28 officers and SNCOs of the Fuerza Aerea Venezolana spent a month at Cottesmore gaining an insight into the type's maintenance procedures.

February 1955 marked the start of a momentous period for RAF Cottesmore. On the 15th the station was placed under Care and Maintenance and 15 and 57 Squadrons departed, followed on the 20th by 44, for Honington, Suffolk. This was not the last that Cottesmore had seen of the Canberra.

Cottesmore then prepared for an onslaught by civil engineers. Monks of Stamford, Lincolnshire, were appointed main contractors for a project which was to again transform the layout of the station and make it suitable for 'V-bomber' operations. The 'V-bombers' were the UK's long range strategic deterrence force, comprising the Vickers Valiant, Handley Page Victor and Avro Vulcan four-jet bombers.

The most radical change envisaged was to the three runways. Gone were the days when these were essential on a military airfield; a single long runway would now suffice. Work commenced in May to extend the main runway to 3,000 yards, with increased load bearing strength. Together with new taxiways and dispersal points, this work was to absorb in the region of 300,000 cubic yards of concrete. Some new buildings were required on both the technical and domestic sites, while improvements were made to many others.

It was not until early March 1958 that the transformation was complete and the station ready to become operational again. In Command was British's leading fighter ace of the Second World War, Group Captain J E 'Johnnie' Johnson DSO DFC.

First of the 'V-bombers' to use the reconstructed airfield was the Vickers Valiant. Four of these aircraft from 90 Squadron and two from 199 Squadron were attached to the station from 5th-26th March while runway servicing work was in progress at their home base at Honington, Suffolk. The detachment provided a perfect opportunity for experience to be gained by everyone concerned in operating all the latest aids with which the base was now equipped.

Cottesmore entered the new era on 9th April 1958, with the arrival of the first Handley Page Victor B.1, XA935, destined for 10 Squadron, captained by Wing Commander C B Owen DSO DFC AFC, officer commanding (OC) 10 Squadron designate. This unit, the first to equip with these crescent-winged aircraft, reformed at Cottesmore on 15th April, gradually coming up to strength as other Victors were received over the next few months. It received its eighth and last aircraft on 9th September. It was joined on 1st September by 15 Squadron, renewing its links with the station, when it too reformed at Cottesmore, to become the second RAF Victor unit. Wing Commander D A Green DSO OBE DFC, OC 15, collected its first aircraft, XA941 on 16th September. The unit received its last aircraft on 29th December.

Overall, September proved a very busy month for the base with its new and potent additions to the 'V-force', rapidly becoming a focus of attention. The Cottesmore-based Victors took part in flypasts during the SBAC Show at Farnborough, featured on a TV programme and were the centre of attraction at a press day. Lastly, the station opened its doors to the general public on the 20th for a Battle of Britain display. Although Cottesmore had on previous occasions staged events in support of this anniversary, the scale of interest in 1958 was quite unprecedented. A crowd estimated at over 40,000 flocked to the station, many no doubt attracted by the thought of seeing the latest bombers. Such a huge influx caused problems on the narrow country roads, and traffic jams developed. At one stage a massive queue of vehicles stretched from the main gates to Uppingham, a distance of ten miles to the south.

While the 'V-bombers' were in residence, these Battle of Britain displays came to be regarded almost as an annual event at Cottesmore, the number of visitors the following year being estimated at over 46,000. Some years, anti-nuclear demonstrators made their presence known outside the base, but their protestations appear to have had little effect on attendances, with figures averaging around 30,000.

Yet another important event occurred on 21st October 1958 when a de Havilland Heron of the Queen's Flight brought Her Royal Highness The Princess Margaret to the station to present 10 Squadron with its Standard. The might of Bomber Command was well represented during the ceremony when 12 aircraft, Valiants, Victors, Vulcans and Canberras, in flights of three, flew past in salute. While at Cottesmore 15 Squadron were also the recipients of a Standard. This was presented on 3rd May 1961, by Her Royal Highness The Duchess of Kent.

By the turn of the year, the two squadrons had begun to flex their muscles with quartets of Victors making practice dispersals to other UK airfields. Several overseas flights

also took place, and on 21st March 1959 during one such exercise, a 15 Squadron Victor, XH594, captained by Group Captain Johnson, flew to Cyprus in 3 hours 46 minutes, breaking the England to Cyprus point-to-point record.

After the winter's lull, spring ushered in a further flurry of distinguished visitors. On 1st April the 41st Anniversary of the founding of the RAF was marked by a visit from Prime Minister Harold MacMillan, accompanied by George Ward, Secretary of State for Air and Marshal of the RAF Sir Dermot Boyle, Chief of the Air Staff. On arrival, the visitors were welcomed by Air Chief Marshal Sir Harry Broadhurst, Air Officer Commanding in Chief Bomber Command, Air Vice-Marshal K B B Cross, Air Officer Commanding 3 Group, and the Station Commander, Group Captain J E Johnson.

During his stay, the Prime Minister was able to see some of the latest operational procedures and was also shown examples of recent additions to the RAF's armoury. A static display allowed him to inspect some of the new aircraft and others in prospect for the service. One aircraft on show was a

Gloster Javelin FAW.7, complete with Firestreak air-to-air missiles, the first time these weapons had been on public view.

Mr MacMillan personally initiated the most impressive event of the day when he gave the signal for a 'V-bomber' scramble. Four Victors, two from each of the resident squadrons, roared off in quick succession, with the last airborne in three minutes 57 seconds. This was the first Victor scramble within four minutes, the warning allowed for an impending missile attack. Later, with improvements in starting equipment and much practice, times of under two minutes became commonplace.

Cottesmore was fast becoming a showcase for the 'V-force', but the station was, by now, quite adept at catering for eminent personages. On 24th April, King Hussein of Jordan received a briefing on Bomber Command and toured the station before viewing a static display which included a Vulcan, Valiant and a Canberra. He later flew in Victor XA938, captained by OC 10 Squadron, and after a flight of 70 minutes, landed at Farnborough. The Shah of Persia visited the station on 13th May.

Canberra B.2 WH920 of 44 Squadron showing off the fine lines of a type that was very much a Cottesmore workhorse. The horseshoe and hunting horn emblem of Rutland are worn on the fin. Eric Watts

The unique format of the crescent-winged Victor shown to advantage on Cottesmore-based B.1 XH588 of 15 Squadron. Ken Ellis collection

The Victors began to range further afield and on 8th July 1959, two from 15 Squadron flew to Vancouver, Canada. There, they took part in anniversary celebrations in support of 50 years of flight in the dominion. Not all sorties to this hemisphere were courtesy visits. Increasing use was made of North America for training where the vast expanses of often snow-covered terrain made for excellent navigational exercises.

Back at home, the two squadrons were engaged in yet more exercises designed to test their readiness and potential. Some were pre-planned dispersals, called 'Kinsman', others known as 'Mayflight' were no-notice exercises, when there was a mass exodus of Victors from their home base. These sorties often ended in a 'Matador' exercise, during which UK defences were probed. A typical training flight from Cottesmore might involve the Victor crew carrying out several simulated bombing runs against a variety of targets in various locations throughout the UK. To these would probably be added navigation tests which could take the aircraft far out over the Atlantic, so base became a welcome sight after long hours in the air.

In the summer of 1960, towards the end of an emergency situation in Malaya, brought about by Communist aspirations, some Cottesmore based Victors were detached to Royal Australian Air Force station Butterworth, Malaya. Known as Exercise 'Profiteer', these excursions continued for some time after the emergency was over, with the aircraft eventually using RAF Tengah, Singapore, after that airfield had been extensively modernised. While in the Far East, these detachments often took the opportunity to practice their conventional bombing skills over the Song Song and China Rock ranges. On at least one occasion, the press were treated to the awesome spectacle created when a Victor released a full load of 35 x 1,000lb bombs. Somewhat closer to home, ranges in Libya. North Africa, were also used for bombing practice with conventional weapons.

No.15 Squadron was the first Victor unit to receive the B.1A, the first example, XH613, being received in July 1960. The B.1A differed from the earlier model by having more sophisticated radar and electronic counter-measures (ECM) equipment. Eventually, both Cottesmore squadrons were to be fully equipped with B.1As, some of them being B.1s modified to the new standard.

When an improved version of the Victor, the B.2, was cleared for squadron service, Cottesmore was chosen, in 1961, as the training base for the crews. The Mk.1 Victors had been powered by four Armstrong Siddeley Sapphire turbojets; the much more capable Mk.2 by four Rolls-Royce Conways. Initially, the B.2 Trials Unit, 'C' Flight of 232 Operational Conversion Unit (OCU), was set up to carry out an extensive period of flying, and to train new crews to form the B.2 squadrons. The crews commenced conversion to the new variant after XL188, the first B.2 to enter service with Bomber Command, arrived on 1st November 1961; the fourth and last aircraft arriving by 19th December. On satisfactory completion of these trials, 'C' Flight 232 OCU began to train crews to fly the Victor B.2, with the first two graduate crews leaving Cottesmore on 26th January 1962 for Wittering, Cambridgeshire, to reform 139 Squadron on 1st February 1962.

Until June 1962, Cottesmore-based Victors had been free of major accidents, but this was to alter when two aircraft were lost within the space of three days. The first incident happened on the 14th when all four engines of 15 Squadron's XH613 failed while on the approach to the airfield. Thankfully, all the crew were successful in leaving the aircraft before it crashed on the disused airfield at North Witham, Lincolnshire.

Unfortunately, the outcome of the second incident, on the 16th, was far more tragic. After take-off from Akrotiri on Cyprus, XA929 of 10 Squadron burst into flames when it crashed half a mile from the end of the runway. There were no survivors from the six man crew.

Shortly after becoming an independent state in September 1963, Malaysia began to receive the unwanted attentions of Indonesia. When Soviet-built Tupolev Tu-16 *Badger* twin-jet bombers of its air force began to make regular nightly flights to within a few miles of Singapore, this was seen as a threatening posture. Once again, Cottesmore's Victors were called upon to play their deterrent role, and in December eight aircraft were detached to the Far East Air Force (FEAF). Stationed at Tengah, these aircraft were under orders to knock out Indonesian airfields, should the confrontation escalate and actual attacks be made. Happily, the need for them to go into action never arose, but their presence no doubt helped to contain a tense situation.

After a six year association, the Victor era at Cottesmore came to an end in 1964. 'C' Flight of 232 OCU, operating the B.2, had already ceased training on 31st March 1963, moving to Wittering where it was redesignated the Victor Training Flight on 1st April 1963. Next to go was 10 Squadron, which disbanded on 1st March 1964, then came the turn of 15 Squadron, on 31st October. Their demise, however, did not sever the station's connections with the 'V-force', for the Victors were quickly replaced.

In November, 9, 12 and 35 Squadrons flew in from Coningsby on the 10th, 17th and 2nd respectively, all equipped with the delta-winged Avro Vulcan B.2s. The arrival of these Vulcan units brought about another change for the station, with a transfer from 3 to 1 Group.

These three squadrons now formed the Cottesmore Wing of the Medium Bomber Force (MBF), all aircraft being maintained centrally, with none of the units having their own aircraft but taking from the 'pool' as needed. All maintained both nuclear and conventional bombing capabilities. Like

Visitors look a bit sparse in this view of the September 1960 Battle of Britain display. Perhaps the show was then over as the tower crew look quite relaxed. In the background is a Victor B.1 with a Chipmunk T.10 in front of it and a Meteor F.8 to the right. R A Forbes

Centralised servicing meant that the Vulcan B.2s of the Cottesmore Wing did not wear squadron markings. The Wing undertook deployments to the Far East and this aircraft, climbing out of Tengah, Singapore, in mid-1968 may have been a Cottesmore machine. Ken Ellis collection

the Victors before them, they spent a considerable amount of time practising the latter art. In many ways the training carried out was similar with frequent exercises, overseas deployments and goodwill visits all part of squadron life.

One overseas duty taken over from the Victors was the periodic rotation of aircraft to the Far East, where friction between Malaysia and Indonesia continued to exist. It was a problem which was to remain unresolved until August 1966. Towards the end of the confrontation, the 'V-bomber' presence was reduced, from eight to four aircraft. From November 1965, these aircraft were drawn from the Cottesmore Wing, with the final four, flown by 35 Squadron crews, returning home in August 1966.

After a long period of stability, the first major change at Cottesmore came on 31st December 1967, when 12 Squadron disbanded. It was though the defence policy changes of 1968 which, while affecting the RAF as a whole, had the most profound effect on the future of the station. On 30th April 1968, Bomber and Fighter Commands combined to become Strike Command. Cottesmore came under the control of the

bomber section, 1 (Bomber) Group. In the re-organisation which followed 9 and 35 Squadrons were to be deployed to Akrotiri. There, with the object of strengthening Britain's commitment to the Central Treaty Organisation (CENTO) and adding to the security of NATO's southern flank, they were to form the Near East Air Force (NEAF) Bomber Wing.

Preparations for the exodus started late in 1968, the first movements taking place in January 1969. The operation became quite a protracted affair, with the last aircraft leaving on 19th March. When previous flights had left, they did so with no formal send off, but the last four Vulcans to go departed with due ceremony. Thick freezing fog shrouded the airfield as the bagpipes of 1 (Bomber) Group pipe band played 'The Last Farewell' while several hundred onlookers strained to catch a last glimpse of the Vulcans. On receipt of the code word 'Barker' from HQ Strike Command, High Wycombe, Bucks, at 11:30 hours the last scramble began. Although the fog was a hindrance, the performance was as impressive as ever. Quickly gaining momentum, the vague shapes of the Vulcans sped along the runway to disappear into the gloom. In less than three minutes, all were airborne and as the crackling roar of 16 Rolls-Royce Olympus engines faded away, a decade of 'V-bomber' operations from Cottesmore came to an end.

But it was not the end of the Vulcan as a newsworthy item as far as the station was concerned. Two aircraft had been left

behind by the departing squadrons, destined to be scrapped. On Sunday, 16th June during the course of this work flame from a cutting torch ignited fuel left in the tanks of one of them. The offending workman just managed to scramble clear as the aircraft burst into flames. Despite liberal amounts of foam being expended by both service and civilian fire crews attempting to subdue the blaze, over 70% of the Vulcan was destroyed.

Within the month replacements began to arrive and their coming brought once again a change in role for the station. During April the aircraft of three specialist units flew in in quick succession. The first of these, on the 17th was 98 Squadron with Canberra B.2s and T.4s, added later was the E.15 calibration variant. Next day it was the turn of some of 115 Squadron's Vickers Varsity T.1 twin-engined calibration aircraft and Armstrong Whitworth Argosies or 'Whistling Wheelbarrows' as they were sometimes affectionately called. (The Argosy being a Leicestershire product, see Chapter Two.) Then, on the 21st, to complete the trio came the Canberra B.2s, T.4s and T.17 ECM trainers of 360 Squadron.

There was one more movement still outstanding before the station's new complement was complete and this was fulfilled on 19th May with the arrival of yet another Canberra unit, 231 Operational Conversion Unit (OCU) with its B.2s and T.4s. By the end of the month aircraft on station strength stood at 56.

A string of redundant airframes have been used for fire crash rescue training at Cottesmore. Swift FR.5 XD976 was issued to the dump in 1961. R Forbes

A line-up of 360 Squadron's Canberra T.17s showing off their distinctive noses. Author

One of 231 OCU's Canberra B.2s, WH919 'V'. Brandon White

Opposite page:

The Canberra 'meet' at Cottesmore held on 13th May 1974 to mark the 25th anniversary of the first flight of the Canberra prototype. The photograph was taken by a Canberra PR.9 of 39 Squadron from Wyton. Note that the airfield denominator by the tower was by then 'CM'. RAF Cottesmore

The previous home of the OCU had been Bassingbourn, Cambridgeshire, while the three squadrons had vacated Watton, Norfolk. There they had been part of 90 (Signals) Group to which Cottesmore was duly transferred from 1 Group. A change of command also took place with Group Captain L G A Bastard AFC, taking over from Group Captain W J H Roberts on 30th May.

No.115 Squadron's allotted task was to carry out calibration and performance checks of all RAF, and later RN, navigational airfield and runway approach aids. No.98 Squadron, in complementary role, engaged in flight checking medium and high level radars. In these capacities aircraft of both units ranged worldwide and were often away from the station for long periods in the course of their duties.

No.360 Squadron was unique in three respects. Not only did it have the distinction of being the RAF's youngest squadron and the only one to fly the T.17, but it was also a joint RAF/RN unit. Staffed on a 75/25% basis with every fourth Commanding Officer drawn from the Senior Service, personnel at all levels were fully integrated, uniform being the only distinction when selecting crews for any duty. The squadron's Canberras were mainly employed in the ECM role with a primary duty of creating problems for military radars throughout the UK and other member countries of the NATO.

With the object of teaching radar operators the possible effect enemy intervention ('jamming') could have on their sets and the opportunity to devise a suitable counter 360's T.17s took part in virtually every major air and sea exercise held. Air defence systems on all flanks of the Alliance were subject to their attentions with a varied range of sophisticated jamming techniques practised. Other devices, such as the input of false information or the creation of spurious radar echoes by distributing 'Window' or 'Chaff' were often introduced to perplex confused operators even further.

The distinction of being the world's first jet bomber conversion unit fell to 231 OCU after it began to receive Canberras in February 1952. At one time the unit operated in excess of 50 aircraft but by 1969 the Canberra force had declined in numbers, as had the strength of the OCU. So it was a much depleted unit by the time of its transfer to Cottesmore, but still with the important duty, the output of trained crews to fly the Canberra.

In the early months of settling in at Cottesmore some difficulties were experienced by all the station's new residents. The centralised system of servicing as practised by the previous occupants did not suit the four units and a more suitable system which met their requirements was soon devised. Also shortage of manpower together with the detachments caused problems and were given as major reasons why monthly targets were not met. Increases in manning levels helped to resolve some of the difficulties.

During 1971 a decision to reallocate all 90 Group aircraft resulted in Cottesmore again becoming a part of 1 (Bomber) Group, Strike Command. Also during February the Varsity was finally phased out of service with 115 Squadron when WJ911 was retired. The unit was then wholly equipped with Argosy C.1s and E.1s. Later in the year one of these aircraft featured in an operation the outcome of which was most rewarding for its crew.

Bitteswell-built Argosy E.1 XP439 of 115 Squadron making an approach to its home base, Cottesmore. From this angle, it is easy to see how it got its 'Whistling Wheelbarrow' nickname. Brandon White

Opposite page:

The changing face of Cottesmore. The left hand diagram shows its status in 1950 with three runways. On the right, the base is shown in 1988 during the Tornado years. The large ASP, built to house the large TTTE fleet was built to the east of the control tower. RAF Cottesmore

While engaged in checking ILS facilities for St Mawgan, Cornwall on 19th May a signal was picked up from a Canberra reporting a patch of disturbed sea some 20 miles south of St Trevose Head. Asked to investigate, the Argosy was heading for the area when a further message from the Canberra stated that it was receiving distress signals from two 'Sarbe' beacons. Taking over control of the search the Argosy then began to direct operations. By the use of ultra violet pictures the general position of the survivors was located and the information passed to two de Havilland Sea Vixen carrier-borne jet fighters and two helicopters which had been dispatched to assist. On arrival in the area the Sea Vixens began their search, one at 500ft the other at 6,000ft with the Argosy in between at 1,500ft.

It was the Argosy crew who spotted the first survivor ten minutes after beginning the search with the second soon afterwards; both were in their dinghies. Circling continuously they passed the position to St Mawgan and the approaching helicopters and when they arrived pinpointed the dinghies. Both men were winched to safety and on return to St Mawgan were able to give an account of their McDonnell Douglas Phantom's crash. The Argosy resumed and completed its ILS check.

In this phase of Cottesmore's life the accident record was good although all three Canberra units were eventually to lose aircraft. The first incident took place on the night of 29th January 1971 and involved 360 Squadron's T.17 WH874 and T.4 WJ862 while engaged in a formation flying exercise a mid-air collision occurred near Mansfield, Nottinghamshire. Both aircraft were destroyed in the resultant crashes, but not before all five crew had ejected or baled out, sustaining only minor injuries. A sec-

ond accident in the year, on 5th October concerned 98 Squadron's E.15 WH973. During a night training exercise problems developed in the aircraft which became insurmountable and the three crew were forced to eject. This they did successfully but WH973 was destroyed when it crashed at Lobthorpe, near South Witham.

Economy measures were introduced by Strike Command from 1st January 1972. No.98 Squadron had its establishment of aircraft cut from ten to seven, aircrew from 25 to 16 and groundcrew from 58 to 44. The squadron's duties were also reduced with the loss of most of their flight checking tasks in the Mediterranean area.

One aircraft the squadron retained though was T.4 WD944 which as a B.2 had been one of the first Canberras allocated to 101 Squadron at Binbrook, Lincolnshire, in 1951. This vintage specimen celebrated 21 years of service with the RAF on the 9th October 1972. It was also in October that Cottesmore received its first 'gate guardian' aircraft in the form of the Canberra PR.7 WH791. This was a type of Canberra which had never served on the station and at first it was repainted with the serial 'WH717' to represent a B.2 of 44 Squadron from the station's first Canberra era. Later it was to acquire its true serial once more. WH791 was to remain 'on guard' at Cottesmore until it was put up for auction on 24th September 1998. It was bought for the princely sum of £2,600 by the 81 Squadron Association and it was moved to the Newark Air Museum during mid-November.

The following year there was another coming of age at Cottesmore when 231 OCU celebrated 21 years of continuous operations with the Canberra on 21st February 1973. It is unfortunate to have to record that two major incidents which

occurred during the year both involved the unit's aircraft.

In the first, on 12th March, a student pilot Flying Officer Andy Miller was engaged on a night exercise when the engines of his Canberra both developed technical problems. Believing a crash distinctly possible his navigator, Flight Lieutenant R E Pocock was ordered to eject. On landing in a ploughed field near Belton, Rutland, he suffered a sprained ankle and extensive bruising, but was able to attract the attention of a searching USAF helicopter by means of his 'Sarbe' beacon and flares. As for Miller, he was able to maintain control of his aircraft to make a safe landing at Cottesmore.

The second accident, on 2nd August, had a far more tragic outcome and again it happened in the course of a night flying exercise. At 23:00 hours 231's Canberra B.2 WJ674 was on the approach to the airfield when it was seen to be in flames. People watching from the Fox Inn on the A1 saw the navigator eject; the parachute barely had time to open before he made a heavy landing in a ploughed field a short distance from the inn. Help was soon at hand. Sadly the pilot, Flight Lieutenant Dennis, was not so fortunate. His ejection was delayed too long, the parachute failed to fully deploy and he was killed.

On September 15th the station opened its gates to the public for Battle of Britain Day, the first time this had happened since 1965. Some 50,000 people flocked to the event, many in the 9,000 cars estimated to have passed through the gates. There were as usual side shows and other attractions to amuse the visitors and to help raise funds for various RAF charities. The afternoon's air display was well up to Cottesmore's previous high standard. One of the highlights was a scintillating performance by the 12 Fouga CM-170 Magisters of the French Air Force aerobatic team, Patrouille de France.

Later in the month 28th September was a memorable occasion, for 360 unique in the unit's already singular history. On that day Commander G Oxley, RN, the first naval CO, received from Air Chief Marshal Sir Andrew

Humphrey KCB CBE DFC AFC, the unit badge. The design of the emblem with its central device of a Melese Laodamia Druce moth superimposed upon a trident together with the motto 'Confundemus' was most apt. A firm naval link was signified by the trident while the moth, a Central American insect, has, in the course of evolution, developed effective radar-type 'countermeasures' to avoid the attentions of hungry bats. As for the motto this translates as 'We Shall Throw Into Confusion', a good indication of the squadron's intentions.

Prospects nationwide during the first two months of 1974 were rather bleak. A strike by coal miners brought fuel stocks to crisis level and saw the introduction of a 3-day working week. Stringent economy measures were introduced which affected civil and service populations alike. Target figures were allocated to service establishments and those set for Cottesmore were not only met but in most instances considerable savings were achieved as the figures show:

	Target	Actual
Aviation Fuel (gallons)	445,300	311,552
'Civgas' (gallons)	3,570	2,965
Diesel (gallons)	1,020	1,142
Furnace Fuel Oil (gals)	88,555	67,430

Electricity consumption was also drastically reduced with 13,482kW/hours used per day compared with a 1973 average of 24,600 kW/hours. Limitations placed on flying hours were in force until March when there was a partial return to normality. Some restrictions remained until May.

Another milestone in the career of the Canberra was reached on 13th May 1974; it was, the 25th Anniversary of the first flight of the prototype, VN799, from Warton, Lancashire. In celebration of this Silver Jubilee a Canberra 'Meet' was held at Cottesmore on 22nd May and for the occasion 12 differ-

ent variants of the aircraft had been brought together on the airfield. Arranged in two parallel lines of six on the threshold of the disused runway, other Canberras from the resident units formed groups on adjacent taxi tracks. In all 33 aircraft were on show with the two lines of representative aircraft proving to be an interesting selection.

To round off the day a reunion dinner was held in the evening and among the many guests were those who had cause to remember the Canberra with affection. Joining test pilot Roland P Beamont, the Guest of Honour, were such distinguished personalities as Marshal of the Royal Air Force Sir Dermot Boyle, Air Chief Marshal Sir Lewis Hodges, Air Marshal Sir John Whitley and Air Vice-Marshal Ivor Broom, all of whom had flown Canberras into the record books. It must have been quite a nostalgic occasion with a great many reminiscences shared.

Government Defence Reviews often announced sweeping changes within the armed forces and none more so than that of 1975. Not only did it reveal that 12 RAF stations were to be closed but that it was planned to deactivate Cottesmore.

A first step in this direction was taken on 5th August when 360 Squadron moved to Wyton, Cambridgeshire, but it was not until February 1976 that the dispersal of the remaining three units took place. Departures began on the 18th when 231 OCU left for Marham, Norfolk. Five days later it was the turn of 115 Squadron bound for Brize Norton, Oxfordshire. Then, on the 27th, in a ceremony which gave an air of finality to the proceedings, 98 Squadron was disbanded and its standard formally laid up in the Air Force Memorial Chapel in Cottesmore's village church of St Nicholas. From the 31st the station again entered a period of Care and Maintenance, lasting for two years.

There were however still five Canberras left on the base, four of these were airframes having major structural problems rectified. Almost a year elapsed before the last of this quartet departed in February 1977. This left only the gate guardian, WH791, as a silent reminder that Cottesmore was once regarded as 'The Home of the Canberra'.

During this period of inactivity at Cottesmore the time came for the Argosy to retire from RAF service. This event was not allowed to pass by unrecorded nor was the past association with the station forgotten. On 24th January 1978 XR143 Omega of 115 Squadron made the last operational sortie of the type from Brize Norton to Cottesmore; on board was the RAF's free-fall parachute team, the Falcons, who jumped over the airfield carrying 1,000 commemorative postal covers. Then, as its final duty XR143 carried out the calibration of the station's approach aids.

When the Panavia Tornado prototype first flew from Manching, West Germany, on 14th August 1974, the event was widely reported but few could have realised the impact this aircraft was to have on Cottesmore in the future. Ordered in quantity to re-equip the air arms of Germany, Italy and the UK and manufactured by a consortium of companies within the three counties, Tornados were expected to make a large contribution to the defence of Europe through the NATO alliance for many years. The initial version of the twin-turbofan, variable-geometry (or 'swing-wing') Tornado was the all-weather Interdictor/Strike (IDS) fighter-bomber for all three participating countries while a stand-off interceptor Air Defence Variant (ADV) version was also developed, initially for just the RAF.

Studies into the possibility of a combined form of training for the Tornado IDS were

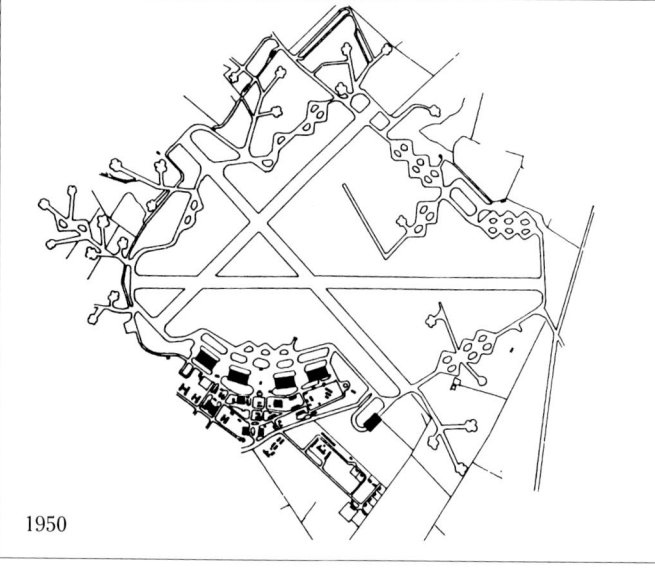

1950

1988

carried out and a March 1975 report recommended Cottesmore as a base. Complete political acceptance followed which led to the Three Nation Memorandum of Understanding being signed on 8th May 1979. This brought into existence the Tri-National Tornado Training Establishment (TTTE).

There was no fanfare of trumpets or wild celebrations when Cottesmore returned to the active list on 1st July 1978; just a simple colour hoisting ceremony, at which the new Station Commander, Wing Commander B N Wanstell took the salute to mark the change in status.

In preparation for its new role the station was once again subjected to a considerable amount of rebuilding and modernisation. Undoubtedly the most striking feature added to the airfield was the ten acres of concrete laid to make a new aircraft servicing platform (ASP), capable of accommodating 28 Tornados. To give quick access to the huge hardstanding a taxi link was added at a central point on the runway. Conversion of one of the four 'C' type hangars provided an engine servicing facility, the largest of its type in Europe, while other noticeable additions were an engine test installation and a de-tuner to lessen the noise impact of engines being ground-run in an airframe. Extra accommodation was obtained by means of extending the annexes on the sides of the hangars and the old Canberra simulator was replaced by a more suitable model.

At an early stage of this activity the Tornado Aircrew Training Course Design Team moved in from HQ Strike Command, High Wycombe. Their task was to create an aircrew training syllabus compatible with the requirements of all three countries. Next to arrive was the Tornado Ground Servicing School, an independent unit controlled by RAF Support Command. Training of personnel at the school began on 22nd October 1979 with the official opening, by Air Vice-Marshal Peter Bairsto, a few days later on the 31st. Other engineering units which followed were the Tornado Engineering, Development and Investigation Team in July 1980 and on 4th August the Tornado In Service Software Maintenance Team, responsible for the computer-based systems in the aircraft.

TTTE received its first Tornados on 1st July 1980 when RAF GR.1s ZA320 and ZA322 were flown in by British Aerospace (BAe) crews. They arrived on a rainy day which seems quite appropriate for an all-weather aircraft but it was probably not appreciated by the welcoming committee headed by the Air Officer Commanding 1 Group, Air Vice-Marshal M W R Knight.

A Tornado in the hands of a TTTE crew first flew from Cottesmore on 22nd August and the flight line began to take on its international appearance with the arrival of a factory-fresh *Luftwaffe* Tornado IDS, 43+01, from Manching, West Germany, on 2nd September.

At a unique ceremony in the presence of four Chiefs of Staff, the TTTE officially came into being on 29th January 1981. Representing the air arms of the participating nations were Air Chief Marshal Sir Michael Beetham, RAF; General Leutnant Friedrich Obleser, *Luftwaffe*; Vize Admiral Gunter Fromm, Bundesmarine (the West German naval air arm); and Generale di Squadra Aerea Lamberto Bartolucci, Aeronautica Militare Italiana (Italian Air Force). Again the Rutland weather was not in tune with the occasion forcing a three-nation flypast to be cancelled. Instead, as a substitute there was a single aircraft flyover which, although it passed by unseen, the sound of its passage was unmistakable.

It was not until 5th May 1982 that the flight

RAF TTTE Tornado, ZA525 'B-03', is dwarfed by the detuner built on the eastern end of the airfield. This huge device takes most of the 'sting' out of the noise generated during an engine test run. Brandon White

line became truly tri-national with the arrival of the first Italian Tornado IDS to join the training programme. By August 1982 the Tornado Operational Conversion Unit's (TOCU) four squadrons had received their full complement of aircraft and consequently there followed a steady increase in flying from the airfield. Output accordingly began to rise to such a scale that in April 1986 above 60 sorties in a day were recorded for the first time. In July there were in excess of 1,000 sorties for the month and by the end of the year some 85,000 movements had been made from the airfield. By September 1987 the 100th Course had begun and over 1,500 pilots and navigators had received training.

In the latter part of 1985 TTTE became, for a time, a four-nation establishment. The first signs that this could happen appeared in August when a fact finding delegation from Saudi Arabia toured the station. Following the announcement in September that the intended purchase of Tornados and BAe Hawks by the Royal Saudi Air Force (RSAF) had been finalised, events moved quite rapidly. The choice of Cottesmore for training was soon confirmed and on 11th October the first Saudi students arrived.

To assist with their training, a detachment of five Hawk T.1s from 2 Tactical Weapons Unit, Chivenor, Devon, arrived on 1st November and were quickly assimilated into their programme, staying for a period of three weeks. By early 1987 four Saudi Arabian courses had passed out and from then on the RSAF became responsible for its own training programme.

Increased activity from Cottesmore had not gone un-noticed by residents of nearby villages for the Tornado is not a quiet aircraft and the amount of noise generated from the airfield has always been a bone of contention in the surrounding area. From the outset, there were complaints which as time went by became more vociferous and often quite acrimonious. Eventually this led to a Noise Compensation Survey Team (NCST) being set up. There followed an investigation into the problem and as this proved to be a rather protracted affair it tended to aggravate the situation further.

The NCST report was finally released on 19th June 1987. It was received with general satisfaction for it recommended generous scales of compensation for residents most affected to enable them to sound proof their homes.

Airfields, with their large expanses of open grassland, attract large flocks of feeding birds and with these visitors comes the problem of possible bird strike. To combat this menace active stations have a small unit whose task is to dissuade these feathered invaders. Cottesmore's Bird Control Unit is a very active one. In the course of its travels round the airfield, operating the Sappho bird scaring apparatus, a considerable mileage is clocked up, while the number of deterrent cartridges fired is no less impressive. When the TTTE was first established the nearby Rutland Water reservoir was still in its infancy but in the interim it has become a site of international importance. This is not only for the large variety of birds which make it their permanent habitat, but also for the huge flocks of migratory wildfowl which overwinter there. The comings and goings of these birds presents a potential hazard to Cottesmore to such an extent that at certain times they lead to circuit restrictions being imposed. A heavily-printed warning 'Caution Bird Hazard' on official flight documents also warns prospective users of the airfield of this possible danger.

As it was during the 'V-bomber' era, so the TTTE has attracted a great many distinguished visitors to the station. Royalty, heads of state, government ministers and politicians, high ranking military personnel

and eminent figures from industry and commerce have all sampled Cottesmore's hospitality. The most prestigious visit must have been on 13th June 1984 when it was the station's privilege to receive an official visit from Her Majesty Queen Elizabeth II. After arriving by air in an Hawker Siddeley Andover CC.2 of the Queen's Flight, she made a tour of the base facilities and the flight line where 26 Tornados flanked her route. Before being entertained to lunch Her Majesty planted a flowering cherry tree in front of the officers mess in commemoration of her visit.

The 50th anniversary of the establishment of Cottesmore came in 1988 and one of the highlights of that year's celebrations took place when the Freedom of Entry into Oakham was granted to the base. This honour meant that a force from the station was permitted to march through the town with drums beating, bands playing, flags flying and bayonets fixed and this they did for the first time on 12th June. Three Tornados, one from each country on the base, staged a representative flypast while officers and men presented a colourful scene as they passed the saluting dais marching to the accompaniment of the band of the RAF College, Cranwell. Group Captain Peter Squire, OC Cottesmore, received the Scroll of Free-

dom, on behalf of the station, from Andrew Makey, Chairman of Rutland District Council, and the Mayor of Oakham Tom Elworth while in a reciprocal gesture both councils were presented with ceremonial swords.

Another event of 1988 was the annual Tornado Symposium, previously held in West Germany. It took place on 15th October and attracted over 200 aircrew and 50 aircraft. Almost every unit operating the Tornado in Europe, at that time, was represented providing a platform for a broad exchange on all subjects relevant to operating the aircraft. One memorable scene recorded during the event was the £558 million photograph, taken when crews and station personnel posed in front of 31 Tornados, each reputed to have cost £18 million.

While the TTTE has been in residence there has been no return to the opening of the station for Battle of Britain anniversary displays; instead 'Families Day' became an annual summer fixture, usually at the beginning of July. This was an occasion when base personnel, their families and invited guests were able to participate in a day with a distinct international flavour. Not only did it provide an opportunity for visitors to gain an insight into the many aspects of station activities not normally on public view, but it also served as a fund raising event from

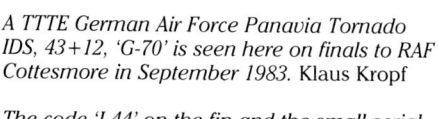

A TTTE German Air Force Panavia Tornado IDS, 43+12, 'G-70' is seen here on finals to RAF Cottesmore in September 1983. Klaus Kropf

The code 'I-44' on the fin and the small serial number MM55004 lower down, reveal it to be an IDS of the Italian Air Force's contribution to the TTTE, touching down on an 'out-and-back' at RAF Coningsby, Lincolnshire, in September 1987. Cottesmore TTTE sorties could ring all the changes, RAF aircraft, German student, Italian instructor and so on. Ron Blenkinsop via Ken Ellis

Where there was once a Canberra 'meet', Cottesmore hosted a similar event for the Tornado on 14th October 1989. This misty view shows a mixture of IDS and ADV variants from British, German and Italian units and gives an excellent view of the huge ASP.
RAF Cottesmore

TTTE held its official stand down ceremony on 24th February 1999 during which air and ground personnel formed the letters 'TTTE' on the huge apron against a backdrop of Tornados from each of the three participating countries.
RAF Cottesmore

which many worthy charities benefited. All the usual ingredients which go to make a successful open day were present, side shows, technical exhibits, a fun fair, static aircraft, food in abundance, all rounded off with an excellent flying display. The last of these very popular events was staged in 1997, though there are hopes that 'Families Day' will make a return in due course.

Since its inception the TTTE maintained a very good safety record. Unfortunately, accidents did occur but the unit sustained only three which involved the loss of life. The fact that in the region of 56,000 hours had been flown before the first of these incidents speaks highly of the accent placed on flight safety.

The first tragedy, which cost the lives of *Luftwaffe* Leutnant Peter Kastner and his RAF navigator Squadron Leader John Towl, happened on 17th June 1986. Bad weather conditions prevailed when their German IDS, 43+24 'G-74', hit a hillside near Claerwen Reservoir in the Elan Valley, Wales.

A view of Cottesmore from the air, looking roughly west in September 1997 when contractors were working on the airfield as part of the work needed to take the Harrier force. In the foreground can be seen the bomb storage area from the 'V-bomber' days. Just beyond the small lake is a large area being used by contractors, containing cement silos etc – all of a temporary nature. Author

It was a totally different set of circumstances which led to the second accident just over two years later. On the evening of 9th August 1988 Flight Lieutenant John Watts with his German navigator Leutnant Ulrich Fayer were engaged on a low level exercise. At dusk, while flying near Appleby, Cumbria, their aircraft, RAF GR.1 ZA329 'B-52', was involved in a mid-air collision with a Tornado of 617 Squadron, from Marham, Norfolk. The crews of both aircraft were killed and their aircraft destroyed.

John Watts was a vibrant pilot who also loved the world of historic aviation and had been instrumental in setting up the successful Fighter Meet air display at North Weald, Essex, and for the import and operation of Consolidated PBY-5A Catalina amphibian G-BLSC *Killer Cat* in 1985. The 'Cat' has, on at least one opportunity, alighted on Rutland Water during one of Anglia Water's annual shows.

The third loss occurred on 21st January 1999 when Tornado GR.1 ZA330 'B-08' was on a low level exercise when it collided with Cessna 152 G-BPZX, a civilian light aircraft, at Everton, near Nottingham. The two on board the Cessna were killed, as were the RAF instructor and Italian student on the Tornado. Wreckage from the Cessna fell very close to the primary school in Everton and the argument about the 'pros' and 'cons' of low level flying training was again brought into play.

Visiting aircraft often frequent Cottesmore's concrete and a quartet in the spring of 1990 were quite outstanding. Over a two week period during April and May the station played host to a detachment of four Boeing KC-135E Stratotankers four-engined jet tankers from the 940th Air Refueling Group, Mather Air Force Base, California, which operated from the airfield in support of the NATO Exercise 'Elder Forest 19'. This was the first time, since 1945 when the 316th TCG were in residence, that heavy fuel tanker aircraft of the USAF had flown from Cottesmore. Short though their stay was the visitors brought back wartime memories for some locals when, during their off duty moments, they managed to sample Rutland hospitality.

By the mid-1990s, TTTE had outstripped all 'opposition' for the title of the longest serving unit to be based at Cottesmore, but in January 1996 plans were disclosed showing that Cottesmore was to be affected by defence cutbacks and the planned drawdown of forces in the recently-established unified Germany. The cutbacks were not just of the homespun variety, but being a tri-national unit, reflected the economies and strategies of Germany and Italy. Force reductions in the two continental European countries lessened the need for the centralised training and plans were brought into being to disband TTTE and for Germany, Italy and the UK to make their own arrangements for future IDS training.

A gentle rundown of the TTTE began in 1997, though the final operational training sortie did not occur until 19th March 1999. (Interestingly, this was flown by RAF GR.1 ZA320 'B-01' – one of the first aircraft taken on charge by the unit, on 1st July 1980). Final departure from the station by Tornados of the German Air Force took place on 31st March 1999 with the last elements of the Italian Air Force and Royal Air Force following suit on 8th April.

The RAF element moved to Lossiemouth, Scotland, where, with effect from 1st April 1999, it linked up with the RAF Tornado Weapons Conversion Unit (operating under 15 [Reserve] Squadron status) to create the National Tornado OCU, with an establishment of 27 aircraft. The Italian Tornados were relocated within their home country while Germany's aircraft and crews set out for the wide open skies of the USAF's Holloman Air Force Base, in New Mexico, USA.

The departure of the multi-national TTTE was a sad moment for many, but it was an era that can always be pointed to in the future as a shining example to all that can be, and was achieved, by co-operation, mutual aims, understanding and trust.

Cottesmore was not to become idle. Following the re-unification of Germany and the agreed withdrawal of RAF units stationed there, Cottesmore's availability saw it designated as a future home for the BAe Harrier GR.7 all-weather vertical/short take-off and landing (V/STOL) strike fighters and T.10 operational trainers, based at Laarbruch.

Just as the station required considerable alteration work to make it suitable for the Tornados, so it needed specialist work to ready it for the Harrier 'jump-jets'. Although this work was largely carried out without closure, the Tornados were 'bolt-holed' to Lossiemouth in Scotland, and to Marham, Norfolk, during the summer of 1996. A new 'STOL-strip' was created that year and work on an increased area ASP began mid-1997. A tie-down pad for ground-running of Harriers plus increased squadron and technician accommodation was also undertaken, with completion scheduled for mid-1999.

The 'bolt-holing' that TTTE required was reciprocated for a month during August 1997 when HP Jetstream T.1 crew trainers of 45(R) Squadron were detached to Cottesmore while their base at Cranwell in Lincolnshire, underwent runway resurfacing.

The UK's 1998 Strategic Defence Review also placed heavy emphasis on the Harrier units and another element of co-operation. Ever since the Falklands conflict of 1982, RAF Harriers have operated alongside the Royal Navy Sea Harriers from aircraft carriers. In February 1999 came the announcement that the concentration of Harriers at Cottesmore and Wittering would increase

Souvenirs of the several legendary Oktoberfests and other interesting occasions held at Cottesmore during TTTE's tenure. Author

Now on display outside the 3 Squadron hangar at Cottesmore, this Harrier GR.3, XW924, is a reminder of the unit's earlier equipment. Mark Young

In February 1999, 4 Squadron were manning the RAF's contribution to Operation 'Deliberate Forge', operating out of Gioia del Colle in Southern Italy. Here, Harrier GR.7, ZD409 '38', armed and complete with crew entrance ladder in situ, is seen at readiness in one of the aircraft shelters erected on the renovated Second World War dispersals. D M Sargent

No.1 Squadron put up their traditional '1' formation, the day they moved their Harrier GR.7s from Wittering to Cottesmore. Flight Sergeantt Rick Brewell, RAFPR.

still further, with the move from RNAS Yeovilton, Somerset, of all the Royal Navy's Sea Harrier F/A.2s and T.8s, under the 'Joint Force 2000' single command initiative.

It is anticipated that the Navy's front-line units, 800 and 801 Squadrons, will fly from Cottesmore, while 899 Squadron, the OTU, will be based at Wittering, alongside the RAF conversion unit, 20 (Reserve) Squadron and the maintenance wing. Cottesmore is, of course, no stranger to RAF-Royal Navy liaison, this going back to the days of 360 Squadron and the English Electric Canberra T.17s.

On 13th April 1999, a new epoch began when the first Harrier GR.7s of 4 Squadron, arrived to take up residence at Cottesmore. Barely a month later, on 11th May, they were joined by 3 Squadron with their GR.7s.

As if having to pack up and re-locate from their long-term base in Northern Germany wasn't difficult enough, both units were, at the same time, involved in 'Allied Force', NATO's 78-day air campaign against Serbia, for which, from March to June, they were detached to Gioia del Colle in Southern Italy, with up to 16 Harriers, as the RAF's contribution to the attack missions.

One side effect of the heavy programme of operational commitments, coupled with the necessity for regular maintenance (by the resident Harrier Maintenance Flight or the MU at RAF St Athan) *and* the need to use aircraft on occasions that have a particular equipment fit, has been the high incidence of airframe inter-change between units. As a consequence there has been a move away from having a fairly settled set of aircraft allocated to each unit towards one of a fleet pooling arrangement.

After a brief respite following the end of 'Allied Force', the newly-resident squadrons were soon busy with training exercises and deployments, during which 4 Squadron had a stint aboard the Royal Navy's aircraft carrier HMS *Illustrious*. Unfortunately, these training exercises have not been without mishap, and both units lost an aircraft during July 1999, but thankfully without loss of life.

Also at Cottesmore is the newly reformed 504 (County of Nottingham) Squadron, a unit which last disappeared with the disbanding of the Royal Auxiliary Air Force flying units in 1957. Previously known as the Offensive Support Role Squadron, it provides a pool of trained, but mainly part-time personnel, to

supplement the Harrier units, as well as the Jaguar units at Coltishall, Norfolk.

On 1st April 2000 a change in the RAF's Command structure saw 'Joint Force Harrier' (as it had by now become known) integrated into a newly resurrected 3 Group, and on 28th July, 1 Squadron, which had been flying Harriers for 31 years from the nearby base at Wittering, made the short move to Cottesmore, the event being marked by its Harrier GR.7s making an eight-ship flypast in the shape of a figure 1, prior to landing.

The close geographic proximity of RAF Cottesmore to Wittering, will allow the air force to bring all of its Harrier force into one environment, providing all the advantages and flexibility of co-locating. The two bases have long operated a combined military air traffic zone to co-ordinate movements in and out of the busy bases and the passing of traffic, both military and civil, through their airspace.

The Royal International Air Tattoo, which can trace its lineage back to 1971, has, in the interim, put on some of the best airshows in the world and at the same time raised much needed revenue for the RAFA and Royal Air Force Benevolent Fund.

Major features of this year's event were a flying tribute to the 60th anniversary of the Battle of Britain and the presentation of pilot's wings and certificates to 12 disabled people by Queen Noor of Jordan – the fruits of a scheme founded in memory of Sir Douglas Bader, famed fighter pilot and former Air Tattoo President.

Spectacular demonstrations of airmanship brought awards to the pilots of an RAF Tornado F.3, a Hungarian Air Force MiG-29, a Swedish Air Force Viggen, also the huge USAF C-17 Globemaster III – four examples of which are to be leased by the Royal Air Force from May 2000, to augment its fleet of C-130 Hercules.

With Harrier units now *in situ* and plans for Cottesmore apparently firm, continued operation of the station seems assured. So, like the Tornado before, the distinctive shape of the Harrier looks likely to be seen in the skies over Leicestershire and Rutland for many years to come.

Beginning at North Weald and progressing over the years via Goodwood, Bassingbourn, Middle Wallop, Greenham Common and Boscombe Down, it was necessary to find a new venue for the 2000 event due to runway renovation work at RAF Fairford, its 'home base' in recent years.

Thus it was that the RIAT, Europe's biggest military air show, came to be staged at RAF Cottesmore over the weekend of 22nd-23rd July, and in spite of unseasonal grey and chilly weather, around 150,000 visitors poured in to witness no less than 351 aircraft representing 49 air arms from 30 nations.

A general view of the eastern end of the public area at Cottesmore, during RIAT 2000, with more than a hundred aircraft visible. Peter March

---

Representative Serials of Cottesmore-based Units

No.35 Squadron
From 20.4.38 to 25.8.39   Code 'WT-'
Avro Anson I   N5264, N5265
Vickers Wellesley I   K7739, L7747, L7749, K7750, K7752, K7754, K7755, K7768, K7770, K8526, K8529, K8530, L2642, L2688
Fairey Battle I   K7588, K7590, K7592, K7593, K7595, K7596, K7597, K7598, K7600, K7619, K7620, K7624, K7629, K7673, K7675, K7677, K7678, K7680, K7693, K7694, K7695, K7705, K7706, K7707, K7708 'N', K7709 'O', K7710, K7711, K7712 'C', K9176 'G', K9177, K9178, K9179, K9180 'X', K9182 'J', K9246, K9330, K9457, K9466, K9469, K9470, K9471 'M', K9472, K9473, K9474, K9475, K9476, K9478, K9479, K9480, K9481, L4974, L4975, L4976, L4977, L4978, L4980, L4981, L5263, L5264, L5265, L5266, L5267, L5268, L5269, L5270, L5271, L5272, L5273.

No.185 Squadron
From 25.8.39 to 17.5.40   Code 'GL-'
Avro Anson I   N5093, N5211, N9830, N9831, N9832, N9833, N9834
Handley Page Hampden I   L4191, L4193, L4196, L4197, L4198, L4200, L4201, L4203, L4205
Handley Page Hereford I   L6005, L6007, L6008, L6012, L6016

No.207 Squadron
From 20.4.38 to 24.8.39   Code 'NJ-'
Avro Anson I   N5266, N5267
Vickers Wellesley I   K7756, K7757, K7758, K7759, K7760, K7761, K7762, K7763, K7764, K7765, K7769, K8531, K8532
Fairey Battle I   K7571, K7573, K7576, K7578, K7580, K7581, K7582, K7583, K7584, K7585, K7601, K7628, K7674, K7684, K7685, K7690, K9181, K9185, K9186, K9187, K9188, K9189, K9190, K9191, K9192, K9193, K9194 'T', K9195, K9196 'A', K9197, K9198, K9200 'Z', K9336, K9448, K9450, K9451,

K9452, K9453, K9454, K9455, K9458, K9459, K9460, K9461, K9462, K9463, K9464, K9465. L4962, L4963, L4964, L4965, L4966, L4967, L5228, L5274, L5275, L5276, L5277, L5278, L5279, L5280, L5281, L5282, L5283, L5284

No.106 Squadron
From 1.8.39 to 6.10.40   Codes 'XS-', 'ZN-'
Avro Anson I   N5162, N5163, N5164, N5166
Handley Page Hampden I   L4149, L4174 'A', L4175 'B', L4176, L4177, L4178, L4180, L4181, L4182, L4183, L4184, L4185 'S', L4186, L4187, L4188, L4189

No.14 Operational Training Unit
From 8.4.40 to 1.8.43   Codes 'AM-', 'GL-', 'VB-'
Avro Anson I   K6186, K8824, L7924, N4911, N4989 'G', N5037, N5064 'W1', N5079, N5093, N5110, N5166 'C', N5169, N5211, N5259, N5323, N5325, N5605, N5608, N5829, N5830, N5831, N5832, N5833, N5834, N5848, N9903, N9905, N9912 'D2', N9991, R3310, R3386 'W1', R3398, R3399, R3445 'Q2', R3587 'Y', R9602 'J2', R9603, R9604 'K', R9605, R9606, N2 N3, R9607, R9608, R9609, R9644, R9645, R9646 'F1', R9647 'L', R9690, R9692, R9718, R9748, R9749, R9750, R9742, R9743, R9744, W1879, AW974 'A', AW978 'G2', AW982 'R2', AX107 'N2', AX108
Handley Page Hampden I   L4038, L4041, L4048, L4070, L4075, L4076, L4086, L4100, L4105, L4108, L4109 'O1', L4110 'N1', L4117 'N', L4131, L4133 'F', L4133 'F', L4162 'X', L4173 'GL-T2', L4193, L4196, L4197, L4198, L4200, L4201 'T', L4204 'GL-H' also 'J2', L6020, L6055, L6063 'GL-P', L6096, N9062 'W3', P1151 'S2', P1155, P1157, P1158, P1167, P1168, P1176, P1185, P1186, P1188 'F1', P1195 'X2', P1196, P1204, P1205, P1209 'AM-H3', P1211, P1213, P1215, P1216, P1217, P1230, P1235 'U1', P1238 'H1', P1240, P1241, P1242, P1243 'P3', P1249, P1254, P1265, P1272, P1273, P1274, P1275 'GL-M', P1276 'AM-M1', P1277, P1278, P1280, P1281, P1282, P1283, P1286 'D', P1289, P1291, P1292, P1293, P1294, P1298, P1300, P1301, P1303, P1305, P1309, P1310, P1312, P1316 'GL-P', P1322, P1335, P1342 'N1', P1343, P1344, P1345, P1346, P1351, P1352,

P1353, P2062, P2064, P2067 'P2', P2072, P2074, P2075, P2076, P2078, P2092, P2112, P2116, P2118, P2119, P2120, P2127, P2128, P2129, P2138, P2139, P4300, P4303, P4306, P4307, P4308, P4309, P4311, P4312, P4313, P4314, P4315, P4316, P4317, P4318, P4391, P4395, P4397, P4418, P5311, P5312, P5320, P5321, P5322, P5344 'Y1', P5387, P5397, P5398, X2972, X2974, X2980, X2989, X2992, X3061, X3116, X3142, AD736, AD740, AD741, AD749, AD751, AD757, AD758, AD766, AD782, AD786, AD787 'C1', AD792, AD798, AD802 'V1', AD838, AD845 'V', AD848, AD851, AD860 'D3', AD906, AD938, AD985, AD988, AE155, AE186, AE190, AE192, AE295, AE312 'Q1', AE386, AE442, AT195, AT222, AT223 'P'.
Handley Page Hereford I   L6008, L6011, L6012, L6014, L6016, L6020, L6035, L6036, L6037, L6047, L6052, L6055, L6061, L6062, L6063, L6065, L6070 'GL-A2', L6073, L6074, L6075, L6088, L6096
Vickers Wellington I /Ia   L4219, L4350, L4380, N2981
Vickers Wellington Ic   L7850 'VB-Y', L7855, L7869, L7895 'Z', L7897, L7898. N2772, N2819 'P' also 'X', N2858 'S' also 'Q', R1019, R1039 'J', R1048, R1077, R1140 'Y', R1224, R1236 'M' also 'D', R1240 'H', R1274 'R', R1295 'P', R1338, R1398, R1401, R1436, R1522 'Q', R1592, R1603, R1621, R1669, R1709 'Q', R1720, R1796 'B', R1797 'S' also 'T', R3206 'J' also 'T', T2511, T2558, T2738, T2887, T2901 'Q', T2914, T2920, W5629, W5667, W5669, X3163, X3165, X9605, X9608, X9680, X9791, X9796 'H' also 'K', X9871 'N' also 'V', X9927, X9944, X9945, X9949, X9953, Z1068, Z1075 'F', Z1092, Z1095, Z1140 'Y', Z1154, Z1169 'Y', Z1171, Z8767, Z8837, Z8856 'P', Z8896, Z8943 'Z' also 'AM-G', Z8970 'Z', Z8977, Z8982 'R', AD594 'O' also 'GL-U', AD600 'B', AD628 'AM-M'. DV435, DV443, DV449, DV479 'A', DV486, DV494, DV565 'Q' also 'R' also 'T', DV666 'Z', DV668, DV678, DV696, DV697 'J', DV719, DV730 'F', DV780, DV822, DV823, DV839, DV842, DV864, DV891 'N', DV897 'P', DV898 'Q', DV917, DV921 'AM-O', DV929, HD943 'K', HD983 'W', HD990 'H'.
Vickers Wellington II   W5352.
Airspeed Oxford I   V3876 'W', W3993, W3994 'R', W3996, W4020, W4021, W4199, W4201, W4203 'S', AT479, AT480, AT481, AT485.

Airspeed Oxford II   AS902, AS903 'K2', AS904, BM833, BM834, BM835.
Boulton Paul Defiant I   N1767.
De Havilland Tiger Moth I   T5983.
Miles Martinet TT.1   HP522 'AM-B', HP523, HP524, JN596.
Westland Lysander III   R9013, T1504, T1553, V9845.
Airspeed Horsa I   DP379, DP603, DP622, DP627, DP663 DP670, DP707, HG736, HG745, HG770, HG798, HG801, HG803, HG835, HG840, HG844, HG846, HG917, HS121, HS125, LG699, LG763, LG765, LG838, LH950, LH962, LJ208, LJ227, LJ229, LJ230, LJ231, LJ232, LJ233, LJ234.

IXth Troop Carrier Command
From 16.10.43 to 1.12.43

No.50th Troop Carrier Wing
From 17.10.43 to 18.11.43

IXth TCC Pathfinder School
From   .2.44 to   .3.44

No.316th Troop Carrier Group   From: 15.2.44 to .5.45
Codes: '4C-' 44th TCS, '6E-' 36th TCS, 'T3-' 45th TCS, 'W7-' 37th TCS.
Douglas C-47 Skytrain   42-23503, -23623, -23639, -23931, -23935, -24181, -24187, -29056, -92056, -92729, -92861, -92884, -93075, -93512, -93753, -93754, -93755, -93780, -100499, -100517, -100883, -100973, -108902, -108909, 43-15106, -15151, -15179, -15185, -15194, -15205, -15207, -15225, -15227, -15258, -15265, -15300, -15305, -15334, -15495, -15614, -15633, 15638, -15641, -15643, -15659, -30652, -47972.
Douglas C-53 Skytrooper   42-68765, -68766, -68769, -68772.
Consolidated C-109   42-51982, -52033 'M'.
Waco CG-4A   42-04881, -07917, -42025, -42678, -47427, -56187, -56194, -56206, -56219, -56226, -56232, -56253, -56254, -56266, -57275, -57279, -56289, -56324, -56488, -56490, 56499, -56507, -56510, -56548, -56556, -56826, -62133, -62733, -73565, -73568, -73838, -73844, -73880, -73884, -73885, -73917, -73952, -74014, -74024, -74029, -74044, -74063, -75880, -77330, -77345, -77355, -77385, -77393, -77447, -77480, -77500, -77538, -77587, -77624, -77627, -77634, -77654, -77663, -77665, -77674, -77695, -77710, -77895, -79081, -79125, -79132, -79133, -79134, -79137, -79142, -79148, -79254, -79451, -79457, -79465, 43-13868, -15254, -19725, -19727, -19735, -19751, -19791, -19824, -19843, -19914, -19915, -19948, -26919, -27348, -27361, -27416, -27441, -27632, -36642, -36654, -36656, -36916, -36935, -36944, -36966, -37287, -37297, -37300, -37322, -37328, -37337, -37382, -37390, -37391, -37399, -37403, -37410, -38804, 38805, -39670, -39678, -39707, -39727, -39781, -39790, -39802, -39804, -39805, -39807, -39808, -39811, -39815, -39844, -39892, -39905, -39944, -39994, -40042, -40051, -40055, -40118, -40119, -40160, -40214, -40244, -40357, -40382, -40386, -40388, -40399, -40421, -40424, -40449, -40451, -40521, -40532, -40535, -40544, -40549, -40551, -40552, -40554, -40569, -40576, -40579, -40583, -40795, -40934, -41035, -41095, -41099, -41101, -41141, -41153, -41163, -41165, -41172, -41180, -41183, -41206, -41207, -41210, -41409, -41439, -41506, -41577, -41582, -41610, -41675, -41689, -41699, -41701, -41865, -41889, -41897, -41898, -41921, -41960, -41963, -42021, -42025, -42030, -42035, -42037, -42044, -42045, -42048, -42049, -42055, -42114, -42117, -42118, -42139, -42159, -43057, -56275, -59190, -73587, -77643, -79114, -79142, -79148, -79457, -87300, -195851, -197510, -405351, -596657, -840214.
Curtiss C-46 Commando   44-77613 'Y'.

No.1668 Heavy Conversion Unit
From 17.9.45 to 7.3.46   Codes: 'J9-', '2K-', 'QY-'
Avro Lancaster I   L7580, R5507 'J9-Y', HK705 'J9-S', HK732, LL795, LM170 '2K-D' also 'X', LM188, LM287, NF968, NG142, NG274, NG295 '2K-N', NG383 '2K-G', NN807, NN811, NN812, PD424 'B', SW252.
Avro Lancaster III   JB551, LM368, LM438, LM717, LM744, ME315 '2K-L', LM329/G 'U', LM569 'D', ND348 '2K-C', ND747, ND749/G '2K-H', ND875, ND877, ND909 'J9-L', ND918, ND965, ND980 'J9-N', NE120, PB375, PB381, PB437, PB487, PB489, PB506, PB508, PB577, PB584, PB611, PB627, PB681, PB867.
Note: The '/G' suffix on ND749 and LM329 denoted that they needed a permanent guard when parked.

Bristol Beaufighter VI   V8615 '2K-T', MM854, ND234.
De Havilland Mosquito XIX   TA342, TA357.
Hawker Hurricane IIc   LF180.
Supermarine Spitfire Vb   W3656, BL328.

No.16 Operational Training Unit
From 1.3.46 to 15.3.47   Codes: 'GA-', 'JS-', 'XG-'
De Havilland Mosquito T.III   HJ835, HJ870, HJ898, HJ985, LR567, RR288, RR289 'GA-L', RR292 'GA-F', RR293, TV976, TW108, VA874.
De Havilland Mosquito FB.VI   SZ973 'GA-S'.
De Havilland Mosquito B.XVI   ML938, ML941, ML974, ML983, ML982 'JS-B', PF483, PF484, PF488 'GA-T', PF492, PF498, PF510, PF512 'JS-E', PF513, PF538, PF540, PF595, PF597, PF601, PF602, PF609, RV307, RV317, RV347, RV360, RV361, RV363, VA874.
Airspeed Oxford I   LX359, PG988, PH468, PH469, PH471, PH474, PH483, PH484, PH485, PH522.

No.204 Advanced Flying School
From 15.3.47 to 1.3.48   Code: 'FMO-'
De Havilland Mosquito T.III   HJ898 'E', HJ985 'D', LR567 'D', LR581 'J', RR288 'C', RR292 'F', RR316 'A', TV959 'B', TV976 'H', TV981, TW112 'G', VA871 'G', VT606 'L'.
De Havilland Mosquito FB.VI   HR175 'Y', HR242 'Y', HR252 'X', HR494, PZ303, RF936 'V', RS551 'O', RS624 'N', RS643, RS644, RS698 'M', SZ973 'S', SZ975 'Z', TA381, TA476, TA546 'T', TE590.

Station Flight
Airspeed Oxford I   LX359 (8.5.47 to 13.10.47).

No.7 Flying Training School
From 16.4.48 to 14.4.54
Codes: 'FBA-', 'FBB-', 'FBC-', 'FBD-', 'FBE-'
De Havilland Tiger Moth I   N9278, N9506 'E', R4833 'L', R4941 'M', R4956, R5083, R5133, R5136, R5139 'A', R5206, T5427 'Y', T5465 'W', T5672 'Z', T5700 'P', T5842, T6043 'T', T6497, T6531, T6562 'Q', T7129 'F', T7332, T7412 'G', T7810, T7867, T7870.
De Havilland Tiger Moth II   DE455, DE482, DE588, DE606, DE615 'K', DE634, DE658 'U', DE853, DE854 'B', DE877 'O', EM814, EM904, EM905 'N', NL993, NM115 'R'.
(All individual letter Tiger Moths above, prefixed 'FBC-'.)
North American Harvard IIB   FE908, FE948 'O-Q', FS739 'O-K', FS757, FS758, FS776 'FBA-L', FS816, FS822, FS849 'FBC-L', FS850, FS894 'O-W', FT153 'FBB-F', FT254 'N-L', FT255, FT258 'N-H', FT303 'N-V', FT319 'O-M', FT321, FT346, FT376, FT393 'FBB-K', FT394 'P-B' also 'N-B', FT412 'FBA-J', FT413, FT418 'FBB-A' also 'N-G', FT431 'FBA-X' also 'N-K', FT435 'O-L', FT436, FT440 'FBB-W', FX220 'N-A', FX226 'FBA-K', FX244 'FBB-L' also 'O-V', FX263 'N-S', FX266, FX284, FX300 'FBC-U', FX324 'FBA-M', FX334 'O-G', FX376, FX388 'O-O', FX397 'FBB-B', FX400, FX428, FX469 'FBA-A', KF142 'N-J', KF153 'FBA-H' also 'P-A', KF156, KF185 'FBA-Q', KF206 'FBD-N', KF224 'FBA-V', KF233, KF238 'FBA-S' also 'P-A', KF243 'N-D', KF265 'FBA-P', KF266 'FBA-G' also 'N-G', KF276, KF288 'O-E' also 'N-F', KF289 'FBA-I', KF290 'O-U', KF300 'FBA-F', KF333 'N-O', KF356, KF362, KF364 'FBA-F' also 'N-C', KF388, KF396, KF472 'FBB-L' also 'O-T', KF481 'FBA-D' also 'N-Q', KF496 'FBA-T', KF565 'O-Y', KF588 'FBB-G' also 'N-R', KF590 'FBA-E' also 'N-E', KF605 'FBA-O', KF633 'FBA-R', F661, KF665 'N-U', KF668, KF688 'FBA-C', KF691, KF695, KF698 'FBA-L', KF714 'N-T', KF725, KF753, KF922, FBB-Z', KF924 'N-K', KF955 'FBB-R', KF959 'FBA-W'.
Boulton Paul Balliol T.2   VR593, VR594, VR595 'Q-C', VR598 'Q-C', WF989 'D-E' also 'Q-Q', WF990, WF991, WF992 'Q-D', WF993 'Q-C', WF995, WF996, WF997 'Q-E', WF998, WG110, WG111, WG112 'Q-A', WG113 'Q-J', WG114 'Q-U', WG115 'Q-V', WG116 'Q-X', WG117, WG118, WG119 'D-O', WG120 'D-Q', WG121 'D-R', WG122 'Q-J', WG123 'D-S', WG124 'D-T', WG126 'D-U', WG127 'D-V', WG128 'D-W', WG129, WG130 'D-C', WG131 'D-A', WG132 'D-B', WG133 'D-C', WG134 'D-D', WG135 'D-E', WG136 'D-F', WG137, WG138 'D-G', WG139 'D-H', WG140, WG141, WG179, WG186, WG187, WG209 'D-K', WN507 'Q-J'.

Percival Prentice T.1   VR219 'FBD-N' also 'M-T', VR220 'FBD-V' also 'M-Y', VR221 'P-Z', VR222, VR223 'FBE-D' also 'M-W' also 'P-Z', VR224 'FBD-A' also 'M-M', VR225 'FBE-H', VR231 'FBD-F', also '-H', 'FBE-J' also 'M-J' and 'M-P', VR234 'FBD-B' also 'FBE-Z', VR268 'FBD-S' also 'M-U', VR278 'FBD-K', VR285 'FBE-K' also 'M-K', VR291 'FBD-B', also 'FBE-A', '-F' and 'M-X', VR294, VR303 'P-X', VR309 'FBE-J', VR310 'FBD-E' also 'M-N', VR311 'FBD-F' also 'M-O', VR312 'FBD-G' also 'M-A', VR317 'FBD-R' also ;M-E', VR318 'FBE-G', VR319 'P-E', VR320 'FBD-Z', VR321 'FBE-F' also 'M-J', VR322 'FBD-Y' also 'M-A', '-G' and '-Q', VR323 'FBE-F', VS247 'FBD-O' also 'M-D', VS272, VS290 'FBE-C', VS318 'P-Y', VS322 'FBD-Q', VS325, VS327 'M-Z', VS354 'FBD-J' also 'M-H', VS357 'FBD-L' also 'M-C', VS359 'FBD-T' also 'M-L', VS365 'FBD-M' also 'M-J' and '-S',VS376 'FDB-X' also 'M-H', VS383 'FBD-U' also '-Y', 'M-F' and 'M-J', VS410 'M-O' also '-Q', VS609 'FBE-J' also 'P-C' and '-E', VS648 'M-B' also '-P', VS649 'M-R'.

No.15 Squadron
From 19.5.54 to 18.2.55
English Electric Canberra B.2   WH724, WH725, WH731, WH907, WJ575, WJ647, WJ717, WJ724, WJ972, WJ974, WJ976, WJ985.

No.44 Squadron
From 20.5.54 to 20.2.55
English Electric Canberra B.2   WH707, WH714, WH717, WH718, WH719, WH856, WH857, WH858, WH920. WJ566, WJ607, WJ981.

No.57 Squadron   From 22.5.54 to 19.2.55
English Electric Canberra B.2   WD996, WH712, WH720, WH859, WH860, WH878, WJ568, WJ574, WJ575, WJ621, WJ645, WJ974, WJ977, WK131.

No.149 Squadron   From 22.5.54 to 24.8.54
English Electric Canberra B.2   WD957, WH711, WH713, WH855, WJ564, WJ567, WJ569, WJ570, WJ612, WJ626, WJ973.

Station Flight
English Electric Canberra T.4   WH850, WJ863 (2.9.54 to 1.11.56).
Avro Anson C.19   VL335 (23.8.54 to 14.8.56). TX196 (12.57 to 3.58), VV306 (11.57 to 6.64).
De Havilland Canada Chipmunk T.10   WP831 (6.57 to 2.58), WB645 (3.58 to 10.58); WG464, (26.6.58 to 3.11.58) WG483, WP783, WP851 (26.6.58 to 17.10.58).

No.90 Squadron   From 5.3.58 to 26.3.58
Vickers Valiant B.1   WP223, WZ393, XD867, XD871.

No.10 Squadron   From 15.4.58 to 1.3.64
Handley Page Victor B.1   XA921, XA924, XA927, XA928, XA929, XA930, XA931, XA932, XA935, XA936, XA937, XA938, XA939, XA940, XA941. *B.1A* XH615.

No.15 Squadron   From 19.9.58 to 1.10.64
Handley Page Victor B.1   XA935, XA938, XA939, XA940, XA941, XH588, XH589, XH590, XH592, XH593, XH594.
Handley Page Victor B.1A   XA925, XH587, XH591, XH613, XH616, XH618, XH620, XH648, XH651.

No.232 Operational Conversion Unit, 'C' Flight
From 1.4.62 to 1.4.63
Handley Page Victor B.2   XL165, XL188, XL189, XL230.

Cottesmore Vulcan Wing:
No.9 Squadron   From 10.11.64 to 26.2.69
No.12 Squadron   From 17.11.64 to 31.12.67
No.35 Squadron   From 2.11.64 to 1.1.69
Avro Vulcan B.2   XH536, XH557, XH560, XH561, XH562, XJ780, XJ782, XJ784, XJ785, XL443. XM569, XM570, XM571, XM597, XM598, XM599, XM602, XM603, XM604, XM605, XM606, XM607, XM608, XM609, XM611, XM612, XM645, XM646, XM647, XM648, XM649, XM650, XM651, XM652, XM653, XM654, XM655, XM656, XM657.

No.98 Squadron From 17.4.69 to 27.2.76
English Electric Canberra B.2 WE113, WE122, WH670, WH911,
WJ603, WJ611, WJ620, WJ635, WJ722, WK144, WK145,
WK162.
English Electric Canberra T.4 WD944, WT488.
English Electric Canberra E.15 WH948, WH957, WH964,
WH972, WH973, WH981, WH983, WJ756.

No.115 Squadron From 9.4.69 to 23.2.76
Vickers Varsity T.1 WF383 'E', WJ911 'X', WJ946 'M',
WL622 'R', WL636 'D', WL678 'C', WL685 'S', WL692 'P'.
Armstrong Whitworth Argosy C.1 XN815, XP412.
Armstrong Whitworth Argosy E.1 XN814, XN816 Iris IV later
Phoenix, XN855 Heleus, XP413, XP439 Iris IV later Theseus,
XP448 Iris IV later Castor, XP449, XR137 Orpheus, XR140
Jason, XR143 Omega.

Trials Flight From 8.12.70 to 5.4.71
Believed to do with ASR role and Lindholme Gear. Two a/cft.
Armstrong Whitworth Argosy C.1 XP450.

No.231 Operational Conversion Unit From 19.5.69 to 12.2.76
English Electric Canberra B.2 WH907 'L', WH914 'U',
WH919 'V', WJ637 'Z', WJ674 'Y', WJ677 'X', WJ681,
WJ728 'J', WJ731 'W'.
English Electric Canberra T.4 WE188 'T', WE192 'A',
WE193, WH843, WH848 'E', WJ861, WJ869, WJ870 'F',
WJ877 'V', WT480 'B', WT482 'C', WT483 'D', WT488.

No.360 Squadron From 21.4.69 to 1.9.75
English Electric Canberra T.4 WD944, WJ862, WJ863 'U' also
'Z', WT488 'Y'.
English Electric Canberra T.17 WD955 'Q'. WF890 'M', WF916
'P', WH646 'G', WH664 'H', WH665 'J', WH740 'K', WH863 'L',
WH872 'W', WH874, WH902 'N',. WJ565 'C', WJ576, WJ581,
WJ607, WJ625 'D', WJ630 'E', WJ633 'F', WJ977 'R', WJ981
'S', WJ986 'T', WK102 'A', WK111 'B'.

No.940th Air Refueling Group, USAF Det. (2 wks) 4.90-5.90
Boeing KC-135E Stratotanker 57-1511, 58-0090, -0053, -0058.

Tri-National Tornado Training Establishment
From 29.1.81 to 31.3.99
Panavia Tornado GR.1 – Royal Air Force
ZA319 'B-11', ZA320 'B-01', ZA321 'B-58' ZA322 'B-50',
ZA323 'B-14', ZA324 'B-02', ZA325 'B-03', ZA327 'B-51',
ZA329 'B-52', ZA330 'B-08', ZA352 'B-04', ZA353 'B-53',
ZA355 'B-54', ZA356 'B-07', ZA357 'B-05', ZA358 'B-06',
ZA359 'B-55', ZA360 'B-56', ZA361 'B-57', ZA362 'B-09',
ZA369 'BR-61', ZA373 'BR-60', ZA405 'BR-62', ZA540 'B-12',
ZA543 'B-59', ZA548 'B-10', ZA562 'B-15', ZA599 'B-16',
ZA602 'B-13'.
Panavia Tornado IDS – West German Air Force
43+01 'G-20', 43+02 'G-21', 43+03 'G-22', 43+04 'G-23',
43+05 'G-24', 43+06 'G-25', 43+07 'G-26', 43+08, 'G-27',
43+09 'G-28', 43+10 'G-29', 43+11 'G-30', 43+12 'G-70',
43+13 'G-71', 43+14 'G-72', 43+15 'G-31', 43+16 'G-32',
43+17 'G-33', 43+18 'G-77', 43+19 'G-78', 43+20 'G-73',
43+23 'G-34', 43+24 'G-74', 43+25 'G-75', 43+26 'G-76',
43+29 'G-35', 43+31 'G-36', 43+36 'G-38', 43+37 'G-37'.
Panavia Tornado IDS – Italian Air Force
MM55000 'I-42', MM55001 'I-40', MM55002 'I-41', MM55003 'I-43'
MM55004 'I-44', MM7002 'I-92', MM7003 'I-93', MM7004 'I-90',
MM7005 'I-91', MM7007 'I-94'.

Miscellaneous Airframes
Battle Damage Repair: Hawker Hunter T. 7 XL618 .
Fire Crash Rescue, airframes have included:
Avro Vulcan B.1 XA910, XH481, XH504, B.2 XM656.
English Electric Lightning F.3 XR716 'AQ' (8904M).
De Havilland Sea Vixen FAW.2 XJ582.
Gloster Javelin FAW.9 XH983.
Gloster Meteor T.7 WG987. F.8 WF654.
Hawker Siddeley Harrier GR.3 XZ966.
Hunting Jet Provost T.3 XM375 (extant July 2000).
Supermarine Swift FR.5 XD976 'B' 79 Sqn.
Vickers Varsity T.1 WL671 'Q' 5FTS.
Gate Guardian:
English Electric Canberra PR.7 WH791 (8187M).
Instructional Airframe:
Panavia GR.1 ZA546.

No.4 Squadron From 13.4.99
BAe Harrier GR.7 ZD323 '04', ZD330 '11', ZD345 '12'
ZD376 '24', ZD379 '27', ZD401 '30', ZD408 '37', ZD409 '38',
ZD435 '47', ZD464 '54', ZD466 '56', ZD469 '59', ZG474 '64',
ZG478 '68', ZG504 '75', ZG505 '76', ZG507 '78', ZG509 '80',
ZG511 '82', ZG530 '84', ZG857 '89', ZG860 '92'.
BAe Harrier T.10 ZH664 '112'.

No.3 Squadron From 11.5.99
BAe Harrier GR.7 ZD322 '03', ZD327 '08', ZD328 '09', ZD329 '10',
ZD376 '24', ZD378 '26', ZD379 '27', ZD380 '28', ZD410 '39',
ZD436 '48', ZD438 '50', ZD470 '60', ZG477 '67', ZG500 '71',
ZG502 '73', ZG503 '74', ZG504 '75', ZG531 '85', ZG532 '86'
BAe Harrier T.10 ZH656 '104'.

No.1 Squadron From 28.7.00
BAe Harrier GR.7 ZD321 '02', ZD323 '04', ZD438 '50', ZD467 '57',
ZG477 '67', ZG502 '73', ZG503 '74', ZG510 '81', ZG862 '94',
BAe Harrier T.10 ZH656 '104'.

The Harrier 'codes' are in effect 'fleet numbers'. There has
already been considerable aircraft movement between the
operational units and this is expected to continue in the future.

Miscellaneous Airframes
Hawker Siddeley Harrier GR.3 XW917 (8975M) -
Gate guardian, arrived 14.7.99.
Hawker Siddeley Harrier GR.3 XW924 (9073M). Arrived from
Laarbruch 15.8.99. Displayed outside 3 Squadron's hangar.
Hawker Hunter F.6A XE606 (8703M). Arrived from Laarbruch
11.99. Painted as 'XJ673' and kept in the 4 Squadron hangar.
McDonnell-Douglas AV-8B Harrier 162068 (9250M) fuselage,
ex-USMC delivered to HMF by road, from Wittering, 26.6.00.
Vickers-Supermarine Spitfire F.21 LA255 'JX-U' (6490M),
owned by 1 Squadron Association, arrived by road from
RAF Wittering, 31st July 2000.

Serious Accidents to Cottesmore-based Aircraft

20.6.38 Battle I K9179 35 Squadron
Engine cut on take-off from Oulton Park, Cheshire. Hit trees
and crashed. To instructional airframe 1126M.

13.12.38 Battle I K7585 207 Squadron
Undershot and hit tree on night approach to Cottesmore. One
killed. To instructional airframe 1787M.

4.1.39 Battle I K7694 35 Squadron
Stalled due to icing and crash landed on approach to
Cottesmore. Became instructional airframe 1341M.

5.5.39 Battle I K9469 35 Squadron
Took off on night training flight from Cottesmore. Engine cut
and aircraft dived in to the ground. Three killed.

22.9.39 Hereford I L6005 185 Squadron
Crashed in forced landing, Stonesby, Melton Mowbray.

28.9.39 Hampden I L4191 185 Squadron
Landed with undercarriage jammed in mid-way position at
Perth, Scotland.

28.10.39 Hereford I L6007 185 Squadron
Crashed on landing, pilot on first solo. Became instructional
airframe 2163M.

30.11.39 Hampden I L4203 185 Squadron
Dived into ground in bad visibility, Hughendon, near High
Wycombe, Bucks.

1.1.40 Hampden I L4205 185 Squadron
Stalled in turn after overshooting airfield, crashed and burnt
four miles north of Cottesmore. One killed.

24.2.40 Hampden I P1279 185 Squadron
Undercarriage collapsed during circuit training.

24.2.40 Hampden I L4198 185 Squadron
Undercarriage failed on landing, Newton Down.

15.4.40 Hampden I L4197 14 OTU
Landed with undercarriage partly raised due to faulty
hydraulics. Written off.

21.4.40 Hampden I L4200 14 OTU
While on practise circuit training at night overshot airfield and
went through hedge. Written off.

6.5.40 Hampden I P1274 14 OTU
Pilot lost control during overshoot and aircraft crashed two
miles NNE of airfield. Four killed, aircraft written off.

9.5.40 Hereford I L6016 14 OTU
Crashed in forced landing at Tugby, 11 miles ESE of Leicester.

13.5.40 Hampden I L6065 14 OTU
Crashed on approach to Aston Down. Became 2969M.

29.5.40 Hampden I P1275 14 OTU
Undershot Cottesmore at 00:30 hours, one injured.

1.6.40 Hampden I P1281 14 OTU
Stalled on take-off from Cottesmore at 00:45 hours.

8.6.40 Anson I N5037 14 OTU
Crashed on approach to Cottesmore.

12.6.40 Hampden I P1280 14 OTU
Undercarriage collapsed at Cottesmore.

13.6.40 Hampden I P4309 14 OTU
Overshot airfield while local flying and ran into hedge.

15.6.40 Hampden I L6008 14 OTU
Crashed half mile south west of Pickworth, Lincs.

7.7.40 Hampden I P1309 14 OTU
Overshot on landing at 23:40 hours and hit pillbox.

9.8.40 Hereford I L6052 14 OTU
Crashed on take-off from Cottesmore.

19.8.40 Hampden I P1305 14 OTU
At 12:30 hours aircraft out of control dived into ground at
Sharnbrook, Beds. Four killed.

24.8.40 Anson I R9752 14 OTU
Ditched three miles south east of Burrow Head, Galloway Bay.

17.9.40 Hampden I P4311 14 OTU
Stalled in attempted forced landing at Kidwelly, Carmarthen.
Four killed.

27.9.40 Hampden I P4308 14 OTU
Pilot on second solo flight lost control, struck tree on Squires
Farm, Langham, near Oakham. One killed.

30.9.40 Hereford I L6036 14 OTU
Forced landing 4 miles NW of Llanelly, Monmouthshire..

5.10.40 Hampden I P2072 14 OTU
Hit hill at Richmond, Yorkshire, in bad visibility during cross
country flight. Two injured, aircraft written off.

Wellington Ic L7850 of 14 OTU came to grief in Exton Park on 2nd December 1942 while on approach to Cottesmore. It had flown a total of 569.05 hours. A salvage crew from 58 Maintenance Unit, Newark, is in attendance.
via N Franklin

16.10.40 Anson I L7924 14 OTU
Landing in bad visibility hit ground near Cottesmore. Five killed.

22.10.40 Hampden I P1343 14 OTU
After encountering poor weather on training flight, force landing attempted at Wittering but the aircraft hit trees on airfield boundary and was written off. One injured.

24.11.40 Anson I R3398 14 OTU
Crashed in forced landing, at Castle Bytham, six miles north east of Cottesmore, after Very light had been fired in cockpit. No serious injuries.

7.12.40 Hampden I P1276 14 OTU
Following engine failure, spiralled to the ground near Cottesmore. Two injured. Written off.

15.1.41 Hampden I P1241 14 OTU
Force landed in field at Barrow, two miles from Cottesmore, due to engine failure.

9.2.41 Hampden I P1342 14 OTU
Aircraft stalled during landing, crashed and burnt out.

23.2.41 Hampden I P1292 14 OTU
Crashed on take-off at Cottesmore.

28.2.41 Anson I R9749 14 OTU
Crashed in forced landing near Haxey, Lincs.

3.3.41 Hampden I P1283 14 OTU
After take-off from base for bombing practice aircraft crashed at 19:35 hours 1½ miles south.

16.3.41 Hampden I P1213 14 OTU
Crashed near Thistleton after control was lost in a turn during air exercise. Three injured.

27.3.41 Hampden I P4313 14 OTU
In bad visibility flew into hillside and struck house at 11:30 hrs, ¾ mile east of Laxey, Isle of Man. Three killed, one injured.

31.3.41 Hampden I P2062 14 OTU
While on high level bombing exercise the aircraft crashed in turn one mile north of Woolfox Lodge at 04:20 hours. Cause unknown, four killed.

8.4.41 Hampden I P1240 14 OTU
Crashed in forced landing ½ mile from Little Bytham after engine failure when on night bombing exercise.

8.4.41 Hampden I P2092 14 OTU
Crashed on LNER railway line at Little Bytham, Stamford. Shot down by German intruder when on practise bombing exercise over Grimsthorpe Range. Three killed.

4.5.41 Hampden I P4307 14 OTU
Swung on take-off, hit Hampden P4312 and burnt.

17.5.41 Hereford I L6047 14 OTU
Crashed on landing at Cottesmore after engine fire.

17.6.41 Hampden I P2088 14 OTU
Stalled on landing approach and crashed one mile north east of airfield. Two killed.

18.6.41 Hampden I P1211 14 OTU
While on ferry flight from Woolfox Lodge, aircraft stalled on approach to Cottesmore at 09:20 hours. Two killed.

21.6.41 Hampden I P4316 14 OTU
After apparently normal take-off for high level bombing detail on Grimsthorpe Range, aircraft dived into ground one mile south east of Cottesmore village. Three killed, one injured.

30.6.41 Hampden I P4300 14 OTU
Failed to return from training flight over North Sea. Four missing.

15.7.41 Hampden I P1289 14 OTU
Hit Anson I R3386 on landing at Cottesmore.

15.7.41 Anson I R3386 14 OTU
Hit by Hampden P1289 while taking off at Cottesmore.

17.7.41 Hampden I P1278 14 OTU
Following an engine fire on take-off aircraft stalled and dived into ground one mile south east of Cottesmore. Two killed.

31.7.41 Hampden I P2128 14 OTU
Crashed on landing at Scampton.

18.8.41 Hampden I L4048 14 OTU
Crashed at Barrow, near base at 02:10 hours after bombing practice. Cause unknown. Five killed.

28.8.41 Hampden I P4391 14 OTU
Exploded in mid-air one mile north east of Akeman Street Landing Ground at 23:00 hours while on cross country exercise. Engines heard to be running erratically before explosion. Wreckage scattered over two fields. Four killed.

12.9.41 Hampden Is P1301 and P4304 14 OTU
Aircraft collided near Saltby. Both crashed and burnt. Eight killed.

3.10.41 Anson I R3310 14 OTU
Abandoned in bad weather half mile west of Sutton St James, Lincs.

30.10.41 Hampden I P1294 14 OTU
While on cross country exercise control was lost in cloud.

Aircraft emerged in vertical dive at 12:30 hours over Llynclys crossroads, Oswestry. Four killed.

27.11.41 Hampden I P1155 14 OTU
On cross country exercise when aircraft stalled and dived in ground half mile north west of Buckminster. Possible cause engine failure. Four killed.

8.12.41 Hampden I P2112 14 OTU
Became lost in bad weather, force-landed on Saltby airfield.

9.12.41 Hampden I P1168 14 OTU
Stalled at low altitude four miles south of Saltby. Two killed.

13.12.41 Hampden I X2992 14 OTU
Stalled, dived into ground and burnt at Blue Point Farm, near Cottesmore airfield while on single engine flying practise. Two killed.

14.12.41 Hampden I AD758 14 OTU
Overshot Jurby, Isle of Man, and crashed into field at 10:50 hours with full bomb load.

15.12.41 Hampden I P2076 14 OTU
Undershot Cottesmore, swung and burnt. Aircraft written off. One injured.

19.12.41 Oxford I V3993 14 OTU
Failed to take-off from Abingdon due to hoar frost on the wings. Three seriously injured. Written off.

23.12.41 Hampden I L6096 14 OTU
Stalled on practise overshoot, spun in one mile south of airfield. Two killed.

26.1.42 Hampden I P1186 14 OTU
Struck ground at high speed in dive half mile north of Pinchbeck Railway Station, Spalding, while on high level bombing detail. Cause obscure, four killed.

10.2.42 Hampden I X2989 14 OTU
Pilot lost control in circuit at Saltby and force landed. Written off.

14.2.42 Hampden I P1316 14 OTU
Caught fire on ground at Cottesmore.

15.2.42 Hampden I L6020 14 OTU
Abandoned at 20:20 hours over Risegate, Lincs, after engine fire while on bombing practice.

4.3.42 Hampden I AD860 14 OTU
Burnt on ground at Cottesmore. Possibly caused by faulty aircraft heater.

8.3.42 Hampden I L4110 14 OTU
Aircraft stalled on landing and crashed two miles north west of Saltby airfield. Two killed, two injured.

16.3.42 Hampden I AD988 14 OTU
While on approach aircraft dived into ground from 400ft at Thistleton, three miles north of airfield. Four killed.

17.3.42 HP Hampden I AD749 14 OTU
Overshot at Newton, Notts, when attempting to land in bad weather at night.

25.3.42 Hampden I P1298 14 OTU
Hit lorry when landing after training flight and caught fire. Written off.

25.3.42 Hampden I P5398 14 OTU
Crashed and burned at Whittle Farm, Brockhampton, Glos. Crew was lost and eight miles off track. Four killed.

27.3.42 Hampden I L4108 14 OTU
Port wing struck ground while doing practise night landing on airfield in poor visibility. Two killed.

27.3.42 Anson I AX107 14 OTU
Caught fire while refuelling at Cottesmore.

19.4.42 Oxford I AS902 14 OTU
Crashed at Cold Overton, ten miles from base, while on night flying. Pilot killed.

29.4.42 Hampden I P1303 14 OTU
During single-engine flying training aircraft dived into ground from 200ft at Gunby, five miles north of Cottesmore. Two killed.

2.5.42 Hampden I P1277 14 OTU
While on training flight overshot Saltby and crashed at 00:15 hours.

5.5.42 Hampden I AE186 14 OTU
Swung on take-off, undercarriage collapsed and aircraft burnt. Written off.

5.5.42 Hampden I P1351 14 OTU
Crash-landed at Stonesby, two miles south west of Saltby after control was lost on take off. Four injured.

15.5.42 Oxford I AT479 14 OTU
Destroyed in collision with Hampden while landing.

31.5.42 Hampden I L4173 'GL-T2' 14 OTU
Ops Cologne. Two survived when aircraft crashed trying to land at Horsham St Faith.

31.5.42 Hampden I P2116 'GL-L2' 14 OTU
Ops Cologne. Shot down by Lt Manfred Meurer III/NJG1 near Diepenveen, Holland. Three killed, one PoW.

31.5.42 Hampden I P5321 'GL-P3' 14 OTU
Ops Cologne. On return collided with 78 Squadron Halifax W1013 and crashed near March, Cambs. Three killed.

3.6.42 Oxford I AS904 14 OTU
Wrecked half mile east of Greetham village, Rutland.

6.6.42 Hampden I L4133 14 OTU
Spun in and burnt near Mere Barn, two miles east of Saltby airfield. Four killed.

16.6.42 Hampden I AD787 14 OTU
Swung on landing at Saltby, undercarriage collapsed and aircraft caught fire. Written off.

18.6.42 Hampden I AT223 14 OTU
Due to engine failure aircraft undershot base and crashed 200 yards short. Four injured. Written off.

26.6.42 Hampden I P5312 'GL-J3' 14 OTU
Ops Bremen. Crashed near Borkum, reason unknown, three dead and one injured - died later.

29.6.42 Hampden I AD848 14 OTU
While on cross country exercise aircraft dived vertically into ground from low altitude at Moorend, nr Doncaster, Yorks. at 23.43 hours. Cause unknown. Four killed.

30.6.42 Hampden I AD802 14 OTU
Spun into ground near Gunthorpe Bridge, Notts., after attempted landing at base. Four killed.

2.7.42 Hampden I P2067 14 OTU
Spitfire IIa P8583, Central Gunnery School, Sutton Bridge on tactical experience flight with a Wellington when it collided head on with P2067 which was flying nearby. Spitfire lost wing and dived vertically into ground at Holmes Farm, Cloot Drove, five miles south of Spalding, pilot killed. P2067 lost starboard engine, flew east for short distance before crash landing in field at Four Mile Bar, Deeping St Nicholas. Crew unhurt. Aircraft repaired.

5.7.42 Hampden I AD766 14 OTU
After taking off at 17:15 hours aircraft stalled and crashed two miles west of Skillington, Lincs. Written off.

13.7.42 Hampden I X2974 14 OTU
Crashed at East Stoke four miles south west of Newark, Notts after collision with Wellington from Finningley.

30.7.42 Hampden I P5397 14 OTU
Mid-air collision while on training exercise. Crew baled out of P5397 which crashed at Wensor Castle Farm, Langtoft, one mile north west of Market Deeping, Lincs. AE192 only damaged. No casualties.

1.8.42 Hampden I L4117 'GL-N' 14 OTU
Ops Düsseldorf. Badly damaged over Germany aircraft crash landed in field at Loddeswell, Devon.

1.8.42 Hampden I N9062 'GL-W3' 14 OTU
Ops Düsseldorf. Shot down by Oblt Heinrich Prinz zu Sayn-Wittgenstein I/NJG1 and crashed near Oisterwijk, Holland. One dead, three PoWs.

1.8.42 Hampden I P1185 'GL-B2' 14 OTU
Ops Düsseldorf. Believed shot down near Ostend. Three died, one PoW.

1.8.42 Hampden I P5322 'GL-U3' 14 OTU
Ops Düsseldorf. Reason for loss unknown. Three dead, one PoW.

1.8.42 Hampden I P2129 14 OTU
Flare ignited in aircraft while on training flight. Pilot lost control and P2129 crashed and burned one mile south-east Cottesmore at 23:30 hours. Four injured.

11.8.42 Hampden I AE155 14 OTU
Crashed at Edenham, Lincs, 03:30 hours, while on low level bombing practice. Three killed.

13.8.42 Anson I R9608 14 OTU
Overshot landing at Cottesmore. Crew minor injuries, Anson written off.

16.8.42 Hampden I P4318 14 OTU
Struck hill on Arkengarthdale Moor at 02:30 hours while on cross country exercise. Two killed, two injured.

28.8.42 Hampden I AE312 14 OTU
While on cross country exercise, due to a possible stall aircraft dived vertically into Thistleton village, two miles north east of Cottesmore. Four killed.

31.8.42 Hampden I P1205 14 OTU
Aircraft yawed, lost height and struck ground on Grimsthorpe Bombing Range, 15:45 hours. Burnt out, one killed, two injured.

2.9.42 Hampden I L4162 14 OTU
Crashed out of control three miles north east of Cottesmore, near Thistleton. Four killed.

11.9.42 Hampden I L4131 14 OTU
Ops Düsseldorf. Failed to return, reason unknown. Crew of four killed.

14.9.42 Hampden I L4109 'GL-S' 14 OTU
Ops Bremen. Crashed near Stadskanaal, Holland. Two dead, two PoWs.

14.9.42 Hampden I AD845 'GL-B' 14 OTU
Ops Bremen. On return, out of fuel, crashed in field near Cottesmore.

15.9.42 Hampden I AD740 14 OTU
Undershot airfield, hit hedge, climbed, stalled over hangar and dived into ground, 23:36 hours. Three killed, one injured.

30.9.42 Wellington Ic T2747 'N' 14 OTU
Crashed 1½ miles north east Market Overton. Burnt out, four killed.

1.10.42 Wellington Ic R1401 14 OTU
Stalled and crashed when landing at Cottesmore.

8.11.42 Hampden I L4100 14 OTU
Undershot Saltby and crashed one mile east of airfield when returning from cross country exercise. Four injured. Written off.

9.11.42 Wellington Ic X3163 14 OTU
Overshot airfield and crashed one mile west at Barrow.

2.12.42 Wellington Ic L7850 14 OTU
Forced landed at Exton Park, three miles south east of airfield.

4.12.42 Wellington Ic DV929 14 OTU
Crashed in Cottesmore village after night take off. All crew killed.

6.12.42 Wellington Ic R1522 'Q' 14 OTU
Crashed on main Cottesmore to Market Overton road near Barrow village. Four crew killed.

17.12.42 Wellington Ic R1603 14 OTU
Crashed in attempted forced landing on edge of Harlaxton Airfield.

21.12.42 Wellington Ic T2887 14 OTU
Forced landed at Millhill Farm, near Bingham, Notts, after engine fire.

9.1.43 Wellington Ic W5629 14 OTU
Crashed near Ashwell, three killed.

11.1.43 Wellington Ic DV449 14 OTU
Aircraft stalled on landing, swung and crashed into lorry. One civilian killed, aircraft written off.

23.1.43 Wellington Ic DV842 14 OTU
Starboard engine failed after take-off, crashed one mile from Harlaxton landing ground.

28.1.43 Wellington Ic Z8896 14 OTU
Crashed attempting landing at Waddington with port engine out, five killed.

After this mishap near Sproxton on 3rd July 1943, Wellington Ic Z8982 of 14 OTU flew again as a Mk.XVI. As it did not involve loss of life nor result in the aircraft being written-off, it does not get a separate mention in the list of serious accidents at this airfield. via Brandon White

6.2.43   Wellington Ic   W5667   14 OTU
Crashed eight miles north-east of Boston, five killed.

17.2.43   Wellington Ic   T2558 'G'   14 OTU
Crashed on overshoot 1 mile north-west of Sproxton, four killed.

10.3.43   Wellington Ic   DV846   14 OTU
Burst into flames after crashing on North Luffenham 'Q' Site, Walk Farm, Pickworth, Rutland. Three killed.

12.3.43   VA Wellington Ic   Z1154   14 OTU
Overshot landing at Holwell Hyde, Herts. Written off.

31.3.43   Wellington Ic   AD628 'M' & X9944   both 14 OTU
AD628 overshot on landing, crashed into stationary Wellington X9944 then hit hangar. Two killed, both aircraft destroyed.

19.4.43   Wellington Ic   W5352   14 OTU
Pilot was unable to maintain height after port propeller fell off and aircraft crashed at Langtoft, near Market Deeping. Crew baled out.

6.5.43   Wellington Ic   Z1068   14 OTU
Aircraft stalled and flew into ground near North Witham. Crew safe, aircraft written off.

19.5.43   Wellington Ic   Z8837   14 OTU
Crashed and burst into flames near south east corner of Cottesmore airfield. One killed.

27.5.43   Anson I   N9829   14 OTU
Broke up in mid-air near Cottesmore while on air test. Pilot and two airmen passengers killed.

11.6.43   Wellington Ic   DV678   14 OTU
Crashed at Chatsworth Park, New Bakewell, Derbys. Aircraft written off, crew safe.

16.6.43   Wellington Ic   DV443   14 OTU
Engine cut on take-off, crash-landed on approach, Oakley, destroyed by fire.

3.8.43   Wellington Ic   DV823   14 OTU
Crash-landed at Langar airfield after engine failed.

Unfortunately, no accident details are available at this time for the period of occupation by the USAAF Troop Carrier Group, between October 1943 and May 1945.

3.10.45   Lancaster I   NG274   1668 HCU
Pilot on initial solo, overshot Cottesmore crashed and burned, all crew killed. Map location given as Burley Bushes, MR 375299.

13.10.45   Lancaster III   ND747   1668 HCU
Crashed. No further details. SoC 2.11.45.

23.10.45   Lancaster I   NN812   1668 HCU
As result of crash was reduced to status of ground instructional airframe, 5909M.

.11.45   Lancaster III   JB551   1668 HCU
Damaged beyond repair. Struck off charge 29.11.45.

26.3.46   Mosquito B.XVI   PF492   16 OTU / 204 AFS
Swung on landing and undercarriage collapsed.

30.3.46   Mosquito T.III   HJ870   16 OTU / 204 AFS
Bounced on landing and swung wrecking aircraft. Crew safe.

2.4.46   Mosquito B.XVI   RV317   16 OTU / 204 AFS
Aircraft swung to port on landing and undercarriage collapsed. Crew safe.

15.5.46   Mosquito B.XVI   RV363   16 OTU / 204 AFS
Landing too fast in bad weather, overshot and turned over. Crew safe.

17.5.46   Mosquito T.III   TW108   16 OTU / 204 AFS
Making forced landing when aircraft struck trees at Bellemore's Farm, Goadby Marwood, near Oadby. One killed.

3.7.46   Mosquito B.XVI   PF538   16 OTU / 204 AFS
Undercarriage collapsed on take-off.

9.9.46   Mosquito B.XVI   PF601   16 OTU / 204 AFS
Crashed on take-off.

7.10.46   Mosquito B.XVI   RV361   16 OTU / 204 AFS
Swung on landing, undercarriage collapsed.

5.11.46   Mosquito T.III   RR289   16 OTU / 204 AFS
Belly-landed on overshoot.

22.11.46   Mosquito B.XVI   VA874   16 OTU / 204 AFS
Swung on landing and undercarriage collapsed.

28.11.46   Mosquito T.III   RR293   16 OTU / 204 AFS
Struck ground 350° 1½ miles from Cottesmore. Flying low while crew were looking for airfield in bad visibility. Both crew killed.

5.5.47   Mosquito FB.VI   RS644   16 OTU / 204 AFS
Hit high ground near Cottesmore at speed. Both crew killed.

19.1.48   Mosquito FB.VI   TA476   16 OTU / 204 AFS
Undershot landing at Cottesmore. Not repaired.

31.1.48   Mosquito FB.VI   HR494   16 OTU / 204 AFS
Flew into ground one mile north of Great Pointon, Lincs., while on night cross country exercise.

6.2.48   Mosquito FB.VI   TE590   16 OTU / 204 AFS
Aircraft dived into ground three minutes after taking off in snow shower. Cause not known, two crew killed. Location given as 1½ miles west of Woolfox Airfield.

9.2.48   Mosquito FB.VI   TA546   16 OTU / 204 AFS
Crashed immediately after night take-off and burned. Both crew killed.

24.8.48   Tiger Moth I   T7412   7 FTS
Crashed on take-off from RAF Wittering.

27.8.48   Tiger Moth I   T7332   7 FTS
Hit by T6043 while taking off at Cottesmore.

5.1.50   Harvard IIb   FT376   7 FTS
Hit tree low flying, Normanby, Lincs.

17.2.51   Prentice T.1   VR309   7 FTS
Flew into ground in snowstorm, Greatham Lodge, Grantham, Lincs. One killed.

20.2.52   Harvard IIb   FT440   7 FTS
Crashed into garden of house in Eastgate, Deeping St James. Pilot killed.

27.2.50   Tiger Moth I   T5700   7 FTS
Caught fire whilst starting up.

14.7.50   Harvard IIb   FT412   7 FTS
Hit tree during forced landing near Barsby, Leics.

28.5.51   Prentice T.1   VR231   7 FTS
Hit tree after engine cut while overshooting practice forced landing one mile south of Grimsthorpe, Lincs.

30.5.51   Prentice T.1   VS290   7 FTS
Spun into ground nr Kirby Underwood, Lincs. One killed.

3.7.51   Prentice T.1   VR323   7 FTS
Stalled on approach to forced landing three miles east of Bourne, Lincs. One killed.

6.12.51   Prentice T.1   VR278   7 FTS
Dived into ground on approach to practice forced landing six miles north east of Bourne, Lincs.

18.5.52   Prentice T.1   VS366   7 FTS
Dived into ground two miles south of Shepshed, two killed.

10.9.52   Prentice T.1   VR234   7 FTS
Bounced on landing and stalled. Cottesmore.

26.9.52   Harvard IIb   KF922   7 FTS
Crashed in forced landing three miles north east of Cottesmore after engine cut.

17.10.52   Harvard IIb   FX388 & KF688   7 FTS
Collided in formation and both abandoned Pickworth, Folkingham, near Grantham, Lincs.

4.11.52   Harvard IIb   FT321   7 FTS
Engine cut whilst in circuit, forced landed two miles north east of Cottesmore.

7.1.53   Balliol T.2   WG113   7 FTS
Hit ground during attempted overshoot at Woolfox Lodge.

28.1.53   Balliol T.2   WG122   7 FTS
Crashed during aerobatics one mile north of Stamford, Lincs. One killed.

8.5.53   Balliol T.2   WG115   7 FTS
Undershot landing at Cottesmore.

26.8.53   Prentice T.1   VR311   7 FTS
Stalled and sank into ground during practice forced landing Thorpe Sachville.

31.12.53   Balliol T.2   WG179   7 FTS
Engine cut due to faulty fuel flow. Crashed landed in field at Pailton, Warks.

2.5.54   Balliol T.2   WG135   7 FTS
Hit ground on night overshoot at Cottesmore.

14.6.62   Victor B.1A   XH613   15 Squadron
Lost power on all engines and abandoned five miles west of Castle Bytham, Lincs, while on approach to Cottesmore.

16.6.62   Victor B.1   XA929   10 Squadron
Failed to become airborne on take-off from RAF Akrotiri, Cyprus. Co-pilot ejected but he and five other crew died.

11.2.66   Vulcan B.2   XH536   Cottesmore Wing
Flew into high ground 20 miles north-west of Swansea while on low-level navigation exercise. 12 Squadron crew of five killed.

30.1.68   Vulcan B.2   XM604   Cottesmore Wing
Suffered fire in No.2 engine after overshooting Cottesmore. Crashed at Cow Close Farm. 9 Squadron crew; four died two ejected safely.

29.1.71   Canberra T.17s   WH874 & WJ862   360 Sqn.
Collided and abandoned 1½ miles south of Mansfield, Notts. All five crew members escaped.

5.10.71   Canberra E.15   WH973   98 Squadron
Rolled and abandoned out of control at Lobthorpe, near Cottesmore. Both crew members ejected and survived.

2.8.73   Canberra T.17   WJ674 'Y'   231 OCU
Yawed on overshoot and abandoned 1½ miles north-east of Cottesmore. Aircraft crashed at South Witham. Both crew ejected, navigator survived but pilot died of injuries.

17.6.86   Tornado IDS   43+24 'G-74'   TTTE
Crashed in Elan Valley, North Wales, while low flying at night. *Luftwaffe* pilot and RAF navigator both killed.

18.8.88   Tornado GR.1   ZA329 'B-52'   TTTE
Destroyed following mid-air collision with GR.1 ZA593 'M' of 617 Squadron, Marham, Norfolk, near Appleby, Cumbria. Both crews killed.

21.1.99   Tornado GR.1   ZA330 'B-08'   TTTE
Crashed between villages of Mattersey and Everton, Notts following a mid-air collision with Cessna 152 G-BPZX. Both members of the crew and the two occupants of the Cessna killed.

9.7.99   Harrier GR.7   ZD345 '12'   4 Squadron
Crashed close to A16 at Surfleet, near Spalding, Lincs., following engine failure while on routine exercise. Pilot ejected with only minor injuries.

14.7.99   Harrier GR.7   ZG532 '86'   3 Squadron
After loss of control during air combat manoeuvring, crashed in the Pallinsburn Estate, near the village of Crookham, between Milfield and Cornhill-on-Tweed, Northumberland. Pilot ejected safely.

Chapter Nine

Desford

A view of the southern area of Desford, the Reid & Sigrist site, c.1980. Running in between the buildings is the Peckleton to Leicester minor road. The junction at right, includes the road north to Desford. via G S M Young

THE ORIGINS of an airfield close to the village of Desford can be traced back to the raids made by German Zeppelins on England during the First World War. In an attempt to combat the menace of these airborne raiders 38 (Home Defence) Squadron, Royal Flying Corps (RFC) moved to Castle Bromwich, Warwickshire in July 1916 from Thetford, Norfolk, where it had formed that April, charged with the defence of the Midlands. At that time it was flying Royal Aircraft Factory BE.2s and BE.12 biplanes. To aid the unit in its task many emergency landing grounds were set up throughout the area of operations. By the end of July one of the first of these, termed a night landing ground, had been established on land farmed by J H Cart close to Desford.

Although nearer to this village, the landing ground was officially referred to as Peckleton, a village a little further away to the south. Several huts were erected on the Peckleton Lane side of the site to house the small staff in charge but, according to local recollection, use of the site was spasmodic and landings few. This situation is said to have suited the sergeant in charge of the detachment as it enabled him to spend a great deal of his time in local inns!

By mid-1917 the landing ground had been downgraded as suitable for day use only. In the following year use of the site was discontinued entirely whereupon the land reverted to farming once more.

The next stage in the history of Desford as an airfield began in 1929 when members of the newly-formed Leicestershire Aero Club (LAC) began to look for a suitable location for an aerodrome. A long and often frustrating search ensued during which many dif-

ferent fields were inspected. All proved unsuitable or unobtainable. A mention by club member J T L Baxter, a prominent Hinckley publisher, that an RFC landing ground had existed at Desford led to the area being examined.

On inspection the site appeared to be suitable for the club's activities so, the owner of the land, who was still John Cart, was approached and proved to be amenable to the LAC's proposals. An agreement was then reached whereby the 18½ acre 'Desford Field' was made available from 21st May 1929. Shortly afterwards this initial

RAF Armstrong Whitworth Siskins performing during Desford's official opening ceremony, 14th September 1929. In the foreground is a de Havilland DH.60X Moth. via N Franklin

The naming ceremony of Leicestershire Aero Club's first aircraft, DH.60M Moth The Quorn, 14th September 1929. As well as the Lady Mayoress of Leicester, Mrs Hand, the Under Secretary of State for Air, F Montague, was also present. A section of the engine cowl including the club's badge and the name, is displayed inside the current LAC clubhouse at Leicester. via N Franklin

venue was also referred to as 'Leicester's Hendon' which was rather an extravagant claim!

Support on the day was good in spite of the fact that the field was over seven miles from Leicester, some distance from a main road and public transport scarce. Amongst the many invited guests present were two prominent people with official engagements to perform. One of these was the Lady Mayoress of Leicester, Mrs Hand, whose pleasant duty it was to christen the club's new Moth, *The Quorn*. This name was adopted after Lindsay Everard, a man with a great love of fox hunting, suggested that club aircraft be named after Leicestershire hunts. The other distinguished person was the Under Secretary of State for Air, Mr F Montague. He had been flown up from Hendon especially to deliver an address to mark the formal opening of the aerodrome.

Like the Under Secretary, quite a few people took the opportunity to fly in and by the start of the main display over 30 visiting aircraft were parked around the field. Although the majority of these were civilian light aircraft the RAF was represented by four Armstrong Whitworth Siskins from 3 Flying Training School, Grantham, Lincolnshire, and two de Havilland DH.9As.

As promised, a varied programme of flying was arranged. Individual and formation aerobatics, a mini air race, flour bag bombing, balloon bursting and a parachute drop were all featured. After his descent the parachutist, John Tranum, remarked that he estimated the crowd at around 30,000, but of these at least half were watching the show free from surrounding lanes and fields.

For many the event of the day was a display by the trio of RAF pilots in their Siskins. This performance was very much appreciated and generated a great deal of excitement amongst the spectators. After the aircraft had landed, in spite of entreaties from the organisers, the crowd swarmed across the aerodrome for a closer look. Eventually the police were obliged to enlist the aid of boy scouts, who formed a barrier with their staves, to help free the aircraft from the throng. When order was more or

area was extended by the addition of a further 13¾ acres and work was soon in hand turning the fields into a flying ground.

Close to the area once occupied by the RFC, a site was prepared for the club's first home. A rather large poultry house was acquired thanks to the initiative shown by a member, Claude Brown and this, after some modification became the clubhouse. Close by a fuel dispensing pump was laid on while a wooden shed, just large enough to house a small aircraft with its wings folded, served as a hangar. These rather rudimentary facilities, although at that time considered to be quite satisfactory for the running of an aero club, would by today's standards be regarded as most unacceptable.

Throughout the summer LAC concentrated on establishing the airfield on a firm basis and by early September considerable headway had been made in this direction.

The amenities at Desford were improved by extensions to the clubhouse, additional hangarage was provided and a further 11 acres added to the rent bill.

In several other respects September 1929 was a memorable month for LAC. Delivery was made of the first club owned aircraft, de Havilland DH.60M Moth G-AAIF, a most generous gift from their president, W L (later Sir Lindsay) Everard. Then, on Saturday 14th, as a fitting climax to the efforts of the summer months, an air display was staged to mark the formal opening of the airfield.

Contemporary advertising of the event urged the public to visit 'Leicestershire's First Great Air Pageant' which would feature 'Crazy Flying, Bombing, Racing, etc by Crack Pilots. Flying from 12 noon. Main Event 3pm - 7.30pm. Admission 1/-, 2/-, 3/- and 10/6' (5p, 10p, 15p and 52½p). The

less restored joy riding was able to commence and continued without interruption until dusk called a halt to the proceedings. This activity was resumed on Sunday 14th with demand sufficient to keep several aircraft engaged for the greater part of the day.

To many reading this account the display will have a certain familiarity for much of its content has been repeated, with various permutations in countless similar events since. On this occasion though for the majority of those present it was all a new and novel experience. Within the club the event was considered overall to have been a success. While results were not startling the small profit of £191-3s-7d (£191.18) was encouraging for the future.

Although the winter months curtailed activities somewhat, progress was such that by early 1930 the club was able to report that membership stood at 902 in three different categories, 125 pilot, 737 observer and 40 honorary. A total of 1,024 instructional flights had been made; 20 trainees, the first of these being J T L Baxter, had attained 'A' License standard and 1,190 hours had been flown without mishap.

At Desford hangarage was being increased by erecting a new building and extending those already on site to house a further two aircraft. The cost of this work was borne by Lindsay Everard. In addition, LAC now owned two DH Moths, the second having been delivered on 7th February. This was G-AASM *The Fernie*, yet another generous gift, this time donated jointly by T T Sawday, H C S Tyler and W A North JP.

Delivery of the club President's own Moth, G-AAUH *Foxhound*, took place at the aerodrome on 16th February. Eager to exploit the commercial aspects of aviation, LAC used the occasion to announce the launch of an air taxi service at a quoted price of sixpence (2½p) per mile. Aimed primarily at Leicestershire's business community it was an enterprise again made possible by the good offices of Lindsay Everard. When not in use by him, he made available his new aircraft together with the services of his personal pilot, Stewart David. Later in the summer the Moth was replaced by de Havilland DH.80A Puss Moth G-AAXM *Leicestershire Fox*. The Puss, being a cabin monoplane, was much more suitable for the carriage of passengers. Again the club benefited from the change as the same terms applied to this aircraft as had previously to the Moth.

Whether the taxi service was a financial success is not known but it is recorded that many commercial flights were made within the year. Notable amongst these were the carriage of granite samples for the Leicestershire Quarry Owner's Federation, delivery of local papers to Skegness, retrieval of the President's son from boarding school, participation in an 'aerial honeymoon' and arranging the advent of 'Santa' to Leicester by air.

A four day flying event staged over the Easter holiday, 19th-21st April, was to have been the club's major show of 1930. However, it ran into trouble from the outset, the culprit, the British weather. On the morning of Saturday 19th, the day of the big display, atrocious conditions prevailed. Everything from brilliant sunshine to hail, sleet and snow was experienced. Following a period of gale force winds and torrential rain, about mid-day the club was compelled to cancel the scheduled programme until Monday in the hope of better conditions.

A few intrepid aviators had braved the elements, amongst whom were several experienced display pilots. So as not to disappoint those hardy souls who remained several of these airmen put on spirited demonstrations. One of those pilots, Flying Officer Snaith, gave what was the first public demonstration of a Comper Swift single-seat sporting monoplane. Many years after he recalled that his flying that day was not quite as planned. As he ran in over the aerodrome boundary to begin his display the engine of the Swift cut out. Had he carried straight on and landed, collision with spectators was inevitable but, he managed to make a steep left hand turn to bring off a curving cross-wind landing, rolling to a stop some 20 yards from another group of people. Thinking that his flying was now over for the day he adjourned to the refreshment

tent where, he admits, he partook of several drinks. Shortly, he was asked to give *another* display, this time in one of the club's Moths! What followed is quoted in his own words:

'*...amongst the most idiotic things I did was to roll through the outside of a tree. I felt a thump and then saw that one side of the mainplane was covered in twigs. Of course I had to get up higher and throw the plane about to get rid of them. The crowd thought it was part of the show. But, when I taxied back to the enclosure my drinking pals were remarkably sober'.*

By Monday, conditions had improved although Saturday's storms plus traffic had left some spectator areas a sea of mud. A notable visitor who flew in from Yorkshire for the display was the Director of Civil Aviation, Sir Sefton Brancker. In his address to the crowd he complimented the club on all that had been achieved in the short time they had been in existence. For the spectators there were to be some disappointments. Unfortunately due to the rearranged schedule there was no RAF presence; also, the parachutist, John Tranum, was unable to give his usual display. He did though give an exhibition of wing-walking which was much appreciated. There was however one unrehearsed item which caused quite a stir.

It involved what was billed as 'The Biggest Aeroplane Ever Seen In Leicester', a Handley Page W.10 airliner of Imperial Airways, which was flown in specially to give pleasure flights. Two types of flight were on offer, a short trip costing ten shillings and six pence (52½p) or a longer circular tour of the city of Leicester for two guineas (£2.10) – a tidy sum in those days.

During the afternoon an Avro Avian biplane, which had just had its engine started, ran away pilotless across the aerodrome heading straight for the Handley Page.

His Royal Highness the Duke of Gloucester (third from left) flew in from Northolt on Friday 13th June 1930, on his way to open the Leicestershire Agricultural Show. Others in the frame are, from the left, Harry Purt, Lindsay Everard, Roy Winn and an unidentified lady.
via N Franklin

A club official supported by some spectators, who sensed the danger, immediately rushed out and by clinging to the errant Avian managed to partly divert it from its course. Thankfully their actions were sufficient to avert what could have been a serious accident as several people were aboard the airliner at the time. Unfortunately their efforts were not enough to prevent a collision in which both aircraft suffered wing damage.

Other features of quite an eventful day were formation and aerobatic displays together with several competitions, while pleasure flights in club and other aircraft continued until dusk intervened.

Desford and the Leicestershire Aero Club were by now becoming very well known in flying circles. The landing ground was, for its day, a very good one while the club had rapidly built up a reputation for their hospitality and excellent social activities.

Aerial visitors to the aerodrome were always welcomed, none more so than His Royal Highness the Duke of Gloucester when he flew in from Northolt, to the west of London on Friday, 13th June on his way to open the Leicestershire Agricultural Show. The Duke arrived in Westland Wapiti I J9095 of 24 Squadron, flown by Squadron Leader Don with a second machine carrying the Duke's equerry, Captain Howard Kerr and his pilot Flying Officer Pearson Rogers. After his official duties were over the Duke returned to Desford departing at 5:20pm on the return journey to Northolt.

In 1930, for the first time, the aerodrome became part of the national air racing scene when it was designated as a turning point in the premier air race of the calendar, The King's Cup. The course of the race, for the trophy presented by His Majesty King George V, was a single 753 mile circuit which started at Hanworth, then in turn took in Hamble, Whitchurch, Birmingham, Hooton Park, Barton, Woodford, Sherburn, Newcastle, and Hedon with the final turning point at Desford. There, the surviving competitors entered the last leg of the race back to Hanworth. Flown on 5th July, LAC capitalised on the event by inviting the public, large numbers of whom paid to watch. Of the 88 starters 62 passed the Desford turn, of these 61 finished the race; Miss Winifred Brown in Avro Avian III G-EBVZ being the eventual winner at 102.7mph. Miss Brown, flying with her fiancé, was the first woman to win the prestigious cup.

Ever keen to bring to public notice the advantages of air travel and its business potentialities the club, ably supported by Lindsay Everard, arranged for a representative collection of commercial aircraft to visit Desford on 13th July. Though the event was aimed primarily at members of Leicester Chamber of Commerce it did not prevent large numbers of the public also being present. Amongst the more interesting aircraft on show were an Avro Five, a three-engined, high-wing, six-seater monoplane, a twin-engined Saro Cutty Sark amphibian, examples of the Junkers Junior, Blackburn Bluebird, Avro Avian two-seaters and, inevitably, several de Havilland types. The offer of trial flights was eagerly taken up by those present, many of whom had never flown before. Demand was so great that by the end of the day quite a few had to be disappointed.

After a full year of operation, LAC had become firmly established at Desford. Their programme of events which had been well received was, with slight variations, to set the pattern for the future.

There followed a period of further consolidation during which activities such as club competitions, at homes, etc, predominated. By June 1931 the two club-owned aircraft had averaged 83 hours per month with only one minor mishap which resulted in a damaged undercarriage. In the July, Desford again featured on the National Air Race calendar when it again became a turning point in the King's Cup air race.

Later in the year their first Moth, G-AAIF, was sold to be replaced by G-ABRF another Moth of the same type. Also added to the club fleet was Lindsay Everard's Puss Moth. Flying activities tended to tail off during winter months but a social calendar which included film shows, lectures, parties and dances served to keep members in touch.

In the summer of 1932 the club entertained another royal visitor when His Royal Highness the Prince of Wales flew in on 6th June on a visit to the Leicestershire Agricultural Show. He was welcomed by Councillor W E Wilford, the Lord Mayor, and with other distinguished guests later took tea in the clubhouse before his return flight.

Just over a week later, on 18th June, a club aircraft featured in the first police flying operation in the UK which resulted in the arrest of a criminal. At the request of the county police one of the Moths was used to make an air search for factory burglars believed to be hiding in wooded farmland near the airfield. Disturbed by the circling aircraft one of the men broke cover. His arrest followed and subsequently he received a prison sentence.

One of the most famous aviation entrepreneurs of the day, Sir Alan Cobham, brought his National Aviation Day touring display to Desford on 14th July. Normally it would have been a day to remember for the show featured a great variety of aircraft, very skilled aviators and spectacular flying. However, the British weather intervened to spoil the event.

The most noteworthy items concerning the club and Desford seem mainly to have occurred during the summer months. In this respect 1933 was no exception. On 17th June Alan Cobham once more visited only to have his display again marred by inclement weather. Several club members were away at this time having flown to take part in the Eastbourne Rally held on the 16th-17th where they met with some success. The first came on the 16th when J T L Baxter won the *Concours d'Élégance* with the club Moth G-ABRF. The next day, in the same aircraft, Baxter came third in the Eastbourne to Bristol race for the Society of British Aircraft Companies' Challenge Cup. In the same race fellow club member Phillip Symington came second in his Comper Swift, G-ABZZ; he also won the prize for the fastest time. It was also during July that LAC's second Moth G-AASM was sold, again to be replaced by a similar aircraft, G-ABTF.

An enthusiastic member of the club and ever keen to exploit the possibilities of using aircraft for police work, Captain C E Lynch-Blosse, Chief Constable of Leicestershire, entertained his deputy and the superintendents of the county force at Desford on 28th July. As part of the entertainment, the visitors were each taken for a flight during the course of which they served as observers and were required to locate a dummy hidden within a mile of the aerodrome. All found it, two of them from a height of over 2,000ft. The Chief Constable was well pleased with his practical demonstration.

For most of 1934 the club was somewhat preoccupied with its impending move to the municipal airport at Braunstone (see Chapter Six), a project which LAC were to manage for the city council. They had expected to be at their new home by the summer, but problems with the landing ground prevented this.

In July the possibilities of co-operation between the police and aircraft were once again shown in a demonstration at Desford. Organised by Captain Lynch-Blosse, the first public showing of a completely mobile range of Marconi radio equipment took place on the 12th. A de Havilland DH.83 Fox Moth biplane of Surrey Flying Services was hired for the occasion to carry the transmitter aloft while in a saloon car equipped with the receiver plus an unwieldy telescopic aerial on the roof were Lynch-Blosse, O J B Cole, Leicester City Chief Constable, and driver.

At the airfield ground-based radio was installed to enable the proceedings to be relayed to spectators. A fake bank robbery was staged and the 'villains' made their escape in a Riley car with a conspicuous white patch on its roof. Elements of farce then began to enter the demonstration. A nearby thunderstorm interfered with transmissions and a car backed into the ground-based aerial which promptly folded up. In spite of these hiccups, the aircraft found its quarry quickly and experienced no difficulty in following it while relaying its movements to the chase car which was then able to intercept the 'miscreants' and make an 'arrest'. Though the trial lacked elements of realism it did serve to illustrate how advances in technology could be used to the advantage of law and order.

To overcome some of the disappointment caused by the postponement of the move to Braunstone some last minute arrangements brought Sir Alan Cobham once more to Desford on 20th September. This time the show fared rather better for, although the morning was quite poor, the weather improved by the afternoon sufficiently for an excellent show to take place.

An 'At Home' was organised at Desford on 29th September 1934 but this too added to the members' frustration. Rain and heavy mist on the day made flying conditions almost impossible, in consequence few guests were able to make the journey. On the plus side though the club were able, from November, to use their purpose-built clubhouse at Braunstone for their winter social activities.

Desford was finally vacated by LAC in favour of Braunstone during March 1935. That the aerodrome was now unused did not go unnoticed by Leicester Air Sports Club who, in April, asked that they be permitted to use it for gliding. Their request was turned down. A month later it was noted that Leicestershire Model Aero Club were now flying model aircraft at the site. They were soon asked to desist.

Under the auspices of the Royal Air Force Expansion Scheme, 13 civilian flying training schools were set up, contracted to train service pilots. Strange to relate, one of these contracts was awarded to a company which, at the time, possessed no airfield. This was Reid and Sigrist Limited (R&S) of New Malden, Surrey, a firm well known for the design and manufacture of aircraft instruments. Their search for a base led to Desford and eventually to the total transformation of the aerodrome.

An inspection of pilots during the official opening of the Reid & Sigrist-operated Civilian Flying Training School, 13th December 1935. With a backdrop of Tiger Moths, left to right: G E Lowdell, Air Commodore A W Tedder, Squadron Leader G Reid, Viscount Swinton, A G Bullmore and five well decked-out pilots. . via R Emmerson

Tiger Moth G-ADPG in an undignified pose at Desford on 7th January 1938. It survived this incident, but was written off in a landing accident in February 1940. via R Emmerson

A view of the pre-war training fleet in the northern hangar complex. via Dr Hugh Thomas

Some very rapid negotiations in late August 1935 between R&S's managing director, Squadron Leader George Reid and John Cart resulted in the latter's farm, together with its existing aerodrome being purchased by the firm. They were then faced with a deadline of three months in which to have the school up and running. This was such a daunting task that Lord Nuffield laid a £10 bet with Reid that it could not be done.

Companies interested in carrying out the work were quickly found and contracts soon agreed. The main recipients of these were En-Tout-Cas Limited of Syston, who were awarded one for the extension of the landing area while the Fairby Construction Co Ltd became responsible for all building work. Operations by both companies began on 12th September.

Creating the new landing area entailed a considerable amount of hedge pulling and tree felling before levelling and drainage of the area could be carried out. It also involved the levelling of *Hallfields*, the Cart family residence since 1884. Some of the materials obtained from this demolition were however later put to good use in other En-Tout-Cas projects. Swithland slates removed from the roof were used during the building of a new church at Mount St Bernard's Abbey near Whitwick, while the bricks are said to have been crushed and the resultant hard-core shipped to the United States where it was incorporated in the building of a hard tennis court for the film star Ginger Rogers.

To meet their commitment to the project, Fairby pulled out all the stops. Their employees worked consecutive days on a shift system, in one week alone 90 tons of crazy paving were laid, merely to enhance the surroundings of one building. While this development of Desford was taking place; the contractors' task was not made any easier by the 10 inches of rain which fell. Nevertheless their combined efforts were sufficient to enable the school to open for business on 25th November 1935 and Reid won the bet.

At this stage, the increased landing area now covered 130 acres, giving a maximum landing run of over 1,000 yards and a minimum of 950 yards. Additionally a further 56 acres had been bought and were available for future extension.

Although such a short time had elapsed since work began a very comprehensive range of buildings were available for use. They comprised of a large hangar 220ft by 70ft with annexes at either end housing lecture rooms, a parachute store, a first aid room together with ambulance fire tender and transport bays. To house the students there were five centrally heated bungalows. Four large lecture rooms, five offices and a photo department were all contained in an administration block which covered 2,500 square feet. But most impressive of all was the stylish clubhouse. On the ground floor was a lounge and dining room each 45ft by 20ft and a kitchen able to feed 120 people. The second floor was a self-contained flat while a small control tower topped off the building.

When this, the ninth of the 13 new RAF Civil Flying Training Schools (CFTS) was officially opened on 13th December 1935, representatives from the press, radio and newsreels were all present to record the event. It fell to the Minister of State for Air, Viscount Swinton of Masham, to do the honours after he arrived appropriately by air. His transport on this occasion was a de Havilland DH.89 Dominie of 24 Squadron, Hendon, escorted by a Hawker Hart of the same unit.

Many other service personalities and civic dignitaries were also present for the occasion. Amongst the former were Air Vice-Marshal F W Bowhill, Air Commodore A W Tedder and Group Captain R Leckie, while the latter included Doctor Bardsley, the Bishop of Leicester, Colonel R E Martin, Chairman of the County Council, O J B Cole, the Chief Constable, W A North, the High Sheriff and Mr Lindsay Everard MP. In his address the Minister was full of praise for both Reid and Sigrist and their contractors. It was hoped, he said, that the speed and efficiency with which the school had been established would characterise the Air Ministry's expansion scheme as a whole.

Choice of the type of training aircraft with which it was to be equipped was the prerogative of each individual school. R&S chose the de Havilland DH.82A Tiger Moth, an aircraft which was to become synonymous with Desford and rarely absent from the skies over and around the airfield for the next 16 years. By the opening date 17 of an expected 21 Tigers had been delivered. Formed up before the new hangar, 12 of these brand new yellow painted machines, together with the first 27 students and their instructors, made an impressive sight on this auspicious, if slightly murky, day.

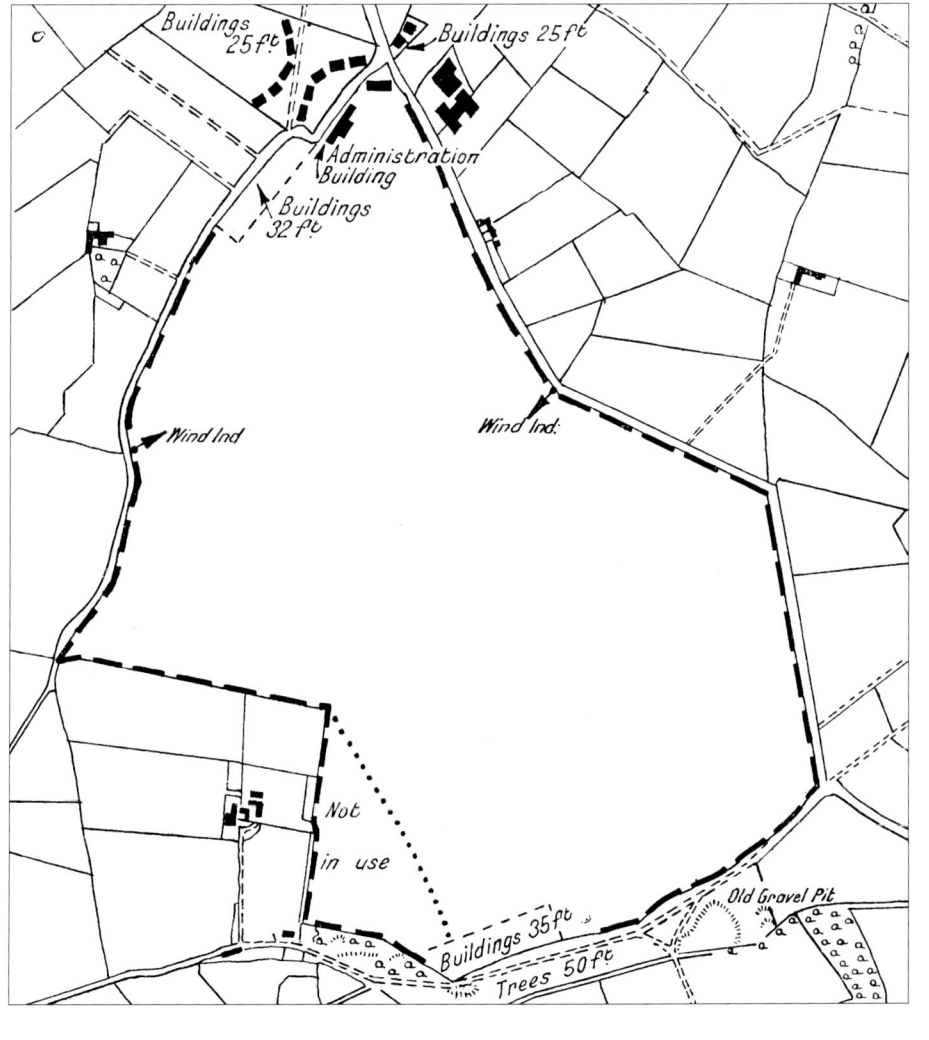

Air Ministry plan of Desford, showing the extent of the flying field, mid-1930s.
Author's collection

After the official opening there followed a period of consolidation. Over the ensuing months the CFTS quietly improved the efficiency of its teaching and the thoroughness of its courses and thousands of pupils were eventually destined to receive the first rudiments of their flying training at Desford. Some went on to achieve great distinction, others high rank, while a very few became known for more dubious activities.

None were to achieve greater notoriety than one of the early students. It is recalled that he was a rather handsome but, said by his instructors, inattentive young man who only managed to scrape through his course with a marginal pass. He is also remembered for his reputation as a ladies' man and certain cheques which bounced! Dismissed from the service in September 1937, he embarked upon a chequered career which was to end at Pentonville on 26th October 1946 when he was hanged for the gruesome murder of Margery Gardner. He was Neville George Clevely Heath.

In order to increase the number of trained pilots available for RAF service the RAF Volunteer Reserve (RAFVR) was created in April 1937. Under the scheme candidates, between the ages of 18 and 25 and educated to the required standard, were enrolled as airman pilots with the rank of sergeant. Enlistment was for five years and reservists undertook to attend a town headquarters on two evenings each week with alternative weekends flying. Also, they had to be available for 15 days continuous training per year. At first ten towns and cities in the UK were selected to house the local branches of this new formation. Leicester was one of these and the headquarters were situated at The Cedars, 197 London Road, under the command of Air Commodore E L Gerrard.

R&S became involved from the inception of this new reserve scheme and Desford was the logical base for the flying element of the training. The fleet of Tiger Moths was then supplemented by aircraft capable of carrying out a more advanced type of training and examples of the Hawker breed of biplanes – the Hart, Hart Special, Hart Trainer, Hind and Audax – soon became part of the Desford scene. To reflect this new role there was also a change in title for the school to 7 Elementary and Reserve Flying Training School (E&RFTS). The RAF already considered this to be the unit's designation although it had not been adopted until this time.

The watch office at Desford. via Author

A three-wheel Thompson Brothers refueller in R&S colours. Taking on fuel is Tiger Moth G-ADXT while in the background is a visiting RAF Tiger Moth, believed to be K2583 from 24 Squadron at Hendon. J Clarke

Also during 1937, memories of Desford's aero club days were briefly revived on 11th September. Once more the sound of finely-tuned aero engines was heard when the airfield again became a turning point during the annual race for the King's Cup. This was to be the last occasion when Desford was to feature in a national air racing event.

As the RAF expanded rapidly towards the end of the 1930s it was realised that in the future the multi-engined aircraft then coming into service would need observers fully trained in the art of navigation. Additionally, if need be, they should also be able to fulfil the duties of bomb aimer and gunner. Prior to December 1937 the trade of observer within the RAF had been of a part time nature, from this date it was decided to dispense with this concept. A syllabus was devised whereby trainees would receive 12 weeks navigation training, then two weeks of discipline and administration at an RAF Depot followed by eight weeks at a service Air Observers School for a bombing and gunnery course.

Direct entry trainees were recruited to swell the numbers required for this new position and to enable the first part of their instruction to be carried out civilian run training units were created. By the early autumn of 1938 the first four of these units, known as Civilian Air Navigation Schools (CANS) had been established. The second of these to begin its training courses in late August was 3 CANS at Desford.

To cater for the new unit and its pupils, extensive building work had taken place. On the north side the number of bungalows had been increased to ten, another hangar complete with office-cum-control tower had been built and a large mess building constructed across the road from the existing clubhouse. The most striking development was on the south, or Peckleton Common side of the airfield where a complex of lecture rooms had been built and hangars erected.

The trainees, 30 at first, 60 for subsequent courses, received elementary ground training followed by practical air navigation. All

flying was carried out in Avro Anson Is. Exercises began with simple cross country flight then progressed on to map reading, interception, long cross country flights and night flying. There were also lessons in aerial photography.

Following the outbreak of hostilities with Germany on 3rd September 1939, all units came onto a war footing, and this soon resulted in a change of title for the CANS. From 1st November 1939 they were all redesignated as Air Observer Navigation Schools (AONS). Under this new title, 3 AONS remained at Desford just a short while before leaving for a new base at Kingstown, near Carlisle, on 24th November.

In 1939 Reid and Sigrist ventured into the field of aircraft manufacture for the first time. The RS.1 Snargasher was the result and a fuller account of this company activity is contained in Chapter Ten.

Wartime activity at Desford can be split into three distinct elements. These were the flying training school, the aircraft repair operation within the Civilian Repair Organisation (CRO) and the assembly of the Supermarine Spitfires by Vickers Armstrong.

The transition from peace to war at Des-

ford appears to have been fairly painless with no drastic upheaval recorded. From 3rd September reserves were mobilised into the armed forces; this was reflected in a change of unit title to 7 Elementary Flying Training School (EFTS). Uniform became the recognised dress with many members of staff sporting officer's or NCO's rank. George Lowdell, the chief flying instructor since the inception of the school, became a Squadron Leader and commanding officer of the unit.

Most noticeable were the aircraft; almost overnight those Tiger Moths still in their overall yellow paint scheme were transformed by the application of a coat of more sombre green and brown camouflage on their upper surfaces. New aircraft began to arrive almost daily and eventually, at their peak, there were around 120 Tigers on strength. On a fine day maybe 90 to 100 of them would be flying, many within a few miles of the airfield. Today it is hard to imagine the amount of aerial activity from such a relatively small airfield.

From September 1939 there was a steady and, for a time, continuous influx of staff; in addition the intakes of trainee pilots began

Left: Flight Lieutenant H A Howes during a solo demonstration of blind flying, showing off the capabilities of the new R&S instrument the Gyrorizon, February 1936. Howes is under the canvas cover completely enveloping the rear cockpit. H A Howes

Top: Heavy snow during the winter of 1939-40 caused the camouflaged main hangar to collapse. Mrs Julien Birchall

Centre: A demonstration of the 'Paraslasher' at Desford. The target on this occasion was a cartoon of a certain Italian dictator, but the intention was to decimate airborne parachutes. R&S

Bottom: The scythe of the 'Paraslasher' in stowed position underneath the fuselage of a Tiger Moth. R&S

to increase in number. This growth meant that extra accommodation was needed and temporary hutments were added on both north and south sides. Those created on the south side formed a separate small camp. They were built off the airfield on land bordering Peckleton Common, either side of the access road to Tooley Park.

*A 7 E&RFTS Hawker biplane formation.
Clockwise, from top left Hart (Special) K3867,
Harts K3007 and K3006 and Audax (note the
extended exhaust pipe) K8321.* J Pickering

Around the airfield perimeter four dispersed flights were established, each with its own accommodation and complement of aircraft. For a time a temporary landing ground was also in use near to Kirkby Mallory. Early in the war Tiger Moths were often dispersed to this site when air raids in the vicinity seemed imminent. On occasion it was also used, with the aid of gooseneck flares, for night flying practice.

In the summer of 1940, when the invasion of England seemed imminent, many stopgap methods were proposed to counter the threat. One of these was to fit EFTS Tigers with two bomb racks, each capable of carrying four 25lb bombs. This idea found favour and the racks were fitted in two ways, either one under each wing, or the two in tandem beneath the fuselage. It was proposed that aircraft so equipped would be flown against an invading force by experienced instructors. Several Tigers at Desford were fitted out and by all accounts

instructors who flew them enjoyed the exercise. In all probability this was due to its novelty, or the fact that it formed a respite from the training round. Targets at both Desford and Braunstone were used during exercises with 8lb practice bombs. These could be released in pairs or all together and when dive bombing the cross bracing wires in the centre section were used as a rudimentary sighting device.

Many strange ways of stopping the invader were also suggested but none can have been more bizarre than one which originated at Desford. Assuming that large numbers of airborne troops would take part in an invasion the fertile mind of George Reid conceived a weapon to combat them. Known as the 'Paraslasher' the operational concept of the weapon was to destroy the enemy paratroops as they descended by slicing open their parachute canopies, or, should they land safely, by carving them up on the ground. Again it was proposed it be fitted to EFTS Tigers and flown into battle by the instructors.

The device consisted of an 8ft length of aircraft tubing with an agricultural scythe blade, honed to razor sharpness, attached

at the 'business end'. It was stowed horizontally beneath the aircraft fuselage and when needed in flight actuated by a lever situated on the port side of the pilot's cockpit. A system of bungee cords then held it in the operational position.

On Reid's instructions, the prototype, and only example of this weird device, was fashioned by Reg Emmerson, one of the school's civilian engineers. It is written that it was fitted to Tiger Moth G-ADPG, but this seems unlikely as records suggest that 'DPG was written off on 27th February 1940.

In the hands of George Lowdell the first flight took place on 12th June 1940. With continued practice he gained considerable expertise with the weapon, despatching canvas screen and straw filled sack targets with ease. Eyewitnesses have said that it was quite a hair-raising experience to see Lowdell in the Tiger suddenly appear from behind a hangar bearing down on the target with blade extended.

A demonstration was arranged for the Ministry officials on 7th July and, although spiritedly flown with the ultimate destruction of the targets, it received a lukewarm reception. It was pointed out that determined

German paratroops, armed with automatic weapons, were likely to be more than a match for Tiger Moths even when flown by experts. So, with no official backing forthcoming, the contraption was removed from the aircraft which then returned to the more mundane task of being the mount for trainee pilots.

Late in 1940, in what appears to have been a short lived exercise, aircraft from 9 Maintenance Unit (MU) at Cosford, Shropshire, were flown in for dispersal at Desford. These obsolete aircraft, which consisted of four Avro Tutors, five Hawker Audax and one Hawker Hector, were picketed out at the Peckleton village end of the airfield with a detachment of 16 airmen and NCOs from the MU in charge. They arrived between 11th and 12th October but by the 25th had begun to leave again, back to their place of origin. By November's end all had departed.

By early March 1941 No.37 Course had begun *ab initio* training. A first hand insight into tuition and life at Desford can be gained from impressions recorded by one of the trainees, J Cheney, in the following extract from his wartime journal:

'At last, after a succession of postponed postings, we got under way for our first Flying Schools. At tea-time on 28th February 1941 trains were leaving Newquay right, left and centre for various parts of the country. Bryan, Ted and myself were posted to 7 EFTS, Desford. At Newquay we said good-bye to Stan, whom we left standing on guard outside St Brannocks.

'We arrived at Desford early the next morning to see the first snow of that winter. It had never snowed in Newquay during the whole of the winter, although it had been severe further north. Of course everyone was thrilled to be on a real aerodrome at last. Tiger Moths at close range was the realisation of a dream.

'We were billeted comfortably in bungalows on the camp, having a room each with all modern conveniences. This was a far different life from the one we had led for the first five months at Newquay. We were living in the lap of luxury at Desford

'As far as work was concerned we had our hands pretty full and time off came only at weekends. We spent half the day on flying instruction, the other half on our ground subjects. These ground subjects were similar to those we had been lapping up at Initial Training Wing (ITW) but were considerably more advanced. There was an addition or two to the curriculum however, these were Airmanship (the Highway Code of the air) and the Study of Aero Engines and Airframes. There is only one outstanding thing worthy of note as far as ground instruction was concerned at Desford, that was the remarkable laziness of the civilian instructors who endeavoured, in their delightfully bored

manner, to teach us the necessary required by Training Command.

'The other half of the programme, the flying training was tons far more interesting and exciting, naturally. My first trip into the air took place on 3rd March and my instructor was Flight Lieutenant Booth, an oldish fellow with grey hair, who had been flying donkey's years. After that, trips came at infrequent intervals due to bad weather and the fact that I did not get on very well with Flight Lieutenant Booth. However, after a few hours I had a change and I must say it was not for the better. This time it was Sergeant Berry, who was very short tempered. The first time I flew with him I was attempting a landing at Braunstone [Leicester Airport, used as a forced-landing ground by pupils of Desford EFTS] and making rather a poor show of it, he asked very politely if I thought I was flying a submarine. Anyway, we got over that and I made a better show of it after that.

'On 2nd April I went up with Flight Lieutenant Baker, who showed me more of flying in the hour I was with him than my other instructors had done on all of my previous flying. He sent me off solo - that was the great day. I did a circuit and a moderate landing. I could manage to take a Tiger off the ground, take her round and land her all in one piece.

'After that I put in a number of hours with various instructors, as one by one they had leave, so I was continually changing around. Sergeant Berry was posted to Canada, he had been on [Fairey] Battles at the beginning of the war and was still alive to tell the tale. Sergeant Griffiths was my next instructor, he had held the rank of Flying Officer in France but had been reduced for low flying. He was a grand bloke and taught me a lot about low flying.

'During my time with Griffiths I learned the various tricks of flying. Blind flying, low flying, aerobatics, forced-landings and how to map read. He sent me on my first cross country solo. I was to go to Cambridge EFTS, have lunch and return. I reached Cambridge quite safely, but couldn't quite make up my mind which aerodrome I should land on. I investigated one which had Wellingtons scattered around and about.

However, I found one which seemed to have an abundance of Tigers in the circuit and I landed. So, it was Cambridge. I had a wizard lunch there and, with an air of self-confidence, set out for Desford. The return journey was managed quite successfully too and old Griffiths breathed a sigh of relief when I stepped out of that aircraft at Desford.

'Griffiths went on leave and I finished the course with Flight Lieutenant Gadd and Pilot Officer Lavender. Both were oldish fellows, Gadd had been with an air circus before the war, I didn't like him at all, Lavender was a very nice bloke and gave me lots of encouragement. I did make quite a hit with Laven-

der, we got on well together.

'During all this time Ted, Bryan and John Lee, who had joined our circle, had been doing the same as me. At the end of the course we took our exams and all the four of us passed rather well. A number of blokes had failed on the flying course and had been posted, but the majority of us got through. Allen, who I had known at Newquay, had been trained on the Reid and Sigrist Snargasher and was invariably airsick until he had done 20 hours or so. Squadron Leader Wardell gave a number of the blokes a CFI [Chief Flying Instructor] test before we left, but I, fortunately, escaped that. He was a holy terror on the ground, what he was like in the air I don't know. I suppose he had reason, really, for his remarkably short temper, the number of pranged Tigers around the aerodrome, on one or two occasions, was colossal.

'On 29th April, 37 Course left Desford. Bryan, John Lee and myself were posted to Kidlington SFTS and were due to report there on 3rd May. We had been recommended for single engine fighters. Ted Burton was to leave us and go to Brize Norton on 10th May. He had been recommended for multi-engined bombers. So Ted left us and we all went away from the smell of petrol and Gipsy Majors for a few days.'

Sadly, Cheney did not survive the war.

Although utilised by R&S for most of the Second World War as a communications hack, the Snargasher was used briefly in its original role in 1941. In what was possibly an attempt to revive interest in the aircraft it was used experimentally by 7 EFTS in its training concept. During the first half of the year it was used to give selected students a full course of training. The results obtained were quite satisfactory, but this method of teaching was not adopted.

In addition to the full *ab initio* tuition, two other types of courses were offered by 7 EFTS. One was a short duration grading course used to assess the suitability of prospective pilots for further training. The other, a refresher course, was primarily for pilots who had undergone their main training abroad, notably in Canada and the USA. Its purpose was to reorientate them with the terrain and reacquaint them with the difficulties that could be experienced while flying once more in the British Isles.

Avro Anson I L7947 'U' of 3 AONS over flooded countryside. via Author

A view of Desford looking approximately eastwards with the village of Peckleton under the wing. This was part of a series of shots taken to illustrate the effectiveness of airfield camouflage - note the dummy hedgerows cutting across the landing area. via Author

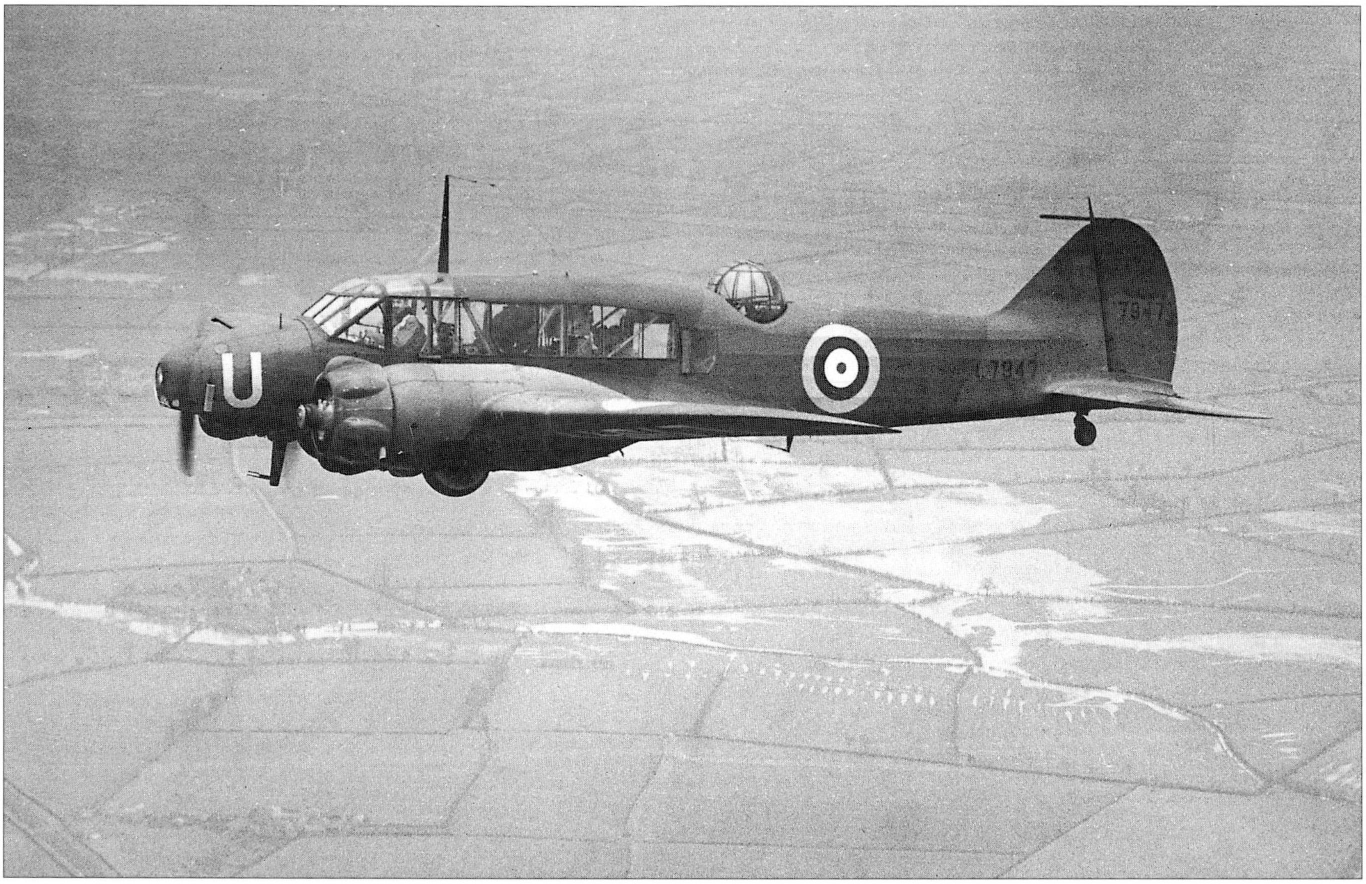
U
L7947

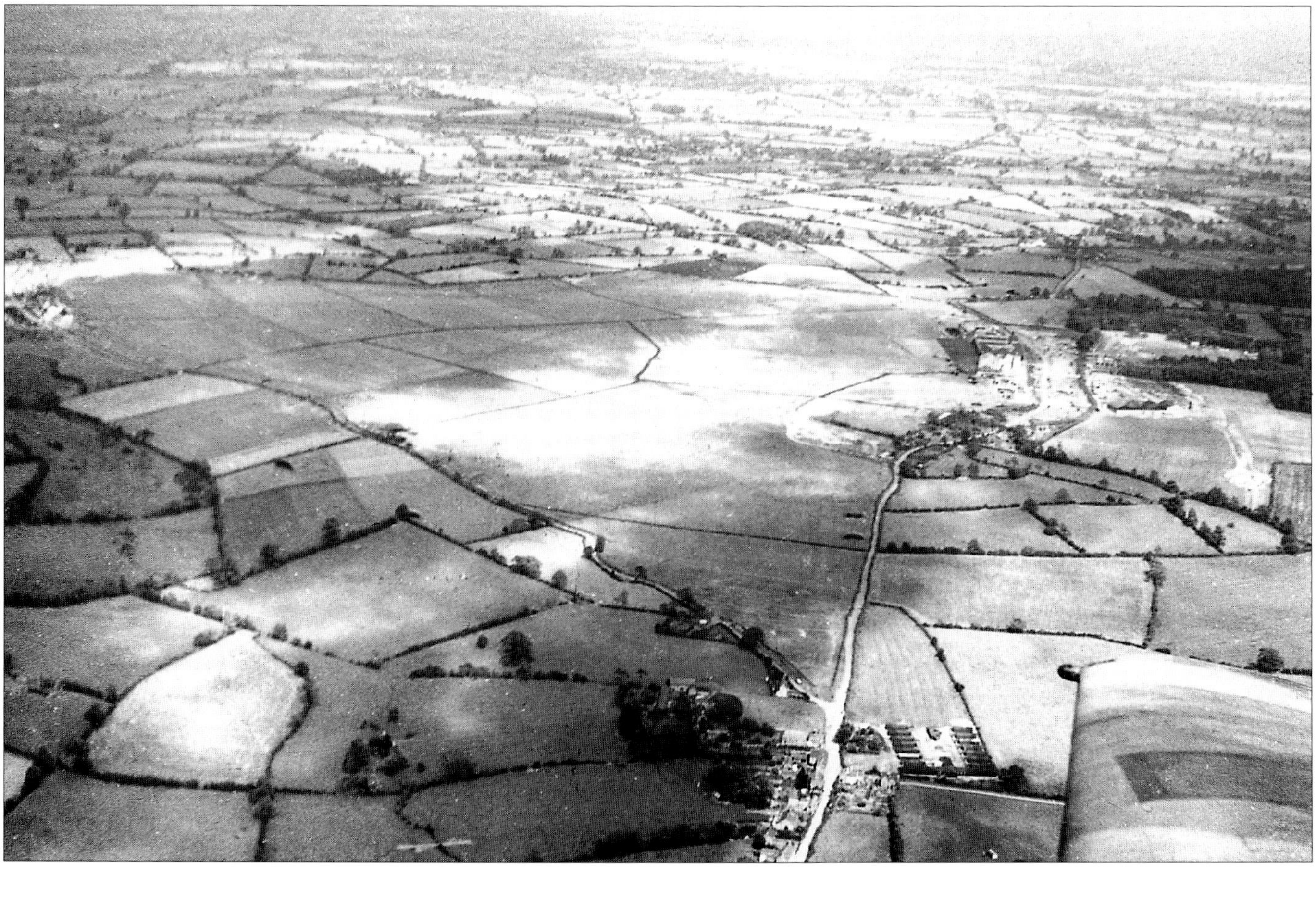

YEAR		AIRCRAFT		PILOT, OR	2ND PILOT, PUPIL	DUTY
MONTH	DATE	Type	No.	1ST PILOT	OR PASSENGER	(INCLUDING RESULTS AND REMARKS)
		—	—	—	—	—— TOTALS BROUGHT FORWARD
APRIL	23	D.H.82	RH905	SELF	R.Ac. AIRES	6.7.8.
	23	"	"	"	" FRENCH.	6.7.8.
	24	"	R6149	"	" CIANO	1).19.
	2?	"	"	"	" CHENEY	14.1).19.
	24	"	"	"	" CIANO	10.19.22.
	2)	"	RH905	"	" CHENEY	19.22.
	?)	"	N95?2	"	" CIANO.	10.19.
	1)	"	"	"	" LIANO	6.).8.
	?)	"	"	"	" CHENEY	19.
	1)	"	"	"	" CHENEY	19 AP12345.
	28	"	"	"	" LIMBERT	6.).9.
	28	"	"	"	" CHENEY	19.
	28	"	"	"	" CHENEY	19.22.
	29	"	"	"	" MONK.	6.).9.

Extract from H P Lavender's logbook showing entries involving J Cheney (see page 80). Included in the exercises flown were: 14 low flying; 17 forced landings; 19 instrument flying; 20 take-offs and landings 'out of wind' (crosswind); and 22 aerobatics. via R W Lavender

On 30th May 1941 there was a change of commanding officer for the station and 7 EFTS. Wing Commander J Beaumont replaced Wing Commander G Lowdell who then went on to join Vickers Armstrong as a test pilot, in due course becoming a valued member of Alex Henshaw's team at the Castle Bromwich works.

Visits to active airfields were always a high spot for cadets of the Air Training Corps (ATC). Those fortunate enough to be taken to Desford invariably considered themselves lucky for they could be virtually guaranteed air experience in one of the many Tiger Moths. Groups of cadets first made their weekend visits from early in the war and so began an association between the airfield and the Corps which was to last almost until Desford closed. From July 1942, the station also began to host annual summer camps for units of the ATC. Usually these were of seven days duration and consisted of four officers and 50 cadets.

Throughout their stay the cadets were introduced to many aspects of service life, including living under canvas when a tented camp became their home for a week. A selected few ATC cadets were also involved in a series of special courses at Desford over two periods of four weeks in December 1942 and February 1943. The two cadets who arrived each week were introduced into the 7 EFTS training programme and for the next six days participated in much the same training as the aircrew cadets. Though not recorded as such, this was probably a study to assess a possible method of reducing their training period on entry into the RAF.

As the war progressed, so the work load of 7 EFTS increased. An indication of the numbers undergoing instruction in the latter half of 1942 is shown in the following monthly summaries.

September	Cadet intake	298
	Output	345
October	Cadet intake	292
	Output	221

Given the flying instruction needed to achieve this throughput and the inexperience of the trainees it is hardly surprising that there were many accidents. In one form or another these happened almost daily. Forced landings, both on and away from the airfield, occurred with monotonous regularity. Often student pilots would become lost, make a successful landing only to be unable to take-off again. This then necessitated a more competent pilot, invariably an instructor, being ferried to retrieve the offending pupil and his aircraft.

Damage, in varying degrees, was inflicted on many aircraft. The frequency of this can be shown by quoting examples from the unit Operational Record Book (ORB):

___

3rd March 1942   'C' Flight, 48 Course

___

LAC Byers   T6953   Lost near Derby. Struck tree during forced landing. Damaged all forward area of aircraft near cockpit.

LAC Clymont   T7849   Damaged port wing, undercarriage and propeller whilst taxying at Desford.

LAC Ferguson   N6483   Caused Category B damage to aircraft at Desford.

___

All this from just from one of 7 EFTS's flights and in one day!

Accidents for March 1943 looked like this:

Day	Serial	Details
3rd	DE298	Struck hedge when landing
4th	N4859	Landed on top of Sgt Lowe in N2900. Extensive damage to both aircraft.
4th	DE400	Damaged night flying.
9th	N6753	Crashed near Bagworth killing pilot Sgt Goodchild.
9th	BB851	Tipped on nose when being started.
9th	BB760	Collided in mid-air with N6488. Only minor damage, both landed safely.
16th	T6189	Struck windsock on landing
22nd	R5254	Taxied into petrol bowser.
23rd	–	Lancaster W4367 landing after ops diversion overshot flarepath and crashed into two Tiger Moths. BB867 written off, N9152 minor damage.

Damage to the Lancaster was limited to the tail and propellers. Repaired, it rejoined 106 Squadron only to be reported missing from a mission to Gelsenkirchen on 26th June 1943.

For some trainees the roofs of buildings around the airfield seemed to have a magnetic quality. In 1942 there were at least two examples of this attraction. On 7th August LAC Jamieson stalled onto a roof on the north side, while for LAC Denton, his first solo in BB868 on 7th October must have been an unforgettable experience when he gave a similar performance on the south side.

In addition to all the repair work needed to restore damaged Tigers to airworthy status, after a scheduled number of hours each aircraft needed to be inspected. To enable both these operations to be carried out efficiently a process similar to a production line system was evolved. Eventually almost 70 people were engaged in this section alone. Many of these were local women who, after tuition, proved particularly adept at fabric repairs.

Visiting aircraft to Desford came in all shapes and sizes; by far the greater proportion left again unscathed, though some did not. Damage to these ranged from superficial through to complete write off.

The following incidents serve to illustrate the worst categories:

5.9.43 Boulton Paul Defiant N3505
10 Air Gunnery School, Barrow. Crashed on the airfield. No casualties. It is probable that N3505 was arriving for attention by R&S. However the damage sustained was sufficient for it to be struck off charge on 30th September.

10.10.43 Boeing B-17 Flying Fortress 42-29557 'SO:S' Yankee Gal
547th BS/384th BG, Grafton Underwood, Northants. Returning from a raid over Germany, lost and short of fuel, at 17:.30 hours attempted to land, overshot and hit a Bellman hangar on south side. Two of the ten crew injured. The aircraft was later dismantled on site.

1.9.44 Miles Magister T9741 ATA
Air Transport Auxiliary. Aircraft crashed due to engine failure on take-off. No injuries. The Magister was being flown by Francis Mary Horsburgh, a Canadian Cadet Officer in the ATA.

Following the successful invasion of Europe, eventual victory became assured and the urgent need for trained aircrew declined. In common with many similar training establishments the workload at Desford decreased. By the time that the end of the war was celebrated in 1945, 7 EFTS had achieved its objective. Several thousand embryo pilots who had passed through its courses now had cause to remember Desford as the place where their first faltering flights had been made on the way to gaining their wings.

Desford – 1st December 1944

Latitude	52° 36' 45" N
Longitude	01° 17' 30" W
Height above Sea Level	425ft
Command	Flying Training (RAF)
Nearest Railway Station	Desford (LMS) 1 mile
Function	Elementary Flying Training School (Parent)
Affiliated Airfields	Braunstone (Relief Landing Ground)

Landing Area

QDM	Dimensions	Extensibility	Remarks
NE – SW	1,200 yards	1,400 yards	Entails removal
E – W	900 yards	1,400 yards	of one house to NW.
Type of Surface	Grass		

Permanent Landmarks

By Day	Lake at Thornton, 3 miles N; Groby Pool 4½ miles NE; Quarry 3 miles S.
By Night	Lake possibly visible.

Permanent Obstructions Factory S side; trees, hangars, factory, near N side.

Facilities

Airfield Lighting	Nil
Flying Control	Nil

Accommodation Semi-permanent buildings, also factory site

Technical	*Hangars:*			
	Civil	2	Bellman (MAP)	1
	Standard Blisters	13		
	Over Blisters	1	EO Blisters	1
	Hardstandings:		Nil	

Domestic	Officers	SNCOs	ORs	Total
RAF	34	69	262	365
WAAF	–	–	–	–

Desford-Based Units and Aircraft

Leicestershire Aero Club (LAC)
De Havilland DH. 60M Moth G-AAIF, G-AASM, G-ABRF, G-ABTF.
De Havilland Puss Moth G-AAZV.

S P Symington
Comper Swift G-ABZZ.

Reid & Sigrist Civil Flying School
No.7 Elementary & Reserve Flying Training School
From 25.11.35 to 3.9.39 No codes.

No.7 Elementary Flying Training School
From 3.9.39 to 9.5.47 No wartime codes.
De Havilland Tiger Moth Post-war 'FHV-' to 'FHY-'
Civil registered examples. Most were later given military serials, and where known these appear in brackets.
G-ADOW (BB856), G-ADOX (BB857), G-ADOY (BB848), G-ADOZ (BB859), G-ADPA (BB851), G-ADPB, G-ADPC (BB852), G-ADPD, G-ADPE, G-ADPF (BB853), G-ADPG (BB854), G-ADPH (BB855), G-ADXT (BB860), G-ADXU (BB861), G-ADXV (BB862), G-ADXW, G-ADXX (BB863), G-AECG, G-AECH (BB864), G-AECI (BB865), G-AECJ (BB866), G-AEID, G-AFAR (BB867), G-AFAS (BB868). K4254, K4260, L6944, L6946, L6947, L6948, N5450, N5473, N5481, N5486, N5489, N6443, N6472, N6475, N6476, N6477, N6478, N6480, N6481, N6482, N6483, N6484, N6485, N6486, N6488, N6526, N6529, N6531, N6580, N6602, N6603, N6615, N6616, N6650, N6651, N6666, N6707, N6719, N6727, N6730, N6740, N6741, N6753, N6771, N6776, N6864, N6865, N6926, N6929, N6938, N6939, N6940, N6942, N6947, N6948, N6967, N9147, N9199, N9200, N9214, N9256, N9272, N9304, N9320, N9335, N9345, N9407, N9408, N9431, N9463, N9502, N9503, N9509, N9510, N9512, N9514, N9516, R4763, R4764, R4770, R4776, R4785, R4832, R4846, R4847, R4850, R4852, R4898, R4900, R4905, R4906, R4922, R4946, R4975, R5020, R5031, R5039, R5109, R5113, R5143, R5149, R5195, R5207, R5208, R5209, R5210, R5214, R5239, R5254, T5416, T5423, T5541, T5564, T5602, T5674, T5689, T5690, T5691, T5692, T5694, T5695, T5696, T5697, T5698, T5700, T5701, T5849, T5883, T5982, T5986, T6178, T6179, T6180, T6189, T6194, T6274, T6288, T6290, T6296, T6399, T6575, T6614, T6615, T6643, T6898, T6901, T6903, T6910, T6911, T6916, T6918, T6953, T6954, T6955, T6957, T7020, T7033, T7036, T7037, T7049, T7089, T7213, T7224, T7242, T7265, T7340, T7350, T7351, T7388, T7605, T7690, T7784, T7791, T7803, T7805, T7809, T7840, T7849, T7964, T7965, T7997, T7999, W7970, X5110, BB800, DE157, DE168, DE248, DE265, DE298, DE314, DE322, DE400, DE410, DE461, DE589, DF120, DF123. EM726, EM926, NL702, NL704, PG686.
(All Tiger Moth IIs except for civilian registered (later military) examples, L6944, L6946, '47, '48, W7970, X5110 and BB800.)
Hawker Hart	K3006, K3007.
Hawker Hart (Special)	K3867, K4428, K4435.
Hawker Hart (Trainer)	K6524, K6526.
Hawker Hind	K5434, K5543, K6641, K6692, K6731, L7175, L7221, L7241.
Hawker Audax	K7421, K8321, K8331.
Miles Magister I	P2403, R1963, T9911.

No.3 Civil Air Navigation School
From .8.38 to 1.11.39

No.3 Air Observer Navigation School
From 1.11.39 to 24.11.39
Avro Anson I K8768, L7947 'U', L7948, L7949, L7951, L7952, L7955 'Z', L7956, N4923, N4940, N5120, N5121, N5338.

No.7 Reserve Flying School
From 9.5.47 to 31.7.53 Code 'RCP-'
De Havilland Tiger Moth II See 7 EFTS list.
Percival Prentice T.1 VN691 '12' later '52', VR197 '10' later '50', VR203 '21', VR264, VR289 '11', VS256, VS273, VS362 '15' later '55', VS366 '14', VS372, VS389 '20', VS547 '17' later '57', VS691, VS697, VS738 '18' later '58', VS745.
Avro Anson I R9809, MG237, MG831, MG964.
Avro Anson T.21 VV297, VV314 'Y' later '71', VV315 '70'.
De Havilland Canada Chipmunk T.10 WG362, WG363.

No.9 Maintenance Unit (Dispersal)
Avro Tutor I	K3254, K3454.
Hawker Audax	K3694, K4400, K5130, K5220, K7339 (K3684 set out but crashed *en route* at Atherstone, Warwickshire, 10.10.40.).
Hawker Hector	K9710.

M44 Gliding School, Air Training Corps
From 4.48 to .50
Slingsby Tutor TX.1	VD167, VD181, VW535.
Slingsby Cadet TX.1	RA897, RA987, RA991, RB135, VW511.
Slingsby Sedbergh TX.1	WB959, WB979.

No.1969 Flight / No.664 Squadron
From 1.9.49 to 17.1.53 Codes 'ROD-'
Auster AOP.5	TJ320.
Auster AOP.6	TW582 'M', TW591 'N'. VW995 'O', VW999 'L', VX128.
Auster T.7	WE559 'P', WE562 'U'.

No.5 Basic Flying Training School
From 1.2.52 to 30.6.53
De Havilland Canada Chipmunk T.10
WB587, WB624, WB718, WD328 '49', WG427, WG478, WG479, WG480, WG482, WG483, WG484, WG485, WG486 '19', WG487 '20', WG488 '21', WG489 '22', WG490, WG491, WK506 '26', WK507 '29', WK508, WK509 '31', WK510, WK511 '33', WK512 '34', WK513 '35', WK514 '36', WK516 '38', WK519, WK520, WK521 '41'. WK522, WK523 '43', WK547, WK548 '26', WK549, WK572, WP896, WP898, WP906 '32'.

Despite this, and probably other mishaps, Tiger Moth G-ADPA went on to enjoy a long career at Desford. After being issued with the military serial BB851 it continued to serve until sold in January 1950. R Emmerson

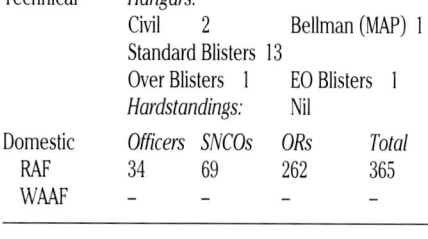

Defiant I T4037 of 256 Squadron with the turret in the 'ready' position with the rear fairing down. It later moved to 287 Squadron and came to R&S on 31st March 1943. It returned again to Desford on 28th June 1944 for conversion to TT.III target tug status, but was recategorised E1 and not proceeded with.

Defiant TT.I DR863 during tests, hence the 'Circle P' marking defining a prototype. Note the under-fuselage fairing that held the sleeve target and the black and yellow high visibility

markings underneath. The cable guide to the winch gear is hardly visible, being directly under the 'P'. This aircraft was at Desford from 6th February to 28th April 1945 for repair and modifications.

Defiant N1697 was converted to TT.III status by R&S between 9th January and 31st March 1944. The water tower and Sergeants Mess can just be seen over the top of the fuselage above the roundel.
All via Author

Civilian Repair Organisation

It was realised, that during the war aircraft casualties would soon far exceed the usual sources ability to repair them. As a solution to this problem attention was focused on the civilian sector and the numerous small companies with the necessary expertise and capacity available. These various businesses were then welded together to form the Civilian Repair Organisation (CRO).

At Desford, R&S were well prepared for this eventuality and were incorporated into the scheme from its outset. To house the repair and conversion work, a large hangar was built off the airfield, on the north side, opposite the two already *in situ*. Later another CRO site was established, again off the airfield but over on the Peckleton Common side. There a T2 hangar and an Over Blister hangar were erected side-by-side and four Super Robins hangars were joined together to make one long workshop.

Contracts for the repair and later conversion of Boulton Paul Defiant two-seat turret fighters were soon signed with the first aircraft arriving in January 1940. Initially deliveries were slow but as these increased the need for a larger workforce arose. Many who were then employed came from surrounding towns and villages and were mainly unskilled. Such were the pressing needs of wartime that they were readily trained in the necessary skills.

From 1940 until the war ended the Defiant became the mainstay of R&S's effort within the CRO. At some time or other all the various marks associated with the type were to be seen on the firm's premises (see table). Many of the aircraft returned to the works several times; circumstances often dictated that second and third visits were commonplace, while one Defiant, N3430, required attention no fewer than five times. The last two to leave the works were DR931 and DR945 on 30th June 1945 bound for 47 MU at Sealand in North Wales. By the time that Defiant contracts ceased in 1945 over 1,000 individual assembly, conversion or repair operations had been carried out.

R&S were also to have been responsible, in conjunction with Air Service Training, Hamble, for airframe repairs to American built Bell P-39 Airacobras. This aircraft was found to be unsuitable for RAF requirements and too few of the type arrived in the UK to warrant setting up repair lines.

Contracts did however materialise for the inspection, repair or modification of North American B-25 Mitchell twin-engined medium bombers. Some of these aircraft were to fly in, but many of the badly damaged specimens to arrive did so in a dismantled state on 'Queen Mary' transport trailers.

The first Mitchells to come to Desford were FL189 and FL671 which arrived from the Aeroplane & Armament Experimental Establishment at Boscombe Down, Wiltshire, on 9th April 1943. Only 16 more had been delivered by the end of the year but this situation was to change in 1944.

It was a delivery in 1944 that well known aerial archaeologist, Jim Pickering of Hinckley, has cause to remember. At the time, Jim was chief test pilot of 511 Forward Repair Unit (FRU), Odiham, Hampshire, and on 10th September he was flying a B-25 to Desford for a major inspection. On coming into land he experienced problems when the undercarriage became stuck half down. A lively session of aerobatics to try to shake it free was to no avail. Neither was the drastic action taken by his passenger, a Sergeant fitter from Leicester, who chopped through hydraulic lines in the hope that the undercarriage would drop and lock. Not an ideal situation but Jim elected to land; after all, the aircraft would be well placed for repair!

After the station duty pilot had managed to clear the many Tiger Moths from the circuit and airfield the B-25 was brought in. It touched down, slithered across the grass and came to a rapid stop with airscrews twisted and cockpit buckled. Both occupants were unhurt and made a speedy exit via the top hatch. Running from the wreck, Jim was almost laid low by a fireman, complete with extinguisher, coming in the opposite direction. Ironically the Mitchell had come to rest at almost the same spot from which Jim had made his first solo flight, in a Tiger Moth, seven years earlier.

R&S staff pose with B-25J 43-27774. This is reputed to have been the 1,000th aircraft to receive attention by the CRO side of the company. via J Grimes

The Mitchell repair and modifications contract took on the look of a production line. The process of refurbishing and repairing B-25s was mostly a case of full strip down, inspection, repair if needed, re-assembly and test flight. P Penney

An increasing number of B-25s found their way to Desford in 1944. By the end of June, 32 had been received but when the year ended the figure had risen to 72. Many of the aircraft required attention due to flying accidents but damage caused by enemy action accounted for a good proportion. In this latter category at least eight Mitchells came to Desford after sustaining damage during the *Luftwaffe's* last major offensive. Known as Operation 'Bodenplatte', it took place on New Years Day 1945 when attacks by German fighters and fighter bombers against Allied airfields on the Continent resulted in many casualties amongst aircraft dispersed on the ground.

At the end of the war in Europe large numbers of aircraft were considered to be no longer worthy of repair. A number of these were awaiting attention at Desford; surveys resulted in them being reclassified as Category E (scrap).

The last large intake of Mitchells was during June 1945 when eight were received. There were no more until what was destined to be the last, FR209, of the Empire Central Flying School (ECFS), arrived from Hullavington, Wiltshire, on 22nd October. The end of an era came on 16th November when FV973 and FW225 left for storage at 12 MU, Kirkbride, Cumberland, and FR209 returned to the ECFS. All that then remained was for R&S to clear away the scrap and bring an end to an interesting chapter of Desford's history.

The third part of the chronicle of Desford's wartime history concerns its association with the Supermarine Spitfire. This largely untold story can be found in Chapter Ten.

Reid & Sigrist, Desford – CRO Aircraft

Boulton Paul Defiant

Official aircraft movement cards record that over 700 of the 931 Defiants built came to Desford either for erection, repair, modification, conversion, or to be reduced to spares. As circumstances dictated that some aircraft required the services of the Desford works on more than one occasion, in excess of 1,000 visits can be traced.

Space precludes a more detailed listing and serial number only will have to suffice. Aircraft are suffixed as follows to denote the number of times they are recorded as visiting the Desford CRO: * twice, + three times, ± four times. Readers wanting more details on individual Defiant histories should refer to *The Defiant File*, by Alec Brew, published by Air-Britain, 1997.

N3436 is recorded as visiting five times, as follows: In on 11.4.41 for SAS (service and storage), despatched to 6 Maintenance Unit (MU), Brize Norton, 1.7.41. Back again 5.8.41 for SAS, leaving 27.8.41 to 60 Operational Training Unit, East Fortune. In again, this time for repair in works (RIW) 6.8.42, being despatched to 44 MU, Edzell, 3.1.43. On 27.11.43 N3436 returned, for conversion to TT.III target tug status. It left on 4.3.44 to join 691 Squadron at Roborough. It made its last appearance at Desford on 29.4.44 for a scheduled RIW, but on 20.5.44 it was recategorised as E1 and struck off charge.

Aircraft prior to AA362 were built as Mk.Is, with conversions to Mk.II and Mk.III status. From AA363 all completed as Mk.IIs. The 'DR' and 'DS' batches were purpose-built as TT.I target tugs.

L6955, L6957, L6963, L6964, L6967*, L6971*, L6976, L6979, L6981, L6983, L6984*, L6986, L6987, L6988, L6989, L6990, L69902, L69904, L69907, L69909, L7000, L7002*, L7003, L7006, L7008, L7011*, L7013, L7014, L7017*, L7020, L7024, L7028, L7029, L7030, L7033, L7035, N1536, N1537, N1538, N1539, N1541, N1542, N1544*, N1545, N1546, N1548*, N1549, N1550, N1552, N1553, N1558+, N1559, N1560, N1561, N1562+, N1563*, N1564, N1566, N1567, N1569*, N1571*, N1572, N1576, N1577*, N1579+, N1581*, N1582*, N1610+, N1613, N1614, N1617, N1618, N1622*, N1623, N1624+, N1626+, N1630*, N1631, N1632*, N1633*, N1634, N1636+, N1638*, N1639+, N1640*, N1642*, N1643*, N1644, N1645, N1646, N1648*, N1649, N1652, N1671*, N1673+, N1674*, N1676, N1681, N1682, N1683*, N1684, N1685, N1687, N1689+, N1690*, N1691, N1693+, N1695+, N1696, N1697, N1698+, N1699±, N1700+, N1701*, N1702, N1704*, N1706, N1725, N1726*, N1727, N1728*, N1729, N1730±, N1733, N1735, N1736+, N1737, N1740*, N1741, N1742+, N1743±, N1744*, N1746, N1747, N1748, N1750, N1751, N1752, N1753, N1755, N1756+, N1758*, N1761, N1763+, N1764+, N1765*, N1767, N1768*, N1770, N1771+, N1772*, N1779+, N1781, N1782, N1783*, N1785, N1786+, N1789, N1800, N1802, N1803*, N1804, N1805+, N1807*, N1808, N1809*, N1810, N1811, N1812*, N3308, N3309, N3310*, N3312*, N3313*, N3314, N3315*, N3316*, N3317, N3318, N3319, N3320*, N3321+, N3322*,

N3323+, N3324*, N3325*, N3326, N3327, N3328, N3329, N3330+, N3331*, N3332, N3334, N3335*, N3336, N3337*, N3338+, N3339, N3340*, N3345, N3346, N3347+, N3370+, N3371, N3372*, N3373*, N3374, N3375, N3379, N3380, N3382, N3384*, N3385, N3386*, N3387, N3393+, N3394, N3395*, N3396, N3399, N3401, N3402, N3403*, N3404*, N3405*, N3421*, N3423*, N3424, N3425+, N3426+, N3427, N3428, N3429, N3430, N3433*, N3434*, N3435*, N3436 see above, N3435, N3437, N3438+, N3440*, N3441, N3448, N3450*, N3452*, N3454*, N3456*, N3457*, N3458, N3459,*, N3479, N3480±, N3481, N3482, N3483, N3484, N3485*, N3486, N3487, N3488, N3489+, N3490, N3491*, N3494, N3497, N3498*, N3499*, N3510, N3511, N3512, N3513, N3515, N3517, N3518, N3519, N3520, T3911, T3913, T3915, T3916*, T3917*, T3918, T3919*, T3920*, T3922, T3923+, T3925*, T3926, T3928*, T3929, T3932*, T3935*, T3936*, T3939, T3941*, T3942+, T3943*, T3945*, T3946, T3947*, T3948+, T3950+, T3951+, T3953, T3954*, T3956, T3957, T3958, T3960*, T3981, T3982+, T3983*, T3984*, T3986*, T3987*, T3988*, T3989, T3990+, T3992+, T3993, T3994, T3995, T3996, T3997*, T3999, T4000, T4001, T4002*, T4005, T4006*, T4007+, T4009+, T4010, T4033, T4034, T4035*, T4036*, T4037*, T4039, T4041*, T4043, T4046*, T4047, T4048*, T4050±, T4052+, T4054, T4055, T4056, T4057, T4059, T4060*, T4062*, T4063, T4065, T4066*, T4067*, T4068*, T4069*, T4070*, T4072*, T4073, T4074, T4076, T4077, T4078, T4111*, T4112*, T4113, T4114, T4115, T4116, T4117, T4119, T4120*, T4121, V1106*, V1107+, V1108+, V1110*, V1111, V1112+, V1114*, V1115+, V1118*, V1119, V1120*, V1122, V1123*, V1124*, V1126+, V1127, V1128, V1129+, V1132, V1133*, V1135+, V1136, V1139+, V1141, V1170, V1172, V1174, V1178*, V1181*, AA282+, AA283, AA285+, AA286*, AA287, AA288*, AA289, AA290, AA291*, AA292, AA294*, AA295+, AA296, AA298, AA300*, AA301*, AA305, AA306±, AA308*, AA310, AA311*, AA312, AA313, AA314*, AA315, AA316, AA317*, AA320, AA321, AA324, AA325, AA326*, AA327, AA328, AA329*, AA330, AA350, AA352, AA354, AA356*, AA357, AA358*, AA359, AA361, AA362, AA363, AA364, AA365, AA366, AA367, AA368, AA370, AA371*, AA372, AA374, AA379, AA380*, AA381, AA382, AA383, AA388*, AA389*, AA401, AA404, AA405*, AA406, AA407, AA409, AA410*, AA411*, AA412, AA413*, AA415, AA416*, AA417, AA418, AA419, AA420, AA421*, AA422*, AA424, AA425, AA427, AA431, AA432*, AA433*, AA434, AA436, AA437*, AA438, AA440, AA441, AA442, AA443, AA444, AA445, AA446, AA447, AA449, AA470, AA471, AA472, AA473, AA474, AA475, AA476, AA477, AA478, AA479, AA480, AA481, AA482, AA483, AA484, AA485, AA486, AA487, AA488, AA489, AA490, AA491, AA492, AA493, AA494, AA495, AA496, AA497, AA498, AA499, AA500, AA501, AA502, AA503, AA504, AA505, AA506, AA507, AA508, AA509, AA510, AA511, AA512, AA513, AA531, AA536, AA537, AA538, AA542, AA544, AA545, AA547, AA549, AA550, AA556*, AA557, AA570, AA573, AA575+, AA576, AA577, AA578, AA579, AA580, AA583, AA587, AA588, AA589, AA591, AA592, AA593, AA594, AA595, AA614, AA615, AA616, AA617, AA618, AA619, AA620, AA621, AA622, AA623, AA624, AA625, AA626, AA627, AA628, AA630, AA631, AA633, AA656*, AA657, AA659, AA660, AA665, AA667*, AA668,

AA669, DR863, DR866, DR869, DR870, DR871, DR872, DR873, DR874, DR877, DR879, DR880, DR883, DR885, DR886, DR888, DR889, DR890, DR891, DR892, DR894, DR915, DR916, DR917, DR918, DR920, DR922, DR923, DR924, DR925, DR926, DR928, DR929, DR930, DR931, DR933, DR935, DR936, DR938, DR939, DR941, DR942, DR945, DR946, DR947, DR949, DR961, DR962, DR963, DR965, DR967, DR968, DR969, DR972, DR973, DR974, DR975, DR976, DR977, DR978, DR979, DR980, DR981, DR982, DR983, DR984, DR986, DR987, DR988, DR990, DR991. DS121, DS122, DS123, DS124, DS125, DS126, DS127, DS128, DS129, DS130, DS131, DS132, DS133, DS134, DS135, DS136, DS137, DS138, DS140, DS141, DS142, DS143, DS144, DS145, DS146, DS147, DS148, DS149, DS150, DS151, DS152, DS153, DS154, DS155, DS156, DS157, DS158, DS159.

North American B-25 Mitchell

Only a handful are recorded as making two visits.

Mitchell II (USAAF equivalent, B-25C and B-25D)
FL166, FL168, FL170, FL171, FL173, FL174, FL176,FL177, FL178, FL182, FL185, FL189, FL201, FL202, FL207, FL215, FL217, FL671, FL676, FL679, FL680, FL681, FL684, FL686, FL688, FL690, FL694, FL695, FL698, FL699, FL701, FL704, FL706, FL709, FR142, FR156, FR159, FR160, FR164, FR167, FR168, FR169, FR170, FR173*, FR175, FR193, FR195, FR197, FR202, FR206, FR209, FR370. (FR209 was one of two B-25Gs in the batch.), FV900, FV901, FV903, FV904, FV906, FV908, FV909, FV913, FV914, FV926, FV927, FV930, FV933, FV935, FV937, FV938, FV947, FV948, FV956, FV957, FV958, FV960, FV961, FV962, FV963, FV965*, FV968, FV973, FV976, FV982, FV995, FW102, FW107, FW108, FW111, FW112, FW114, FW115, FW116, FW126, FW128, FW130, FW131, FW134, FW155, FW157, FW160, FW162, FW164, FW180, FW190, FW192, FW197*, FW201, FW202, FW204, FW213, FW214, FW215, FW217, FW219, FW223, FW225, FW226, FW238, FW250, FW252, FW254, FW256, FW257, FW262, FW264, FW266, FW269, FW271, FW275, FW276, HD303, HD304, HD321, HD328.

Mitchell III (USAAF equivalent, B-25J)
HD356, HD371, HD373, HD375, HD377, HD382, HD387. KJ562, KJ569, KJ578, KJ586, KJ691, plus B-25J 43-27774.

Reid & Sigrist Civil Fleet

Airspeed Oxford I	G-AIUH (previously NM277) Modified by R&S for use by Hunting Aerosurveys.
De Havilland Tiger Moth	G-AJHS, G-AJHT, G-AJHU
De Havilland Rapide	G-ACYR, G-AIYR, G-AIYY, G-AIZI
Percival Proctor 1	G-AIIW, G-AIKK
RS.1 Snargasher	G-AEOD
RS.3 Desford	G-AGOS
RS.4 Bobsleigh/Desford	VZ728, later G-AGOS Full details in Chapter Ten.

Opposite top: An air-to-ground of the southern site at Desford during the summer of 1945. Camouflaging of the buildings is evident. Four Mitchells, two Spitfiress and the Desford on the operational area. The centre section with wings of another Mitchell is dumped on the ground between the hangars and the 'factory' buildings to the rear. R R Leader

Opposite bottom: An early post-war view of buildings on the north side of the airfield, Sergeants Mess in the centre foreground. This photograph was taken during a sortie to test an early model of the Reid F2 camera which was manufactured at Braunstone. J Hart

Right: An early post-war visitor, Mustang III FZ124 of 309 (Polish) Squadron, RAF. Author

An Air Cadet of 1F (City of Leicester) Squadron, ATC, awaits his turn for an air experience flight aboard Tiger Moth II N9272 'RCP-F' at 7 RFS, Desford, 14th March 1948. John Collier

Opposite: *Vertical survey shot of Desford, on 8th December 1948. A handful of aircraft can be seen outside of the northern hangars, but the southern area is deserted.* DoE

Post-War Years

The end of military repair contracts and the rapid reduction in size of the RAF in the immediate post-war years brought problems for R&S and 7 EFTS. As repair work dwindled, the workforce associated with the CRO activity quickly became redundant. Reductions in staff on the training side although more gradual, the eventual effect was the same.

In the summer of 1945 the second aircraft to be designed by R&S was unveiled. This was the RS.3 Desford; the story of this aircraft and similar company projects is also covered in more detail in Chapter Ten.

For a brief period, beginning in late 1945, a type of training aircraft not normally associated with 7 EFTS was to be seen at Desford. These were three Miles Magisters attached to the unit for temporary duty of an unspecified nature. It could possibly have been in connection with two Chinese officers who were also on attachment around this time. The reasons given for their presence was refresher flying and to gain an insight into the running of an EFTS.

The sad sight of the demise of Avro York I MW259 at Desford, August 1948. via Author

Throughout 1946 and into 1947 the size of 7 EFTS continued to ebb. By 30th May 1947 only five officers and 15 other ranks plus three training officers remained on permanent staff which, in turn, led to only a nucleus of skilled staff being retained by R&S.

In an attempt to diversify and to generate further income R&S obtained several former military aircraft which they then converted to civil standards. The intention was to operate these Percival Proctors and de Havilland Rapides on charter services. Although launched with some publicity in the summer of 1947 the venture met with little success for in this time of restrictions and austerity passengers requiring this type of service were few. As a result the aircraft were frequently idle. To bring in some revenue, they were often employed in pleasure flying at Desford and air displays.

One of R&S's Rapides, G-ACYR, had an interesting past. In 1936, while owned by Olley Air Services, it was used to fly General Franco from the Canary Islands to further the Republican cause in the Spanish Civil War. After leaving R&S employ it returned to Spain where it is now preserved in the Museo del Aire at Cuatro Vientos, near Madrid.

An upturn in fortune for Desford began in 1947 following an increase in reservist train-

ing. From 9th May control of the airfield passed to 64 Group, Reserve Command. No.69 Reserve Centre was established and 7 EFTS reflected this change by becoming 7 Reserve Flying School (RFS). The training pattern was much the same, but with a marked increase in flying. For several more years the ubiquitous Tiger Moth continued to serve the unit until finally retired from RAF service in 1951. As replacements, in common with other reserve schools, 7 RFS received Percival Prentices and, following the addition of two Avro Ansons to the unit inventory, navigator training also became part of the curriculum.

Between the end of the Second World War and the close of the airfield the most spectacular accident to happen to an aircraft at Desford occurred on 11th August 1948. Avro York I, MW259, a four-engined transport, was on air test from Abingdon, Oxfordshire, when the propeller of No.4 engine oversped. While attempting a forced landing, with the undercarriage retracted, the York hit a bump on the airfield which broke its back. Six crew members on board received injuries and MW259 was declared Category E Scrap. Although reputed to have belonged to 242 Squadron, at the time of the crash it still bore the unit markings of 51 Squadron.

A further selection of Desford-based aircraft: Percival Prentice T.1 VR203 of 7 RFS, Slingsby Sedbergh TX.1 WB979 of M44 Gliding School and Auster T.7 WE562 'U' of 1969 AOP Flight, 664 Squadron. J M G Gradidge / Jim Morrow

No.1969 Flight stayed at Desford for over three years before returning to Hucknall in January 1953.

Another unit at Desford during this period was 5 Basic Flying Training School (BFTS). Formed in January 1952 and equipped with de Havilland Canada DHC-1 Chipmunk T.10s its primary role was in the tuition of National Service pilots. In what proved to be a fairly brief but busy existence, 5 BFTS lost four Chipmunks to accidents. One of these led to the unit's only fatal casualty when WK506 crashed at Kirby Muxloe on 28th April 1953 following a mid-air collision.

Unfortunately it was all too good to last and it was a statement made in Parliament on 19th December 1952 by the then Under Secretary of State for Air, George Ward, that was to decide Desfords' destiny in aviation. In his speech he said that in future less aircrew would be needed and numbers of National Servicemen accepted for aircrew training would be substantially reduced. This meant that the seven schools set up for their basic training and operated by civilian contractors would soon be closed. In addition seven of the existing RFS's were also to be closed within the next six months. This announcement became Desford's death knell for it affected both 5 BFTS and 7 RFS.

Following the cancellation of government contracts George Reid decided to retire and break his ties with Desford. He then entered into negotiations for the sale of the airfield. By the end of May severance notices had been sent to flying staff informing them that their employment with R&S would cease on 30th June 1953.

All that remained was to tidy up ready for the new owners but even this operation was not without incident. On 13th July Avro Anson C.19 VL335 of 187 Squadron, Transport Command, based at Aston Down in Gloucestershire, brought in pilots to ferry redundant aircraft away. Landing in gusty, showery conditions the Anson swung to starboard. On being corrected it developed into a skid which continued for about 350 yards before VL335 struck a grass bank on the airfield boundary. Damage was caused to the port undercarriage. Although the pilot, Flight Lieutenant S F Cooper, came in for censure, R&S were not considered altogether blameless. They had removed the wind indicator and allowed the grass to become rather unkempt. This accident caused only a minor delay in the winding up procedure. On 31st July 1953, 7 RFS officially disbanded, Desford closed and brought an end to flying after 24 years.

Post-war many ATC squadrons continued their association with Desford. There were still frequent visits for air experience flights and in April 1948 a new dimension was added to their flying activities when M44 Gliding School left Bruntingthorpe to be based on the airfield. Most weekends, weather permitting, the unit's Slingsby Cadets, Tutors and Sedberghs would be airborne following a winch launch. In 1950 this activity came to an end when the gliding school was disbanded.

An expansion of the RAF brought about first by the Berlin blockade in 1948-49 and then by war in Korea resulted in further units being activated at Desford. On 1st September 1949, 1969 Air Observation Post (AOP) Flight was formed as a detached element of 664 (AOP) Squadron whose headquarters were at Hucknall, Notts. Flying locally-built Auster AOP.6s and T.7s the main duties of these units entailed working with army formations in the role of spotter aircraft, observing the results of artillery fire.

Shortly after this the new owners, Caterpillar Tractor Company, began to occupy the site. Gradually over the next two years they moved in their parts distribution facility which had outgrown premises in Coalville. For over 20 years little development was done to the site. Use was made of existing buildings on both north and south sides while land in between was used for agriculture. Then the company embarked upon two ambitious projects which, when finished, were to change the entire face of the former airfield. The first of these schemes, on the south side, in 1975-76, entailed the construction of buildings covering 432,000 square feet to house a new lift truck assembly plant. During this development, the former lecture rooms and ancillary buildings disappeared but the three types of hangar still exist, absorbed into the works complex.

Some four years later the north side was transformed by an even larger building. This was to house a parts warehousing facility and occupied some 600,000 square feet. Up until this phase of the development the majority of the buildings from the R&S era, both on and off the airfield still remained. Progress took its toll and most were either dismantled or demolished. The only significant wartime building now remaining is the former CRO hangar.

As an added feature of this expansion Caterpillar (UK) Limited carried out an extensive landscaping programme which now enhances the site. This in turn makes it even harder for a stranger to realise that this was once the location of one of Leicestershire's busiest airfields.

For 46 years there has been little or no aeronautical activity at Desford, bar one or two unscheduled landings and the occasional helicopter visit. However, on 10th June 1999, as the highlight of a celebration to mark the completion of the 100,000th Backhoe Loader – a type of earth-moving machine that has been assembled at the Desford

plant in recent years – nine BAe Hawks of the RAF's 'Red Arrows' aerobatic team, and a Battle of Britain Memorial Flight Spitfire, (the Mk.IIa, P7350 'XT-D'), performed over the former airfield for the assembled throng of Caterpillar employees.

Although it is doubtful whether Desford airfield had witnessed anything quite like the 'Red Arrows' at first hand before, it was no stranger to the Spitfire, as the following Chapter will reveal.

Chipmunk T.10s WK514 and WG489 of 5 BFTS, thought to be taking part in a final 'farewell' formation before disbanding, June 1953.
F Lewin

Serious Accidents to Desford-based Aircraft

Reid & Sigrist Civil Flying School, 7 E&RFTS, 7 EFTS, and 7 RFS
De Havilland Tiger Moth

5.3.36	G-ADPD	Crashed at Desford.
29.5.37	G-AECG	Crashed, no details.
18.6.37	G-ADXW	Crashed, no details.
15.4.38	L6948	Stalled and hit tree landing at Desford.
27.2.40	G-ADPG	Crashed at Desford.
10.5.40	G-ADPE	Crashed at Kirkbymoorside, Yorks.
27.5.40	G-ADPB	Damaged beyond repair in landing at Stoughton.
27.5.40	N6939	Crashed in forced landing at Welford.
27.6.40	N6942	Abandoned in spin near Desford.
28.8.40	T5694	Crashed in forced landing at Markfield.
30.8.40	N6472	Crashed in forced landing at Oakley.
27.9.40	G-AEID	Crashed at Desford.
2.10.40	T5689	Hit cables on approach at Desford.
16.12.40	R5039	Crashed in forced-landing at Waltham on the Wolds.
27.3.41	T5602	Spun into ground after take-off at Braunstone.
8.4.41	T5691	Abandoned in spin near Newtown Linford.
19.6.41	R5030	Abandoned after controls jammed near Ellistown.
23.6.41	R5020	Crashed in forced landing four miles east of Lutterworth.
24.7.41	T5564	Spun into ground after take-off at Braunstone.
2.8.41	T5350	Hit tree, low flying at Thornton.
6.8.41	T7242	Overturned on landing at Desford.
15.8.41	N9256	Hit tree in bad weather at Market Bosworth.

22.8.41	BB866	Pilot on second solo spun-in from 150ft, Braunstone. A/c written-off, pilot injured.
25.8.41	N6603	Hit cables in attempted forced landing at Market Bosworth.
25.8.41	N6602	Crashed. No further details.
6.9.41	T7224	Crashed on take-off following forced landing at Wiston Leics. (Or Wistow or Western?)
19.9.41	T5416	Hit obstruction landing at Braunstone.
11.11.41	N6650	Hit tree in forced landing near Knutsford, Cheshire.
22.11.41	L6946	Stalled at low altitude and crashed at Coleshill, Warwicks.
8.12.41	N6938	Crashed in forced landing Wythall, Worcestershire.
9.5.42	N6481	Crashed during overshoot, Desford.
16.2.43	DE461	Engine cut, crashed near Sutton Cheney.
9.3.43	N6753	Spun into ground near Desford.
12.4.43	N9214	Dived into ground, Tamworth, Staffordshire.
27.5.43	BB855	Crew baled out after collision with R4906 over Northampton. Aircraft spun-in and destroyed by fire.
6.9.43	T7036	Abandoned after controls jammed near Ratcliffe.
17.11.43	N6484	Crashed on approach at Desford.
12.5.44	T7964	Crashed on landing at Braunstone.
27.5.44	T7999	Collided with T6954 and crashed 1½ miles south east of Groby.
27.5.44	T6954	Collided with T7999, as above.
21.3.45	T5674	Crashed in forced-landing at Markfield.
10.4.45	X5110	Crashed in forced landing at Chalfont St Peter, Bucks.
5.5.45	BB861	Spun off turn and crashed from 1,000ft, Attleborough, Warwickshire.

11.5.45	T5982	Collided with T6910 and crashed at Elmdon, Warwickshire.
11.5.45	T6910	Collided with T5982 and crashed at Elmdon, Warks.
28.9.45	DF120	Aileron jammed aircraft abandoned, crashed at Sutton Elms near Broughton Astley.
9.10.45	T7049	Crashed in forced landing near Braunstone.
26.11.45	N9345	Crashed on take-off following forced landing at Baginton, Warks.
15.3.46	N9304	Dived into ground, Odstone, Leics.
20.12.46	PG686	Stalled on take-off at Braunstone and damaged beyond repair.
23.4.50	N9272	Hit hut on landing.

Hawker Hind

23.6.39	L7241	Stalled and dived into ground near Desford.

Percival Prentice T.1

18.5.52	VS366	Dived into ground 2 miles south of Shepshed.

No.5 Basic Flying Training School
De Havilland Canada Chipmunk T.10s

29.7.52	WK547	Collided with WK519 on take-off at Desford.
29.7.52	WK519	Hit by WK547 while parked.
23.10.52	WK510	Hit tree during practice forced landing, Broombriggs Farm, Leics.
28.4.53	WK506	Collided with WG478 and lost tail. Crashed near Kirby Muxloe, one killed.

Extensive development of the northern part of Desford in progress during 1980. The greater proportion of the buildings seen in the bottom half of the picture were soon to be either dismantled or demolished. Caterpillar via H Webster

Dismantling the second of Desford's two pre-war hangars. They were both re-erected at Tollerton, Nottingham. Author

Chapter Ten

Desford's Spitfires and the 'Twins'

Famed Spitfire test pilot Alex Henshaw performed the first flight in Spitfire Vb EN821 from Desford on 15th May 1942. Following 'sign off' it was accepted by 45 Maintenance Unit at Kinloss, Scotland, the following day. It joined 243 Squadron (illustrated) at Ouston, Northumberland, on 27th June 1942 and later served with 65 Squadron. By February 1944, EN821 was at Lee-on-Solent, Hampshire, and joined the Fleet Air Arm as an operational conversion trainer for Seafires, initially with 886 Squadron. On D-Day, 6th June 1944, Squadron Leader H A Coghill was flying as part of 808 Squadron in EN821. The Spitfire was either hit by gunfire or in collision with an enemy aircraft and it was seen to dive in to the sea near Le Havre, killing Coghill. via Author

FOLLOWING German air attacks against the huge Vickers Armstrong works at Castle Bromwich in the Midlands, dispersal of a considerable amount of component manufacture and construction took place. Chapter One has outlined the factories and workshops in Leicestershire that turned their hand to the production of vital Spitfire sub-assembles and components. Two additional assembly works were also established, one at Cosford, near Wolverhampton and the other at Desford.

Heavy snowfalls in the winter of 1939-40 severely damaged the hangar 3 AONS had previously occupied on the south side of the airfield – see Chapter Nine. Repairs were carried out and this, together with a newly-erected Bellman hangar, became No.8 Factory in the dispersal scheme.

Components for the assembly of complete aircraft began to be brought in and by February 1941 finished Spitfires were leaving these assembly shops. Initially they were of the Mk.IIa type but progressively Mk.Vs and Mk.IXs were produced. While most aircraft assembled at Desford were built from components supplied by the main works, later a good proportion of locally-fabricated wings, fuselages and undercarriages all helped to feed the production line.

Before delivery each completed Spitfire was subjected to at least one test flight by one of the Castle Bromwich team of test pilots. In charge of this team was Alex Henshaw, already a legendary figure from his pre-war air racing and record breaking exploits. While in his capacity of chief test

Above: *A view of the Spitfire assembly line at Desford. In the foreground are the fuselages of Mk.IXs TA977, TA978 and TA979. TA977 was issued to 33 Maintenance Unit at Lyneham, Wiltshire, on 25th November 1944. All three were eventually supplied to the Soviet Union.*

Below: *No.8 Factory, Desford, flight shed. Mk.IXs under final assembly. In the foreground is TA930 which was despatched to 33 Maintenance Unit at Lyneham on 28th November 1944 and was later shipped to the Soviet Union.* Both via R R Leader

A grouping from No.8 Factory, Desford, with one of their products. Left to right: W H Sparrow, foreman; A Roberts; F Hayward, assistant foreman, flight shed; L G Cooney, stores; Flight Lieutenant Phillips, test pilot; E L Wardel, works inspector; G Bird, Aeronautical Inspection Department; F G Wills, works manager. via F Hayward

pilot he further enhanced his reputation for his undoubted expertise when flying the Spitfire. He is still remembered by many for his scintillating aerobatic displays when called upon to demonstrate these aircraft.

When his services were required he would often arrive at Desford in a Hawker Tomtit which had Leicestershire connections. He acquired three (G-AFIB, G-AFTA and G-AFVV) from their previous owners, Leicestershire Aero Club, for use as a means of commuting between the various airfields where Spitfires needed his expert attention. Ultimately he was to be responsible for carrying out test flying on over 150 Desford-built aircraft. (Tomtit G-AFTA survives in airworthy condition, flying in military markings with the Shuttleworth Trust at Old Warden, Bedfordshire.)

With the exception of two, his flights in these Spitfires appear to have been fairly routine. One troublesome incident was due to failure of the skewgear in the Merlin engine of Mk.V EP353 on 17th June 1942. With the engine dead, Alex glided back to Desford. Then after skilfully avoiding the many Tiger Moths in circuit he managed, to his great relief, to make a good landing on the airfield with wheels and flaps down. On the other occasion he admits to experiencing his worst-ever case of blackout. It happened quite suddenly while in a vertical spiral dive from altitude. When he came to he was shaking uncontrollably but managed to make a recovery with the airfield just a few hundred feet below.

To date it has not been possible to trace accurate figures for the output of No.8 Factory but it is believed that in the region of 20 aircraft per month were turned out by a workforce of around 60. A list of over 200 Spitfires known to have been assembled at Desford has been compiled from various sources and is given in a table.

Vickers-Armstrong, Desford Spitfire Assembly

Serial numbers have been collated mainly from the logbooks of Alex Henshaw and various ATA pilots.

Mk.IIa   P8132, P8133, P8192, P8193, P8205, P8277, P8424, P8425, P8427, P8430, P8437, P8442, P8446, P8460, P8476.

Mk.Vb   P8561, AB853, AB858, AB961, AB964, AD123, AD126, AD128, AD134, AD179, AD193, AD195, AD196 AD249, AD273, AD301, AD307, AD308, AD319, AD350, AD381, AD411, AD450, AD451, AD472, AD537, AD555, BL265, BL368, BL625, BL647, BM513, BM639, EN821, EN822, EN945, EN824, EP108, EP109, EP111, EP112, EP114, EP276, EP277, EP280, EP282, EP284, EP353, EP388, EP487, EP521, EP596, EP598, EP600, EP601, EP603, EP728, EP729, EP748, EP756, EP760, EP772, EP783, EP791, EP793, EP816, EP873, EP875, EP881, EP882, ER115, ER117, ER120, ER301, ER594, ER724, ER726, ER728, ER791, ER832, ER924, ER945, ER961, ER965, ER967, ER968, ER969, ER971, ER975, ES137, ES179, ES186, ES187, ES192, ES193, ES194, ES246, ES262, ES276.

Mk.Vc   ES145, ES236, ES281, JK214, JK219, JK336, JK367, JK370, JK374, JK375, JK377, JK380, JK836, JL363, JL389, JL391, LZ868, MA295, MA354, MA684, MA686, MA692, MA702, MA850, MA852, MA893, MH568, H585, MH587.

Mk.IX   JL109, JL239, MH602, MH927, MJ218, MJ220, MJ222, MJ555, MJ560, MJ562, MJ569, MJ964, MK504, MK552, MK585, ML310, NH308, NH361, NH371, NH377, PL169, PL351, PT929, TA930, TA961, TA962, TA965, TA977, TA978, TA979, TA995, TA998, TB127, TB128, TB448, TB466, TB470, TB479, TB485, TB488, TB490, TB803, TB805, TB824, TB825, TB826, TB854, TE129, TE137, TE140, TE141, TE142, TE143, TE144, TE147, TE148, TE528, TE529, TE534, TE535, TE549, TE553, TE563, TE575

Mk.XVI   TB487, TD197, SM399.

By the time the works closed in September 1945 it is highly probable that in excess of 1,000 Spitfires had been produced by No.8 Factory. This represented a not unimportant part of the overall production of this classic fighter.

Desford's 'Twins'

Already renowned as pioneers and makers of aircraft instruments, Reid & Sigrist's (R&S) first venture into aircraft construction began during 1938-39 when the RS.1 Trainer was designed at the company's main works at Shannon Corner, New Malden, Surrey and built close by. When ready, the aircraft was brought to Desford for final assembly and flight trials where, at an early stage, workers jokingly called it the 'Snargasher'. Although it had no specific meaning the nickname stuck and became a popular appellation for the aircraft.

The RS.1 was a three-seat tandem trainer of plywood-covered wooden construction with a fixed cantilever undercarriage. In the design stage specific attention was given to possible mass production. With this in mind specialised knowledge from experts in the motor car industry was sought.

Powered by two 205hp de Havilland Gipsy Six II inverted air-cooled engines driving de Havilland two position controllable airscrews, it was primarily intended to serve as an advanced trainer for the conversion of pilots from single to twin-engined aircraft. The design also made provision for the teaching of navigation, bombing, wireless telephony and gunnery. Under the continuous canopy the pupil sat forward, the instructor or observer immediately behind, with the radio operator or gunner aft. The rear end of the canopy was fitted with a tip-up cowl underneath which was a special R5 mounting for a Lewis gun. This mounting enabled the gun to be traversed through 180°, have 90° of elevation and be fired almost vertically over the sides. For use in the bombing role, a prone aiming position was provided in the belly beneath the two cockpits.

Flown for the first time early in 1939 by G E Lowdell and registered G-AEOD (constructor's number 1) it made its public debut at the Royal Aeronautical Society's Garden Party at Heathrow on 14th May, receiving its Certificate of Airworthiness shortly afterwards on 3rd June. The RS.1 was given extensive tests and trials, including a series witnessed by representatives of the Royal Aircraft Establishment at Farnborough, Hampshire. Throughout the test period the aircraft disclosed no real vices and was a pleasant machine to fly. It was not accepted by the RAF as no requirement existed for an aircraft in this category at this time.

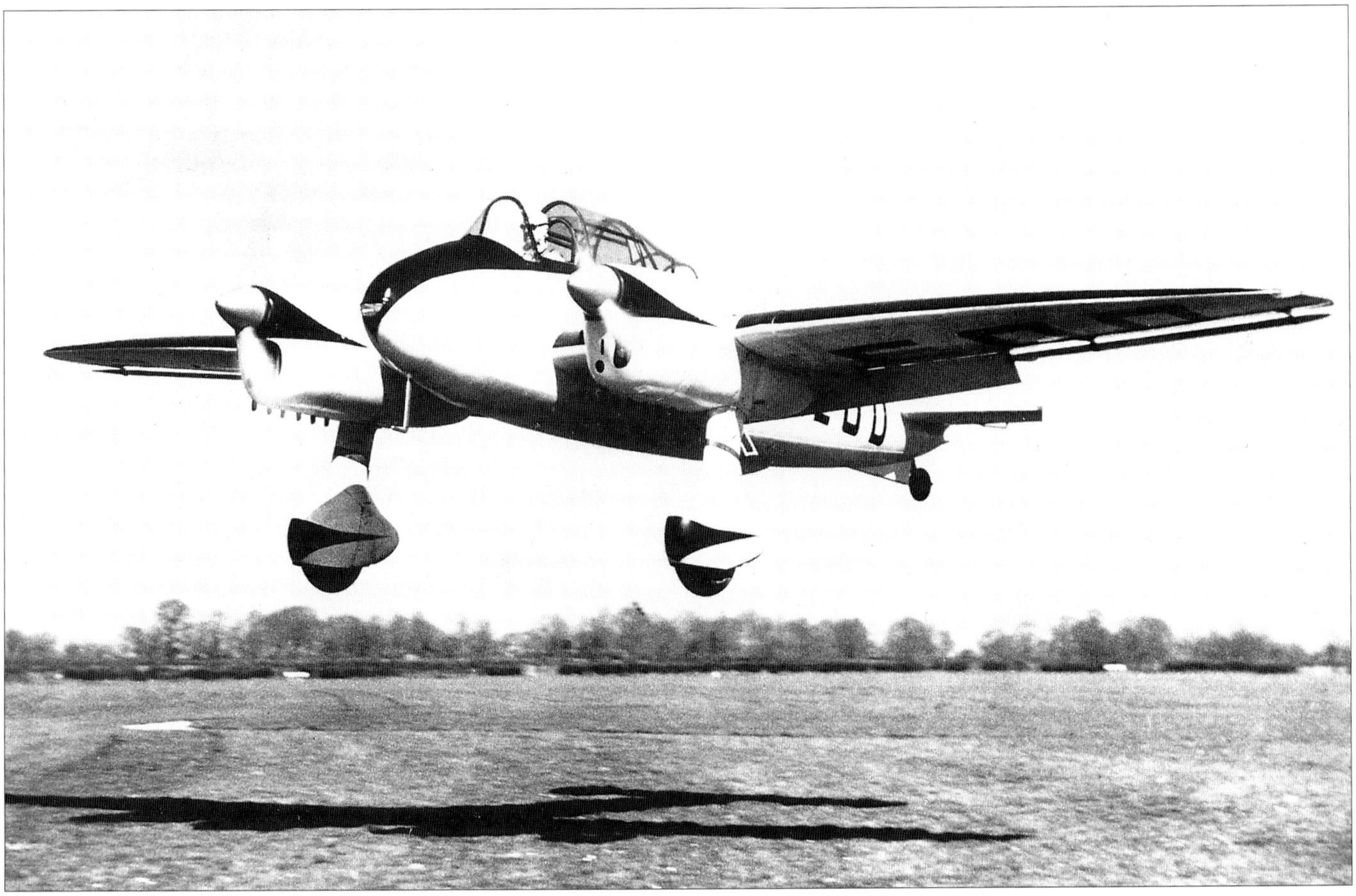

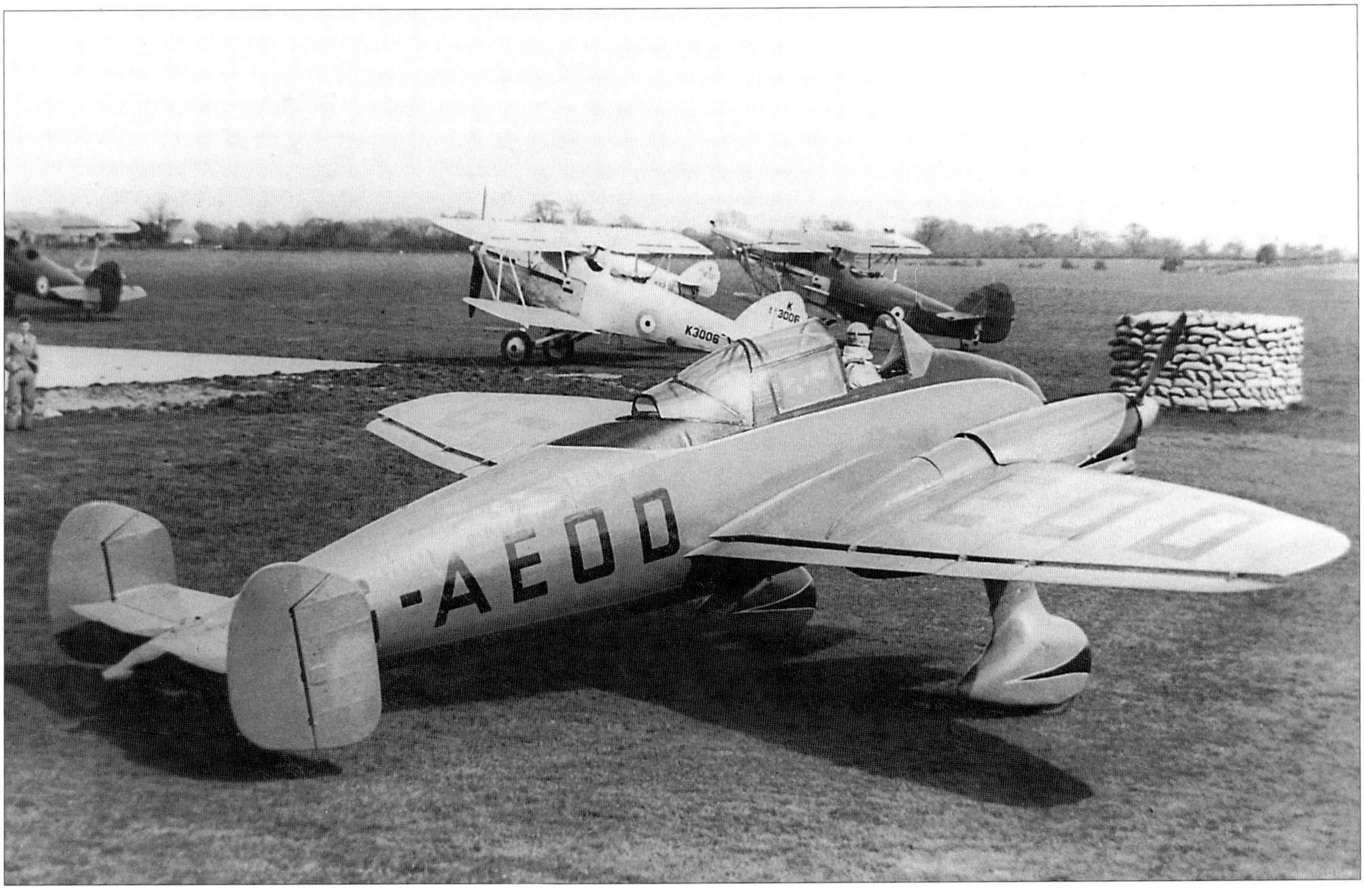
-AEOD
K3006
K
3006

RS.1 Snargasher

Dimensions

Span	36ft 4in.
Length	25ft, 4in.
Height	8ft 11in.
Wing area	212 square feet.

Weights

Empty	3,000lb.
Loaded	4,900lb.

Performance

Maximum speed	205mph at sea level.
Cruising speed	190mph at 75% power at 6,000ft.
Stalling speed	65mph.
Initial rate of climb	1,330ft per minute.
Service ceiling	18,000ft.
Absolute ceiling	20,000ft.

Range

Fuel consumption	21.8 gallons per hour normal duration.
Endurance	4¼ hours at 190mph.
Range	800 miles.

Opposite page:

G-AEOD during a very low fly-by during a demonstration at Desford. The attractive lines of the aircraft are evident. via Author

A good view of the 'Snargasher' at Desford in its original scheme. Note the 7 E&RFTS Harts and Audaxes behind and the sandbagged airfield defence point. via Author

This page:

With the advent of war, the 'Snargasher' took on camouflage and RAF markings and was used for company communications work and training experiments. Note the generous area of flap and the lack of undercarriage fairings and spats. Peter Green collection

An R&S advert that appeared in the aviation press in mid-1940. It shows two proposed versions, assumed to be the RS.2, both with retractable undercarriage for use as a fighter or bomber trainer. Engines were quoted as being of 240/260hp with a top speed of 230mph. Author's collection

In July 1939 the Snargasher was taken aboard for exhibition at the Second International Salon of Aeronautics in Brussels and although interest was shown and praise high no orders resulted. It is also worthy of note that had war not intervened the RS.1 could well have been seen on the air racing circuit for it was an entry in the King's Cup Air Race which was to have been run at Birmingham on 2nd September 1939.

Throughout the Second World War the Snargasher was used by R&S mainly for communication duties, but during 1941 it was utilised by 7 Elementary Flying Training School at Desford in a training experiment. Over a four month period from March to June selected pupils were given a full *ab initio* training course; results obtained were quite satisfactory but this method of training was not adopted. Only the one example of the Snargasher was produced and a projected development of the design known as the RS.2 was shelved during the war.

As to the fate of the RS.1 most accounts state that it was written off during 1944. Former employees have said that this was due to a landing accident and that the guilty party on the occasion is reputed to have been a Canadian pilot named Gilliver. The company did have hopes that the aircraft might be resurrected but damage was too substantial. Much of the Snargasher was then scrapped, but the fuselage was retained to linger on for some years. A spotter's report in the magazine *Air-Britain Digest* for July 1950 confirms that it was still to be seen gathering dust in a hangar at Desford at that time. On a final note, information from three separate sources indicates that the fuselage was still present when the airfield and buildings were sold in 1953. During clearing up operations it was consigned to a bonfire.

During 1939 the company's aircraft design department was transferred from Shannon Corner to Desford; this was primarily in order that it might be on hand to deal with the increasing work associated with military contracts centred at the company airfield. It was from this design office that R&S's second aircraft originated, appearing in completed form during the summer of 1945.

Designed by Charles Bower, the aircraft was built in conditions of secrecy at Desford during the closing stages of the Second World War. Once again the company chose to have major sections of the airframe manufactured away from the airfield. This contract was undertaken by the Austin Veneer Company of London, one of many similar concerns within the furniture industry at this time, which been impressed into work associated with wooden aircraft. After completion, the wings, fuselage and tail unit came by road to Desford for assembly

followed by the installation of engines, flying controls and ancillary equipment.

An interesting story concerns the assembly of the machine which was done in a former lecture block on the south side of the airfield. The building comprised two rooms one of which housed the design department, the other the experimental workshop. This was an excellent arrangement as work on the project could be easily supervised by the design office and at the same time secrecy maintained.

The workshop had a double door type of emergency exit which was also the only means of access from outside. This door proved to be an adequate way of entry for the large components mentioned above, but when the aircraft was ready to emerge it was a different story. It was a relatively easy matter to remove the fuselage from the wing and detach the tail unit after the flying controls had been disconnected, these components then went readily out through the emergency doors. This was not the case with the wing which was a one piece structure, complete with engines and undercarriage – additions that made it impossible for the wing unit to go out though the doorway in the manner by which it had been brought in. So, two strong wooden cradles were made to fit around each engine and undercarriage leg, castors were fitted to the cradles which then allowed the whole unit to be manoeuvred while still maintaining a horizontal 'flying' position.

One night after working hours, efforts began to solve the problem of removal. First the door frame was taken out, then large sections of brickwork were removed. This enlarged hole then enabled the wing unit to be manhandled out. Immediately this had been done the doorway was re-installed, the brickwork restored and then camouflaged. Work continued throughout the night so that by starting time next day everything appeared normal with the aircraft relocated in an out-of-the-way corner of the flight test shed ready for final re-assembly and subsequent test flying.

The aircraft was given the company designation RS.3 and named after its birth place, Desford. It showed some family resemblance to the RS.1 and probably to a greater extent the shelved RS.2 project, but evidence is lacking to prove this. The design concept can be traced back to early in the war from advertisements appearing in *Flight* magazine. These depict an aircraft of similar layout to the RS.1 but with much finer lines and two-seat tandem accommodation. Although purporting to illustrate the Reid and Sigrist Trainer (the RS.1 Snargasher) to all intents and purposes the aircraft shown is the RS.3 Desford. The illustration in the advertisement was taken from a photograph of a model which remained in

company hands at Braunstone until 1971 when it was presented to Leicester Museums. The model is now held by the Leicestershire Museum of Technology, who have a small aeronautical display within the Snibston Discovery Park at Coalville.

Like its predecessor, the RS.1, the RS.3 Desford was of wooden construction with a fixed cantilever undercarriage. The wing was a one piece, two-spar structure bolted to the monocoque fuselage while the all wood strut braced tailplane had twin fins and rudders mounted as end plates. Intended to serve as an *ab initio* and intermediate trainer the crew of two were seated in separate tandem cockpits, the pupil in front, with full blind flying equipment and the instructor aft. Both cockpits were enclosed by a one-piece moulded sliding canopy which could be jettisoned and the windscreen structure was strengthened to form a crash bar should the aircraft turn over.

Registered G-AGOS (constructor's number 3) the RS.3 flew for the first time on 9th July 1945, powered by two 130hp de Havilland Gipsy Major Series Is. Following the initial flight, the Desford embarked upon an intensive test programme in which no major snags were encountered. Reports indicate that, like its predecessor the Snargasher, it possessed admirable flying characteristics. When shown to representatives of the aviation press early in 1946 it received excellent reviews being variously described as 'the complete trainer' and 'an instructor's aeroplane'. It received a full Certificate of Airworthiness on 30th May 1946.

Throughout the late 1940s, a vigorous sales campaign was mounted in an effort to find buyers for the Desford. It participated in several major exhibitions and was a welcome addition to airshows.

RS.3 Desford

Dimensions

Span	34ft.
Length	25ft 6in.
Height	8ft 2in.

Weights

Empty	2,413lb.
Loaded	3,300lb.

Performance

Maximum speed	162mph at sea level.
Cruising speed	148mph.
Initial rate of climb	1,100ft per minute.
Service ceiling	17,730ft.
Absolute ceiling	19,200ft.

Range

At cruising speed	463 miles.
With belly tank	1,500 miles.

Fully aerobatic, its sparkling performances in the hands of company pilots C F French and J A Hart were often the highlight of the display. Interest in the basic trainer version was shown by several foreign countries including the Argentine, Egypt and Spain and during May 1947 a 12-day visit was made to the latter country, demonstrations being given to government representatives at Madrid.

The need to diversify the RS.3's role and so attract a wider market led to an experiment being carried out to assess its suitability for agricultural crop dusting. For test purposes a R&S designed belly pannier was fitted and although the Desford is known to have flown in this configuration, no record of the trials has been found. In 1946 the company had announced that they proposed to develop the RS.4, which was to be a luxury four/five seat private owners version of the RS.3, but due to lack of outside interest these plans were allowed to lapse.

Unfortunately, in spite of all efforts made, no customers could be found for any version of the Desford so, like the RS.1, it was destined to be the sole example of its type. As interest in the aircraft declined it gradually spent more and more time idle at the company airfield until eventually it was tucked away at the back of a hangar and almost forgotten. Then in May 1949 it gained a new lease of life when it was acquired by the Air Council to be used for experimental purposes, investigating the concept of the prone position pilot.

After purchase, the RS.3 remained at Desford where, eventually, a conversion was carried out to enable it to participate in service experiments. Alterations to the aircraft involved a drastic redesign of the forward fuselage which resulted in the deletion of the front cockpit, the aft cockpit being provided with a windscreen and sliding canopy. An extended nose section was fitted to house a pilot in the prone position, this resulted in an increase in the overall length to 26ft 6in. This new extension was not roomy enough to permit rudder pedals to be fitted so the controls for all three axes were incorporated in a specially designed twin grip control with 3° of freedom.

With increasing experience of turbojet aircraft, particularly fighters, and a wealth of material gained from German experiments and designs, the 'race' was on for ever-faster performance. Turbojet or rocket power allowed for particularly smooth aircraft, but the surface area required to accommodate a pilot seated in the conventional manner often dictated the depth of the fuselage. The concept of a prone pilot, got around this problem, allowing an aircraft to be designed that had a fuselage not much deeper than the height of its jet engine and offering a considerably reduced

Early picture of the RS.3 on a somewhat unkempt Desford airfield. Left to right: Dennis Harben, stress calculations; 'Chas' Bower, designer; and T Newton.

View from above of the RS.3, complete with 'Prototype P' marking behind the roundel. Both R&S

cross-section offering less drag and a both smaller target and radar image when encountered head-on.

Following modification the RS.3 received the reallocated company designation of RS.4 and named the Bobsleigh – from the position of the experimental pilot – the civil registration was cancelled and it reappeared bearing the military serial VZ728. The first flight as the RS.4 Bobsleigh took place on 13th June 1951 with Squadron Leader A G Bullmore AFC, at the controls. Bullmore's logbook entry for the occasion reads 'Initial test - very tail heavy'. Attempts were made to rectify the fault but after being flown the next morning the following comment is recorded, 'Tail heavy and sits right wing low', later that day after further attention another test revealed that while the tail heaviness had been cured the fault affecting the starboard wing was still present. By the time of the next flight on 21st June remedial action had been taken resulting in a satisfactory flying attitude being achieved. During July and August test

flying continued, including some flights with Squadron Leader H A Howes occupying the prone position. All passed without incident and on 23rd August the Bobsleigh was taken on strength at the Royal Aircraft Establishment, Farnborough, Hampshire.

While at the RAE, the RS.4 was used mainly by the Institute of Aviation Medicine (IAM) in a programme to determine the feasibility of operating aircraft in the prone flying position. It is reported that the unconventional method of control made the aircraft somewhat difficult to fly in this mode. During May 1953. the series of tests was completed but the Bobsleigh stayed on at Farnborough until 3rd March 1955 when it departed to 15 Maintenance Unit at Wroughton in Wiltshire.

The tests with the Bobsleigh paved the way for a more radical assessment of the prone pilot concept. Armstrong Whitworth Aircraft (AWA) were given a contract by the Ministry of Supply to convert a Meteor twin-jet fighter to take a prone cockpit in the nose. F.8 WK935 was so converted, the work including the fitting of a larger tail unit from a NF.12 variant as well as the elongated second cockpit. Eric Franklin made the first flight from Baginton, Coventry, to Bitteswell, on 10th February 1954. The IAM made a large series of flights with this aircraft which today can be seen at the RAF Museum, Cosford, Shropshire. (WK935 was built by AWA – see Chapter Three.)

The RS.3 in flight, showing its very pleasing lines. Mounted on the nose is a pitot tube for airspeed calibration. Between the 'A' and the 'G' of the underwing registration, between the engines, can be seen the hatch area for possible use in the bomb aimer trainer role or for air survey work. via Author

During 1946-47 preliminary design studies were carried out on yet another 'twin', but the proposed layout of the aircraft bore no resemblance to any previous R&S design. Surviving sketches and drawings show that this time a composite structure of wood and stressed skin metal was favoured for the construction. In configuration the aircraft was to be a low wing monoplane with a twin boom fuselage, similar in style to that of the de Havilland Vampire, and a fixed tricycle undercarriage. Intended principally for the private owner, pilot and passengers were to be carried in the forward section of the central nacelle with the engine, driving a pusher propeller, mounted at the rear. The powerplant under consideration at this early stage was the new and untried Fedden Flat Six which Roy Fedden Limited intended to manufacture at Stoke Orchard, near Bristol. No company designation was allocated to the project which, due to the economic climate prevailing, was allowed to lapse after a minimal amount of work had been carried out.

To return to the languishing RS.4; eventually it was put up for sale by the Air Ministry and purchased by Air Courier (Transport) Limited and restored to the British civil register in January 1956 as the Reid and Sigrist RS.4 Desford Trainer, receiving its previous registration letters G-AGOS. During overhaul at Croydon, south of London, it was re-engined with two 145hp de Havilland Gipsy Major 10 Mk.2 engines, which, in addition to enhancing its performance, increased the empty and loaded weights to 2,557lb and 3,480lb respectively.

A renewed Certificate of Airworthiness was issued in January 1958 and shortly afterwards in March the RS.4 was sold to Captain John Crewdson's company, Film Aviation Services, subsequently being used by them as a photographic aircraft until September 1958. The aircraft made an excellent camera platform and was used again in this role from 1963 to 1972 by Kemps Aerial Services of Thruxton, Hampshire. While with Kemps, the Desford returned briefly to Leicestershire during 1968 when it was based at Castle Donington to carry out aerial survey work over the Midlands.

After Kemps went into liquidation in 1972 it was hoped that the aircraft might return to Leicestershire as a museum exhibit but in June 1973 it was acquired by well-known historic aircraft restorer and operator Nick Grace. Refurbished, it was later flown at the Cranfield Air Pageant in September of that year wearing its former military markings and a totally inappropriate camouflage colour scheme. Nick decided to sell the Desford and *reportedly* offered it to Leicester Museum for the sum of £8,000, but it was a case of no sale. Eventually it was bought in November 1974 by Sir William J D Roberts and flown north to join the Strathallan Aircraft Collection housed on his estate near Auchterarder, Perthshire, Scotland. While at Strathallan the Desford was kept airworthy and participated in several of the collection's air displays.

In 1981 circumstances forced Sir William Roberts to put 25 of the collection's aircraft up for auction, amongst these was the Desford. It was estimated that it would realise a figure in the region of £20,000 and it was hoped that with public support this sum could be raised to try and bring the aircraft home to Leicestershire once more. Unfortunately Leicestershire Museums Service, into whose care the Desford was expected to go, found the problem of storage and display insoluble so no further steps were taken to acquire the aircraft. When the auction was held by Christie's on 14th July some of the aircraft under the hammer attained very high prices, but not so the Desford. It was knocked down to Victor Gauntlett of Pace Petroleum, Farnham, Surrey, for £5,500.

After the sale Victor in turn presented it to the Scottish Aircraft Collection Trust who intended to put this unique aircraft on display at Scone Airport, Perth, Tayside. Events did not transpire as the Trust had envisaged and eventually the Desford was made available, via the Museum of Flight, East Fortune, to the Leicestershire Museums Service.

A team journeyed north in January 1991, dismantled the aircraft and brought it back to the county for potential display.

Unfortunately, for several reasons, this has not yet taken place and currently the Desford languishes, still dismantled, in a store at Snibston Discovery Park, near Coalville. It is hoped that before too long this significant example of Leicestershire's aviation heritage, and a pioneering research and development airframe, will be placed on public display.

Squadron Leader H A Howes tests a mock-up of the prone pilot layout with the aid of a modified Reid Pilot Testing Apparatus (also referred to as the Reid Aptitude Indicator) first used in the early 1930s. via H A Howes

The prone pilot's instrument panel.
H A Webster

A view from the conventionally-seated pilot's cockpit, looking forward to the prone pilot cradle and controls. In the foreground can be seen the pilot's control column and rudder pedals – the instrument panel has yet to be installed. H A Webster

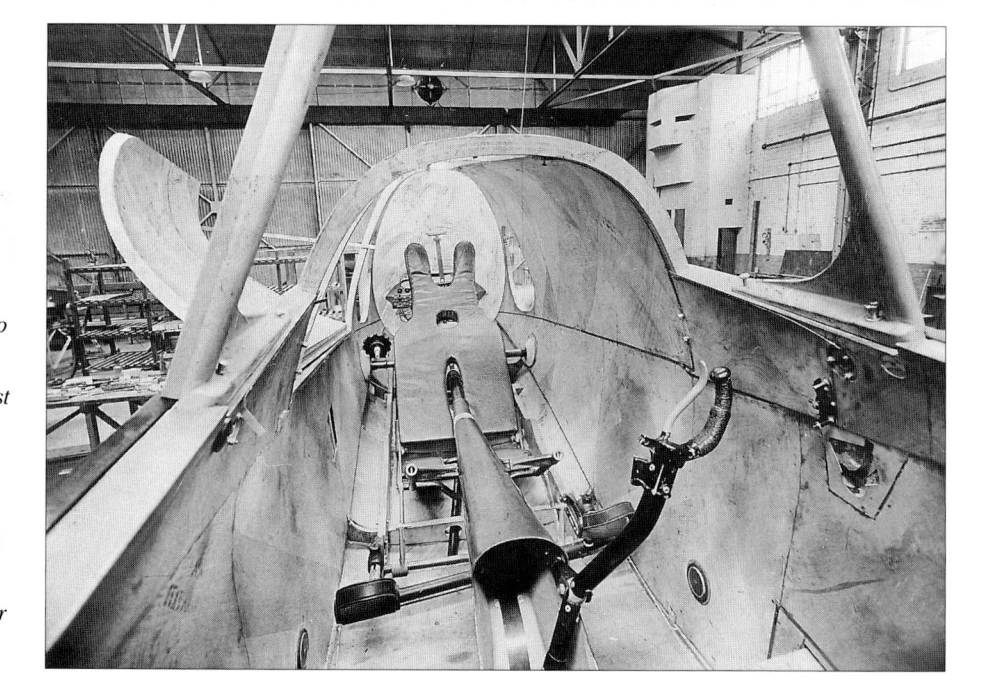

In an attempt to widen the possible market base for the RS.3, a mock-up of a crop-dusting pannier with airflow-driven pump was installed under the centre section. via Author

The Bobsleigh at the Royal Aircraft Establishment, Farnborough, with a pilot in the prone position. via Author

Following the trials with the Bobsleigh, a Meteor F.8 was radically modified to test the concept at higher speed. Armstrong Whitworth at Coventry and Bitteswell were charged with the design, conversion and flight test of the test-bed. It is fascinating that Leicestershire gave rise to both of the aircraft involved in the UK's experimentation into prone pilot aircraft and that both are still extant. AWA via Ken Ellis

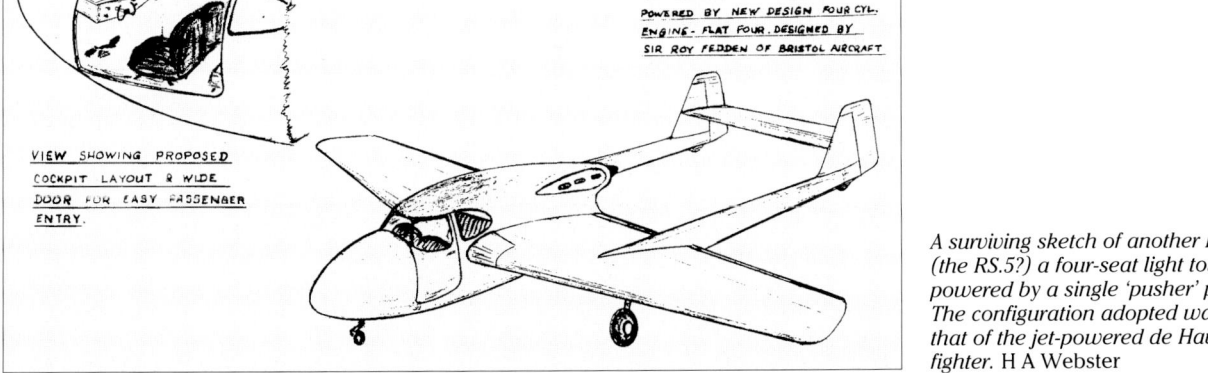

A surviving sketch of another R&S design (the RS.5?) a four-seat light touring aircraft powered by a single 'pusher' piston engine. The configuration adopted was very similar to that of the jet-powered de Havilland Vampire fighter. H A Webster

Chapter Eleven

Husbands Bosworth

High performance sailplanes lined up awaiting launch at Husbands Bosworth. To the left is a length of original perimeter track. Running across the picture is a narrow access track, all that remains of the 04/22 runway.
The Soaring Centre

CONSTRUCTION began in late 1941 when the main contractors, George Wimpey & Company Limited, moved onto the site. Originally planned as an operational station it was allocated to 8 (Pathfinder) Group, RAF, as a satellite airfield for Bruntingthorpe in November 1941. Not required by them it was reallocated to 5 Group, Bomber Command, in June 1942 and in July of that year an official visit was made to the site to assess whether it would be suitable as a base for an Operational Training Unit (OTU). Investigation proved favourable and the as yet unfinished airfield passed into the hands of 92 Bomber OTU Group for this purpose on 7th August 1942.

The building of the airfield naturally made a considerable impact on the surrounding area for not only did it absorb the usual quota of farmland, but road closures also meant inconvenience to several villages in the vicinity. Sibbertoft to the east was one badly affected in this way for the location of the airfield resulted in the connecting road to Husbands Bosworth and Welford being severed so making detours necessary via Theddingworth and Naseby respectively, to reach these places.

Preparations by 92 Group for the opening of the station began on 1st June 1943 and early in August it became a satellite of 14 OTU, Market Harborough. The main purpose of 14 OTU was to train crews for 5 Group, Bomber Command, and Husbands Bosworth housed 'A' and 'B' Flights of this unit. By 17th August the station had received its complement of Vickers Wellingtons and was fully operational in the role of converting men who had been individually trained in the various aircrew duties, into well-knit bomber crews. Included in the intensive training programme

were navigation and fighter affiliation exercises, air firing (usually over the Wash or open sea), and practice bombing. Frequently this latter exercise was carried out on a range situated in open country near Mowsley to the north of the airfield and, unfortunately, occasional bombs missed their intended target, falling outside the designated danger area. These incidents brought forth loud protests from the local inhabitants who accepted that they may be bombed by the *Luftwaffe* but *not* the RAF!

Training sorties at Husbands Bosworth were not entirely without incident, in common with other similar units accidents happened with considerable frequency. Thankfully most were of a minor nature with no loss of life or injury to personnel. The first incident involving a unit aircraft in a fatal accident occurred on 22nd October 1943 when a Wellington Ic W5688 'O', which had been recalled from the bombing range, arrived in the vicinity of the airfield and suddenly dived into the ground from 1,500ft, killing all five crew members.

Dinghy drill by personnel from 85 OTU, Husbands Bosworth, at Naseby Reservoir, 1944. via F B Aggas

An 85 OTU crew in front of a Wellington III at Husbands Bosworth. The aircraft, very probably X3821, is carrying the 'FQ-' codes of its previous 'owner', 12 OTU, Chipping Warden, Northamptonshire. OTUs frequently sourced aircraft from other units to bring them up to strength. Left to right: Sergeant Peterson BEM, wireless op; Sergeant Petrie, bomb aimer; Pilot Officer Benton, pilot; Sergeant Hartle, mid-upper gunner; Sergeant Woods, rear gunner; Pilot Officer Bibby, navigator. via F B Aggas

The association between the station and 14 OTU lasted until 16th June 1944 when the OTU was officially reclassified as a three-quarter strength unit, becoming a parent station with the formation of 85 OTU under the command of Group Captain D J Eayrs DFC. As the purpose of the new unit was to remain unchanged, except that the output of crews would now be mainly for 3 Group, it retained 14 of 14 OTU's Wellington Xs as initial equipment and training was carried out with a minimum of interruption. Most of the personnel resident on the station were posted to remain *in situ* and their numbers increased to cope with the demands made by the uprated unit. Many new buildings were erected to house the influx of new personnel while others were, in the course of time, altered or extended to serve new functions.

It did not take the new unit long to lose its first aircraft due to a flying accident. This occurred on 23rd June 1944, when Wellington LN589, piloted by pupil pilot Flight Sergeant Barnes, crashed in a field at Aston near Stevenage, Hertfordshire. Short of fuel and in rapidly deteriorating weather the pilot elected to crash-land with undercarriage retracted. On touching down the aircraft broke its back, burst into flames and was totally destroyed, the crew escaping with only minor injuries to two members.

By the end of June the first aircrew to be posted direct to the unit for operational training had arrived and formed No.3 Course which became the first complete programme to receive training at 85 OTU. By now more aircraft had arrived and the total Wellington Xs on strength at this time was 38. It is interesting to note how these

additional aircraft had to be culled from various sources to help bring the new unit up to strength. The makers, Vickers-Armstrong, supplied seven, all of which needed considerable modifications; 16, 26, 29 and 84 OTUs provided two each, 12 and 17 OTUs three each, with single aircraft coming from 8, 23 and 48 Maintenance Units.

Crew training progressed satisfactorily and by the end of July special diversionary exercises were being flown as far as the continental coastlines by advanced crews. During one of these, on the 28th two of the aircraft taking part were engaged on three occasions in combat with enemy aircraft; no damage was inflicted on the Wellingtons but a Junkers Ju 88 was claimed as damaged.

Another type of enemy aircraft featured in an interesting unit report for July was the Fieseler Fi 103, or FZG-76, more commonly known as the V-1, 'Doodle Bug', or 'Flying-Bomb'. On the 22nd of the month at 22:53 hours, HQ 92 Group informed Flying Control at Husbands Bosworth that one of these missiles was on a north west course heading straight for the airfield. The Intruder Telling Line was kept open and four minutes later group reported the incident closed as the bomb had fallen near the village of Creaton, Northamptonshire, ten miles south-east of the base.

Training of a different type was carried out on the airfield during early August when 13 Douglas C-47 Skytrains of the United States Army Air Force (USAAF) were resident from the 5th to the 14th. These were from the 313th Troop Carrier Group then stationed at Folkingham, Lincolnshire, and were used by troops of the 82nd Airborne Division, US Army, who were housed at various locations in Leicestershire for many practice exercises in preparation for participation in Operation 'Market', the airborne assault by Allied forces on the bridges at Grave, Nijmegen, and Arnhem. Also resident on the airfield around this time were eight Piper L-4 Grasshoppers. Two each of these liaison and artillery spotter aircraft were on the strength of the 319th and 320th Glider Field Artillery Battalions and the 376th and 456th Parachute Field Artillery Battalions of the 82nd Airborne.

During August the first 'Nickel'-ing operation by 85 OTU was carried out when two Wellingtons were despatched on the 16th. They successfully dropped their cargoes of leaflets over Chateauroux and Bourges.

From now until the end of the year much time and effort was devoted to improving the amenities and general appearance of the station as a whole. To help with the many tasks involved Italian prisoners of war were employed, eventually reaching a peak of over 70 men. Their work, for which payment in sterling was made, included the laying of paths and improving drainage on domestic sites, planting shrubs and evergreens and making garden areas. Emphasis was also placed on interior decoration, resulting in many of the camps communal buildings being made more habitable as time passed.

Towards the end of September, 85 OTU suffered what was to be its only accident involving the loss of an aircraft and its crew. On the night of the 24th at 23:30 hours, Wellington X LP826 dived out of control from high altitude and crashed at Althorp Park, Northamptonshire. The aircraft was completely burnt out in the subsequent fire and all the crew perished. Although seven other accidents involving unit aircraft occurred during the month, none were of a serious nature, while on the credit side over 2,338 flying hours were amassed and 21 crews completed their course.

October was a much better period for the OTU for in spite of a reduction in flying hours to 1,650, 30 crews completed training and the month was accident free. This latter achievement brought congratulations from the AOC of 92 Group, Air Vice-Marshal H K Thorold CBE, DSC, DFC, AFC.

During the autumn and early winter mists and fog often interfered with the flying programme. Not only did they reduce the hours flown, but frequently developed so rapidly that aircraft returning from training sorties had to divert to other airfields. Many of the fogs were so local that there was no need for diversions further afield than Market Harborough or Bruntingthorpe.

The pattern of life at Husbands Bosworth for the last two months of 1944 altered little. Early in November the Bomber Command WAAF Senior NCO School was formed on the station with an initial pupil population of 20. An opening address was given by the AOC on the 11th.

As with many other isolated RAF stations, sport often played a big part in relieving the boredom of off-duty hours. Football was always popular and it is recorded by 85 OTU that the first match in the Midlands under Australian rules was played on the station on 2nd November. The 18 members of the opposing side came from Australian personnel stationed at nearby Bruntingthorpe.

Reportable accidents for the month totalled two, one of which is worthy of mention in view of the airmanship involved. While climbing to take part in a night-fighter affiliation exercise on the 21st, Hawker Hurricane I P2733, and Wellington X LN177 collided at 4,000ft. Despite a shattered airscrew and serious damage to fin and rudder, the Hurricane pilot, Flight Sergeant Butcher, recovered control, managed to pump down the undercarriage and land safely. The Wellington, piloted by Flying Officer Hindercks, received extensive damage to the underside of the fuselage, in addition the hydraulic system was severed, but in spite of this a landing was effected without further damage.

Also during November major alterations were carried out to improve the target on the practice bombing range at Mowsley. The original 60ft equilateral concrete triangle was enclosed by one measuring 100ft on all sides and incorporating a north pointing arrow and pyramid. A generator-powered triangle of nine electric lights was installed to facilitate night bombing, and 29 danger boards were also erected around the range perimeter.

Crash and fire crews at the station were often called upon to assist at disasters involving aircraft from units other than their own. The worst tragedy of this kind which

they attended took place on the night of 5th December 1944. At 18:55 hours two operational aircraft, Avro Lancaster X KB768 of 428 Squadron, Middleton St George, and Handley Page Halifax VII LW200 of 426 Squadron, Linton on Ouse, collided and fell about one mile east of Yelvertoft, Northants, six miles from the airfield. All 14 crew members lost their lives.

Festivities over Christmas were much enjoyed at the station, the interiors of all messes and many huts being specially decorated for the occasion. A happy note was struck to end the year for December was another month devoid of accidents. The AOC marked the achievement with another signal, the text of which read: '*I again send to you my congratulations on having completed a second accident free month in 1944. Although your total flying hours for December represents a figure well below normal the achievement reflects the greater credit on all concerned and I wish my appreciation conveyed to all ranks who have made this good record possible.*'

Weather presented Husbands Bosworth with many problems in the first two months of 1945; severe frosts which began at the end of December 1944 played havoc with water and sewage systems. Water supplies to essential sites such as mess halls and station sick quarters were only maintained with great difficulty. As a result of pipe damage latrine accommodation was totally inadequate and primitive arrangements using Elsan closets and buckets had to be adopted.

A shortage of fuel made life even more miserable in the living quarters for as an economy measure all unauthorised electrical equipment was removed and low

Certificate awarded to the top crew on each course with 85 OTU. via F B Aggas

Another crew pause for a photograph in front of their Wellington Mk.X of 85 OTU, 1944.
Bill Clay via Dr Hugh Thomas

amperage fuses fitted to all huts. This effectively prevented the occupants from using electric fires to boost the heat output of the solid fuel stoves and cut out the use of boiling rings and irons.

Owing to the weather all external work on repairs and improvements was suspended, only minor internal repairs being carried out. From the middle of January snow effected the serviceability of the airfield and snow ploughs were in use to clear the perimeter tracks and runways. Consequently flying hours were very restricted. Many men made idle by the weather were employed on emergency frost repairs to dispersals.

As soon as the weather improved, steps were taken to make good the ravages of winter. By early March repairs had been carried out to water services on all sites but it was not until April that the sewage system was fully restored.

The flying programme was almost back to normal by the end of the month, the only inconvenience being caused by the resumption of work on the relaying of the perimeter track, an operation which had commenced in mid-December 1944.

Mention has already been made of the need to divert aircraft from the airfield, in turn the station was often called upon to accept diversions from other bases. These visits usually involved no more than one or two aircraft, but at times many aircraft of types not common to the airfield were involved. In late winter and early spring of 1945 this occurrence was quite prevalent, two examples being as follows.

'*March 4th:* at 01:53 hours ten Lancasters of 44 Squadron, Spilsby, landed on a "Scram" [enemy intruders over home base] diversion after attacking Ladbergen. All but one left for home next day.

'*April 9th:* 15 Halifaxes of 426 Squadron, Linton on Ouse, diverted to the station after returning from an attack on Hamburg. All aircraft returned to base later the same day'.

Visits of this nature gave rise to speculation in the vicinity that the airfield was being used for operational purposes; however, official records examined contained no evidence that it was ever used as a base other than by 14 and 85 OTUs.

After the war in Europe ended on 8th May 1945, the airfield did not remain active for long; on 3rd June all flying training came to an end. From then on flights by 85 OTU were restricted to observation tours over the Ruhr, 12 of which were successfully completed, and the ferrying of aircraft away from the station. Aircraft on charge and disposed of in this way were 28 Wellingtons, three Hawker Hurricanes, three Miles Martinets, two Miles Masters and several Airspeed Oxfords.

On 14th June 1945 the establishment of the OTU was cancelled; two days later the bombing range at Mowsley was closed and all equipment removed. Also during the month over 500 personnel were posted to other stations. Even though flying had ceased, maintenance work on the airfield continued right up to the end of June, contracts not being terminated until the 25th. By this time 19,000 square yards of perimeter track had been relaid and the spraying of the Nissen Huts and hangars with a bituminous compound had just been completed. As of the 18th July the airfield was reduced to Care and Maintenance status.

Although the station no longer carried out its original function, RAF personnel continued to be very much in evidence within the camp for some time. From 21st August the dispersed sites were used to house elements of 26 Aircrew Holding Unit until 15th November 1945 when it became a part of 7 Personnel Reception Centre until August 1946. These two units dealt with personnel awaiting reassignment or demobilisation and the parent station of both for this period was Market Harborough.

For varying periods of time in 1945 and 1946 the airfield was transferred to 21 and 54 Groups of Flying Training Command, but this brought no further flying to the disused airfield. On 13th November 1946 however, there was one unscheduled flying visitor when Gloster Meteor F.3 EE337 was forced to make an emergency landing here. After receiving a faulty homing signal from Bramcote, insufficient fuel was left for the aircraft to return to its home base at Bitteswell. A supply of fuel was brought to Husbands Bosworth and the pilot, Wing Commander McDowell, was then able to take-off and complete his journey.

After the RAF vacated them, many of the hutments on the domestic site became homes for displaced persons, a large number of whom were Polish ex-servicemen who had elected to stay in Britain rather than return to their homeland. By the late 1950s alternative accommodation had been found for these expatriates and buildings fell into disuse.

From September 1945 until July 1950, 216 Maintenance Unit, Sutton Coldfield, Warwickshire, used the airfield and many of its buildings as a sub-site to store quantities of redundant ground equipment. Later, government departments found the four T2 hangars useful as a repository for various stores, including large stocks of stationery. Eventually these stores were transferred elsewhere and the empty hangars advertised for sale by tender. Vickers-Armstrong made the successful bid and all four were dismantled and removed from the airfield. Most of the other buildings were also sold, many going to local farmers.

The road to Sibbertoft was reopened, but instead of reverting to its pre-war course it followed the route of the airfield perimeter track. A story told locally in Sibbertoft concerns a villager who, while cycling home one night across the airfield in dense fog, became totally disorientated and was there until first light next morning.

Eventually a new road was built which follows the line of the old east-west main runway.

A view of the now demolished observation tower on the Mowsley bombing range. The 'X' marks the approximate position of the target marker. F B Aggas

Vertical survey photograph of Husbands Bosworth, dated 10th August 1945. Construction involved closing the Husbands Bosworth to Sibbertoft minor road (A and B) which was swallowed by the East to West runway. The former A50 (now the A5199) from Husbands Bosworth to Welford is at (C), the substantial Wheler Lodge (D) and the Sulby Reservoir (E) are other landmarks. The control tower, signals square and the airfield denominator 'HZ' are at (F). DoE

DFS Grunau Baby glider BGA.1409 about to
touch down at Husbands Bosworth, 1973.
Author

Air-to-ground view of Husbands Bosworth in
1985, looking north-west. Husbands Bosworth
village is at the right (A), with the A50 – since
renumbered A5199 – running across the background (B). The gliding site is on the northern
part of the former airfield (C) while the
Husbands Bosworth to Sibbertoft road runs
along the course of the east-west runway (D).
Author

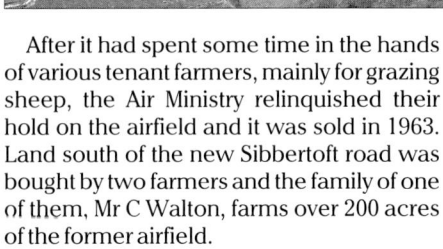

opened by the Home Secretary, Michael Howard, in June 1994, it had, by the end of the first year of operation, proved a great success. In 950 hours flying, 1,695 incidents were responded to, 12 missing persons traced, 225 suspects arrested, almost £300,000 of property and many stolen vehicles recovered.

Sadly, such operations are not without risk; G-EMAU was destroyed when it crashed into a wooded area close to its base on 9th October 1998 killing PC Stuart Ross and injuring two others. The combined forces were committed to the continuation of the East Midlands Air Support Unit as it had proven beyond all doubt that it was a major benefit to the region. Accordingly, a replacement helicopter, a Eurocopter EC.135T, G-EMAS, was delivered in October 1999, and is now carrying out its duties.

Of the wartime airfield little remains to be seen today. What was once the area occupied by the bomb stores can still be identified close to the gliding site while on Walton family land stand most of the important buildings that remain including the derelict control tower. Dense thickets of scrub and saplings all but obscure what were once domestic and communal areas of the camp. Only the gutted shells of buildings, cracked and eroded concrete hut bases and the crumbling remains of air raid shelters serve as a reminder of the past. As to the runways, little trace of these is to be found for they, along with most of the perimeter track and hardstandings, disappeared during the 1960s when they were bought by the St Ives Sand and Gravel Company and removed for use as hardcore. Much of the rubble obtained from the site was used in the construction of the Crick to Lutterworth extension of the M1 Motorway.

Doubtless the other tangible links with the Second World War which are still to be seen will disappear as years pass, leaving only memories.

After it had spent some time in the hands of various tenant farmers, mainly for grazing sheep, the Air Ministry relinquished their hold on the airfield and it was sold in 1963. Land south of the new Sibbertoft road was bought by two farmers and the family of one of them, Mr C Walton, farms over 200 acres of the former airfield.

Land to the north of the Sibbertoft Road was acquired by Coventry Gliding Club who moved their activities from Coventry Airport, Baginton, to the airfield in 1964. Since then, the land has been progressively developed into a very active and popular gliding site. On many occasions it has been the venue for international competitions at regional and national level. To mark their 40th Anniversary in 1992 and in keeping with the club's nationally recognised status the site became known as 'The Soaring Centre'. Hopefully the club will continue to enjoy the success it deserves and sport flying of this nature will flourish at Husbands Bosworth for many years to come.

In 1988 the threat that hangs over many former Leicestershire airfields seemed about to materialise. Proposals were made to develop 72 acres of land south of the Sibbertoft Road into a new village of 450 homes and amenities. Following mounting pressure from villages in the surrounding area the developers, David Wilson Estates Limited, withdrew their planning application in February 1989. To date there have been no further proposals in this direction.

It was also on the south side that the most recent development at Husbands Bosworth has taken place. A short distance from some of the old wartime buildings a purpose-built hangar and control centre now house the East Midlands Air Support Unit initially equipped with Eurocopter AS.355N Twin Squirrel helicopter, G-EMAU. Shared jointly between the police forces of Leicestershire, Northamptonshire and Warwickshire this helicopter served as a fast response vehicle to help combat crime.

Set up at a cost of £2,000,000 and officially

Members of The Soaring Centre prepare for the resumption of another week-day training session as they position Lycoming re-engined DHC Chipmunk 22 tug G-BBNA to provide aerotows for SZD-50-3 Puchacz sailplanes 'FWT'/BGA.3589 and 'FXQ'(sic)/BGA.3658 .

Possibly a lunch break scene, around the hangars during a Coventry Gliding Club open day on 24th April 1983. In the foreground is a Scheibe SF-27A Zugvogel V, marked 'EKS', which identifies it as BGA 1252 in the British Gliding Association's register. The club uses both aero-tow and winch tow for launching.

The East Midlands Air Support Unit hangar on the southern side of Husbands Bosworth, September 1996. Sadly, this Twin Squirrel helicopter, G-EMAU, was involved in a fatal accident in October 1998. All Author

RAF Husbands Bosworth – 1st December 1944

Latitude	52° 26' 00" N
Longitude	01° 02' 30" W
Height at Sea Level	505ft
Command	Bomber (RAF)
Nearest Railway Station	Welford and Kilworth, LMS
Function	Operational Training Unit (Parent)
Affiliated Airfields	Nil

Landing Area – Runways

QDM	Dimensions	Extensibility	Remarks
223°	1,400 x 50 yds	1,600 yds	Entails control of
343°	1,400 x 50 yds	1,800 yds	main road and
273°	2,000 x 50 yds	2,300 yds	demolition of a
			pair of cottages
			& farm buildings.

Type of Surface: Concrete, surface tar and wood chips.

Permanent Landmarks

By Day:	Two large reservoirs, one 3 miles WSW and the other 1 mile S of airfield.
By Night:	Nil

Permanent Obstructions Rugby Wireless Masts 8 miles SW of airfield. All illuminated.

Facilities

Airfield Lighting	Mk.II
Beam Approach	–
Radio	–
QDM	–
Flying Control	Yes

Accommodation

All buildings temporary.

Technical	Hangars		Hardstandings	
	Type	No	Type	No
	T2	4	Spectacle	36

Domestic	Officers	SNCOs	ORs	Total
RAF	213	469	854	1,536
WAAF	10	48	300	358

Husbands Bosworth-based Units and Aircraft

No.14 Operational Training Unit
See under the parent station, Market Harborough.
From 28.7.43 to 15.6.44   Codes 'AM-', 'GL-' and 'VB-'

No.85 Operational Training Unit
From 15.6.44 to 14.6.45   Codes '9P-' and '2X-'
Vickers Wellington Ic   T2468, DV844
Vickers Wellington X   HE151, HE473, HE731, HE770,
HF568, HZ482, JA115, JA449, JA458, JA465, JA498 'U', LN177,
LN230, LN447, LN589, LN649, LN739, LN758, LN933, LN934 'F',
LP151, LP176, LP230, LP287, LP336, LP498, LP506, LP513,
LP553, LP640, LP699, LP701, LP703, LP813, LP815, LP826,
LP838, LP839, LP848, LP869, LR130, LR132, ME883, MF424,
MF514, NA798, NA922, NA975, NC431, NC432, NC619, NC679,
NC680, NC682, PG 119, PG293, PG394
Hawker Hurricane II   LF698, PG518, PG580, PG582,
PZ733
Miles Martinet TT.I   HN864, HP523, HP524, JN508,
JN582, JN596, MS901
Miles Master II   DK927, DL118
Airspeed Oxford I   PH122

Serious Aircraft Accidents to Based Units

No.14 Operational Training Unit
See under parent station - Market Harborough.

No.85 Operational Training Unit
23.6.44   Wellington X   LN589
Aircraft short of fuel, weather deteriorating so pilot crash-landed in field at Aston, near Stevenage, Herts. Aircraft broke its back, burst into flames and was totally destroyed. No fatal injuries.

24.9.44   Wellington X   LP826
Althorp Park, Northampton. Aircraft dived from a considerable height and completely burnt out in crash. All 7 crew killed.

21.1.45   Wellington X   ME883
Crew baled out after aircraft became uncontrollable due to broken elevator controls. All landed safely and only minor injuries were sustained. Aircraft crashed in Slough, Berks.

3.2.45   Wellington X   LP640
Engine cut and aircraft crashed in forced-landing near Market Harborough.

28.4.45   Wellington X   NA798
Low on fuel after cross country flight and unable to land at base due to bad weather, cloud base below 200ft. Pilot climbed aircraft to 8,000ft and ordered crew to bale out. All landed safely. When remaining fuel exhausted, aircraft crashed at Whittlesey Wash, near Peterborough.

Husbands Bosworth Civil Aircraft Accidents

3.4.80   Cessna F.150L   G-AZWU   D W Walton
Damaged beyond repair at Husbands Bosworth.

22.9.87   DHC.1 Chipmunk   G-BDID   Coventry Gliding Club
Crashed on airfield killing both occupants. Destroyed by fire.

24.10.90   Bocian Glider   BGA.1900   Coventry Gliding Club
Spun-in near Mill Farm, North Kilworth, while instructor trying to land in bad visibility after being towed above the cloudbase.

Once the station gymnasium and chapel, this building went on to serve as a cattle barn. It is now converted for use as a stable block. Author

Husbands Bosworth's ruined control tower – still serving as a poignant monument. Author

Chapter Twelve

Leicester East –
Leicester Airport

A view of the 1980 Popular Flying Association rally which was held at Leicester for three years before out-growing the venue.
W J Bushell

To BUILD THIS wartime airfield the Air Ministry requisitioned 490 acres of good farmland, most of which belonged to the Co-operative Wholesale Society. It is possible that some of the acreage involved had been envisaged as a probable site for a small aerodrome long before the outbreak of the Second World War, for in the 1932 Regional Planning Report for Leicestershire, a proposal was made for an aerodrome to serve Humberstone and North East Leicester to be situated on the east of the city. No progress was made in this respect, at that time.

Most service airfields are named after the nearest village or town, so this one should have been called Stoughton, as indeed it is often referred to locally, but the official title adopted was RAF Leicester East. Possibly the reason for this was to avoid confusion with RAF Little Staughton, Bedfordshire, or it could just have been that an aerodrome already existed to the west of the city at Braunstone. Originally intended to serve as a base for two operational squadrons of Bomber Command, this requirement was cancelled and it was re-allotted for Operational Training Unit (OTU) use.

Following instructions contained in Bomber Command letter BC/S30582/ORG, dated 7th September 1943, stating that the airfield would be required to house a 'three-quarter' OTU and that the station would be placed within 93 Group as of 15th October 1943, an indent party under the command of Squadron Leader J B Connolly arrived from Headquarters, Bomber Command on

Despite an intensive search, wartime views of aircraft at Leicester East are elusive. Short Stirling '7T-E' of 196 Squadron, possibly while operating from Leicester East. via D J Smith

Supreme Commander, Allied Forces Europe, General Dwight D Eisenhower, addresses the men of the 82nd Airborne Division at Leicester East, 10th August 1944. via Derek Wills

Elements of the 82nd Airborne pass the saluting base at Leicester East on 10th August 1944 prior to participation in Operation 'Market'. Among the high-ranking officers on the dais are Generals Brereton, Eisenhower, Gavin and Ridgeway. via Derek Wills

8th October and proceeded to open up the station. On 16th October a further Command note (BC/S30638/ORG) arrived. It stated that a decision had been made that 25 (MB) OTU which was to have formed at Leicester East on 1st November was now considered unnecessary and therefore the instructions contained in the previous letter were cancelled.

A new letter arrived on 30th October instructing that the station be placed on a care and maintenance (C&M) footing with effect from 15th November. This letter further stated that Leicester East would be required for the temporary accommodation, on a lodger basis, by a Troop Carrier Group of the United States Army Air Force (USAAF) on, or about 1st April 1944. In the meantime the station was to remain in Bomber Command and be used as a relief airfield.

No sooner had these instructions been assimilated when a further signal was received on 14th November, containing the information that the opening of the station was to be completed immediately for the reception of two heavy bomber squadrons belonging to 3 Group. Both units were to be housed on a lodger basis only, pending their transfer to 38 Group (Airborne Forces), and the eventual allocation of new bases.

Two days after this signal the advance party of 196 Squadron arrived from Witchford, Cambridgeshire, under the command of Wing Commander N Alexander, closely followed on the 20th by elements of 620 Squadron from Chedburgh, Suffolk, with Wing Commander D H Lee in charge. The majority of the Short Stirling four-engined heavy bombers belonging to the two units arrived on the 18th and 23rd respectively.

Both squadrons experienced some difficulty settling in on the new, and as yet untried, station and during what proved to be rather a brief stay, little use was made of the airfield by No.196. Recorded air activity was limited to odd cross country flights and local circuits. Over the Christmas period of 1943 the unit stood down from all duties and many personnel were able to take advantage of numerous offers of hospitality received from the people of Leicester and surrounding area. Early in the new year the squadron received orders to move out and it left Leicester East by road, rail and air on 7th January 1944, bound for a new home at Tarrant Rushton, Dorset.

The space left by the departure of 196 was soon filled when on 5th January Air Ministry Signal 02483 authorised the re-formation of 190 Squadron. This unit was to be equipped with Stirling IVs with an establishment of 16 aircraft plus four in reserve. On 20th January the first of the new squadron's aircraft arrived, LJ823 and LJ827 being delivered direct from the makers and by the time commanding officer, Wing Commander Harrison arrived at the base on 25th January, the majority of the unit's complement had been delivered. No.190 Squadron existed for almost two months before any flying was possible, due mainly to the lack of ground crews. The first of these reported for duty on 31st January and from then on most of February was spent getting the unit up to full strength and improving ground organisation. By the end of the month personnel attached to the squadron totalled 739 in the following categories:

Officers SNCOs (Flying)	55
SNCOs (Ground)	133
Glider Pilots	25
Airmen	80
WAAFs	276
Petty Officers	176
Naval Ratings	147

A detachment of three NCOs and 133 airmen from the Heavy Glider Maintenance Unit were also included.

The first unit aircraft airborne from Leicester East was LJ833 on 1st March and from that date activity centred around an impending move to a new base. In connection with this move unit aircraft were despatched on occasions to Marham, Norfolk, for the purpose of collecting Airspeed Horsa assault gliders and on 25th March the air party compete with fully-laden gliders, departed from Leicester East *en route* for Fairford, Gloucestershire, where 620 Squadron were already in residence.

Of the three Stirling squadrons to use Leicester East, 620 was the most active during its stay, local flying being carried out within two days of arrival. In addition to intensive flying training the unit also carried out, in February 1944, several sorties on behalf of the Special Operations Executive (SOE). This organisation was responsible for clandestine activities against the enemy and utilised 38 Group aircraft to deliver agents and to supply drop arms, ammunition and explosives to resistance groups within enemy occupied territory. Despite several views held locally, 620's operations on behalf of SOE at this time were *not* carried out from Leicester East. Between 2nd and 16th February five unit aircraft were detached to Hurn, near Bournemouth, for this purpose. While there, the sorties they carried out over occupied France were not without incident. Several aircraft suffered damage from enemy anti-aircraft fire, others came under attack from hostile nightfighters and one, Stirling LK395 failed to return from an operation on 4th February.

By the end of February a change of base was in the offing for the unit and on 14th March an advance party left for Fairford, Gloucestershire, with the rest of the squadron joining them there on the 23rd.

Following the departure of 190 and 620 Squadrons the airfield was once again placed in the hands of a care and maintenance party from RAF Wymeswold (Chapter Twenty-Four). This state of affairs lasted until May 1944 but although officially on C&M the airfield was not devoid of activity for the entire period, five Vickers Wellingtons belonging to 93 Group (Screened) Pilots' School (GSPS) being resident from 19th to 30th April. This unit was given the task of carrying out the day conversion of a surplus of pupils which had accumulated at 82 OTU, Ossington, Nottinghamshire. One of 93 GSPS's former pilots, Eric Walker, wrote 'Flying started early in the morning and continued until late evening. Weather must have been fine because my logbook shows I was in the air every day from 20th to 30th April inclusive. During this period some 20 pupil crews were converted to Wellingtons and a visit from the AOC 93 Group, Air Vice-Marshal Boyd resulted in an appreciative letter being received. However, those most deserving of praise were of course the maintenance crews who worked from dawn (preparing) to dusk (refuelling) every day. Their efforts were appreciated though for at the end they were all awarded a 48 hour pass.'

Late in April 1944, the station was transferred to 46 Group, Transport Command and on 3rd May 107 OTU was formed there under the command of Wing Commander G R Howie DSO. Douglas Dakota twin-engined transports, Airspeed Oxford general purpose twins and Horsa assault gliders equipped the new unit which was to be responsible for training Dakota aircrews to be proficient in all air transport roles including the dropping of paratroops, supplies and glider towing. In order to accomplish this task a course of approximately six weeks duration was laid down during which, in addition to intensive flying experience and instruction, lessons and lectures were given which included such subjects as airmanship, crew procedure, intelligence, airborne operations, navigation, Link trainer, meteorology, radar, armament, aircraft recognition, night vision, signals and physical training. The average number of crews per course was 20.

The tempo of training increased as more aircraft were taken on strength and by the end of the month 14 Dakotas, 9 Oxfords and 3 Horsas had been delivered. By mid-June the first course was well into its training period, most aspects of air supply had been practised and unit routine was settling down nicely. An inspection tour of training and camp facilities was made on 16th June by Air Chief Marshal Sir Frederick W Bowhill, Air Officer Commanding, 46 Group, Transport Command.

Variety was often injected into the train-

ing programme by staging such diversions as evasion and escape exercises carried out in co-operation with local Home Guard units and county police. Personnel were transported and dropped off at various points within a ten mile radius of the station and getting back to base, undetected, was often quite a feat of ingenuity especially when one bears in mind the fact that most signposts had been removed as part of anti-invasion measures. During one such exercise on the night of 17th/18th June, of the 144 men taking part, 52 were 'captured'.

Personnel from RAF Leicester East often added their support to schemes in aid of the war effort. An example of this occurred on 8th July, when a contingent of 200 airmen and WAAF's from the station took part in a parade at Oadby in aid of 'Salute the Soldier Week'. Group Captain Howie, accompanied by Colonels Norton and Williams, took the salute and while the parade was in progress three Dakota–Horsa combinations from 107 OTU flew over.

It can be well imagined that with the amount of airborne exercises being carried out daily, a great many parachutes were in use. Re-packing such large quantities was beyond unit capabilities so civilian packers were employed on this work in a Leicester factory. As an exercise in good relations a special demonstration of supply and pannier dropping was staged at a local drop zone on 30th July for the benefit of these packers. Almost 300 employees, mostly girls, were present and showed extreme pleasure at seeing such a practical demonstration of their work.

Some measure of the air activity from the airfield at this time is shown by 107 OTU's flying hours for July which totalled 2,289. The majority of these were amassed on conversion flying but included 417 hours by the Oxford Flight, 140 paratroop dropping, 183 supply dropping and 95 glider tugging.

A considerable contribution was also made on the station to the training of other branches of the Allied armed forces. These included many men of the US 82nd Airborne Division who were, in the summer of 1944, encamped in and around Leicester after having been heavily engaged in battle with German forces attempting to counter the allied invasion of Europe. No.107 OTU was responsible for many of these American paratroopers gaining added air experience in preparation for their next assault on enemy held territory. Dakotas of the unit were also utilised, both on the ground and in the air, to train men of the Royal Army Service Corps in the role of airborne despatchers. In addition local squadrons of the Air Training Corps were catered for, all types of aircraft on the unit inventory being used to give air experience flights to upwards of 300 cadets each Sunday.

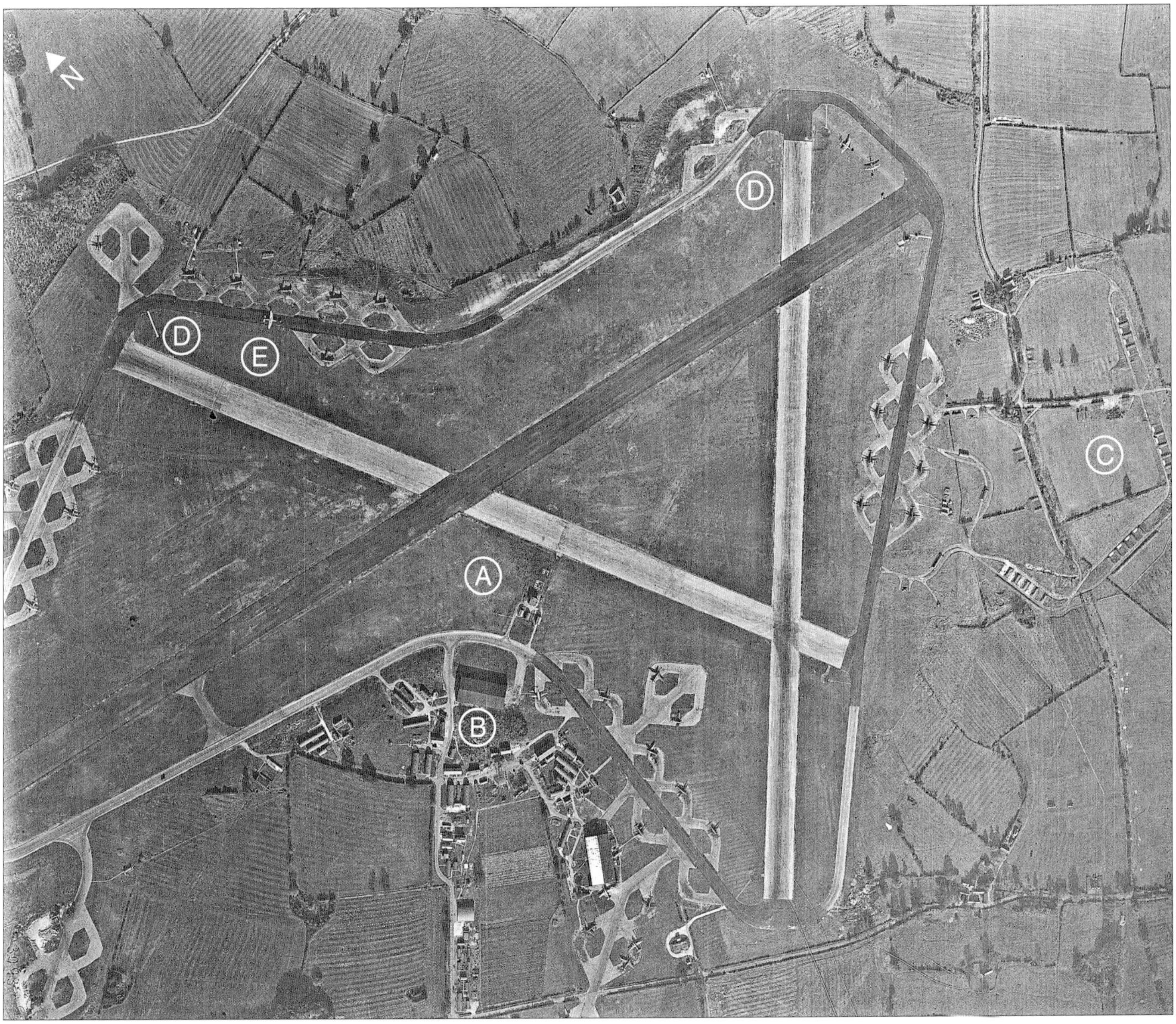

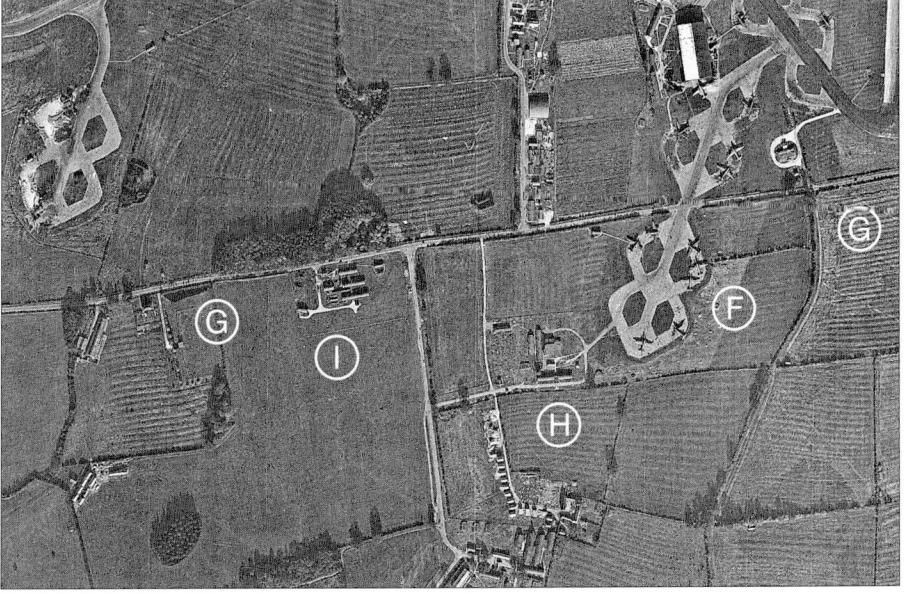

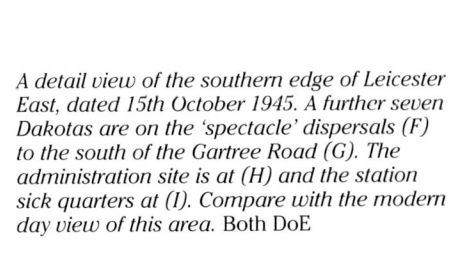

An aerial survey view of Leicester East, dated 15th October 1945. A total of 28 Dakotas, nine Horsas and a single Oxford can be seen. The control tower, which still exists in modified form, plus the signals square and airfield denominator 'LE', are at (A) and the surviving T2 hangar at (B). The present day King's Norton road was then consumed within the bomb dump complex (C). The current Gaulby Lane, running along the northern boundary of the airfield, follows the perimeter track (D). A Horsa glider, under tow can be seen at (E) on this track.

A detail view of the southern edge of Leicester East, dated 15th October 1945. A further seven Dakotas are on the 'spectacle' dispersals (F) to the south of the Gartree Road (G). The administration site is at (H) and the station sick quarters at (I). Compare with the modern day view of this area. Both DoE

On 5th August 1944, the airfield was closed to all traffic and used as a parade ground by elements of the 82nd Airborne Division. The Commanding General, Matthew Ridgway, presented decorations to a number of officers and men, afterwards taking the salute at the march past, 1,400 men paraded and several formations of Dakotas flew over. This parade was actually only a rehearsal for a much larger one of greater importance which was held four days later on the 9th. On that day the men of the 82nd were reviewed by the Supreme Commander, Allied Forces Europe, General Dwight D Eisenhower. After the parade the men formed a solid square behind the saluting base and the General delivered an impromptu speech in which he praised them for their valour in Normandy but warned them that even greater things would be expected of them in the forthcoming months.

By the end of August training within the confines of the airfield had become more hectic; in addition to the normal syllabus such activities as mass parachute drops by the US Airborne and experiments with pannier and container delivery added to the congestion. In an effort to relieve this situation the use of a satellite airfield was sought. The first site investigated was at RAF Sutton Bridge, Lincolnshire, on 2nd September 1944 but this was found to be unsuitable. Consultations nearer home resulted in facilities at RAF Melton Mowbray (Chapter Sixteen) being made available and from 10th September detachments were able to carry out conversion training from this airfield.

During September, 107 OTU suffered its first aircraft loss when a Dakota on glide approach training failed to check on reaching the runway and flew straight in; as a result the undercarriage collapsed and the aircraft was written off, thankfully without serious injuries.

In the latter half of September six crews from the OTU assisted on operations in support of the Allied forces in Europe by flying from Lyneham, Wiltshire, to airfield B.19, Brussels, with urgent freight and bringing home a full load of casualties on return.

Throughout the remainder of the year the tempo of training activity showed no decrease, only the intervention of inclement weather slowing the pace. Another training commitment for which the station became responsible came about on 9th November when the Air Ambulance Training School was established. Nursing orderlies posted to the school received a week long course which included intensive training in general air ambulance duties and familiarisation flights involving ten hours in the air.

To begin 1945 another new unit came into being at Leicester East, on 5th January the Glider Pick-Up Training Flight (GPUTF)

Cracked and eroded 'spectacle' dispersals to the south of the Gartree Road – compare with the wartime shot. Patches of concrete near the browsing cattle to the left are all that remains of the administration site. At the top of the picture in front of the trees to either side of the road, the rough ground marks the location of the station sick quarters. Author

was formed to develop glider snatching techniques. Initial equipment for the flight was five Dakotas and 16 Waco CG-4A Hadrian gliders. The new unit was destined not to stay long on the station, the first detachment of 26 men leaving for Zeals, Somerset, on 21st January and by early February the GPUTF was in operation at that station. Several special conversion courses began in January also, one which involved 30 crews, was so urgent that the resident 12 Course was sent on leave in the middle of their training to enable 107 OTU staff to cope with this added burden.

On 2nd February a milestone was passed by the glider flight of the OTU when it completed the 2,500th tow since the formation of the unit. During this month there occurred the greatest tragedy to involve station personnel. On the 19th, Dakota III TS436 crashed into high ground at 15:30 hours approximately 1¼ miles north of Zeals while on a return flight to Leicester East. On board were 21 crew and passengers including 16 aircrew, the sole survivor was the seriously injured pilot, Flight Lieutenant Mackay.

With the end of the European conflict in sight, emphasis was given to problems of air supply raised by operations in South East Asia Command (SEAC) and a drop zone more suited to the terrain in this area was sought.

The first sites investigated early in February 1945 were in the vicinity of Ashbourne, Derbyshire, but they were found to be unsuitable. Later though, in March, SEAC drops were carried out by unit aircraft at an unspecified location in the Pennines.

RAF Leicester East – 1st December 1944

Latitude	52° 36' 23" N
Longitude	01° 02' 00" W
Height at Sea Level	455ft
Command	Transport (RAF)
Nearest Railway Station	Leicester, LMS and LNER
Function	Operational Training Unit (Parent)
Affiliated Airfields	Nil

Landing Area – Runways

QDM	Dimensions	Extensibility	Remarks
107°	2,000 x 50 yds	2,000 yds	Entails
051°	1,400 x 50 yds	1,400 yds	diversion of
165°	1,400 x 50 yds	1,500 yds	Roman road.
Type of Surface	Concrete.		

Permanent Landmarks

By Day	Leicester City
By Night	Nil

Permanent Obstructions Houghton-on-the-Hill church steeple on approach to runway 231°

Facilities

Airfield Lightning	Mk.II		
Beam Approach	–		
Radio	–	QDM	–
Flying Control	Yes		

Accommodation All buildings temporary.

Technical	Hangars		Hardstandings	
	Type	No	Type	No
	T2	4	Spectacle	48
Domestic	Officers	SNCOs	ORs	Total
RAF	116	283	1,152	1,551
WAAF	10	16	340	366

On 25th March 1945 notification was given that 107 OTU had ceased to exist and the unit was to be renamed 1333 (Transport Support) Conversion Unit (TSCU). Only the unit title changed, the training mixture remained the same and carried on without pause. Allied to this undiminished activity was the usual crop of training accidents which, thankfully, included no major catastrophes. Typical examples of the mishaps which did occur throughout the unit's life are illustrated by the following entries taken from the unit Operations Record Book:

'06.05.45 – Horsa RJ351 (Staff Sergeant Kendall) while carrying ten passengers, nine of whom were ATC cadets, undershot on landing. The glider crashed wrecking the front and centre fuselage. No injuries to passengers.

'13.05.45 – At 23:59 hours, while taxiing to take off, Dakota KG405 (Warrant Officer Broose) struck Dakota FL631 (Flight Lieutenant Hindson). Propeller of former aircraft damaged, as was port elevator and tailplane of the latter.

'25.06.45 – Ambulance called to DZ to collect Driver Turner, RASC, who had been hit on the head by a falling canister.

'17.07.45 – While taxiing on the perimeter track Dakota KG513 (Pilot Officer Booth) struck a steam roller with starboard wing. Extensive damage caused to the starboard aileron and slight damage to wing.

'22.08.45 – Horsa RN560 made a heavy landing while night flying and sustained serious damage to nosewheel structure.

'21.09.45 – While taking off for a tugging exercise, the co-pilot of Dakota KG652 (Flying Officer Shrimpton) retracted undercarriage prematurely. Considerable damage to engines and propellers of the aircraft but the glider made a successful landing ahead of the Dakota.'

Many of the rapidly-built wartime airfields suffered, after a short time of intensive operation, from deterioration of the often hastily laid concrete runways and perimeter track. In this respect Leicester East was no exception. Extensive repairs to all the concrete surfaces had to be carried out between May and August 1945. Throughout this situation the station was in full operation and in August alone 4,078 movements including 172 visiting aircraft, were recorded. When repair work tended to hamper the large flying programme, unit aircraft made use of the neighbouring airfields at Bruntingthorpe and Market Harborough.

Almost as soon as the airfield returned to normal a re-organisation of training units led to a change of base and composition for 1333 TSCU. The unit was to be split with the main element going to Syerston, Nottinghamshire, while the Radar Flight with its Oxfords was bound for Snaith, Yorkshire.

These major changes at Leicester East began on 10th October from which date the Air Ambulance Training School ceased to operate. Then on the 20th a shuttle service was initiated to ferry stores and equipment to Syerston in Conversion Unit aircraft. This continued until the 25th when the main air party left but without the gliders, which were grounded due to high winds. Blustery weather persisted until the 27th and on that day the Dakotas returned and ferried the Horsas to Syerston. The Radar Flight lingered four more days before departing for Snaith on the 31st. On that day Dakotas of 1333 TSCU returned to Leicester East and in what might be termed a parting gesture, used their old home as a drop zone.

From early November the airfield was placed on C&M before being transferred to 40 Group, Maintenance Command. On the 15th of the month it began to be used as a Sub-Storage Site of 216 Maintenance Unit (MU), Sutton Coldfield, Warwickshire, for a time and from 21st January 1946 until 5th May 1948 it served the same purpose for 255 MU, Fulbeck, Lincolnshire. Three Motor Transport Companies, Nos.2, 3, and 8 were the next RAF units to move onto the station where, following the arrival of No.2 in mid-March 1946, all three combined into one unit. During its stay at Leicester East 2 MTC was engaged in the movement of stores and personnel from various locations spread over a very wide area. One particular task in which the unit was concerned were the logistics involved with the preparations for the Victory Parade held in London in June 1946. The company left the station for Warton, Lancashire on 12th December 1947 leaving only a C&M party behind. This contingent duly left to rejoin the main unit on 14th January 1948, and with their departure Leicester East closed. Then the RAF relinquished their control of the airfield which was taken over by the Army to be used as a camp and training area until 1949.

After the Army departed, areas of the airfield reverted to agriculture again and in late 1950 aircraft once more began to use the runways. This time though they were light aircraft in the hands of civilian pilots belonging to the Leicestershire Aero Club (LAC). The Club, which until April 1950, had enjoyed the use of Ratcliffe aerodrome, were forced by the death of Sir Lindsay Everard and the subsequent sale of his private aerodrome, to seek a new home. After searching for several months the club was able to negotiate a lease for the use of Leicester East which included the use of a hangar and the control tower. This latter building was soon modified so that in addition to serving its original function it doubled as a clubhouse. By mid-December 1950 the club were in residence and able to

announce that visiting private or club aircraft were welcome, no landing charges would be levied and that limited repair and fuelling arrangements were available.

The club continued to lead a fairly placid existence at Leicester East over the coming years, the pattern following that of many other aero clubs in post-war Britain. In 1958 the airfield was put up for disposal by the Government and the land sold back to its original owners, but LAC were able to retain the use of the area they already occupied.

On 9th May 1958 Leicester East received the most illustrious visitors ever to land there when Her Majesty Queen Elizabeth II and His Royal Highness the Duke of Edinburgh arrived to fulfil an official engagement in Leicester. After the de Havilland Heron of the Queen's Flight landed the Royal couple stepped out onto a red carpet to be met by the Lord Lieutenant of Leicestershire, Lord Cromwell, and as they left the airfield to proceed to the city they received a great ovation from 2,000 children lining the route to the entrance.

In the 1970s LAC emerged from the doldrums to become one of the premier organisations of its type in the British Isles. Progressively equipped with the most modern Cessna two-seaters for flying training and a variety of other types for touring and instrument training the club became renowned for the standard of its flying tuition. This reputation was acknowledged during the 1970s and 1980s when, for several years in succession LAC was awarded a Ministry of Defence contract to provide flight training for a number of air cadets who had qualified for flying scholarships. Today the club continues to be held in high regard for the proficiency of its courses.

Since their arrival at Leicester East the aero club endeavoured to hold an annual air show. From very humble beginnings this was developed into a major event enjoyed by thousands. (See Chapter One.) For many years the show was second to none in the Midlands but in the mid-1990s it had a rival in 'Big Thunder' displays at Bruntingthorpe. A reluctant decision was taken in 1997 that that year's Leicester International Air Display would probably be the last.

In recent years the airfield has been the venue for several prestigious events including both the British Parachute and Aerobatic Championships. For three years, 1979, 1980, and 1981, the Popular Flying Association (PFA) held their annual international fly-in at Leicester East. This event, the largest of its kind in Europe, attracted hundreds of visiting aircraft from home and abroad. On several occasions the airfield was filled to capacity.

Over the years, LAC members and other individuals have built aircraft from kits or plans to the highest of standards, winning awards at various PFA rallies and other events. Homebuilding in the counties owes its origins to the 'Flying Fleas' of the 1930s and has carried on ever since. Two aircraft completed at Leicester East have become PFA champions in recognition of their excellence; Pitts S-1S Special single-seat aerobatic biplane G-FLIK (taking the award twice) and Sequoia F8L Falco two-seat monoplane G-OCAD receiving the accolade in 1997.

For some years now Leicester East has become a firmly established venue on the British air racing calendar. From 1988, the airfield has hosted the Royal Aero Club Records, Racing and Rally Association and the final heat in the British Air Racing Championship, the Steward's Cup.

Held early each September, the Steward's Cup was followed by the prestigious King's Cup, a trophy competed for by British pilots since 1922. Competed over four laps with a handicap start to take into account aircraft of different performances, the races provide an exciting spectacle. It seems rather unfortunate that audiences at these historic events are not greater. King's Cup results at Leicester have been as follows:

1988 *Squadron Leader Mike Baker*
    SAL Bulldog T.1   XX631   142.8mph
1989 *Roger Hayes =*
    Beagle Pup 150   G-AXPN   134.2mph
    Dick Nesbit-Dufort =
    Forney Aircoupe   G-ARHF   117.2mph
1990 *Alf Hawley*
    MS Rallye   G-BKUT   108.1mph
1991 *Steve Jones*
    Cassutt IIIM   G-RUNT   192.0mph
1992 *Peter Crispe*
    Cessna 337F   G-AZKO   186.4mph
1993 *Roger Hayes*
    SAL Bulldog 128   G-BPCL   144.7mph
1994 *Geoffrey Boot*
    Cessna 340   N66SW   210.7mph
1995 *David Soul*
    Rockwell 114   G-LADS   198.1mph
1996 *Eddie Coventry*
    CAARP CAP 10B   G-BLVK   168.0mph
1997 *Mel Willies*
    Cessna 120   G-BTBW   119.5mph
1999 *Roger Hayes*
    SAL Bulldog 128   G-BPCL   141.6mph
2000 *Mish Konstantinovic*
    Cessna 182R   G-MISH   154.7mph

Air displays at Leicester East always packed in the crowds. Vickers-Supermarine Seafire FR.47 VP474 '156-BR' of 1833 RNVR Squadron, Fleet Air Arm, from HMS Gamecock, *RNAS Bramcote, Warwickshire, demonstrates the use of rocket-assisted take-off, circa 1953.* via Author

Link trainer instruction with the newly-established Leicestershire Aero Club. J Stubbs

A one time resident at Leicester East was Vickers Varsity G-BDFT, here on approach to Runway 28. On 19th August 1984 the aircraft crashed at Marchington, near Uttoxeter, killing 12. A memorial plaque was displayed inside the control tower at Leicester East. Author

For many years the prototype Auster J/1 Autocrat G-AGOH was a familiar sight at Leicester East. It was used as a working museum piece, part of Leicestershire Museums, but operating aerial survey work for various departments within the County Council. G-AGOH was retired on 12th July 1995 when it was ferried to the Newark Air Museum, Nottinghamshire, where it is kept in ground-running condition.

Leicester East's wartime control tower is now the headquarters of the Leicestershire Aero Club. It has been continually modified and updated and now includes a fully double-glazed and covered balcony area offering a commanding view of aerial activity, no matter what the weather is! Both Author

In anticipation of another superb LAC air display, lines of cars grow in number, ready for the show. This view is looking south east, the remains of some of the eastern boundary 'spectacle' dispersals are apparent. W Mallord

How low can you go? The famous B-17G Flying Fortress Sally B *during a spirited display at a Leicestershire Aero Club air display. Such flying was the hallmark of Don Bullock, who died while flying a B-26 Invader in a semi-aerobatic routine at Biggin Hill in September 1980.* Author

Opposite page:

Some of the contestants at the 1997 King's Cup air race, staged at Leicester East in September. In the foreground is the local entrant, Cassutt IIIM G-BOMB One Jump Ahead *flown by Mark Simpson.* Author

A beaming Rob Millinship with his Pitts S-1S Special G-FLIK at the Popular Flying Association's rally at Cranfield, Bedfordshire, 1986. Rob has taken the top PFA award twice for this superb machine. Ken Ellis

Leicestershire Aero Club's latest addition, Reims-built Cessna F.152 Series II G-IBRO prior to a photographic sortie for this book, June 1998. In the background is a microlight from the recently established school. Author

Sadly the 1998 King's Cup was not competed. With the increasing stature of the sport the Formula Air Racing Association (FARA) had agreed to stage their end-of-season event also at Leicester – the British Grand Prix. FARA compete in single-seat midget racing aircraft, all built to the same specification and therefore not requiring a staggered start.

Two British and four French aircraft provided a superb spectacle racing around the eight-lap circuit on 6th September 1998. Having won the race, architect Andrew Chadwick, racing in his Cassutt Speed One G-AXDZ *White Lightning* encountered difficulties and crashed on the airfield. The response of the LAC fire crews was both immediate and decisive, Andrew recovered well from his accident. Because of the incident, the King's Cup, in what would have been its tenth anniversary at Leicester, was not staged.

With many airfields the threat of development from non-aviation sources is ever present. It was Leicester East's turn in 1989 when the Co-operative Wholesale Society, owners of the airfield and much of the surrounding land, announced plans to develop 1,300 acres of this, at a cost of £400 million, to create the village of Stretton Magna. This ambitious scheme, which was revised a year later to absorb a further 350 acres, featured a pioneering energy system and electronic network. It also included 2,400 homes, a 1.6 million square feet office park and a two course golf complex. Although a start date of 1991 was envisaged, to date the threat has not materialised.

Over the years large sections of the airfield have been returned to agriculture by the removal of a considerable amount of concrete from runways, hardstandings and perimeter track. A large section of the perimeter track on the airfield's northern border has been incorporated into Gaulby Lane while on the eastern side a section of Houghton Mere is built along what was once a road within the station bomb dump. Apart from the T2 hangar and control tower few wartime buildings of any significance still remain on the airfield. Many, admittedly beginning to look rather shabby, disappeared during tidying up operations prior to Her Majesty the Queen's visit in 1958.

Until 1995 only 3,000 feet of hard surfaced runway was available, using the east-west runway (28/10). Two grass runways, parallel to the former RAF runways 16/34 or 24/06 had operated for many years, but are subject to winter bogging. During 1995 the old runways were resurfaced and the airfield returned to a full three-runway state. The new runways were officially opened on 3rd November 1995 when, among others, a Harrier GR.7 from Wittering took part in the ceremony.

In addition to the thriving aero club, the airfield has housed privately owned and business and executive aircraft. The latter have included Fox's Mints DH.89A G-AIDL, several DH Doves, and the Nuclear Power Group DH Herons G-ASUU and G-ANUO. In recent years Aerostar 601P G-MOVE of A1 Hydraulics has been based at Leicester.

Another long-term resident is Ron Neal, a former Auster employee who undertakes painstaking restorations of Austers when not attending to the maintenance requirements of the more modern resident aircraft.

On the area once occupied by the RAF technical site a test facility was established by Marconi Radar. The towers for this were demolished in 1994 as Marconi pulled out.

Leicester Airport, as it was officially renamed in 1975, though it is still more often referred to as Stoughton or Leicester East, is currently in a buoyant state. Hopefully it will continue to remain active and in the coming years be developed to realise its full potential.

A view of Leicester Airport in 1998, looking north-east, showing the newly-established 'triangle' of surfaced runways. Note the traces of 'spectacle' dispersals to the west, east and south. Author

Leicester East-based Units and Aircraft

No.196 Squadron
From 18.11.43 to 7.1.44   Codes 'ZO-', '7T-'
Short Stirling III   BK771.
Short Stirling IV   EE874, EE892, EF178, EF190, EF210, EF468, EF469, EF492, EF516, EH932, EH981, EJ110, LK403.

No.620 Squadron
From: 22.11.43 to: 18.3.44   Codes 'Q5-', 'D4-'
Short Stirling III   BF503 'H', BF580.
Short Stirling IV   EE945, EE971 'A', EF117 'C', EF121 'F', EF134 'E', EF143, EF197, EF203, EF256, EF275, EF293, EF295, EF303, EF433, EF440, EF456, EH890, EH894 'K', EH983, LJ440, LJ445, LJ446 'D', LJ449 'E', LJ463, LJ847, LJ849, LJ850, LJ864, LJ865, LJ866, LJ867, LJ869, LJ872, LJ873, LJ875, LJ880, LK395 'B'.

No.190 Squadron
From: 5.1.44 to: 25.3.44   Codes 'G5-', 'L9-'
Short Stirling IV   EF213, EF260, EF270, EF298, LJ816, LJ818, LJ820, LJ822, LJ823, LJ824, LJ825, LJ826, LJ827, LJ828, LJ829, LJ830, LJ831, LJ832, LJ833, LK335, LK336, LK363, LK431.

No.93 Group (Screened) Pilots School
From 19.4.44 to 30.4.44   No unit codes
Vickers Wellington III   X3479, X3565, BJ975 or ME975, ME992, ND112 or JA112.

No.107 Operational Training Unit
From 3.5.44 to 12.3.45   Code 'CM-'

No.1333 (Transport Support) Conversion Unit
From 12.3.45 to 25.10.45   Code 'ZR-'
Douglas Dakota III   FD782, FD864, FL519, FL584, FL604, FL608, FL609, FL613, FL626, FL629, FL631, FL634, FL635, FZ578, FZ591, FZ593, FZ629, FZ636, FZ664, FZ666, FZ672, FZ691, FZ693, FZ697, KG360, KG405, KG438, KG442, KG450, KG454, KG513, KG527, KG547, KG578, KG584, KG595, KG597, KG601, KG604, KG606, KG608, KG609, KG612, KG614, KG617, KG618, KG629, KG640, KG643, KG644, KG648, KG652, KG662, KG665, KG670, KG671, KG728. TS424, TS435, TS436.
Mk.III (C-47A)   42-24068 (instructional airframe 4844M) allotted to 107 OTU direct from USA.

Airspeed Horsa I   DP750, PF809, RJ139, RJ151, RJ158, RJ161, RJ175, RJ279, RJ297, RJ300, RJ351.
Airspeed Horsa II   PW845, PW881, PW886, RN516, RN556, RN560, RX551, RX823, RX905, RX984, RZ286, RZ380.
Airspeed Oxford I   R6363, W6630, W6634, T1105, T1256, V3849, T4204, AB659, AB687, AB763, AP390, EB971, ED189.
Taylorcraft Auster III   NX488.

Glider Pick-Up Training Flight
From 8.1.45 to 21.1.45   Codes 'IB-', 'W4-'
Douglas Dakota III   TS433, TS434.
WACO CG-4A Hadrian   No serials known.

Leicester East-based Serious Aircraft Accidents

No.107 OTU / No.1333 (TS)CU

16.8.44 Oxford I AB687. Damaged beyond repair.

3.9.44 Dakota III KG547. Aircraft on glide approach landing failed to check on reaching runway. Flew in causing undercarriage to collapse. Aircraft written off.

29.11.44 Dakota III KG527. Took off with elevators locked and belly-landed at Biggin Hill, Kent. Became instructional airframe 4989M.

19.2.45 Dakota III TS 436. After take-off from Zeals, Somerset, aircraft flew into hill, two miles to north-east.

6.5.45 Horsa I RJ351. Stalled on approach and hit ground.

18.6.45 Auster III NX488. Caught fire when starting up, at Leicester East.

2.10.45 Dakota III KG 513. Hit by FZ691 while parked at Leicester East and damaged beyond repair.

22.10.45 Horsa I RJ175. Crash-landed and hit pole after tow rope parted on take-off.

Civil Aircraft

3.4.55 BAC Drone G-ADPJ
Crashed at Leicester East.

15.6.71 Stampe SV-4C G-AXPK
Nose-dived steeply from 30ft and crashed on the runway. Both occupants injured.

24.6.71 Piel Emeraude G-AWXP
Ditched in the Channel off Dungeness *en route* L.East-Calais.

4.10.80 Cessna (Reims) FA.152 Aerobat G-BFZN LAC
Crashed in forced landing near Croft. On leisurely rebuild.

28.9.84 Cessna (Reims) F.152 II G-BHHJ LAC
Stalled on take-off at Leicester East and came to rest inverted.

1.10.85 Rockwell Commander 112A G-BHOC
Struck power lines and crashed near Leicester East. Pilot killed.

5.5.89 Cessna (Reims) F.152 II G-BHJW LAC
Badly damaged in forced landing shortly after take-off from Leicester East.

29.1.93 Robinson R-22 Beta G-BSRG Meridian Helicopters
Damaged in heavy landing at Leicester.

19.4.95 Westland Bell 47G-4A G-OEMH
Crashed while hovering during a local flight from Leicester.

19.4.98 Robinson R-44 G-POWE Hired from Leicester.
Took off from Desford for dinner party at Shearsby Hotel. On return, weather deteriorated. Crashed in wooded area between Laughton and Gumley. Four on board killed.

23.5.98 Cessna F.152 II G-BIIJ Leicestershire Aero Club.
On flight Leicester to Blackpool. Crashed 200ft from the summit of the 3,010ft Tryfan, Snowdonia. Both occupants killed.

Leicestershire Aero Club Fleet

Aircraft used while at Leicester East (2000 fleet).*

Auster J/1 Autocrat	G-AIGR
Auster J/4	G-AIJK
Auster J/5F Aiglet Trainer	G-AMTD
Beagle Terrier II	G-ASOY, G-ATBU
Cessna (Reims) F.150L	G-BAMC
Cessna (Reims) F.150M	G-BCUJ
Cessna (Reims) F.152 II	G-BGBP, G-BHHJ, G-BHJW, G-BIIJ, G-BKGW*, G-BMCV*, G-IBRO*
Cessna (Reims) F.152 Aerobat	G-BFZN, G-BHEN*, G-LEIC*
Cessna (Reims) F.172N Skyhawk II	G-ECGC
De Havilland Tiger Moth	3 examples
Piper PA-28-161 Cadet	G-FOXA*
Piper PA-28-181 Archer II	G-BPAY*, G-EFIR*

Chapter Thirteen

Loughborough

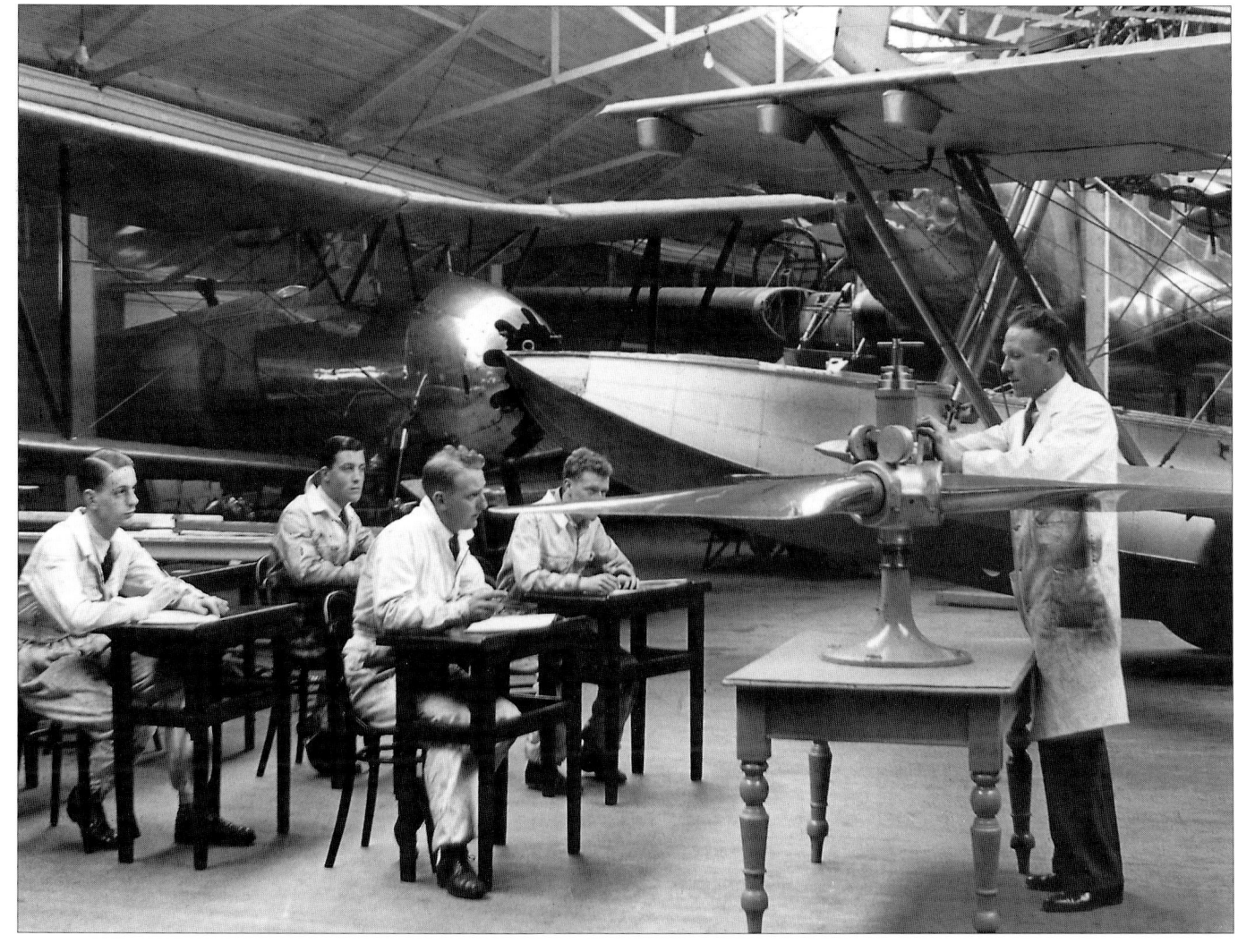

The sole examples of the Fairey S9/30 (fuselage frame attached to the large float at right), Bristol Bullpup (biplane to left) and the Blackburn HST.10 form a backdrop to a class in progress in the old Premier Dance Hall. The propeller in use as a teaching aid is now installed on the airworthy Bristol Blenheim based at Duxford, Cambridgeshire.
via P Geary

DURING the First World War, Brush Electrical Engineering Company built a large number of aeroplanes for both the Royal Flying Corps and the Royal Naval Air Service between 1915 and 1919. Close to Brush's Falcon Works was a large expanse of ground known as Loughborough Meadows and this was where the landplane types were tested. Occasionally, delivery flights would also be made from the Meadows, but most types were delivered in crates by road. (For a full examination of Brush's aircraft production, see Chapter Fourteen, *Brush-Built*.)

After the end of the First World War horse racing became a part of the Loughborough sporting scene once more and for many years meetings were held, in the spring, on a course laid out in fields situated between the River Soar and Derby Road (the A6). The major event on the calendar in those days was called the Quorn Hunt Steeplechases and so popular did these races become that during the 1920s they were invariably regarded as an excuse for an annual holiday by many Leicestershire folk. For example, over 25,000 people are reputed to have attended the 1923 meeting. Prior to the 1924

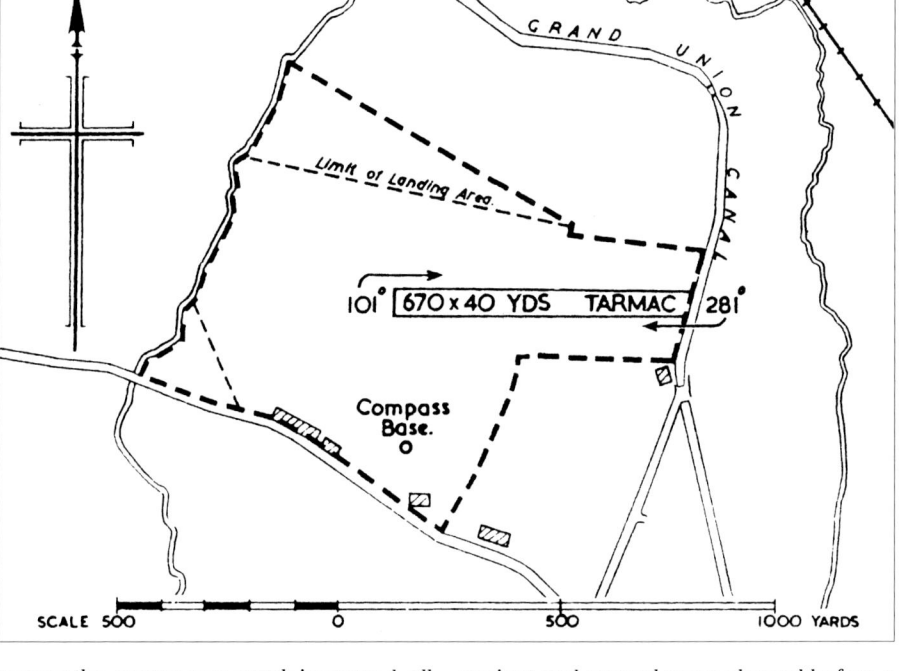

season the course was much improved, all arable land was levelled and reseeded, operations which in all probability had an influence in later years when other decisions were being made regarding future use of the area. Eventually, interest in races declined to a point where they became impracticable and were discontinued.

When civil flying began to increase in popularity during the late 1920s many local government bodies considered that the addition of an aerodrome to their community amenities would be a decided asset in the future and began to earmark sites for eventual development. Loughborough was one of the corporations with an eye to the future and during 1929 a site adjacent to the racecourse, known as Bishop's Meadow, was given consideration. In spite of initial enthusiasm little progress was made on the

project and several years elapsed before a more detailed survey of the area was carried out.

This next inspection was made by Ivor McClure of the Automobile Association Aviation Department and in his report dated 6th May 1933 the following observations were made. Although a larger site to the west of Bishop's Meadow was in many respects eminently more suitable for airfield development it was subjected to down currents from a ridge nearby called Bellevue Hill. So, for this reason alone, Bishop's Meadow was to be preferred and it was the only other reasonable site near the town worthy of development.

Maximum dimensions available for landing strips on the proposed aerodrome site at this time were given as north/south 700ft, north-east/south-west 800ft, east/west 750ft

and south east-north west 850ft. A major hazard noted was a 160,000 volt power line running north to south 850 yards from the eastern perimeter. Little immediate progress was apparent following McClure's report and a further eight months elapsed before another examination of the site was carried out. This time, on 23rd January 1934 when Mr Granger, the borough surveyor, accompanied W A Campbell who represented the Director of Civil Aviation.

The next milestone in the airfield project was reached some 14 months later, in May 1936, when Loughborough Corporation finally acquired the Derby Road site, at a cost of £17,000 from a Mr de Lisle. About this time the corporation were first approached by Dr Herbert Schofield MBE, principal of Loughborough College. He enquired into the possibility of the establishment either leasing or buying a piece of frontage land on the proposed airfield for the purpose of erecting buildings for the use of the College's Department of Aeronautical Engineering.

Although the land had been secured, the project went ahead at a snail's pace and the next noteworthy event occurred in June 1938 when a public meeting was convened on the 6th, to discuss the question of the Corporation borrowing £20,086 for the purpose of building the airfield. A satisfactory conclusion was reached and at last things began to move.

By November 1938 plans had been drawn up by Boulton & Paul Limited for an aircraft hangar 135ft x 60ft, an aeroplane assembly and rigging shop 185ft x 70ft and a 45ft x 20ft engine test building, all for the use of Loughborough College. Preparations for the erection of these buildings were well under way by the end of January 1939 but no start had been made on the aerodrome surface. Work on this eventually got under way but was incomplete by the time of the outbreak of war in September 1939. Although all civilian flying ceased for the duration of hostilities the project was allowed to proceed and to be finally completed early in 1940.

Loughborough College had negotiated with Leicestershire County Council and Loughborough Corporation and obtained a lease of the airfield to run for 21 years. The buildings which had been erected for the use of the College were soon occupied by

A plan of Loughborough airfield, showing the tarmac strip.

A view of the instructional airframes in the old Premier Dance Hall, Loughborough. Left foreground, Bristol Bullpup; middle Blackburn Baffin; right foreground Armstrong Whitworth Atlas. via Author

the Department of Aeronautical Engineering and several of their instructional airframes which had previously been housed in the old Premier Dance Hall on Ashby Road, were installed in the hangar, together with engines and other ancillary equipment for student use.

The aerodrome was still unused at this time and because of fears of possible invasion by airborne troops it was felt that action was necessary to prevent the enemy having easy access to the landing area. During May and June 1940 the Trent Motor Company were approached and steps were taken for them to supply derelict vehicles to obstruct any possible landing by glider-borne troops on the aerodrome.

A disused airfield is not much use in wartime and Loughborough was not allowed to stay in this state for long. The Ministry of Aircraft Production (MAP) realised the potential of the site, requisitioned it later in 1940, and earmarked it for future use. Airwork was the company eventually selected to occupy the airfield and develop it into a repair base for RAF aircraft. R W Cantello was put in charge of the project and the story of his company's early association with Loughborough is perhaps best told in his own words.

'Airwork, a leading aircraft repair firm during the Second World War, had a large number of factories in various parts of the country. They were asked to visit Loughborough to survey yet another site in 1941. Yours truly accompanied by his director set off by car from London with only a compass to navigate. Owing to the invasion scare all road signposts had been removed so we set off hopefully on a northern bearing. Being ignorant of compasses my companion, L A Lafone, was the navigator. 'LAL' had done a lot of pioneering flying in the Middle East in the early 1930s for Airwork so he was an expert. He made a pin-point arrival in Loughborough but on finding the alleged airfield found a tiny building belonging to Loughborough College and a pocket handkerchief airfield. We had some vague MAP maps which showed six fields earmarked for requisitioning. No one had told the farmers of this so our arrival was not greeted with any patriotic enthusiasm. However, difficulties were overcome and a year later an aerodrome had been established complete with new hangars of 60,000 square feet. We then started operations.'

What 'RWC' omits to say at this time was that in spite of the College building being 'tiny' it did not prevent him from commandeering the major portion of it while his own hangars were being erected. The College students, very few at that time, were allowed to stay on in one corner provided they were neither seen nor heard. Also, use of the requisitioned fields, some of which

had previously been part of the racecourse, enabled approximately 3,300ft of runway to be established. Of this 2,040ft at the eastern end was paved to a width of 120ft, the remainder was grass.

The contract which Airwork undertook was for the repair and modification of an American-built aircraft, the Douglas DB-7 or A-20, then in service in considerable numbers with the RAF. A medium twin-engined bomber-intruder version was known in British circles as the Boston while the nightfighter variant was called the Havoc. Both these types passed through the Loughborough workshops and eventually over 400 men and women were employed on the work. In the main, the aircraft were brought in by road in a dismantled state and placed in storage around the hangars until they were required.

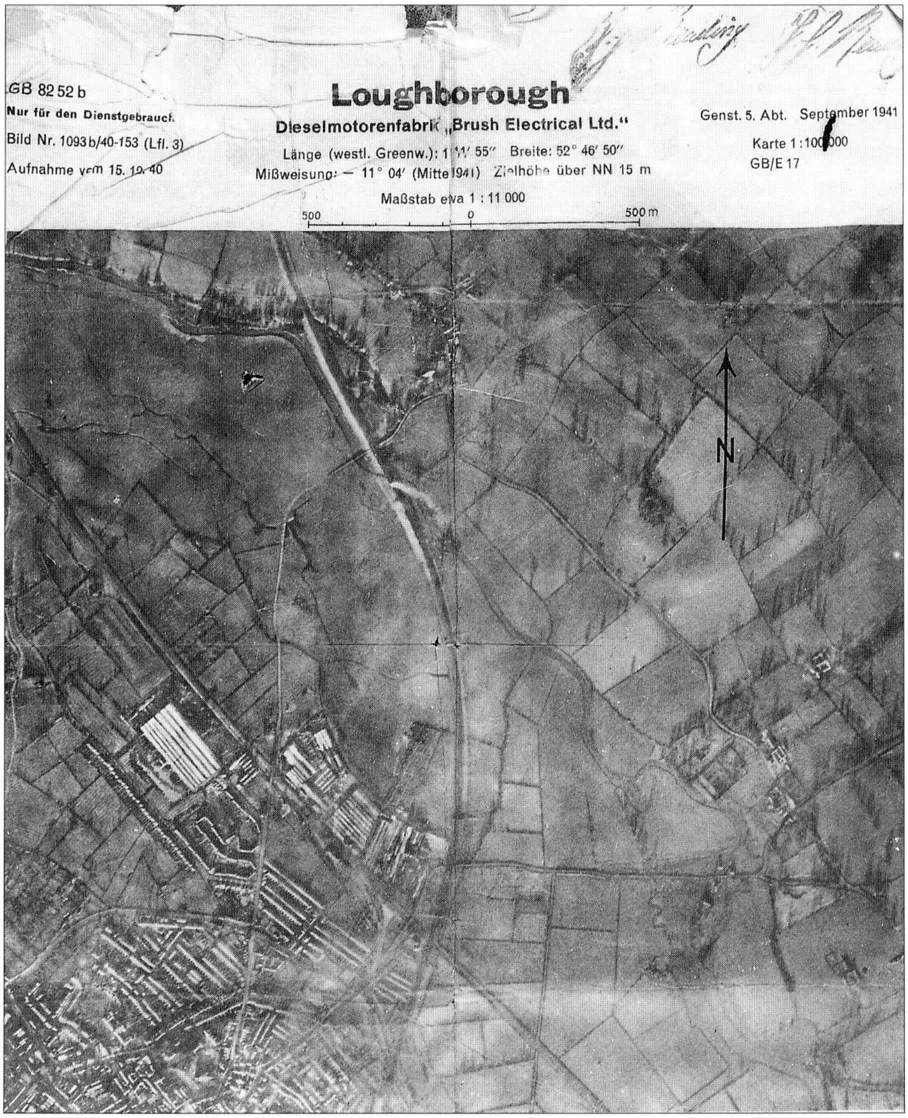

A Luftwaffe target photograph of the Brush works, dated 15th December 1940.
via A P Jarram

When an overhaul was completed the aircraft was test flown from the airfield by a Loughborough man, named Peter Clifford. Some of his spectacular take-offs from the short runway and the flying which followed are still well remembered locally. Some of his personal recollections were as follows:

'I carried out the first flight at Loughborough on 8th June 1943 and the last test I did was on 29th June 1945. During that period I tested 72 different Bostons.

'When testing commenced on these aircraft we operated a left hand circuit and when approaching from the eastern end this necessitated flying low over the town. After a while we were requested by the authorities to fly right hand circuits to avoid low flying over Loughborough. From memory we always did from that time onwards.

'There is one interesting fact that during the period when we were testing Bostons on one occasion an aircraft was being collected by an RAF pilot. He obviously was not accustomed to operating from such a short

GB 82 52 b
Nur für den Dienstgebrauch.
Bild Nr. 1093 b/40-153 (Lfl. 3)
Aufnahme vom 15. 12. 40

Loughborough
Dieselmotorenfabrik „Brush Electrical Ltd."
Länge (westl. Greenw.): 1° 11' 55"   Breite: 52° 46' 50"
Mißweisung: — 11° 04' (Mitte 1941) Zielhöhe über NN 15 m
Maßstab etwa 1 : 11 000

Genst. 5. Abt.   September 1941
Karte 1 : 100 000
GB/E 17

N

What a treasure trove this would have been for today's aircraft preservationists! A veritable feast of aero engines in the College engineering hangar. Norman Hayes

Fleet Air Arm engineering officers of the third course, 1943-1944, at Loughborough, with Grumman Martlet I AL246 in the background. J Oates

strip and abandoned take-off, finishing up in the small brook at the western end of the airfield. After this episode, instructions were received from the Civilian Repair Organisation that only I should operate Bostons from the airfield.'

Another viewpoint on the same period comes from Ron Redfern, then a teenager and an aviation enthusiast:

'The aerodrome being near my home enabled me to keep an eye on things. I also delivered a church magazine to Bishop's Meadow farm and was glad of the opportunities to cross the aerodrome legally, but nothing ever flew during my journeys. There was a small control hut and warning notices at the point where the lane to the farm crossed the runway.

'Airwork occupied the first and second hangars from Loughborough on the Derby Road. Here they refurbished and converted old Bostons. Many were of the Turbinlite* variety and these matt black, flat-nosed Havocs arrived by road in anything from poor to terrible condition. I remember the day I heard the roar of engines and cycled quickly to the aerodrome to find the first conversion doing engine runs. It was stand-ing on the circular concrete pad between the second and third hangars. I witnessed some test flights and the short runway made the necessary low approach over the sewage farm, canal, towpath, hedge, lane and boundary fence look a very hairy business. Once I saw the main wheels of one aircraft brush through the top of the hedge. One Boston, I remember finished up nose down in the Black Brook with its nose and the Derby Road, Dishley Mill Bridge, mutually damaged.'

(* In the early phase of the war, when the art of radar interception was still in its infancy, the Douglas twins were modified to carry a high intensity searchlight in the nose. In company with a Hawker Hurricane night-fighter, the Turbinlite Havocs would be vectored onto a suspect aircraft by RAF ground controllers and then illuminate it. With identity confirmed and the target in view, in theory the Hurricane could attack.)

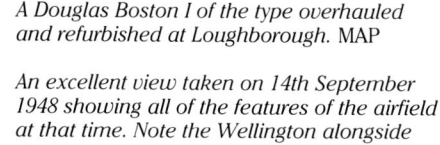

A Douglas Boston I of the type overhauled and refurbished at Loughborough. MAP

An excellent view taken on 14th September 1948 showing all of the features of the airfield at that time. Note the Wellington alongside the hangar. Loughborough University

Airwork General Trading – Aircraft Repairs etc

Douglas Boston I	AE464. AX928. BD117.
Douglas Boston II	AH431, AH434, AH435, AH446,

AH447, AH451, AH457, AH472, AH478, AH489, AH518.
Douglas Boston III   W8253, W8260, W8262, W8269,
  W8271, W8273, W8274, W8275, W8277, W8279, W8294,
  W8303, W8306, W8307, W8308, W8309, W8313, W8317,
  W8323, W8324, W8327, W8330, W8339, W8343, W8352,
  W8353, W8357, W8367, W8368, W8370, W8379, W8389,
  W8393, W8397, W8398, Z2169, Z2205, Z2214, Z2239, Z2246,
  Z2270, Z2280, Z2284, AL271, AL458, AL707, AL760, AL774.
Douglas Boston IIIA   BZ199, BZ208, BZ211, BZ212,
  BZ214, BZ221, BZ236, BZ240, BZ241, BZ248, BZ253, BZ254,
  BZ259, BZ275, BZ280, BZ290, BZ291, BZ308, BZ312, BZ320,
  BZ328, BZ332, BZ346, BZ352, BZ358, BZ362, BZ374, BZ376,
  BZ381, BZ389, BZ395, BZ397.
Douglas Boston IV   BZ429, BZ448.
Douglas Havoc IA   AW401, BJ469, BJ490.

Note:
Some Boston Mk.Is were converted to Havoc or to trainer status. Some Boston Mk.IIs were converted to Turbinlite or Havoc status. Some Boston Mk.IIIs were converted to Intruder, Turbinlite and NF.II status. It is not known at which modification stage the aircraft came to Loughborough and aircraft are referred to simply as 'Mk.Is', 'Mk.IIs' or 'Mk.IIIs' here.

Finally, Ron made the following observation with regard to Peter Clifford's flying: *'The test pilot for Airwork gained quite a reputation locally, good or bad depending on your viewpoint, his 'beat-ups' used to include the town as well as the aerodrome.' Peter Clifford went on to establish a well-known civil aviation operation at Oxford Airport and, amongst other achievements, won the 1955 King's Cup air race.'*

Before the Second World War ended the Boston programme began to tail off and the work force then progressively turned their attention to the repair of Avro Lancaster wing sections. In the town, Brush Coachworks were also engaged on this type of repair at their Falcon Works. Previously, between March 1941 and December 1943, they had repaired Handley Page Hampden fuselages, but neither of these contracts had any direct connection with the airfield. From 1942, Brush took over the contract to build de Havilland Dominie twin-engined biplanes – see Chapter Fourteen.

Dominies began to leave the works in March 1943. From there the fuselage sections were towed tail-first through the town, out along the Derby Road (A6), before turn-ing right into Swingbridge Road. A short distance inside the road an entrance led to a hangar which had been built on the airfield close to the eastern end of the runway. Here the Dominies were finally assembled and rigged prior to flight testing and delivery. The last Brush-built aircraft left in July 1946.

In addition to Airwork and Brush, the College Aeronautical Department made their own contribution to the war effort. The completion of Airwork's hangars allowed them full use of their own building once more. To make up for the deficiency in students a contract was obtained to teach members of the Fleet Air Arm. Courses which began in October 1942 were of approximately one year's duration for an entry of up to 50 midshipmen. Thorough tuition in aeronautical engineering enabled successful trainees to be ranked as engineering officers on completion. The final course left the College late in 1945 and staff were then able to revert once more to teaching civilian students.

During October-November 1942 the airfield was utilised even further when a gliding school was established for the benefit of local Air Training Corps (ATC) units. Several of the College staff took an active interest devoting a considerable amount of their free time to this activity. Plans were also formulated for College students to build a glider for the ATC's use, but this idea was shelved after a gross error was found in their drawings. In late May 1944 the gliding school was required to vacate Loughborough and move over to Rearsby (Chapter Twenty).

A view of the instructional airframes in and around the hangar. Left to right: Wellington, Martlet, Hurricanes (one inside and one out), Spitfire.

Students gaining practical experience on the Spitfire V and the Martlet. Behind are visiting Tiger Moths of Nottingham University Air Squadron.

Aeronca 100 G-AEVT following a mishap on take-off from Loughborough, 14th July 1950. It was written off. Many of the College buildings are visible in the background.

One of the Hurricanes on the College campus in June 1958. It had been dismantled and transported from the airfield by high-spirited students. All J Oates

With the ending of the war Airwork's military contracts tapered off, the company then vacated the centre hangar and concentrated all their activities in the first and largest building. For a time they retained a contact with aircraft as at least 12 former RAF Dominies were converted into civilian Dragon Rapides. It is also known that at least one Percival Proctor received similar treatment. Mk.II G-AGLJ was civilianised for the Ministry of Civil Aviation in 1944.

A complete break with aviation came when the works were taken over by the War Office for vehicle maintenance and an Airwork subsidiary company known as Dishley Engineering Limited, was awarded a contract worth £2,000,000 to manage a motor spares unit. Over 100 staff were employed on the task of sending spares to various army depots. A new contract which started in 1955 involved stripping to the base chassis and reconditioning, as new, all components on Commer three-tonners. Staff increased to over 400 and the weekly output was six completely overhauled lorries. In excess of 2,500 of these passed through the works before the requirement ceased in 1963, bringing to an end Airwork's association with the airfield after 20 years.

The hangar vacated by Airwork when the war finished was not allowed to remain empty for long; its new tenants were the College Aeronautical Engineering Department. They soon transferred the Grumman Martlet and Hawker Hurricanes, their main instructional airframes at this time, over from the Boulton Paul hangar which then became the aero engine shop. Many other parts kept from aircraft which had passed through the Department's hands over the years also made the short journey. With more space available other airframes were gradually acquired and these included a Vickers-Supermarine Spitfire, a Douglas Boston and a Vickers Wellington.

A rather amusing story concerns the acquisition of the Boston. In 1945 Airwork had several of these aircraft which had been declared Category E which meant that they were fit for scrap only. Instructions were given that they should be reduced to produce and disposed of accordingly. Aeronautical Department staff, made aware of the situation, persuaded the person responsible that it was highly unlikely that anyone could tell exactly how many aircraft constituted a scrap heap. One dark night, a flat tin of 50 Players cigarettes changed hands and a Boston was towed over to join the other airframes in the College hangar, where it remained until it was finally scrapped shortly before the Department left the airfield.

Another aircraft which should have appeared on the College inventory was Handley Page Halifax B.VI NP884. When being delivered on 4th July 1946, by a crew from 4 Ferry Unit, it overshot the runway, removed its main undercarriage in the Black Brook and belly-landed in a ploughed field beyond. College staff, instructed to show no interest in the wreck, stayed well clear for fear they might be asked to accept it *in situ*. It was eventually removed by an RAF salvage crew. Over the years many interesting aircraft have been utilised as teaching aids at Loughborough. (See table.)

Following de-requisitioning of the airfield in 1947, applications were made for an operating licence. This was granted by the Ministry of Civil Aviation in 1949 but the hoped for influx of traffic did not materialise. There were no scheduled services from the airfield although it was used on infrequent occasions by charter companies such as Olley Air Services. Landings by private aircraft were also sparse, the most numerous visitors were de Havilland Tiger Moths of Nottingham University Air Squadron which came to give air experience to College students affiliated to the unit.

Sections of the airfield were turned over to agriculture. The main crop produced was hay but sizeable areas were tilled and potatoes grown. Students were induced to harvest this latter crop for cigarettes as payment. College catering benefited most from the potato crop but they were also made available to staff at ten shillings (50p) per bag, delivery free by the airfield ambulance. On one occasion, in an attempt to alleviate the problem of tobacco shortage, a quantity of these plants were grown around the control hut and the crop when harvested was processed in a press constructed by the students. By all accounts the resulting product was foul and only smoked, in any quantity, by one member of staff. It is said that with his pipe stoked up and going full blast his presence could be detected up to 100 yards downwind!

An unusual use of the airfield occurred during the 1950s when it became the venue of the All England Sheepdog Trials. It was not a popular choice as the terrain was considered too flat.

When the College's lease finally expired in 1961 the fate of the airfield was sealed and what had been envisaged, in the 1930s as becoming Leicestershire's second municipal airport closed to flying. Soon the Aeronautical Department cleared their hangar, and in so doing disposed of the bulk of the contents including the four Second World War fighter aircraft, which all found homes either with historic collections or in museums. The faculty then severed the link with what had been its home for over two decades and took up residence in new buildings on the main campus.

After moving to their new premises, the Aeronautical Department still required instructional airframes. Having disposed of many relics from an earlier age, more modern replacements were sought. Space was more limited and accommodation could only be found for two airframes.

The first of these, Hawker Hunter F.4 XE677, was acquired from Hawker Siddeley while the second, Hunting Jet Provost G-AOBU, came on extended loan from the Shuttleworth Trust. This duo became long serving residents catering to the needs of student classes for over 25 years. Further reductions in space allocated for 'hands on' teaching brought about their disposal.

After a short period on loan to the Lincolnshire Aviation Society, the Hunter was returned to the University and sold to Jet Heritage while the Jet Provost was also sold on after return to Shuttleworth. Since then, both aircraft have been restored to flying condition, made possible, no doubt to the care and attention which they received while at Loughborough. (See the listing of Instructional Airframes overleaf.)

Following their departure and the reorganisation of the Aeronautical Department, there was space for only one airframe. Arriving in January 1991 was SEPECAT Jaguar GR.1 (mod), XX765, from British Aerospace at Warton, Lancashire. This was a one-off test-bed for Active Control Technology, all of the controls being what is called 'fly-by-wire'. On 20th September 1981 XX765 had the distinction of being the first aircraft in the world to fly with no reversionary control, relying only on fly-by-wire inputs. It went on to play an important role in the development of EAP and EF2000 before retiring.

The Jaguar was retained at Loughborough until an even more exotic aircraft arrived in June 1996. Also coming from Warton, this was the British Aerospace EAP, ZF534, a twin-engined single-seater used as a technology demonstrator to pave the way for the four-nation Eurofighter EF2000 programme (named Typhoon in 1998). The EAP currently allows students to become familiar with many of the advanced technologies of today's aerospace industry. Having larger dimensions than the somewhat diminutive Jaguar, the EAP's starboard wing remains partially dismantled.

With the passage of time, the acreage which once made up the airfield has undergone a total transformation and has now become the home of a modern industrial park. None of the buildings once occupied by Airwork or the College, now a University, have survived the onslaught of progress. No trace is to be found of the runway although a short stretch of Bakewell Road does follow the direct line of the approach.

Only one building exists that can be associated with the airfield era. This is the old Brush hangar off Swingbridge Road but this is unrecognisable for what it was and has been absorbed into the industrial complex.

Loughborough College & University Instructional Airframes

Armstrong Whitworth Atlas   Two-seat general purpose military biplane. Fuselage finally converted into gantry for servicing hangar roof lighting.

Blackburn Baffin   Two/three-seat naval torpedo biplane. No further details.

Blackburn Shark   Two/three-seat naval torpedo biplane. Thought returned to Fleet Air Arm circa 1945.

Bristol Bullpup   J9051   Single-seat biplane fighter. Withdrawn from use at Filton in mid-1935.

Fairey S9/30   S1706   Two-three-seat naval reconnaissance floatplane. Believed acquired in 1936.

Gloster AS.31 Survey   K2602   Twin-engined aerial survey and general duties biplane. Ex Royal Aircraft Establishment, Farnborough. Struck off service charge in March 1937.

Blackburn HST.10   B-9   Twin-engined 12-seater airliner. Donated in 1938, scrapped in 1946.

Fairey Long Range Monoplane   K1991   Single-engined monoplane designed for ultra-long range record-breaking flights. Dismantled at Farnborough and brought to the College, circa 1938. Scrapped.

Hawker Hart (T)   K6469 'O'   Two-seat, single-engined biplane advanced trainer. Damaged in heavy landing at Grantham, Lincs, 14th November 1939. Became instructional airframe 2045M. Fuselage and other parts to Loughborough circa 1943. Scrapped circa 1946/1947.

Hawker Sea Hurricane Ib   Z7015   Single-seat ship-borne fighter. Allocated November 1943. To the Shuttleworth Trust, Old Warden, Bedfordshire, 21st February 1961. First flown following restoration at Duxford, Cambridgeshire, on 16th September 1995. Civil registration G-BKTH. Currently airworthy.

Douglas Boston   See main text. Known to have served with USAAF also said to have been formerly French Air Force (or ordered by them and not delivered). Bore the name *Shoo Shoo Baby* and individual names by crew positions. Scrapped.

Grumman Martlet I   AL246   Single-seat ship-borne fighter. Ex Fleet Air Arm, late 1944/early 1945. To the Fleet Air Arm Museum, Yeovilton, Somerset, in 1965.

Vickers Wellington XVI   R3237   Twin-engined medium bomber. Records show that aircraft crashed in forced-landing in Cumberland while being flown by a crew

The engine test shed, to the left, was the last of the old College buildings to be demolished.

The Brush hangar, spring 1998. Both Author

Students working on the Gloster AS.31 Survey (right) with the engineless AW Atlas behind. Loughborough Echo

The Blackburn HST.10 at Brough. It is believed not to have left the old Dance Hall and was scrapped there in 1946. Hawker Siddeley Aviation

from 5 Ferry Pool on 1st February 1945, but reported to have flown into Loughborough. Modified as a transport with seats in fuselage also long range tanks in bomb bay.

Hawker Hurricane IV KX829 Single-seat fighter. Flown in on loan from 22 Maintenance Unit, Silloth. Authorisation dated 20th February 1946. Left in 1961 for the Birmingham Museum of Science and Industry. Currently in store awaiting new museum building.

Supermarine Spitfire Vc AR501 Single-seat fighter. Delivered 21st March 1946. Removed to Shuttleworth Trust, Old Warden, Bedfordshire and used in the film *The Battle of Britain*, 1967. Civil registration G-AWII. Restored to flying condition at Duxford, Cambridgeshire, and first flown 27th June 1975. Currently airworthy.

Handley Page Halifax B.VI NP884 Four-engined heavy bomber. Not truly an instructional airframe, even though allotted to College. 'Arrived' 4th July 1946. See main text.

Hunting Jet Provost T.1 G-AOBU Two-seat basic jet trainer. On loan from the Shuttleworth Trust, Old Warden, Bedfordshire, arrived April 1961. Sold to private collector and eventually restored to flying condition at Cranfield, Bedfordshire, making its first flight on 22nd May 1994. Currently airworthy.

Hawker Hunter F.4 XE677 Single-seat jet fighter. Arrived from Dunsfold, Surrey, 9th January 1962. On loan to Lincolnshire Aviation Society, East Kirkby, 1988. Returned to the University and sold to Jet Heritage Ltd of Bournemouth, Dorset, October 1989. Registered G-HHUN, following restoration reflown in January 1994. Fatal crash near Dunsfold, 5th June 1998.

Payne Knight Twister Single-seat sporting biplane of US design. Uncovered fuselage frame only. Brought by students from London area circa 1983. Thought to be either G-APXZ or G-ARGJ, both of which were not completed and stored at Biggin Hill. To East Kirkby, Lincs, and now stored at Breighton, Yorkshire.

British Aerospace (SEPECAT) Jaguar GR.1 (mod) XX765 Single-seat, twin-engined jet strike fighter modified to test 'fly-by-wire' (Active Control Technology) controls. (No mechanical or hydraulic linkage to the controls, all electrically-actuated.) Arrived from BAe at Warton, Lancs, on loan January 1991. Departed prior to the arrival of the EAP (see below) and now on display at the RAF Museum, Cosford, Shropshire.

British Aerospace EAP ZF534 Single-seat technology demonstrator aircraft, leading to the British-German-Italian-Spanish Eurofighter EF2000 Typhoon. Arrived on loan from BAe June 1996.

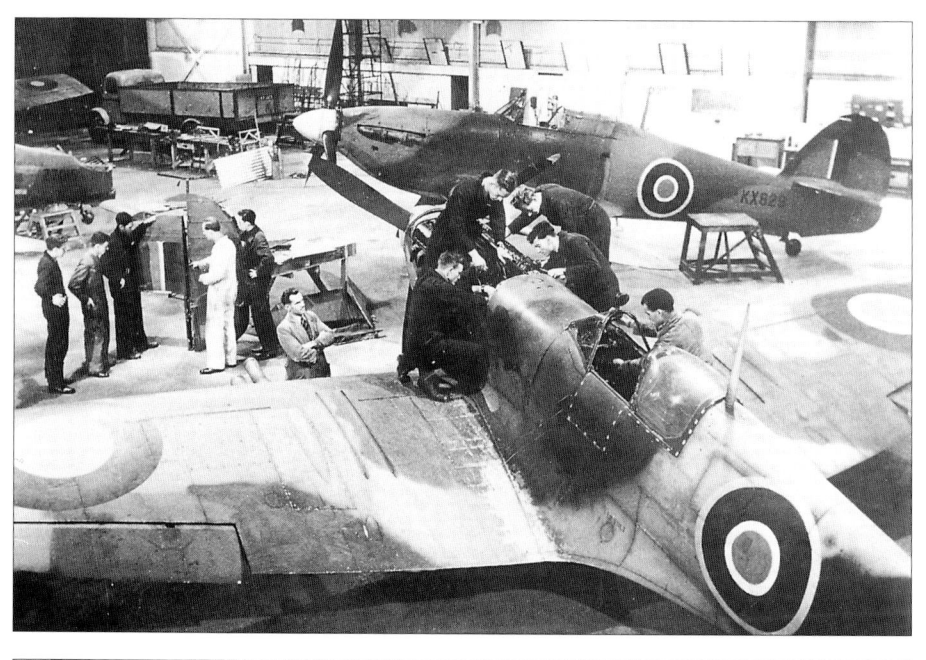

The Hart (T) in the College hangar with the Martlet in the foreground.

A busy scene in the College hangar. Spitfire AR501 in the foreground with Hurricane KX829 behind and the rear fuselage and fin/rudder of Z7015 to the left.

Following the move to the University campus there was a need for more modern airframes to act as teaching aids. Initially fulfilled by the Jet Provost, rear, and the Hunter. All J Oates

Arrival of the fly-by-wire Jaguar at the University, January 1991. Author

Latest in a long line of student teaching aids, the British Aerospace EAP, ZF534. Author

Spitfire Vc AR501 takes off from Old Warden, Bedfordshire. Since its return to flying status it has given pleasure to countless numbers of people. Author

Chapter Fourteen

Brush-Built

Superb view of a Short 184 floatplane, complete with bombs, on the manoeuvring tracks at Loughborough. Such aircraft were dismantled and despatched to their destination by road. via W A Baguley

THE NAME BRUSH is a link with Charles Francis Brush of Cleveland, USA. Brush, like Edison and Swan, was associated with the early years of the electrical industry and among his inventions were the Brush arc lamp and dynamo.

It is believed that moves were made to set up an office in London in 1878. The 'Brush' nomenclature appeared the following year when the Brush Anglo Electric Light Company was established in Lambeth. In the early 1880s, the company played a prominent role at electrical exhibitions, with the new arc lamp being considered a sensational development. Rapid growth followed as the market for the generation and utilisation of electrical energy was exploited. This

growth prompted a merger with the Falcon Engine & Car Works Limited in 1889 and a move into the Falcon Works at Loughborough; this was followed by a change in company name to Brush Electrical Engineering Company Limited.

By this time, products included rotating electrical machines; transformers (first built in 1880); steam trams and locomotives. At the turn of the century, when the horse-drawn omnibus gave way to the electric tram, Brush were again involved, and built trams in large numbers. By 1907 the company had also built the first all metal 'bus. Brush railway locomotives were also to be found all over the world.

Early in 1915 the first Sea Lord of the Admiralty, Winston Churchill, approved a paper for the expansion of the Royal Naval Air Service (RNAS). The result of this expansion was for the required building of naval aircraft and the need for private factories; with high standards of workmanship, to

contribute towards the war effort. Brush was selected as one such factory and went on to build aircraft for both the RNAS and the Royal Flying Corps (RFC).

Initial orders were placed for the production of a number of different types of aircraft, including the Avro 504C, Short 827 seaplane and Maurice Farman S.7 'Longhorn' trainers. Between late 1915 and April 1919 a total of 651 aircraft were built by the firm. This figure would have been increased by several hundred more had not some orders been curtailed due to the ending of the war.

Close to the Falcon Works, Brush were fortunate to have a large expanse of flat ground known as Loughborough Meadows. This land proved to be excellent for flying purposes and was used by the company to flight test many of the newly-built landplanes. On occasion direct delivery flights were also made from what was then regarded as a temporary aerodrome.

Maurice Farman S.7 'Longhorn'

The S.7 was designed to carry out reconnaissance, bombing and training duties but after early use in the First World War in the first of these roles it was relegated solely to the latter duty with the RFC and the RNAS. The S.7's long outriggers soon earned it the nickname 'Longhorn' but many Brush employees called them 'Birdcages'.

An initial contract for 12 was received by Brush and the first of these, 3001, was completed in late 1915. It was officially photographed on the Loughborough Meadows before leaving for Hendon in north west London, for acceptance trials. These aircraft and also a further 20 which were delivered in 1916 were all powered by 70hp Renault engines.

A further 25 'Longhorns' were ordered in 1916 which were to be built from quantities of spares held by two other aircraft contractors, Robey & Co Ltd of Lincoln and Phoenix Dynamo Manufacturing Co of Bradford. When completed, US-designed Curtiss OX engines were installed in these aircraft.

In 1916, inclement weather delayed deliveries to such an extent that purchase of a motor lorry and trailer was considered. As no record of such an acquisition exists, the weather must have improved in the end.

'Longhorns' (and later the Astral and the Avro 504s) were all reputed to have flown from Loughborough Meadows.

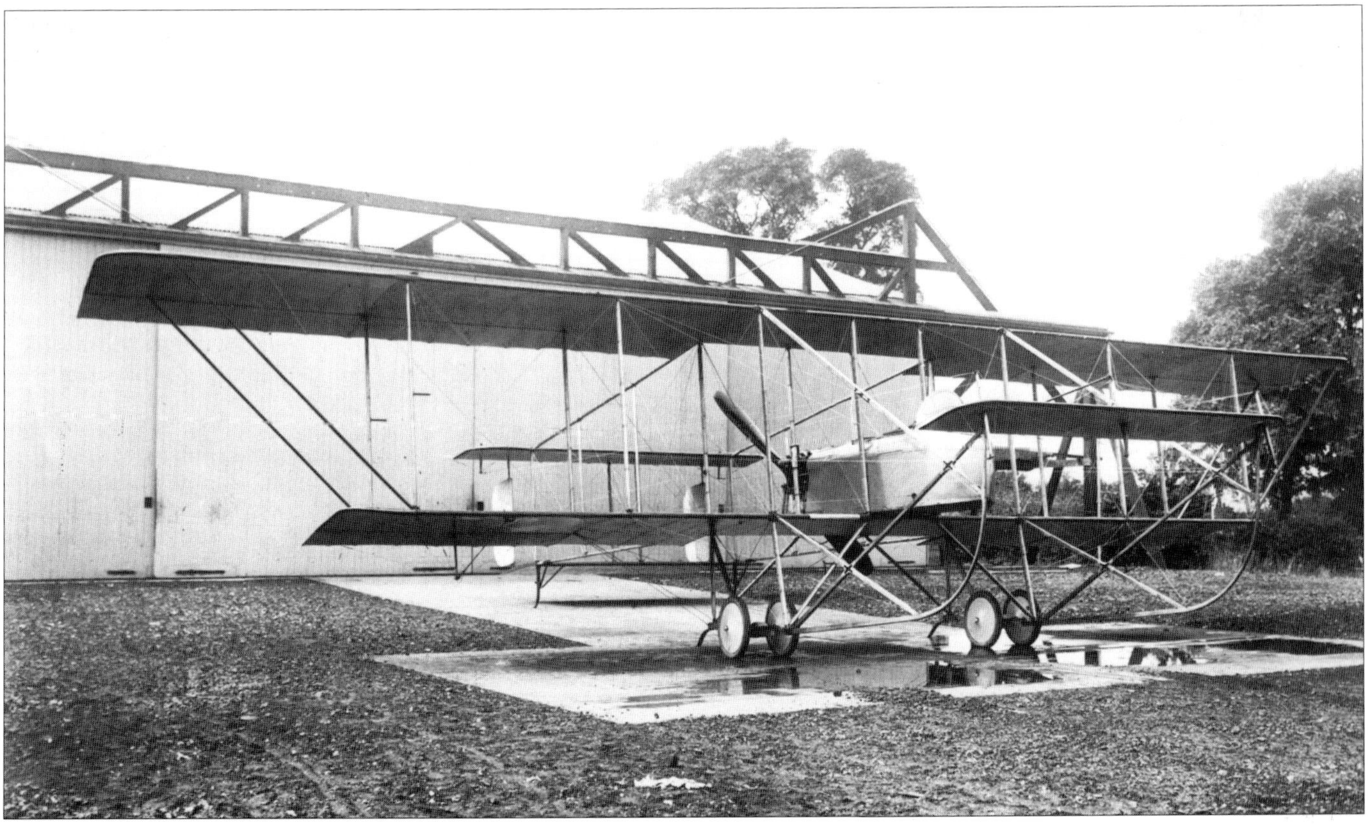

When delivery flights were necessary, the ferry pilot on these occasions is said to have been a Mr Teddy Barrs.

During 1916-1917 the company received two further orders, each of which called for 30 Renault-engined 'Longhorns'. Although the first batch was duly completed, no record has been found of the second.

Avro 504

The Avro 504 biplane first flew in prototype form at Brooklands, Surrey, on 18th September 1913 and was the forerunner of over 8,000 of the type which were to be produced in many versions. Throughout the First World War its many variants gave sterling service and the 504 then went on to have an extended life with the RAF until finally retired in 1933.

The 504 family also proved popular in the civilian market and was extensively flown as a light aircraft in post war years. They earned a considerable reputation as a 'joyriding' aircraft – see Chapter One.

Although most of those built were used as two-seat *ab initio* trainers some early examples saw limited active service in France. Notable amongst the exploits of the Avro 504 was the bombing of the Zeppelin airship sheds at Friedrichshafen on 21st November 1914.

Of the various sub-types of Avro 504 Brush became the only sub-contractor to build the 504C, a single-seater for the RNAS in whose service it was known as the Avro Scout. The 504C was originally designed to combat enemy Zeppelin airship attacks and for this purpose it was equipped with an upward-firing Lewis gun. The type was also suitable for long range reconnaissance work.

The neat lines of the 504C included a fixed fin and a plain, rounded rudder in place of the comma-shaped rudder-only configuration of other models. This new tail became a feature of future Naval models. In all Brush were to build 50 504Cs, all with 80hp Gnome rotary engines.

All of the rest of the Avro 504s built by the company were basic trainer versions. The first contract was for 150 aircraft which

Opposite page:

Brush directors pose with the first aircraft to be delivered, 'Longhorn' 3001.

'Longhorn' 8939, one of a batch of 20 delivered in 1916.

This page:

Avro 504C fuselages awaiting despatch. Note the tramcar body in the background.

Detailed portrait of Avro 504C 3315, complete with single bomb underwing. All via W A Baguley

were delivered as a mixture of 504As, 504Js and 504Ks. Two further orders followed for 100 and 150 aircraft respectively, all to be built as 504Ks. On 9th August 1919 the last contract was reduced by 100 aircraft. All had been delivered by the spring of 1919.

Henri Farman Astral

In 1916 the RNAS had a requirement for a twin-engined bomber and it is understood that representatives visited France to study the possibility of Farman or Nieuport designs fitting the bill. Little is known about any moves towards Nieuport, but a Farman type was built by Brush.

Named Astral, this Henri Farman design was powered by two 100hp Anzani engines. The propellers turned in opposite directions to decrease any tendency to yaw. Photographed on Loughborough Meadows, the finished article bore no markings other than the Brush falcon badge on the nose, although its serial number was 9251. It was sent to Hendon for trials on 12th March 1917 but these proved to be unsuccessful and the order for the remaining nine was cancelled.

Short Seaplanes

Two of this company's designs were built at the Falcon Works, the Types 827 and 184. Brush were only responsible for the construction of 20 of the Type 827 two seat bomber and reconnaissance seaplanes during 1916-1917.

Brush's major contribution to seaborne naval aviation in the First World War was in the building of Type 184s. This aircraft, again a bomber and reconnaissance seaplane, was one of the main types to serve in this role during the war and in many respects can be compared to the Fairey Swordfish of the Second World War. The 184 had an endurance of 2 hours 45 minutes and frequently used up every second of this on long patrols in search of U-boats.

Of the 900 Type 184s built, Brush received orders for 240 but of these only 142 were completed due to cancellations. Construction of the 184s was not without difficulties; varied engine fitments led to complications which, in turn, caused some delay in delivery of finished aircraft. A decision by the Air Board to standardise on the 260hp Sunbeam Maori solved much of this problem.

Following the end of the war, seaplane production was swiftly cut back but it was not until 9th April 1919 that the last Brush-built 184 left the works.

Opposite page:

*One of the many Avro 504Ks built by Brush,
seen on Loughborough Meadows.*
via W A Baguley

*The one and only Henri Farman Astral on
Loughborough Meadows.*
via W A Baguley

Bare bones of a Short Type 184 fuselage.
via W A Baguley

Summary of First World War Production

Maurice Farman	Serial Numbers	Qty	Date
S.7 'Longhorn'	3001 to 3012	12	1915-1916
	8921 to 8940	20	1916
	C9311 to C9335	24	1916
	C4279	1	1916
	N5050 to N5059	30	1916-1917
	N5720 to N5749	30	*see Note 1*
Avro 504C	1467 to 1496	30	1917
	3301 to 3320	20	1917
Avro 504A, 504J and 504K			
	D6251 to D6400	150	1918
Avro 504K	F2233 to F2332	100	1918
	H2946 to H3195	250	*see Note 2*
Henri Farman	9251	1	1917
Astral	9252 to 9260	9	Cancelled
Short Type 827	3321 to 3332	20	1916-1917
Short Type 184	N1660 to N1689	30	1916-1917
	N2630 to N2659	30	1918
	N2790 to N2819	30	1918
	N9060 to N9099	50	1918
	N9260 to N9289	30	*see Note 3*
	N9350 to N9399	50	Cancelled

Notes. 1: No evidence that the final batch of 'Longhorns' was
either completed, or even started. 2: Order reduced to 100 acft,
all delivered by the spring of 1919. 3: Order reduced to 12 acft.

Handley Page Hampden I Overhauls

L4076, L4086, L4144, L4145, L4165, L4170, L4193, L6069, L6089,
L6090. N9096, N9106. P1147, P1158, P1164, P1176, P1177,
P1195, P1196, P1200, P1204, P1219, P1265, P1282, P1291, P1293,
P1298, P1311, P1322, P1339, P1352, P1355, P2073, P2074, P2091,
P2093, P2130, P2145, P4296, P4321, P4401, P4415, P4418, P5311,
P5343. X2905, X2912, X3057, X3061, X3123. AD752, AD754,
AD757, AD758, AD764, AD794, AD829, AD842, AD848, AD850,
AD852, AD857, AD920, AD938, AD961, AD963, AD964, AD968,
AD970, AD973. AE116, AE122, AE123, AE132, AE156, AE192,
AE198, AE201, AE228, AE246, AE248, AE258, AE293, AE309,
AE357, AE366, AE370, AE372, AE375, AE401. AN149. AT147,
AT150, AT152, AT179, AT180, AT182, AT225, AT250.

Notes: L4144 arrived on 14.7.41 from 16 OTU, Upper Heyford,
and was despatched back to them on 30.8.41. It returned from
16 OTU 31.12.41 and returned to them on 30.7.42. It is the only
Hampden documented as coming to Loughborough twice.
Work on L6090 was abandoned on 28.9.43 and scrapped on
site. The following were abandoned on the dates given: 8.12.43
AD852; 16.12.43 AD757, AD764; 20.12.43 P1158, P5311, X2905,
AN149. P2093 is the first documented arrival at Loughborough,
coming in from 50 Squadron at Lindholme on 27.3.41; it was
returned to service on 17.6.41. Last documented aircraft
coming to Loughborough and having work completed on it
was AT225 which came in from 1404 Flight at St Eval on 14.9.43
and returned to service on 24.11.43.

Second World War

With the advent of the Second World war it
was hardly surprising that Brush with their
diverse skills and experience in light metal
fabrication should again become involved
with the war effort, namely in the repair and
eventually the construction of aircraft.

Repair work commenced in 1941, as a
result of sub-contracts being received from
the Derby Locomotive Works for the repair
and overhaul of twin-engined Handley Page
Hampden bombers. Later, similar work
was also undertaken which involved Avro
Lancaster wing sections.

Between March 1941 and December 1943
Brush worked on the Hampden fuselages
brought to the works on 'Queen Mary' trailers. These transporters also brought loads
in other combinations such as centre wing
sections complete with landing gear and
outer wing sections. Another local recipient
of this work, Willowbrook Coachworks, took
delivery of tail sections.

Although the majority of the Hampdens
dealt with by Brush came for major overhaul or refurbishing, several of the 100 aircraft that eventually passed through the
works arrived as a result of enemy action or
flying accidents. (Individual aircraft totalled
99 as L4144 made two visits.)

Only one of the Hampdens received
(L6090) was broken up as being beyond
economical repair. When the type was
withdrawn from service, work on seven
aircraft ceased, although one of these was
later given a further lease of life as an
instructional airframe at RAF Cosford,
Shropshire.

It is believed that all the completed Hampdens were re-assembled at Tollerton, near
Nottingham, by Tollerton Aircraft Services
before being flown by a test pilot from Croydon. When returned to the RAF they usually
went to Operational Training Units although
two put in store were scrapped in February
1943 without seeing further service.

De Havilland Dominie

During 1942 Brush became involved in the
production of the Armstrong Whitworth
Albemarle, a twin-engined bomber which
was to be built from sub-assemblies fabricated by over 1,000 sub-contractors spread
countrywide.

The Loughborough works undertook
production of the nose section and although
some progress was made in this direction
problems arose which saw all work on the
project transferred to MG Motors at Abingdon, Oxfordshire.

This, in all probability, had a bearing on
what transpired with regard to the Dominie,
for it was also in 1942 that the need arose for
production of this aircraft to be transferred
from the de Havilland works at Hatfield,
Hertfordshire, to enable the company to
concentrate on output of Mosquito fighters
and fighter-bombers. Brush had the capacity and the workforce available so a production line was established at the Falcon
Works, thus renewing the company's association with the manufacture of complete
aircraft.

The aircraft which came to be called the
Dominie was designed in late 1933 as a
scaled down twin-engined version of the
DH.86 four-engined airliner. Originally
called the DH.89 Dragon Six and powered
by two 200hp DH Gipsy Six engines, it was
renamed Dragon Rapide in February 1935.
The prototype first flew on 17th April 1934
and was to be followed by over 700 more
during its production run.

Known as the Dominie while in service
with the RAF and the Fleet Air Arm, it was
used for communications (Mk.II) air ambulance and crew training (Mk.I). Some of the
aircraft continued in military use for a considerable time after the end of the war; for
instance some examples served with the
Fleet Air Arm into the late 1950s.

At the Falcon Works no new permanent
buildings were built to house aircraft production during the Second World War
although some temporary wooden structures were erected.

Continued on page 238.

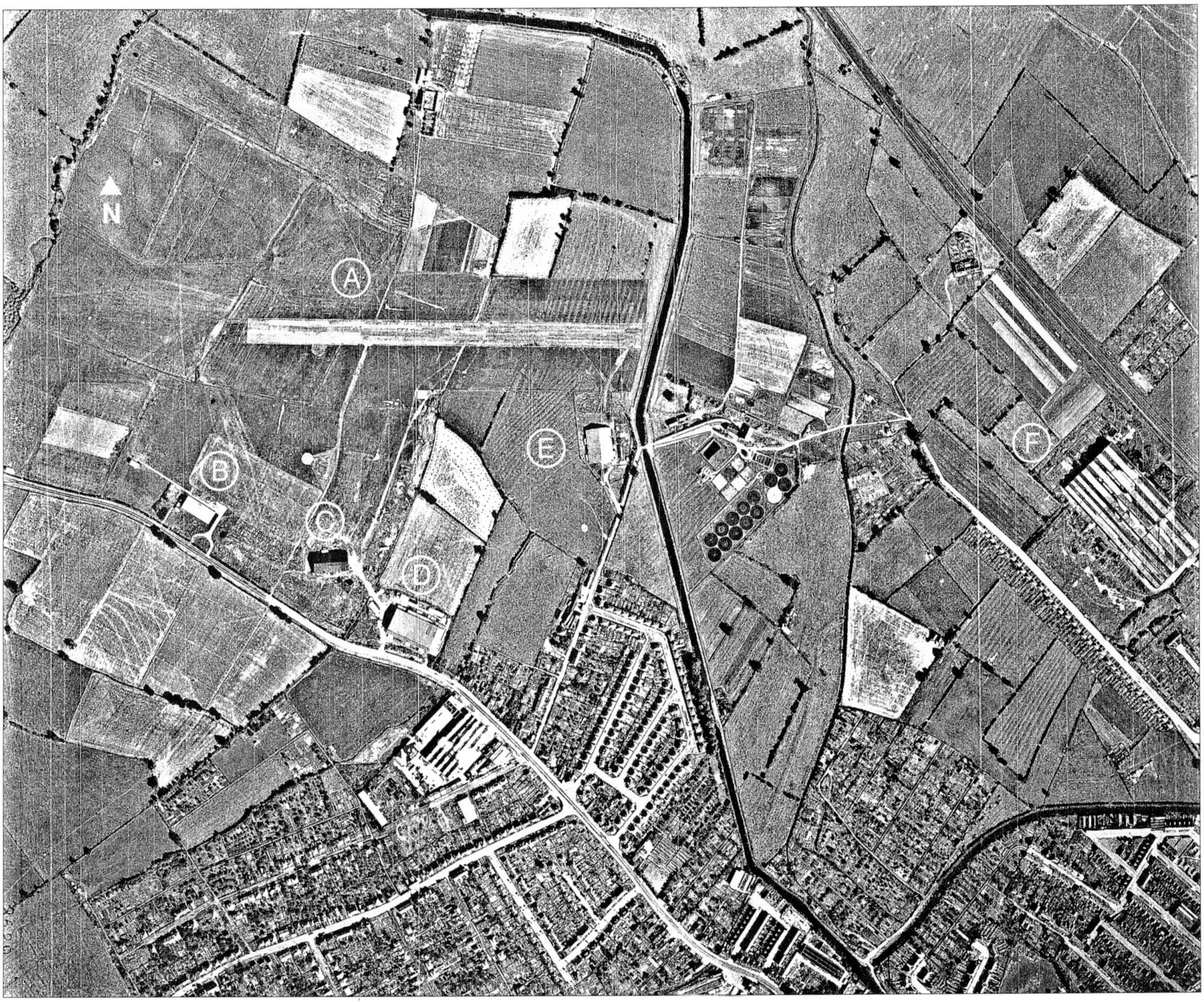

Vertical survey of Loughborough, dated 27th August 1945, taken by a 541 Squadron Spitfire PR.XI. The metalled surface of the east-west runway (A) stands out. The College hangars are (B) and (C) while the Airwork General Trading works is at (D). At least three Bostons can be seen around this area in the original print. The Brush flight shed (E) is close to the runway while the Falcon Works is off to the east at (F). DoE

Lancaster outer wing sections under repair at the Falcon Works. Brush, via Dr Hugh Thomas

A view inside the Falcon Works, showing newly repainted (in primer) Hampden fuselages. Note the purpose-built two-wheeled 'dolly' to help move them around the works. via N Franklin

De Havilland Dominie Mk.I production underway at Loughborough. The aircraft in the foreground, HG719, was accepted at 18MU Dumfries on 1st March 1944 and served the RAF until it was sold off in March 1948. After several operators in the UK, it was last heard of when it was exported to Zaire in late 1964. Brush, via Leicester Museums

Dominie Mk.I NR680 was delivered to de Havillands at Hatfield on 14th August 1944 and served with them and the Royal Aircraft Establishment until being sold off in January 1948 and civilianised as G-AKSC. via Ken Ellis

Many operations which the Dominie entailed were integrated with existing fabrication work alongside the manufacture of buses, airfield crash tenders, night navigation training cars and the usual electrical generating machinery. After the war the 'Aircraft Shops' as they were now referred to remained at the Meadows Lane end of the site and although erected as 'temporary' accommodation only, some of the buildings remained in use well into the 1970s with locomotive construction taking place in them.

Dominies began to leave the Falcon Works in March 1943. From there the fuselage sections were towed tail first through the town, out along the Derby Road (the A6) before turning right into Swingbridge Road. A short distance inside the road an entrance led to a hangar which had been built on the airfield close to the eastern end of the runway. Here Dominies were finally assembled and rigged prior to flight testing and delivery.

Brush received contracts for a total of 455 aircraft but the end of the war led to cancellations which resulted in only 335 being built. Production of Dominies finally ceased and the last Brush-built example left Loughborough airfield in July 1946.

Post war many Dominies, now surplus, were put up for disposal and after conversion found ready customers in airlines and aero clubs worldwide. Today a number of Loughborough-built aircraft still survive; several are still airworthy while others are preserved in museum collections.

Note:

Material in this chapter is adapted from *Brush Aircraft, Production at Loughborough*, (ISBN 0 904597 07 5) by A P Jarram, published by Midland Counties Publications in 1978 and now out of print. Many thanks to the author, Tony Jarram, for his help.

The former HG721 is now preserved as F-BHCD, at the Musée de l'Air at Le Bourget, near Paris. It is shown in the guise that many Dragon Rapides adopted post-war, that of a parachute platform. Author

Still earning its keep is the former HG691 – one of the last Brush-built Dominies. As G-AIYR Classic Lady, Classic Wings conduct pleasure flights out of Duxford, Cambridgeshire, and from their base at Clacton, Essex, in her. via Ken Ellis

Summary of Dominie Production

Serial Nos	Qty	From	To
HG644 to HG674	31	3.43	11.43
HG689 to HG732	44	11.43	4.44
NF847 to NF896	50	4.44	6.44
NF669 to NF701	33	7.44	10.44
NR713 to NR756	44	11.44	1.45
NR769 to NR815	47	1.45	6.45
NR828 to NR853	26	6.45	8.45
RL936 to RL946	11	9.45	3.46
RL947 to RL968*	22	9.45	3.46
RL980 to RL986*	7	9.45	3.46
RL987 to RL999	–	Cancelled	
RM112 to RM158	–	Cancelled	
TX300 to TX319	20	3.46	7.46
TX300 to TX339	–	Cancelled	
TX361 to TX370	–	Cancelled	

All Mk.Is except for Mk.IIs, indicated *

Brush-built Dominies

Serial	TOC*	By
HG644	3.5.43	J Park & Son
HG645	5.3.45	de Havilland, Hatfield
HG646	20.3.43	de Havilland, Hatfield
HG647	1.4.43	de Havilland, Hatfield
HG648	13.5.43	76 MU, Cosford
HG650	3.6.43	76 MU, Cosford
HG651	3.6.43	76 MU, Cosford
HG652	11.6.43	76 MU, Cosford
HG653	23.6.43	76 MU, Cosford
HG654	3.7.43	76 MU, Cosford
HG655	22.7.43	76 MU, Cosford
HG656	23.7.43	76 MU, Cosford
HG657		no record
HG658	23.8.43	76 MU, Cosford
HG659	16.8.43	de Havilland, Hatfield
HG660	13.8.43	de Havilland, Hatfield
HG661	1.9.43	de Havilland, Hatfield
HG662	14.9.43	76 MU, Cosford
HG663	14.9.43	76 MU, Cosford
HG664	2.10.43	76 MU, Cosford
HG665	11.10.43	76 MU, Cosford
HG666	2.10.43	de Havilland, Hatfield
HG667	19.10.43	de Havilland, Hatfield
HG668	7.11.43	de Havilland, Hatfield
HG669	5.11.43	76 MU, Cosford
HG670	15.11.43	76 MU, Cosford
HG671	28.12.43	de Havilland, Hatfield
HG672	23.11.43	76 MU, Cosford
HG673	2.12.43	18 MU, Dumfries
HG674	10.11.43	76 MU, Cosford
HG689	26.11.43	76 MU, Cosford
HG690	11.12.43	18 MU, Dumfries
HG691	11.12.43	18 MU, Dumfries
HG692	13.12.43	18 MU, Dumfries
HG693	4.1.44	18 MU, Dumfries
HG694	28.12.43	18 MU, Dumfries
HG695	10.1.44	76 MU, Cosford
HG696	10.1.44	76 MU, Cosford
HG697	21.1.44	18 MU, Dumfries
HG698	21.1.44	18 MU, Dumfries
HG699	21.1.44	18 MU, Dumfries
HG700	21.1.44	18 MU, Dumfries
HG701	24.1.44	de Havilland, Hatfield
HG702	31.1.44	de Havilland, Hatfield
HG703	1.2.44	de Havilland, Hatfield
HG704	1.2.44	de Havilland, Hatfield
HG705	28.1.44	18 MU, Dumfries
HG706	8.2.44	18 MU, Dumfries
HG707	8.2.44	de Havilland, Hatfield
HG708	8.2.44	18 MU, Dumfries
HG709	15.2.44	18 MU, Dumfries
HG710	8.2.44	de Havilland, Hatfield
HG711	12.2.44	de Havilland, Hatfield
HG712	19.2.44	18 MU, Dumfries
HG713	12.2.44	18 MU, Dumfries
HG714	25.2.44	18 MU, Dumfries
HG715	3.3.44	18 MU, Dumfries
HG716	11.3.44	18 MU, Dumfries
HG717	29.2.44	18 MU, Dumfries
HG718	3.3.44	18 MU, Dumfries
HG719	1.3.44	18 MU, Dumfries
HG720	11.3.44	18 MU, Dumfries
HG721	11.3.44	18 MU, Dumfries
HG722	10.3.44	18 MU, Dumfries
HG723	18.3.44	18 MU, Dumfries
HG724	18.3.44	18 MU, Dumfries
HG725	21.3.44	782 Sqn, Donibristle
HG726	21.3.44	782 Sqn, Donibristle
HG727	22.3.44	782 Sqn, Donibristle
HG728	31.3.44	18 MU, Dumfries
HG729	30.3.44	1 RS, Cranwell
HG730	6.4.44	18 MU, Dumfries
HG731	15.4.44	de Havilland, Hatfield
HG732	12.4.44	76 MU, Cosford
NF847	7.4.44	18 MU, Dumfries
NF848	6.4.44	18 MU, Dumfries
NF849	7..4.44	18 MU, Dumfries
NF850	14.4.44	18 MU, Dumfries
NF851	23.4.44	18 MU, Dumfries
NF852	24.4.44	18 MU, Dumfries
NF853	22.4.44	18 MU, Dumfries
NF854	26.4.44	18 MU, Dumfries
NF855	21.4.44	18 MU, Dumfries
NF856	28.4.44	18 MU, Dumfries
NF857	30.4.44	18 MU, Dumfries
NF858	30.4.44	18 MU, Dumfries
NF859	8.5.44	de Havilland, Hatfield
NF860	5.5.44	18 MU, Dumfries
NF861	8.5.44	18 MU, Dumfries
NF862	11.5.44	18 MU, Dumfries
NF863	11.5.44	18 MU, Dumfries
NF864	9.5.44	18 MU, Dumfries
NF865	12.5.44	18 MU, Dumfries
NF866	15.5.44	18 MU, Dumfries
NF867	15.5.44	18 MU, Dumfries
NF868	18.5.44	18 MU, Dumfries
NF869	22.5.44	18 MU, Dumfries
NF870	22.5.44	18 MU, Dumfries
NF871	23.5.44	18 MU, Dumfries
NF872	20.5.44	18 MU, Dumfries
NF873	26.5.44	18 MU, Dumfries
NF874	30.5.44	18 MU, Dumfries
NF875	26.5.44	18 MU, Dumfries
NF876	30.5.44	de Havilland, Hatfield
NF877	9.6.44	18 MU, Dumfries
NF878	3.6.44	18 MU, Dumfries
NF879	31.5.44	787 Sqn, Wittering
NF880	31.5.44	782 Sqn, Donibristle
NF881	9.6.44	782 Sqn, Donibristle
NF882	9.6.44	4 RS, Madley
NF883	13.6.44	ATA, White Waltham
NF884	13.4.44	13 GCF, Inverness
NF885	14.6.44	4 DF, Clifton
NF886	16.6.44	ATA, White Waltham
NF887	23.7.44	Heston Aircraft Co.
NF888	19.6.44	ATA, White Waltham
NF889	19.6.44	1 RS, Cranwell
NF890	21.6.44	76 MU, Cosford
NF891	24.6.44	76 MU, Cosford
NF892	23.6.44	ADGB, Northolt
NF893	24.6.44	TTC, White Waltham
NF894	29.6.44	TTC, White Waltham
NF895	29.6.44	TTC, White Waltham
NF896	30.6.64	16 GCF, Detling
NR669	4.7.44	18 MU, Dumfries
NR670	7.7.44	18 MU, Dumfries
NR671	7.12.44	de Havilland, Witney
NR672	1.7.44	18 MU, Dumfries
NR673	6.7.44	18 MU, Dumfries
NR674	11.7.44	18 MU, Dumfries
NR675	12.7.44	5 MU, Kemble
NR676	12.7.44	5 MU, Kemble
NR677	15.7.44	18 MU, Dumfries
NR678	17.7.44	1 RS, Cranwell
NR679	17.7.44	18 MU, Dumfries
NR680	14.8.44	de Havilland, Hatfield
NR681	11.8.44	de Havilland, Witney
NR682	–	de Havilland, Witney
NR683	28.7.44	5 MU, Kemble
NR684	28.7.44	5 MU, Kemble
NR685	28.7.44	5 MU, Kemble
NR686	15.8.44	MCS, Hendon
NR687	9.9.44	15 GCS, Speke
NR688	18.8.44	24 Sqn, Hendon
NR689	23.8.44	76 MU, Cosford
NR690	16.9.44	ATA, White Waltham
NR691	23.7.44	ATA, White Waltham
NR692	23.9.44	ATA, White Waltham
NR693	1.12.44	5 MU, Kemble
NR694	29.9.44	76 MU, Cosford
NR695	28.9.44	76 MU, Cosford
NR696	27.9.44	Airwork
NR697	1.10.44	12 (P)AFU, Spittlegate
NR698	6.10.44	5 MU, Kemble
NR699	6.10.44	5 MU, Kemble
NR700	19.10.44	76 MU, Cosford
NR701	17.10.44	5 MU, Kemble
NR713	1.11.44	18 MU, Dumfries
NR714	3.11.44	18 MU, Dumfries
NR715	4.11.44	18 MU, Dumfries
NR716	4.11.44	5 MU, Kemble
NR717	9.11.44	5 MU, Kemble
NR718	6.11.44	5 MU, Kemble
NR719	6.11.44	5 MU, Kemble
NR720	10.11.44	5 MU, Kemble
NR721	15.11.44	5 MU, Kemble
NR722	13.11.44	5 MU, Kemble
NR723	15.11.44	5 MU, Kemble
NR724	15.11.44	5 MU, Kemble
NR725	24.11.44	5 MU, Kemble
NR726	28.11.44	5 MU, Kemble
NR727	1.12.44	5 MU, Kemble
NR728	2.12.44	5 MU, Kemble
NR729	10.1.45	4 RS, Madley
NR730	8.12.44	5 MU, Kemble
NR731	31.12.44	MCS, Hendon
NR732	14.1.45	de Havilland, Witney
NR733	10.1.45	Old Sarum SF
NR734	7.2.45	CCCF, Northolt
NR735	23.11.44	5 MU, Kemble
NR736	15.11.44	5 MU, Kemble

Brush-built Dragon Rapide G-ALAX, the former RL948, was in a silver and blue trim scheme when photographed at East Midlands Airport in April 1967. G-ALAX was last heard of in store in the Andover area in 1987.
Chris Salter

NR737	20.1144	5 MU, Kemble
NR738	7.12.44	de Havilland, Witney
NR739	7.12.44	de Havilland, Witney
NR740	17.1.45	5 MU, Kemble
NR741	14.1.45	18 MU, Dumfries
NR742	10.145	Skaebrae SF
NR743	10.1.45	4 RS, Madley
NR744	14.1.45	de Havilland, Witney
NR745	18.12.44	de Havilland, Witney
NR746	18.12.44	de Havilland, Witney
NR747	12.12.44	de Havilland, Witney
NR748	12.12.44	de Havilland, Witney
NR749	14.1.45	2 RS, Yatesbury
NR750	9.1.45	Halton SF
NR751	14.1.45	18 MU, Dumfries
NR752	14.1.45	18 MU, Dumfries
NR753	14.1.45	18 MU, Dumfries
NR754	17.1.45	18 MU, Dumfries
NR755	17.1.45	18 MU, Dumfries
NR756	19.1.45	18 MU, Dumfries
NR769	20.1.45	18 MU, Dumfries
NR770	14.2.45	de Havilland, Witney
NR771	14.2.45	de Havilland, Witney
NR772	20.2.45	de Havilland, Witney
NR773	20.2.45	de Havilland, Witney
NR774	20.2.45	de Havilland, Witney
NR775	30.1.45	18 MU, Dumfries
NR776	22.2.45	Belgian Air Force
NR777	22.2.45	Belgian Air Force
NR778	15.2.45	18 MU, Dumfries
NR779	20.2.45	18 MU, Dumfries
NR780	27.2.45	de Havilland, Hatfield
NR781	23.2.45	18 MU, Dumfries
NR782	1.3.45	18 MU, Dumfries
NR783	1.3.45	18 MU, Dumfries
NR784	7.3.45	57 OTU, Hawarden
NR785	5.3.45	18 MU, Dumfries
NR786	29.3.45	18 MU, Dumfries
NR787	8.3.45	18 MU, Dumfries
NR788	15.3.45	ATA, White Waltham
NR789	16.3.45	13 GCF, Inverness
NR790	16.3.45	18 MU, Dumfries
NR791	16.3.45	18 MU, Dumfries
NR792	20.3.45	18 MU, Dumfries
NR793	20.3.45	76 MU, Cosford
NR794	23.3.45	Peterhead CF
NR795	26.3.45	Skaebrae SF
NR796	29.3.45	18 MU, Dumfries
NR797	10.4.45	de Havilland, Witney
NR798	10.4.45	de Havilland, Witney
NR799	12.4.45	de Havilland, Witney
NR800	12.4.45	de Havilland, Witney
NR801	18.4.45	de Havilland, Witney
NR802	22.4.45	18 MU, Dumfries
NR803	24.4.45	Talbenny SF
NR804	20.4.45	4 DF, Clifton
NR805	25.4.45	18 MU, Dumfries
NR806	27.4.45	18 MU, Dumfries
NR807	27.4.45	18 MU, Dumfries
NR808	25.5.45	de Havilland, Witney
NR809	7.5.45	80 OTU, Morpeth
NR810	15.5.45	de Havilland, Witney
NR811	18.5.45	de Havilland, Witney
NR812	17.5.45	de Havilland, Witney
NR813	29.5.45	de Havilland, Witney
NR814	31.5.45	de Havilland, Witney
NR815	31.5.45	de Havilland, Witney
NR828	28.5.45	18 MU, Dumfries
NR829	30.5.45	de Havilland, Witney
NR830	18.6.45	de Havilland, Witney
NR831	15.6.45	de Havilland, Witney
NR832	18.6.45	de Havilland, Witney
NR833	13.6.45	de Havilland, Witney
NR834	18.6.45	de Havilland, Witney
NR835	20.6.45	de Havilland, Witney

NR836	21.6.45	de Havilland, Witney
NR837	21.6.45	de Havilland, Witney
NR838	.6.45	de Havilland, Witney
NR839	.46	de Havilland, Witney
NR840	25.7.46	de Havilland, Witney
NR841	20.7.45	de Havilland, Witney
NR842	25.7.45	de Havilland, Witney
NR843	25.7.45	de Havilland, Witney
NR844	28.7.45	de Havilland, Witney
NR845	20.7.45	de Havilland, Witney
NR846	20.7.45	de Havilland, Witney
NR847	3.8.45	de Havilland, Witney
NR848	8.8.45	de Havilland, Witney
NR849	10.8.45	de Havilland, Witney
NR850	14.8.45	de Havilland, Witney
NR851	22.8.45	de Havilland, Witney
NR852	23.8.45	de Havilland, Witney
NR853	31.8.45	de Havilland, Witney
RL936	31.8.45	de Havilland, Witney
RL937	5.9.45	de Havilland, Witney
RL938	12.9.45	de Havilland, Witney
RL939	17.9.45	de Havilland, Witney
RL940	9.10.45	de Havilland, Witney
RL942	30.10.45	de Havilland, Witney
RL943	20.10.45	de Havilland, Witney
RL944	31.10.45	de Havilland, Witney
RL945	13.11.45	de Havilland, Witney
RL946	31.10.45	de Havilland, Witney
RL947	1.1.46	18 MU, Dumfries
RL948	1.1.46	18 MU, Dumfries
RL949	2.1.46	18 MU, Dumfries
RL950	2.1.46	18 MU, Dumfries
RL951	4.2.46	18 MU, Dumfries
RL952	22.12.45	de Havilland, Witney
RL953	2.1.46	de Havilland, Witney
RL954	1.1.46	de Havilland, Witney
RL955	2.1.46	de Havilland, Witney
RL956	2.1.46	de Havilland, Witney
RL957	10.1.46	18 MU, Dumfries
RL958	4.2.46	18 MU, Dumfries
RL959	4.2.46	18 MU, Dumfries
RL960	4.2.46	18 MU, Dumfries
RL961	28.2.46	18 MU, Dumfries
RL962	18.2.46	de Havilland, Witney
RL963	18.2.46	de Havilland, Witney
RL964	18.12.46	de Havilland, Witney
RL965	4.2.46	de Havilland, Witney
RL966	4.2.46	de Havilland, Witney
RL967	11.3.46	18 MU, Dumfries
RL968	11.3.46	18 MU, Dumfries
RL980	11.3.46	18 MU, Dumfries
RL981	5.3.46	18 MU, Dumfries
RL982	21.2.46	de Havilland, Witney
RL983	28.2.46	de Havilland, Witney
RL984	14.5.46	de Havilland, Witney
RL985	14.3.46	de Havilland, Witney
RL986	14.3.46	de Havilland, Witney
TX300	19.3.46	de Havilland, Witney
TX301	19.3.46	de Havilland, Witney
TX302	22.3.46	de Havilland, Witney
TX303	22.3.46	de Havilland, Witney
TX304	28.3.46	de Havilland, Witney
TX305	28.3.46	de Havilland, Witney
TX306	1.4.46	de Havilland, Witney
TX307	1.4.46	de Havilland, Witney
TX308	4.4.46	de Havilland, Witney
TX309	8.4.46	de Havilland, Witney
TX310	7.5.46	de Havilland, Witney
TX311	15.4.46	de Havilland, Witney
TX312	15.4.46	de Havilland, Witney
TX313	7.5.46	de Havilland, Witney
TX314	20.5.46	de Havilland, Witney
TX315	20.5.46	de Havilland, Witney
TX316	28.5.46	de Havilland, Witney
TX317	14.6.46	de Havilland, Witney

TX318	19.6.46	de Havilland, Witney
TX319	2.7.46	de Havilland, Witney

* Research has failed to uncover first flight or despatch dates for Brush Dominies. The date given here is that on which the aircraft was taken on charge (TOC), generally the date when it was accepted at a unit or occasionally when the aircraft was accepted at the point of origin for delivery.

Decode of units and other organisations receiving Dominies from Brush:

ADGB — Air Defence of Great Britain Communications Squadron, Northolt;
Airwork — Contractor, likely base Gatwick;
ATA — Air Transport Auxiliary Headquarters, White Waltham;
CCCF — Coastal Command Communications Flight, Northolt;
Heston Aircraft Co. — Contractor;
JP — J Park & Son. Contractor specialising in packing for overseas shipment;
MCS — Metropolitan Communications Squadron, Hendon;
SF — Station Flight, prefixed by the airfield involved;
TTC — Technical Training Command Communications Flight, White Waltham.
1 RS — No.1 Radio School, Cranwell;
2 RS — No.2 Radio School, Yatesbury;
4 DF — No.4 Delivery Flight, Clifton;
4 RS — No.4 Radio School, Madley;
5 MU — No.5 Maintenance Unit, Kemble;
12 (P)AFU — No.12 (Pilot) Advanced Flying Unit, Spittlegate;
13 GCF — No.13 Group Communications Flight, Inverness;
15 GCF — No.15 Group Communications Flight, Speke;
16 GCF — No.16 Group Communications Flight, Detling;
18 MU — No.18 Maintenance Unit, Dumfries;
24 Sqn — No.24 Squadron, Hendon;
57 OTU — No.57 Operational Training Unit, Hawarden;
76 MU — No.76 Maintenance Unit, Cosford;
80 OTU — No.80 Operational Flight, Morpeth;
782 Sqn — No.782 Squadron, Fleet Air Arm, Donibristle;
787 Sqn — No.787 Squadron, Fleet Air Arm, Wittering.

Examples of surviving, Brush-built Dominies include:

HG691 — Airworthy, Duxford, Cambs as G-AIYR.
HG721 — On display, Musée de l'Air, Le Bourget, France as F-BHCD.
NF865 — Science Museum, Wroughton, Wilts as G-ALXT.
NF869 — Displayed in the Royal Netherlands Air Force Museum, Soesterberg as PH-OTA.
NF875 — Airworthy, Kemble, Glos as G-AGTM.
NR676 — Stored in Denmark, as OY-AAO.
NR743 — Airworthy in South Africa as ZS-JGV.
TX310 — Airworthy, Coventry, Warks as G-AIDL.

The Fleet Air Arm used Dominies in small numbers. HG708, was originally delivered to Dumfries on 8th February 1944. It entered service with 701 Squadron at Lee-on-Solent in April 1945.
Ken Ellis collection

Chapter Fifteen

Market Harborough

Atmospheric view summing up the present state of many former wartime airfields across Britain. Building No.136, the bomb fusing hut, hanging on to a skeletal existence at Market Harborough in the late 1980s. F B Aggas

THE EARLY HISTORY of RAF Market Harborough, often referred to locally as Lubenham, follows a pattern similar in many respects to that set by several of Leicestershire's other wartime airfields. Planned originally as a base for operational bomber units, it was constructed during 1942-1943, the main contractors of the project being J R Mowlem & Co. While work on the site was at an early stage an official visit was made in July 1942 by representatives of 92 Group, Bomber Command, to assess whether the airfield, when completed, would be suitable to house an Operational Training Unit (OTU). Their report proved favourable so, accordingly, RAF Market Harborough became part of 92 Group with effect from 7th August 1942.

Following the arrival of the first detachment of RAF personnel on 1st June 1943 the station was opened up and preparations begun in readiness to receive 14 OTU which was under orders to vacate Cottesmore and Saltby (Chapters Eight and Twenty-Two respectively). Movement of the unit was initially scheduled for early July, but accommodation at the new airfield was insufficiently advanced so the event was postponed for a fortnight. The transfer was eventually accomplished between 28th July and 7th August. A contributory factor to the timespread of the operation was the lack of motor transport available and, in order to complete the movement, ten vehicles had to be borrowed from other units. Even at this stage the WAAF domestic site was incomplete, so temporary accommodation had to be found for most of them at Husbands Bosworth (Chapter Eleven) which had been designated as 14 OTU's satellite airfield.

After day and night flying began in earnest on 16th August, the rural peace was shattered as RAF Market Harborough became yet another of Leicestershire's airfields to experience the constant comings and goings of Vickers Wellingtons, 61 Mk.Ics being on unit strength at this time.

The training syllabus followed a sequence familiar to that of other bomber OTUs – type conversion, circuits and bumps, more

The girls of 'Admin View', officially known as Hut 310-P, 14 OTU, Market Harborough, 1944.

Groundcrew in front of a 14 OTU Wellington, circa 1943. Both via F B Aggas

spite of help from the Desborough crash crew and a National Fire Service detachment, nothing could be done for the bomber's crew of nine, who were all killed.

In addition to the Wellingtons, other types of aircraft were used by 14 OTU for various purposes. An Avro Anson and later Airspeed Oxfords, were used for communication purposes, Miles Martinets and Masters carried out various ancillary training roles, while cine-gunnery – fighter affiliation exercises – were catered for by using Hawker Hurricane IIc fighters.

Before the OTU received their own complement of this latter type of aircraft, affiliation duties were carried out by 1683 Bomber Defence Training (BDT) Flight which was in residence for a time at nearby Bruntingthorpe (Chapter Six). This unit transferred to Market Harborough on 3rd February 1944, and operated from the station until it was disbanded in August of that year. Curtiss Tomahawks equipped the unit when it first arrived, but early in April Hurricanes were also taken on strength. Eventually, the Tomahawks were phased out but for a time, during the middle of the month, six of each type were being operated by the Flight. The main function of the unit remained the same as at Bruntingthorpe; to simulate enemy fighter attack on OTU Wellingtons, thus enabling trainee pilots to practise evasion tactics while the gunners attempted to 'shoot' the attacker down on film. In addition to 14 OTU, the Flight served other units, exercises being regularly carried out for the benefit of 29 OTU, Bruntingthorpe, and 84 OTU, Desborough, and 12 OTU, Chipping Warden, both in Northamptonshire.

The flights at the Husbands Bosworth satellite were detached from the parent unit in June 1944 and used to form the basis of 85 OTU. This split also meant a change of status for 14 OTU and from the 16th of the month it was reclassified as a 'three-quarter' OTU.

Often the daily routine of an RAF camp in wartime was enlivened by incidents of a very diverse nature and in this respect Market Harborough had a share, as is shown by the accounts which follow.

A 'classic cops and robbers' scene was enacted on 26th July 1944, when armed car thieves in a stolen Vauxhall, careered through the station. They smashed their way out through a fence and disappeared into the fields to the north. Although civil

circuits and bumps, then exercises – day and night cross country, navigation, fighter affiliation, night bombing, 'Bullseye', 'Nickels' and, to add some variation to the never ending round – ground instruction, lectures, visits to the bombing teacher, Link and turret trainers, dinghy drill, both wet and dry and so on until at the end of the course a successful crew emerged competent and ready to pass on for further training, usually with a Heavy Conversion Unit.

From December 1943 the OTU began to dispose of its weary Mk.Ics and receive, as was usual, Mk.Xs as replacements. It took until May 1944 before the transition to this variant was complete and No.87 course was the first to be wholly trained, by the unit, on this type.

It would be nice to note that following the

change of aircraft a significant improvement in the accident rate occurred, but this was not the case and 14 OTU's record while at Market Harborough was at no time exemplary. In fact a stint of duty for the station crash crew was often quite hectic as many accidents, both major and minor, happened. In addition, frequent calls were made for them to assist at incidents away from the station, which often took them over the borders into neighbouring counties. One tragic accident of this nature concerned Short Stirling III EE956 of 1661 HCU, Winthorpe, Nottinghamshire, which crashed into a quarry near Kelmarsh, Northamptonshire, at 23:55 hours, on 17th May 1944. When the crash tender reached the scene it was found that the quarry was so deep that it was impossible to reach the aircraft and in

Vertical survey view of Market Harborough, dated 10th August 1945. The control tower, signals square and airfield denominator 'MB' (now site of the maximum security prison) are at (A). The northern taxi track (B) is now largely the course of the Foxton to Great Bowden minor road. To the north is the Grand Union Canal (C) and to the south-west is the *village of Lubenham (D). Straggling at (E) is the bomb dump.* DoE

A former officer, who shall be nameless, also recalled an embarrassing duty during an evening stint as Orderly Officer. Accompanied by his WAAF counterpart a tour was made of haystacks close to the base to clear away airmen and airwomen. This followed a complaint from a local farmer that his haystacks were taking on a mushroom-like appearance because so much had been pulled from the bottoms for the offending parties to lie on!

Apart from heralding in the New Year, 1st January 1945 was also a red letter day for 14 OTU. His Majesty King George VI approved the award of the unit's own distinctive badge. The central motif was a hound's head superimposed on a hunting horn and riding whip and crop with the motto 'Keep Up With The Pack' at its base.

RAF Market Harborough – 1st December 1944

Latitude	52° 29' 30" N
Longitude	00° 57' 00" W
Height at Sea Level	360ft
Locality	2 miles NW of Market Harborough
Command	Bomber (RAF)
Nearest Railway Station	Market Harborough, LMS (3 miles)
Function	Operational Training Unit (Parent)
Affiliated Airfields	Nil

Landing Area – Runways

QDM	Dimensions	Extensibility	Remarks
180°	1,400 x 50 yards	1,600 yards	Entails
140°	1,900 x 50 yards	2,000 yards	diversion of
290°	1,400 x 50 yards	1,400 yards	Roman road.

Type of Surface – Concrete.

Permanent Landmarks

By Day	Town of Market Harborough
By Night	Rugby Wireless Masts 17 miles SW of airfield.

Permanent Obstructions Nil

Facilities

Airfield Lightning	Mk.II
Beam Approach	–
Radio	–
QDM	–
Flying Control	Yes

Accommodation   All buildings temporary.

Technical	Hangars		Hardstandings	
	Type	No	Type	No
	T2	4	Loop	11
	B1	1	Spectacle	48
Domestic	Officers	SNCOs	ORs	Total
RAF	171	628	892	1,691
WAAF	10	15	427	452

police gave chase they failed to apprehend the suspects and the car was later found abandoned near the Grand Union Canal.

On 10th May 1945, Flying Officer G M Buchanan was taxying his Hurricane IIc, MW341, along the perimeter track when he experienced braking problems and overran a small van driven by LACW E Huntsman. The Hurricane's propeller sliced through the van and entered the cab, narrowly missing the occupant. She was extricated from the vehicle and taken to the station sick quarters in a state of shock, but suffering from physical injuries no greater than bruising of the right, lower ribs. This near miraculous escape makes one wonder if the WAAF involved still occasionally has nightmares about the event.

On occasions aircrew also deviated from routine, as recalled by Les Pooley, a former air gunner. It was noticed, while on one of his training trips, that the Italian Prisoners of War working in the fields directly under the

Formal grouping inside the Warrant Officers and Sergeants Mess, 14 OTU, Market Harborough. The fireplace on the right was built by Italian PoWs.

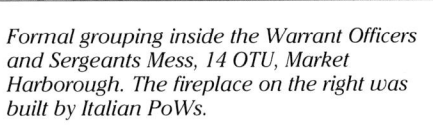

The Warrant Officers and Sergeants Mess in recent times, a sheep pen! The fireplace can just be discerned at the right.
Both via F B Aggas

runway approach would often shake their fists as the aircraft passed overhead. Next time out, assorted brickbats were loaded into their Wellingtons and at a signal from the bomb aimer, bottles, bricks and pieces of wood made a rapid exit through various hatches. After several of these 'missions' it was noted that the rain of debris had had the desired effect and the Italians were seen to lie face down, covering their heads with their hands, whenever an aircraft approached.

After the war in Europe ended in May 1945, it was inevitable that cutbacks of certain types of training units would follow. The axe fell swiftly on 14 OTU and on 26th June 1945 it was amongst the first of the bomber OTUs to be disbanded. A rapid rundown of the station then began, with both aircraft and personnel leaving at a steady rate. Records compiled show that while at Market Harborough the output of trained personnel from 14 OTU was 516 pilots, 484 navigators, 480 bomb aimers, 497 wireless operator/airgunners and 931 air gunners. To achieve these totals flying took place on 510 days and 372 nights during which 45,835 flying hours were amassed. In the course of training exercises 61 aircrew lost their lives.

On 1st July the station was transferred to 91 Group, Bomber Command. Not that this meant a return to bomber crew training was imminent; on the contrary, the base became a temporary satellite of No.1333 (TS)CU – (Transport Support) Conversion Unit, Leicester East (Chapter Twelve) and Douglas Dakotas of that unit used the airfield for approximately a month from 17th July, for circuit training. Market Harborough closed as an active airfield on 18th August and from that date was reduced to care and maintenance.

No.54 Group, Flying Training Command became the next custodian of the station on 20th August, but again the change brought no resident flying units. Instead, on 21st August 26 Aircrew Holding Unit was formed there. Its purpose was to accommodate redundant aircrew on the strength of 7 Personnel Reception Centre, Harrogate, Yorkshire, until such a time as they could be found alternative employment within the forces or were demobilised. This unit had a rather brief existence and was disbanded on 15th November.

The airfield next became 113 Sub Storage Site (SSS), an offshoot of 273 Maintenance Unit, Polebrook, Northamptonshire, in February 1946. This did result in aircraft once more being seen on the airfield as it was used for the storage and dismantling of Airspeed Horsa assault gliders and Miles aircraft such as the Queen Martinet, a radio controlled pilotless target version of the single-engined Martinet, and Monitor twin-engined target tugs.

Only 20 of this latter type of aircraft were built and as ten of these never saw service it is thought these were the examples which came to Market Harborough. Following a period of storage the Monitors were overhauled and over a six week period made return flights to the Miles company airfield at Woodley, Berkshire. This seems to have been a rather futile exercise for all were subsequently broken up and scrapped.

No.21 Group, Flying Training Command became responsible for the station on 15th June 1946, but it meant no change in status. After the personnel of 113 SSS were withdrawn on 28th April 1947, the station closed. At that time, 62 Horsas still remained on the site but these were later removed to 6 Maintenance Unit, Brize Norton, Oxfordshire.

In 1948 the Army took over the station and it became known as 72 BVD (Brigade Vehicle Depot), Royal Army Ordnance Corps. Hundreds of surplus War Department vehicles of all descriptions were then delivered to the airfield where they were stored pending disposal. Eventually, many of them found a ready sale onto the transport starved market of post-war Britain, via one of the frequent auction sales held at the camp. As the years passed these vast surplus stocks ran down and the Army vacated Market Harborough in the late 1950s. While the Army occupied the airfield some of the land was leased for farming and this policy was continued and increased after they left.

By the early 1960s the runways and other concrete areas had begun to deteriorate and there appeared little prospect that Market Harborough would ever be used as an airfield again. Even the remote possibility of this happening was finally settled on 30th January 1961 when it was announced that the Home Secretary had approved the site for the building of a new closed prison. As is usual following a controversial decision such as this, protests were made and meetings held, but to no avail; the project went ahead on the 95 acres reserved for the purpose. Built at a cost of £1,000,000, by Lavender, McMillan (Contractors) Limited, of Worcester Park, Surrey, Gartree Prison, as it is now called, opened during the first week of April 1966. Accommodation for both prisoners and staff now occupies what was once the RAF Station technical site.

Aftermath of the contretemps between a Hurricane and a Ford Utility at Market Harborough, 10th May 1945. The WAAF driving the Ford had an incredible escape. via F B Aggas

One of the stored Miles Monitor TT.Is (NP418) undergoing servicing prior to despatch to Woodley. G Bedding via Julian Temple

Where possible all of the airfield land not occupied by the prison has now reverted to agriculture, only one third width sections of the runways and perimeter track remain in place as access roads. The missing areas of concrete were removed during the early 1960s and converted into hardcore for use in civil engineering projects such as the Crick-Lutterworth section of the M1 motorway.

Most of the camp's domestic and communal sites, situated to the west of the Lubenham to Foxton road, are now derelict. When their service life was over several were used to provide temporary homes for displaced persons, many of Polish origin, but now in most cases, little remains to show they ever existed. Several buildings of note are still to be seen on what was once No.2 Communal Site, an area which is now part of Chapel Farm. Close to the road is the former gymnasium and chapel, which gave the farm its name, now used as a store and to house farm animals. Also on the same site, clinging to a tenuous existence, is the one time sergeants mess.

Further into the site, along a private road, is a building which once housed the station standby set, a self-contained generating plant to be used in the event of a failure of the main electricity supply. This building now serves an entirely different purpose which is probably unique on former RAF airfield sites. Known as the 'Fortress Works' it has been converted to become the business premises and home of the owner J R Burbidge. A little further along the Lubenham-Foxton road is a recently-established livestock market. This stands on what was once No. 3 WAAF Site but apart from a solitary air raid shelter all trace of this has now disappeared.

To give easier access to the prison, and Foxton village from the A6, a new road was laid which closely followed, for much of its distance, the line previously taken by a large section of the old perimeter track. On a slight rise, a few yards from this road, in what was the north east corner of the airfield is another very interesting wartime relic. At first glance it appears to be a military pill box of very low profile, but it was the station battle headquarters intended to serve as a control centre in the event of emergency such as imminent arrival of enemy airborne troops. The reason it still survives, in splendid isolation, is probably due to the fact that it is heavily constructed of reinforced concrete and descends on two levels approximately 20ft below the ground.

Whether further relics of interest to aviation archaeologists still exist within the boundaries of the prison is doubtful, but in any case unauthorised close scrutiny of a penal establishment of any type is not advised. (Because of the sensitive nature of the prison, no contemporary air-to-ground views of the former will be illustrated here.)

Although it had long ceased to be an airfield there was one very brief aeronautical interlude at Market Harborough on 10th December 1987 during the course of a daring jailbreak. A Bell 206L Long Ranger helicopter, hired ostensibly for a business trip, was hijacked at gunpoint when near Market Harborough and the pilot ordered to fly to Gartree Prison. After circling the prison three times the pilot was directed to land on the all weather football pitch inside the jail's perimeter fence. While other inmates formed a human barrier keeping prison officers back, two convicts dashed out and boarded the helicopter. Thirty seconds after landing the helicopter was airborne again heading towards Market Harborough. It landed near an industrial estate on the outskirts of the town where the fugitives left the aircraft and commandeered first a van and then a car in which they made good their escape. It is probably an episode best forgotten by the prison service.

Over the years developers have become interested in many of Leicestershire's former airfields. Market Harborough is no exception. Recent proposals concern some 200 acres of Airfield Farm which borders the A6 and Foxton Road. Plans include 70 to 80 acres to be established as a permanent home for Leicestershire County Show with the remainder being allocated for a mix of office, industrial and leisure use. Should they eventually favour the developers plans then the outcome can be no worse than has been the fate of several of the counties other old airfields.

Market Harborough-based Units and Aircraft

No.14 Operational Training Unit

From 1.8.43 to 24.6.45   Codes 'AM-', 'GL-', 'VB-'.

Vickers Wellington Ic   L7897, N2858, R1669, T2738, T2739, T2914, W5688 'O', W5716, X3196, X9680, X9823, X9871, X9874, X9945, X9949 'F', Z1075, Z1169 'J', AD594, AD600, DV431, DV432, DV435, DV479, DV486, DV494, DV596, DV666, DV668, DV697, DV719, DV730, DV780, DV822, DV823, DV839 'D', DV891, DV897, DV898, DV917, DV953, HD943, HD945, HD946, HD983, HD990.

Vickers Wellington III   BK145, DF625.

Vickers Wellington X   HE277, HE301, HE579, HE587, HE705, HE846, HE918, HE978, HF484 'B', HF541 'Y', HF599 'T'. HZ479, JA132, JA349, JA475, JA498, LN169, LN235 'O', LN281, LN394, LN399 'F', LN428, LN457, LN458, LN459, LN509, LN510, LN511, LN555, LN600, LN637, LN649, LN654 'X', LN655 'P', LN675 'Y', LN689, LN697, LN701, LN709, LN739, LN758, LN838 'R', LN876, LN911, LN933 'H', LN934 'C', LN935 'U', LN936, LN948 'Y', LN971 'B', LN973 'S', LN986, LP151 'D', LP169, LP176, LP308, LP312, LP346, LP462, LP498, LP504, LP506 'W', LP513, LP553, LP598, LP600, LP627, LP866, LP867, LR124, LR125, LR126, LR138, LR139, ME883, ME978 'J', MF115, MF424, MF425, MF439, MF441, MF514 'S', MF518, MF529 'X', MF533, MF561, MF562, MF563, NA796, NA620, NA621, NC728, NC729, NC732.

Airspeed Oxford I   NM767. PH122.

Hawker Hurricane IIc   MW341, MW354, MW373. PG513, PG523.

Miles Martinet TT.I   HN864, HP434, HP435, HP436, HP522 'AM-B', HP523, HP524, JN596, MS901.

Miles Master II   DL840.

No.1683 Bomber Defence Training Flight (14 OTU)

From 3.2.44 to 1.8.44
(* Aircraft marked thus were later transferred to 14 OTU)

Curtiss Tomahawk I   AH753, AH775, AH836, AH853, AH882, AH899, AH929*, AK101, AK116, AK136*, AK190*, AK276.

Hawker Hurricane IIc   LF741, LF744, LF746, LF750, LF755. MW341*.

No.26 Aircrew Holding Unit

From 21.8.45 to 15.11.45

No.113 Sub Storage Site (273 MU)

From .2.46 to 28.4.47   Storage and/or dismantling.
Airspeed Horsa, Miles Queen Martinet and Miles Monitor

The Gymnasium and Chancel on No.2 Communal site. F B Aggas

Serious Accidents to Mkt Harboro'-based A/cft

3.8.43   Wellington Ic   DV823   14 OTU
Engine cut, crash landing made at Langar, Notts.

16.9.43   Wellington Ic   L7897   14 OTU
Starboard engine cut; aircraft crashed and caught fire in forced landing two miles south of Husbands Bosworth.

16.9.43   Wellington Ic   DV479   14 OTU
Bounced on landing, attempted overshoot, but sank back and belly-landed near Welford, Northants.

26.9.43   Wellington Ic   DV697   14 OTU
Port engine failed on final approach to land at Husbands Bosworth. Aircraft damaged beyond repair, four killed.

22.10.43   Wellington Ic   W5688 'O'   14 OTU
Aircraft was returning from bombing range and when in vicinity of Husbands Bosworth airfield it dived into the ground from 1,500ft. All five crew killed. Written off.

24.10.43   Wellington Ic   DV839 'D'   14 OTU
Control difficulty encountered during descent through cloud to check position. Aircraft came out in shallow dive and crashed near Wittering. Four killed.

24.11.43   Wellington Ic   DV435   14 OTU
Crashed in Derbyshire, while on a 'Bullseye' exercise. Crew baled out and landed safely, except for an air gunner who was killed.

25.11.43   Wellington Ic   X9680   14 OTU
Crashed at Orton four miles south of Desborough. One crew member killed, rest admitted to hospital.

20.12.43   Wellington Ic   X9823   14 OTU
After crew had baled out, aircraft crashed on airfield under construction 2½ miles south west of Folkingham.

20.12.43   Wellington Ic   HD983   14 OTU
Port engine failed, made belly-landing at Desborough.

21.12.43   Wellington Ic   T2738   14 OTU
Lost propeller, belly landed at base.

2.1.44   Wellington Ic   Z1169 'J'   14 OTU
Starboard engine failed and aircraft crashed at Upper Middleton Lodge, Northants. Crew bailed out safely.

24.1.44   Wellington X   LN948 'Y'   14 OTU
Starboard engine and wing caught fire, pilot made an unsuc-cessful belly-landing at Braybrooke, Northants. The aircraft was written off, three crew killed, three seriously injured.

4.2.44   Tomahawk I   AH899   1683 BDTF
Crashed in emergency landing at Market Harborough.

19.2.44   Tomahawk I   AH929   1683 BDTF
Crashed in emergency landing at Harrington.

24.2.44   Wellington Ic   DV668   14 OTU
Caught fire while unoccupied on a dispersal at Market Harborough. Despite efforts of both fire tenders aircraft burnt out and destroyed.

2.3.44   Wellington Ic   DV719   14 OTU
Port engine failed seven minutes after take-off, aircraft crashed at Weston by Welland, Northants. No casualties. Written off.

19.3.44   Wellington Ic   X9949 'F'   14 OTU
Engines cut due to misuse of fuel cocks, aircraft crashed at Oxenden (?), rear gunner killed. Written off.

27.3.44   Wellington Ic   R1669   14 OTU
Crashed on approach to Market Harborough. Flight Sergeant Ferguson and crew all killed.

28.3.44   Tomahawk I   AH853   1683 BDTF
Damaged beyond repair.

28.5.44   Wellington Ic   HE846   14 OTU
Engine failure; crashed on runway at Bruntingthorpe. Five crew injured. Written off.

1.7.44   Wellington X   LN689   14 OTU
After port engine failure pilot attempted forced landing in field two miles west of Clipston, but hit tree with port wing and crashed. All crew, except pilot injured, one fatally.

13.7.44   Wellington Xs   LN509 and LP627   14 OTU
Collided while flying in formation near East Farndon, Northants. Both crashed and written off. Four crew killed.

1.8.44   Wellington X   LN511   14 OTU
When overshooting, starboard engine failed. Pilot could not hold height and forced landed in field half mile north north east of Church Langton, Leicestershire. Aircraft touched down and then struck tree. Crew all injured. Written off.

13.8.44   Wellington X   LN281   14 OTU
Attempted forced landing in field four miles north of Melton Mowbray airfield, but aircraft blew up on impact and was finally destroyed by fire. Seven crew killed, one seriously injured.

17.8.44   Wellington X   LN 600   14 OTU
Overshot when landing at night at Market Harborough.

30.8.44   Wellington X   LN 394   14 OTU
Collided with a high voltage electricity pylon and crashed near the railway sidings south east of Welham, Leicestershire. Five killed, rear gunner survived but was injured.

8.9.44   Wellington X   MF562   14 OTU
Aircraft was returning from a night cross-country exercise when it suddenly dived into the ground at high speed and at a steep angle, half mile east of Keyham, Leicestershire. Eight killed.

11.9.44   Wellington X   MF425   14 OTU
Engine cut on approach, overshot landing.

11.9.44   Wellington X   MF439   14 OTU
Damaged beyond repair in accident.

21.9.44   Wellington X   LN876   14 OTU
While circling airfield starboard engine lost all power, pilot feathered prop and jettisoned petrol but could not maintain height. Sight of the airfield was lost in poor visibility so forced landed in field and crashed through hedge near Thedding-worth, Leicestershire. Jettison switch was not in 'off' position and fire broke out which destroyed the aircraft. No casualties.

12.10.44   Wellington X   JA475   14 OTU
Aircraft was on solo cross country when it dived almost vertically into the ground half mile South of Guilsborough Church, Coton, Northants. All crew of six killed. Believed due to thunderstorm.

16.10.44   Wellington X   MF518   14 OTU
Pilot carrying out solo circuits and bumps following dual instruction. Seen to climb away safely but crashed shortly afterwards at Marston Trussell, Northampton. All six crew killed.

20.11.44   Wellington X   LN428   14 OTU
Aircraft was on a cross-country flight when it crashed in flames near the Red House Inn, Lilleshall, Shropshire. Five crew killed.

20.11.44   Wellington X   HF484 'B'   14 OTU
Forced landed in heavy rain at Farnborough, overshot runway and hit obstruction. No casualties. Aircraft written off.

31.12.44   Wellington X   LN973   14 OTU
On a check dual exercise prior to practice bombing, aircraft made normal circuit and approach but belly-landed on runway and caught fire. No casualties. Written off.

3.2.45   Wellington X   LN838   14 OTU
Crashed near Flore, between Daventry and Northampton when returning from cross-country navigation exercise. All crew killed.

5.2.45   Wellington X   ME978 'J'   14 OTU
Aircraft got out of control and crashed at Blease Farm, Knutsford, Cheshire, after crew baled out. One crew member was killed.

10.5.45   Hurricane II   MW341   1683 BDTF
Taxied into van, Market Harborough. Became instructional airframe 5311M.

A group of personnel from the 14 OTU MT Section. F B Aggas

Top left: *Buildings on the former airfield at Market Harborough in the late 1980s include the Stand-by Set House on No.2 Communal site. Now, much modified, it is the home of Mr and Mrs Burbidge.*

Top right: *The Battle Headquarters, another survivor, offered 360° viewing through the observation slit. In the foreground is the emergency exit to the underground rooms.*

Left and below: *One of the buildings on the Chapel Farm communal site, the former Building 161, the Airmen's showers, ablutions and gas decontamination centre.* All Author

Chapter Sixteen

Melton Mowbray

L ANDING GROUNDS and airfields have, at various times existed to the north, west and south of this town. The association with powered flight goes back to the pioneer days of aviation and the *Daily Mail* 'Circuit of Britain' air race in 1911. An account of this has been given in Chapter One.

During the First World War several landing grounds were set up in Leicestershire for the use of 38 (Home Defence) Squadron, Royal Flying Corps. Two of them were in the vicinity of Melton Mowbray. The first was at Brentingby on a 30 acre site located between the village and Gravel Hole Spinney. It was only used for a short time during 1916 as a night landing ground and later in the year it was closed in favour of a much larger site to the north of Melton.

Called Scalford, this landing ground was actually very much nearer to Melton Mowbray than the village after which it was named. Situated off the A606 Nottingham Road opposite Sysonby Lodge Farm this landing ground became one of the largest in Leicestershire during the First World War. Although the area was said officially to be 45 acres it did in fact measure closer to 60. Initially designated a night landing ground, as had been Brentingby, a major factor which in all probability influenced the change and choice of site was the movement of 38 Squadron headquarters from Castle Bromwich, Warwickshire, in October 1916 to a new home on Scalford Road, Melton Mowbray. Therefore, the use of a landing ground in close proximity to

For security purposes, photographs of Thor IRBM sites were almost always at night, therefore concealing vital details. This could well be any of the bases converted to take the nuclear-tipped missiles, but is perfectly representative of the final role that Melton Mowbray played out for the RAF.
Ken Ellis collection

unit headquarters would be of great value for communication and liaison purposes, especially as the three Flight Stations of the squadron were some distance away in Lincolnshire.

The field was used by the squadron from late 1916 until the unit departed for a tour of duty in France in May 1918. To fill the gap left by this move, 90 Squadron was formed at

Founder members of the Leicestershire Flying Pou Club, which later became the County Flying Club. Left to right: Doree, Fraser, Farrell, Harris, Hall, Miss B Peberdy (later Mrs K F Tunnicliffe), A H Rawnsley, K F Tunnicliffe; remainder unknown. V Doree

LFPC's Flea fuselage at Frog Island, Leicester. V Doree

J S Squires in the cockpit of his Flea G-AEIO. This machine beat the LFPC's example into the air. J S Squires

Buckminster and this unit assumed responsibility for Scalford until it was closed down following the German capitulation. (See Chapter One for details of First World War landing grounds.)

In the early 1930s Brentingby again returned to the aviation scene. The area gained a new lease of life when the landing ground was re-established. For a time it became part of Register of Temporary Landing Grounds set up under the auspices of the Aviation Department of the Automobile Association. These landing grounds were an attempt to overcome a shortage of airfields which existed in many locations throughout Britain at this time.

It is probably true to say that Henri Mignet, a Frenchman, was responsible, in a way, for an area close to Melton Mowbray being used for flying activities. In 1933 he first flew an aircraft of his own design which was completely unorthodox in most aspects. Mignet had been developing a series of light aircraft that he called 'alternative aviation' while looking for an aircraft that could afforded, built and flown by the man-in-the-street within minimum intervention from others, especially the authorities! He went on record as saying that all that was required to build his aircraft, which he called the Pou du Ciel, or Flying Flea, was a rudimentary knowledge of carpentry and metalwork, approximately £20 for materials plus a further sum for the purchase of a suitable engine. Following demonstrations by Mignet in England the flood gates opened and a spate of Flea homebuilding swept the country. Caught up in this wave of instant aviation were a group of enthusiasts in Leicester who met and formed the Leicestershire Flying Pou Club for the purposes of building their own Flea.

The club's aircraft was acquired in kit form and built in premises on Frog Island near Leicester city centre. While building was in progress, thought was given to obtaining a site from which to fly; first steps taken in this direction centred on Braunstone Airport, but when enquiries were made a negative answer was received. Eventually, in the spring of 1936, a large field of suitable area was found off Sandy Lane, near Melton Mowbray, and for a nominal sum permission was granted for it to be used as a flying ground.

By now the Flea was nearing completion but as yet lacked an engine and due to a financial crisis within the club no funds were available to purchase one. To overcome this difficulty an enterprising committee member, Harry Rawnsley, suggested that the club hold a flying display at their Sandy Lane field, charge spectators for admission and thereby, hopefully, alleviate the cash problem. The idea found immediate favour with the members and plans were formulated which included invitations being sent to Stephen Villiers Appleby and Robert Kronfeld, both of whom were prominent exponents of the day in the field of ultra-light aviation, to attend and demonstrate their aircraft.

Prior to the show a wooden hangar, 50ft by 30ft was acquired and thanks to energetic teamwork by club members on 27th April 1936 it was completely erected at Sandy Lane on that day.

On the date set for the show, 3rd May, the day dawned fine and the weather turned out to be perfect. Appleby gave a fine demonstration in his Flea but the great attraction proved to be Kronfeld's Drone; additionally the arrival of several visiting aircraft from other clubs helped to add interest. Amongst the latter was another Flea (G-AEEC) flown by a young man named Bernard Collins who was later to become manager and chief flying instructor at Rearsby Aerodrome. His flight from Heston to Melton, a distance of 87 miles, was covered in approximately 2½ hours and at that time constituted a Flea record.

For two other visitors, a Mr Peach and his son, from Stoke-on-Trent the event proved even more memorable in a totally different way. They had flown in for the event in a North Staffs Aero Club Miles Hawk two-seater monoplane and after the display while taking off to return to Meir, Staffordshire, their machine crashed. It had been noted that prior to take-off no attempt had been made to warm up the engine and that it was firing unevenly. When the aircraft had reached a height of about ten feet it stalled, a wing tip touched the ground and the machine turned over. Thankfully both occupants were able to crawl from the wreckage with only minor cuts and bruises.

Financially the show proved a great success for the club and the gate receipts from the spectators, who numbered in the region of 2,400, amply justified the members' efforts. Indirectly the display also had an unexpected effect on the future of the club; member's enthusiasm and enterprise so impressed one distinguished visitor, Mr Lindsay Everard (later Sir Lindsay), President of Leicestershire Aero Club, that he agreed to become President of the Leicestershire Flying Pou Club also. Furthermore after commenting that he saw little future in the Flea as a club aircraft, he suggested the Kronfeld Drone as an alternative and offered to help the club to obtain one. Needless

to say his offer was accepted with alacrity and being the great benefactor that he undoubtedly was Sir Lindsay was not only instrumental in the club receiving the Drone but a Kronfeld Ground Trainer in addition.

The club's Flea was eventually completed but the rather dubious honour of being the first Leicestershire-built Pou to fly fell to another machine which was constructed by a club member from Barrow on Soar, J S 'Steve' Squires. Costing £110, inclusive of £60 for the engine, this Flea (G-AEIO) was built in the Squires' garage on South Street, the builder following instructions contained in a step-by-step do it yourself manual, the last pages of which carried directions on how to fly the finished article. A bus driver by trade, Steve Squires spent over a year of his spare time building his Flea, often working on the project until the early hours of the morning. By the spring of 1936 the aircraft was finished and after engine testing, initial taxi trials were carried out at Ashby Pastures, near Ashby Folville. Permission to use this site was withdrawn following an incident during which the antics of the Pou dashing madly around the field delayed the landing of an aircraft bringing His Royal Highness The Prince of Wales on a private visit to the area.

Trials were resumed at Sandy Lane on 18th May and by the evening of Thursday, 28th May, Steve felt proficient enough to attempt the first flight, so with the manual on his lap and undeterred by recent reports of several fatal accidents involving Fleas, he proceeded to put his creation to the test. The maiden flight was approached with some caution, a height of no more than 20ft was attained, landing proved rather difficult owing to the Flea's tendency to float and was only achieved following a series of decreasing bounces down the field. As for the second flight of the evening, that proved disastrous. With engine roaring, the Flea tore down the field, rose at a very step angle attempting to clear trees at the end. The inevitable happened, the aircraft stalled, struck the trees and in the crash which followed G-AEIO was written off. Contemporary newspaper reports of the mishap, no doubt toned down in an attempt to avoid embarrassment to the club and further adverse publicity for the aircraft, state that the pilot suffered only a twisted ankle when in actual fact both were broken. These injuries served only as a temporary curb to Steve's aspirations to pilot his own aircraft and later on he constructed and flew with great success, the first homebuilt Luton

LFPC's Flea, G-AEHG, inside the hangar at Sandy Lane.

Activity at Sandy Lane. Left to right: A E Coltman's Drone G-ADMU, LFPC's Drone G-AEJS and the unmarked Flea. Both K Tunnicliffe

A Drone, thought to be G-ADMU, in flight at Sandy Lane. K Tunnicliffe

Over 80 aircraft could be seen in the original print of this survey photograph of Melton Mowbray, dated 22nd April 1944.
Peter Green collection

LA-4 Minor single-seat parasol monoplane, G-AFIR.

To return to the club's Flea, in spite of many attempts to get it airborne it seemed to prefer to emulate a motor mower and only once is it believed to have left the ground. The pilot on this 'historic' occasion was a petite female member of the club, Miss Bettina Peberdy, who managed to coax G-AEHG into the air for a very short

hop one July evening. Frustration ultimately overcame enthusiasm and members interest in the Flea waned until eventually it was dismantled. Finally, to bring a futile career to an end it was cremated with due ceremony as part of the club's Guy Fawkes celebrations in November 1937 after they had moved to Rearsby.

Lindsay Everard's promise to the club materialised in July 1936 when the BAC /

Kronfeld Drone G-AEJS arrived at Sandy Lane. On the evening of the delivery day the aircraft carried out its first flight from the field and at the controls was the Leicestershire Flying Pou Club's founder V H Doree. Some years ago he recalled that the occasion was approached with some trepidation owing to the fact that due to financial circumstances he had only managed 30 minutes solo flying in the previous year and also had never flown a Drone before. However, gentle persuasion by his friend, Harry Rawnsley, prevailed and following engine testing, taxying practice was embarked upon. Inevitably, after several fast runs down the field the urge to fly overcame Victor Doree's nervousness and turning into wind, he opened up the throttle and took off. During the initial stages of the flight which followed he admitted to being thoroughly frightened, but he gradually regained his confidence and eventually executed a passable landing. After this, subsequent flights were carried out with much more confidence and with experience Victor grew to enjoy flying the Drone.

In the summer of 1936 only two or three members of the club were licensed pilots but the arrival of the Ground Trainer in August 1936, was expected to rectify this situation. It was envisaged that primary tuition on the Ground Trainer would enable embryo pilots to progress on to the Drone without fear of serious accidents. Fortunately it was soon realised that the Sandy Lane field was inadequate for this teach-yourself type of flying, for while the surface was fairly level too many trees and high hedges surrounded the site. Therefore wheels were put in motion to find a more suitable venue for club operations and thanks once more to Lindsay Everard, land was made available at Rearsby, the County Flying Club as it became known, taking up residence there from the spring of 1937. (See Chapter Twenty.)

Use of the Sandy Lane field tailed off in the autumn of 1936, ultimately the hangar was dismantled to be re-erected at Rearsby and so with its departure the last tangible evidence of occupation of the field by a flying club disappeared. During the Second World War flying of a vastly different nature returned to this area when an airfield for the RAF was established.

Leicestershire Flying Pou Club

Mignet HM.14 Pou Du Ciel	G-AEHG
BAC/Kronfeld Drone	G-AEJS
Kronfeld Ground Trainer	Unregistered

Private Aircraft based at the Sandy Lane field

Mignet HM.14 Pou Du Ciel	G-AEIO	J S Squires
BAC/Kronfeld Drone	G-ADMU	A E Coltman

RAF Melton Mowbray was built during 1942-1943 within 2½ miles of the town. Situated about 300ft above sea level it stood out above most of the surrounding countryside, particularly the Wreake Valley on the south western side. Construction of the airfield entailed the demolition of several houses and farm buildings and a main road was obliterated, while the removal also of natural wind breaks such as hedges and trees meant that it could be a very cold, bleak site during winter months.

It is reputed that this was an airfield no one really wanted to accept. The main reasons given for this are that it was built on steeply contoured land with the main runway out of line of the prevailing wind. Yet during its short active life of just over two years, a greater variety of aircraft were to use this airfield than any other RAF station within Leicestershire and Rutland.

Bomber Command are said to have shown little or no interest in Melton Mowbray even though in September 1942, while in the early stages of construction, it was on the inventory of 93 Group. On 1st August 1943 it was transferred to 44 Group, Transport Command and completed during that month.

Officially Melton Mowbray opened on 31st July 1943 with the arrival of an indent party from Headquarters, 44 Group. In charge was Squadron Leader R J Sancean who then assumed command of the station. As in many similar situations during the Second World War these early arrivals were faced with the task of organising the various services and sections essential for the running of a new station. Throughout August the number of personnel on the station remained small; by the end of the month Melton Mowbray's complement had only risen to 12 officers and 123 airmen and airwomen. Even so, in these early weeks Melton attracted its fair share of VIP visits. The Air Officer Commanding (AOC), Transport Command, Sir Frederick W Bowhill made two tours of inspection on 6th August and 11th September, while in between, Air Commodore Kingston-McCloughry, AOC, 44 Group, came on 1st September for the same purpose.

In September also, command of the station passed to Wing Commander B A Oakley; at the same time he became OC of 4 Overseas Aircraft Preparation Unit (OAPU) which formed at Melton Mowbray during the first week of the month. While the OAPU was working up to strength two more units with complementary duties were posted to the station. These were 306 and 307 Ferry Training Units (FTU) both of which began to arrive during the second week of October. By the end of the month the movement of the two units, which had come from Long Kesh, Co Down, Northern Ireland and Finmere, Buckinghamshire, respectively, was complete.

At about the same time as the two FTU's began to move in aircraft started to arrive for 4 OAPU to work on. The first of these were three Vickers Wellington twin-engined medium bombers which flew in on 17th October but none of this trio was to be the first aircraft to be processed and completed by the unit. This distinction fell to Douglas Boston IIIA BZ257 which was despatched to the FTU on 30th October.

As a whole RAF Melton Mowbray had little time to get firmly established before autumn turned into winter with all its attendant problems. Land disturbed during construction had had no time to consolidate again before rain, frosts and snow turned it into a glutinous mess. On the airfield and domestic sites alike winter caused many difficulties which were compounded by shortages of both personnel and equipment. Station and unit Operational Record Books contain entries which serve to highlight some of the many problems encountered in the closing months of the year:

'*November 1943* - Lack of tractors for towing aircraft to dispersal points results in numerous cases of bogging down. This was due to pilots attempting to taxi aircraft to hardstandings.

December 1943 - Considerable inconvenience caused by bogging down of aircraft by Air Transport Auxiliary pilots.

December 11th - Boston BZ386, 4 (O)APU overshot runway and became bogged down. It was subsequently hit by Boston W8357 which was also overshooting when landing.

December 20th - Boston BZ197, 4 (O)APU overshot runway and slewed round on soggy ground. Nosewheel struck edge of perimeter track and collapsed.

December 23rd - Boston W8395, 307 FTU made a belly-landing due to the pilot being unable to lower the undercarriage. The selector lever had broken off in his hand!'

The advent of a new year is said to be a time of change and this is certainly what happened at Melton Mowbray in January 1944. During the first two weeks of the month 304 FTU moved to the station from Port Ellen, Strathclyde, and by the 13th the transfer was complete. Two days later 306 and 307 FTU's disbanded and combined with 304 to form one large unit. While this was taking place, 1 Ferry Crew Pool (FCP) was also in the process of moving in from Lyneham, Wiltshire, and by the 17th the last of this unit had taken up residence. From this date units at Melton Mowbray were capable of preparing an aircraft for delivery overseas, providing a crew trained to fly a specific type of aircraft and of instructing that aircrew in the various problems to be faced on long range ferry flights.

At this time 1 FCP was not only responsible for the supply of crews to 304 FTU but also to 301, 303 and 311. A list of crews on unit strength at the end of February gives a fair indication of the main aircraft types being ferried for overseas service in early 1944: Wellington 94, Beaufighter 26, Hudson 22, Boston 3, Blenheim 1, Spitfire 3, Halifax 3, and Beaufort 11.

Change, evident early in February with the posting of Wing Commander Oakley to

Pages from the logbook of Albert Mettam, which illustrate well the transient nature of visits to RAF Melton Mowbray by many aircrew. via Peter Green

Opposite page: Melton's control tower in a state of dereliction before being demolished. The design appears to be a 12779/41 with an additional floor. The building at the right is thought to be the floodlight tractor and trailer shed. Presumably the night flying equipment store and fire tender were housed in the bottom floor of the tower. The site plan does not show this layout, it has the much more conventional three buildings plus control tower format. Rigby Graham

Down Ampney, Gloucestershire. His place was taken by Group Captain C F H Grace who assumed command of Melton Mowbray from 9th February.

What must have been the first major crisis to affect the station following his appointment can once again be blamed on the weather. On 27th February a very heavy snowfall blanketed the area covering the airfield to a depth of 6-12 inches. All available resources were marshalled to clear the runways and perimeter track so that the airfield might return to operational status. Although some snowploughs were used, manpower was relied upon to get the job done. It took three days before the airfield was finally cleared and on two of these days everyone who could be spared was employed on snow clearance. The main runway was open again by 15:00 hours on the 27th and the other two by 16:00 hours next day. Thanks to the efforts of all concerned, Melton Mowbray was the first station in the district to be cleared. Doubtless the crews of the three USAAF Boeing B-17 Flying Fortresses were also thankful for this when they were unable to land at their own base.

After only two months at Melton 1 FCP moved out again on 16th March, this time to Pershore, Worcestershire. A change in policy must have dictated the move as two days later the unit disbanded and merged with 301 FTU to form 1 Ferry Unit. Although 1 FCP's stay in the county was brief it was not without incident; three Wellingtons were lost while being flown by crews from the unit. On 4th February HF289 crashed while on a flight between Talbenny and Hurn, all the crew of LP199 perished when the aircraft crashed at Gibraltar on 8th March and again there were no survivors when MN775 was destroyed on Dartmoor in the same month.

With the approach of spring Melton began to shake off the rigours of winter. Despite conditions in the previous months some progress had been made in certain areas but in others improvement was definitely lacking. Confirmation of this is given in the monthly resume, for March, on the state of affairs within the station:

'A notable month in having shown a record output from 4 OAPU and 304 FTU with a total of 105 aircraft despatched, this is over double any previous figure. The improvement in the weather towards the end of the month enabled the station generally to begin to shake off its coating of winter mud and filth. All sections have been and are still smartening up their various sites. In conjunction with the advice of the local Agricultural Committee the unit food promotion scheme has gone to work and some 30 acres will soon be under cultivation, most of this area has already been ploughed. The AOC, 44 Group, Air Commodore G R Beamish CBE, visited the station on 17th/18th and congratulated 4 OAPU on their work, he was not however satisfied with much else that he saw and neither is the Station Commander. Steps were and still are being taken to improve general cleanliness and efficiency of the unit as a whole.'

During the next few months the measures taken began to have a marked effect on the continued improvement of the station. Officers in charge were able to report that the great deal of self-help work which had been carried out by their respective sections had made a significant contribution to conditions in general. In addition the employment on various tasks within the camp of 50 Italian Prisoners of War, or Co-Operators as they were by then referred to, was also of considerable help.

There were still some problems though. In June the Station Medical Officer stated that the lack of leave was beginning to tell on all personnel. WAAF's in particular seemed to be affected, complaints of nerves, run-down, insomnia and anorexia were quite common and were often accompanied by emotional outbursts. Even incoming aircrew presented the MO with difficulties. Usually their short but intensive course lasted eight days, four spent on ground subjects, four flying, which meant that they had little time to acquire the inoculations and vaccinations necessary for overseas service.

Despite the many other pressing needs the welfare and social demands of station personnel were not entirely neglected. During May the Station Dramatic Society was able to give the first performance in the newly-completed theatre. Visits by touring shows also made a welcome diversion, often providing an enjoyable evening's entertainment. Opportunities to take part in sporting activities both on and off the station were always popular. Football and cricket were naturally firm favourites, in the latter sport the 1944 season proved to be a very successful one for the station team. Not only were they runners-up in the Melton and District League but also winners of the District and Red Cross Cup together with Melton and District Nursing Cup. For some time another off duty recreation which found favour was horse riding lessons. These were made available to all ranks by courtesy of Lieutenant Colonel Sparling, Officer Commanding an Army Remount Depot at Melton Mowbray.

It is perhaps appropriate to include here an account of an amusing incident with a sporting theme which befell John P Wells, a former engine fitter with 4 OAPU. In the early days there was no barbers shop on the station so John had been into Melton for a haircut; he was returning to camp when a car driven by the Commanding Officer pulled up alongside. The CO asked if John was on his way back to camp to which he replied 'Yes Sir', hoping for a lift. Instead the CO requested him to take his golf clubs back in order to make more room in the car as he had passengers to pick up. It was a request that could not be refused so off John set with the bag of clubs over his shoulder. As he approached the camp gate the Orderly Officer was on duty checking airmen in and out of camp, on seeing John he remarked, 'Ah, airman have you been playing golf?', 'No, Sir' came the reply 'I've been for a haircut'. Without waiting for further explanation a guard was called and John was placed under arrest for being insolent. Further attempts to explain fell on deaf ears so John and the golf clubs were forced to remain in the guard room until the CO arrived to confirm his story. Recalling the incident afterwards caused many a laugh, but the look on the Orderly Officer's face at the time was enough for John to make every effort to avoid him in the future.

Problems there may have been throughout the early life of the station but the major one which had beset the OAPU and FTU seem to have been largely overcome by the summer months of 1944. To permit much safer and more efficient parking of aircraft, McAlpines, the civil engineering firm which had carried out the main contract for the building of the airfield, began work in April to fill in the spaces between the spectacle type hardstandings at the southern end of the airfield. Additionally as a further aid to working conditions concrete aprons were laid outside Nos.1 and 3 hangars.

By the end of the month 52 aircraft had been prepared and despatched by 4 OAPU. Of these machines 90% had been passed on to 304 FTU. This was the highest output figure so far achieved by the unit and it was to remain so for the next four months. That it was not improved upon in this time is no reflection on the ability of the OAPU as

monthly intakes of aircraft received during this period were on a much lower scale. It was noted in unit records that more could have been dealt with had they been available.

In preparation for multi-engined aircraft being added to unit commitments, ground personnel had been sent on Short Stirling airframe courses during March. Then on 26th and 27th April one of these aircraft, possibly belonging to the Empire Central Flying School, visited the station from Hullavington, Wiltshire, to give a short conversion course on the type to two unit pilots. The OAPU was provided with a Stirling 'hack' of its own and this was flown in on 23rd May the same day that others began to arrive for the unit to work on. From then on these four-engined bombers became a regular addition to 4 OAPU's workload and for several months in succession a quota of ten aircraft was completed.

On 16th June another change in command took place at Melton when Wing Commander Grace was replaced by Wing Commander P S Gomez. In turn, he was soon faced with considerable reorganisation within the station.

It was decided on 28th June that 4 OAPU and 304 FTU would be combined into one composite unit. A further directive received from Headquarters, 44 Group on 10th July confirmed that initially the union was to be for a trial period of one month but both units would keep their individual identities. Dur-

ing the month there was one change, the word 'Overseas' was dropped from the OAPU's title and it then became 4 APU. All arrangements were expected to be completed by 14th July ready for the new combination to begin to function from 09:00 hours next day.

No major hold ups are recorded so the transition must have been fairly snag free but perhaps the changeover did help contribute to scheduled output being slightly in arrears by eight aircraft at the end of August. It was noted however that difficulties were experienced with a batch of 25 Douglas Boston IVs and also with some Bristol Beaufighters so it is probable that these were mainly responsible for the deficit. Whatever problems there may have been August was still a good month for the APU. The unit achieved its highest output yet, beating the previous best performance by one aircraft.

Owing to the nature of the flying exercises carried out congestion was often a major obstacle experienced at many training airfields throughout the Second World War. Towards the end of 1944 this problem began to affect movements at Leicester East where the situation was further aggravated by the lack of a satellite airfield. But, thanks to the fact that Melton Mowbray's circuit was not overloaded with aircraft a solution was found. Early in September an agreement was reached whereby from the 10th Dakotas of 107 OTU were able to use the airfield to carry out conversion training.

RAF Melton Mowbray – 1st December 1944

Latitude	52° 44' 00" N
Longitude	00° 53' 30" W
Height at Sea Level	400ft
Locality	2 miles south of Melton Mowbray
Command	Transport (RAF)
Nearest Railway Station	Melton Mowbray, LMS
Function	Parent Station.
Subsidiary Function	OAPU
Affiliated Airfields	Nil

Landing Area – Runways

QDM	Dimensions	Extensibility	Remarks
157°	2,000 x 50 yds	2,500 yds	But not
296°	1,400 x 50 yds	1,400 yds	recommended.
035°	1,300 x 50 yds	1,300 yds	

Type of Surface – Concrete.

Permanent Landmarks

By Day	Melton Mowbray, north, 1 mile.
By Night	Nil

Permanent Obstructions Nil

Facilities

Airfield Lightning	Mk.II
Beam Approach	–
Radio	–
QDM	–
Flying Control	Yes.

Accommodation   All buildings temporary.

Technical	Hangars		Hardstandings	
	Type	No	Type	No
	T2	4	Spectacle	12
			Apron	18

Domestic	Officers	SNCOs	ORs	Total
RAF	115	414	1,472	2,001
WAAF	10	24	288	322

The temporary amalgamation of the OAPU and FTU extended well beyond the original one month trial and evidently the arrangement worked very well for both units were officially disbanded on 9th October only to be reformed immediately as 12 Ferry Unit (FU). The aircraft establishment for the unit was three Beaufighters, two Boston IIIAs two Wellingtons, two Airspeed Oxfords and two Avro Ansons and one Percival Proctor.

Output by the FU during the autumn months was rather disappointing but small commitments coupled with late deliveries of aircraft helped to explain the reasons for this. In October, of the 42 aircraft scheduled to be completed, only 34 left the unit while in November the total was even less with only 25 being despatched. The bulk of this last figure was made up of Mosquitos (15) followed by Beaufighters (6), Hurricanes (3) and single examples of Stirling and Anson.

To finish a very poor month an accident on the last day cost the unit not only an aircraft but also the life of a crew member. It was a typical November day with very poor visibility and after take-off the undercarriage of de Havilland Mosquito NF.30 MM783 failed to retract. While in a turn to line up with the runway to land again the aircraft sideslipped into the ground near the airfield and burst into flames. Although injured, the pilot, Flight Sergeant Higgins, managed to escape. His navigator, Pilot Officer Boudreau, was not so fortunate, he was extricated from the wreckage badly burned and subsequently died of his injuries.

It would seem that Melton Mowbray was a popular choice when 46 Group, Transport Command, needed assistance. Not only were 107 OTU Dakotas using the airfield but following a decision taken late in October the station became a winter home and staging post for Field Signals Units (FSU) belonging to the Group. Agreement was reached that accommodation be provided, under canvas, to enable these units to stay for an indefinite time. Nos 5, 6 and 7 FSU's were all housed on the station for varying periods between 21st November 1944 and 28th February 1945.

The greater proportion of the personnel and equipment belonging to these three FSU's was airlifted out to the Continent between 16th and 29th January 1945 but not every movement order went according to plan. Most of 7 FSU was scheduled to leave on 28th January for Le Bourget in five Dakotas which had flown up from Blakehill Farm, Gloucestershire. When the leading aircraft taxied out to position for take-off it slewed off the runway edge, got badly bogged down, blocked the runway and prevented the rest from taking off. Even with the join efforts of station and FSU personnel it took 1½ hours of hard work to retrieve the aircraft from deep snow. By the time the runway was clear once more it was too late for the journey to be made so departure was postponed until the 29th when all aircraft left, this time without a hitch.

The opening months of 1945 proved to be another bad operating period for Melton Mowbray's resident unit. Once more weather was chiefly to blame; in January flying was possible on only nine days and out of the 134 aircraft due for delivery by 12 FU only 53 were despatched. Beginning this month the delivery of single-engined, single-seat fighters became a major commitment for the Ferry Unit and it was the first time that a 44 Group unit had despatched this type of aircraft overseas. Spitfires formed the bulk of the month's output, 35 of these aircraft being delivered of which 30 were Mk.Vbs assigned to the French Air Force at Bordeaux.

For February it was almost a repeat story, short supply of aircraft and atrocious weather for two thirds of the month. But, in spite of this, the unit processed 100 of the 130 aircraft received. Again the major part of these were Spitfires, 69 leaving the station, but also for the first time naval fighters were despatched in the form of 16 Grumman Hellcats.

Two interesting commitments for the month concerned a Stirling III bound for the USSR and a batch of ten North American Harvard advanced trainers destined for Yugoslavia. The Stirling was only allowed to proceed after it had been inspected by members of the Russian Mission in the UK while the Harvards were held up throughout the month with no explanation, though the reasons were believed to be political. Whatever the problem it was resolved in March and they were duly delivered.

March was the first of several notable months for the Ferry Unit. It received orders to despatch 190 aircraft, its highest total, and although this figure was not achieved deliveries exceeded receipts by 135 to 134 respectively. Vought Corsairs, North American Mustangs and Vultee Vengeances were all part of unit output for the first time. April's turnover was even better with the despatch of 142 aircraft, exceeding those received by 32 and although this was to be the peak month for 12 FU, May proved equally successful in that the total output of 103 aircraft was more than had been requested. Doubtless this figure could have been improved upon had it not been for slack periods caused by discrepancies in aircraft delivered to the station and celebrations in support of VE Day.

Commitments for the despatch of large numbers of single-engined fighters ceased in June and thereafter 12 FU reverted to its more normal twin and multi-engined output. Most of the single-engined ferry pilots were then posted out to RAF Filton and a big influx of multi-engined crews took their place with the resultant strain on messing facilities.

Once more the station Medical Officer came under pressure and he noted that since hostilities ended in Europe the station had, to use his words, 'gone haywire'. His chief problem was the inoculation of the hundreds of aircrew, many of whom had arrived to ferry aircraft to South East Asia Command. He intimated in his report that if

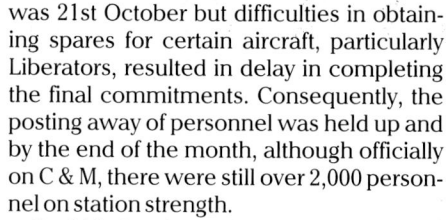

inoculations were not completed before crews arrived on the station then he envisaged delays occurring in the despatch of aircraft. As it transpired, his fears were short-lived, for victory over Japan in August brought about a rapid reduction in monthly requirements.

After they had been relieved of their fighter commitments in June an increasing number of multi-engined aircraft passed through 12 FU's hands during the remaining summer months. In addition to a considerable quantity of Handley Page Halifaxes and Consolidated Liberators, between 28th June and 3rd October over 70 Avro Lancasters were processed. The majority of these were Canadian-built B.Mk Xs, which had arrived in this country during the spring and early summer of 1945, too late for active service. Many of those which passed through Melton Mowbray during July and August were prepared for a return trip back across the Atlantic to serve with the Royal Canadian Air Force. In the later weeks, many were delivered direct from Melton Mowbray for storage at maintenance units at Colerne, Wiltshire and Aston Down, Gloucestershire, where the majority were to remain until they were scrapped a few months hence.

During 1945 several small units were formed to undertake specialised duties overseas. Three of these, 1341 (Special Duties) Flight and 1588 and 1589 (Heavy Freighter) Flights, were all associated with the station for brief periods while they received their aircraft and made preparations to depart for their respective theatres of operation.

No.1589 (HF) Flight's record is a fairly typical account of the activities of these transitory formations while at Melton. The unit began its career under Squadron Leader H F Johnson on 28th September 1945. It had an establishment of eight aircrew and 96

ground personnel with five Short Stirling Vs as main equipment. Aircrews were drawn from 295 and 570 Squadrons of 38 (Airborne Forces) Group and the ground crews from 44 Group.

Destined to serve in the Middle East the object of the flight was to help support trunk routes throughout the area covered by 216 Group. Also it was to provide spares and repair parties whenever and wherever an aircraft was unserviceable. To this end the ground crews were formed into specialised groups each capable of dealing with a specific type so parties were available to maintain the Stirlings, Halifaxes, Liberators and Avro Yorks then in service with the Group.

On 1st October an aircraft of the Flight was airborne for the first time when Stirling V PJ979 carried out initial tests. Over the next few days the rest received their checks, by the 4th all had been completed and preparations made to depart.

Four unit aircraft left Melton Mowbray for St Mawgan, Cornwall on 5th October on the first stage of their journey to the Middle East. Each was fully loaded carrying 20 ground crew in addition to stores. The remaining aircraft, PJ975, cleared Melton for St Mawgan next day and by 10th October the Flight had arrived safely at Cairo West.

As has already been mentioned, from August the urgent need for the despatch of aircraft to the Far East ceased. No.12 Ferry Unit's workload then contracted swiftly and during September the unit received movement orders for only 26 aircraft.

It became known that in order to concentrate their ferry commitments in as few FUs as possible 44 Group had decided to close Melton Mowbray. The two main reasons given for this were that it was the farthest north and that it had the highest incidence of bad weather. The date officially set to transfer the station to Care & Maintenance

was 21st October but difficulties in obtaining spares for certain aircraft, particularly Liberators, resulted in delay in completing the final commitments. Consequently, the posting away of personnel was held up and by the end of the month, although officially on C & M, there were still over 2,000 personnel on station strength.

On 26th October Wing Commander D H Sutton took over command of 12 FU for what proved to be a very short period in authority for 12 days later on 7th November the unit was disbanded. Transport Command wound up its activities at Melton Mowbray and on 1st February 1946 the station was transferred to 22 Group, Technical Training Command. No.22 Group soon made use of the camp and it became the home of 14 Recruits Centre from 15th February when this unit moved in from Hereford, but 14 RC did not have a very long life on the station, being disbanded on 27th September.

From then Melton Mowbray took on another new role; the camp was prepared ready to accommodate dependants of Polish service personnel who were to settle in Britain. No.9 Resettlement Unit (Polish) was formed at Melton Mowbray on 5th October 1946 and the first contingent of temporary residents arrived on 26th November.

In the coming months these Polish expatriates passing through were given assistance in settling down in the country of their adoption; many found a home in the immediate area. On 4th June 1947 6 RU(P) moved in from Hucknall, Nottinghamshire; this unit was immediately disbanded and taken over by 9 RU(P). For a further year 9 RU(P) remained at Melton then on 10th June 1948 the unit moved out to Dunholme Lodge, Lincolnshire, where it too was disbanded three weeks later.

While 14 RC and 9 RU(P) mainly utilised the many buildings and dispersed sites during their stay, the airfield was not allowed to remain idle. Early in February 1946 a visit was made by the Air Ministry and Agricultural Executive Committee to assess the site prior to its transfer to agricultural use. The area in question covered approximately 500 acres of which 150 were taken up with concrete runways and hardstandings, leaving 350 acres available for farming. Of this it was agreed to transfer 200 acres and one of the four hangars was allocated as the only building at this time to be used in connection with farming operations.

Responsibility for farming the airfield was left to the District Committee of the AEC and cultivation started in May 1946. Many difficulties were encountered, not least of these being buried wires, manhole covers, boulders and stone which caused a fair amount of damage to ploughs. Roughly 50 acres of the allocated area had once been the bomb dump and a large force of PoWs awaiting repatriation were employed in clearing this section during 1946. At first it was considered that owing to the many mounds and roads with which it was covered that this area would be suitable only for afforestation. However, a week's work by a bulldozer during 1947 enabled this land to be returned to productive use also.

For the first year land reclaimed was allowed to lie fallow but by the end of 1947 crops of wheat and flax had been harvested from the 250 acres then under cultivation. Progressive reclamation of various sections of the airfield continued and by 1950 the acreage yielding produce had been increased to 380. Various cereals formed the main crops but substantial areas of potatoes, beans, peas and mangolds were also grown and in April 1947 cattle were reintroduced onto sections of the land.

Following the departure of 9 RU(P) in June 1948 RAF Melton Mowbray had closed, but this was not to be the end of the service's association with the airfield. Farming continued to be the major activity until 1958 when the RAF once more became interested in the site and it came under the control of 3 Group, Bomber Command. A central section of what still remained of the wartime airfield was then significantly altered to play an active role once more.

When in 1958 Her Majesty's Government accepted the US Government's offer to supply Britain with Intermediate Range Ballistic Missiles (IRBM) one of the provisos of the agreement was that Britain would provide the operating bases. It was accepted that the RAF would put the missiles into service and supply these bases. Four launch complexes were set up, each comprising of a main base on a permanent RAF station, and

four satellite bases which, with one exception, were all sited on disused wartime airfields. North Luffenham was selected as one of the main bases and in turn Melton Mowbray became one of its four satellites.

Launch pads for three Douglas SM75 Thor IRBMs were built roughly in the centre of the old airfield. Each T-shaped pad was able to house a missile, its shelter, and fuel tanks for liquid oxygen, kerosene and nitrogen. Other buildings on the site included crew rooms, a powerhouse and stores and the whole area was surrounded by a screen of 'unclimbable' security fencing.

As the missiles were to be transported in by lorry from North Luffenham access roads to the camp were improved; the B6047 connecting Melton to Great Dalby was re-routed taking in a long stretch of the old perimeter track before following the line of a former runway.

Each base of three missiles was classified as a squadron and Melton Mowbray's trio were allocated the number of an old Second World War Coastal Command strike unit. No.254 (Strategic Missile) Squadron was reformed at Melton on 1st December 1959 and the North Luffenham complex was declared fully operational in May 1960.

As with all bases which have contained nuclear deterrents, Melton's missiles attracted several protest marches but they were to no avail; the Thors stayed *in situ* until 1963. It was finally realised that these fixed sites were extremely vulnerable to attack and in August 1962 it was announced that the missiles were to be withdrawn and returned to the United States.

Last of the four to be completed, North Luffenham's complex was also the last to go when its squadrons were disbanded during August and September 1963. No.254 (SM) Squadron's turn came on 23rd August, the installation was dismantled and once again RAF Melton Mowbray lapsed into disuse. In 1966 the land was sold and much of it has since reverted to agriculture.

Plans to turn the airfield into a new township at a cost of some £100 million were unveiled in March 1980. Envisaged were 2,500 Scandinavian-type houses together with a light industrial estate. It was hoped that with planning permission a start could be made in 1981. Although it was reported at the time that discussions had taken place with Melton Borough Council they cannot have been very fruitful for nothing came of this project.

Yet another ambitious scheme of a similar nature, was revealed by David Wilson Estates of Ibstock in May 1988. This company proposed to create a new village of 1,100 homes together with a high-tech business park on 450 acres of the site. To be called Kettleby Magna, the village was to include community amenities such as shops, a

church and leisure centre. In addition, to enhance the road network a southern bypass connecting the Leicester to Oakham roads would be built. After lengthy negotiations and a green light from the Department of the Environment in April 1990 the project looked set to proceed but no progress was made, probably due to a slump in the housing market. In June 1994 Leicestershire County Council asked Melton Council to rethink the plans but it was not until July 1999 that David Wilson Estates put forward revised proposals. The latter prompted concern in the neighbouring villages of Burton Lazars, Great and Little Dalby, primarily about the increased traffic the 1,200 homes in the new village would bring. Doubtless the developers will endeavour to allay these and other fears and Kettleby Magna may yet become a reality.

Over two thirds of the main runway still exists and in the early 1970s this was the venue of a very controversial Sunday market. Trading on a regular basis was eventually stopped but in recent years conditions have become more relaxed and trading has resumed. During the late 1970s this runway did see very limited use once more by an aircraft belonging to Shetland Line, a company with shipping interests and a base in Melton Mowbray. More recently microlight aircraft have been noted flying from the site. A section of the No.2 runway also exists and alongside this, at its western end, a number of small businesses have now become established. As a reminder of its more recent use, the massive reinforced concrete blast walls on the airfield still provide tangible evidence of the missile era.

Of the important buildings which once stood on the former Technical Site, alongside the B6047 road, only the gaunt shell of an AML Bombing Teacher is to be seen. A little further on, just off this road, are the area district offices and road salt storage depot of Leicestershire County Council Highways Department. Here, still existing from the days when this was the station Administration Site, is the building which was once the station offices and two others which served as the operations block.

As for the dispersed domestic sites the encroaching environs of Melton Mowbray have obliterated those which were nearest to the town. On others only hut bases or isolated buildings still remain. There is one exception. On what was No.2 Mess Site, situated off Sandy Lane and now occupied by Sandy Lane Poultry Farm and Storers, several of the original Nissen type buildings may still be seen. Doubtless with the passing years, more, if not all of these relics of the past will disappear, leaving only photographs and fading memories.

The runways and dispersals stand out in stark relief in this oblique photograph taken in 1944 from an aircraft of 105 OTU. Note the many aircraft present. Peter Green collection

Melton Mowbray-based Units and Aircraft

No.4 Overseas Aircraft Preparation Unit
From 1.9.43 to 5.7.44
Douglas Boston III	W8357, BZ197, BZ386
Vickers Wellington XIII	JA183, JA316, JA569.

No.306 Ferry Training Unit
From 13.10.43 to 15.1.44
Bristol Beaufort II	LS136, LS143.
Bristol Beaufighter X	NE257 (unconfirmed)

No.307 Ferry Training Unit
From 14.10.43 to 15.1.44
Douglas Boston III W8259, W8267, W8287, W8290, W8295, W8327, W8332, W8334, W8346, W8349, W8353, W8363, W8370, W8373, W8391, W8395, W8398, W8399, Z2214, Z2281, Z2286.

No.304 Ferry Training Unit
From 1.12.43 to 9.10.44
Airspeed Oxford I	R5948, R6025.
Avro Anson I	MG557, MG588.
Bristol Beaufighter I	T5111.
Bristol Beaufighter VI	V8449, V8827, X7898, X8100. KW170, KW199.
Bristol Beaufighter X	KW282, KW283, KW340, KW342, KW346, KW347, KW348, KW350, KW378, KW383, KW391, KW394, KW396, KW397, KW398, KW400, LX846.
Bristol Beaufort I	AW312
Bristol Beaufort II	AW347.
De Havilland Mosquito VI	HR365.
De Havilland Mosquito XIII	MM506, MM532, MM533, MM579, MM581, MM582, MM583.
Martin Marauder I	FK109, FK137.
Short Stirling III	LJ512.
Vickers Wellington X	MF246, MF251.
Vickers Wellington XI	MP563.
Vickers Wellington XIII	HZ762.

No.1 Ferry Crew Pool
From 14.1.44 to 16.3.44

No.4 Aircraft Preparation Unit
From 5.7.44 to 5.10.44

Mk.X AI Conversion Flight
From .8.44 to .9.44

No.12 Ferry Unit
From 9.10.44 to 7.11.45
Airspeed Oxford I	P8931, R6025, X7396.
Avro Anson I	MG557, MG588.
Avro Lancaster I	PD281, PD348, SW244.
Avro Lancaster III	PB992.
Avro Lancaster X	FM101, FM102, FM103, FM105, FM106, FM108, FM111, FM113, FM114, FM117, FM118, FM121, FM123, FM124, FM125, FM126, FM127, FM128, FM129, FM131, FM132, FM134, FM136, FM137, FM138, FM140, FM144, FM145, FM146, FM148, FM149, FM150, FM151, FM153, FM154, FM155, FM156, FM159, FM160, FM161, FM165, FM166, FM169, FM170, FM171, FM174, FM176, FM178, KB170, KB790, KB897, KB906, KB935, KB940, KB943, KB953, KB958, KB966, KB969, KB974, KB975, KB978, KB980, KB981, KB982, KB983, KB984, KB986, KB988, KB989, KB990.
Avro York I	MW173.
Bristol Beaufighter X	KW282, LX846, NE823, NV308, NV309, RD164, RD214, RD223, RD240, RD272, RD360, RD477, RD513, RD725, RD747, RD749.
Chance Vought Corsair IV	KD184, KD187, KD196, KD197, KD207, KD219, KD269, KD386, KD397, KD411, KD433, KD493, KD750, KD782.
Consolidated Liberator VI	EV948, EV962, KH279, KH348, KL390, KL472, KL486, KL494, KL499, KL503, KL517, KL520, KL529, KL550, KL558, KL559, KL562, KL567, KL576, KL578, KL593, KL643, KN726, KN730, KN732, TW768.
De Havilland Dominie I	R5922, X7396, V4725.
De Havilland Mosquito VI	HR575, RF584, RF604, RF614, RF616, RF619, RF650, RF654, RF661, RF699, RF732, RF758, RF765, RF766, RF779, RF891, RF947, RF952. TE598.

De Havilland Mosquito XIX	TA155, TA218, TA232, TA282.
De Havilland Mosquito XXX	MM752, MM783. MV569.
Grumman Hellcat II	JV238, JV286, JW717, JX691, JX731, JX740, JX742, JX744, JX746, JX748, JX749, JX751, JX752, JX753, JX755, JX765, JX766, JX769, JX771, JX773, JX775, JX777, JX779, JX781, JX782, JX784, JX786, JX787, JX788, JX790, JX791, JX795, JX796, JX797, JX798, JX799, JX800, JX804, JX812, JX821, JX824, JX825, JX826, JX827, JX828, JX830, JX831, JX833, JX836, JX837, JX838, JX840, JX841, JX842, JX843, JX845, JX846, JX848, JX852, JX853, JX855, JX856, JX858, JX861, JX862, JX863, JX864, JX865, JX866, JX867, JX868, JX871, JX872, JX873, JX875, JX877, JX878, JX879, JX880, JX881, JX894, JX896,.JX898, JX900, JX903, JX909, JX930, JX933, JX934, JX935, JX937, JX940, JX941, JX942, JX946, JX949, JX951, JX953, JX954, JX955, JX957, JX958, JX959, JX962, JX963, JX964.
Handley Page Halifax III	PN369, PN371, PN384, PN388, PN390, PN406, PN424, PN439, PN443.
Hawker Hurricane IIc	PZ862.
Lockheed Hudson I	P5149.
Miles Master II	DL121, DL285, DM140, DM162.
North American Harvard III	FT174, FT152, FT339, KF283, KF302, KF305, KF429, KF471, KF474, KF477.
North American Mustang III	FX862, FX872, FZ128, FZ130.
North American Mustang IV	KH713, KH719, KH720, KH762, KH763, KH774, KH780, KH811, KH826, KM162, KM262.
Short Stirling IV	LJ938, LJ941, LJ953, LJ969, LJ972, LJ974, LJ978, LJ981, LJ984, LJ987, LK152, LK172, LK173, LK174, LK175, LK176, LK177, LK178, LK179, LK180, LK181, LK182, LK183, LK184, LK185, LK186, LK187, LK188, LK189, LK211, LK226, LK227, LK228, LK229, LK230, LK231, LK233, LK234, LK235, LK240, LK243, LK248, LK249, LK251, LK252, LK253, LK255, LK615, LK618.

Short Stirling V PJ888, PJ897, PJ947, PJ975, PJ989, PJ996, PJ999, PK143, PK150, PK151.
Vickers Warwick I BV273, BV529.
Vickers Warwick III HG130, HG241, HG273.
Vickers Wellington X LP512, LP749, NC849.
Vickers-Supermarine Spitfire V EP179.
Vickers-Supermarine Spitfire IX JL355, MH298, MH371, MH454, MH499, MH568, MH581, MH713, MH716, MH724, MH941, MJ118, MJ237, MJ293, MJ295, MJ333, MJ365, MJ402, MJ404, MJ424, MJ557, MJ729, MJ774, MJ823, MJ886, MK319, MK378, MK636, MK811, MK882, MK951, MK981, MK989, MK991, ML142, ML146, ML239, ML307, ML400, ML404, ML409, NH182, NH276, NH346, NH355, NH363, NH370, NH378, NH407, NH423, NH453, NH483, PT360, PV142, PV314, RR258, SM143, TA791, TA808, TA821.
Vultee Vengeance IV FD277, FD290, FD360, FD364, FD367, FD372, FD374, FD379, FD383, FD393, HB302, HB318, HB327, HB337, HB348, HB370, HB403, HB441, HB507, HB527.
Westland Lysander I R1991, T1445.

No. 1341 (Special Duties) Flight
From late 1944 to 7.11.45
Handley Page Halifax B III PN369, PN381, PN382, PN383.

Nos. 5, 6 and 7 Field Signals Units
From 21.11.44 to 28.2.45

No.1588 (Heavy Freighter) Flight ('K' Flight)
From 16.9.45 to ?
Short Stirling V PJ973, PJ996. PK150, PK151, PK178.

No. 1589 (Heavy Freighter) Flight ('J' Flight)
From 28.9.45 to 5.10.45
Short Stirling V PJ975, PJ979, PJ989, PJ994, PK143.

No. 154 Recruits Centre
From 15.2.46 to 27.9.46

No. 9 Resettlement Unit (Polish)
From 5.10.46 to 10.6.48
No. 6 Resettlement Unit (Polish)
From 4.6.47 (immediately incorporated into 9 RU(P).

No. 254 (Strategic Missile) Squadron
From 1.12.59 to 23.8.63
Douglas SM75 Thor IRBM

Serious Melton Mowbray-based Unit Accidents

11.12.43 Boston III W8357 4 OAPU
Overshot runway on landing at Melton Mowbray and hit Boston BZ386 which had also overshot runway and become bogged down.

19.12.43 Beaufort II LS136 306 FTU
Force-landed at RAF Wyton due to loss of power on starboard engine. No casualties.

28.12.43 Beaufort II LS143 306 FTU
Damaged by shrapnel from range at St Agnes Head.

17.1.44 Wellington XIII JA569 4 OAPU
Engine cut, belly-landed near Braunston, Rutland.

28.1.44 WellingtonXIII JA316 4 OAPU
Engine ran away, hit cables recovering from dive and crashed, Odstone.

10.4.44 Beaufighter NE480 304 FTU
Engines cut at 1,000ft due to failure to change tanks and aircraft crashed in attempting to land on Denton Relief Landing Ground, Northants.

1.5.44 Beaufighter VI KW199 304 FTU
Starboard engine cut and control was lost. Crashed at Kirby Bellars, near Melton Mowbray.

28.6.44 Beaufighter VI KW170 304 FTU
Engine caught fire while taxying at Habbaniya, Iraq. Damaged beyond repair.

30.11.44 Mosquito XXX MM783 12 FU
Landing in bad weather aircraft side-slipped into ground during a turn to line up with runway. Crashed near airfield, caught fire and burnt out. Two occupants injured, one died later.

12.12.44 Hurricane IIc PZ834 304 FTU
Lost radio contact and belly landed at Mauseladron, Cornwall while lost.

15.1.45 Oxford I R6025 12 FU
Aircraft overshot landing at Braunston, Lincs. Collided with hedge and nose dropped into ditch.

26.1.45 Beaufighter X RD360 12 FU
Damaged beyond repair in belly-landing at Heliopolis, Egypt.

3.2.45 Spitfire IX MJ295 12 FU
Crashed near Marseille in south of France. Pilot killed.

3.2.45 Spitfire IX PV142 12 FU
Crashed into mountainside near Point Tangone on coast of Sardinia. Pilot killed.

5.2.45 Beaufighter X LX846 12 FU
Port undercarriage failed to lock and collapsed on landing. Became instructional airframe 5756M.

10.2.45 Spitfire IX NH483 12 FU
Crashed at Littleton on Severn during snow shower.

17.2.45 Spitfire IXs NH276 and PT360 12 FU
Lost valley in formation and flew into cliff top, Kimmeridge, Dorset. One pilot killed.

23.2.45 Hellcat II JX784 12 FU
Missing on a flight to Portreath.

7.3. 45 Spitfire IX NH378 12 FU
Engine cut while on ferry flight, belly-landed near Toulouse/Blagnac, France.

23.3.45 Vengeance IV FD364 12 FU
Undercarriage leg jammed, landed on one wheel.

25.3.45 Beaufighter X NE823 12 FU
Collided with Stirling BK615. Became instructional airframe 5757M.

25.3.45 Stirling V BK615 12 FU
Hit by Beaufighter X NE823 of 12 FU.

27.3.45 Vengeance IV FD393 12 FU
Undershot landing and undercarriage collapsed.

12.5.45 Vengeance IV FD277 12 FU
Abandoned after engine failure near Ajaccio, Corsica.

21.6.45 Mosquito XIX TA282 12 FU
Aircraft was beating up the airfield at Cranfield, Beds, when it lost speed in a turn. Stalled and crashed into four Mosquitos on the ground. Pilot and airman passenger killed. Aircraft written off, as was KH356. DZ260, HK253, NT237 were damaged.

11.8.45 Lancaster X FM106 12 FU
Overstressed recovering from a dive.

21.8.45 Mosquito VI RF952 12 FU
Undercarriage leg collapsed on landing, swung and hit steamroller at Drigh Road, India. Destroyed by fire.

31.8.45 Beaufighter X RD725 12 FU
Starboard engine cut on take-off, aircraft swung through 180° and crashed near airfield. Pilot and navigator killed.

A view of Melton Mowbray from the air during the summer of 1997, looking west. In the foreground and then turning north west is the B6047 Great Dalby to Melton road. Author

Chapter Seventeen

North Luffenham

CONSTRUCTION of this airfield began in 1940, the main contractor for the project being the civil engineering firm Laings. By January 1941 the airfield was considered fit for use and the station then came under the control of 51 Group, RAF Flying Training Command. On 6th January North Luffenham's first resident unit, 17 Elementary Flying Training School (EFTS) began to form and on the 18th the initial intake of 60 pupils arrived to begin basic flying training. Not that this appeared likely to start in the immediate future for the whole area was under a deepening blanket of snow and in addition there were no aircraft. Neither were domestic facilities within the camp all that might be desired with many buildings not yet completed.

By the end of the month both the weather and domestic situation had improved considerably. The first de Havilland Tiger Moth biplanes had been delivered, the never-ending round of circuits and bumps was under way and by the 28th February the pupils of No.1 Course were ready for their final exams. When the 90 trainees of No.7 Course reported in on 23rd June the camp had begun to take on an air of permanency and their arrival helped swell the strength of personnel to 998. But a change was in the offing and in July 17 EFTS vacated North Luffenham; by the 17th the complete transfer of personnel had taken place and all aircraft had flown to their new station at Peterborough.

On 21st June 1941 a 5 Group letter had informed 61 and 144 Squadrons at Hemswell, Lincolnshire, of an impending move

Sabre 19102 was the second Canadian-built example, making its first flight in January 1951. It served with both 410 (Cougar) and 441 (Silver Fox) Squadrons, RCAF, almost certainly from North Luffenham. This pre-acceptance air-to-air photo session shows to advantage the type's elegant lines. via Author

to North Luffenham. This order was duly executed with both units taking up residence by the time the last elements of 17 EFTS left on 17th July. These were operational squadrons equipped with Handley Page Hampden twin-engined medium bombers and had been in action since the beginning of the war. They soon resumed their forays against the enemy with both squadrons often participating in the same operation.

The first sorties from North Luffenham took place on the night of 19th/20th July with a 'Gardening' (mining) operation. Five Hampdens from 61 planted 'Vegetables' (mines) in the sea area coded 'Eglantine' while 10 from 144 delivered theirs to 'Yam'. Two nights later on 21st/22nd Frankfurt was the target for the first bombing raid. Five aircraft from 61 Squadron took part but only three felt confident enough to report attacking the primary target. On the next night Frankfurt was again the objective of 34 Hampdens and amongst these were 9 from 61 and 11 from 144. The main post office and telephone exchange were designated as the target and despite heavy rain and 10/10ths cloud 14 North Luffenham aircraft reported locating Frankfurt. Whether they succeeded in disrupting the postal services to any degree is not known. Those Hampdens which failed to find Frankfurt resorted to targets of opportunity at Cologne, Koblenz and Vogelsang airfield.

On the following day, the 24th, 144 Squadron were again in action taking part in a daylight raid against the battleships *Prinz Eugen* and *Gneisenau* lying in the harbour at Brest. Bombing in formation from 13,000ft the six Hampdens easily identified the target; they also encountered intense flak. All five of the Hampdens which returned bore scars as testimony to the accuracy of this anti-aircraft fire. The missing aircraft was AE225, shot down by fighters off Brest.

For the third night in succession, on the 24th/25th, 61 Squadron were engaged on operations. Eight Hampdens left North Luffenham bound for North Germany and Kiel shipyards in particular. One aircraft failed to return, believed shot down by a night fighter off the Dutch coast. Three of 144s aircraft were also active planting some more 'Vegetables'. Success attended their efforts, all returned safe.

To end the month, on the night of the 30th/31st, the station sent out its largest bombing force yet for an attack on the railway marshalling yards at Cologne. The aircraft, 11 from 61 and 15 from 144 constituted more than half the Hampdens taking part. Weather conditions over Germany were very unfavourable and only 15 aircraft bombed the main target or its estimated position, but many bomb bursts and fires were observed. Even on return to England the aircraft were dogged by bad weather; only one of 61's Hampdens managed to return to base. As for others, one of 144's aircraft, AD784, crashed into the sea off the Dutch coast; another, AE252, was believed lost due to icing up. P4399 of 61 Squadron crashed during a thunderstorm at Dartford, Kent, and AE266 was destroyed after undershooting a diversionary landing at Upwood, Huntingdonshire. From these four aircraft there were only two crew who survived.

August began badly with losses for both squadrons. Two of 144's Hampdens were lost on the 6th/7th while on a bombing raid to Karlsruhe; two nights later 61's X3127 and AE263 were missing following an attack on Kiel shipyards. On return a third squadron aircraft, AE259, was on the receiving end of some accurate anti-aircraft fire from an Allied convoy off Spurn Head, all the crew managed to bail out safely but the Hampden was destroyed when it crashed at Fosdyke, Lincolnshire. On this occasion 61 Squadron had operated from Woolfox Lodge (Chapter Twenty-Three) which had become North Luffenham's satellite airfield from 1st August.

For the rest of the month both squadrons fared somewhat better, with 61 losing one more Hampden and 144 two. Brunswick, Cologne, Düsseldorf, Frankfurt, Hanover, Krefeld, Magdeburg, Mannheim and Rotterdam were all attacked and although these cities were the designated target many aircraft failed to find their primary objective, alternative targets serving as substitutes.

Aerial activity during August was not entirely all one way; on two occasions single enemy aircraft paid North Luffenham a visit. Nine bombs fell on the airfield on the 9th, but apart from cratering caused no further damage. A further five were dropped on the 30th; one made a direct hit on the motor transport bay damaging several vehicles, craters on the airfield were again the end product of the rest.

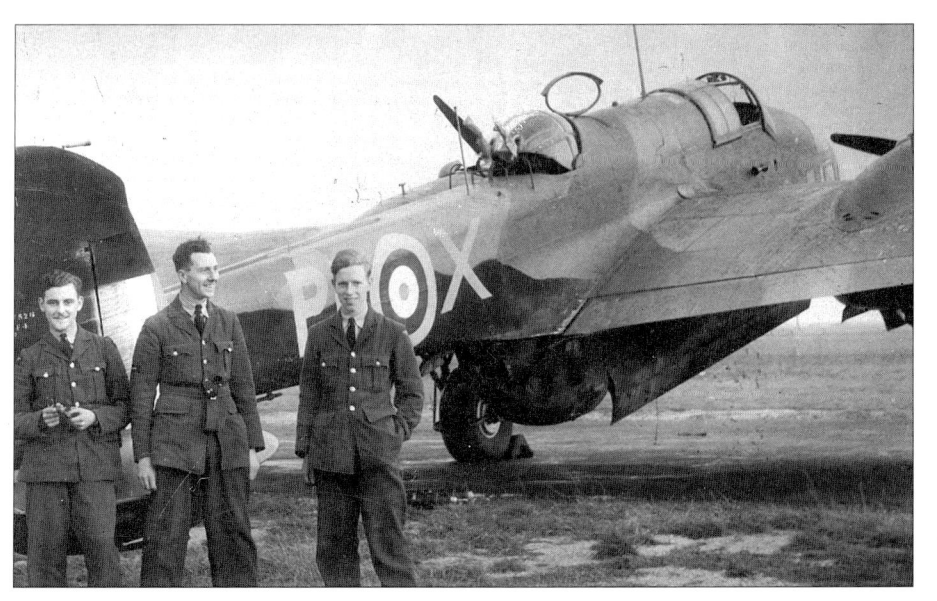

Hampdens of 408 (Goose) Squadron, RCAF, formating above the clouds. The lead aircraft, P1166, also served with 144 Squadron.
Peter Green collection

Airmen of North Luffenham's photographic section in front of 144 Squadron Hampden 'PL-X'. H Stretton

A grouping outside the Sergeants' Mess at North Luffenham, August 1941. Left to right: Gurd, Donovan, Leyshon, McGregor, Rowe. L Boot

A formal gathering outside the Officers' Mess, circa 1942. In the centre is Group Captain Walker. H Stretton

While at Hemswell 61 Squadron had operated a number of Avro Manchester twin-engined heavy bombers and it had been hoped that it would become the third unit to be wholly equipped with these aircraft. Continual teething troubles prevented this but the squadron still had a flight of Manchesters when it came to North Luffenham and training exercises were carried out when serviceability permitted.

On 14th/15th August Wing Commander G E Valentine, the squadron commanding officer, flew L7388 on an offensive mission to Magdeburg, successfully bombing the city from 1,500ft. When a further sortie, to Berlin, took place on 2nd/3rd September the Wing Commander made it clear that he intended to fly at low level, climbing only to safe bombing height when he reached the target area. The Manchester reached Berlin but fell foul of the flak defences and was shot down in the Schönefeld district of the city. The crew, which included on this occasion the station commander Group Captain J F T Barratt, were all killed.

Following this disaster orders were given that station and squadron commanders were no longer allowed to fly on operations without special permission. No.61 temporarily relinquished its remaining Manchesters and the crews were attached to 97 and 207 Squadrons for the purposes of continuation training.

Throughout September the station's Hampdens continued with their forays into Germany. For 144 Squadron it was to be a bad month, ten aircraft being lost in the course of six operations. The night of 21st/22nd was the worst of these occasions, of the eleven Hampdens despatched only two successfully identified and attacked the main target in Frankfurt. No aircraft was lost over enemy territory but it was a different story on their return to England. AD922, which had already been damaged by flak, ran out of fuel and crashed near Foulsham, Norfolk. Three of the crew baled out safely but the pilot, Sergeant E C W Turner, was killed. Fuel shortage also led to the loss of AD923 near Dishforth, Yorkshire, thankfully with no loss of life. Worse tragedies were to occur when AD872 was destroyed near Coningsby, Lincolnshire, and X3030 suffered the same fate near Morcott after undershooting North Luffenham and hitting high tension cables. There were no survivors from either crew.

Perhaps 144 could have considered that fate dealt the unit a very cruel blow for no aircraft was lost from any of the 37 Hampden sorties carried out by 61 Squadron during that month. From the beginning of October 144 Squadron became the only flying unit on the station after 61 Squadron left for the Woolfox Lodge satellite where it was to re-equip with Avro Manchesters.

Throughout the remaining months of 1941 144 continued to make its contribution to Bomber Command's war effort. Bombing attacks were mounted against many major cities in Germany, mines were laid with regularity and several shipping strikes were carried out.

It was during one of these operations that an attack by a lone North Luffenham Hampden resulted in the death of a senior German commander. On 3rd November Flight Lieutenant J F Craig RNZAF, piloting AE309

on an offensive patrol came across a ten ship convoy off the Frisian Islands. An attack was carried out at low level during which four 500lb and two 250lb bombs were dropped. Direct hits were observed on the largest vessel which was left burning and apparently sinking. It was later learned that Major General Felix Varda, chief of the western anti-aircraft defence system, was amongst many other casualties.

Although this operation gained a plus mark the one which followed on 5th/6th November was definitely a big minus. Nine Hampdens were despatched with shipping and other targets as their objectives. Of these three failed to return, all as a result of enemy fire after attacking a convoy off the Dutch coast. Only three crew members survived to become prisoners of war.

Two nights later AE238 crashed on return from a raid on Cologne. The next casualties sustained by North Luffenham personnel occurred following an incident on the night of 9th/10th November when AE311, flown by Sergeant A Nightingale, returned from bombing the Blohm und Voss shipyards at Hamburg. Enemy flak had damaged the aircraft and on landing the port undercarriage collapsed. The Hampden swung round, hit the Chance light caravan, caught fire and was burnt out. Fortunately the crew managed to escape uninjured but not so the flarepath party, two of whom were killed and others injured.

During December the squadron was to lose five more aircraft. Two of these failed to return from consecutive daylight raids against the German capital ships at Brest on the 12th and 13th while another two were lost on what was to be 144's last operation of the year. On 28th/29th ten Hampdens were despatched as part of a large force of Bomber Command aircraft to bomb targets at Huls. Only eight Hampdens returned to North Luffenham; P1295 was reported missing and AD804 damaged by flak crash landed at Doetinchem, with one crew member killed and the rest taken prisoner.

Throughout the war increases in personnel frequently placed a burden on the available living quarters within many RAF stations. To alleviate the problem buildings which had never been intended for service use were often requisitioned as added accommodation. Popular amongst these were large mansions in close proximity to the airfields. In this respect North Luffenham was fortunate and during the first year of operation Edith Weston, Lyndon, Preston and South Luffenham Halls were all impressed as dispersed accommodation.

The pattern for 1942 was unchanged as far as 144 Squadron was concerned. Attacks on major cities in Germany, minelaying and the inevitable sorties against Brest harbour installations were all carried out. During the month North Luffenham became a two squadron station once more when a detachment of 408 (Goose) Squadron, Royal Canadian Air Force (RCAF), began to operate from there. This move became necessary when their home airfield at Balderton, Nottinghamshire, was declared unserviceable for operational flying owing to large amounts of snow and surface water.

For the unit's first two outings to Brest on the 25th and 26th and 27th/28th, their Hampdens operated from North Luffenham, only to return to Balderton next day. This arrangement proved unsatisfactory and from the 29th the operational echelon was detached until such a time as Balderton was considered serviceable once more.

Their third operation on the 31st/1st, when they were joined by 144, was yet another visit to Brest. All their aircraft came

home safely but this target was to cost 144 yet another two Hampdens with five crew killed and three captured. German flak is believed to have claimed AT149 while AE359 crashed into the sea off the French coast. Losses continued to mount for 144 Squadron and another pair of Hampdens, AD824 and AE392, were lost during a daylight mining operation off the Frisian Islands on 7th February. Both were shot down west of Terschelling by a Messerschmitt Bf 109 of II./JG1 flown by Oberfeldwebel Detlef Luth. There were no survivors.

The ever-present threat that German warships at Brest could break out into the Atlantic and there wreak havoc amongst the convoys bringing in vital supplies was of paramount importance to the British High Command. Unfortunately the many bombing raids against the French port failed to disable the Scharnhorst, Gneisenau and Prinz Eugen. Despite what were considered to be stringent surveillance measures the three ships managed to slip out unobserved during the night of 12th February.

With a large force of escorting ships and in atrocious weather conditions they proceeded to make a high speed run through the English Channel, heading for ports in North Germany. The first visual sightings were made when the force was off Le Touquet and by the time Bomber Command was able to take action, the enemy ships, now with fighter cover, were well into the North Sea. At 11:30 hours all bomber groups were ordered to stand by to make an attack. In all 244 aircraft were detailed for take-off in three separate waves, the first at 13:30 hours with fighter escort, the second which involved North Luffenham's contribution to Operation 'Fuller' of eight Hampdens from 408 and nine from 144 began to get airborne at 14:45 hours and had no fighter escort.

Weather conditions in the target area were extremely poor, 8-10/10ths cloud with a base as low as 700ft and intermittent heavy rain. Three of 408's aircraft failed to locate the enemy; two found them but were unable to attack due to low cloud and so brought their bombs back. The remaining three managed to release their loads of 4 x 500lb general purpose bombs on the ships but due to the poor visibility were unable to observe the results. In this trio was AT154 flown by Squadron Leader Constance who had the unnerving experience of having the port aileron shot away plus considerable other flak damage. After bringing his aircraft home under extreme difficulties he was awarded the Distinguished Flying Cross.

As for 144 the outcome of the operation was much worse. Early returns due to engine trouble, bombs brought back or jettisoned when unable to find the target and two attacks with no result observed. In addition the unit lost two aircraft. AT175

vanished without trace, believed to have been the victim of either flak or fighters while AE141 with its starboard engine out of action and heavy flak damage, crashed at Mousehold, near Norwich, Norfolk. Three crew members were safe but the pilot, Sergeant E I Nightingale DFM, died in hospital that evening from injuries received.

Overall the operation was a dismal failure for Bomber Command. Of the aircraft involved, 15 were missing, two crashed on return and no significant damage was done to the German ships. During the course of their voyage though, both the Scharnhorst and Gneisenau did suffer damage from mines. The possibility exists that North Luffenham aircraft were responsible for this as both squadrons were active in the area where this occurred in the days preceding the 'Channel Dash'.

Following the action 408 Squadron continued to operate from the station until midMarch. During this period unit aircraft carried on with their bombing and mining sorties, most of the former being against targets in Germany. While at North Luffenham the unit was to lose only two aircraft, one happening at this time. Neither was due to enemy action and occurred in similar circumstances. Both Hampdens were scheduled for operations and crashed on take-off, AD782 on the squadron's first operation from the station on the 25th/26th January and AD842 on leaving for a mining sortie on 8th/9th March. Balderton was finally declared fit for their return and the detachment left for their Nottinghamshire base on 17th March.

Before the month of March closed 144 Squadron were destined to lose a further three Hampdens. Two of these unfortunates were engaged on a minelaying operation off Heligoland when they fell to the guns of a night-fighter flown by Prinz zur Lippe-Weisenfeld. Only 13 minutes elapsed between the two combats and the cold North Sea claiming another eight lives.

March proved to be a much better month for the squadron. Although still very active both bombing and mining only two Hampdens were lost, both while on the latter type of operations. A change was in the offing for 144. A communication received from HQ Bomber Command on 1st April contained the information that it was proposed to transfer North Luffenham and its satellite to 7 (Training) Group. The signal further stated that 144 Squadron would then move to Swinderby, Nottinghamshire, on the 18th.

In the meantime it was business as usual. Raids between 1st/2nd and 14th/15th April, mainly against major German cities cost the unit dear. Four Hampdens failed to return, one while en route for Dortmund, crashed near Bognor Regis with the loss of all on board, engine failure resulted in another

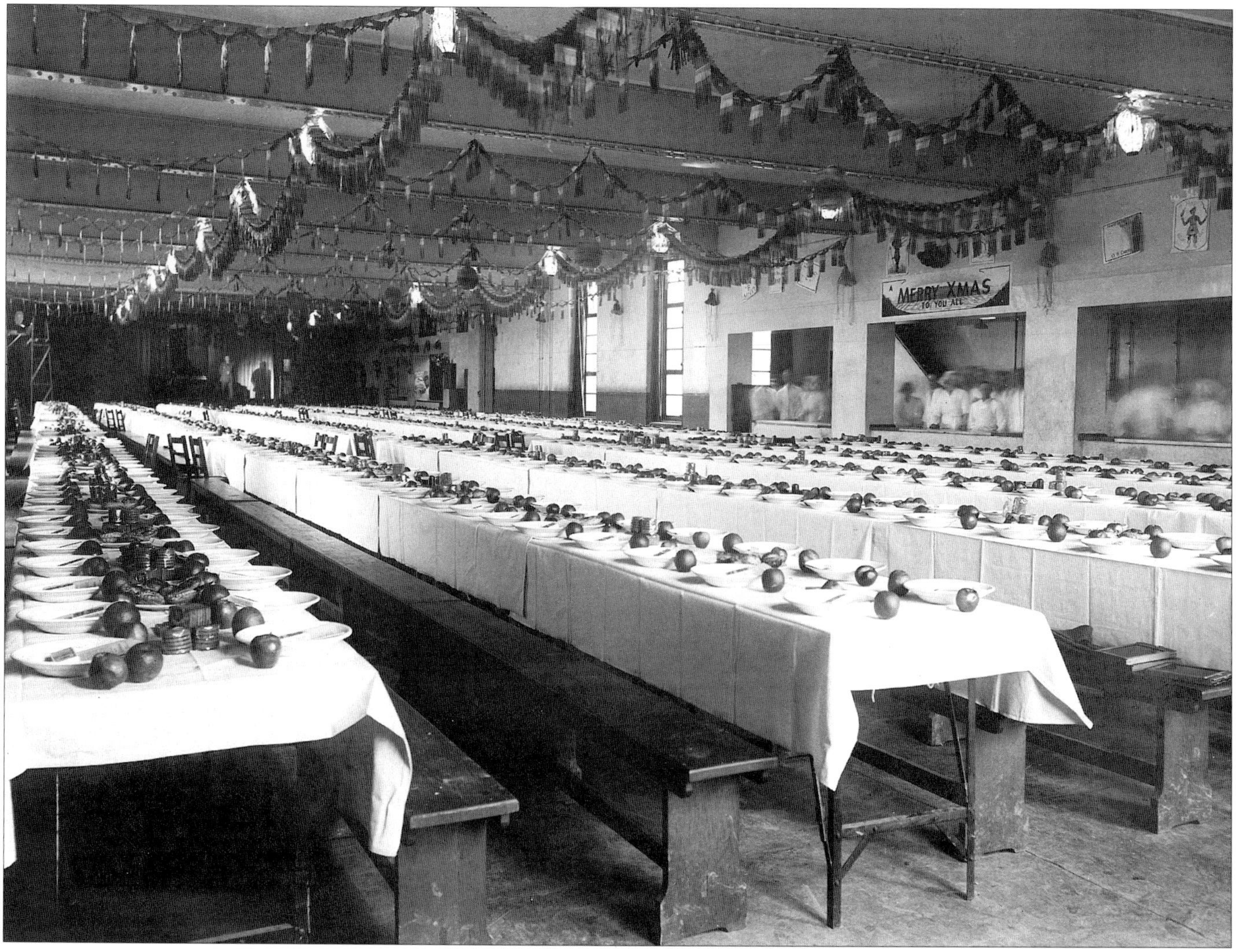

The Airmen's Mess with the kitchen staff ready and waiting, Christmas 1942.
H Stretton

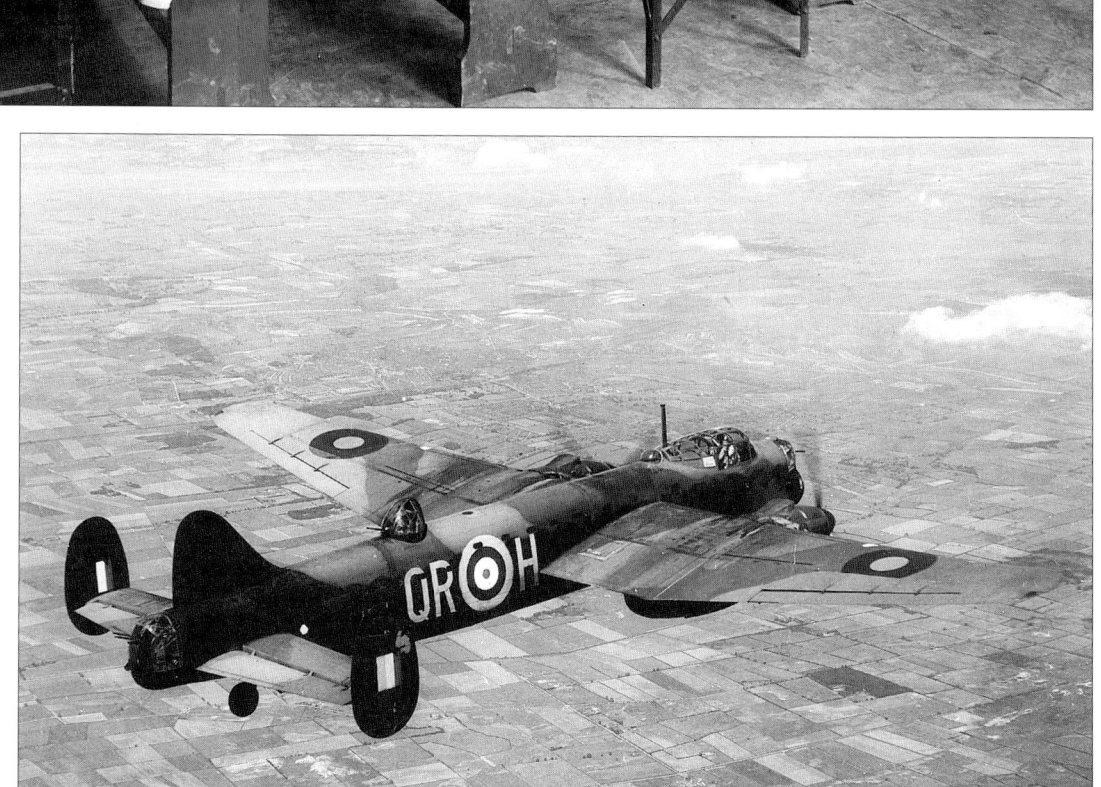

Avro Manchester 'QR-H' of 61 Squadron, 1941.
H Stretton

Vertical view of North Luffenham, dated June 1942. The main camp area is at (A) while the southern complex of dispersals can be seen at (B). To the east lies Witchley Warren Farm (C). The flying field (D) has been effectively camouflaged with painted-on hedgerows etc. MoD

It took some time for the new unit to become established and it was not until 10th June that the first course began its training. At the end of the month, in addition to their tutorial role, aircraft and crews were called upon to partake in operations.

During the late spring and summer of 1942 a series of heavy raids took place against major German cities. Known as the 'Thousand Plan' the aim was to assemble the greatest concentrations of bombers yet seen at this stage of the war and despatch them against a single specific target. To enable a force of this magnitude to be mounted the C-in-C, Bomber Command, Air Chief Marshal Sir Arthur T Harris KCB MC DFC was called upon to utilise aircraft from many sources including the training OTUs of his command.

The first two of these huge raids took place against Cologne on 30th/31st May and Essen on 1st/2nd June. Bremen was the objective of the third raid in the series and on this occasion 29 OTU were amongst the 1,006 bombers taking part.

Eight of North Luffenham's Wellingtons were detailed for the operation and all took off successfully between 23:02 and 23:14 hours on the night of the 25th/26th June. Engine malfunctions caused three aircraft to return early, two with their bomb loads intact, the other safely jettisoned. The remaining aircraft continued on to the target where they encountered heavy cloud cover. Despite this they were able to release their incendiary bomb loads on fires already started by preceding bombers. At interrogation, on return, the five crews were all confident that they had been successful in bombing the primary target.

It had been hoped to mount raids of this type on a regular basis over several months but Bremen was to be the last on this scale for some considerable time. Before the autumn though 29 OTU were to participate in three more major operations. Of the ten aircraft detailed to attack Dusseldorf on 31st July/1st August seven were successful and against the same target on 10th/11th September all eleven Wellingtons engaged completed the operation. Finally Bremen on 13th/14th September was to be the last major raid in which 29 OTU took part. Eight aircraft were detailed and of these seven completed their task. The remaining Wellington, R1459, took off at 23:47 hours and crash-landed at Empingham three min-

crash near Sutton Bridge. While the circumstances which led to the destruction of AT226 are unusual, they are by no means an isolated case. Returning from Cologne, lost and out of fuel the Hampden crash landed. Believing themselves to be in enemy territory the crew set fire to the aircraft. There must have been some very red faces when they found that their landing place was near Grendon Underwood, Buckinghamshire.

No.144 Squadron flew its last bombing operation from North Luffenham on 15th/16th April when five Hampdens once more bombed Dortmund and for their final sorties, next night two aircraft went 'Gardening' off Lorient. The proposed move to Swinderby never came about. Instead an urgent need for a Hampden torpedo bomber squadron led to the choice of 144. The unit then left the station on 21st April bound for Leuchars, Fife, where they were

to convert to this role. With their departure a most eventful period of North Luffenham history came to an end.

On the 24th April the station passed from the control of 5 to 7 Group and 29 Operational Training Unit (OTU) was formed. Shortly afterwards, on 11th May, another change was initiated when 7 Group was renumbered to become 92 Group. Not that this made any difference to the function of the OTU; it was still required to train bomber crews up to operational standard.

Originally it was planned to equip 29 OTU with 40 Vickers Wellington twin-engined medium bombers plus 14 in reserve, but on 22nd May, Headquarters Bomber Command notified the unit that as an interim measure this figure was to be halved and for a time the unit considered a 'half' OTU. A number of Avro Ansons and two target towing aircraft were also on strength.

utes later. Lack of engine power was stated to be the cause and all of the crew were uninjured. This was the OTU's only casualty during this series of raids though other similar units did sustain rather heavy losses.

It was also on the 14th September that information was received from Headquarters, Bomber Command, that presaged a further interruption to training schedules. The communication stated that it was intended to transfer 29 OTU to the as yet unoccupied airfield at Bruntingthorpe, also in Leicestershire (Chapter Six).

As a first move in this direction 'D' Flight was brought back to North Luffenham from the satellite at Woolfox Lodge on 10th October. The next stage in the proceedings came on the 20th when a detachment of an officer, an NCO and 12 airmen left to prepare Bruntingthorpe for the arrival of the OTU. On the 6th November the transfer of 'A' Flight took place and Bruntingthorpe then became a temporary satellite of North Luffenham.

Although the flight was able to carry out some training exercises from the new airfield the situation was far from ideal. Before Bruntingthorpe was in a fit state to receive the complete unit further work needed to be carried out. To enable this to take place without hindrance 'A' Flight was withdrawn, returning to Woolfox Lodge on 30th January 1943.

In the interim the training of crews had carried on and was set to continue. But, an indication that the time for the transfer of the entire OTU was getting ever closer came on 7th April when Air Commodore Darley visited North Luffenham to decide on the positioning of the concrete runways.

The transfer of 29 OTU finally began on 24th May and by the 3rd June it was complete. Both North Luffenham and its satellite had been vacated and the OTU was in residence at Bruntingthorpe and Bitteswell. On 15th June North Luffenham was handed over to the civilian contractors, Wimpeys, in readiness for the reconstruction of the airfield. While this work was in progress their employees were to be housed in the RAF barrack blocks and given the use of the airmen's messing facilities. An RAF presence was still maintained and during this period several anti-aircraft units of the RAF Regiment were briefly based on the station for the purpose of reforming and completing their training.

During the autumn North Luffenham, along with other RAF airfields in the area, was allocated for use in future operations by troop carrier units of the United States 9th Air Force. Although it became Station 477 in their inventory and a small contingent of American personnel were stationed on the camp for a time, it was not required and remained in RAF hands.

In preparation for the airborne operations in support of the liberation of Europe sites were required for the erection, modification and storage of the many gliders which were to be used. Early in the winter facilities at North Luffenham were made available to the Ministry of Aircraft Production (MAP) for this purpose. Hangars on the station then became one of the main locations for the assembly and modification of General Aircraft Hamilcar assault gliders. This was the largest and heaviest glider employed by the Allied forces in the Second World War. Many Hamilcars arrived at the station in kit form while others were flown in, often towed by Handley Page Halifax bombers converted for the purpose. In the initial stages the MAP teams engaged on the work were assisted by a force of United States servicemen but after an American requirement for these gliders was cancelled they were withdrawn. Although the MAP were due to vacate the station by 1st March 1944 their operations were to carry on long after.

By March 1944 the airfield was ready for use once more, 92 Group had relinquished their control and the station passed into the hands of 23 Group, Flying Training Command. The unit designated to be the new tenant of North Luffenham was the Heavy Glider Conversion Unit (HGCU) which transferred from Brize Norton, Oxfordshire, during the first two weeks of March. They began to occupy the station from the 1st and the advance party arrived in style when they were ferried up from Brize Norton in 12 Airspeed Horsa gliders towed by the unit's Armstrong Whitworth Whitleys.

Flying training commenced on the 6th but it was not without its interruptions and anxious moments. On the 8th five Douglas Dakotas circled the airfield while training was in progress. Despite red warning flares two landed. They were American aircraft from nearby Cottesmore whose pilots had mistaken the airfield for their own.

A new type was to be seen in the circuit during 17th-25th March when Armstrong Whitworth Albemarle P1605 was attached to evaluate the suitability of the type for glider towing operations. A successful outcome was reported. By the end of the month 80 of the HGCUs aircraft had now arrived. They consisted of 40 Whitleys, 36 Horsas, three

Lancaster I ME375 'A3-D' of 1653 HCU plus airmen at North Luffenham, October 1945.
via Andy Thomas

Airspeed Oxfords and one Miles Magister.

During April another experiment was carried out which involved Dakotas of 233 Squadron, Blakehill Farm, Wiltshire. Beginning on the 12th four of these aircraft were engaged in night circuits and landings. By the 22nd it was decided to discontinue this practise as it resulted in the HGCU falling behind in their night flying schedules.

But problems apart the unit was settling in well and visits by examining officers of the Empire Central Flying School brought favourable comments. Their impressions were that although the HGCU was operating in under far from ideal conditions it was to be congratulated on the smooth way in which the training programme was carried out. The rapid retrieval of gliders and the preparation of tow trains was the outcome of excellent ground organisation.

It seems that North Luffenham was being used by all and sundry for trials at this time. In May the United States Army Air Force (USAAF) at Cottesmore requested permission to use the airfield to practice glider snatch take-offs. The request was granted and quite a number of these spectacular glider tows were successfully achieved using the Dakota and Waco CG-4A Hadrian combinations.

During July 1944 the HGCU received its first Albemarles and the venerable Whitleys were gradually phased out. These old one-

Halifax A.VII NA423 'FE-PL' of 21 HGCU; note the glider towing gear under the rear fuselage. F M Taylor via Andy Thomas

Airspeed Horsa II 'FERV' of 12 HGCU being towed across the airfield, 1947. via N Franklin

time bombers had been involved in many accidents, often due to engine failure or wheels-up landings, but none reported as involving loss of life. The Horsas too had their fair share of incidents; heavy landings, premature release and overshooting were just a few of the causes.

After just over six months at North Luffenham the unit was given orders to move back to Brize Norton between the 16th-18th September. On the 14th a month's stay of execution was given and in order to finish No.1 RAF Course on time, arrangements were made to use Woolfox Lodge as a relief landing ground. On 13th October the HGCU began to move out and by the 15th North Luffenham was ready for a new unit.

Once again a drastic change was about to happen. From 16th October North Luffenham ceased to be answerable to 23 Group when control passed to a reformed 7 Group now responsible for heavy bomber conversion units. As part of a new system North Luffenham was to become the controlling

element in a group of three Avro Lancaster four-engined heavy bomber training stations known as 73 Base. Woolfox Lodge was another and Spanhoe, Northamptonshire, should have been the third but at this time it was under American control.

Nevertheless, reorganisation and preparation of the station began on this basis and for the reception of 1653 Heavy Conversion Unit (HCU) from Chedburgh, Suffolk. Then between 16th and 27th November the HCU moved in and as the unit was in the process of converting from Short Stirlings to Lancasters the 40 crews under training were all sent on leave. This enabled the instructors at the HCU to complete their own conversion in readiness for the pupils on their return.

When fully re-equipped the unit was to have a strength of 32 Lancasters together with a miscellany of Bristol Beaufighters, de Havilland Mosquitos, Hawker Hurricanes and Vickers-Supermarine Spitfires for fighter affiliation purposes.

RAF North Luffenham – 1st December 1944

Latitude	52° 37' 53" N
Longitude	00° 36' 15" W
Height at Sea Level	350ft
Locality	6 miles SW of Oakham
Command	Bomber (RAF)
Nearest Railway Station	Luffenham, LMS, 2½ miles
Function	Operational Base
Affiliated Airfields	Spanhoe (Sub-station)
	Woolfox Lodge (Sub-station)

Runways – Landing Area

QDM	Dimensions	Extensibility	Remarks
190°	1,400 x 50 yds	2,000 yds	Entails demolit-
260°	2,000 x 50 yds	2,050 yds	ion of two huts
320°	1,400 x 50 yds	2,500 yds	and diversion of
Type of Surface – Concrete.			one road.

Permanent Landmarks

By Day	Ketton Chimney.
By Night	Nil

Permanent Obstructions Nil

Facilities

Airfield Lightning	Mk.II
Beam Approach	–
Radio	–
QDM	–
Flying Control	Yes

Accommodation	Permanent technical and communal buildings.

Technical	Hangars		Hardstandings	
	Type	No	Type	No
	J	2	Loop	32
	T2	3	Frying Pan	18

Domestic	Officers	SNCOs	ORs	Total
RAF	108	182	1,828	2,118
WAAF	11	10	290	311

Initially trainee crews were involved in the tedium of circuits and bumps while their pilots became familiar with handling four-engined bombers. As soon as progress permitted, sorties which involved the various crew members were undertaken. Exercises in navigation, gunnery and bombing practise and fighter affiliation, by day and night, all helped the crews to hone their skills and become a tight-knit unit in readiness for operational flying.

It would be nice to relate that all went smoothly but alas this was not the case. During the first four months of 1945 four Lancasters and a Spitfire were lost by the HCU, each time in fatal circumstances.

To commemorate the end of the war in Europe the station enjoyed a two day stand-down on 8th/9th May and many of North Luffenham's occupants took it as an opportunity to celebrate in style. The training round was soon resumed but the surrender of Japanese forces in August brought a relaxation and aircrews began to look to the future with greater optimism.

On 15th September the station opened its gates to the general public for the first time as part of countrywide open days in commemoration of the Battle of Britain. Almost 13,000 people and over 1,800 cars are reported to have attended the event which contained many of the ingredients which became standard at future open days. There were ground displays of aircraft and equipment, one exhibit being a captured German glider bomb. In the air Lancaster formations, Spitfire aerobatics, a Gloster Meteor jet fighter flypast and a Hurricane dropping practise bombs all helped to give the public an enjoyable day.

The HCU continued its allotted task and continued to lose several aircraft in accidents. Far more were disposed of as tired and weary old warriors and consigned to be scrapped. Decreases in both personnel and equipment were beginning to take place and from 6th December the HCU's complement of Lancasters was reduced to 18. In the same month the station became part of 91 Group, a change in title only for the Group was still responsible for bomber crew training.

The opening months of 1946 proved to be rather a difficult period for the station. Demobilisation of RAF personnel and the repatriation of Italian Prisoners of War placed a severe strain on manning levels. Flying hours suffered and the servicing wing was hard pressed to keep four aircraft available for flying at all times. Evidence of the difficult situation is given in a summary for February. During the month the training intake was just two crews and the output 12; flying was only possible on 16 days and 14 nights when 413 hours were flown. All this was mainly due to a shortage of aircraft.

The HCU shouldered its burden and carried on making the most of these difficulties associated with peacetime and the run-down of the RAF. It continued to operate from the station throughout the summer and into the autumn, then after two years in residence a change of scene was ordered. On 28th October 1946, 1653 HCU vacated North Luffenham to move further north and become established at RAF Lindholme in Yorkshire.

North Luffenham's next unit was to be no stranger to the station for two years earlier it had been in residence as the Heavy Glider Conversion Unit (HGCU). Now with a number prefixed to its title it had become 21 HGCU. Owing to the poor state of the camp at Elsham Wolds, Lincolnshire, the decision was made to transfer to North Luffenham. Accordingly control of the station was passed to 23 Group, Flying Training Command on 25th November.

Although the type of training was to be the same and the gliders were still Horsas the tow aircraft had changed and were now Handley Page Halifaxes. On 5th December the main party of the HGCU arrived and five days later flying recommenced. In the near future it was to come to an abrupt halt.

Bad weather which began during January 1947 was to develop into one of the worst winters Rutland had ever experienced. Between 28th January and 28th February there was a period of heavy snowfalls and hard frosts. No flying of any description could be carried out and the station's main effort was concentrated on keeping the road to North Luffenham open. Snow-ploughs were in constant operation but suffered from frequent breakdowns. To clear many large drifts over six feet deep it was necessary to resort to manual labour.

Owing to the shortage of many essentials, including solid fuel, and the urgent necessity for economy, large numbers of personnel

Dakota 'NU-C' of 240 OCU, parked outside of one of North Luffenham's Type 'J' hangars. R Handley

No.240 OCU Valetta C.1 VW807 'NU-T' draws little attention during one of the station's open days. via Andy Thomas

Pleasing air-to-air of a pair of Spitfire F.22s (the rear example in camouflage) of 102 FRS, November 1951. In the foreground is PK399 'M-50'.

No.102 FRS had only a brief life at North Luffenham. One of the unit's Vampire FB.5s, WA455, during November 1951.
Both Alan Holt via Peter Green

were sent on leave, reducing camp staff to a minimum. After a short lull terrible weather returned again on 4th March. Very heavy snowfalls accompanied by strong winds blocked all camp roads and drifts over seven feet high cut the road to North Luffenham railway station. By the 5th all roads were blocked, snow ploughs were unable to cope so all available men were engaged in clearing the road to the station. On the 8th the road was finally cleared enabling rations to be collected from Peterborough. The nearby villages of Edith Weston and North Luffenham were also suffering but were helped by sales from the NAAFI.

All roads were at last open by the 11th but it was some time before the thaw set in. By the 27th the runways and airfield were clear once more but bad weather still persisted and although aircraft flew for the first time next day activity was still limited for some time. As the weather improved so did the HGCU's output, the Halifaxes with Horsas in tow becoming a familiar sight.

At the end of June a visit was made to the station by a delegation from a French airborne division. This unit was in the process of being equipped for the training of glider pilots and 21 HGCU's advice and expertise were sought. The visit was quite a success and in consequence the division's Commandant requested that aircraft from the HGCU pay a visit to his airfield at Mont de

Marsan to demonstrate glider flying to a wider audience. Also it would be an opportunity for his unit to reciprocate the hospitality shown to his men while at North Luffenham.

The invitation received official blessing and three Halifax and Horsa combinations left on 3rd July. All arrived safely, various demonstrations were given and by special request, on one flight, a Horsa (TL424) was towed by a Junkers Ju52 three-engined transport. In appreciation of this reciprocal visit their French hosts treated the RAF personnel to an all too brief outing for rest and relaxation at Biarritz. All good things must come to an end and a return to the UK was made on 6th July. Again the flights were without incident, the combinations landing at North Luffenham in the afternoon and early evening.

Continuing with the demonstration theme the unit assisted at five RAF stations during the Battle of Britain displays on 9th

September. At each, exhibitions of landing and take-off techniques were given by single Halifax and Horsa combinations. Next day contingents of personnel from North Luffenham took part in parades at Leicester and Stamford.

Into the autumn the training continued; the scale of this is illustrated by the figures for October when a total of 310:45 hours were flown by the following aircraft: Halifax 176:35, Horsa 123:20 and Oxford 10:50 hours. As glider training was due to be reduced the days of the unit were numbered. After receiving confirmation during November that 21 HGCU was to disband, this directive came into effect from 3rd December. North Luffenham was then taken over by Transport Command and consequently became the base of a completely different type of unit.

From 10th December 1947, 1382 (Transport) Conversion Unit began to move in from Wymeswold (Chapter Twenty-Four). Engaged in medium range conversion training and equipped with Douglas Dakotas, the unit continued its flying programme without any major break.

Apart from the unit being renamed 240 Operational Conversion Unit (OCU) on 5th January 1948, little change in its activities were noted until 28th June when all flying and much of the ground training came to an abrupt halt. The cause of this unusual procedure was the Russian blockade of Berlin which had begun on 26th June and the urgent need to fly essential supplies to the beleaguered city. Aircraft and crews from North Luffenham were amongst the first detailed to take part in these freight flights, initially known as Operation 'Carter Patterson' but later renamed 'Plainfare'. From humble beginnings this was to develop into that massive air operation, the Berlin Airlift.

By 5th August, in just over a month of operations, 240 OCU and crews under its control flew 1,023 sorties and carried 3,250 tons of freight. While engaged in support of 'Plainfare' the unit's Dakotas returned periodically to North Luffenham for all major servicing. Full involvement in the operation continued until 20th September when training was recommenced at half its intended scale. A gradual release of instructors and crews from airlift duties then eventually allowed the OCU to return to normality and fulfil its allotted commitments. It was not until 23rd March 1949 that the last crews returned to North Luffenham.

Towards the end of 1948 two new types of transport aircraft entered service with the RAF, the de Havilland Devon and Vickers Valetta. Conversion courses on both these types were introduced to become part of the OCU's syllabus. Eventually the Valetta was to supplant the Dakota in Transport Command.

From a safety aspect 1948 was an extremely successful year for 240 OCU and in recognition, on 8th February 1949 the unit was presented with the Transport Command Accident Prevention Trophy. Many high ranking officers were attracted to the occasion. They included Marshal of the RAF Lord Tedder, four Air Marshals, four Air Vice-Marshals and two Air Commodores, added to these were various civic dignitaries and personalities including Sir Frederick Handley Page.

Quite a large flying display was staged on the day which featured mainly aircraft of Transport Command. The scale of the influx of people for the event can be judged by the fact that there were 38 visiting aircraft. Not everyone appreciated the event; personnel returning from airlift duties found no transport available and the camp much depleted. Many staff had been given a 72 hours pass in celebration.

During the summer months the training schedules were frequently interrupted when the OCU was required to supply aircraft for various displays and exercises. On many occasions unit aircraft were deployed to Netheravon, Wiltshire, where they took part in the training of airborne forces, which mainly involved the dropping of paratroops over Salisbury Plain. When engaged on these exercises the side doors of the Dakotas were removed and the edges of the opening then padded with felt. Rex Handley, one time radar mechanic, recalled that this material had another very important use. Cut into foot size pieces it was attached to the 'erks' boots who then skated round the billet floors keeping them well polished to pass inspection.

Although the OCU had won the Accident Prevention Trophy in 1948 there was to be no repeat performance in 1949. During the year too many reportable accidents occurred, mainly to Dakotas, as the following selection of incidents shows:

23rd May While parked KP276 was struck by KJ810 and written off.

July Between 7th–18th there were three forced landings and two taxying accidents. Only one of these incidents took place at North Luffenham; the others occurred at airfields the Dakotas were visiting.

29th August While night flying KN544 crash landed on the airfield. Both propellers had been feathered in error.

13th September On taking off for a night exercise at Netheravon KJ865 sank back and hit the ground. The aircraft was written off.

There was little change in 240 OCU's activities throughout 1950. Training followed the established pattern apart from the introduction, in June, of longer range exercises which took crews on occasion to Germany and Malta. The Battle of Britain was celebrated with an open day but attendance was rather sparse with just over 2,000 visitors. One thing that did alter during the year was the accident rate. This fell to such a degree that once again the OCU was awarded the Command Accident Prevention Trophy, presented on 14th March 1951 by Air Chief Marshal Sir Ralph Cochrane.

This was the last big ceremonial occasion for 240 OCU at North Luffenham as a change was scheduled. On 20th March the OCU and most of its aircraft moved to Dishforth, Yorkshire, and North Luffenham prepared to receive a new resident unit.

At this time, following an act of Parliament, certain members of the Royal Air Force Volunteer Reserve were required to undertake three months continuous service in order to convert from the elementary types of aircraft they normally flew to higher speed aircraft then in service. The first half of these reservist's course was spent at either Ternhill, Shropshire, or Oakington, Cambridgeshire, flying the North American Harvard to familiarise themselves with a heavier type of aircraft. They then went on to carry out the high speed conversion element of the training.

One of two new units established to perform this function, 102 Flying Refresher School (FRS), part of the recently formed 25 Group, Flying Training Command, was North Luffenham's new resident. On its inception the FRS was organised into two squadrons, No.1 equipped with 32 Supermarine Spitfires and No.2 with 9 de Havilland Vampire F.1s, although the latter were quickly superseded by 24 Vampire FB.5s. Several Gloster Meteor T.7s and Harvards were also available for dual tuition. Each course consisted of an average of 36 students who were each given a dual check in a Harvard before they joined 1 Squadron for three weeks to spend 20 hours flying Spitfires. They transferred to 2 Squadron for the remainder of their course where a further 15 hours were spent airborne in the Vampires.

In addition to flying, each student was required to attend almost 20 hours of lectures and spend a minimum of four hours in Link Training Tuition. Due to the intensive nature of the course flying began at 06:30 hours and invariably continued until 21:00. In order to keep to the tight schedules involved both air and ground crews worked to a shift system.

For several months North Luffenham was a very busy station but this new type of training was destined to have a very short life. In October 102 FRS was disbanded and on the 29th the main party of the now defunct unit left North Luffenham for Oakington, Cambridgeshire, where it became an integral part of 206 Advanced Flying School.

Following the demise of 102 FRS a new era was to dawn for North Luffenham. Due to the outbreak of the Korean war relations between Western Europe and the Eastern Bloc were at a very low ebb. It became imperative that the forces of the North Atlantic Treaty Organisation (NATO) were strengthened. Canada responded and signified its intention to deploy an Air Division of four Fighter Groups, each with three squadrons, to bolster the West's defences.

As suitable bases on mainland Europe were not yet ready, the first squadrons were housed temporarily on a British base. This was North Luffenham.

The station was transferred from RAF control on 15th November 1951 to become the headquarters of No.1 Fighter Wing, Royal Canadian Air Force, and the base for three squadrons equipped with Canadair Sabre 2 swept-wing jet fighters. Although one of the station's hangars had to be pressed into service when bad weather forced the parade and handing-over to be held indoors, it was carried out with due ceremony. Present were the Canadian High Commissioner, the Hon L D Wilgress and the Vice Chief of Air Staff, Air Chief Marshal The Hon Sir Ralph Cochrane, together with other senior officers from Fighter and Flying Training Commands. Group Captain R A Ramsey Rae OBE relinquished control of the station which was then officially accepted by Group Captain E B Hale DFC the new officer commanding RCAF North Luffenham.

After lunch a short flying display was staged and it had been hoped that this would be given by 410 (Cougar) Squadron RCAF the first of station's units to arrive. However, the aircraft carrier HMCS *Magnificent* which had transported the squadron across the Atlantic had only docked the previous day and although the pilots were able to attend, their aircraft still awaited unloading in Scotland. In the event the display was given by 421 (Red Indian) Squadron RCAF, flying de Havilland Vampire FB.5s. This unit had been stationed at RAF Odiham, Hampshire, training with Fighter Command since January and was about to return to Canada to re-equip with Sabres.

In March 1952, 441 (Silver Fox) Squadron became the second of the Wing's units to arrive. Their aircraft were brought over in HMCS *Magnificent* but the personnel travelled in style aboard the *Empress of France*.

It was left to 439 (Tiger) Squadron to complete No.1 Fighter Wing and their arrival at North Luffenham went down in aviation history after they made the first large scale ferry flight of Canadair Sabres across the Atlantic. The squadron's 21 aircraft embarked upon Operation 'Leapfrog 1' on 30th May 1952, with refuelling stops scheduled at Bagotville, Goose Bay, Bluie West 1, Keflavik, Kinloss and thence to North Luffenham.

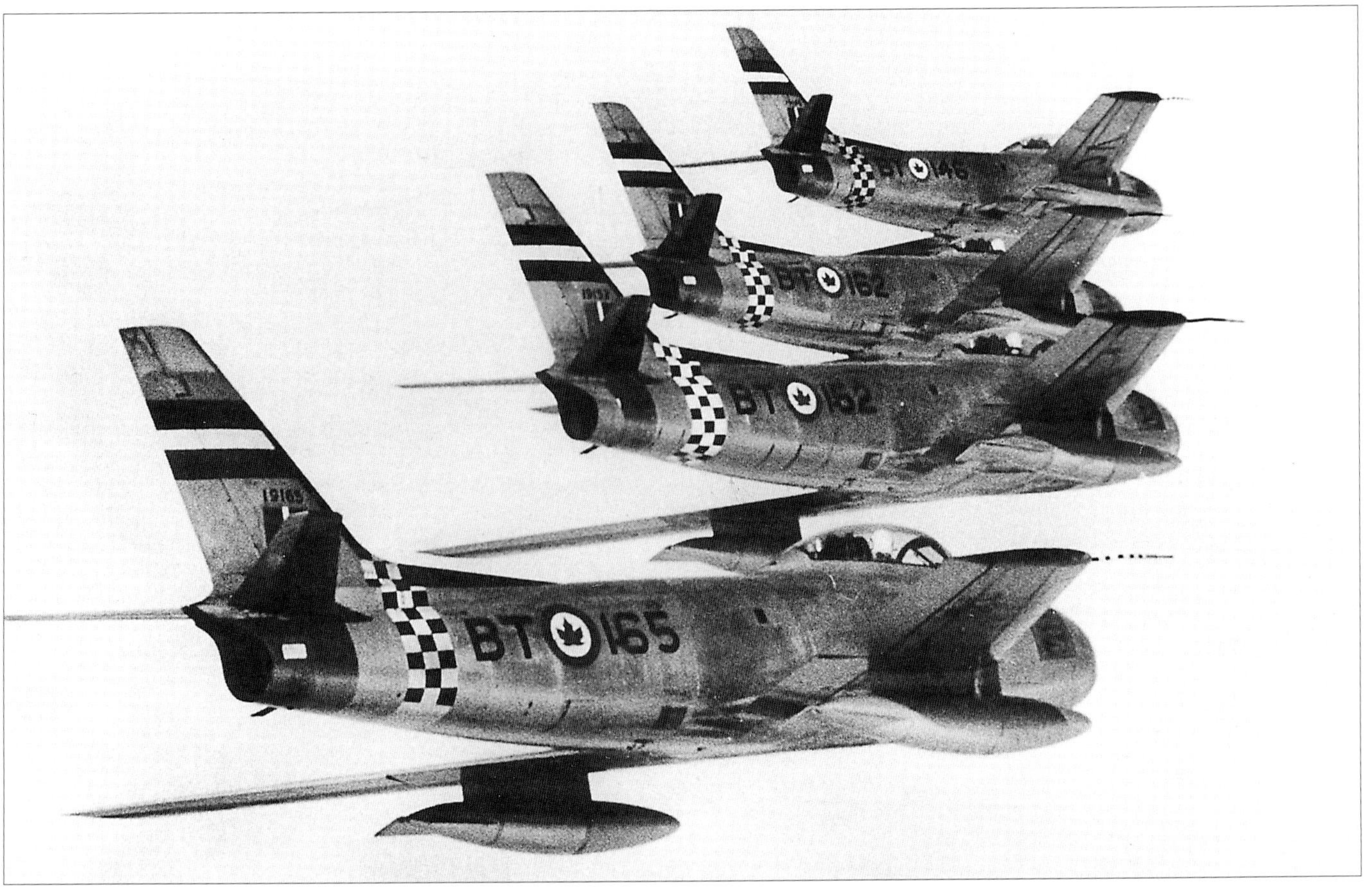
BT 165
BT 162
BT 162
19165

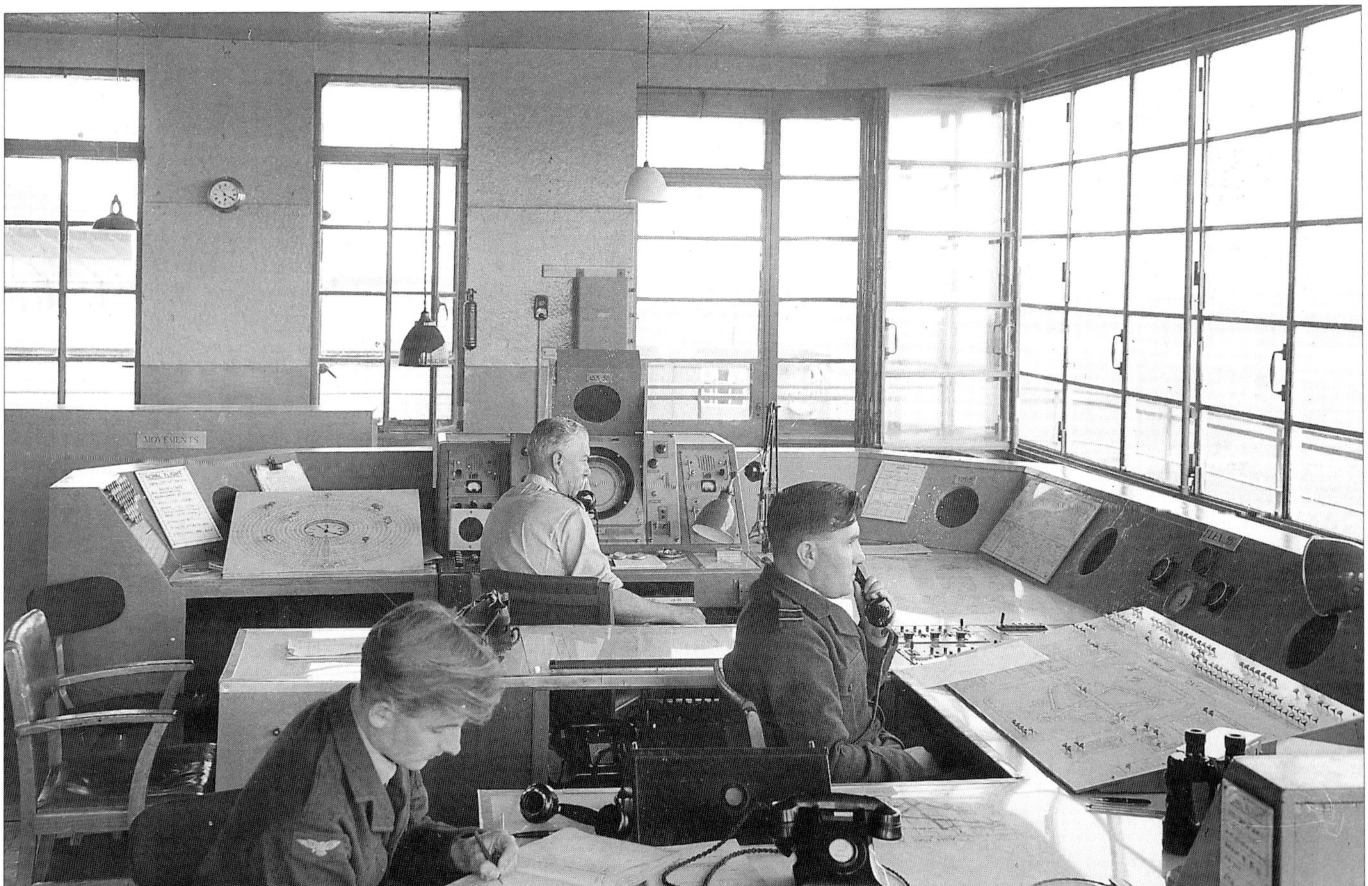
MOVEMENTS

Opposite page:

A neat echelon of chequerboarded Sabres of 441 (Silver Fox) Squadron. via J Smith

A view inside the North Luffenham control tower, August 1955. via Author

Not all went to plan and what was intended to be a four day trip extended to 16 due to the weather. To add to the problems, while *en route*, the CO Squadron Leader C D Bricker came down with appendicitis making necessary a temporary command for Flight Lieutenant W Bliss. Problems apart, the trip was a success and the squadron flew in to its new home tired and weary on 15th June. The week's leave in London which followed their arrival soon helped rejuvenate the Tigers.

One other unit was to become resident at North Luffenham during 1952 but only for a brief period. Operation 'Leapfrog 2', which left Canada on 28th September, was the first mass ferry flight of RCAF Sabres to the European mainland. Three squadrons undertook the trip and flying with them were the first three Sabre F.2s destined for RAF service. After reaching the UK early in October they were sent to North Luffenham where they formed No.1 Long Range Ferry Unit (LRFU). These aircraft were then used in the conversion of pilots who were to make the first all-RAF ferry flight of Sabres during December. At the same time about 50 groundcrew were also detached to the station to undergo training in servicing this new type on the RAF inventory. The LRFU, its initial purpose fulfilled, left the station on 4th December to continue its activities at Abingdon, Oxfordshire. While the RCAF were to remain at North Luffenham, there was continued close collaboration on all matters technical and operational in respect of the Sabre.

The arrival of the Canadians, accompanied in many cases by their dependents, placed quite a strain on camp facilities. Some families found accommodation in surrounding villages while others were housed in a caravan site established on the airfield. Later the situation was further eased by more permanent quarters being built.

A pair of RCAF 410 (Cougar) Squadron Sabres lift off from North Luffenham.

A misty morning at North Luffenham with a line-up of RCAF 439 (Tiger) Squadron Sabres on the operational apron. The aircraft in the foreground, 19166, served with both 439 and 441 Squadrons, but the relevance of the code 'EB-H' and the fuselage striping, is unknown.

Pilots from 439 (Tiger) Squadron pose in front of one of their Sabres. All via J Smith

From the outset the Sabres quickly made their presence felt. They acquitted themselves extremely well during air exercises and in mock combat against other NATO aircraft. They were frequent and popular attractions at air displays countrywide, while the station also made its own contribution to Battle of Britain open days. Many memorable aerobatic displays were performed by this most agile of fighters in the hands of some extremely skilled pilots. The Wing was also well represented on several prestigious occasions. Twenty-four Sabres from North Luffenham were amongst the aircraft taking part in the flypast to celebrate the Coronation of Her Majesty Queen Elizabeth II and later a formation of 36 aircraft participated in the Review of the Royal Air Force by Her Majesty at Odiham, Hamp-

shire, on 15th July 1953. No.1 Wing also formed an aerobatic team. This four Sabre formation was in great demand and toured the UK and the continent.

Unfortunately, the intense air activity generated by the North Luffenham units was not sustained without mishap. One unusual way of trying to reduce flying accidents was introduced which involved a goat. This animal was ceremonially awarded monthly to the squadron with the worst accident record. The pilot then found guilty of the worst flying mistake was then made responsible for the animal and its welfare until the next luckless individual took over a month later. On a more serious note, during their stay in Rutland the squadrons were to write off 17 Sabres and six pilots were to forfeit their lives.

From contemporary accounts the Canadians seem to have enjoyed their stay in Rutland. Locally they were well liked with a result that many lasting friendships were formed. No.1 Wing began to leave North Luffenham towards the end of 1954. Departing in the order in which they arrived: 410 left for Baden-Sollingen, Germany, on 14th November; 441 followed on 21st December, bound for Zweibrucken, Germany; and finally on 1st April 1955, 439 flew out to Marville, France. The station then reverted to RAF control.

An advance party had been making preparations for this change since February and during April a new unit, the All-Weather Operational Conversion Unit (AWOCU) was formed. Equipped mainly with Gloster Meteor NF.12s and NF.14s it was to specialise in training crews destined to fly these night-fighters equipped with AI Mk.21 airborne interception radar. Prior to arriving at North Luffenham trainees had undergone the initial part of their course flying in Bristol Brigands at Colerne, Wiltshire, and now it was the task of the AWOCU to take them through the advanced phase.

As its title suggests crews were to be trained to fly in all weathers, day or night, a situation not without hazard. While engaged on a night interception exercise on 21st September 1955, two Meteors collided in mid-air over Derbyshire. Both aircraft were abandoned by their crews two of whom lost their lives. On 11th January 1956 another Meteor was written off when it crashed near the Ketton Cement Works after hitting a tree while on a night approach to North Luffenham. This time both occupants walked away from the incident. The crew of WS661 were not so fortunate, nine days later. While low flying near Wadhurst, Surrey, this aircraft also hit trees before crashing into a bungalow; both the pilot and observer were killed. Thankfully there were no more tragedies of this nature to affect the unit.

In January 1957, following a decision to rationalise night fighter training 238 OCU at Colerne was split. Its Brigand T.4s journeyed north to join 228 OCU at Leeming, Yorkshire, while the Brigand T.5s, together with the remainder of the Boulton Paul Balliols came to North Luffenham. Following their arrival the AWOCU and 238 OCU merged, the latter's title being adopted.

A Meteor F.8 touches down on North Luffenham's runway while a line of AWOCU NF.12s await their turn. via N Franklin

The night shift in progress in one of North Luffenham's Type 'J' hangars. The Vampire T.11, Meteor F.8 and two Meteor NF.14s look lost in the vast interior. N Franklin

Brigand T.5s of 238 OCU flying westwards towards their base, over the township of Ketton, with the cement works visible bottom left. Lumbers Collection, Leicestershire Museums

Balliol T.2 WG116 'D' of 238 OCU awaiting the day's assignments. MAP via R C B Ashworth

A Meteor NF.12, (possibly WS610) undergoing servicing in the ASF hangar at North Luffenham, 1958. Eric Sharpe via Ken Ellis

A graphic invitation from 238 OCU!
P Richardson

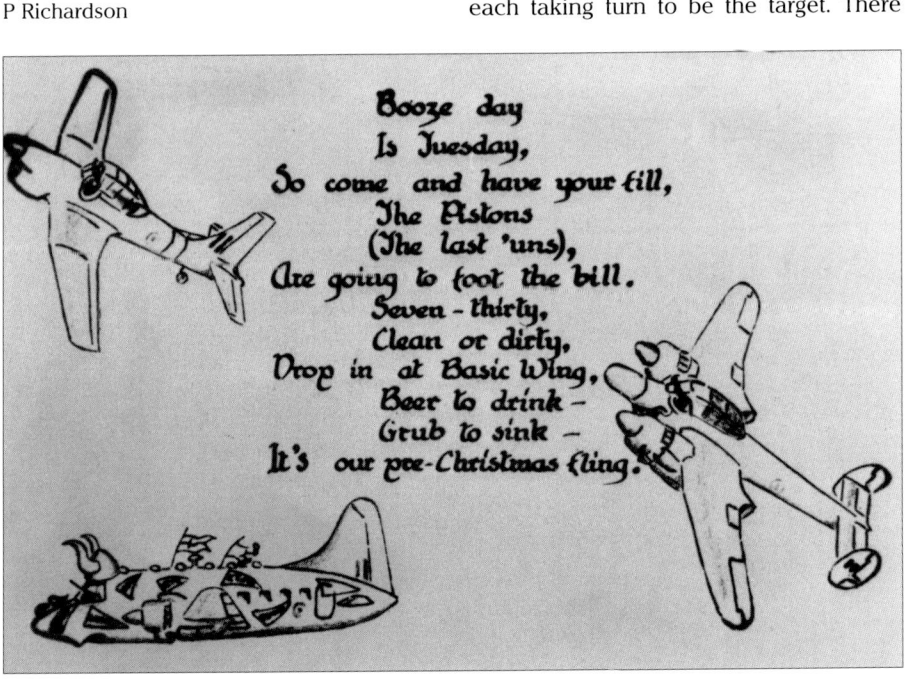

With the new regime installed trainees spent the first part of their course with the Basic Flying Wing where they mastered the fundamentals of their trade. At this stage unit Balliols acted as target aircraft for the trainee operators in the Brigands. Basics over, they then passed to the Advanced Flying Wing for the final stages of their course. The aircraft usually operated in pairs with each taking turn to be the target. There were, however, frequent exercises involving the interception of other RAF aircraft.

Training by the OCU was not just limited to RAF crews. Fleet Air Arm pilots and observers destined to fly de Havilland Sea Venoms also came to North Luffenham where they received a 12 week course. This consisted of two weeks ground school, eight weeks interception training and two weeks of gunnery. For this latter exercise drogue-towing Gloster Meteor F.8s were used. In addition the unit was also responsible for the training of navigators for some foreign air forces.

On 19th February 1958, for the first and as it transpired, the only time, the station became the base of a front line fighter squadron when repairs to the runways at North Weald, Essex, made a move necessary for 111 Squadron. Being the unit from which the RAF's premier aerobatic team, the Black Arrows, was drawn they were expected to arrive with panache and style. Instead, it was a very subdued affair with the Hawker Hunter F.6s slipping in out of cloud in pairs. Next day they made up for it with a spectacular beat-up of the station.

As the need for trained crews for the Meteor NF.12 and NF.14 squadrons grew less so the role of 238 OCU declined. On 13th March 1958, as part of the closing down ceremonies, a formation of nine Brigands made a farewell flypast over the station. Four days later the OCU disbanded.

Throughout the spring and early summer of 1958 the Black Arrows continued to hone and perfect their aerobatic routines in the skies over Rutland. During this time several of their Hunters were to be seen in experimental paint schemes but in the end the overall gloss black finish was retained. 'Treble One' left North Luffenham on the 18th June for their new operating base at Wattisham, Suffolk. Their departure was to leave a void which would never be filled. The station's days as a base for flying units was at an end for it was on the verge of entering the missile age.

It was announced in a Defence White Paper on 13th February 1958 that HM Government had accepted a US Government offer to supply Britain with a nuclear deterrent in the form of Douglas SM75 Thor Intermediate Range Ballistic Missiles (IRBM). To house these there were to be four main bases each with four satellite stations. Each site would house three of the nuclear-tipped delivery system weapons. North Luffenham was the last of the main bases and four, long disused, Second World War airfields at Folkingham, Harrington, Polebrook and Melton Mowbray (Chapter Sixteen) became its satellites.

The station had been placed on care and maintenance in June 1958 and work began to prepare it for its new role. On the 31st October, North Luffenham became part of 3 Group, Bomber Command and events progressed rapidly. Less than a year later in September 1959 operational and technical RAF personnel who had been trained in the USA began to be posted in. United States Air Force and Douglas Aircraft Corporation personnel also began to arrive, presenting yet again an accommodation problem. As with the Canadians before, a solution was found by establishing a large trailer camp.

During October the first missile for the North Luffenham complex arrived and the last, the RAFs 60th, was disgorged from a Douglas C-124 Globemaster II transport after a flight from the USA on 10th March 1960. All 15 Thors for the North Luffenham group were delivered to the airfield in this way, either in the aforementioned type of aircraft or in Douglas C-133 Cargomasters of the US Air Force Military Air Transport Service. Onward distribution to the outstations was then completed by road.

The station and its missiles was declared fully operational in May 1960. Each group of three IRBMs was allocated the number of a reformed RAF unit; North Luffenham's trio became 144 Squadron. One shudders to think of the destructive power of the Thor's two megaton warheads when compared to the puny bombloads carried by the Hampdens which the squadron had previously operated from the airfield in 1941-1942.

Concurrent with the missile complex the station also became the Headquarters of 151 Wing, Fighter Command, and as such was responsible for the control of two Bristol Bloodhound Mk I surface-to-air (SAM) missile batteries which were intended as a defence against enemy attack not only on the Thor sites but also the V-bomber bases. Eleven of these anti-aircraft missile units were positioned throughout eastern England, each was allocated a squadron number and the two under North Luffenham's jurisdiction were 257 Squadron at Warboys, Huntingdonshire and 62 Squadron at Woolfox Lodge.

Control of these SAM batteries was divided into four separate areas each equipped with a Type 82 radar. One of the distinctive three storey buildings to house this equipment with its large radar aerial and adjacent Tactical Control Centre (TCC) was built on the airfield. Following the receipt of information passed on after an intruder had been located by a coast based Master Radar the task of the TCC was to then assign targets to the appropriate missile battery.

While the Thors were *in situ* there were frequent 'Combat Training Launches'. These were exercises intended to test that the system was in operational readiness. There were also three practise launches of North Luffenham Thors but these took place from Vandenburg Air Base, California, after a missile had been withdrawn from service. Because of their nuclear capability IRBMs were also the target of 'Ban The Bomb' agitators and in common with other similarly equipped stations North Luffenham had to cope with demonstrations in support of this aim.

The life of the Thor force, as a whole, was rather short. Her Majesty's Government announced on 1st August 1962 that owing to the vulnerability of these fixed sites the IRBM squadrons were to be disbanded and the missiles returned to the USA. Following this decision the rundown of the force was rapid and within the space of six months during 1963 all Thor units were de-activated. Those in North Luffenham's complex, the last to be activated, were also the last in service. First to go during August were 144 Squadron, North Luffenham, 223 Squadron, Folkingham and 254 Squadron, Melton Mowbray. They were closely followed by the remaining pair, 130 Squadron at Polebrook and 218 Squadron at Harrington, during September. The Thor force then ceased to exist.

Following this the rundown of the Bloodhound I units was almost as swift as had been the demise of the Thors. All units so equipped were disbanded between June 1963 and September 1964. Of the pair controlled by North Luffenham the first to go, on

31st December 1963, was 257 Squadron, Warboys, while at Woolfox Lodge 62 Squadron continued in service until 30th September 1964 when it became one of the last two to be disbanded.

Prior to the expiry of 151 (SAM) Wing Bomber Command had already handed over the station to Signals Command on 1st November 1963 and the pattern was set with North Luffenham becoming a major electronics and associated skills school. In turn, Strike, Support and Logistics Commands were to be the umbrella organisations up to its closure as a RAF station.

On 1st November the Ground Radio Servicing Unit (GRSU) was formed at the station. After absorbing several detachments with allied duties the unit adopted a new title on 1st October 1964 and became the Ground Radio Servicing Centre (GRSC). The GRSC provided a repair and servicing facility for a wide range of ground based communications and electronic equipment including most large radars, then in service. This facility was available not only to the RAF but also the Army, Royal Navy and some civil organisations throughout the UK and overseas.

From 2nd December 1963, after vacating Upwood, in Huntingdonshire at that time, the Radio Technical Publications Squadron (RTPS) was the next unit to become resident at North Luffenham. Responsible for the writing and publication of servicing schedules associated with new ground radio installations, it was logical that the unit came to the station where it could work in close collaboration with the GRSU. Following amalgamation with the Radio Introduction Unit (RIU) on 26th April 1976 it became the RIU Detachment (RTPS).

Also from Upwood, on 23rd March 1964 came the Aviation Medicine Training Centre. One of the main tasks of this unit was to train aircrew to cope with airborne emergencies. To achieve this the centre was equipped with several specialised pieces of apparatus. These included decompression chambers, a spacial disorientation familiarisation training device and a 60ft high ejection training tower. The AMTC also gave lectures in aviation medicine and was responsible for the issue and fitting of aircrew flight equipment. About 3,500 personnel passed through the centre annually.

North Luffenham was also the home of the Communications Analysis Training School (CATS), which formed there on 1st October 1964 following the amalgamation of the Joint Services Language School and the Wireless Telegraphy (A) School. It was then known as the Training Wing but following restructuring it became CATS from 1st July 1988. The unit was responsible for teaching Russian, Polish and other languages up to interpreter level.

The Type 82 Radars controlling the Bloodhound SAM batteries had an extremely short life. Due mainly to their susceptibility to jamming and weather clutter, all were taken out of service in January 1961 and mothballed. In January 1966 three of these installations were given a new lease of life and returned to service in an entirely new role as part of the military air traffic control system.

North Luffenham's Type 82 was one of those re-activated and with the title Midland Radar it became responsible for the control of military and to a smaller degree, civil aircraft transiting eastern England. Midland Radar was the last of its type to operate and had for 24 years given an outstanding service until it was finally closed down on 12th January 1990.

The Leicestershire & Rutland Wing of the Air Training Corps had merged with the Northamptonshire Wing in January 1966 to create a South Midlands Wing. Initially they continued to use the former L&R premises over the RAF recruiting office on London Road, Leicester, but were moved to North Luffenham in 1978. There they were housed in the old control tower until around October 1996 when transferred to RAF Wittering.

In addition to what might be termed its permanent residents the station and the airfield have been used on occasion by several transient units and organisations. During the 1970s units of the RAF Regiment were present while re-equipping and training with the Rapier ground defence missile system. Time expired aircraft, the remains of the Thor sites and other airfield installations have been used for exercises in connection with anti-terrorist activities.

A use has also been found for the station's disused runways. Sections of these have been liberally peppered with craters by members of the Explosive Ordnance Disposal (EOD) Squadron from nearby Wittering. This unit, in addition to operations involving the clearance of explosive ordnance, is also responsible for RAF trials and training concerning these devices. A series of airframes have been used in this training role.

An aerial view of the two Type 'J' hangars with the tower and apron in the foreground, taken during September 1997. The dome-like structure between the control tower and the left hand 'J' is unexplained. At the top of the picture is a domestic area and to the right the base's famed golf course, long since shared with the local community.

Also in September 1997, the former Thor IRBM sites at the eastern end. Witchley Warren Farm is in the background.

A further September 1997 view: most of the airfield, looking south west. All Author

In the past North Luffenham faced the axe in 1977 and 1987, but on both occasions the station escaped. It was again decreed in 1993 that the base was to close on 1st October 1996, but even this date slipped by and North Luffenham remained on an extended stay of execution. Finally, a closing date did not slip by and on 1st April 1998 the base commenced a rapid wind-down. By early 1999, the base had been renamed as St George's Barracks, with the first major deployments of men and vehicles occurring by May.

One of the main external changes was the removal from the main gate of Gloster Meteor NF.14 WS776 and a Bloodhound missile in March 1998. These two were auctioned on 26th February 1998 and moved to the Lincolnshire airfield of North Coates for what turned out to be an abortive museum project. Both Meteor and Bloodhound had moved on to Sandtoft airfield in Lincolnshire, by the end of 1999.

The resident RAF units had been relocating for some time, but the EOD section will remain, working as before as a satellite from Wittering and will eventually establish as an enclave working within the Army base. It is interesting to note that aircraft will now feature much more in the life of North Luffenham than in its recent RAF past, as helipads for transport helicopters will be established for use in both exercises and communication flights.

Whatever the level of activity at the North Luffenham of the future, nothing can detract from the fact that throughout its life as an RAF station it has had a distinguished and diverse history.

North Luffenham-based Units and Aircraft

No.17 Elementary Flying Training School
From 18.1.41 to 15.7.41
De Havilland Tiger Moth II   T5825, N9334.

No.61 Squadron
From 17.7.41 to .9.41   Code 'QR-'
Handley Page Hampden I   P4399, X3127, X3138, X3140, AE142, AE189, AE200, AE202, AE235, AE247, AE259, AE263, AE266, AD804, AD826.
Avro Manchester I   L7307, L7315, L7385, L7387, L7388.

No.144 Squadron
From 17.7.41 to 22.4.42   Code 'PL-'
Handley Page Hampden I   N9086, P1295 'L', L2063, L4347, L4399, L4415, X2903, X2969, X3030, X3130, AD752, AD765, AD767, AD784, AD791, AD804, AD832, AD846, AD872, AD903 'A', AD905, AD918, AD921, AD922, AD923, AD959, AD965, AE118, AE119, AE121, AE122, AE125, AE140, AE141, AE143, AE158, AE225, AE235, AE252, AE253, AE304, AE311, AE316, AE353, AE359, AE392, AE440, AE441, AT110, AT116 'F', AT117, AT145, AT149, AT155, AT187, AT188, AT194, AT218, AT226.

No.408 (Goose) Squadron, RCAF
From 25.1.42 to 17.3.42   Code 'EQ-'
Handley Page Hampden I   L4140, L4204, P5321, X4201, AD842, AD963, AD982, AE139, AE150, AE154, AE156, AE179, AE190, AE197, AE217, AE219, AE244, AE288, AE297, AE360, AE418, AE439, AT120, AT154, AT176, AT220, AT224, AT234.

No.29 Operational Training Unit
From 21.4.42 to 24.5.43   Codes 'NT-', 'TF-'
Vickers Wellington I   L7869, L7895, L9802, N2751. T2558, T6307, R1042, R1297, R1459, R1779, R3286, X3816, X9802.
Vickers Wellington III   BJ760, BJ779, BJ782, BJ791, BJ832, BK210, BK212, DF614, DF634, DF674, DV578, DV833, DV834, DV836, DV864, DV877, DV879, DV880, DV881, DV891, DV896, DV897, DV898, DV914, DV917, DV923, DV926, DV929, DV987.
Avro Anson I   N5164, N5191, N5323, R3313, R3445, R9606, R9647, R9693, R9716, R9717, W1879, AX108.
Boulton Paul Defiant I   N1768, AA327.
De Havilland Tiger Moth   N6581, T6307.
Armstrong Whitworth Whitley V   T4210, instructional airframe 3058M.

General Aircraft Glider Assembly & Modification Unit
General Aircraft Hamilcar   HH926, HH927, HH928, HH931, HH932, HH934, HH935, HH957, HH958, HH965, HH968, HH969, HH970, HH971, HH972, LA637, LA638, LA639, LA640, LA641, LA642, LA644, LA645, LA650, LA651, LA652, LA653, LA654, LA655, LA656, LA670, LA671, LA672, LA673, LA674, LA675, LA676, LA677, LA678, LA679, LA680, LA681, LA682, LA683, LA684, LA685, LA686, LA687, LA688, LA689, LA690, LA691, LA704, LA705, LA706, LA707, LA708, LA709, LA710, LA711, LA712, LA713, LA714, LA715, LA717, LA718, LA719, LA720, LA721, LA722, LA723, LA724, LA725, LA726, LA727, LA728, LA729, LA730, LA731, LA732, LA733, LA734, LA735, LA736, LA737, LA738, LA739, LA740, LA741, LA742, LA743, LA744, LA745, LA746, LA747, LA748, LA749, LA750, NX805, NX806, NX807, NX808, NX809, NX810, NX811, NX812, NX813, NX814, NX815, NX816, NX817, NX818, NX819, NX820, NX821, NX822, NX823, NX824, NX825, NX826, NX827, NX828, NX829, NX830.
Handley Page Halifax III   LL222, NR192.

Heavy Glider Conversion Unit
From 2.3.44 to 16.10.44
Armstrong Whitworth Whitley VII   BD508, BD537, BD545, BD546, BD547, BD549, BD557, BD559, BD602, BD627, BD628, BD630, BD631, BD632, BD633, BD635, BD638, BD657, BD659, BD660, BD661, BD662, BD663, BD664, BD665. BL537, EB307, EB332, EB333, EB336, LA774, LA791, LA874, LA875, LA884, LA885, LA888, LA894, LA917, LA926.
Armstrong Whitworth Albemarle I   P1605, V1642, V1742, V1783.
Airspeed Horsa   DF391, DP283, DP307, DP334, DP337, DP348, DP371, DP389, DP499, DP620, DP761, DP803, DP807, DP810, HS105, LG749.

Station Flight
Airspeed Oxford I   V3669 (11.44)

No.1653 Heavy Conversion Unit
From 16.11.44 to 28.10.46   Codes 'A3-', 'H4-'
Avro Lancaster I   HK549, HK702, HK703, HK704, HK706 'A3-J', HK707, HK708, HK728 'A3-K', HK733, ME315, ME331, ME375 'A3-D', NG118, NG272, NG437, NN813, NN816, PD392, PD431, SW258.
Avro Lancaster III   DV161, LL907 'H4-Q', LM524, LM719, LM741, ND647 'H4-P', ND898, NE132, PB149, PB288, PB342, PB507, PB681.
Airspeed Oxford I   HN426, HN433, PG971, PG972, PG973, PG974.
Bristol Beaufighter VI   KV928.
De Havilland Mosquito XIX   TA296, TA306, TA342, TA343, TA356.
Hawker Hurricane II   HW917, LF632.
Vickers-Supermarine Spitfire I   W3656.
Vickers-Supermarine Spitfire V   AR395, BM593.

No.21 Heavy Glider Conversion Unit
From 5.12.46 to 3.12.47   Codes 'FEP-', 'FER-', 'FET-'.
Handley Page Halifax III   MZ580, MZ637, MZ965, NA104, NA132, NA365, NA368, NA389, NA371, NA375, NA398, NA413, NA422, NA423.
Handley Page Halifax VII   PP364, PP377, PP373, PP374, PP367, PP378, PP383.
Airspeed Horsa   RX799, RX807, RX813, RX821, RZ323, TL181, TL392, TL424.

No.1382 (Transport) Conversion Unit
From 10.12.47 to 5.1.48   Code 'NU-'   Renamed 240 OCU

No.240 Operational Conversion Unit
From 5.1.48 to 28.3.51   Code 'NU-'
Douglas Dakota IV   KJ810 'O', KJ838, KJ861, KJ865, KJ972, KJ978, KJ983, KJ995, KK129, KK133, KK134, KK141, KK197, KK198, KN252, KN268, KN312, KN347, KN355, KN375, KN380, KN408, KN431, KN438, KN449, KN462, KN488, KN494, KN521, KN528, KN531, KN544, KN564, KN629, KN631, KN634, KP233, KP251 'G', KP276, KP279.
Avro Anson I   W1792, DJ678, EF861, LT342, LT452, LT502, LV317, MG589, MG862, NK147, NK213, NK391, NK396, NK531, NK565.
Avro Anson XII   PH756.
Avro Anson C.19   PH845, TX219, TX230, VM380, VM394.
Airspeed Oxford I   HN426, HN433.
De Havilland Tiger Moth   N6858, T7016.
De Havilland Devon C.1   VP963, VP964, VP972, VP974.
Vickers Valetta C.1   VL274, VW141, VW142 'Z', VW152, VW194, VW807, VW808, VW809, VW825, VW828, VW830, VW849, VW857, VW859, VW860, VW862, VW863, VW864.

No.102 Flying Refresher School
From 1.5.51 to 15.11.51
Vickers-Supermarine Spitfire XVI   RW346, SM410, SM482, SM512, TB245, TB302, TB675, TB702, TB747, TB758, TB861, TD257, TD261, TD343, TE120, TE187, TE204, TE257, TE352, TE358, TE396, TE397, TE464.
Vickers-Supermarine Spitfire F.22   PK316, PK328, PK331, PK334, PK336, PK340, PK347, PK353, PK371, PK373, PK377, PK399, PK406, PK426, PK429, PK430,PK43 1, PK491, PK499, PK549, PK552, PK561, PK567, PK574, PK580, PK581, PK609, PK615, PK620, PK622, PK651, PK657, PK668, PK676.
De Havilland Vampire F.1   TG300, TG307, TG370, TG373, TG381, TG384, TG427, TG440, VF282.
De Havilland Vampire FB.5   VV467, VV477, VV547, VZ851, VZ867, VZ868, VZ876, WA231, WA307, WA314, WA333, WA335, WA336, WA338, WA339, WA344, WA346, WA347, WA374, WA375, WA400, WA413, WA416, WA417, WA418, WA425, WA454, WA456, WG795, WG797.
De Havilland Mosquito VI   HX803.
Gloster Meteor T.7   VW419, WF844, WG946.
North American Harvard III   KF396, KF580, KF986.

No.410 (Cougar) Squadron, RCAF
From 15.11.51 to 14.11.54
Canadair Sabre 2   19102, 19107, 19115, 19116, 19119, 19120, 19121, 19122, 19123, 19125, 19128, 19129, 19134, 19135, 19142, 19143, 19144, 19145, 19147, 19148, 19150, 19153, 19154, 19156, 19157, 19159, 19160, 19161, 19162, 19169, 19170, 19171, 19172, 19173, 19175, 19176, 19177, 19178, 19179, 19180, 19181, 19182, 19184, 19186, 19193, 19194, 19195.

No.441 (Silver Fox) Squadron, RCAF
From 1.3.52 to 21.12.54
Canadair Sabre 2 19108, 19115, 19116, 19119, 19127, 19131, 19132, 19143, 19150, 19151, 19152, 19153, 19158, 19164, 19165, 19166, 19167, 19168, 19172, 19177, 19183, 19184, 19185, 19189, 19194, 19198, 19199.

No.439 (Tiger) Squadron, RCAF
From 15.6.52 to 1.4.55
Canadair Sabre 2 19112, 19114, 19139, 19150, 19155, 19164, 19166, 19168, 19172, 19174, 19175, 19177, 19180, 19187, 19188, 19190, 19191, 19192, 19193, 19194, 19195, 19196, 19198, 19199.

No.1 Long Range Ferry Unit
From .10.52 to 4.12.52
Canadair Sabre F.2 XB530, XB531, XB532

All Weather Operational Conversion Unit
From .4.55. to 31.12.56 Merged with 238 OCU 1.1.57

No.238 Operational Conversion Unit
From: 1.1.57 to: 17.3.58
Gloster Meteor NF.12 WS590, WS592 'A', WS593 'B', WS594 'C', WS598, WS599, WS604, WS605, WS610'D', WS615 'E', WS617, WS619, WS621, WS625 'F', WS627 'G', WS629, WS630 'I', WS632, WS636, WS639, WS661, WS666 'J', WS667, WS668, WS672 'K', WS673 'L', WS679 'M', WS681, WS682, WS683, WS684 'N', WS687 'O', WS721 'P'.
Gloster Meteor NF.14 WS742 'R', WS760, WS774 'S', WS801 'T', WS811 'U', WS829 'M', WS832 'W' also 'N', WS838 'X' also 'C', WS839 'Y', WS842 'Z', WS847 'HMT'.

Gloster Meteor T.7 VW456, VZ638, WA653, WA740, WF768 'E'.
De Havilland Vampire T.11 WZ588.
Avro Anson T.21 VV889.
Boulton Paul Balliol T.2 WG116 'D', WG118 'C', WG141, WG220 'M', WN138 'F', WN152 'P', WN162, WN163 'F', WN167, WN169, WN170, WN511 'T', WN525, WN527, WN529, WN531 'B', WN532.
Bristol Brigand T.4 RH807, VS837 'N', WA568.
Bristol Brigand T.5 RH757 'M', RH758, RH765 'X', RH774 'C', RH797 'D', RH800 'R', RH804 'S', RH813, RH826 'Z', RH829, RH832. VS833 'H', VS855, VS865, VS866 'K', WA561 'L', WA565, WA566 'B', .
Vickers Valetta C.1 VW814, VX512, VX542 'B'.
Vickers Valetta T.3 WJ462, WJ480.
De Havilland Vampire T.11 XE883.
Gloster Meteor NF.12 WS594, WS625.
Gloster Meteor NF.14 WS731.

No.111 Squadron
From 19.2.58 to 18.6.58
On temporary detachment from North Weald. Departed to Wattisham, Suffolk.
Hawker Hunter F.6 XE592 'P', XE653 'S', XF416 'T', XF430 'V', XF446 'R', XF506 'J', XG129 'F', XG160 'U', XG170 'G', XG171 'E', XG189 'D', XG190 'C', XG193 'A', XG194 'N', XG200 'Q', XG201 'B', XJ715 'H',

No.144 (Strategic Missile) Squadron
From 1.12.59 to 23.8.63

Explosive Ordnance Training Airframes
Hawker Siddeley Harrier GR.3 XV804.
Hawker Siddeley Harrier T.4 XZ146 'S'.
Hunting Jet Provost T.3 XM410, XN554.
Hunting Jet Provost T.3A XN579.
Hunting Jet Provost T.4 XP629, XP686, XS186.
De Havilland Sea Vixen FAW.2 XJ608, XP699, XP921.
Hawker Hunter FGA.9 XG194.
Westland Whirlwind HAR.10 XP344.
McDD Phantom FGR.2 XT905.

Gate Guardians
Gloster Meteor NF.14 WS776.
Bristol Bloodhound I –

Serious Accidents to North Luffenham-based Aircraft

5.3.41 Tiger Moth II N9334 17 EFTS
Crashed in forced landing Rollaston, Rutland.

24.7.41 Hampden I AE225 144 Squadron
Ops Brest. Shot down by fighters near Ploudalmezeau, north west of Brest. Three dead, two PoWs.

25.7.41 Hampden I AE189 61 Squadron
Ops to Kiel. Shot down by night fighter and crashed in sea off Den Helder.

31.7.41 Hampden I AD784 144 Squadron
Ops Cologne. Crashed into sea off Dutch coast. No survivors.

31.7.41 Hampden I P4399 61 Squadron
Ops to Cologne. Pilot lost control while flying in violent electrical storm. Crashed 04:00 at Deast Hill, Dartford, Kent.

31.7.41 Hampden I AE266 61 Squadron
Ops to Cologne. Crashed at 04:50 on return while trying to land at Upwood, Cambs.

31.7.41 Hampden I AE252 144 Squadron
Ops Cologne. Crashed near Cambrai, France. No survivors.

7.8.41 Hampden I AD903 'A' 144 Squadron
Ops Calais. Lost without trace.

7.8.41 Hampden I AE140 144 Squadron
Ops Karlsruhe. Lost without trace.

9.8.41 Hampden I AE263 61 Squadron
Ops Kiel. Lost without trace.

9.8.41 Hampden I X3127 61 Squadron
Ops Kiel. Believed crashed near Kiel. One killed, three PoWs.

9.8.41 Hampden I AE259 61 Squadron
Ops Kiel. On return hit by AA fire from Allied convoy off Spurn Head. Aircraft damaged and crash landed at 05:30 near Fosdyke, Lincs. All safe.

26.8.41 Hampden I AD918 144 Squadron
Ops Mannheim. Crashed near Brussels. Three killed, one PoW.

26.8.41 Hampden I AE265 144 Squadron
Ops Mannheim. Force landed on Ypenburg airfield, Holland. All crew PoWs.

30.8.41 Hampden I AE247 61 Squadron
Ops Frankfurt. Lost without trace.

Long term gate guardian (1961-1998) at North Luffenham, Meteor NF.14 WS776. Author

Sea Vixen FAW.2 XN699 being reduced to scrap on one of the former Thor missile sites. On the skyline can be seen a line-up of Jet Provosts, also used for EOD training. Author

2.9.41 Hampden I AD905 144 Squadron
Ops Cologne. Crashed near target city. Three died, one PoW.

7.9.41 Hampden I AE304 144 Squadron
Ops Berlin. Three minutes after take-off, probably due to stalling, aircraft crashed on Empingham to Ketton road near Stamford at 20:55 hours. Four killed, aircraft destroyed.

8.9.41 Hampden I AD936 144 Squadron
Ops Berlin. Hit by flak and crashed south-east of Amsterdam. One dead, three PoWs.

12.9.41 Hampden I AE118 144 Squadron
Ops Rostock. Crash landed at 06:15 hours into trees at Barn Farm, Billesdon, on return. Aircraft low on fuel and lost. Hampden written off. Two injured.

12.9.41 Hampden I AE121 144 Squadron
Ops Rostock. When returning short of fuel aircraft force landed at 06:00 hours near Isolation Camp, Empingham. Two killed, one injured, Hampden written off.

20.9.41 Hampden I X3030 144 Squadron
Ops Frankfurt. On return undershot airfield struck high tension cables and crashed on Morcott to Uppingham road at 22:50 hours. Four killed, aircraft written off.

21.9.41 Hampden I AD872 144 Squadron
Ops Frankfurt. Following an engine failure aircraft crashed at 02:50 hours four miles north east, Coningsby, Lincs. Four killed, aircraft written off.

21.9.41 Hampden I AD922 144 Squadron
Ops Frankfurt. At 04:20 hours ran out of fuel and abandoned, except for pilot, near Swanton Morley. Hampden crashed near Foulsham, Norfolk, pilot killed.

21.9.41 Hampden I AD923 144 Squadron
Ops Frankfurt. Force landed at 04:30 on Hutton Moor, Yorks following fuel shortage after being diverted to Dishforth due to fog. All crew safe.

30.9.41 Hampden I AE143 144 Squadron
Ops Hamburg. Ran out of fuel and crash landed in garden of house at Sunnyside near Driffield, Yorks. Crew safe.

13.10.41 Hampden I AD965 144 Squadron
Ops Huls. Shot down by Oblt Helmut Lent 4/NJG1 and crashed into the Ijsselmeer. No survivors.

25.10.41 Hampden I AE316 144 Squadron
Ops Frankfurt. Thought to have ditched off Belgian coast. Two dead, two PoWs.

6.11.41 Hampden I AD846 144 Squadron
Ops Anti-shipping. Hit by flak and crashed into sea off Terschelling. Two killed, two PoWs.

6.11.41 Hampden I AE253 144 Squadron
Ops Anti-shipping. Fate as AD846 above. Three killed, one PoW.

6.11.41 Hampden I AE424 144 Squadron
Ops Anti-shipping. Lost without trace.

8.11.41 Hampden I AE238 144 Squadron
Ops Cologne. Hit by flak, crash landed near Lichfield, Staffs on return.

9.11.41 Hampden I AE311 144 Squadron
Ops Hamburg. When landing at 23:43 Hampden swung, collided with airfield control caravan and written off. Crew safe but two airmen killed and one injured in caravan.

28.11.41 Hampden I AE440 144 Squadron
Ops Düsseldorf. Struck high ground at Birdlip, Glos, after descending through cloud to pinpoint position on return from ops. One killed, one injured.

8.12.41 Hampden I AD791 144 Squadron
Ops Aachen. Cause of loss not known.

11.12.41 Hampden I AE353 144 Squadron
Ops Brest. Thought damaged by flak over target, later crashed in sea off Sussex coast. No survivors.

29.12.41 Hampden I P1295 'L' 144 Squadron
Ops Huls. Believed crashed in sea. No survivors.

29.12.41 Hampden I AD804 144 Squadron
Ops Huls. Crash-landed at Doetincham, Holland. One dead, three PoWs.

9.1.42 Hampden I AD752 144 Squadron
While on circuit training, crashed and burnt at Duddington, Northants, at 06:15 hours. Cause obscure. Two killed.

15.1.42 Hampden I AE441 144 Squadron
Ops Hamburg. Ran out of fuel, clipped chimney stack and crashed at Field Dalling, Norfolk. Crew safe.

25.1.42 Hampden I AD782 'A' 408 Squadron, RCAF
Ops Brest. Took off, climbed away very steeply, stalled, nosed over and dived straight in from 1,500ft. All crew killed instantly.

26.1.42 Hampden I AD765 144 Squadron
On take-off for training sortie aircraft swung and crashed. Pilot thrown out of cockpit and killed.

1.2.42 Hampden I AE359 144 Squadron
Ops Brest. Crashed at Creances, France. One killed, three PoWs.

1.2.42 Hampden I AT149 144 Squadron
Ops Brest. Crashed in target area, no survivors.

7.2.42 Hampden I AD824 144 Squadron
Ops 'Gardening'. Shot down by Ofw Detlef Luth II/JG1. Crashed into sea off Terschelling. No survivors.

7.2.42 Hampden I AE392 144 Squadron
Ops 'Gardening'. Shot down in similar circumstances to AD824 above. Again no survivors.

12.2.42 Hampden I AE141 'J' 144 Squadron
Ops 'Fuller'. Hit by flak and later wrecked in emergency landing at Norwich. One killed.

12.2.42 Hampden I AT175 144 Squadron
Ops 'Fuller'. Lost without trace.

17.2.42 Hampden I AD832 144 Squadron
Written off in forced landing at 13:25 hours five miles east of Harringworth, Northants, following engine failure while on air firing exercise.

25.2.42 Hampden I X2969 144 Squadron
Ops 'Gardening'. Lost without trace.

25.2.42 Hampden I AT194 144 Squadron
Ops 'Gardening'. Believed lost over the sea.

27.2.42 Hampden I L4178 144 Squadron
Ops Kiel. Crashed at 03:30 hours, Hexthorpe railway cutting near Doncaster, Yorks, following engine failure due to lack of fuel. No survivors.

9.3.42 Hampden I AD842 408 Squadron, RCAF
Ops 'Gardening'. Took off at 01:52 hours, stalled, struck 'Armadillo' on edge of airfield and caught fire. Three killed, one injured.

22.3.42 Hampden I AT116 'F' 144 Squadron
Ops 'Gardening'. Landed 23:26 hours at Exeter, hit tail of Stirling N3674 which had become bogged down. Hampden wrecked.

27.3.42 Hampden I AE200 144 Squadron
Ops 'Gardening'. Lost without trace.

2.4.42 Hampden I AD959 144 Squadron
Ops NW Germany. Shot down at 00:17 near Gross Roscharden, Germany. One dead, 3 PoWs.

6.4.42 Hampden I AT226 144 Squadron
Ops Cologne. Lost and low on fuel on return force landed on a bombing range at Grendon Underwood, Bucks. at 07:37 hours. Believing themselves to be in enemy territory crew destroyed aircraft after landing.

11.4.42 Hampden I AT187 144 Squadron
Ops Essen. Crashed on return in forced landing at Wrights Farm, Gedney Marsh, Holbeach, Lincs after engine failure. Three killed, one injured.

11.4.42 Hampden I AT218 144 Squadron
Ops Essen. Cause of loss unknown, three dead, one PoW.

12.4.42 Hampden I AT155 144 Squadron
Crashed and burst into flames 15:40 hours at Ridlington, near Oakham, following a stall while on night flying test. Two killed.

14.4.42 Hampden I AT110 144 Squadron
Ops Dortmund. Crashed at 22:15 at Felpham, Sussex. No survivors.

15.4.42 Hampden I AT157 144 Squadron
Ops Dortmund. Cause of loss not known. Two dead, two PoWs.

5.7.42 Tiger Moth T6307 29 OTU
Dived into ground at Alconbury, Hunts, while flying inverted.

19.8.42 Wellington Ic DV881 29 OTU
Landed at an angle to flarepath at Woolfox Lodge, skidded and undercarriage collapsed.

28.8.42 Wellington Ic DV834 29 OTU
Crashed on take-off from North Luffenham.

13.9.42 Wellington Ic R1459 29 OTU
Ops Bremen. Crashed at Empingham shortly after take-off due to engine problems.

25.10.42 Wellington III BJ896 29 OTU
Crashed on take-off from North Luffenham.

15.1.43 Wellington X DF614 29 OTU
Ops 'Nickel'. Tasked to drop leaflets in vicinity of Nancy but crashed near Dieppe. All crew killed.

26.1.43 Wellington III BJ779 29 OTU
Dived into ground one mile east of Wyton, Hunts, while night flying. Five killed.

27.2.43 Wellington III BJ760 29 OTU
Swung on take-off and undercarriage collapsed.

5.3.43 Wellington III BK390 29 OTU
Aircraft was on a high and low level bombing exercise at Whittlesey Range, Cambs., when after low level run it crashed in village street at Coates, near Whittlesey. Crew all killed plus four civilians. A house was also destroyed.

10.3.43 Wellington III BK543 29 OTU
Undercarriage collapsed on landing at Woolfox Lodge.

25.4.43 Wellington Ic X3816 29 OTU
Engaged on cross country exercise when it crashed at Stocking Farm, Belgrave, Leics.

5.5.43 Wellington III BK210 29 OTU
Engine cut when overshooting at North Luffenham.

7.5.43 Wellington III BK441 29 OTU
Flew into hill in cloud, Greenhow Farm, Durham.

12.5.43 Wellington III BK123 29 OTU
Following a starboard engine failure while doing circuits and bumps aircraft crash landed at Scottlethorpe near Bourne, Lincs. Three killed.

24.3.44 Whitley V LA774 HGCU
On night flying training pilot was unable to unfeather a propeller and was baulked on approach to land. Aircraft force-landed near Empingham.

13.8.44 Horsa I DP348 HGCU
Stalled while in circuit at North Luffenham and hit ground. Became instructional airframe 4873M.

16.1.45 Lancaster III DV161 1653 HCU
After take-off flew into ground at Morcott, Rutland.

6.2.45 Lancaster III NE132 1653 HCU
Broke up in cloud while on navigational exercise. Crashed on the Rhinogs, North Wales, seven killed.

4.3.45 Lancaster I PD431 1653 HCU
Hit van and tree when overshooting North Luffenham.
Destroyed by fire.

20.3.45 Spitfire V AR395 1653 HCU
On fighter affiliation exercise with a Lancaster when it collided
at 5,000ft with Dominie NE889, from 1 Radio School, Cranwell.
Spitfire crashed at Easton on the Hill near Stamford. Pilot's fate
unknown, but all occupants of Dominie killed.

8.4.45 Lancaster III ND647 1653 HCU
Crashed at Scraptoft, Leics., at 15:15 hours during a fighter
affiliation exercise. All crew killed.

28.4.45 Lancaster III LM719 'H4-M' 1653 HCU
Control lost in blizzard conditions while on cross country
exercise. Crashed near Spitalgate. All crew killed.

7.5.45 Lancaster I HK709 1653 HCU
Crashed at North Luffenham.

18.9.45 Lancaster I HK703 'H4-Z' 1653 HCU
Belly-landed near North Luffenham. Written off.

18.10.45 Lancaster III PB681 1653 HCU
Airframe overstressed after stalling in cloud. Struck off charge.

25.10.45 Lancaster I NG118 1653 HCU
Written off following an accident at North Luffenham.

30.10.45 Lancaster I NN813 1653 HCU
Missing on training flight.

17.1.46 Hurricane IIc LF632 1653 HCU
Belly-landed at North Luffenham after undercarriage jammed
up. Written off.

18.3.46 Lancaster I NG437 1653 HCU
Stalled and crashed just outside boundary of North Luffenham
airfield. Aircraft burst into flames and was burnt out. All seven
on board killed.

12.7.46 Mosquito XIX TA306 1653 HCU
Overshot landing and undercarriage collapsed. Written off.

15.8.46 Lancaster III LM524 1653 HCU
Hit hut on overshoot at North Luffenham.

17.5.47 Halifax VII PP373 21 HGCU
Elevator failed on take-off, undercarriage retracted to abort.

26.5.48 Dakota IV KN375 240 OCU
Hit by KK198 while parked.

24.7.48 Dakota IV KN252 240 OCU
Crashed at Fassberg, Germany, in force-landing after an engine
caught fire.

20.4.49 Anson I LT602 'NU-D' 240 OCU
Pilot lost control when seat slid back on take-off at North
Luffenham.

23.5.49 Dakota IV KP276 240 OCU
Hit by KJ810 while awaiting take off.

29.8.49 Dakota IV KN544 240 OCU
Both propellers feathered in error. Aircraft belly-landed.

13.9.49 Dakota IV KJ865 240 OCU
Sank back on take-off at Netheravon while towing a glider.

25.7.51 Vampire FB.5 WA400 102 FRS
Lost and short of fuel belly-landed on moor near Great
Longstone, Derbyshire.

12.6.52 Sabre II 19189 441 Squadron, RCAF
Written off following wheels up, deadstick landing into potato
field, Thurlby Fen, near Bourne. Cause - engine trouble.

18.4.52 Sabre IIs 19177 and 19181 410 Squadron, RCAF
Mid-air collision over The Wash. The two pilots, F/O's J A L Kerr
and A B Rayner, killed.

24.6.52 Sabre II 19156 410 Squadron, RCAF
Written off in emergency landing near Stamford following a fire
in the ammunition bay.

1.7.52 Sabre II 19187 439 Squadron, RCAF
Ran out of fuel and crashed into sea. F/O R J Conti killed.

8.7.52 Sabre II 19112 439 Squadron, RCAF
Pilot ejected over The Wash following engine failure.

25.8.52 Sabre II 19178 410 Squadron, RCAF
Crash landed while overshooting at North Luffenham.

21.2.53 Sabre II 19122 410 Squadron, RCAF
Landed short during night flying at North Luffenham. Pilot
F/O Knox-Leete.

3.6.53 Sabre II 19193 439 Squadron, RCAF
Dived straight into ground near Boston, F/O J J R Bedard killed.

20.8.53 Sabre II 19158 441 Squadron, RCAF
Fuel exhausted, pilot ejected into sea off Cromer.

6.10.53 Sabre II 19167 441 Squadron, RCAF
No details of cause of write off. Location given as North
Luffenham.

26.11.53 Sabre II 19152 441 Squadron, RCAF
Unable to recover from spin, pilot ejected near Wells.

2.12.53 Sabre II 19185 441 Squadron, RCAF
Landed short at North Luffenham.

16.12.53 Sabre II 19137 439 Squadron, RCAF
With fuel exhausted and unable to eject pilot, F/O D G Tracey,
attempted to bale out but was unsuccessful and died when the
aircraft crashed near Long Whatton, Leics.

21.2.54 Sabre II 19159 410 Squadron, RCAF
Landed short at North Luffenham. F/O Knox-Leete.

8.4.54 Sabre II 19155 439 Squadron, RCAF
Experienced engine trouble and landed short of runway at
North Luffenham.

17.5.54 Sabre II 19163 441 Squadron, RCAF
Aircraft flown by W/C W F Parks failed to return, believed
crashed in North Sea.

21.9.55 Meteor NF12s WS621 and WS683 AWOCU
Collided while on night interception exercise. Both aircraft
abandoned and crashed in Derbyshire, WS621 at Church
Broughton, WS683 at Great Cubley. One fatality from each
aircraft.

11.1.56 Meteor NF.12 WS619 AWOCU
Hit tree while on night approach two miles east of North
Luffenham.

20.1.56 Meteor NF12 WS661 AWOCU
Hit house while low flying and crashed at Wadhurst, East
Sussex. Two killed.

29.4.57 Balliol T.2 WN162 238 OCU
Pilot affected by fumes, undercarriage retracted on landing.

*A nice study of a 238 OCU Bristol Brigand T.4.
Note blacked-out rear portion of cockpit hood,
for radar operator training.* Author's collection

*A four-ship formation of Sabres overflies
17505, one of the many RCAF Canadair North
Stars to visit North Luffenham.* via J Smith

Chapter Eighteen

Nuneaton

The roof of Nuneaton's Type 'T2' hangar being reclad in May 1959. This operation was not without incident; one workman fell and was seriously injured. via R J Nutt

WHEN talked of locally, this airfield is invariably called 'Lindley' and even semi-official documents of the wartime period are known to refer to it in this way. The use of the name is probably appropriate and understandable when it is known that in medieval times a long vanished settlement called Lindle existed in the vicinity. Additionally, a look at a modern map shows much evidence to support the use of this name with a wood, park, lodge, grange, house and hall farm, each bearing the prefix Lindley, appearing close to the former airfield. However, even though officialdom settled for the name of a Warwickshire town, the area concerned is all within Leicestershire's boundary.

A survey of the land involved was made during 1940 and no doubt the team engaged were well pleased with the site as it entailed making no road diversions or the demolition of any major obstacles. A considerable amount of land belonging to several farms was affected but only one, Valley Farm, was eventually to disappear entirely.

The main contract for the airfield went to Trollope and Colls of London and in turn several sub-contractors were appointed. In the spring of 1941 the first of these, Sutton Land Clearance Company of Sutton Coldfield, Warwickshire, arrived on the site and proceeded to carry out the preliminary work of removing trees and grubbing out hedgerows. Local workmen employed by the company on this job, recall that the newly cleared area must have looked inviting to a single-engined aircraft which was apparently in trouble. Thought to be either a Spitfire or Hurricane, it attempted to make a forced landing but unfortunately success did not attend the venture, the aircraft crashed and blew up on impact. Not a very auspicious 'christening' for an embryo airfield!

Before the main work on the project got under way the Furniss family of Higham Fields Farm, on the north eastern edge of the site had quite a shock when, in the spring of 1942, they received six weeks notice to quit after being informed that their farm buildings encroached upon the line of the proposed main runway. Quite naturally they complained and objected strongly to this situation and an official named Maxwell duly arrived from London to attempt to resolve the problem. Evidently he was a reasonable man who saw sense in the family's argument as the plans were altered, with the runway re-aligned slightly, so saving their home, but over 50 acres of the farm were swallowed.

When work was well advanced on the airfield, it was seen that one major obstruction did exist in the vicinity; this was the 120ft spire of St Margaret's Church in the village of Stoke Golding.

In January 1943 the Air Ministry notified the Bishop of Leicester that the spire would constitute a danger to aircraft operating from the airfield and that demolition was considered necessary. After protracted negotiations, which lasted for six months, it was finally agreed to remove the first 60ft, number and store the stones as taken down and rebuild as soon as practicable when the war was over. After the contract for the job was awarded to W J Furse & Company, of Nottingham, the dismantling began on 27th August and by 24th September it was down to the required height. The truncated spire was then capped with a reinforced concrete slab and after a red obstruction light had been fixed, it no longer presented a hazard to aircraft as they thundered over on the approach to the runway.

The station was opened within 93 Group, Bomber Command, on 7th February 1943, when a detachment of NCOs and airmen under the command of Squadron Leader L G Blomfield, arrived from Bitteswell. It was intended to serve as a satellite airfield for nearby Bramcote, Warwickshire, where 18 (Polish) Operational Training Unit (OTU) were then in residence. Whether this unit's Vickers Wellingtons made any use of the airfield is open to doubt as the OTU was, at this time, in the throes of moving to Finningley, Yorkshire, and Nuneaton was in a very unfinished state.

On 5th April 1943, the airfield was once more transferred, this time to 44 Group, Transport Command again to be used as a satellite of Bramcote, where 105 OTU had been formed. The Wellington Ic, an aircraft type usually associated with bomber crews, was initially used by this unit, but the crews trained were destined to join transport squadrons. The OTU began to show real interest in the satellite in June 1943, when Wing Commander B A Oakley was posted in as Officer Commanding and Wing Commander, Flying.

Unit aircraft began to arrive at Nuneaton towards the end of June and continued through into early July, at this stage they were dispersed to the airfield for picketing and general maintenance only as the station was, as yet, not quite ready to begin operations. Although the runways, perimeter track and dispersals were finally accepted from the Air Ministry Works Department on 26th July, over three more weeks elapsed before flying training commenced on 18th August.

Before this day arrived unit Wellingtons on the station had undergone a major modification which resulted in their appearance differing considerably to those flying from other bases within the county at this time. As 105's commitment was to provide crews for transport aircraft, air gunnery training formed no part of the curriculum, so in consequence the front and rear turrets on the Wellingtons were declared surplus to requirements and removed. The positions they had occupied were then faired over so giving a much more streamlined shape to the portly-looking 'Wimpeys'.

Records indicate that for a considerable time a state of flux existed with regard to many aspects of life at Nuneaton. This situation is well illustrated by the frequent changes of station Commanding Officer during the first year of the OTU's residence. In this period no fewer than six different officers were appointed to this position, which they held for periods of time ranging from seven months to a matter of days. May 1944 must have been an especially difficult month for the station administration with three changes in a very short period of time.

Included in the build up of United States forces prior to the invasion of Europe in

Opposite page: *An aerial view of Nuneaton,
dated April 1944. At least 26 Wellingtons can
be seen on the dispersals and perimeter track.
The A5 is in the bottom left hand corner.*
Peter Green collection

Above: *Vertical survey view of Nuneaton,
dated 10th August 1945. Ten Dakotas and
25 Wellingtons can be seen at dispersal.
On the dispersal, just north of the tower,
signals square and airfield denominator 'NU',
(A) is an unidentified twin-engined type.
The approximate crash site of Spitfire IX*

*RR237 on 11th October 1944 is at (B).
The LMS railway line (C) parallels runway
06/24. The village of Stoke Golding and its
truncated church are directly under the
approach of Runway 24 (D). The village
of Higham on the Hill (E) is to the south.*
DoE

A 1381 (T)CU Dakota, coded '7Z-, in the background in the Airwork General Trading's compound at Gatwick, awaiting civilian conversion. Despite a considerable search, this is the only 'close-up' of a Nuneaton-based aircraft that has surfaced. via Author

Nuneaton's watch office/control tower, a Type 13726/41 for Bomber satellite and OTU satellite stations, illustrated in March 1958. The visual control room 'glass top' is now to be found on the top of the tower at Duxford. via R J Nutt

RAF Nuneaton – 1st December 1944

Latitude	52° 33' 45" N
Longitude	01° 26' 45" W
Height above Sea Level	378ft
Locality:	4½ miles north-north-east of Nuneaton
Command	Transport (RAF)
Nearest Railway Station	Nuneaton, Trent Valley, LMS (2 miles)
Function	Operational Training Unit (Satellite)
Affiliated Airfields	Bramcote (Parent)

Landing Area – Runways

QDM	Dimensions	Extensibility	Remarks
130°	1,400 x 50 yds	2,200 yds	See below
240°	2,000 x 50 yds	2,700 yds	
180°	1,400 x 50 yds	2,200 yds	

Type of Surface – Concrete.
The runway extensions would entail demolition of two houses, four cottages and diversion of a secondary road.

Permanent Landmarks

By Day	Slag heap, 2½ miles SSW
By Night	Nil

Permanent Obstructions Church tower in circuit

Facilities

Airfield Lightning	Mk.II
Beam Approach	–
Radio	–
QDM	–
Flying Control	Yes

Accommodation		All temporary.	
Technical	Hangars		Hardstandings
	Type	No	Type No
	T2	1	Spectacle 27

Domestic	Officers	SNCOs	ORs	Total
RAF	87	286	928	1,301
WAAF	2	18	140	160

1944 were many artillery units. One of these, the 250th Field Artillery Battalion, was housed for a time at a camp close to Merevale, near Atherstone, Warwickshire. It was usual for units of this type to have a section of spotter/liaison aircraft in support and arrangements were made for this element of the 250th to be based at RAF Nuneaton.

The first of their Piper L-4H Grasshoppers arrived on 11th March but such was the demand that delivery of a second aircraft was delayed until 20th April. Grasshoppers were absent from the airfield during May and June when they accompanied the Battalion on field exercises in Yorkshire and Wales. They did find time though on 23rd April to take part in an escape and evasion exercise held in conjunction with RAF per-

sonnel, the local Home Guard and police. Of the 42 airmen masquerading as the enemy only six managed to elude the searchers.

Early in June the 250th moved out to take up duties in the north of England. The air section then left Nuneaton to occupy an airstrip close to the unit's Headquarters at Swanwick, near Ripley, Derbyshire.

After operating Wellington Ics for a year, the OTU progressively changed them for Mk.Xs, again with turrets removed, over a four month period starting in June 1944. Training seems to have run to a fairly even pattern, but several interchanges of flights did take place between Nuneaton and the parent station, Bramcote, during the first 14 months of operation, causing an occasional hiccup.

The position stabilised somewhat in November 1944 after Bitteswell was reallocated as an additional satellite; from then on 'A' and 'C' Navigation Flights were established at Nuneaton. To give crews on this part of the course a more authentic insight into their future role, a shuttle service was inaugurated in January 1945 between Nuneaton and Nutts Corner, Northern Ireland.

This exercise not only gave experience in longer range navigation, but additionally provided a useful service in the carriage of passengers and freight. After operating for approximately six months this service was discontinued and replaced on 9th July 1945 by a round trip route from Nuneaton which daily visited Valley, Anglesey, Crosby, Cumberland, and Riccall, Yorkshire.

Accidents unfortunately form an integral part of any airfield history and on the afternoon of 11th October 1944, Nuneaton was the scene of a tragic incident, the exact cause of which will, in all probability, never be known. Flight Lieutenant J R Brew DFC, a test pilot working for the Ministry of Aircraft Production, had cleared several aircraft earlier in the day before he took off from the airfield at Castle Bromwich, Warwickshire, at approximately 15.20 hours, to carry out the first test flight since assembly on Vickers-Supermarine Spitfire IX RR237. The weather at the time was particularly bad – 8-10/10ths cloud cover with a base at 500ft. Almost an hour later the duty crew at a Royal Observer Corps post situated ¾ mile to the north-east of the airfield near Stoke Golding, sound plotted an aircraft as it

approached from the south west at an estimated height of 8,000 to 9,000ft. When the aircraft was almost overhead the engine note was heard to change and emit a noise as if in a power dive. Within seconds RR237 was seen to dive vertically out of the low cloud base and with the engine full on, crash into the centre of the airfield. An eye witness stated that one wing broke off immediately prior to impact and later examination of the wreckage proved this to be correct. The badly fragmented aircraft did not catch fire and the remains of the pilot were found amongst the wreckage.

An investigator's report on the incident revealed that it had been observed by several people that Flight Lieutenant Brew had appeared unwell for some ten days before the crash and just prior to take-off ground personnel had noted that he seemed very off colour. The conclusions of the inquiry were that the circumstances of the accident suggested loss of control due to incapacity of the pilot, probably caused by a lack of oxygen, coupled to a below normal physical condition.

While 105 OTU aircraft were operating from the airfield their accident record was

by no means exemplary. There were a fair number of minor incidents and several forced landings on and in the vicinity of the airfield. Although casualties occurred in some of these most of the accidents involving unit aircraft in loss of life or serious injury happened during the course of the many long distance navigation exercises.

Concern over the possibility of accidents happening was shown by the London, Midland and Scottish Railway Company, when the airfield first opened and this prompted a visit by a delegation of their officials on 14th July 1943, to discuss the consequences of an aircraft crash affecting one of their branch lines which ran by the airfield, parallel to the main runway.

Their fears were not unfounded, for on 13th October 1944, Wellington X, MF515, experienced a burst tyre during take-off, on a night flying exercise. Although the pupil pilot, Flight Lieutenant Evans, retracted the undercarriage and managed to hold the aircraft straight, it overshot the end of the runway and came to rest on the railway lines. No fire broke out and thanks to his skilful handling of the situation, what might have been a very serious accident was averted.

The truncated spire at St Margaret's Church, Stoke Golding. Author's collection

St Margaret's Church restored to its former glory. Note the concrete band denoting the level of dismantling. Author

A view from the control tower of Nuneaton in the early 1950s. Left to right: 'T2' hangar, crew rest, locker and drying rooms. via R J Nutt

Early days at MIRA, one of the former RAF buildings utilised as a vehicle workshop. via R J Nutt

By far the worst incident involving a Nuneaton-based aircraft occurred in the early hours (03:15) of 20th February 1945, Flight Lieutenant Billett was returning to base in Wellington X, LP654, when it hit a high tension pole in low cloud and crashed into a small housing estate at Corley, north of Coventry. The accident resulted in all three crew members losing their lives and in the deaths of five civilians on the estate where extensive damage was done to several properties. Considerable publicity was given to the tragedy at the time.

Unlike many other county airfields, Nuneaton does not seem to have attracted any major diversions of aircraft returning from operations over Europe. At times it did provide a very welcome refuge for individual machines in trouble. Two examples of these occasions occurred in March 1945. In the first, on the 7th, Lancaster 'HK-G' of 57 Squadron, East Kirkby, Lincolnshire, with Flying Officer Dimond at the controls, force-landed on the airfield after becoming lost following a failure of the Loran equipment while returning from a raid over Germany. When they found Nuneaton their fuel situation was extremely critical, so the pilot elected to try a wheels-down landing on the grass beside the runway. Unfortunately, while attempting this the undercarriage collapsed and the aircraft crashed at the runway's end. Thankfully there was no fire and injuries to the crew were confined to the pilot receiving slight head wounds while

the Flight Engineer, Sergeant Shorey, was taken to Nuneaton Hospital with a suspected broken leg.

In the second incident, which happened on the 29th, the landing was not so spectacular, but Lieutenant Rosenbauer of the USAAF's 1st Scouting Force, 857th Bombardment Squadron, from Bassingbourn in Cambridgeshire, was no doubt no less grateful to ease his North American Mustang down onto the main runway after he too had become lost, this time in low cloud and bad visibility when returning from a meteorological flight over France.

March 1945 was an eventful month in other ways too. During the early afternoon of the 21st, three German Prisoners of War who had escaped from a camp at Atherstone on the 16th, were recaptured at a farm about half a mile west of the airfield by Sergeants Hay and Dalziel of the Station Police. The PoWs had not fared well while at liberty for five days and when apprehended offered no resistance. After spending some time in the station guardroom, they were collected and returned to their camp.

Throughout RAF Nuneaton's active life alterations and additions were constantly being made to airfield facilities. In April a new Visual Control Room (VCR) was built on top of the control tower which afforded staff a panoramic view over the airfield and surrounding area, and as an added navigational aid a mobile radio range was installed at Kirkby Mallory.

No.105 OTU and the station were transferred and came under the control of 4 Group, Transport Command, in June 1945. During the same month the unit began to re-equip with Douglas Dakotas. Initially, type conversion training was carried out at Bitteswell, but when that station closed in July 'B' and 'D' Flights moved back to Nuneaton on the 17th. Not too much congestion occurred as a result of this move as 'C' Flight left Nuneaton on the same day and headed for Crosby-on-Eden, Cumberland.

At this time in 1945 a great many changes were being made to RAF units; in this respect 105 OTU was not ignored and on 10th August it was retitled to become 1381 Transport Conversion Unit – (T)CU. Not that this made any change to the role of the unit and for a time Wellingtons and Dakotas operated side by side from Nuneaton until eventually they became wholly equipped with the latter type. For several months training continued, but on a reduced scale.

The winds of change had not ceased to blow over the station and by the autumn of 1945, its closure was imminent. In November it was announced that 1381 (T)CU would vacate the base on the 21st and move to a new home at Desborough, Northants.

When that day came the weather was so atrocious that the proposed airlift had to be cancelled and the move made by road. The bad weather offered only a temporary respite and eventually the aircraft were able to leave. Their departure signalled the end of RAF Nuneaton as an active airfield and it was placed on care and maintenance from 30th November.

By the following spring the parishioners of Stoke Golding considered that the war had been over and the airfield inactive long enough to warrant their church spire being re-instated so they prevailed upon the Air Ministry to honour the long standing agreement. Although sympathetic to a certain extent the Air Ministry were not, as yet, ready to give way to local pressure so for a time stalemate existed. Unknown to the villagers, ideas were being formulated in an entirely different sphere which would eventually materialise to decide the future of the airfield and in turn allow the cropped steeple to be restored to its former glory.

During 1946 the question of establishing a vehicle proving ground was first raised within MIRA – the Motor Industry Research

Association. As the minimum area considered essential for such a project was one square mile the acquisition of a tract of agricultural land first came to mind but in view of government policy this was not feasible. The best chance offered seemed to be to persuade the Air Ministry to release one of its disused wartime airfields. An agreement was reached and the possibilities of 15 former airfields in different parts of the country were investigated before Nuneaton/Lindley was finally chosen.

So with the future use of the former RAF station settled and the Air Ministry having no further interest in the site, permission was given for St Margaret's spire to be re-erected. W J Furse & Company were engaged once more, this time to reverse the process which they had carried out in 1943. Rebuilding work began on 18th August 1947 and aided by a long period of fine weather, progress was so rapid that by mid-November restoration was complete and Stoke Golding could once more lay claim to having the most beautiful village church in Leicestershire.

MIRA's choice of Lindley, as it is always referred to today, was governed by both the geographical aspect and also the suitability of the site to form a basis upon which the majority of desirable facilities could eventually be constructed. Initially a 99 year lease of the site (later converted to outright purchase in 1963) was negotiated and the condition of the three runway system and perimeter track was so good that they were available almost immediately for simple testing, the first recorded use of the new proving ground taking place in early October 1948. It was during these early days that observers saw a package fall from an unidentified light aircraft as it swooped low over the airfield. Before anyone was aware of what was happening the package was retrieved by the occupants of a car which departed the scene at high speed. HM Customs were extremely interested in the incident, the outcome of which is unknown.

Over the years since the test facility was first established extensive remodelling has drastically altered the appearance of this one time airfield. Notable amongst these changed features from an airfield historian's point of view, are the 2.8 mile high speed circuit which utilises much of the old perimeter track and the various sections of differing types of road surfaces and test environments which have been built using the existing runways as a base.

Major wartime buildings which remain *in situ* are the solitary T2 hangar and the control tower. A site was cleared during the Second World War for another T2 hangar in the north-west corner of the airfield but it was never erected. The T2 hangar is now the home of two wind tunnels, one a quarter scale model and the other a full scale version in which wind speeds up to 80mph can be achieved and which is large enough to accommodate a double-decker bus.

As for the tower, this still serves much in its original role but instead of aircraft it now exercises control over almost 650 acres of proving ground. The tower carries out this function without the benefit of the original VCR. As this item was no longer used, a decision was made in May 1986 to dismantle and dispose of it. Thanks to the forethought of Richard J Nutt of the Boston-Havoc Preservation Trust of Barwell, it was rescued and currently serves in its intended role. Restored and re-erected in the summer of 1989 it now crowns the control tower at Duxford, the Imperial War Museum's airfield in Cambridgeshire.

Nuneaton-based Units and Aircraft

No.18 Operational Training Unit
From 7.2.43 to 27.3.43   Code 'LD-'
Vickers Wellington Ic   Use of airfield at this time unlikely.

No.105 Operational Training Unit
From 25.6.43 to 10.8.43   Code '8F-'   Re-titled 1381 (T)CU

No.1381 (Transport) Conversion Unit
From 10.8.43 to 21.11.45   Codes 'I5-', '7Z-'
Vickers Wellington Ic   L7854, R1652, T2617, X9915, Z1087, DV429, DV501, DV558, DV559, DV572, DV577, DV578, DV695, DV696, DV706, DV758, DV766, DV774, DV807, DV865, DV925, HD968, HD987, HD988, HF911, HX371,
Vickers Wellington X   HE219, HE242, HE734, HE848, HE907, HE908, HZ256, LN619, LP351, LP356, LP410, LP444, LP447, LP448, LP654, LP655, LP656, LP665, LP669, LP671, LP673, LP675, LP677, LP679, LP751, LP761, LP771, LP816, LP817, LP819, LP820, LP821, LP823, LP824, LP907, MF513, MF515, MF517, MF521, MF568, MF569, MF570, MF699, MF701, MF702, MF703, MF704, MF706, NA717, NA733, NA734, NA805, NA869, NA930, NC532, NC547, NC548, NC549, NC551, NC553, NC664, NC665, NC666, NC690, NC691, NC692, NC707, NC708, NC709, NC710, NC711, NC712, NC856, NC857, NC901, NC954.
Hawker Hurricane II   PG297, PG306, PG308, PG309, PZ832.
Douglas Dakota III   FD789, FD869, FD904, FD940, FD944, FL517, FL518, FL547, FL559, FL562, FL586, FL634, KG451, KG583, KG584, KG646, KG656, KG731, KG744, KG751, KG773.

Air Echelon, 250th Field Artillery Battalion, US Army
From .3.44 to .6.44
Piper L-4H Grasshopper   43-29849, 43-30109

Serious Accidents to Nuneaton-based Aircraft

4.12.43   Wellington Ic   DV925   1381 (T)CU
Caught fire and abandoned near Tilstock, Shropshire.

14.1.44   Wellington Ic   DV577   1381 (T)CU
Engine caught fire on take-off, crash landed at Nuneaton and destroyed by fire.

21.1.44   Wellington Ic   DV695   1381 (T)CU
Missing on navigation exercise over North Sea.

27.1.44   Wellington Ic   HF911   1381 (T)CU
Flew into Moel Fodair at night while on navigation exercise.

22.3.44   Wellington Ic   HD987   1381 (T)CU
Crashed Mill Lane, Digbeth, Birmingham. Signal had been received that an engine had failed. Crew of three killed.

18.6.44   Wellington Ic   T2617   1381 (T)CU
Crashed on landing at Nuneaton, caught fire and burnt out. Crew injured.

26.6.44   Wellington X   MF704   1381 (T)CU
Missing on night navigation exercise.

19.8.44   Wellington X   MF568   1381 (T)CU
Overshot on wet runway and undercarriage raised to stop.

22.8.44   Wellington X   MF517   1381 (T)CU
Flew into ground out of cloud and crashed near Halesowen, Worcs, while on night navigation exercise.

26.8.44   Wellington X   LP675   1381 (T)CU
Engine failed, aircraft crashed in forced landing near Kinver, Worcs., and destroyed by fire.

13.10.44   Wellington X   MF515   1381 (T)CU
Tyre burst on take-off, u/c retracted, slid into railway cutting.

28.10.44   Wellington X   LP665   1381 (T)CU
Destroyed by fire in crash at Eagles Green, Northumberland, after control had been lost due to icing and fabric had stripped from wing.

27.11.44   Wellington X   LP671   1381 (T)CU
Overshot landing and hit ditch which removed undercarriage, Valley, Anglesey.

8.1.45   Wellington X   LP761   1381 (T)CU
Missing near Bardsey Island while on navigation exercise.

8.1.45   Wellington X   NC954   1381 (T)CU
Engine caught fire, hit pole in forced landing near Wootton Brigg, Lincs. Destroyed by fire.

5.2.45   Wellington X   LP351   1381 (T)CU
Dived into sea out of cloud off Kilberry Head, Argyll.

20.2.45   Wellington X   LP654   1381 (T)CU
Hit high tension pole in cloud. Crashed into small housing estate at Corley near Coventry. Crew of three killed plus five civilians.

22.2.45   Wellington X   NC692   1381 (T)CU
Engine failed overshot night landing at Acklington, Northumberland, hit bank and damaged beyond repair.

24.3.45   Wellington X   NC691   1381 (T)CU
Crashed in Irish Sea while on night navigation exercise.

29.4.45   Wellington X   LP410   1381 (T)CU
Flew into high ground, Moccas Park, Hereford, after elevators failed in thunderstorm.

25.6.45   Wellington X   MF706   1381 (T)CU
When taking off escape hatch flew off, undercarriage retracted to stop.

29.7.45   Wellington X   HE734   1381 (T)CU
Overshot landing and damaged beyond repair.

2.8.45   Wellington X   NC547   1381 (T)CU
Hit trees in practice overshot 1½ miles north of Nuneaton. Later caught fire while being salvaged.

17.8.45   Wellington X   HZ256   1381 (T)CU
Belly landed at Nuneaton after undercarriage jammed.

An aerial view of Nuneaton, looking north-west, June 1998. The airfield layout has lent itself perfectly to its new role.

Another view of the MIRA site, June 1998, this time looking east, towards Hinckley. In the foreground are the MIRA headquarters buildings and the A5. The former LMS railway line can be seen to the right. Both Author

Chapter Nineteen

Ratcliffe

TRAVELLING north from Leicester on the Fosse Way (the A46), if one looks to the left shortly after passing the entrance gateway to Ratcliffe College – the view is not very impressive – a rather untidy clutter of buildings in the centre of a large tract of farmland. Hardly a scene to warrant a second glance, yet, a closer look will reveal that several military-style buildings and small hangars are a part of the farm.

This 'island' complex and the land surrounding it was once a Mecca of aviation. Here, in the 1930s a private aerodrome second to none in the British Isles was established and one which later became a key airfield in the Air Transport Auxiliary delivery system during the Second World War.

The founder and owner of the airfield was Sir William Lindsay Everard, a member of the Leicestershire brewing family, who was for many years a patron of light aviation

and an outstanding benefactor to flying clubs within the county. During his lifetime he held various positions of prestige connected with the light aviation movement.

Both Leicestershire Aero Club and the County Flying Club were indeed fortunate in their choice of president. He was never content to be just a figurehead but was extremely active in office, expending a great amount of time and energy in the interest of both organisations. Within the Royal Aero Club he wielded considerable influence as Chairman 1936-1940, Racing Committee Chairman 1932-1939 and as the Vice-President of the Club from 1946-1948. As Unionist Member of Parliament for the Melton Mowbray constituency for many years, he was able to speak with authority on matters of aeronautical interest and in addition between 1938 and 1947 he held a commission as honorary Air Commodore

An incredible assembly of aircraft visiting Ratcliffe for the closing down ceremony on 6th October 1945, as viewed from the control tower. Left hand row, from the foreground: Handley Page Halifax, Douglas Dakota, Hawker Tempest, North American Mustang, Vickers Warwick, Fairey Barracuda, Lockheed Hudson, Hawker Hurricane, Airspeed Oxford, Grumman Hellcat, Vickers Wellington, Fairchild Argus, Avro Anson. Middle row, from the front: Stinson Reliant, De Havilland Dominie, Supermarine Sea Otter. In front of the hangar: Spitfire. Behind hangar, from the front: Fairey Firefly, Armstrong Whitworth Albemarle, North American Mitchell, De Havilland Mosquito. W W Storer

Airfield layout of Ratcliffe, circa 1935, showing the exceptional level of equipment, particularly for night flying.

Advert for the 1930 Air Pageant at Ratcliffe. Both via Author

of 605 (County of Warwick) Squadron, Royal Auxiliary Air Force. A knighthood was bestowed upon him in 1939.

James Hunter Limited of Chester was the company given the contract for preparing the site for Lindsay Everard's aerodrome and work began early in 1930. At first the land was very undulating with a great deal of ridge and furrow pasture but after repeated grading and consolidation it was possible to motor across the surface at 50mph with a minimum of discomfort. To ensure

adequate drainage of the site a system of mole drains, to a total length of 40 miles was laid below the surface. By the second week of June the airfield had been sown, a landing circle with the word 'Ratcliffe' laid and work had started on converting existing farm buildings and erecting a hangar. Favourable weather encouraged grass growth and this, together with satisfactory progress on the buildings, led to an application being made on 12th August for a licence to operate. When this was granted

eight days later it was in a restricted category for Avro 504 type training biplanes and light aircraft only.

At this time facilities on the 60 acre L-shaped airfield comprised one brick hangar 50 x 50 x 12ft, three lockups 30 x 50 x 10ft, petrol and oil storage tanks for 1,000 and 50 gallons respectively, together with an office and club room. The landing area offered a maximum grass runway length of 620 yards north to south and a minimum of 510 yards east to west.

The official opening of Ratcliffe was planned for Saturday, 6th September 1930 and to mark the occasion a Gala Weekend of flying was organised by Leicestershire Aero Club on their President's behalf. Air racing, aerobatics, formation flying, a parachute descent and other attractions were all advertised as part of the entertainment. On the big day, at first, the weather was kind and an unprecedented number of visitors arrived by air; at one time well in excess of 100 aircraft were parked on the airfield. The afternoon's proceedings began after lunch with the race for the Society of British Aircraft Constructors' Cup. This was staged over a 33 mile triangular course which took the competitors around the city of Leicester via Desford, Glen Gorse, and back to Ratcliffe. Although the eventual winner was Oliver Tapper of the London Aero Club in de Havilland DH.60G Moth G-AAEX at 99.5 mph, local entrants did well with J T L Baxter flying Leicestershire Aero Club's Moth, G-AASM, into second place while another club member, H P Lavender came in fourth.

Then followed the opening ceremony at which it had been anticipated Miss Amy Johnson, the most celebrated aviatrix of the day, would officiate. On doctors orders she had asked, on 4th September, to be relieved of the duty and although she did attend the meeting it was in the capacity of honoured guest only. After accepting the invitation at very short notice, the distinction of making the formal declaration fell to another notable personality, Sir Sefton Brancker, the Director of Civil Aviation.

Shortly after the ceremony rain began to fall and continued intermittently for the next 24 hours. At one stage it was commented that baptism might have been a better description of the occasion. Nevertheless, despite the unco-operative elements the crowd of spectators, variously estimated to number between 5,000 and 10,000, were treated to excellent entertainment. Included in the event was a superb display of aerobatics, both tied together and individual, by a flight of three Armstrong Whitworth Siskin biplane fighters of 43 Squadron from Tangmere, Sussex. An anonymous gentleman from the Household Brigade Flying Club

baled out of a de Havilland Moth and made an eight second delayed drop before opening his Russel Lobe parachute to land safely on the airfield. As a grand finale a set piece was staged which involved 'kidnapped missionaries' escaping from 'evil Chinese pirates'. These 'villains' ultimately paid for their crimes and were bombed into oblivion along with their dummy ship by the gallant pilots of 43 Squadron.

Weather apart, the day overall was considered a success although two incidents did occur which could have had serious results. During the morning a tradesman on the airfield was struck a glancing blow by the tail skid of an aircraft as it came into land. Several other people were forced to throw themselves to the ground to avoid this machine which was so dangerously low that it cut one of the rope barriers before touching down. After the show

another accident almost proved fatal for the occupants of Simmonds Spartan G-AAGN. Captain A R P Kirby and his wife had just taken off when the engine failed and the aircraft crashed, narrowly missing crowds leaving the aerodrome. The Spartan was written off and Captain Kirby was fortunate enough to be thrown clear, unhurt, but his wife was trapped in the wreckage sustaining leg and facial injuries which needed attention at Leicester Royal Infirmary.

After Saturday's crowds Sunday was some-thing of an anti-climax. Very few members of the general public were present for the flying which was devoted to the competition for the Grosvenor Cup. The eliminating heats which began about 11am took place in anything but ideal weather, the pilots having to contend with bumpy conditions and rain storms as they flew a short course to the north of the airfield.

Only the one hangar has been built in this early photograph. Everything is new and spotless. Note the running fox wind indicator. A Codling

Westland Wallaces and Avro 504Ns of 504 (County of Nottinghamshire) Squadron in evidence among the 30 aircraft which arrived for a garden party at Ratcliffe on 28th July 1935. C H T Brown

By afternoon there had been some improvement for which the six finalists were thankful. The eventual winner of the trophy was L Turnbull of Newcastle Aero Club flying de Havilland Moth G-EBQV at 95mph, closely followed by W Runciman in G-AAWW, a Klemm L27a, while the third competitor to cross the finish line was Captain Edgar Percival piloting the Hendy 302 G-AAVT. It had also been intended to run a race for the Air League Challenge Cup but this was abandoned due to the weather and the mass exodus of aircraft following the finish of the Grosvenor Cup. So on a rather disappointing note ended the first of many eventful gatherings to be held at Ratcliffe.

From the incidents that occurred at this meeting it would appear that airfield control was rather rudimentary and discipline somewhat lax, but this situation was not confined solely to Ratcliffe. Indeed, during the early 1930s when most club flying was in its infancy the state of affairs concerning these matters often left a great deal to be desired. As far as Lindsay Everard was concerned it was totally unsatisfactory and he became something of a pioneer in this field. Safety precautions together with the general efficiency in the running of Ratcliffe became a byword in aviation circles.

Although Ratcliffe was, from the outset, a private aerodrome other aviators benefited from its existence at an early stage. In March 1931 it was offered, together with all ancillary services, as an emergency landing ground for both RAF and civilian aircraft. At this time cross country flying was still very much an adventure for the average club pilot who frequently relied on good visibility to enable him to reach his destination by following main roads and railway lines. This method of navigation was often referred to as 'flying by Bradshaw' after a railway timetable of that name. A visual navigational aid, which was both novel and practical, for which Lindsay Everard can take credit began to appear in the county from the late spring of that year. He successfully negotiated with several local and municipal authorities to have their respective names painted on the tops of their gasometers, in many cases then the most prominent landmark in the area. Both the aviation press and aviators at that time were quite enthusiastic about these aerial signposts.

During 1931 the airfield was further improved in many ways with the result that when a second operating licence was issued on 28th August, Ratcliffe was declared suitable for all types of aircraft. Probably the most interesting addition made at this time was the installation of comprehensive night flying equipment which included a 630,000 candle power mobile flood light, which was mounted on the chassis of one of Lindsay Everard's old Rolls-Royce cars,

and a flashing beacon which, under normal conditions, was visible from the air for over 15 miles. Ratcliffe, at this time was one of the few airfields in the country equipped with these aids.

These facilities received a fair trial on 1st August when a night flying meeting was held. This rather unusual event although not publicly advertised still drew a considerable number of spectators many of whom watched the proceedings from outside the airfield's perimeter. Police estimated that well over 1,000 cars were present and these, together with other forms of transport, led to quite a congested situation. Naturally the flying programme was somewhat limited in scope but it did feature a formation of three aircraft one of which was outlined underneath with small electric lights. Another aircraft flew round sporting a large motor car headlight with which the crowd and parked cars were spotlighted. An illuminated parachute descent caused considerable excitement and to round off the evening the inevitable set piece was staged. This item involved intrepid pilots rescuing a young lady from the clutches of cannibal tribesmen. Rarely held elsewhere in the county night flying meetings became a regular fixture at the airfield in the years before the Second World War.

A full and varied calendar of events was always featured at Ratcliffe throughout the 1930s. As part of the social scene many dates were set aside for small private parties but gliding displays, model aircraft competitions, charity events and public open days such as Empire Air Day were all held, many on an annual basis. International gatherings also formed a memorable part of the Ratcliffe scene prior to 1939 and Lindsay Everard's excellent reputation as a host always ensured that on these occasions many distinguished guests flew in to sample his hospitality. Two notable examples of this type of meeting were on 26th July 1936 when participants in the Weekend Aérien were his guests and on 27th June 1937 when delegates to the Fédération Aeronautique Internationale conference were entertained.

Some idea of the popularity of Ratcliffe as a venue in the 1930s aviation circles can be deduced from the fact that 97 visiting aircraft were attracted to the 1936 gathering while over 50 were present on the airfield in 1937. Aircraft ranged in size from the then giant Handley Page HP.42 airliner *Heracles* down to the smallest single-engined monoplane of the day and as a result of the international nature of these meetings many rare and exotic foreign machines were present. Frequently numbered among the visiting pilots were individuals noted for their flying ability with a result that impromptu flying displays often featured as an added

attraction on these occasions.

Strange though it may seem in spite of his obvious love of flying Lindsay Everard never became a pilot. His aircraft, of which he invariably owned several at a time, were flown for him by a personal pilot who doubled in employment as resident aerodrome manager. Flight Lieutenant Stewart David, Flying Officer A H Hole, Miss Winifred Spooner, Lieutenant Commander Chris Philips and W D MacPherson were all engaged at various times in this capacity. Like the aerodrome, his aircraft were always maintained to the highest standards and impeccably turned out by full-time staff.

Winifred Spooner was a fine pilot with an excellent reputation in competitive flying and foreign tours and no doubt it was her influence which stimulated in Lindsay Everard such a keen interest in similar events. Aircraft were frequently entered in his name in air races throughout the British Isles and notable amongst the touring competitions in which he personally took part was the Circuit of the Oases in Egypt in 1933 when his de Havilland Dragon G-ACKU was the winning aircraft.

Contemporary articles in the aeronautical press during the mid-1930s were always loud in their praise of Ratcliffe. Statements such as 'The best equipped private field in Great Britain' and 'Its completeness is a thing to marvel at and its organisation unequalled' were extremely complimentary but not entirely unwarranted for since its inception the aerodrome had seen almost continuous improvement. Between 1935 and the summer of 1936 a large area of land to the south was incorporated into the flying area. This enabled the available north-south landing run to be increased to 1,050 yards; it also added a further 250 yards to the north-east south-west grass runway bringing this up to 800 yards in length. By this time several significant additions had also been made to the centre complex, these included a second hangar 58 x 31 x 12ft, an open air swimming pool and a small control tower.

Further refinements to the night flying equipment had also taken place. A permanent system of Loverage boundary lights was now installed; the operation of a single switch activated these together with red lights on every major obstruction in the immediate vicinity of the airfield and illuminated the landing 'T'. Hourly weather reports were received from Heston, Middlesex, crash and fire fighting equipment was in excess of the standard laid down by the Air Ministry and a qualified engineer with a fully equipped workshop was capable of carrying our major overhauls.

After they had vacated their field near Melton Mowbray (Chapter Sixteen) in the autumn of 1936 the members of the County

Members of the Leicestershire Flying Pou Club / County Flying Club pose as a flying helmeted Robert Kronfeld explains aspects of his Flight Trainer.

One of the many glittering gala occasions at pre-war Ratcliffe. Delegates to the FAI conference in London and other guests arrived for lunch with Sir Lindsay, 27th June 1937. The large biplane is Handley Page HP.42W G-AAXC Heracles *of Imperial Airways. Note the landing ground marker circle and the name 'RATCLIFFE'.*
Both A Codling

Members of the Leicestershire Flying Pou Club / County Flying Club pose as a flying helmeted Robert Kronfeld explains aspects of his Flight Trainer.

One of the many glittering gala occasions at pre-war Ratcliffe. Delegates to the FAI conference in London and other guests arrived for lunch with Sir Lindsay, 27th June 1937. The large biplane is Handley Page HP.42W G-AAXC Heracles *of Imperial Airways. Note the landing ground marker circle and the name 'RATCLIFFE'.*
Both A Codling

Flying Club (CFC) must have considered themselves very fortunate when Lindsay Everard extended to them the privilege of the temporary use of the airfield. Most activity in the winter months of 1936/1937 was confined to ground training but Robert Kronfeld visited Ratcliffe during this period to deliver and demonstrate one of his flying trainers which Lindsay Everard had been instrumental in obtaining for the Club. It was difficult to ascertain whether CFC utilised this machine to any extent, but if the recollections of surviving club members are to be relied upon, it would appear not. Club activities began to cause some inconvenience by the spring of 1937 but this was short lived for as soon as conditions permitted they moved over to their new home nearby at Rearsby (Chapter Twenty).

Ratcliffe also played a part in the advancement of law and order within the county. For a considerable period during 1936-37 facilities were made available on the aerodrome to enable a radio amateur, William W Storer to carry out experiments with VHF radio. These proved to be so successful that they eventually led to some of Leicestershire County Police cars being amongst the first in the country to be equipped with radio communication.

During the first decade of its existence there were many memorable happenings at Ratcliffe, but in the course of events none was to prove of greater importance to British light aviation, not only in the county but eventually worldwide, than one that took place in the spring of 1939.

In February of that year the newly-formed company of Taylorcraft Aeroplanes (England) Limited began to manufacture aircraft at their Britannia Works in Thurmaston. At this time the company possessed no airfield from which to test fly the finished product but Sir Lindsay Everard solved this problem by giving permission for Ratcliffe to be used for this purpose. On 24th April the prototype Taylorcraft Model Plus C left the Britannia Works, and minus wings it was hitched to the back of a lorry and towed tail first along the A46 to the aerodrome. Upon arrival, Sir Lindsay's engineer, Albert Codling completed the assembly and rigging in readiness for the first test flight. G Winn-Eaton was at the controls for the maiden flight which took place on 3rd May and the initial test of G-AFNW was such a complete success that almost immediately a second flight was made. This time A L Wykes, Taylorcraft's managing director, took over the controls and with another director, Percy Wykes, as passenger, displayed absolute confidence in the company product by taking off and proceeding to loop the aircraft.

Production at Thurmaston built up to average about one aircraft per week and with the Plus Cs finding a ready sale all continued to be towed to Ratcliffe for final erection and test flying. In mid August, owing to the worsening situation in Europe, the company made the decision to run down production but to finish the airframes then under construction. In all 24 aircraft had been completed by 31st August, but only two of these, one of which was the prototype of a new model, the Plus D, remained at Ratcliffe when war was declared three days later on 3rd September. From then, an immediate ban on all civil flying and the manufacture of aircraft for the civilian market effectively terminated all company activity at Thurmaston and Ratcliffe, but as it later transpired it was only the end of the first chapter of the Taylorcraft/Auster story. (See Chapters Twenty and Twenty-One.)

For over a year following the outbreak of war little, apart from grazing animals, moved on the airfield. On 5th May 1940 a request was made that the licence (P89 343461/35/CA2(c)) be cancelled as Ratcliffe had not been used since September 1939 and was currently only being used for agricultural purposes. Then, in the late summer of 1940, there began what Sir Lindsay was often heard to refer to as 'the battle of the Light and Dark Blues'. One morning an official RAF party turned up armed with a permit to inspect the airfield with a view to

ATA Ferry Pilot Pools were redesignated Ferry Pools with effect from 1st May 1942. Two of 6 FPP's pilots pose with one of their charges, a Spitfire II, while Ratcliffe's tower looms over the fin and a Hudson can be seen, left, in the trees. B V Hewes

Ansty	Standard Motors	Airspeed Oxford, De Havilland Mosquito
Baginton	Armstrong Whitworth	AW Whitley, Avro Lancaster
Bitteswell	Armstrong Whitworth	Avro Lancaster. *(Chapter Three)*
Castle Bromwich	Vickers	Supermarine Spitfire, Avro Lancaster
Desford	Reid & Sigrist	Boulton Paul Defiant, Nth American Mitchell. *(Chapter Nine)*
	Vickers	Supermarine Spitfire *(Chapter Ten)*
Elmdon	Austin Motors	Short Stirling, Avro Lancaster.
Loughborough	Brush Coachworks Airwork	De Havilland Dominie. *(Chapter Fourteen)* Douglas Boston. *(Chapter Fifteen)*
Rearsby	Taylorcraft	DH Tiger Moth, Hawker Hurricane, Hawker Typhoon. *(Chapter Twenty)* Auster. *(Chapter Twenty-One)*
Wolverhampton	Boulton Paul	Boulton Paul Defiant, Fairey Barracuda.

taking it over. No sooner had they left when Captain Norman Edgar, representing the Air Transport Auxiliary (ATA) arrived and requested the keys that he too might view the place with a similar purpose in mind. This state of affairs continued for several days, both parties spending a great deal of time commuting between their respective headquarters and Ratcliffe.

The RAF must have been very confident in acquiring the use of the aerodrome for an entry made on 16th October 1940 in the operations record book of the Central Landing Establishment (CLE) intimates that both Ratcliffe and Rearsby had been allocated to the CLE for the purpose of forming a glider training squadron. This statement was proved to be premature as the Ministry of Aircraft Production won the 'battle' by being the first to guarantee the initial rent, so 6 Ferry Pilot Pool (FPP) was duly formed and installed at Ratcliffe in October 1940.

From then on the ATA were to remain the sole occupant of the airfield for over five years and it became for 6 FPP what was virtually a self-contained base. This enabled the Pool to acquire an individual character and in many ways it retained an atmosphere of the pre-war flying club. Not that this in any way detracted from its efficiency for in this respect it was second to none. The reputation that the Pool was also a very happy one survives to this day, perhaps factors which helped to contribute to this were the close proximity of Ratcliffe Hall and the Everard family. Right from the start Sir Lindsay proved himself a true friend to the ATA; his first gesture, an act typical of the man, was to throw open his home to Pool personnel. This privilege he never withdrew and while the ATA occupied the airfield a proportion of the staff were always found a home at the hall.

In November 1941, initially on a trial basis, 6 FPP became a mixed Pool when four female pilots were posted in to join their male counterparts. There were minor difficulties but on the whole the arrangement worked very well and Ratcliffe continued to be staffed in this way until operations were finally wound up. Over the years pilots of many nationalities served with the Pool, at times the differing shoulder flashes on the dark blue uniforms in the mess presented quite a cosmopolitan appearance. From the beginning, Americans seemed to gravitate to Ratcliffe and the hall always contained a strong contingent from that country.

By enjoying such a central position within the Midlands, Ratcliffe was well placed to deal with movements which were required by the many aircraft factories, repair works and RAF Maintenance Units (MU) scattered throughout the area. Additionally the location also made it an excellent staging post for aircraft in transit north or south. At least one example of every type of aircraft operated by the RAF during the Second World War landed and took off from the airfield.

Flying-boats are the only types excluded, but even they formed part of 6 FP's history. Strange though it may seem for such a landlocked unit it was one of only three within the ATA organisation to be given the responsibility of these aircraft. The main activity of the pool in this respect centred on the clearance of Sunderlands from Short Brothers works at Rochester, Kent, and the dispersal of American 'boats such as the many Consolidated Catalinas which staged through Beaumaris, Anglesey, for modification by Saunders-Roe Limited.

The major concern of 6 FPP/FP remained in the Midlands however, and a list of the principal factories and repair works which it served is quite impressive:

To these must be added the various Maintenance Units (MUs) covered by the pool. Considerable numbers of aircraft to be ferried to and from these establishments, which included Lichfield, Cosford, Ternhill, High Ercall and Shawbury, ensured that the pool received and carried out, weather permitting, a sizeable daily allocation of collections and deliveries.

During winter months, Ratcliffe received its fair share of snow and fog but the opinion was held that when the tower of nearby Ratcliffe College was visible from the watch office then flying was 'on'. Taxi Avro Ansons and Fairchild Arguses then proceeded to take-off and grope their way around to deposit the pilots, flight engineers and sometimes Air Training Corps or Sea Cadets who flew as supernumerary crew, at the airfield where the aircraft awaited collection. Reaching some destinations caused problems, and in these conditions collection of Spitfires from Castle Bromwich was never very popular. As well as having to cope with the heavy blanket of industrial smog which invariably hung over the area there was the additional hazard of an extensive balloon barrage to contend with.

That selected members of the Cadet Corps formed a small but active part of the ATA is a little publicised fact, Geoff Cooke, one of Ratcliffe's contingent recalls his past experience.

'During school holidays in August 1942 a friend and I journeyed to Ratcliffe complete with binoculars and notebooks to look at and record the many aircraft on the airfield. We were so engrossed in our observations that we failed to see an armed soldier approach. He didn't appreciate that we were pursuing an innocent pastime, arrested us and marched us across the airfield to the buildings in the centre. We were brought before the adjutant who proved to be an understanding man for, after mildly admonishing us asked just how interested we were in aircraft. My immediate reply was "Very" following which he gave me a short aircraft recognition test from a copy of Flight which lay on his desk. I must have impressed him for the upshot was that he asked if I would like a job there when I left school. My answer was "Yes", but I needed my parents' permission. After considerable badgering on my part they eventually agreed and I left school at Christmas 1942, shortly before my 16th birthday.

'So, from January 1943 to September 1945, a time which proved to be the busiest period in 6 FPP's history, I became one of eight ATC cadets to be employed by the ATA at Ratcliffe.

'Our duties were varied but one of the main ones was to fly either as Pilots' Assistants or "Wheelwinders". In the former category we flew in aircraft which, when being ferried, did not warrant the presence of a flight engineer, but could not be flown solo by the pilot as the emergency undercarriage lowering system, should it be required, was not within the reach of his seat. This is where we came in. The aircraft involved were the [AW] Whitley, [Lockheed] Hudson, [Lockheed] Ventura, [AW] Albemarle and [Short] Stirling. This last was an exception to the rule though for it also carried a flight engineer.

'As "Wheelwinders" we were required (or volunteered) to go on Anson taxi flights to wind the undercarriage up or down as needed. This operation necessitated about a hundred turns of a handwheel by the side of the pilot's seat and as several airfields were usually visited in the course of a round trip it could turn out to be a rather irksome and tiring business.

'When 6 FPP began to ferry flying-boats (Sunderlands from Rochester to Wig Bay and Catalinas from Beaumaris mainly to Oban) five Sea Cadets joined us, the ferry crew for a boat being 1st and 2nd pilots, flight engineer and two cadets.

'There were other more mundane duties, which for me proved just as interesting.

They included the operation of a rudimentary flying control system from the "greenhouse" at the top of Ratcliffe's spidery steel tower, acting as "duty pilot" (or cadet) for the purpose of logging all daylight aircraft movements on the airfield and also serving as relief night operations officer once a week. The main purpose of this duty was to receive and record the following day's programme of aircraft movements for the pool which were despatched via a telephone link from Ferry Control at Andover.

'A rota system was operated and out of the seven cadets usually on duty on any one day two would generally be available for flying, four allocated ground duties while the odd man would be available for duty as required.

'There was always an element of competition amongst us with regard to amassing flying hours and new types and in this respect I was very fortunate. By the end of my time at Ratcliffe I had logged 536 flying hours in 39 different types of aircraft and been paid for the pleasure of doing so.

'All in all this employment with the ATA was a wonderful and unique experience for us young lads. Nothing like it had ever occurred before and is hardly likely to again'.

When activity was at its peak over 140 staff were employed in the many different trades which were needed to allow the unit to function efficiently. At first when the ATA took over, existing buildings on the airfield proved adequate for their needs but the increases in both staff and workload made great demands on the available space so consequently more accommodation had to be provided. During the course of the war many new buildings were added to the central area and, to enable servicing to be carried out on the pool's fleet of taxi aircraft, additional hangarage was provided. In October 1941 the Ministry of Aircraft Production proposed that a hangar 90 x 80 x 18ft together with an equipment store be built on the eastern boundary of the airfield. Although approved, the scheme was not carried through; instead, when they were erected the site chosen was on the northern side of the central group of buildings. It has been said that had the war continued much longer then the ever-expanding 'island' in the middle of the airfield would have left very little room around it for flying to take place.

Overall the contribution made by the ATA to the Allied war effort was both vital and immense. Between 15th February 1940 and 13th June 1945 deliveries totalling 300,056 aircraft were made by the organisation – a truly remarkable figure when one considers that even in the peak year of 1944/1945 on an average only 427 operational personnel were available. As for Ratcliffe's share, it

has been estimated that while 6 FPP / 6 FP were in residence about 50,000 ferry flights originated from the airfield.

When the services of the ATA were no longer required the exit of the organisation, like its entrance, was unheralded and unsung. Throughout the war its activities received little publicity and at the end few awards came the way of its personnel. Officially the ATA ceased to exist on 15th December 1945 but prior to this date individual pools held their own displays and parties not only to mark the passing of a unique organisation but also to raise money for the ATA Benevolent Fund.

No.6 Ferry Pool's own show was held on 6th October and for the occasion a fantastic array of over 30 different types of aircraft had been assembled on the airfield. They ranged in size from locally-produced Austers to examples of the Handley Page Halifax and Short Stirling four-engined bombers. Sideshows, equipment displays and rescue demonstrations were all laid on as public entertainment together with an excellent flying display. A notable item in this event was a superlative display of aerobatics given by a Vickers-Supermarine Spitfire flown by that acknowledged master of the aircraft, Alex Henshaw. Undoubtedly the high spot of the day for most spectators was the appearance of two jet aircraft, a Gloster Meteor and a DH Vampire, the latter being flown by Geoffrey de Havilland.

After such a successful show it is sad to relate that the day ended on a very sombre note. In the evening, to round off the proceedings a farewell party was held in the Officers Mess on the airfield. There, following an incident in the bar, one of the guests, First Officer H E Spain, received a very serious eye injury. Spain, who had at one time served as a pilot with 6 FPP was rushed to Leicester Royal Infirmary where, following an emergency operation, he collapsed and died.

Even after the farewells had been said the pool continued to operate for over a month with staff diminishing in numbers and the workload decreasing as the base was gradually run down. One of the last flights to be made was on 9th November when one of the unit's Fairchild Argus I FK313, was flown south to ATA headquarters at White Waltham piloted by Flight Captain A E Coltman. So, finally, after five eventful years of almost constant activity, 6 Ferry Pool, ATA, closed down; Ratcliffe once more became a peaceful backwater and for a time returned to agriculture.

Postwar austerity measures inhibited the immediate return of private flying but after restrictions were relaxed during 1946 the light aviation movement soon began to flourish once more.

O.P.S.	A. T. A.	SPECIAL INSTRUCTIONS TO PILOT

PRIORITY AIRCRAFT COLLECTION CHIT

To the official in charge of the undermentioned aircraft :—
This document hereby authorises the undermentioned pilot to collect.

P. 1.

PILOT'S NAME F/O J. E. Nayler   Chit ref. number 6/253   2nd January 1945
                                                                    Date

Aircraft Type	Aircraft number	Allotment number	Consignor	and	Aerodrome
Mosquito VI	RF 603		Ansty		

Consignee   and   Aerodrome
   328 Sq. Banff

He will hand over the air-   to complete delivery
craft to the Ferry Pool at :   wiring out action if
                                              taken by you should
                                              be to that station.

Collected with/without logbooks | ....Sealed Package(s) | Covers | ....Watch(es)

*Signature of Officer issuing instructions
(to be signed in indelible pencil)*

A wartime view, showing the many buildings that were added to the central complex.

A Blackburn Botha at the northern end of Ratcliffe. B V Hewes

A priority collection chit for 2nd January 1945, for Joan Naylor to pick up the

DH Mosquito VI, RF603, from Ansty, near Coventry, for delivery to 328 Squadron at Banff in northern Scotland. The 'Mossie' was successfully delivered by Joan, but on 24th February it broke up in mid-air and crashed onto Macduff golf course. Strangely, 328 did not operate Mosquitos; RF603 only served with 248 Sqn at Banff until lost in the accident. via Geoff Cooke

Although he still retained his interest in flying, ill health restricted Sir Lindsay Everard from resuming his once active role. Ratcliffe gained a new lease of life following the amalgamation of the County Flying and Leicestershire Aero Clubs in August 1946. As neither of the airfields which the two clubs had occupied was available, (Rearsby had become a company airfield and Braunstone was still requisitioned by the Air Ministry), Sir Lindsay placed Ratcliffe at the reconstituted clubs disposal on very generous terms for an initial period of two years. The same facility was also offered to the Leicestershire Gliding Club and after leaving Rearsby they too took up residence at the airfield.

Although at the time it was reported that Ratcliffe was immediately available for flying, 1st April 1947 was officially the date upon which Leicestershire Aero Club commenced its activities. They were soon in a position to entertain guests and on 1st June their first post-war 'At Home' was held. It was quite a modest affair attracting some 250 members and friends along with over 20 visiting aircraft. The day's programme took on a familiar format with the usual type of club competitions and informal displays being staged.

The arrival competition produced a very interesting winner in Squadron Leader Wright who brought in the largest aircraft present, a Douglas Dakota, from 1382 (T)CU stationed at nearby Wymeswold. Another visitor, a DH Mosquito of 605 Squadron Royal Auxiliary Air Force (RAuxAF), thrilled the spectators with some very low level, high speed runs across the airfield.

In common with many other flying organisations LAC found the going hard; they had high hopes of government assistance but this did not materialise. At this time they would have found it difficult to purchase aircraft of their own but they were very fortunate in being able to use machines supplied by Auster Aircraft Limited for most of the year, at the very low rate of £2 per hour. After the continual movements of ATA days club activity must have appeared very minimal. According to their committee report in the first year of operation club controlled aircraft flew a total of 192 hours 45 minutes, 7 pilots were trained to 'A' licence standard and overall 571 flights were made from Ratcliffe, this from a membership of 179.

The pattern of the club's activities for their second year at Ratcliffe deviated little from 1947 to 1948. Again the only flying event was the 'At Home' held on 4th July. Similar numbers of members attended but this time bad weather hampered the proceedings it did not however prevent the Royal Navy Volunteer Reserve Squadron from Bramcote carrying out a display of formation flying and aerobatics.

During 1948 and 1949 there was a quite definite upturn in club flying. Although membership showed only a slight increase at 190, flying hours were up to 484.50, 'A' licences obtained totalled 18 while flights from the airfield had more than doubled to 1,413. It appeared to augur well for the future, but the death of Sir Lindsay Everard, which occurred on 11th May 1949, was later to have a marked effect on the affairs of the club for with his passing they had not only lost their long time president but also their most generous patron.

When the initial lease of Ratcliffe expired on 31st May 1949 the club were able to secure an extension of their tenancy for a further year. By the time the club entered this third year social and flying activity at Ratcliffe had adopted an almost familiar routine. For their flying event of 1949 they deviated from the pattern set in previous years to stage a public display. Held on 29th May it was a very modest promotion when compared to the sophisticated international display later organised annually by the club. Demonstrations by individual light aircraft formed the backbone of the eleven item show while service participation was drawn from Volunteer Reserve units based in the locality.

The early part of the show was distinctly military in content. No.504 Squadron, RAux-AF, stationed at Wymeswold provided a formation of Spitfires; from Bramcote came their naval counterparts, Seafires belonging

to 1833 Squadron RNVR and 7 RFS at Desford completed the services formation by supplying a flight of Tiger Moths. Although conditions were rather turbulent they seemed to have little effect on this latter formation which carried out tied together aerobatics with apparent ease, not that these same conditions were entirely to the liking of the parachutist, Major T W Willans, who encountered some difficulty from the erratic wind.

A diverse assortment of single aircraft, including examples of the BAC Drone, Chilton DW.1, Miles M.18, Percival Proctor and Prentice all performed in the second half of the show. At the end of the day the organisers must have been well pleased by their effort which had attracted a crowd estimated at around 10,000. Non-paying spectators still posed a problem and at times traffic on the A46 running parallel to the airfield was almost at a standstill due to the congestion.

On 21st June communication was received which precipitated a crisis within the club. Captain Anthony Everard, Sir Lindsay's son, notified them of the intention to dispose of the airfield, but, at the same time offering the club the opportunity to purchase the site for the sum of £15,000. Unfortunately this figure proved to be beyond the reach of their finances so they were forced to forego the offer and eventually the land and buildings were sold to Ratcliffe College.

Faced with no prospect of a further extension of their lease the club began a frantic search for another home. Several avenues were explored but by the time their tenancy expired in March 1950, they had still not secured another base. Leicestershire Gliding Club were rather more fortunate. They managed to obtain permission to use the airfield at Bruntingthorpe. There lease of a hangar allowed them to move their equipment and resume their activities without too much delay.

A view from the tower of the former swimming pool being put to good use with an airborne lifeboat and a dinghy display. W W Storer

Most of the staff of 6 Ferry Pool arranged for a formal photograph, circa 1944. A pair of Argus 'taxies' are behind. G Cooke

As part of the winding up procedure a farewell party was held at Ratcliffe on 25th March. Some 30 visiting aircraft arrived from airfields scattered all over England. A short flying display was staged which in the main was devoted to demonstrations by several different types of Austers in the hands of company pilots. To conclude the programme, 16 aircraft made an aerial tour of the Leicester area before returning to a well attended and most successful party. On 31st March 1950 after almost two decades of aeronautical activity Ratcliffe was finally closed to flying.

Since that date farming has been the sole occupation of the land. All the pre-war accommodation and many of the smaller buildings erected during the Second World War still serve useful purposes to the farm. Two main buildings no longer dominate the site; the first, the MAP hangar was removed in either 1947 or 1948 while the second, that most prominent landmark, the control tower remained standing until 1974. By that time disuse and the ravages of time had taken their toll of the structure making it unsafe, so it too was dismantled.

The name Ratcliffe did not, however, disappear entirely from the aeronautical scene. In March 1966, only a short distance away from the old family airfield, Anthony Everard established, in the grounds of his home at Ratcliffe Hall, his own private heliport complete with its own small hangar and landing pad bearing the legend 'RATCLIFFE'. For several years a succession of helicopters used extensively by him for business and pleasure were housed on the site. Following Mr Everard's retirement in the 1980s, the heliport began to be used less and less. On occasion the hangar was used to house sheep and with the passing of time the name on the landing pad began to erode away and so as it faded, the association between Ratcliffe and aviation became history.

(As an aside, Everard's plant at Fosse Park, close to the M1/M69 junction west of Leicester still has a helipad and small hangar for the company's Robinson R-22 helicopter, thus keeping the family name and aviation firmly linked.)

A vertical survey view of a deserted Ratcliffe, dated 3rd January 1947. The airfield marker circle is just visible at (A). Ratcliffe College (B) lies to the south, while the eastern boundary is the A46 (C). DoE

Vic Hewes and his parachutist passenger Bernard Lynch take-off respectively in and on DH Tiger Moth G-AHRX at LAC's 1947 show. H E Batchelor

Ratcliffe-based Aircraft

Sir Lindsay Everard

DH.60G III Moth	G-ACBX	28.1.33	
		.5.36	To LAC
DH.80A Puss Moth	G-AAXM		Leicestershire Fox.
DH.84 Dragon	G-ACEK	11.5.33	Leicestershire Vixen.
		.6.36	To Olley Air Services
	G-ACKU	24.11.33	
		.2.34	To Wrightways
DH.85 Leopard	G-ACKM	2.2.34	
Moth		.12.36	To Household Brigade Flying Club
DH.87 Hornet	G-ADLY	4.11.35	
Moth		.2.40	Impressed as W9388.

Served with 3 & 4 Coastal patrol Flights; 2 Radio Maintenance Unit; 2 Repair and Salvage Section; 71 Wing and 526 Sqdn. Sold in 1946 and restored to civil register. Still airworthy.

DH.90 Dragonfly	G-ADXM		Leicestershire Vixen II.
		.2.40	Impressed as X9327.

Served with 110 Wing; 4 & 6 AA Co-operation Units; Army Co-op Command Com Flt; 2nd Tactical Air Force Com Flt. Struck off charge 22.7.44.

Percival Gull 4	G-ACAL	10.11.32	Sold 1933.
Percival Vega Gull	G-AELE	19.5.36	Leicestershire Fox IV.
		26.6.39	Ditched nr Le Touquet.

No.6 Ferry Pilot Pool (Air Transport Auxiliary)

From .10.40 to 1.5.42   Renamed No.6 Ferry Pool

No.6 Ferry Pool (Air Transport Auxiliary)

From 1.5.42 to .11.45

Avro Anson I   L9165, N1339, N4860, N4872, N4877, N4929, N4954, N5314, N9536, N9598, N9674, N9726, N9977, R3323, R9696, AX319, AX581, DG802, DJ229, DJ385, EG120, EG373, EG377, LV314.

De Havilland Tiger Moth II   N9150, N9198, T5604.
(All allocated new to Ratcliffe then to Central Landing Establishment.)

De Havilland Dominie I   X7322, X7338, X7455.

Fairchild Argus I   EV750, EV751, EV767, EV768, FK313, FK315, FK332, FK334, FK335, FK336, FK338, FK348, FK350, FK356, HM183, HM184.

Fairchild Argus II   EV770, EV771, EV772, EV775, EV783, EV787, EV788, EV790, EV792, EV799, EV800, EV801, EV806, EV811.

Post-war Civil

Auster J/4	G-AIPS	30.07.47 P A W B Everard
Auster –		Leicestershire Aero Club, Used Auster types supplied from Rearsby

No.6 Ferry Pilot Pool and No.6 Ferry Pool (ATA) – Serious Accidents

15.11.40   Hector I   K9733
On ferry flight from Brize Norton, landed on soft ground and overturned at Henlow, Beds.

5.1.41   Hampden I   L6070
Engine failed belly landed at Thornton le Moor, Lincs. First Officer Emmett Eugene Beville, USA, unhurt.

29.4.41   Dominie I   X7322
Damaged by enemy action.

12.8.41   Spitfire V   AB866
Wheel struck rut while landing at Little Rissington. Port undercarriage leg broke off and aircraft tipped on nose.

14.9.41   Oxford I   X6969
Dived into ground in bad visibility four miles from Stafford.

11.11.41   Anson I   N4872
Overshot landing at Walsall in poor visibility went through hedge and crashed in Longwood Lane.

10.12.41   Spitfire V   BL498
Crashed in forced landing Bisley, Glos.

16.12.41   Spitfire V   BL387
Crashed, no further details.

30.1.42   Defiant I   N3337
Crashed in forced landing ten miles north-east of Ternhill.

9.1.42   Mohawk IV   BJ445
Crashed in forced landing, Astley, Lancs.

15.3.42   Oxford I   X7190
While on ferry flight Ratcliffe-Edzell crashed near Wigtown.

16.4.42   Spitfire V   BM478
Overshot landing at Burtonwood, Lancs.

15.5.42   Spitfire I   K9961
Crashed in forced landing near Leicester.

12.8.42   Spitfire V   EP748
Missing on ferry flight.

13.10.42   Spitfire IV   BR371
Crashed on take-off from Hucknall.

7.11.42   Spitfire V   ER947
Undershot landing at Sherburn in Elmet.

10.12.42   Botha I   W5103
Crashed on air test five miles north-east of Glossop.

14.2.43   Defiant II   N1551
Abandoned after control lost. Crashed Lindel, Lancs.

9.3.43   Typhoon I   DN446
Crashed in forced landing at Henlow after engine cut.

20.6.43   Boston III   W8266
Overshot landing at Tollerton, Notts.

20.8.43   Spitfire VIII   JF844
Crashed in bad weather at Luckley Farm, Stow on the Wold, due to pilot's inability to fly on instruments.

6.10.44   Lancaster I   NG198
Collided with Blenheim V AZ946 of 12 (P)AFU, Spittlegate, Lincs. Crashed 1½ miles north-east of Spittlegate.

30.3.45   Mosquito VI   RF847
Believed to be on fire and abandoned, ten miles south-east of Jedburgh, Scotland.

31.5.45   Spitfire IX   TB357
Undercarriage jammed, belly landed at Brize Norton.

Ratcliffe's hangar compex shortly before dismantling of the control tower. Note that the running fox wind indicator had by now disappeared. Peter Stoddart

Miles Monarch G-AFCR and a 1382 (T)CU Dakota from Wymeswold at Ratcliffe on 1st June 1947. Peter Green collection

Although some sub-division of the land has taken place, the layout of Ratcliffe is still evident in this July 1997 view, looking east with the A46 in the mid-ground. Author

Ratcliffe Hall with the adjacent helicopter hangar and landing pad, July 1997. Author

Chapter Twenty

Rearsby

Some of the visiting aircraft at the official opening of Rearsby on 23rd July 1938. In the middle is Alex Henshaw's Percival Vega Gull G-AFEA and, to the right, G-ADEH an Avro Cadet of the Tollerton Aero Club.
R Townsend.

AFTER they had achieved a distinguished record in wartime operations, light aircraft manufactured at this airfield went on to consolidate their reputation in peacetime and attain great popularity on a worldwide basis. Yet, strange as it may seem, this aerodrome owed its existence, indirectly, to the erratic and unstable flying characteristics of an ultra-light aircraft, the Mignet Pou du Ciel, or to give its more popular name, the Flying Flea.

The story of Rearsby really begins with the formation of the Leicestershire Flying Pou Club whose object was to build one of these aircraft. In readiness for when their Pou was finished the club obtained permission to use a rather inaccessible field off Sandy Lane, near Melton Mowbray (Chapter Sixteen). Here, in an effort to raise funds to further the Flea project, the club held a small flying display in May 1936.

One of the invited guests on that day was W Lindsay Everard (later Sir Lindsay) a prominent figure in light aviation circles not only within Leicestershire but in the country as a whole. Members' obvious dedication and enthusiasm had a marked effect upon him and he agreed to become the club's

President. He intimated though that he saw no future in the Flea as a club aircraft, offering financial assistance if it was abandoned in favour of a safer and more suitable ultralight, the Kronfeld Drone. Agreement was reached and after one of these aircraft, G-AEJS, was delivered to the Sandy Lane field in July 1936, members soon realised just how inadequate their flying ground was for their activities, so a search began for a new home.

Once again their president came to the rescue by making land available off Gaddesby Lane, Rearsby. Mr W W Storer who was, at the time, carrying out radio experiments at Ratcliffe Aerodrome recalled that Sir Lindsay gave him the task of finding a suitable area of land. Several possible locations were investigated including one near Kibworth Beauchamp, but the Gaddesby Lane site eventually gained approval, ease of access proving to be the deciding factor.

Lindsay Everard engaged the local firm of En-Tout-Cas Ltd, Syston, to prepare the land and early in 1937 levelling and drainage operations were in progress. By the summer, after the expenditure in the region of £1,000, Rearsby was ready and to quote a

club publicity brochure gave 'an area of 86 acres of beautiful level flying ground'.

The County Flying Club Limited (CFC), as it had now become, negotiated terms for the use of the aerodrome on a year to year basis and then began the process of making the new field habitable. As a first measure in this direction the wooden hangar which had stood at Sandy Lane was dismantled and re-erected at Rearsby; also, a small shed was assembled to serve as a temporary clubhouse. With these rudimentary amenities in place flying began using the club's existing equipment.

The system of tuition whereby prospective pilots progressed from the Kronfeld Ground Trainer to the Drone was still not ideally suited to club operation. A new type of aircraft, the American-built Taylor J2 Cub was soon introduced to Rearsby thanks to

V H Doree, a prominent member of the club, who arranged for a demonstration at the aerodrome after he had seen one of these aircraft while on a visit to Braunstone. CFC took delivery of their first Cub, G-AEXY, in July 1937 and from the outset it proved very popular; eventually they were to own three of this type. Throughout the summer of 1937 Rearsby was operated as an unlicensed aerodrome, a state of affairs which was eventually brought to the notice of the County Police. Following a visit to the airfield by members of the force in August, an application was made to the Ministry of Civil Aviation (MCA) to ensure that complaints could not be raised regarding this situation in the future.

When the first temporary licence came into effect in September it had been issued subject to the following requirements being met: 'Provided crash equipment is readily available, telephone installed, landing area marked with 'A' type markers and trees adjacent to the site are removed. Rearsby Aerodrome, excluding the eastern portion is licensed for light aircraft only for the period 7th September 1937 to 6th November 1937'.

Apparently some of these conditions were either ignored or forgotten by CFC for when the time came to renew the licence a report made by the MCA inspector, John Grierson, contained some very uncomplimentary observations: 'Licencees appear to have been very lax in the administration of their aerodrome in allowing cart ruts to develop, buildings put up without reference to us and in failing to cut down the trees which we had asked for. Therefore, permanent licence cannot be recommended with the aerodrome in its present state and we can only recommend the continuation of the present temporary licence'. Steps were taken to rectify omissions and to correct the faults, but it was a slow process and almost a year was to elapse before a permanent licence was forthcoming.

Work on a new and well appointed clubhouse began in 1938. Construction was undertaken by Walker Brothers of Sileby

Remembered by many for the amount of noise it made as well as its 'flying dragon' paint job, BAC Drone VII G-ADSB belonged to Bernard Collins. K F Tunnicliff

A proud J S Squires poses with his Luton Minor G-AFIR. He had already successfully built and flown a Flying Flea - see Chapter Sixteen. via J S Squires

Rearsby aerodrome staff in front of a Taylorcraft. Manager Bernard Collins, wearing the 'teddy bear' coat, ready for cold weather flying. His assistant, 'Mac' Love is on the far right. K F Tunnicliff

and, aided by club members, the building was made ready in time for the official opening of the aerodrome on Saturday, 23rd July 1938. Air Commodore J A Chamier, Secretary General of the Air League of the British Empire, performed the opening ceremony while the Lord Mayor of Leicester, Councillor F Acton, followed up by formally opening the clubhouse. To celebrate the event flying displays were staged throughout the weekend. Saturday's festivities attracted over 30 visiting aircraft and several distinguished personalities flew in for the occasion. Notable amongst these were Alex Henshaw, the popular winner of the 1938 Kings Cup Air Race, while a party of French dignitaries led by Baron De La Grange, President of the Aero Club de France, arrived in what proved to be the largest aircraft, Farman F.193 F-AMPD.

In his opening address Air Commodore Chamier took the opportunity to announce the formation of the Civil Air Guard (CAG). Under this government-sponsored scheme people were taught to fly at the low cost of two shillings and sixpence (12½p) per hour and for each pilot completing training the club to which they belonged received a subsidy of between £30 and £50. From the outset response was quite tremendous; on one day alone the CFC received over 80 applications from aspiring pilots wishing to enrol in the scheme.

Participation in the CAG project from October 1938 enabled the club to acquire further aircraft, one of these was another American-built type, a Taylorcraft Model A G-AFJW. One member, A L (Lance) Wykes, was so impressed with this new purchase that he decided to diversify his existing textile machine building business (Crowther Ltd) and enter the world of aircraft manufacture. His decision was, at a later date, to have a far reaching effect on the future of Rearsby aerodrome.

It was also in October 1938 that the first permanent licence was issued for the airfield. Although it had taken some time to achieve the club had by now made considerable progress in their administration of Rearsby. This is well illustrated by the content of the inspectors report dated 11th May 1939:

Landing Circle	Yes, clean. Name, no.
Boundary Markings	'A' type – to be erected on posts.
Bad Ground	None.
Wind Indicators	Three socks, one wind 'T'.
Other Markings	None.
Surface Conditions	Good, well drained.
Obstructions: North	Power cables, very well marked.
Obstructions: South	Farm buildings, occasional trees.
Boundaries	Well defined hedges.
Medical and Crash Equipment	Up to standard, mounted on vehicle.
Night Flying	Nil.

General Observations:

New hangar and CAG hut have been erected west of the original hangar. Bad ground in west is now in good condition. This aerodrome now appears to be well maintained and controlled.

Following up his decision to build aircraft, A L Wykes concluded an agreement with the American Taylor-Young Corporation to licence build to their designs. In partnership with F Bates and P Wykes he founded the company of Taylorcraft Aeroplanes (England) Limited in November 1938 and a production line was set up in buildings at the rear of Britannia Works, Thurmaston.

The first machine completed left the works in April 1939 and as it incorporated many improvements on the American design it was named the Taylorcraft Plus Model C. Possessing no company airfield at this time, final assembly and test flying took place at nearby Ratcliffe (Chapter Nineteen). A link with the company and Rearsby was established as their demonstration aircraft, an imported Taylorcraft B, G-AFKO, was based there.

The firm prospered, their product proving very popular with both private owners and flying clubs and by August five aircraft per week were being produced. Another link with Rearsby was established when, over a

Official plan showing the layout of Rearsby, the northern boundary being the Rearsby to Gaddesby road. via Author

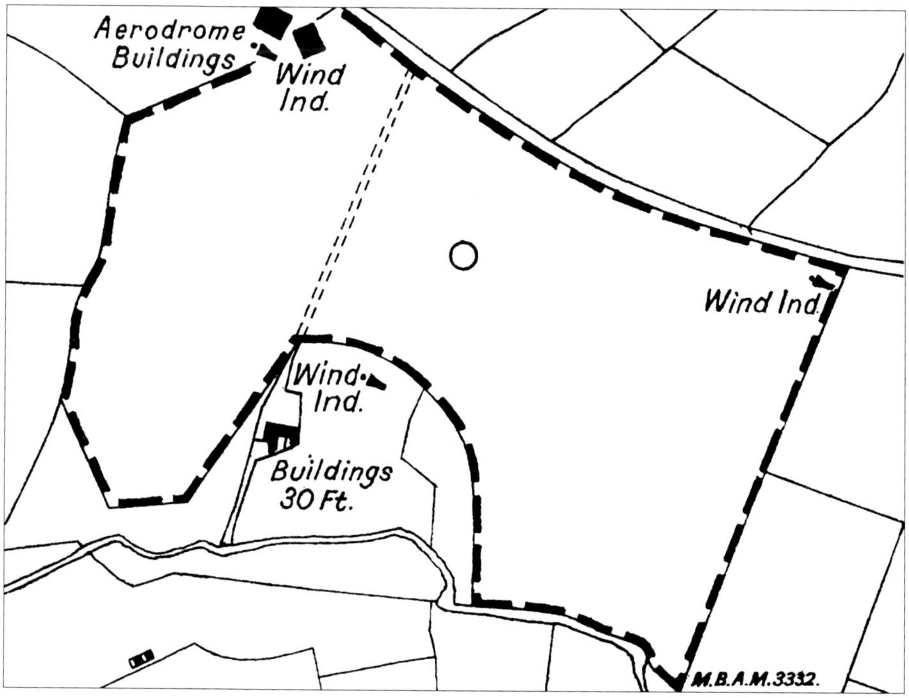

period of time, three of their Plus Cs were added to the flying club's fleet. The company also had plans to introduce a new model fitted with a British 90hp Cirrus Minor I engine. This was to be the Plus D.

In mid-1939 another company became associated with the airfield in what is believed to have been a short-lived operation. This was the Midland Aircraft Company (Rearsby) Ltd who were claiming to be able to deliver Piper J-4A Cubs, with a choice of either a 60 or 65hp engine, within three weeks of an order being placed. As far as sales are concerned the Cub was in direct competition with the locally-built Taylorcraft and Midland were offering to supply J-3 trainers for £425 and J-4As, with a comprehensive accessories fit for £625.

J-4A G-AFTE was registered to the company on 16th June 1939 but its life was rather brief as it was written off in a crash near Leicester on 8th August. After this event nothing further is known of the company.

Throughout 1939 CAG flying formed the major part of activity at Rearsby; in April of that year 140 trainees were reported to be receiving tuition at the airfield. During week days a large proportion of the visiting traffic consisted of de Havilland Tiger Moths belonging to 7 Elementary & Reserve Flying School at Desford. It was noted that bar profits benefited considerably from these visits.

On the whole life at the airfield appears to have passed fairly smoothly during 1939 until the outbreak of war in September brought things to an abrupt halt. Staff employed at the airfield were aware that something was about to happen following the visit, towards the end of August, of a camouflaged Avro Anson. Its passenger, Group Captain Probyn, delivered a sealed envelope together with instructions that it was only to be opened on receipt of a specific telephone call sometime hence. The call duly came and the content of the letter stated briefly that the airfield and buildings were to be camouflaged and the white landing circle markings to be painted green.

The Air Navigation (Restriction in Time of War) Order 1939 came into force. Amongst other things this order invoked a complete ban on private and club flying. Operations at Rearsby ceased immediately, employees were dismissed with one week's notice and eventually the club aircraft were dismantled to be stored in the garage of Crawford, Prince and Johnson Limited at Queniborough and Rearsby, as an airfield, closed.

In spite of the official closure, it is known that Rearsby was used afterwards on two occasions for illegal flying activity. Although the airfield was, by now, very unkempt with grass almost a foot high, during the Easter and Whitsun holidays of 1940 a group of enthusiastic young men managed to fly a Dixon Primary glider which they had rebuilt. By using a car to provide launch power a considerable number of long hops and ground slides were made. Unfortunately the glider was rather badly bent during the Whit session, terminating the proceedings. It was not the end of the glider however, for eventually it was repaired to serve as the initial equipment for M42 Gliding School at Loughborough.

The outbreak of war and the Restriction Order soon altered the outlook for Taylorcraft. Production ceased, there being no civil outlet for the aircraft. The firm was hard put to survive but small subcontract orders from other firms engaged on military aircraft production saved the day. Things began to look up when a contract was received to repair de Havilland Tiger Moths and also, when in the first half 1940, eight of the new Plus Ds were produced. These were mainly for Army use to enable them to be evaluated in the liaison and artillery spotting roles.

With their reputation for repair work growing Taylorcraft were asked, in the Autumn of 1940, to undertake repairs to Hawker Hurricanes. Having no experience of high speed fighter aircraft it was with some trepidation that they accepted the challenge. Needing additional working space for the contract they took over several empty premises in the area, permission was also received for them to use Rearsby aerodrome, and so began an association which was to last for almost three decades.

So urgent was the need for aircraft that

hangars and ancillary buildings were rapidly erected and to cope with the Hurricanes the airfield was extended towards Gaddesby. Taylorcraft were in occupation by the end of the year. At first there were many problems and improvisation was the order of the day but repaired Hurricanes were soon leaving the works. The first was Mk.I V7338 in February 1941.

Throughout the war Taylorcraft maintained a steady output of repaired aircraft. In early 1943 the Hawker Typhoon began to replace the Hurricane on the repair lines, the first leaving the works in May of that year. Eventually, after the departure of the last repaired Tiger Moth in March 1944, the Typhoon occupied the greater part of Rearsby's repair facilities, the last of this type being returned to the RAF in November 1945. A contract for the repair of Kirby Cadet gliders which followed was completed in April 1946 after eleven of these aircraft had been repaired.

Some controversy exists regarding totals of various types repaired during the Second World War, but to quote a company press release of December 1945 the figures were, Tiger Moth 339; Hurricane 406; Typhoon 281. Solitary examples of other aircraft passed through the repair sections hands and included a de Havilland Hornet Moth, a Piper Cub Coupe and a Handley Page Harrow which was converted to a Sparrow unarmed transport. Additionally, a salvage section on the airfield dealing with crashed aircraft deemed too badly damaged to warrant repair, handled 326 aircraft. Most of these aircraft were of types being repaired by the company but they did include a number of Harrows.

Taylorcraft also manufactured parts for various types of aircraft including the Albemarle, Audax, Hurricane, Oxford, Spitfire and Tiger Moth. This, together with their involvement in the Civilian Repair Organisation, was of considerable help to the war effort but the company's most significant contribution came from the development and building of their own aircraft. The Army was impressed with their Taylorcraft and a dynasty of aircraft respected the world over was about to be launched. The story of Taylorcraft, Auster and Beagle and their impressive line of products, is told in Chapter Twenty-One.

It was in the spring of 1944 that the company suffered a severe blow with the tragic death of its founder and managing director, A L Wykes. On 14th May while he was giving an AOP demonstration at a 'Salute the Soldier' rally held in aid of the National Savings Movement in Abbey Park, Leicester, the Auster he was flying dived to the ground from only about 300ft and crashed just outside the park boundary. Wykes, the sole occupant, was killed instantly.

Towards the end of 1946 large numbers of ex-service aircraft began to be released for public sale which ultimately led to a decline in orders for Rearsby's new products. Consequently, a large number of aircraft awaiting sale or delivery were picketed out at Rearsby in the early months of 1947. During the night of Sunday 16th March disaster struck when a violent gale raged across the airfield. Next morning widespread damage was revealed, aircraft had been torn from their moorings and flung about like toys. Two had been deposited on the roof of the main drawing office, others over the hedge into Gaddesby Lane, while one had travelled right over the road into a field on the opposite side. In all 72 aircraft received damage and several were completely destroyed. The company had been dealt a severe blow at a time when the situation was beginning to look rather precarious.

Even though it was now a company airfield, air displays and club flying, both features of pre-war Rearsby, returned at the end of the war. The first flying display for six years took place on 1st September 1945 when Leicestershire Gliding Club staged a Victory Flying Display. Various aspects of Air Training Corps (ATC) Gliding activities formed a major part of the event but cadets were shown what they might aspire to by Prince Bira of Siam in his displays of a Slingsby Gull III high performance sailplane. Despite fuel restrictions the programme contained several notable items of powered flying. Geoffrey Edwards, Auster's chief test pilot, ably demonstrated the flying characteristics of a captured German Fieseler Storch while another company test pilot, Mr Derbyshire, put a newly-repaired Typhoon through its paces. Quite naturally both military and civil versions of the Auster were included in the display.

Gliding had become a part of the Rearsby scene in the autumn of 1943 when M44 Elementary Gliding School of the ATC became established on the airfield. On the south side of the airfield, near Benskins Barn, a blister hangar had been erected to house them. This was to be their home until the summer of 1947 when the unit moved once more, this time to resume its operations from Bruntingthorpe.

At Easter 1946 a large gliding meeting was held at Rearsby which attracted many personalities associated with the British gliding movement. Although the gathering had quite an informal atmosphere it was regarded as the first post-war National Gliding Championships.

Club flying was re-introduced during 1946 with the formation of the Auster Flying Club. Company sponsored, it was able to offer tuition and flying at reduced rates.

At their first flying display held on 21st July, the Auster Flying Club played host to the County and Leicestershire Flying Clubs both of which were without a home. This problem was solved by the successful merger of the two clubs and Sir Lindsay Everard's offer of the use of Ratcliffe to the reconstituted Leicestershire Aero Club. This offer was extended to Leicestershire Gliding Club who took advantage of this and moved out to Ratcliffe.

Following this 1946 event, air displays held under the auspices of the Auster Flying Club became an annual feature for many years at Rearsby. Invariably well attended they provided the host company with an excellent opportunity to display their latest products as well as including a varied programme of both military and civilian flying.

It was during 1960 that gliding returned to Rearsby with the founding of the East Midlands Gliding Club (EMGC). One of its gliders, a Slingsby T.21, came to Leicestershire by a very circuitous route. Bought in Sweden it was then aero-towed via Denmark, Holland, Belgium across the English Channel eventually arriving at Rearsby. During 1962 the EMGC amalgamated with Leicestershire Gliding Club which, following its demise at Bruntingthorpe, had continued a shared existence with the Coventry Gliding Club. The title of Leicestershire Gliding Club was then adopted. It became a very successful club owning as many as five gliders to cater for a sizeable membership. Club activity, allied to a number of privately owned gliders, meant that Rearsby became a very busy site on most suitable weekends.

On 20th May 1962, Rearsby was the venue for one of the Redhill Tiger Club displays, complete with Druine Turbulents and the like. Among many visitors was the LeVier Cosmic Wind, G-ARUL, a diminutive racing aircraft, newly imported to the UK. Locally-built products on view included numerous civil and military Austers, two Beagle Terriers and seven of the new Beagle Airedales. Also present was the Beagle company's 'hack', the resplendent DH.84 Dragon I, G-ACIT.

Sadly, the demise of Beagle, as the company had now become, came about in March 1970 following a period of financial problems. Although the works had closed the airfield was still used by the Leicestershire Gliding Club for their activities but in May 1971 even this ceased. The club was then wound up with many of its members joining either the Buckminster or Coventry Gliding Clubs. After over 30 eventful years another segment of Leicestershire's aviation passed into history.

The factory was eventually disposed of to Rearsby Automotive Limited, a British Leyland company manufacturing car components. Though now no longer a subsidiary of British Leyland, Rearsby Automotive continue their association with the automobile industry. Now trading under the Adwest

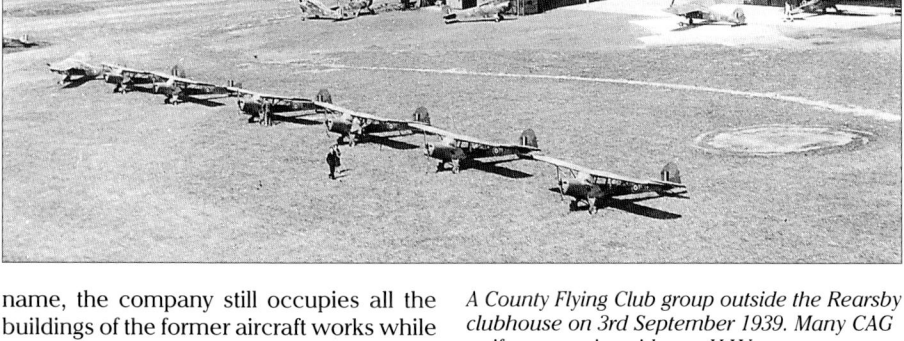

name, the company still occupies all the buildings of the former aircraft works while the surrounding land, which was once such an active airfield has long since returned to agriculture.

Since the closure and sale of the airfield there have been two brief interludes when Austers flew once more from Rearsby. Both have been made possible due to the co-operation between Rearsby Automotive on the first occasion and Adwest, the present site owners on the second; the International Auster Pilot Club (now named the International Auster Club); and Peter Palmer who now farms the former airfield.

The first event was a fly-in arranged to celebrate the 50th Anniversary of the formation of Taylorcraft Aeroplanes (England) Limited in 1938. Held on 10th September 1988 the event was blessed by fine weather.

In place of grass the landing area was now the close cut stubble left by the harvest. The surface was still both firm and level presenting no problems for the 28 Austers which came back to their birth-

A County Flying Club group outside the Rearsby clubhouse on 3rd September 1939. Many CAG uniforms are in evidence. H Warren

The Rearsby end of the field, showing the Auster sheds and a large number of AOP.Vs, with and without wings. Taylorcraft

place for the day. Many former Auster employees attracted to the event seized the opportunity to renew old acquaintances and exchange reminiscences of times past during this nostalgic visit to their one-time place of employment.

Nine years were to elapse before a similar gathering was held on 20th September 1997. Though there was little prior publicity, the grapevine and the 'old boys' network' must have been quite active for the visitors book contained 300 entries at the end of the day. As in 1988, the weather was again favourable, but this time visiting aircraft exceeded expectations. No fewer than 49 Austers of various types returned, albeit fleetingly, to their ancestral home.

Lady workers moving a shrouded Tiger Moth fuselage (T6298 ?) for a publicity picture, almost certainly at Thurmaston.

Tiger Moth BD170 trestled on the aerodrome, prior to flight test. This was an impressed example, having previously been in civilian hands as G-AFJM. Both Chris Salter collection

Work underway on the overhaul of Hawker Hurricanes. Each aircraft is carefully placarded with its status and identity and according to the boards, the aircraft on the left is Mk.II Z2483 which was shipped to Russia in January 1942. The next one along is Mk.I L1695 which was destroyed when it flew into cables near Shrewsbury, also in January 1942. via Author

Many former employees who made yet another pilgrimage to their old workplace noted that in the interim several changes had occurred. Notable among these was the disappearance of the old County Flying Club clubhouse-cum-works canteen. This had been demolished following the change of ownership of the site.

The Leicester Museums Service (LMS) has been instrumental in preserving many items of historical importance relating to the days of Taylorcraft, Auster and Beagle and their products. Central to this has been the saving of the production plans and diagrams by the Arts and Records Service. Over a long period of time, this department has been instrumental in helping owners and operators of Austers worldwide to maintain and restore their aircraft.

Additionally, a large amount of Auster and associated hardware has been collected, including five whole aircraft. At Leicester Airport, restoration work continues for LMS on Taylorcraft Plus C2 G-AFTN, found in a barn in Devon. Stored at another location is J/4 G-AIJK. Chapter Twelve charted the operation of J/1 G-AGOH and it can currently be found in the Newark Air Museum at Winthorpe, Nottinghamshire.

Auster AOP.9 XP280 'flies' from the ceiling inside the Snibston Discovery Park, Coalville, having previously been in store at the Abbey Pumping Station in Leicester and until recently was the only Auster type to be displayed within the county of its birth. During April 1999 the Charnwood Museum at Loughborough helped to correct this by placing LMS J/1N Alpha G-AJRH on display in the Newcastle Aero Club markings and race No.7 that it wore when it won the King's Cup air race at Coventry in 1956.

It is a great pity that space restrictions prevent the display of the other airframes and items, particularly as they relate to a county product that is known and revered the world over.

Rearsby-based Aircraft

County Flying Club

Taylor J-2 Cub	G-AEIK, G-AEXY, G-AEXZ
Taylorcraft A	G-AFJW
Taylorcraft Plus C	G-AFNW, FUZ, FWM
Piper J-3 Cub	G-AFFJ
Kronfeld Drone	G-AEJS

Other Owners and Operators

Avro Avian	G-ACKE	V H Doree
De Havilland Leopard Moth	G-ACHC	
Kronfeld Drone	G-ADSB	B H Collins
Luton Minor	G-AFIR	J S Squires
Piper J-4A Cub Coupé	G-AFTE	Midland A/c Co
Taylorcraft B	G-AFKO	Taylorcraft Ltd
Taylorcraft Plus C	G-AFWK	W G Turnbull

Post-1945

Percival Proctor III	LZ570	Auster Aircraft Ltd
Auster D4/108	G-ARLG	Auster Flying Club
Auster J/4	G-AIJP	Auster Flying Club
Auster J/4	G-AIZP	Auster Flying Club

Serious Accidents to Rearsby-based Aircraft

. . . .39	Taylorcraft A Crashed at Rearsby.	G-AFJW
8.8.39	Piper J-4A Cub Coupé Crashed at Leicester.	G-AFTE
19.7.46	Taylorcraft Plus D Crashed at Rearsby.	G-AGZN
16.3.47	Auster J/2 Arrow Destroyed by a gale.	G-AGPS
2.9.47	Taylorcraft Plus D Damaged beyond repair at Rearsby.	G-AHSF
15.5.49	Auster 5 Crashed Humberstone.	G-AHGV
19.11.49	Auster J/4 Crashed at Shardlow, Derbyshire, while in use by Auster Flying Club.	G-AIZP
2.8.50	Auster Avis Damaged beyond repair in forced landing at Queniborough.	G-AJYF
22.4.51	Auster J/4 Crashed near Melton Mowbray after pilotless take-off from Rearsby.	G-AJYX
2.12.56	Auster J/4 Destroyed by fire in fatal crash at Gaddesby.	G-AIZT
23.5.64	Terrier 2 Fatal crash at Rearsby while glider towing.	G-ASFM
27.12.65	Terrier 2 Damaged beyond repair following loss of propeller when taking off on glider tow.	G-ATKJ

Taylorcraft – Civilian Repair Organisation

De Havilland Tiger Moth I   K2598, K4248, K4256, K4279, L6923, L6926, L6929, L6940.

De Havilland Tiger Moth II   N5448, N5451, N5452, N5460, N5466, N5480, N5489, N6445, N6457, N6464, N6472, N6476, N6483, N6485, N6525, N6535, N6539, N6545, N6551, N6577, N6581, N6591, N6595, N6598, N6602, N6603, N6637, N6638, N6651, N6662, N6667, N6707, N6710, N6716, N6723, N6730, N6732, N6733*, N6741, N6744, N6754, N6770, N6778, N6780, N6789*, N6792, N6798, N6804, N6852, N6863, N6874, N6880, N6908, N6912, N6926, N6931, N6934*, N6948, N6969, N6973, N9115, N9148, N9177*, N9184, N9189, N9190, N9191, N9193, N9199, N9208, N9212, N9244, N9256, N9314, N9315, N9326, N9332, N9347, N9370, N9380, N9385, N9402, N9406, N9408, N9454, N9499, N9509, N9514, R4749, R4753, R4757, R4764, R4771, R4773, R4775, R4783, R4832, R4845, R4855, R4856, R4923, R4948*, R4963, R5015, R5023, R5025, R5028, R5029, R5081, R5086*, R5103, R5112, R5138*, R5142, R5143, R5145, R5147, R5236, T5370, T5382, T5416, T5427, T5468, T5533, T5535, T5538, T5603, T5607, T5612, T5621, T5622, T5630, T5673, T5674, T5678, T5682, T5698, T5716, T5717, T5809, T5811, T5832, T5833, T5836, T5840, T5841, T5842, T5844, T5970, T6026, T6059, T6099, T6104, T6125, T6177, T6179, T6180, T6184, T6193, T6250, T6265, T6271, T6273, T6288, T6293, T6298, T6311, T6363, T6364, T6371, T6401, T6443, T6464, T6465, T6534, T6547, T6559, T6582, T6683, T6685, T6686, T6708, T6709, T6750, T6766, T6767, T6806, T6811*, T6859, T6876, T6963, T6980, T6986, T7043, T7051, T7054, T7086, T7088*, T7104, T7120, T7142, T7161, T7166, T7176, T7181, T7188, T7210, T7215, T7223, T7224, T7232, T7237, T7271, T7259, T7283, T7287, T7288, T7294, T7295, T7329, T7332, T7351, T7352*, T7408, T7414, T7443, T7445, T7602, T7605, T7730*, T7735, T7744, T7747, T7748, T7752, T7753, T7790, T7809, T7846, T7912, T8252, T8255, T8261, W6418, W6419, W7954, X5108, BB679, BB698, BB703, BB723, BB728, BB729, BB735, BB741, BB742, BB755, BB759, BB791, BB800, BB806, BB810, BB814*, BB867, BD170. DE132, DE171, DE249, DE258, DE319, DE370, DE398, DE482, DE518, DE560, DE569, DE571, DE582, DE606, DE622, DE623, DE632, DE659, DE663, DE685, DE734, DE745, DE774, DE779, DE785, DE809, DE899, DE982, NL690.

Hawker Hurricane I   L1555, L1563, L1574, L1594, L1601, L1638*, L1695, L1704, L1731, L1777, L1796, L1825, L1864, L1917, L1934, L1973, L2063, L2064, L2070, L2089, L2091, L2100, N2329*, N2338, N2399, N2436, N2469, N2471, N2591, N2647, N2666, N2706, P2575, P2630, P2681, P2799, P2805, P2860, P2909*, P2918, P2993, P3146*, P3161*, P3211, P3217, P3265, P3385, P3396, P3416, P3475, P3620, P3641, P3675, P3715, P3814, P3854, P3861, P3863, P3868, P3881, P3884, P3886, P3901, P3937, P5196, P5197, R2681, R2688, R4077, R4113, R4118, R4178, R4196, R4217, T9519, T9523, T9524, T9332, T9333, V6552, V6558, V6573, V6635, V6637, V6680, V6723, V6727, V6728, V6731, V6732, V6738, V6743, V6808, V6845, V6856, V6869, V6878, V6887, V6918, V6926, V6956, V7005, V7010, V7012, V7058, V7077, V7080, V7081, V7131, V7135, V7137, V7159, V7160, V7173, V7184, V7256, V7285, V7316, V7318, V7338, V7366, V7401, V7411*, V7416, V7425, V7436, V7462, V7464, V7466, V7496, V7508, V7607, V7613, V7618, V7627, V7645, V7682, V7743, V7744, V7751, W9111, W9115, W9128, W9136, W9138, W9151, W9153, W9187*, W9225, W9294, Z2312, Z2321, Z2322, Z2325, Z2334, Z2384, Z2389, Z2424, Z2446, Z2448, Z2463, Z2465, Z2483, Z2504, Z2506, Z2577, Z2640, Z2641, Z2685, Z2691, Z2696, Z2744, Z2760, Z2791, Z2792, Z2800, Z2802, Z2803, Z2804, Z2808, Z2816, Z2828, Z2886, Z2891, Z2960, Z2966, Z2979, Z2985, Z2993, Z3018, Z3025, Z3031, Z3078, Z3080, Z3084, Z3097, Z3147, Z3148, Z3151, Z3154, Z3165, Z3178, Z3227, Z3231, Z3265, Z3312, Z3323, Z3333, Z3336, Z3348, Z3390, Z3395, Z3432, Z3434, Z3502, Z3559, Z3568, Z3572*, Z3581, Z3584, Z3588, Z3595, Z3663, Z3684, Z3784, Z3833, Z3888, Z3914, Z3919, Z4045, Z4049, Z4501, Z4575*, Z4631, Z4924, Z5051, Z5072, Z5126, Z5215, Z5217, Z5256, Z5258, Z5261, Z5346, Z7049, Z7058, Z7059, Z7080, Z7146, AF972, AF979, AF980, AF995, AG101, AG105, AG132, AG141, AG153, AG166, AG175, AG179, AG208, AG213, AG225, AG253, AG259, AG289, AG665.

Hawker Hurricane II   BE161, BE354, BE404, BE500, BE503, BE505, BE512, BE551, BE635, BE645, BE668, BE693. BH119. BN105, BN188, BN206, BN230, BN234, BN287, BN292, BN360, BN411, BN965. BP769, BP772. BV172. DG621. HL588, HL603, HL728, HL862, HL864, HL865, HL937, HL938. HV286, HV301, HV730. HW557, HW596, HW731. JS281, JS347. KX176.

Hawker Hurricane X   AM293, AM353, BD788, BD833, BD872, BD875.

Hawker Typhoon I   R7588, R7589, R7591, R7595, R7599, R7613, R7627, R7631, R7643, R7646, R7673, R7679, R7683, R7693, R7698, R7713, R7800, R7803, R7873, R7879, R7922, R7923, R8220, R8225, R8636, R8651, R8652, R8653, R8694, R8702, R8718, R8722, R8745, R8749, R8750, R8753, R8757, R8761, R8762, R8763, R8768, R8770, R8771, R8774, R8776, R8777, R8778, R8779, R8819, R8820, R8821, R8830, R8843, R8869, R8871, R8872, R8878, R8890, R8969, R8977*, DN252, DN269, DN298, DN301, DN304, DN308, DN322, DN328, DN329, DN330, DN332, DN339, DN359, DN365, DN379, DN380, DN385, DN413, DN414, DN422, DN423, DN426, DN437, DN441, DN467, DN480, DN482, DN485, DN488, DN490, DN491, DN492, DN505, DN538, DN550, DN554, DN556, DN561, DN562, DN586, DN597, DN618, EJ910, EJ913, EJ930*, EJ978, EJ979, EJ983*, EJ991, EJ995, EK136*, EK149, EK187, EK194, EK211, EK218, EK232, EK269, EK285, EK324, EK371, EK500*, JP383, JP384, JP394, JP442, JP443, JP445, JP497, JP504, JP515, JP580, JP596, JP598, JP601, JP610, JP654, JP666, JP667*, JP669, JP672, JP687*, JP726, JP744, JP753, JP789, JP795, JP802, JP861, JP917, JP920, JP936, JP938, JP963, JP964, JP974, JR140, JR141, JR205, JR208, JR212, JR259, JR261, JR291, JR308, JR312, JR320, JR337, JR363, JR379, JR380, JR429, JR437, JR506, JR514, JR516, MM955, MM958, MM976, MM978, MM987, MM988, MM990, MN119, MN142, MN148, MN179, MN202, MN234, MN243, MN244, MN251, MN253, MN260, MN291, MN301, MN304, MN311, MN315, MN320, MN344, MN349, MN353, MN364, MN365, MN371, MN378, MN427, MN435, MN482, MN485, MN517, MN528, MN530, MN533, MN549, MN550, MN551, MN573, MN593, MN598, MN626, MN632, MN698, MN712, MN738, MN744, MN745, MN757, MN758, MN777, MN802, MN858, MN873, MN886, MN893, MN926, MN937, MN952, MN968, MN969, MN971, MN978, MN982, MN985, MN988, MM994, MM996, MP117, MP140, MP147, MP182, PD455, PD463, PD500, PD501, PD504, PD507, PD522, PD527, PD529, PD531, PD535, PD548, PD557, PD562, PD569, PD571, PD589, PD590, PD600, PD610, RB197, RB212, RB249, RB257, RB281, RB305, RB309, RB334, RB365, RB368, RB375, RB388, RB403, RB450, RB457, RB459, RB490, RB499, RB500, RB507, SW405, SW410, SW416, SW419, SW420.

Note: Aircraft marked * visited twice.

View of part of the production line at Rearsby in the early 1950s. Norman Hayes

Hurricane I V7338, reputed to be the first of the type repaired by the Rearsby CRO.
N Ellison

A Typhoon Ib parked out, ready for assessment at Rearsby. It is likely to be either R8830 or R8871, both previously with 181 Squadron. Both of these aircraft were not refurbished but reduced to spares.
via Dr Hugh Thomas

The scrap dump was located close to the road to Gaddesby on the east of the airfield. The remains of Typhoons and Austers can be readily identified. The Typhoon Ib fuselage that dominates the dump is believed to be MN698 'FM-P' formerly of 257 Squadron which was struck off charge on 23rd October 1945.
J H Collier

Top left: *A portrait of ATA ferry pilot Toni Strodl in the cockpit of a Mustang I or II. Danish-born Toni was based 'over the road' at Ratcliffe, and is believed to have test flown for Austers as well as delivered the type for the ATA. The photo is inscribed 'Best wishes to Taylorcraft' and dated 1945.* Chris Salter collection

Top right: *Famous post-war radio personality Caroll Levis, poses with the Fieseler Fi156 Storch evaluated by Taylorcraft at Rearsby.* Taylorcraft.

Right: *Vertical view of Rearsby dated 17th January 1947, with 63 Austers visible around the main buildings and one out on the flying field. The pre-war airfield identity circle (A) is barely visible, having been obscured during the war years.* DoE

Below left: *Prince Bira in the cockpit of a Slingsby Gull III during the 1st September 1945 flying display. Note his passenger, his West Highland white terrier Titch, behind his head. The boy second from left looks very like a covert aircraft spotter!* J Collier

Below right: *A gathering at Rearsby, under the watch of the tower. In the foreground is Auster J/4 G-AIPG while at the rear is J/1 G-AGYJ which was exported to Australia in January 1952.* J Collier

Top left: *Aerial view of Rearsby, September 1997, looking approximately north-west with the village of Rearsby in the background and, beyond that, Ratcliffe. The airfield buildings are now hedged in and the flying field devoted to arable farming.*

Top right: *A close-up of the former Auster buildings. A car park now exists on the area where the clubhouse once was.*

Above left: *The 50th anniversary cake, with its illustrations in full colour, was a good size as the knife to the right gives testament!*

Above right: *G-AFTN, the oldest surviving Auster type, is owned by Leicestershire Museums Service and under slow restoration to display condition.*

Centre left: *Three local products at rest on the stubble that once was Rearsby aerodrome, during the 50th anniversary fly-in, on 10th September 1988. Left to right: J/1N Alpha G-AJYB, D5/180 Husky G-AXBF and AOP.9 WZ662 (G-BKVK).* All Author

Bottom: *AOP.9 XP280 is displayed inside the Snibston Discovery Park, Coalville.* Ken Ellis

Chapter Twenty-One

Taylorcraft - Auster - Beagle

WITHOUT a doubt, the family of aircraft produced at Rearsby have created a worldwide affection and interest. As shown in Chapter Twenty, proud owners operate 'Austers' in many countries; those that built and maintained them foster a great sense of camaraderie; and thousands of enthusiasts take great delight every time they see one, be it in the air, on the ground, or in a museum.

In the same manner as Chapters Two and Three were linked to chart the history of Bitteswell as an airfield and then as a production centre, so this chapter serves to provide an overview of the output of the Taylorcraft, Auster and Beagle concerns to complement the history of Rearsby aerodrome that appeared in Chapter Twenty.

The choice of the word 'overview' is deliberate. The story of 'Austers' (that name having become generic for all of the products, many regarding even the 'big' Beagles as coming under the 'Auster' umbrella) has yet to be told fully and satisfactorily in print and richly deserves to be the subject of a book in its own right. Research into this task in on-going by a variety of specialists and even today there is much to refine and discover relating to the at times, complex production history.

In terms of previously published material on 'Auster', four works (all long out of print) remain as important building blocks on the route to a comprehensive study of the dynasty. In June 1965, Norman H Ellison ARAeS and (the late) Richard O Macdemitria AMIED AMIBE compiled *Auster Aircraft – Aircraft Production List*, published by Air-Britain as No.4 in a monograph series. Produced on a duplicator, this valued work was reprinted in October 1965 and again in January 1966.

In 1974, Midland Counties Publications (sister company to the publishers of this book) produced the booklet *Beagle Aircraft – A Production History*, compiled by the Midland Counties Aviation Research Group. This told the whole of the Beagle story up to that point and a supplement produced in October of that same year listed the initial

Fine portrait of G-ASBV, the demonstrator D5/180. The D5/180 was eventually renamed the Husky and represented the ultimate development of the classic 'Auster' format.
Ken Ellis collection

production by Scottish Aviation at Prestwick of the Bulldog military trainer, a development of the B.121 Pup trainer/tourer.

In the spring of 1975 Mike Draper embarked upon the the deeply-researched and well-illustrated *Auster Quarterly*, dealing with all aspects of Auster production, history and operation. Publication ceased with the sixth example, dated Winter/Spring 1977.

In 1979 the International Auster Pilot Club (now the International Auster Club), produced a booklet by Auster luminary Ambrose Hitchman entitled *The History of the Auster Aeroplane*. (Revised and updated in 1989 by Roy Houghton on behalf of Ambrose.)

To date this remains the best and most readable history of the companies. Since its formation in November 1973, the IAPC/IAC has continued to publish the excellent *Auster News* which also deals with matters of history as well as the activities of its many members.

This chapter aims to outline the history of the three concerns and to provide a survey of the aircraft that were built at Rearsby, allowing the reader to appreciate the scope of activity and level of aeronautical ingenuity that was to be found within Leicestershire. As well as the Author's own studies using a wide range of original source material, the works mentioned above have proved invaluable in the creation of this chapter. Perhaps the appearance of this book may help to encourage 'The Book' on this great subject of Auster to emerge at long last!

Taylorcraft

Taylorcraft Aeroplanes (England) Ltd was formed in 1938 by A L (Lance) Wykes, Managing Director of Crowther Ltd and a member of the County Flying Club at Rearsby and the Civil Air Guard. Crowthers made textile machinery at the Britannia Works, Thurmaston, Leicester and a building on this site was converted for the production of the US-designed two-seat light aircraft. As well as the production rights to the aircraft in the United Kingdom, Taylorcraft imported a Model B (G-AFKO) from the Taylor Young Airplane Corporation of Alliance, Ohio, USA to familiarise themselves with the product.

Work began on the first British-built aircraft, which was designated the Plus C as it incorporated several improvements and a 'beefed-up' structure over the US versions, was started in February 1939 by a small nucleus of staff who later called themselves the '39 Club'. This aircraft, G-AFNW, was towed to Ratcliffe on 24th April and made its first flight on 3rd May powered by a US-built 55hp Lycoming.

Increasing interest by the Army in the use of light aircraft of observation and artillery gun-laying purposes led to one of the small production batch of Plus Cs being fitted with a 90hp Blackburn Cirrus Minor 1 and this was evaluated in June 1939. The Cirrus Minor variant was built in small numbers for the civil market, as the Plus D.

Impressed by the usefulness and reliability of the Plus Ds it had evaluated the Army decided to use the type as an Air Observation Post (AOP). More development work resulted in an order for 100 of the military version being placed towards the end of 1941 and most of the Plus Cs, now impressed into wartime service, were brought up to Plus D standard under the designation Plus C/2.

When a name was sought for the new aircraft the company suggested 'Icarus'. It was pointed out however that according to Greek mythology this gentleman flew too near the sun on waxen wings which melted resulting in a fatal crash – hardly an appropriate name for an aircraft. As an alternative 'Auster' was put forward, this being a warm and gentle Mediterranean wind. Thought suitable, Auster was adopted and was eventually to become a name synonymous with Rearsby.

The Auster I flew for the first time in May 1942 and by the end of the year the contract for 100 was complete. Progressive development of the basic airframe resulted in more and more orders being received for improved models. Rearsby facilities alone could not have coped with this output, but thanks to their system of dispersed factories feeding sub-assemblies, quotas were met. Peak output at the airfield occurred in the period just prior to the D-Day landings in June 1944 when a target of 28 aircraft per week was reached. There were ten sites undertaking wartime Auster work:

No.1 Crowther Ltd, Britannia Works, Thurmaston. Machine shop.
No.2 Original Taylorcraft works alongside Crowther's, Thurmaston. Tiger Moth re-assembly
No.3 Factory, Victoria Street, Thurmaston. Welding and detail fitting.
No.4 Allen's garage, Mountsorrel Part used for sheet metal work
No.5 En-Tout-Cas works, Syston –
No.6 Aerodrome, Rearsby Flight test and delivery
No.7 Rice's shoe factory, St Peters Street, Syston Main assembly shop
No.8 Ward's, Broad Street, Syston Woodworking
No.9 Factory in Brookside, Syston Experimental shop
No.10 Wadd's garage, Syston Tube store
'No.11' The Horse and Groom, Rearsby!

Site 'No.11' was a well-used 'code' by Taylorcraft workers!

During the course of production several interesting variations and modifications to military Austers were made. One of these was the ski-equipped version. Early in 1945 heavy snow blanketed the continent grounding virtually all wheeled aircraft including the Austers which had become essential for the operation of heavy artillery. Skis were developed at Rearsby, test flown and 12 sets manufactured and flown to France within seven days of the request being received. Other modifications carried out and tested at Rearsby included the fitting of mail and message pick-up gear, provision in an aircraft for a stretcher case in

addition to the pilot and an attendant and the installation of telephone cable laying gear. This latter innovation enabled cables to be laid automatically over treetops for jungle operations. Eventually an Auster could lay four miles of continuous cable without ground aid and telephone communication could be established within five minutes.

By the end of the war in 1945 over 1,500 Austers of Mks.I to VI had been produced and a further 235 had been repaired. They had seen action and given sterling service in all theatres of operation and had, in no small way, helped in the bringing of peace.

Model Plus C
Prototype G-AFNW first flown, at Ratcliffe, 24th April 1939. Powered by a 55hp Lycoming O-145-A2. Total of 23 produced, all for the British market. Sixteen were converted to Plus C/2 status by fitting a 90hp Blackburn Cirrus Minor 1. Plus C2 G-AFTN is preserved by Leicestershire Museums Service – see Chapter Twenty.

Model Plus D Auster I
The 11th Plus C airframe was converted for military AOP trials with a 90hp Blackburn Cirrus Minor 1, June 1939, as T9120. This was effectively the Model D/1 Auster I prototype. G-AFWN appeared in August 1939, also with a Cirrus Minor as the prototype civilian Plus D. This was followed by eight production examples, all British registered.

A major order for 100 Model D/1 Auster Is was met between May and December 1941: LB263 to LB299, LB311 to LB352, LB365 to LB385. Many were civilianised post war, under the designation Taylorcraft Plus D. Several extant, including G-AHGW (LB375) based at Shenington, Warwickshire and the newly restored G-AIXA (LB264) at Spanhoe.

Model E Auster III
As experience of operational use of the Auster I grew, it became apparent that it needed greater power for some of the theatres it was expected to operate in, including North Africa, the Middle East and the Far East. The Model E was a developed Plus D, with a 130hp de Havilland Gipsy Major I and equipped with split flaps. The prototype first flew on 28th September 1942.

The Model E entered large scale production as the Auster III in 1943 with 470 built plus several spare fuselages for major repairs. Production as follows:

64 units, July and August 1943
  MT368 and MT369, MT382 to MT419, MT431 to MT454;
132 units, January to May 1943
  MZ100 to MZ145, MZ157 to MZ198, MZ212 to MZ255;
224 units, June to September 1943
  NJ747 to NJ758, NJ771 to NJ818,

NJ830 to NJ876, NJ889 to NJ935,
NJ947 to NJ995, NK112 to NK132;
50 units, June and July 1943
NX484 to NX509, NX522 to NX545.
Post-war supplies from these batches to the Czechoslovak Air Force; Royal Australian Air Force, Royal Hellenic Air Force and Royal Netherlands Air Force. MT454 converted to Mk.IV. MZ105 and MZ110 laid down as Mk.IIIs, converted to Mk.II prior to first flight, later reverted to Mk.III status. Many conversions to civil status post war.

Few Mk.IIIs survive as such; examples are G-AREI (MT438), currently airworthy and flies from a strip at Petersfield, Hampshire and R-11 (MZ236) stored by the military museum at Soesterberg, Netherlands.

Model F Auster II

Another attempt to give the Auster I greater power, this time with the US-built 125hp Lycoming O-290-3, designated Auster II. Two Mk.IIIs converted prior to first flight, MZ105 and MZ110, later returned to Mk.III status. The first example flew on 30th December 1942. Worries about the supply of Lycomings, because of the U-Boat threat, meant that the US-engined version was not proceeded with.

Model G Auster IV

It was clear by early 1943 that supplies across the Atlantic were becoming more and more stable and that the Lycoming 'flat-four' engine could be used for mass produced Austers. Following on from the experience of the two converted Mk.IIs and taking into account further operational experience, the prototype Auster IV, MT454 first flew on 3rd May 1943. As well as the 130hp Lycoming O-290-3/1 engine, the Mk.IV was principally characterised by the greatly increased area of glazing at the rear of the cockpit, allowing the observer a considerably enhanced view.

A total of 254 Mk.IVs were built, with deliveries being completed between March and May 1944. Batches were as follows:
MS934 to MS981, MT100 to MT145,
MT158 to MT199, MT213 to MT256,
MT269 to MT314 and MT328 to MT355.
Many Mk.IVs were civilianised in the post-war years, some being converted to Auster 5 status. A small number of Auster IVs survive in original guise, including G-ANHS (MT197) which flies from Spanhoe Lodge, Northants.

Model H

During 1943 Taylorcraft built a two-seat training glider, the Model H, using components from the production line. The area occupied by the engine was replaced by a second seat and a streamlined glazed fairing. With a rapidly increased need for gliders to train pilots for the troop carrying

G-AFNW, the first Taylorcraft Plus C leaves the Britannia Works at Thurmaston bound for Ratcliffe and its first flight, 1939.

Production of the first Plus Cs under way at the Britannia Works, early 1939.
Both Leicestershire Museums Service / Sharp collection

A line-up of the 'founding fathers', the so-called '39 Club', the photograph having been signed by A L Wykes, 1941. Left to right: Joe Eames (assistant inspector); Albert Codling, Ken Sharp, Herbert Thompson, Bob Jeffreys,

Ernie Facey (who welded the first fuselages), Bob Burrows, Frank Bates (director), Harold Gooding (sheet metal worker), Jack Humphries (labourer), Mrs Waile (covering), Phil Coleman, Albert Morris, E C 'Jim' Harrison, Reg Hill, Toni Strodl, Lewis 'Guss' Morris, John Grant (latter killed in action), Mr Williams (publicity, formerly with Raleigh), George Potterton, Jack Hunter (first works manager), Harold Chatwind (sprayer), Bill Waile (sprayer), A L Wykes (managing director), Harold Prestwell (cashier), Reg Barrowdale (wing ribs), 'Uncle' Percy Wykes, David Webster. Chris Salter collection

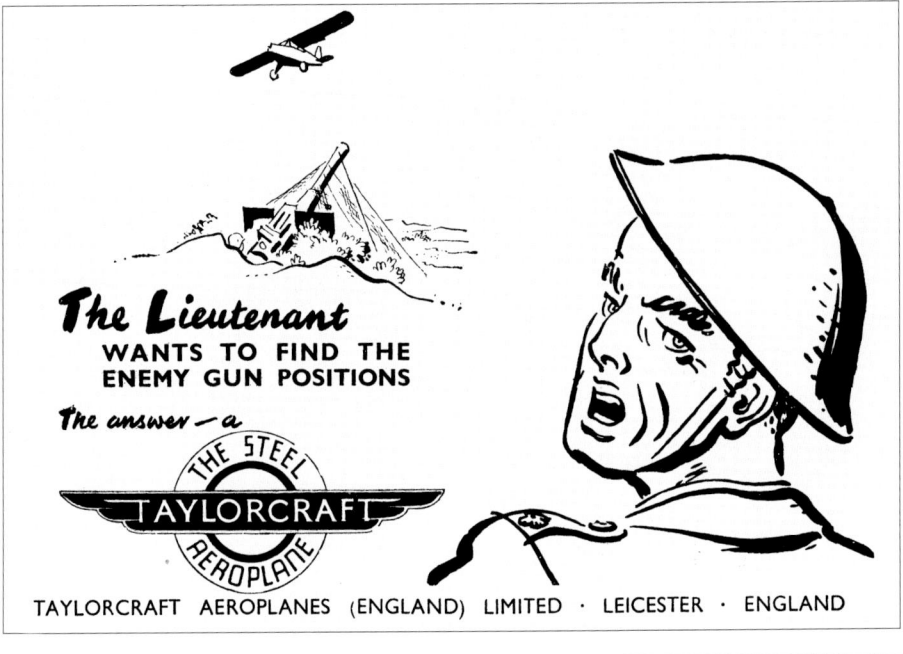

assault gliders, it was felt that the quickly available Model H would find a niche. The conversion followed the lines of the Taylorcraft TG-6, built for similar purposes for the US forces. The anonymous glider made its first flight at Rearsby on 8th July 1943. The design was taken no further, the General Aircraft Hotspur meeting the training needs.

Model J Auster V

Further refining of the Mk.IV gave rise to Auster V, which was produced in the largest numbers. Among the changes introduced with the Mk.V were a blind flying panel and a tailwheel in place of the skid (many previous marks were fitted with a tailwheel following the introduction of the Model J). A moving assembly line for Mk.V fuselages was introduced at Rearsby so that the run of over 800 airframes (including spare fuselages) could be achieved. The first Mk.V appeared in May 1944 and the electric-powered production line came on stream on 14th July 1944.

Production batches were as follows:
12 units, May to June 1944:
    MT356 to MT367;
114 units, June to August 1944
    NJ609 to NJ651, NJ664 to NJ703,
    NJ716 to NJ746;
150 units, August to November 1944
    RT458 to RT499, RT513 to RT540,
    RT553 to RT582, RT595 to RT644;
399 units October 1944 to December 1945
    TJ187 to TJ228, TJ241 to TJ276,
    TJ290 to TJ325, TJ338 to TJ380,
    TJ394 to TJ438, TJ451 to TJ487,
    TJ504 to TJ546, TJ563 to TJ607,
    TJ621 to TJ657, TJ672 to TJ706, TJ708;
112 units August 1945 to February 1946
    TW362 to TW402, TW433 to TW478,
    TW496 to TW520;
2 units April and May 1946, delivered as
    floatplanes, TW522 and TW521.
Large numbers were converted post-war to civilian Auster 5 and other sub-variant status. Large numbers survive in airworthy condition worldwide.

From 1957 to 1959, 14 purely civilian Model Js were built at Rearsby as the Auster Alpha 5. Essentially similar to the original Mk.V, only the smaller area of glazing in the rear of the cabin serves to identify them. Several survive, an example being G-APBE, currently registered to a Norwich resident.

Note that the Model J designation was developed much further with the extensive civilian 'J' series, these are dealt with under the 'Auster' heading, which follows. Likewise, the final wartime AOP development was the Model K, or Auster VI. As the bulk of its production was undertaken after the name change from Taylorcraft to Auster, this is also dealt with below.

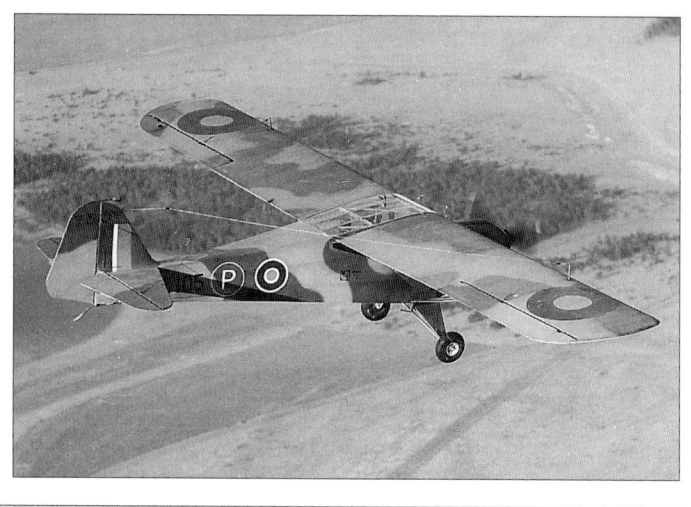

Opposite page, top to bottom:

Taylorcraft advert, August 1944. via Author

Plus C G-AFNW, the first of 23 produced.
Chris Salter collection

Fitted with a Cirrus Minor engine, G-AFWN was the Plus prototype. via Author

Taylorcraft Plus D G-AHGW restored into its Auster I markings as LB375 and currently flies from Shenington, Warwickshire. Ken Ellis

This page:

Top left: *Auster I in the paint bay.* F B Aggas

Top right: *Auster II MZ105 in flight over Salisbury Plain.* Ken Ellis collection

Right: *An Auster IV performing for press cameras at Rearsby.* Ken Ellis collection

Bottom: *Portrait of Mk.IV MT225, 1944. It survived the war and was retired in November 1947.* Ken Ellis collection

Top left: *The one-off Model H training glider based on the Auster airframe.* N H Ellison collection

Top right: *In the late 1950s the Auster V witnessed a brief renaissance as a purely civil type with the construction of a batch of Auster Alpha 5s. G-APBE still flies.* Alan Curry

Below left: *A view of the production line.* via Author

Above: *Auster 5M G-AOSL carrying a neon array for advertising purposes, operated by Overseas Aviation Ltd in the Netherlands, 1957-1959.* Chris Salter collection

Below right: *Careful use of hangar space allowed many more airframes to be squeezed into the Rearsby flight sheds when production of the J/1 Autocrat was at its height. In the foreground is G-AHAR, while stacked up are G-AGXB, G-AGXC, G-AGXG and Danish-registered OY-DGI.* Dr Hugh Thomas collection

Auster

Although constant development of the AOP Austers occupied most of the design staff's time, the successful outcome of the war assured, thoughts were given to peacetime production. They led to the adoption of a design for a three-seater aircraft for private owner and club use. The new type was known initially as the Taylorcraft Auster 5 Series J/1. This name changed on 8th March 1946 when the company, whose aircraft were now far divorced from the original American designs, dropped Taylorcraft from their title, becoming Auster Aircraft Limited. The J/1, which was eventually named Autocrat, flew for the first time in April 1945 at Rearsby and became the first British post-war light aircraft. It sold readily both at home and abroad carrying on in series production at Rearsby until the end of 1947. From the Autocrat stemmed designs which were to be the mainstay of Rearsby's civil production for many years. These variants and sub-variants are outlined below.

By the summer of 1947 the demand for light aircraft had become so low that Auster's workforce was reduced to just over 200 people. At the end of the year only two factories, the main works and offices at Rearsby and the original No.7 works at Syston, were still retained by the company, a far cry from the ten works and some 1,600 employees of just three years before. Post-war, the volume of work at Rearsby fluctuated considerably resulting in several mass lay offs of employees, but the company always managed to retain a nucleus of skilled staff.

Although much reduced after the war military contracts continued to provide employment at Rearsby and undoubtedly helped the company to survive. Continuing development of the AOP series resulted in the Mk.VI, or Model K. This was first flown in prototype form at Rearsby on 1st May 1945. Orders for the type were forthcoming and it was placed in quantity production in 1947 and continued until 1953. By this time 304 aircraft had been built for service with the military air arms which included the Royal Air Force, Arab Legion, South African, Australian, Belgian and Royal Canadian Air Forces.

Always in search of ways to increase sales of their products in civilian markets Austers tried many variations and aircraft were often to be seen at Rearsby with different appendages attached. Over a period of time these included neon light apparatus for aerial advertising at night, loudspeaker equipment, glider towing hooks and the fitting of crop spraying and dusting gear. When used in this latter agricultural role Auster variants proved very successful eventually achieving worldwide use in this

sphere. Efforts were also made by the company at various times to diversify their products in a bid to nullify the effects of fluctuations in aircraft sales. Ventures included the manufacture of a portable saw bench, industrial scales and automobile components. Of these the latter proved most successful.

Following on from the AOP.6, Auster's next contender for this role was a completely new design. This was the AOP.9 which made its maiden flight on 19th March 1954. Its introduction into service in 1955 led, eventually, to the remaining AOP.6s and the trainer version, the T.7, being declared redundant. Subsequently most of these were repurchased by Auster Aircraft for conversion to civilian standards. The feasibility of this project being already realised as many conversions of wartime Austers had previously been carried out by the company. Although completely successful in carrying out its duties, the AOP.9 was to be the last true Auster to see military service, the Army Air Corps (which was formed as an independent force out of the RAF's AOP units in September 1957) indicating that future requirements in the AOP role would be met by helicopters.

The other major airframe of this time was the B8 Agricola, a purpose-built agricultural aircraft aimed at what seemed to be a large and expanding market. The development of such a large and complex aircraft must have taken considerable resources of time and money and the small production run that ensued must have been of considerable disappointment to the company.

Model J Civil Variants

As related above, as it became clear that the war was drawing to a close, Taylorcraft (Austers from 8th March 1946) began to look ahead to the prospect of producing variants of the famed AOP aircraft for civilian use. It was decided to base the new machine upon the Mk.V but to substitute a lower-powered, and British-built, engine. To this end there were effectively two prototypes for what became known, somewhat ponderously, as the Taylorcraft Auster 5 Series J/1 Autocrat.

The chosen powerplant was the Blackburn Cirrus Minor 2 in-line of 100hp. Blackburns undertook the conversion of a Mk.V airframe and this appeared in April 1945 as G-AGOH, a one-off test-bed for engine and airframe. (As related in Chapters Twelve and Twenty, G-AGOH was maintained in airworthy condition by Leicestershire Museums Service and based at Leicester East. It is now on display at the Newark Air Museum, Winthorpe, Nottinghamshire). At the same time as G-AGOH was emerging, Austers took the damaged hulk of Plus D G-AFWN, gave it a slightly modified Mk.V fuselage and

this became the true J/1 prototype.

With the name change to Auster Aircraft, the designation of the type became the much more compact Auster J/1 Autocrat. As will be seen from the table of Auster Model J civil variants (page 322), while the company name change helped to keep overall designations easier to handle, the number of sub-types meant that Auster nomenclature has always been a subject of confusion and debate!

The J/1 Autocrat was a three-seater, with the third seat arranged sideways under modified rear cabin framing and glazing; the windscreen was of one-piece Perspex. The first production J/1, G-AGTO, was delivered to a customer at Tollerton, Nottinghamshire, in December 1945. In 1999 it was still in existence, albeit as a bare frame, at Duxford, Cambridgeshire.

Several other J/1 versions were produced including the J/1A conversion allowing for two seats in the rear and the one-off J/1S with a 145hp de Havilland Gipsy Major installed. Austers offered a conversion of the J/1 with a 120hp DH Gipsy Major 1 installed; this was known as the J/1N Alpha and over 40 were built from new at Rearsby. The J/1N also featured an enlarged fin and rudder. Many J/1s were converted to a variety of configurations and powerplants by owners and operators as the years went by.

Prior to the J/1N Alpha, Austers had been examining a Gipsy Major 1 version aimed specifically at the blossoming agricultural market. The prototype of this was a converted J/1, G-AJUW, appearing in 1950 as the J/1B Aiglet. The bulk of J/1B production was for overseas, although only a small proportion were used for agricultural work.

The final J/1s were very different in appearance from the others that shared the designation. The J/1U Workmaster was developed specifically for Crop Culture (Aerial) Ltd for agricultural spraying operations, mostly in Africa. With wings from the J/5R, provision for two spray atomisers under each wing, 'balloon' tyres, extended fin fillet and a 180hp Lycoming O-360 'flat-four' engine, just ten were built. The broadly similar J/1W, with 'B' Condition (or 'trade-plate') markings G-25-6, of 1959 led to the later D5 series.

As will be seen from the table, over 500 J/1s of several sub-variants were built for civilian customers the world over. Space precludes a detailed analysis of individual aircraft, but the countries involved (by initial registration) were: Algeria, Argentina, Australia, Belgium, Brazil, Ceylon, Denmark, Finland, France, India, Iraq, Ireland, Italy, Kenya, Madagascar, Netherlands, New Zealand, Nigeria, Norway, Pakistan, Portugal, Rhodesia and Nyasaland, Sarawak, South Africa, Sudan, Sweden, Switzerland, Transjordan, Trinidad and Tobago, Uganda and of course the UK. J/1s are still operated by private owners in many countries and many others are to be found in museums or private collections.

To meet the two-seat trainer/tourer market, Auster designer Ken Sharp produced a one-off aircraft in 1945 powered by a Lycoming O-145-B3 of 65hp. This aircraft was registered as G-AGPS and never aspired to a designation, being known as the 'Sharp's Special'. It was wrecked in a gale at Rearsby on 16th March 1947.

G-AGPS paved the way for the production J/2 Arrow, powered by a Continental A75 'flat-four' engine. Wearing the 'B' Condition markings Z-1, the prototype first flew in July 1946. Import restrictions prevented the US-engined J/2 from attracting many UK orders, but the type did find some favour overseas, particularly in Australia. The J/3A Atom economical trainer/tourer with a 65hp Continental 'flat-four' failed to find any orders and only the prototype, G-AHSY was built in 1946. A version of the J/2 with a 90hp Cirrus Minor 1, the J/4 was put into production and was known as the Archer for the Australian market. The prototype J/4 G-AIGZ, appearing in late 1946.

Several J/2s and J/4s are still operational and others were later converted to other powerplants by their owners.

In 1947 a slightly more developed version of the J/1 for the Australian market, the J/5 Autocrat appeared in the form of G-AJER. Available in three-seat or four-seat versions – the latter with a more rounded rear cabin top – the type was marketed in Australia as the Adventurer. The J/5 was powered by a 130hp Gipsy Major 1 and featured a strengthened undercarriage.

The J/5 series took on a more different look with the appearance of the first J/5B Autocar, G-AJYK, in August 1949. This had a built-up rear fuselage making it a more spacious four-seater and was again powered by the popular Gipsy Major 1 with additional fuel tankage.

A one-off short wingspan version of the J/5B, J/5E G-AJYS appeared in 1950, powered by a 155hp Cirrus Major 3. This was not successful, but led to the J/5G Cirrus Autocar aimed essentially at the agricultural and overseas market. The prototype J/5G was G-AMKG, first flown in July 1951. A higher powered version, the J/5P with a 145hp Gipsy Major 10-2 also found limited appeal. The first J/5P was G-ANXZ in 1955.

The name Aiglet was revived again within the J/5 series. The Aiglet Trainer was the first genuinely aerobatic model of the civil versions and boasted a slightly wider fuselage and four seats. Wingspan was reduced

from 36ft to 32ft. The prototype J/5F first flew in mid-1951 with the 'B' Condition marking G-25-1 (later G-AMKF) and over 90 were produced followed by a smaller batch of the more powerful J/5L.

Final J/5 versions to see limited production were the J/5Q and J/5R Alpines, offering a blend of Aiglet Trainer fuselage and tail with Autocar wings. Further development of the J/5 line was intended via the one-off J/5T (G-25-4) and the J/5V (G-APUW), but this line of thought was to emerge in the D4 and D6 series respectively – see under Beagle below.

As will be seen from the table, nearly 400 J/5s of several sub-variants were built for civilian and military customers the world over. Military customers were: the Arab Legion Air Force, two J/5Fs, A408 and A409; the Royal Australian Navy, two J/5Gs A11-300 and -301; the New Zealand Air Force, six J/5s, NZ1701 to NZ1706; the Pakistan Air Force, 17 J/5Fs, W4100 to W4116; and the Southern Rhodesian Air Force, four J/5s SR-53 to SR-56. Space precludes a detailed analysis of individual civilian examples, but the countries involved (by initial registration) were even greater than those of the J/1 series, as follows: Argentina, Australia, Austria, Belgium, Brazil, British Cameroons, British Guiana, Chile, France, French Indo-

Left: *The Australian market was a particularly important one for Auster and several types were developed specifically to appeal there. J/1 Autocrat VH-ASI illustrated.* via Author

Bottom left: *J/1 G-AIBH during trials with a ski undercarriage.* Chris Salter collection

Bottom right: *J/1N G-APAR carrying wing-mounted atomisers for agricultural work.* via Author

Top left: *The one-off 'Sharp's Special' G-AGPS following the gales at Rearsby on 16th March 1947. The 'Special' paved the way for the J/2 Arrow.* Ian O'Neill

Top right: *The J/2 Arrow prototype, wearing 'B' condition markings as Z-1, July 1946.* J Collier

Centre left: *Auster J/4 G-AIZP had only a brief career. Built in early 1947, it crashed at Shardlow in Derbyshire on 19th November 1949.* via Author

Centre right: *J/5B Autocar F-DAAP was delivered to a company operating in Saigon, French Indo-China.* via Author

Above left: *Leicestershire Aero Club has had a long association with Austers. Their last (to date!) was J/5F Aiglet Trainer G-AMTD operated in the early 1990s.* Ken Ellis

Above right: *W4104, one of 17 J/5F Aiglet Trainers operated by the Pakistan Air Force.* Ken Ellis collection

Right: *Swedish-registered J/5G Cirrus Autocar SE-BYT on floats.* Chris Salter collection

Bottom right: *J/5P Autocar G-ARLY, one of 24 built during 1955 to 1961.* Ken Ellis collection

Army Air Corps Auster AOP.6, VF618, taken a Rearsby Open Day. **Author**

A line-up of Royal Canadian Air Force AOP.6s at Rearsby. Note the extra tall undercarriage fitted. **Ken Ellis collection**

China, Gabon, India, Indonesia, Iran, Iraq, Ivory Coast, Japan, Morocco, Netherlands, New Zealand, Pakistan, Portugal, Portuguese West Africa, Rhodesia and Nyasaland, Singapore, Spain, Sudan, Sweden, Switzerland, Trinidad and Tobago, Tunisia, Venezuela, West Germany and of course the UK. J/5s are still operated by private owners in many countries and many others are to be found in museums or private collections.

Model K Auster VI (AOP.6) and T.10

Further development of the Model J Auster V led to the 145hp de Havilland Gipsy Major 7 powered Model K which also featured external flaps. The prototype, TJ707 (originally intended as a production Mk.V) first flew on May 1st 1945. The Mk.6 became the standard post war AOP and attracted a series of export orders, production running through to 1953. In no small way the AOP.6 provided Auster with the means of staying in business during the lean years immediately post-war.

Breakdown of Model J Austers

Series	Name	hp	Engine	Produced	Quantity	Notes
J/1	Autocrat	100hp	Cirrus Minor 2	1946–1952	414	1
J/1A	Autocrat	100hp	Cirrus Minor 2	1949	–	2
J/1B	Aiglet	130hp	Gipsy Major 1	1950–1954	87	
J/1N	Alpha	120hp	Gipsy Major 1	1956–1959	43	
J/1S		145hp	Gipsy Major 10-2/2	1954	1	3
J/1U	Workmaster	180hp	Lycoming O-360-A1A	1958–1961	10	
J/1W		160hp	Lycoming O-320	1959	1	
J/2	Arrow	75hp	Continental A75-12	1946–1952	44	4
J/3A	Atom	65hp	Continental A65-12	1946	1	
J/4		90hp	Cirrus Minor 1	1946–1952	26	5
J/5	Autocrat	130hp	Gipsy Major 1	1947–1952	59	6
J/5B	Autocar	130hp	Gipsy Major 1	1950–1957	82	
J/5E	Autocar	155hp	Cirrus Major 3	1950	1	7
J/5F	Aiglet Trainer	130hp	Gipsy Major 1	1951–1956	92	8
J/5G	Cirrus Autocar	155hp	Cirrus Major 3	1952–1963	94	
J/5H	Cirrus Autocar	145hp	Cirrus Major 2	1953	–	9
J/5K	Aiglet Trainer	155hp	Cirrus Major 3	1953	1	
J/5L	Aiglet Trainer	145hp	Gipsy Major 10-2/1	1954–1960	27	10
J/5P	Autocar	145hp	Gipsy Major 10-2	1955–1961	24	
J/5Q	Alpine	130hp	Gipsy Major 1	1956–1957	4	
J/5R	Alpine	145hp	Gipsy Major 10-2/1	1956–1957	6	
J/5T		108hp	Lycoming O-235	1959	1	
J/5V	Autocar	160hp	Lycoming O-320	1959	1	
J/8F		155hp	Cirrus Major 3	1959	–	11
J/8L		130hp	Gipsy Major 1	1959	–	12

Notes:
1   Conversions to J/1N (many); J/1B (1); J/1S (1).
2   Four-seater conversions of J/1, small number undertaken.
3   One-off conversion with former DHC Chipmunk engine.
4   Four converted to J/4.
5   Marketed as the Archer in Australia.
6   Marketed as the Adventurer in Australia.
7   Short wingspan version for air racing.
8   Conversions to J/5K (1); J/8L (1).
9   One-off conversion of J/5B with a 145hp Cirrus Major 2, undertaken in Australia.
10   One converted to J/5R.
11   (J/6 and J/7 were design studies only.) G-ANVJ, not completed.
12   One conversion, from J/5F.

Batches for the RAF were as follows:
86 units between May and September 1946
    TW523 to TW540, TW561 to TW598,
    TW613 to TW642;
144 units between Sept 1946 and April 1948
    VF482 to VF530, VF543 to VF582,
    VF600 to VF648, VF660 to VF664.
    (Further batches, VF666 to VF700,
    VF713 to VF733, VP628 to VP646 and
    VP653 to VP669 were cancelled.).
40 units between June and August 1948
    VW985 to VW999, VX106 to VX130.
    (Of these VX126 and VX127 served with
    some modifications in the Antarctic.)
4 units, between May and July 1949
    VX922 to VX925.
1 unit, VX942, delivered February 1950.
36 units between Nov 1951 and March 1953
    WJ354 to WJ378, WJ398 to WJ408
A further batch, WJ409 to '412, was cancelled. Ten aircraft were later converted by Auster to interim trainer standard as T.10s.

The following overseas air arms took delivery of AOP.6s: Belgian Air Force, 22 units as A1 to A22 (allocated RAF serials VT976 to VT997 but not in that order); Royal Canadian Air Force 36 units, 16651 to 16682 – these aircraft had extra tall undercarriage and the ability to operate off skis; South African Air Force four units, 5407 to 5411; Trans Jordan Air Force (Arab League) three units, A403, A404 and A405.

With the advent of the Auster AOP.9, Auster AOP.6s, T.7s (see Model Q opposite) and T.10s were sold off, many going to

Auster and to other concerns for conversion to civil status as the Auster 6, or with enlarged tail surfaces and a 145hp Gipsy Major 10-1/1 as the Auster 6A. Similar conversions carried out in Australia and Belgium. Further conversion of the Auster 6 was carried out under the name Terrier by Beagle-Auster and later Beagle, see below. Many Mk.6s and their derivatives are still operational with private owners.

Models M and N, A2/45

The Auster Model L was a design study, a low wing two-seater that got as far as mock-up stage only. The Model M witnessed the first use of yet another designation system for Auster, the so-called 'standardised' system brought in by the Society of British Aircraft Manufacturers (SBAC) to make British aircraft designations more easy to understand. Each SBAC member company was supposed to run design numbers from 'A1' to 'A9', then 'B1' to 'B9' and so on. Additionally, each design should have had a letter prefix, denoting the manufacturer, but Austers for one did not apply this.

Design A1 was the Model M with a 160hp Gipsy Major 1. It was not finished and did not aspire to a registration or serial. The Model N, the largest high-wing design ever to bear the Auster name, was the A2. Chapter Twenty illustrated the captured German Fieseler Fi 156 Storch evaluated by Austers. When Specification A2/45 was issued for a new AOP type, Auster responded with a large high wing aircraft very much in the Storch mould. Two examples were built for a 'play off' evaluation against the very much more radical Heston JC.6, a low-wing type with a 'pusher' engine set between two slender booms that held the tail surfaces – a layout made famous by the de Havilland Vampire jet fighter.

The first A2 was VL522, powered by a 160hp Gipsy Major 31 and this first flew in April 1948. It was followed by VL523, powered by a 250hp Gipsy Queen 32. Both aircraft were evaluated by the Aeroplane and Armament Experimental Establishment at Boscombe Down, Wiltshire, but neither the Model N nor the Heston rival were accepted as the entire requirement was cancelled in March 1950 and AOP was to remain the domain of the Auster AOP.6 for the time being.

Type P Avis

Using the experience of the Model K Auster AOP.6, Auster designed a 'dedicated' four-seater in 1947 and this was named the Avis.

Using an early example of an 'out-of-sequence' registration the Automobile Association operated J/5R Alpine G-APAA on 'roadwatch' duties. Ken Ellis collection

Powered by a 145hp Gipsy Major 10-3, the Avis had the external flaps of the AOP.6 but featured a rounder, more tapering rear fuselage. The most interesting design feature of this aircraft was the four separate entry doors.

Flown in 'B' Condition markings as Z-2, the prototype Avis took to the air for the first time in 1947; it later became G-AJXW. Flight trials were somewhat protracted (for an Auster type!) being completed the following year. By that time, it was clear that the Avis was not attracting interest and it was dismantled.

By 1950, the Army was expressing informal interest in an aircraft capable of carrying a standard issue stretcher, with patient and an orderly in and out of confined spaces. Interest in the Avis was rekindled at Rearsby as the multi-door fuselage lent itself to conversion with a large hatch on the starboard side suitable to take a stretcher and the orderly located in a seat behind the pilot. The Model P was rebuilt, becoming Mk.2 Avis G-AJYF. In this guise it was test flying at Rearsby by August 1950. On the 2nd, the propeller detached in flight and the aircraft was destroyed in the subsequent force-landing at Queniborough. The project was shelved.

Model Q Auster T.7

With the increasing numbers of AOP.6s in use, there was a need for a dual-control trainer variant. The prototype T.7, VF665, was first flown on 20th April 1948. (VF665 was later converted by Marshalls of Cambridge to becoming the MA.4 suction wing research aircraft.)

Batches for the RAF were as follows:
VF665 – prototype.
7 units between Dec 1949 and Feb 1950
    VX926 to VX929, VX934 to VX936;
69 units, between Feb 1950 and Jan 1952
    WE534 to WE572, WE587 to WE616.
(Batch WJ452 to WJ455 cancelled.)

Additionally, three overseas air arms took export examples: Union of Burma Air Force, three aircraft, no identities known; Royal Canadian Air Force, six aircraft, 16687 to 16692; Trans Jordan Air Force (Arab League) two aircraft, A410 and A411.

Left: *Design of the large Model N (the first example, VL522, illustrated) took advantage of Auster's trials of the captured Fieseler Fi 156 Storch.* via Author

Below left: *The prototype Auster T.7, VF665. This aircraft was later drastically modified into the Marshall MA.4 suction wing research test-bed.* Ken Ellis collection

Centre left: *A Christmas card from the Auster design office, almost certainly showing the C4 'Antarctic' version.* via Author

Below right: *The Model S WJ316 helped to prove the utility of the Bombardier engine.* MAP

Bottom left: *One of the two Auster C4s, WE600 survives and is displayed at the RAF Museum, Cosford.* Ken Ellis collection

Bottom right: *The B3 target drone. Auster built not only the drone but its launch ramp.* via Author

Christmas Greetings

Two of these aircraft were converted by Auster to Model C4 status, for the Trans-Antarctica Expedition (WE563 and WE600). These aircraft had special fits to allow them to be readily converted from conventional undercarriage, to skis or floats. WE600 is displayed today in the RAF Museum Cosford, Shropshire.

Some former Canadian T.7s were converted for civilian use and a number of T.7s were converted by Auster upon 'demob' to Terrier 1 and Terrier 2 status and are further outlined under Beagle below.

Model S

Projecting the continued development of the AOP line of aircraft, AOP.6 VX125 was re-engined to test the Blackburn Bombardier 702 in-line engine of 180hp in 1950. The Auster and Bombardier proved to be a promising combination and the Model S was developed to extend the concept further. The prototype, WJ316, first flew in 1951, being struck off charge on 13th September 1955. The Bombardier-engined Auster was to crystallise as a completely new design, the Type B5, see below.

Model B3

While the Model N was the largest of the Auster designs the smallest also achieved one of the highest production runs. The B3 was an unmanned, radio-controlled target drone for the British Army, based upon the US-designed OQ-3. The contract involved the development and manufacture of both the miniature aircraft and its portable launch ramp. Beyond the prototypes, 149 units were delivered and while the little craft seemed 'small beer' in comparison to its full-size companions, the production contract, which ran from 1951 to 1953 was very welcome by the company at the time.

Model B4 'Ambulance'

Further thinking around Army requirements that evolved the Model P Avis, and again using the Bombardier engine, gave rise to another highly individual Auster type. The B4 was specifically built around the needs for casualty evacuation and with an eye on the light freighter market. While looking very different from the Model S, the types were very much aimed as a 'package' with as many spares as possible being common to both types.

A completely new fuselage was designed around the well-tried 'pod-and-boom' concept with a four-seat cabin behind which was a large fairing-cum-door which could swing to the side, allowing unhindered access to the cabin for stretchers, or bulky loads. The tail surfaces were carried above all of this on a boom-like slim fuselage. The single tailwheel was replaced by a pair of castoring units, one either side of the fuse-lage, attached to the large rear door frame. The rear fairing could be totally removed, prior to flight, allowing parachute drops to be made directly from the B4's fuselage.

The prototype first flew as G-AMKL on 7th September 1951. It was evaluated at the Aeroplane & Armament Experimental Establishment at Boscombe Down as XA177. The type failed to attract orders from either the civil market, or the military and the B4 was dismantled and placed into storage at Rearsby in 1956, where it languished until removed to the Beagle-Auster Broom Lane store at East Goscote in 1962.

Model B5 Auster AOP.9

The final AOP type to achieve production status was the entirely new B5, or AOP.9. This took the opportunities offered by the Bombardier engine and experience gained in operating the AOP.6s and in developing types such as the N and the S. The cockpit area offered extensive glazing and ease of access to the two/three-seat interior. The robust undercarriage used a single main leg and the wing bracing was also by a single unit. To enhance the characteristic Auster short-field performance, this AOP model featured differential (or 'drooping') ailerons, which were effective as additional flaps in the landing regime.

The prototype AOP.9 (WZ662) made its first flight at Rearsby on 19th March 1954 and production ran until 1962. Units produced for the RAF/Army Air Corps were as follows:

56 units, July 1954 to December 1955
    WZ662 to WZ679, WZ694 to WZ731;
25 units February 1956 to March 1957
    XK374 to XK382, XK406 to XK421;
15 units September 1959 to April 1960
    XN407 to XN412, XN435 to XN443;
33 units November 1960 to November 1961
    XP232 to XP253, XP277 to XP286;
16 units November 1961 to April 1962
    XR236 to XR246, XR267 to XR271.
1 unit April 1962, XS238.
(XP254 was taken off contract and completed as the E3 or 'AOP.11', see page 326. It was replaced by XS238.) Many AOP.9s survive, operated by private owners or with museums.

Export of the B5 was limited to two countries, the Indian Air Force received 35 units (IN755 to IN764 and IN1659 to IN1683) and the South African Air Force took just two, 5412 and 5413.

Type B8 Agricola

Although several projects adopted low or mid-wing layouts, the large B8 Agricola was the only low wing design to be produced by Auster. It was clear that the agricultural top-dressing and crop spraying market showed great potential for expansion. Contacts established in New Zealand by Auster designer R E Bird, where this 'new' market was particularly vibrant, helped to formulate a specification and a large low wing monoplane of 42ft wingspan, powered by a 240hp Continental O-470-B capable of lifting ¾ ton of fertiliser came about. The hopper area could be readily converted to take two passengers for ferry and transfer work.

The prototype was first flown on 8th December 1955 as G-25-3, just over a year after the design was formulated. A batch of 14 was laid down beyond the prototype, but in the end only another seven were produced up to 1959, all for New Zealand other than one going to British Guiana. (In March 1971 another Agricola flew in New Zealand, having been assembled from the extensive spares holdings produced to support what was initially seen as a large New Zealand fleet.) One Agricola is still airworthy in New Zealand and as this book went to press, moves were being made to bring the survivor back to the UK for preservation.

Construction of a further refined Series 1A Agricola was started but this aircraft was not completed. A wide range of design projects were drawn up around the B8 airframe, for both civilian and military markets. Civilian uses included light freighter (with the fuselage arranged in a similar pod-and-boom layout as adopted by the B4 'Ambulance'; a three-seat floatplane and a four/five seater cabin monoplane. Military applications included an AOP version, casualty evacuation, cable-laying, light ground attack and forward air controller and glider towing. All came to nought.

Model C6 Atlantic

The naming of the C6 was prophetic as Auster was coming under increasing pressure from the rapidly expanding US general aviation market, offering a wider range of types aimed at the expanding club operators and private owners of the late 1950s and early 1960s. The tried and trusted 'tail-dragger' traditional Auster layout was no longer fashionable and tricycle undercarriage layout with wider cabins were the main sales thrust. The C6 was a genuine four seater with tricycle undercarriage and powered by a 185hp Continental E185-10 'flat-four' engine. The prototype, G-APHT (but allocated the 'B' condition marking G-25-5) appeared in 1957 and was exhibited statically at that year's Farnborough airshow. The C6 was not developed and the prototype was dismantled at Rearsby in 1959.

Beagle

Late in 1960 Austers and the Shoreham, Sussex, company of F G Miles Limited were acquired by the Pressed Steel Company of Oxford. They were used to form a subsidiary which came into being on 7th October 1960 and was known as British Executive and General Aviation Limited (Beagle). The Managing Director of the new company was Peter (later Sir Peter) Masefield.

At the Rearsby end of operations, known as Beagle-Auster Limited, the initial products were of true Auster origin. These were rebuilt versions of surplus AOP.6s and T.7s already acquired and known as 6A Tugmaster and A.61 Terrier series. Also versions of the D series evolved, mainly for the use of the Portuguese Air Force.

Another change in company title occurred on 10th May 1962 when consolidation of the Auster and Miles companies brought into being Beagle Aircraft Limited; following this it was envisaged that building of all future company designs would be jointly undertaken at Rearsby and Shoreham.

In the early 1960s, in efforts to diversify and help balance the books, Rearsby also undertook aircraft overhauls and rebuilds, as well as sub-contract work on Jet Provost and TSR.2 components for the BAC Group, but by the end of 1964 the company faced serious cash problems; putting the twin-engined Beagle 206 into production was proving particularly expensive. The parent company, Pressed Steel Fisher as it had now become, approached the government and during February 1965 development costs of the 206 to the tune of £600,000 were met. Shortly afterwards Pressed Steel Fisher was absorbed into the British Motor Corporation and the aviation side was again reviewed. In March 1966 talks began with the government with a view to further financial support for Beagle. Talks escalated and on 12th December 1966 it was announced that the government had acquired the company for £1,000,000, excluding the auto side.

Under state ownership problems still persisted. These came to a head in 1969 when the government refused to grant £6 million needed for development and expansion and Beagle was placed in the hands of a receiver. Under the receivership of K R Cork the company was renamed Beagle Aircraft (1969) Limited and efforts were made to dispose of it as a going concern. When no prospective buyer had come forward by January 1970 there was no alternative but to liquidate the assets of the company.

At Rearsby the production line, which had only been ticking over, ground to a halt and an official closure of the works took place on 13th March 1970. Many of the unfinished Beagle Pups which were then being built, were transported to Shoreham, some for eventual completion and, after lying empty for several months, the factory was eventually disposed of to Rearsby Automotive Limited, a British Leyland company manufacturing car components.

Apart from a few Pups which were completed, only the Bulldog military trainer design went forward. The design rights were acquired by Scottish Aviation Limited and the Bulldog was put into production at Prestwick in Scotland to meet a large order from Sweden. Beyond this the type was ordered in quantity by the Royal Air Force and proved to be a considerable export success. All of this lies beyond the story of Taylorcraft - Auster - Beagle and Rearsby.

Model A.61 Terrier

As related under the Auster Model J series above, former Auster AOP.6s and T.7s were converted (by the Repair & Service Dept) for civil use by Auster under the designation Auster 6A for glider towing and the Auster 6B two/three seat tourer.

Under the aegis of Beagle, the 6A became the Beagle-Auster Tugmaster and the 6B the Beagle-Auster A.61 Terrier 1. The first true Terrier 1 was G-ARLH, which was first flown on 7th April 1961, a conversion of AOP.6 VX109. The conversion was further refined with the A.61 Terrier 2 which had a large tail unit, improved undercarriage and other changes. The first Series 2 example, G-ARLR, first flew on 3rd April 1962.

One Terrier was completed at Heathrow Airport by the Apprentice School of British European Airways with a Lycoming O-320B, first flying on 31st December 1968 as the only Series 3. Two Terrier 2s were completed in 1970, beyond the collapse of Beagle. A number of these conversions are still flying.

In all, Beagle produced 79 Tugmaster and A.61 conversions, the last being completed in 1967. Space precludes a detailed analysis of individual aircraft, but the countries involved (by initial registration) were as follows: Finland, Ireland, New Zealand, Norway, Sweden, Switzerland, West Germany and of course the UK.

Models D4, D5 and D6 and Husky

Respectively the ultimate developments of the J/5T, J/1W and J/5V designs, the Beagle-Auster 'D' series owed its development to the needs of the Portuguese Air Force and their Air Ministry for a liaison and training aircraft to be produced under licence by Oficinas Gerais de Material Aeronautico (OGMA), the aeronautical workshops at Alverca, near Lisbon.

A contract to produce 150 aircraft was signed on 4th November 1959. The 'D' series used a J/1 fuselage, all-metal fabric-covered 'Auster' wing, the tail and undercarriage of the J/1U Workmaster all mated to a Lycoming 'flat-four' engine. The D4 had a 108hp O-235C-1 and the D5 and D6 the 160hp or 180 hp O-320A. The prototype of the series was D5/160 G-25-7 which first flew on 10th January 1960, eventually becoming 3512 with the Portuguese Air Force. The first D.4/108 was G-25-8 (later CS-AME with the Director General of Civil Aeronautics) which first flew on 12th February 1960. The first D.6, was a 160hp model for a Norwegian customer, first flying on 9th May 1960 as LN-BWB.

In all, six D4/108s were supplied to Portugal for aero club or governmental use and G-ARLG was assembled from spares and flown by the Auster Flying Club at Rearsby. Twenty-two D5/160s were supplied to Portugal (eight for aero club or governmental use and 14 for the Air Force as 3501 to 3511 and 3513 to 3515) and three went to the Congolese Air Force (as WL-05, WL-06 and WL-07). The D5/180 was produced in small batches from 1961 through to 5th March 1969 when the final example, OE-DEW for the Asko Flugsport Club of Vienna, first flew – the last 'Auster' to be flown from Rearsby. Fifteen D5/180s were built, all but one being built or refurbished to the lightened up Husky standard, as follows: one to OGMA, eight for British customers, one for Ghana, one for Tanzania, three for the Burmese government, one for Thailand and the very last for Austria. The single Norwegian D6/160 has already been mentioned; it was followed by three D6/180s in 1960, two for UK customers and one for Denmark.

A further development of the 'D' series was the D8/180, three of which were started at Rearsby, but not completed as such. A rethink of the C6 Atlantic, this project was to emerge as the A.109 Airedale - see below.

Model E3 'Auster AOP.11'

A production Model B5 Auster AOP.9 (XP254) was taken off the production line and re-engineered in an attempt to extend the type's usefulness for the Army Air Corps. Dramatically increasing the power by installing a Rolls-Royce-built Continental IO-470D of 260hp with airframe and cockpit improvements, the Beagle E3 first flew at Rearsby in August 1961. The aircraft was evaluated by the Army and several recommendations were made regarding further modifications, although it was very obvious that the future of Army aviation lay with helicopters. The private venture aircraft was unofficially designated 'AOP.11' and there were further plans for what is tentatively referred to as the 'AOP.12' boasting automatic leading edge slats and new tail surfaces. Put on the civilian register as G-ASCC, the E3 undertook a series of demonstrations to other potential customers, but it failed to attract orders. It was put into storage in 1967, but later sold and restored to flying condition in private hands.

Top left: *Distinctive layout of the B4 'Ambulance' G-AMKL. The rear fairing/door was removable to allow loads or people to parachuted.* J M G Gradidge

Top right: *The AOP.9 was a new design, relying on its predecessors only in layout. IN757 from the first batch acquired by the Indian Air Force.* Ken Ellis collection

Centre left: *An early AOP.9 for the Army Air Corps flying at Rearsby.* Ken Ellis collection

Centre right: *The prototype Agricola ZK-BMI.* Chris Salter collection

Lower left: *While the tricycle undercarriage offered by the one-off C6 Atlantic may have been becoming very much in demand by the marketplace, it proved a little difficult to adapt to at Rearsby! This ungainly attitude is thought to have been the result of the nosewheel failing to cope with the old farmtrack that bisected the airfield at Rearsby.* Chris Salter collection

Right: *Auster carried out considerable work to 'stretch' the Agricola design into other applications. Design sketches showing armament options on one of the military versions.* via Author

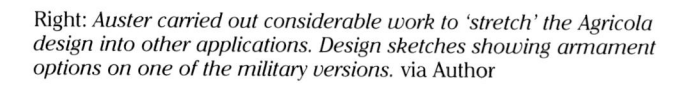

Originating as AOP.6 VF527, G-ARRN was the development prototype of the Terrier Series 1. It first flew on 23rd June 1961 and was used for trials at both Rearsby and Shoreham. It was rebuilt as a Series 2 in 1964. via Author

Right, second down: *The prototype Auster D4/108, wearing G-25-8, first flew on 12th February 1960.* Ken Ellis collection

Left, third down: *D5/160s CS-LED, CS-LEC, CS-LEA and CS-LEB on a formation flight over Leicestershire, October 1961.* via Author

Right, third down: *The last 'traditional' Auster to be built at Rearsby, Husky OE-DEW.* Ken Ellis collection

Bottom left: *Norwegian D6/160 LN-BWB, first flew at Rearsby on 9th May 1960.* Chris Salter collection

The ultimate AOP Auster, the E3 or AOP.11 XP254 at the 1961 Farnborough airshow.
Ken Ellis collection

Airedales (rear) and Terriers (foreground) on the Rearsby production line, circa 1962.
N H Ellison

A.109 Airedale

Following on from the unsuccessful C6 Atlantic and the stillborn D8/180, Beagle finally managed to get a tricycle undercarriage, much-modernised development of the 'classic' Auster layout into production with the appearance of the A.109 Airedale four-seater in 1961. G-ARKE, the first example, powered by a 180hp Lycoming O-360A, first flew at Rearsby during the evening of Sunday 16th April 1961. During the July and August of 1961 Marshall's of Cambridge re-engined this aircraft to become the one-off A.111 by fitting a 185hp Continental GO-300. The A.109 went into production in 1962 but it was soon realised that it required lightening and from the ninth example, all were built to this new specification. Despite vigorous sales campaigns, including promoting the type for general duties and casualty evacuation for the military, the Airedale failed to penetrate a market already largely dominated by mass produced American light aircraft. Production was completed in June 1963 when the 43rd example was finished. Initial customers for the type were to be found in the following countries: Australia 5; Denmark 2; Ireland 1; Italy 2, Netherlands 1; New Zealand 1; Pakistan 1; Portugal 1, Sweden 1; Switzerland 1; West Germany 1 and the UK 26. A small number of Airedales remain airworthy in the UK.

Beagle 206 and Basset

The twin-engined Beagle 206 originated with Bristol Aircraft at Filton as the Type 220. When Peter (now Sir Peter) Masefield set up Beagle, the Type 220 design came with him and was to evolve into the large 206 five/ seven seater executive twin. The design was completed by George Miles at Shoreham and throughout its evolution, it was to remain a Shoreham-based project, although largely produced at Rearsby. Powered by two 260hp Continental IO-470As, the prototype, B.206X G-ARRM, first flew at Shoreham on 11th August 1961. This aircraft was followed by B.206Y G-ARXM (wearing 'B' condition markings as G-35-5) on 12th August 1962 which was far more representative of the intended production standard. (G-ARRM is preserved today by the Bristol Aero Collection at Kemble, Gloucestershire).

The enlarged second aircraft was aimed at an RAF requirement for up to 80 aircraft to replace the venerable Avro Anson as a communications aircraft, particularly with a view to ferrying V-Bomber crews to dispersed locations in the event of a nuclear alert. Principal competitor in this requirement was the DH Devon, the military variant of the Dove which had first flown in 1945 but was still in production in the early 1960s. Two interim aircraft, designated B.206Zs, were ordered for evaluation. The second of these was the first aircraft to be wholly completed at Rearsby.

The military B.206R with large entry door, airstair and other modifications was ordered into production, but the total of 20 was disappointing. In RAF service the type was designated the Beagle 206 Basset CC.1 and it faced considerable problems in its early career, requiring a string of modifications before it became acceptable. The civilian model initially on offer was the B.206C, or the Series 1 and this began to find orders from a series of operators. Development work on the type continued and B.206C was eventually replaced by the more capable B.206S or Series 2 which featured 340hp Continental GTSIO-520Cs, a larger wing and the entrance door and air-stair of the Basset.

During the short production history of the Beagle 206, the company found itself building airframes ahead of orders and some were to remain in store through the life of the company, only being sold on to customers for the first time upon liquidation. East Midlands Airport (Castle Donington, see Chapter Seven) was used as a point of medium to long term storage, as were Nottingham Airport (Tollerton) and Hemswell, Lincolnshire. When the Basset contract was looming, Beagle were negotiating to use Wymeswold (Chapter Twenty-Four) for flight test and modification purposes, but it is believed this did not come about.

There were continued attempts to widen the market for the Beagle 206, which was always being fought for in the face of vibrant competition from a whole series of designs

The prototype A.109 Airedale, G-ARKE.
Ken Ellis collection

A view of the Airedale production line.
via Author

the Series 1 (or Pup 100) two-seater with a 100hp Rolls-Royce Continental O-200A and the 2+2 Series 2 (or Pup 150) with a 150hp Lycoming O-320A-2B. A genuine four-seater was to follow as was a fully aerobatic two-seater with military trainer potential. This was known initially as the Bullpup, but was to eventually appear as the Bulldog.

Fuselage shells, wings and tail units for the Pup were built at Rearsby, the remainder being produced, assembled and flight tested at Shoreham. Additionally, painting and some customer fitting out was carried out at Rearsby, but this situation was somewhat hand-to-mouth with other centres also being involved as production got under way, only for it all to falter with the collapse of Beagle in 1969. During the initial set up of production, eight Pups were assembled and test flown at Rearsby, as follows:

C/n	Model	Regn	First flight
011	1	G-AWDZ	8.8.68
012	1	G-AWEA	27.8.68
014	1	G-AWEC	17.9.68
017	1	G-AWKM	29.9.68
019	1	G-AWKO	15.10.68
026	1	G-AWVC	13.12.68
027	2	G-AWRW	8.1.69
028	2	G-AWRX	21.1.69

Despite its very short production history and early teething troubles, the Pup quickly established itself as a much sought-after 'classic' and it remains that way today with a large number cherished by owners, particularly in the UK. The Beagle Pup Club has a strong membership and now includes an increasing number of owners of demobbed overseas-operated Scottish Aviation Bulldogs with the addition of the wholesale disposal of the RAF's Bulldog fleet beginning in 2000.

produced in the USA. The South African Air Force were interested in the type for maritime patrol, but this potential order was lost to the Italian company Piaggio with their P.166S Albatross. The only other military order accrued was for an air survey version for Syria.

In an attempt to further expand the market a major modification was air tested on 29th May 1968 (as G-35-28, later G-AXPV) featuring an enlarged rear fuselage designed to accommodate up to ten seats. This was the Series 3 for which the name 'Commuter' was tentatively put forward. The first Series 3 was an aerodynamic testbed only, having the airframe shape built-up over the existing fuselage. It reverted to Series 2 status following tests. A single 'true' Series 3 was built, but it did not get through to certification before the collapse of the firm. When Beagle folded, four B.206 air-frames were on the production line, these were not completed.

The B.206 was the most advanced and largest aircraft built at Rearsby and because of this a brief production summary follows. A small number of Beagle 206s and former Bassets are still operated by individuals and companies and the Empire Test Pilots School at Boscombe Down, Wiltshire, still flies Beagle 206Z2 XS743 fitted with special control systems.

Beagle 121 Pup

The B.121 Pup two-seat and four-seater all-metal light aircraft were designed at Shoreham and intended as the starting point of a whole series of light aircraft, including twins. The prototype, G-AVDF, first flew at Shoreham on 8th April 1967 and the shapely Pup very quickly met a good reaction from the marketplace. Two versions were offered,

Beagle 206 Production

C/no	Model	First flt	1st customer, identity
001	X	15.8.61*	Prototype, UK, G-ARRM
002	Y	12.8.62*	Prototype, UK, G-ARXM
003	Z	24.1.64*	Ministry of Aviation, UK, XS742
004	Z	20.2.64§	Ministry of Aviation, UK, XS743
005	C	17.7.64	Demonstrator, UK, G-ASMK
006	R	28.12.64	RAF, UK, XS765
007	C	22.10.64	Demonstrator, UK, G-ASOF
008	R	10.2.65	RAF, UK, XS766
009	C	20.3.65	Rolls-Royce, UK, G-ASWJ
010	R	5.3.65	RAF, UK, XS767
011	R	2.4.65	RAF, UK, XS768
012	R	30.4.65	RAF, UK, XS769
013	C	12.5.65	Demonstrator, UK, G-ATDD
014	R	29.5.65	RAF, UK, XS770
015	C	27.7.65	Demonstrator, UK, G-ATEU
016	R	25.6.65	RAF, UK, XS771
017	R	3.8.65	RAF, UK, XS772
018	R	1.7.65	RAF, UK, XS773
019	C	21.9.65	Maidenhead Organ Studios, UK G-ATHO
020	R	9.9.65	RAF, UK, XS774
021	R	30.9.65	RAF, UK, XS775
022	C	16.11.65	Imperial Tobacco, UK, G-ATKO
023	S	27.1.66	Demonstrator, Australia, G-ATLF
024	R	25.10.65	RAF, UK, XS776
025	R	11.11.65	RAF, UK, XS777
026	C	3.12.65	Demonstrator, UK, G-ATKP
027	S	15.4.66	Aviones Taxis, Spain, EC-BES
028	S	27.4.66	BIASA, Brazil, LV-DMR
029	S	10.6.66	Southern Aviation, South Africa ZS-EMI
030	R	14.1.66	RAF, UK, XS778
031	R	24.2.66	RAF, UK, XS780
032	S	10.5.66	Sayed el Imam de Hadi, Sudan ST-ADA
033	R	20.4.66	RAF, UK, XS781
034	R	2.2.66	RAF, UK, XS779
035	S	29.9.66	Aviones Taxis, Spain, EC-BFR
036	R	23.5.66	RAF, UK, XS782
037	–	–	Not completed, Srs 3 mock-up
038	C	22.9.66	Sold at liquidation, UK, G-ATYW
039	C	27.7.66	Air London, UK, G-ATYC
040	S	12.8.66	Demonstrator, UK, G-ATYD
041	S	19.8.66	Demonstrator, UK, G-ATYE
042	R	22.6.66	RAF, UK, XS783
043	S	23.9.66	Aviones Taxis, Spain, EC-BJF
044	C	11.10.66	Irish Air services, Ireland, EI-APO
045	R	8.8.66	RAF, UK, XS784
046	S	29.9.66	Demonstrator, UK, G-ATZP
047	S	20.10.66	Demonstrator, Australia, G-ATZR
048	S	1.11.66	GKN Ltd, UK, G-AVAL
049	S	15.11.66	Bouley Investments, UK, G-AVAM
050	S	25.11.66	Royal Flying Doctor Service, Australia, VH-FDA
051	S	7.12.66	Hunting Surveys, UK, G-AVCG
052	S	22.12.66	Royal Flying Doctor Service, Australia, VH-FDB
053	S	17.1.67	British Ropes, UK, G-AVCI
054	S	15.2.67	Imperial Tobacco, UK, G-AVCJ
055	S	22.2.67	Butler Aviation, USA, N1008B
056	S	6.3.67	Sold at liquidation, UK, G-AVHR
057	S	16.3.67	Butler Aviation, USA, N966B

C/no	Model	First flt	1st customer, identity
058	S	23.6.67	British Aircraft Corp, UK, G-AVHO
059	S	16.5.67	Sold at liquidation, UK, G-AVLK
060	S	2.6.67	Government of Nigeria, 5N-AGW
061	S	14.6.67	Royal Flying Doctor Service, Australia, VH-FDF
062	S	21.6.67	Sold at liquidation, UK, G-AXZL
063	S	24.7.67	Miami Aviation, USA, N592MA
064	S	3.8.67	Miami Aviation, USA, N552MA
065	S	10.8.67	Miami Aviation, USA, N539MA
066	S	22.8.67	Miami Aviation, USA, N568MA
067	S	16.10.67	Syrian Arab Air Force, YK-AMA
068	S	13.11.67	Miami Aviation, USA, N477EC
069	S	16.10.67	Miami Aviation, USA, N569MA
070	S	23.10.67	Kode Ltd, UK, G-AWRM
071	S	30.10.67	Sold at liquidation, UK, G-AWRN
072	S	15.11.67	Sold at liquidation, UK, G-AWRO
073	S	14.12.67	Miami Aviation, USA, N584MA
074	S	8.5.68	Became Series 3 prototype, UK G-35-28

C/no	Model	First flt	1st customer, identity
075	S	31.1.68	Groupair Ltd, Australia, VH-KCA
076	S	29.2.68	Miami Aviation, USA, N587MA
077	S	13.6.68	Miami Aviation, USA, N662MA
078	S	2.5.69	Miami Aviation, USA, N663MA
079	S	14.5.69	Miami Aviation, USA, N664MA
080	S	21.8.69	Demonstrator - Series 3, UK, G-AWLN

* Built and flown at Shoreham.
§ Built at Shoreham, assembled and first flown at Rearsby, all remainder Rearsby-built. This aircraft and all subsequent had their wings built by Boulton & Paul Ltd at Wolverhampton.

Dramatic view of Pup 150 G-AVLN in its element. via Author

Above: *Basset CC.1s XS777 and XS778.*
Both via Author

Below: *A trio of Beagle 206Ss destined for Argentinean operator Aero Camahue at Rearsby in late summer 1968.*

The deal fell through. Previously stored at Castle Donington, they went on to another period of storage, this time at Hemswell.

Chapter Twenty-Two

Saltby

A fine (and rare) portrait of a Consolidated C-109 flying fuel tanker. 449359 'S2-U' was operated by the 32nd TCS, 314th TCG from Saltby. Behind is a 'CE-' coded Avro Lancaster of 5 Lancaster Finishing School. Rolls-Royce

Established in open countryside on the Leicestershire and Lincolnshire border, Saltby opened as a satellite of 14 Operational Training Unit (OTU), Cottesmore, in August 1941 and began to be used by the unit's Handley Page Hampden twin-engined medium bombers and Avro Anson crew trainers. Apparently the *Luftwaffe* was fully aware that this new grass airfield was in full use and within the first month it was 'visited' by German aircraft on three separate occasions. Each time a lone aircraft carried out the attack and in all 18 high explosive bombs were dropped. Of these, 17 caused only two minor casualties and no real damage. As for the odd one out, this was dealt with by a Bomb Disposal Unit.

These interruptions apart, the station settled into its allotted task. Constant circuit training, by day and night, frequent accidents, occasional ground exercises and the inevitable battle against the vagaries of the British weather all became part of the Saltby scene.

During the satellite's first four months of existence at least 12 aircraft sustained reportable damage during the course of activities. At the lowest end of the scale were those capable of being repaired by the unit while at the other extreme were aircraft completely destroyed. Five of the Hampdens from Saltby fell into this latter category and 14 aircrew paid the ultimate price.

In the opening months of 1942 atrocious winter conditions played havoc at airfields throughout the two counties. While combating heavy snowfalls the situation at Saltby was not helped when a complete failure of the power supply meant that the station had to resort to paraffin lamps during the first four days of February. Conditions cannot have been so bad as those which prevailed at Cottesmore (Chapter Eight). There such a state of unserviceability was reached that in order to continue training 'A' Flight was detached to Saltby where it remained from the 7th to 20th.

Shortage of food during wartime led to many RAF stations adopting their own self-help schemes to increase a camp's supply. One way often chosen was to establish a vegetable garden and the contribution from the one at Saltby in the autumn of 1942 was no mean effort. Included in the crops raised were over 18,000 cabbages of various types and 35 tons of potatoes. Shortage of labour meant that local farmers also appreciated help. In this respect, during the same period, camp personnel devoted almost 3,000 man hours to help bring in the harvest.

With Vickers Wellingtons now in use the accident rate did improve slightly. One tragic incident serves to illustrate that it was not only service personnel who were at risk. On 11th January 1943, while coming in to land Mk.Ic DV449 undershot the runway. In so doing the aircraft collided with a lorry which civilian workmen were unloading. Four of their number were killed; there were no injuries amongst the Wellington crew although the aircraft was a write-off.

In preparation for the eventual invasion of Europe many airfields were used as storage areas for the hundreds of assault gliders which were to take part. Saltby was one which served such a purpose. These gliders began to arrive on the 15th May when three

Airspeed Horsas landed after being towed to the airfield by Armstrong Whitworth aircraft, two Albemarles and a Whitley. Horsas continued to arrive at intervals until by the end of the month 15 were on charge.

That a change of role for the station was on the cards had been intimated for some time. As early as January 1943 a conference had been held to discuss plans for a new technical site. From late June elements of 5352 Airfield Construction Wing began to move to Saltby and they, together with the civilian contractor, G Wimpey & Co., were to be responsible for a virtual reconstruction of the airfield and its environment.

In August 14 OTU vacated both Cottesmore and Saltby, bound for airfields at Market Harborough and Husbands Bosworth (Chapters Fifteen and Eleven, respectively). Saltby was then relegated to care and maintenance status and work began in earnest to create a Class A type airfield capable of operating heavy bomber units. It then transferred from 92 Group to 5 Group, Bomber Command, on 1st September 1943. The Horsa gliders, which eventually numbered 32, remained *in situ* and passed into the care of 32 Heavy Glider Maintenance Section, part of 2 Heavy Glider Maintenance Unit, Snailwell, Cambridgeshire.

For the rest of 1943 and into 1944 Saltby remained in a state of flux. During this time three concrete runways, connecting perimeter track and allied hard standings were laid down while many extra buildings for accommodation and other purposes were erected or built. But, bomber squadrons were not, eventually, to occupy Saltby. In

August, US engineers had already made a preliminary visit with a view to the United States Army Air Force (USAAF) taking over the station. This duly came about, when on 18th December 1943 control passed form 5 Group to the US 9th Air Force Troop Carrier Command (TCC) and Saltby then became USAAF Station 538.

The unit chosen to occupy the airfield was the 314th Troop Carrier Group (TCG), part of the 52nd Troop Carrier Wing. Headquarters for the Wing, which had previously been part of the US 12th Air Force and had seen action in the Mediterranean theatre, were situated in Grantham, Lincolnshire, from where it controlled bases throughout the East Midlands. Four Troop Carrier Squadrons (TCS) made up the Group and these, the 32nd, 50th, 61st and 62nd TCSs arrived between 20th February and 6th March 1944.

Equipped with 80 Douglas C-47 Skytrain and C-53 Skytrooper twin-engined transports (both of these were Dakotas to the British), the wing was given little time to settle in before work began in earnest. Practice and more practice was the name of the game in an effort to perfect techniques already familiar from their North African sojourn, including formation flying by both day and night. Glider towing involved Waco CG-4As and Horsas – those at Saltby had already been assigned to the USAAF on 17th February. Exercises often involved men of the 82nd Airborne Division, who were deployed in the Leicester area.

One practice that did not go exactly according to plan for the 314th was Exercise

Stirlings of 196 Squadron, Shepherds Grove, Suffolk, wait at Saltby to carry men of the 1st British Airborne Division to Copenhagen, in May 1945. via D J Smith

'Eagle', a large scale rehearsal for the coming invasion. It was staged on the night of 11th May and when the aircraft of the 314th reached their designated drop zone in southern England the marker beacons and lights were not operating. Most went round for a second try and this time the aids were on. Most of the aircraft dropped their parachutists successfully but nine had given up and gone back to Saltby while another nine made their drops by guesswork and were far off target.

On the eve of D-Day, the night of 5th/6th June, the time came for the 314th to go into action once more. Sixty aircraft took off carrying part of the airborne army bound for occupied France. On board the 51 C-47s and 9 C-53s were men of the 508th Parachute Infantry Regiment and a detachment of the 82nd Division headquarters. Their destination was an area of land, bounded by the Merderet and Douave rivers, designated drop zone 'N'. In their number were the divisional paratroop commander, General James M Gavin and the regimental commander Colonel Roy Lindquist.

The two serials (formations) of 36 and 24 aircraft were in good order until they reached the French coast. Shortly after crossing they ran into a cloud bank which caused them to become disorganised; also, on nearing the drop zone (DZ), flak and heavy machine gun fire was encountered.

As a result the drop was fragmented, with many paratroops and much equipment widely scattered.

The 314th returned to Saltby either singly or in small groups. Eighteen aircraft had suffered damage from enemy fire, one had been shot down in flames while making a third pass to drop its cargo, but the crew survived and reached Allied lines that night. In another aircraft the pilot was killed but the co-pilot completed the mission.

Next day 52 aircraft took off from Saltby as part of Operation 'Freeport', a parachute resupply mission in support of the 82nd Airborne Division. The operation began well before dawn under a sky blanketed in heavy cloud, the base of which was down to 1,500ft at times. Assured during briefing that they would not need to fly on instruments the crews set out into the murk. Instead of improving, conditions gradually grew worse as they reached the command assembly point in southern England and although they attempted to continue individually on instruments many became lost. Thirteen 314th aircraft aborted the mission; one of these was induced to return after coming under fire from Allied shipping.

Although the others were able to continue the mission was not a great success as the Germans controlled the drop zone and many supplies fell into their hands. At the end of the day the 314th had suffered badly, three aircraft were missing, 30 had suffered battle damage, 14 crew members were missing and four others were wounded.

After the D-Day operations the 314th carried out many flights in support of the invading armies. Practice exercises were also flown and the TCG was also scheduled to take part in several airborne operations, but in each case these were stillborn due to the rapid advances made by the Allies.

On 14th September troop carrier units were again placed on alert and their bases restricted. Airborne troops began moving into tented accommodation and the stage was set for Operation 'Market', the airlift element of the Arnhem operation. The 314th provided 72 aircraft in the first lift on 17th September delivering 1,172 men of the 2nd and 3rd Battalions of the 1st Parachute Brigade to DZ 'X' on Renkum Heath.

Take-off began at around 11:20 hours and by 11:30 hours all aircraft were airborne. Assembly with the 61st TCG from Barkston Heath went smoothly and in fine weather

the four serials made good progress over the northern route. Only light and mainly ineffectual flak was encountered and Rebecca-Eureka beacons were effective in guiding the formations to the DZ. There, ground signals were clearly visible and between 13:53 and 14:08 hours a near perfect drop took place. All 72 aircraft returned to Saltby unscathed. This was not to be the case next day.

For the second lift, on the 18th, the 314th again supplied 72 aircraft this time to transport elements of the 4th Parachute Brigade, destination DZ 'Y' on Ginkel Heath. All went well until the formations were about 25 miles from the DZ when they began to come under enemy fire. Small arms and light flak began to take their toll and when about five miles short of their DZ concentrated fire from Wageringen claimed several victims. In spite of this 90% of the survivors made very accurate drops. Although the mission was considered a success, four aircraft from Saltby failed to return, six received damage and two crew were wounded.

A third lift scheduled to take the 1st Polish Parachute Brigade into action on the 19th ran into difficulties when the weather

decided to take a hand. For two days impenetrable overcast over the 52nd's bases prevented any attempt being made even though aircraft were loaded and marshalled on the runways with engines warmed up ready to go. On the 21st conditions were far from good, but the situation in Holland was so desperate that the mission was authorised to go ahead.

It consisted of four serials, the first two of 27 aircraft each were flown by the 315th TCG, Spanhoe, Northamptonshire, while the third and fourth of 27 and 33 aircraft respectively were drawn from the 314th. The first serial's attempt to get under way was unsuccessful when thick cloud forced it to disperse; in so doing 25 pilots lost contact and returned to base. After adopting different tactics the second serial from Spanhoe and those of the 314th had a greater measure of success and only six aircraft became separated during the process of forming up.

Those remaining set course for Holland but while crossing the Channel a flight leader of the 314th received garbled messages which he decided must be recall signals and, acting on this assumption, returned to Saltby with his ten aircraft. The

A Douglas Skytrain of the 62nd TCS, coded 'E5-S', airborne from Saltby. via Buckminster Gliding Club

An engine or prop change on a Skytrain of the 32nd TCS. Note the unit code 'S2-', the name 'Marguerite' and the mission markings on the upper fuselage. via Buckminster Gliding Club

Above left: One of a small number of Curtiss C-46 Commando transport aircraft issued to the USAAF 62nd Troop Carrier Squadron at Saltby, late 1944. via Buckminster Gliding Club

Above right: Although taken at Prestwick this is a rare view of a 'Q9-' coded Douglas Skytrain of the USAAF 61st Troop Carrier Squadron, such as was based at Saltby. A Pearcy collection

Below: Survey photograph of Saltby, dated 17th January 1947. Two runways (A) and (B) are already marked with an 'X' to show they are unusable. The control tower, signals square and airfield denominator 'SY' (C) are to the south of the almost square wooded area, called Herring Gorse. The south-west/north-east runway cut through a field road (D) running from Harston to Sewstern. The Buckminster Gliding Club buildings are located on the site of the 'B1' hangar (E). DoE

others continued to fly on at almost 10,000ft but after crossing the Belgian coast thinning cloud enabled them to descend to 1,500ft.

En route some ground fire was encountered and this increased in intensity as they approached DZ 'K' south of Arnhem. The Poles jumped successfully, but were unable to play a decisive part in the battle. Afterwards their commander, Major General Stanislaw Sosabowski, who had departed from Saltby, praised the troop carrier crews for their skill in the face of enemy anti-aircraft fire.

Few aircraft engaged in this mission made it back to their bases that day, damage and thickening fog being the principal reasons. When a final tally was taken the 314th had not come off as badly as had first been thought. Of the 60 of their aircraft taking part 14 had aborted but none had been lost, although there were nine damaged and two men wounded.

The Group was to have one last mission in support of Operation 'Market-Garden'. This took place on the 26th when 29 aircraft of the 314th landed on a grass airstrip at Oud Keent near Grave to deliver troops and much-needed supplies.

As before, the Group then resumed its practice sessions, it also continued to fly many sorties delivering freight and personnel to the Continent, sometimes evacuating casualties on return. Between 25th and 29th December, during the German offensive through the Ardennes, it also flew several missions carrying reinforcements to France.

It also began to receive a few examples of two new types of aircraft. One was the Curtiss C-46 Commando, a twin-engined transport with a greater carrying capacity than the C-47 or C-53. The other was a flying fuel tanker, the Consolidated C-109, converted B-24 Liberator bombers. It was intended that these would make rapid deliveries of fuel to Europe. Their success was somewhat limited due to the runways of many Continental airfields being unable to stand up to the weight of a C-109 landing with a full load.

Early in 1945 the progress of the Allied advance through France meant that airfields were liberated which were suitable for the operation of TCGs. One of these, B.44 at Poix, was allocated to the 314th and the Group began leaving Saltby late in February. By the beginning of March movement was complete and the 314th prepared for the final large scale airborne assault of the war operation 'Varsity', the crossing of the River Rhine.

The station soon reverted to RAF control. This began on 12th March when a group of officers arrived in connection with the impending transfer of 1665 Heavy Conversion Unit (HCU) from Tilstock, in Shropshire. An advance party followed by rail on the 23rd and two days later the aircraft flew in. By the 30th, the conversion training of aircrew had begun using Short Stirlings and Handley Page Halifaxes. It seems strange that while Saltby housed heavy bombers, control of the station was vested in Fighter Command.

In addition to the HCU, other units began to make use of the airfield. This started on 5th May with the arrival of 38 Stirlings from Shepherds Grove, Suffolk. Two days later 33 of these aircraft left for Copenhagen carrying men of the 1st British Airborne Division leaving the five spares to return to their home base.

Later in the month, on the 14th/15th, the 349th TCG flew in with 48 C-46s to begin operations from Saltby. Over the next 15 days in 224 lifts they carried 1,163 troops of the 1st Airborne Division and delivered almost 660 tons of freight to Oslo, Stavanger and Copenhagen.

The stay of this unit was marred by one serious accident. At 23:50 hours on the 29th Stirling PW386 'T' swung off the runway on take-off. It collided with dispersed C-46s and burst into flames. The Stirling and two C-46s (44-7854 and -77857) were destroyed and another damaged. An American serviceman sleeping on one C-46 was trapped and lost his life; the Stirling crew, with the exception of the pilot who sustained serious burns and lacerations, were unhurt.

Next day, its duties at Saltby over, the 349th left for A.73, the airfield at Roye-Amie, France. Despite all the extra traffic during May the HCU still managed to complete 907 hours flying by day and 467 at night.

From 1st June control of the station changed hands and it became part of 38 Group, Transport Command. Very early in the month concern was voiced with regard to the runways which appeared to be

unable to cope with the continuous 'circuits and bumps' of the HCU and the constant comings and goings of other traffic. The ends of two runways were found to be disintegrating and in order to limit further damage the HCU began to use Barkston Heath, Lincolnshire, on a daily basis. It is highly probable that the state of the runways had an effect on matters that were to transpire some weeks later.

A rapid sequence of events began on 1st August following the receipt of a signal from 38 Group headquarters, it instructed that 1665 HCU was to move to Marston Moor, Yorkshire. The advance party made their departure on the 3rd, closely followed by most of the remainder of the unit two days later. It was then left to the rear echelon to tidy up and Saltby was then reduced to care and maintenance. Responsibility was at first assumed by Melton Mowbray, but when this station also closed Wymeswold took over from 21st October.

Although its military flying activities were at an end the station still had a useful function to perform. From 28th November Saltby was transferred to 40 Group, Maintenance Command. It was then used over a period of several years, for varying lengths of time, by 216, 255 and 256 Maintenance Units for storage. The station was finally derequisitioned in September 1955.

Agriculture again began to take over but the airfield was on occasion used for activities connected with autosport. The Owen Organisation made use of it briefly during the testing of their BRM racing car and in the past autocross meetings have also taken place making use of some of the more overgrown areas such as that which surrounded the prominent wooded area called Herring Gorse.

Saltby again came under public scrutiny in the 1980s after proposals were made by the Coal Board to establish a new coalfield in the Vale of Belvoir. One mine was to be sited within a mile of the old airfield which, in turn, was to become a dump for colliery waste. In preparation for this those derelict

The gliding site occupies what was the base of the 'B1' hangar. Author

Autocross racing in progress on the airfield. In the background is Saltby's Type 12779/41 and 15371/41 control tower, the second built on the airfield and now demolished.

Ruined remains of Saltby's AML Bombing Teacher with an emergency water supply reservoir in the foreground.

Aerial view of Saltby, looking south west. The site of the original control is at (A) while the second was at (B). The gliding club area is located within the wooded area on the extreme right (C). All Author

buildings which still remained, including the control tower were flattened. Despite fears in the local community and although some mining has taken place in the Vale the plans for Saltby were not put into operation.

After an absence of 25 years, a transport aircraft of the USAF once again landed at Saltby but only for a fleeting visit. In 1970 the 62nd Tactical Airlift Squadron (TAS), based at Mildenhall, Suffolk, obtained permission to pay a goodwill visit to the former wartime home of its predecessor, the 62nd TCS. News of the impending arrival was made known and villagers from the locality turned out in force on the morning of 31st August to greet the Americans who arrived in style in one of their Lockheed C-130E Hercules (68-10948 'SR'). Dubbed Operation 'Sentimental Journey', the main object of the visit was to enable the unit to express its thanks for the way their wartime counterparts had been treated by the locals.

Aboard the C-130, in addition to other squadron personnel were the commanding officer of the 62nd TAS, Lieutenant Colonel Carl E Stone and the guest of honour Colonel Richard Gibney, the only man in the party who had served at Saltby during the war. Then commanding the 64th Tactical Airlift Wing, Colonel Gibney had flown in from the USA in order to be present. Also amongst the crowd was William Bennett, former publican of the Crown Inn, Sproxton, a popular watering place with USAAF and RAF alike during the war. He and his wife were asked to receive a commemorative plaque on behalf of the villages of Saltby and Sproxton. Part of the inscription on this token admirably conveys the sentiments of the Americans for it reads: *'In deep appreciation to the people of Leicestershire for their hospitality and friendship to the Squadron. May the bonds of friendship founded in wartime continue in peace'.*

It was hoped that the plaque would be placed in Saltby church, but this was not to be and it is now in the safe keeping of a resident of Sproxton.

Although agriculture and forestry occupy most of the site, Saltby today is one of the few airfields in Leicestershire where organised flying still takes place, if only on a small scale. Thanks to the fact that good sections of runway have been allowed to remain it has, since about 1971 been the home of Buckminster Gliding Club. A clubhouse and a much smaller hangar now occupy the site of the wartime 'B1' hangar. In addition to club activities, over the years, the airfield has also been the venue for several regional gliding championships.

For many years, BGC members have been able to enjoy their flying virtually undisturbed in this peaceful, fairly remote corner of the county. Long may they continue to do so.

Saltby – 1st December 1944

Latitude	52° 49' 45" N
Longitude	00° 42' 30" W
Height at Sea Level	475ft
Locality	8 miles NE of Melton Mowbray
Command	USAAF Troop Carrier Group
Nearest Railway Station	Great Ponton, LNER, 5 miles
Function	Operational Station
Affiliated Airfields	Bottesford (Base)

Landing Area – Runways

QDM	Dimensions	Extensibility	Remarks
196°	1,400 x 50 yds	2,000 yds	–
255°	2,000 x 50 yds	2,000 yds	–
314°	1,400 x 50 yds	2,100 yds	–
Type of Surface	Tarmac.		

Permanent Landmarks

By Day	Kimpton Reservoir.
	Saltby, 300°, 3 miles.
By Night	Nil

Permanent Obstructions House on NE side of airfield

Facilities

Airfield Lighting	Mk.II
Beam Approach	–
Radio	–
QDM	–
Flying Control	Yes

Accommodation

All buildings temporary.

Technical	Hangars		Hardstandings	
	Type	No	Type	No
	T2	4	Hvy Bmbr	50
	B1	1		

Domestic	Officers	SNCOs	ORs	Total
RAF	61	325	608	994
WAAF	2	8	102	112

Saltby-based Units and Aircraft

No.14 Operational Training Unit
From 1.8.41 to 10.9.43   Codes 'AM-', 'GL-', 'VB-'
See parent station – Cottesmore.

No.2 Heavy Glider Maintenance Unit
From .8.43 to .10.43

No.32 Glider Maintenance Section
From .10.43 to 15.3.44
Airspeed Horsa I   DP503, DP568, DP835, DP838,
HG741, HG769, HG800, HG834, HG839, HG852, HG942,
HS123, HS138, LF894, LF937, LF955, LG692, LG726, LG762,
LG777, LG840, LG885, LG938, LG973, LG974, LH139, LJ110,
LJ123, LJ173, LJ189, LJ190, LJ193, LJ215.
These gliders initially assigned to the care of 14 OTU,
reassignment to 2 Heavy Glider Maintenance Unit followed i
n August 1943. Then in October they became the responsibility
of 32 Heavy Glider Maintenance Section before eventually
being transferred to the USAAF in February 1944.

No.314th Troop Carrier Group, USAAF
From 20.2.44 to .3.45
    32nd TCS, code 'S2-'
    50th TCS, code '2R-'
    61st TCS, code 'Q9-'
    62nd TCS, code 'E5-'
Douglas C-47 Skytrain   42-23368, 42-23910, 42-32873,
42-92903, 42-100892, 42-100976, 43-15146, 43-30715.
Douglas C-53 Skytrooper   –
Curtiss C-46 Commando   –
Consolidated C-109   44-49359.

No.1665 Heavy Conversion Unit
From 26.3.45 to 1.8.45   Codes 'FO-', 'NY-', 'OG-'
Short Stirling I   BF341, BF349, BF436.
Short Stirling III   BF520, BK652, EE874, EF178,
EF433, EF511, EH899, EH954, EH981, LJ461, LJ622, LJ828,
LK544, PK232, PW386.
Handley Page Halifax III   LW161, LW554, MZ582, MZ950,
NA124, NA312, NA527, NA559, NA565, NA703.
Supermarine Spitfire V   BL957.

No.349th Troop Carrier Group, USAAF
From 14.5.45 to 30.5.45   Codes '9E-', 'Q8-', '3F-'
Curtiss C-46 Commando   44-77854, 44-77857.

Buckminster Flying Club
Various types of aircraft employed as tugs, including
Auster J/5F Aiglet Trainer G-AMRF and Beagle Terrier 2 G-ATMS.

Serious Accidents to Saltby-based Aircraft

For No.14 Operational Training Unit accidents
see parent station – Cottesmore.

6.12.44   C-47 42-100892   314th TCG
Crashed into 300ft high slag heap on approach to forward
airfield A.93 at Liege, Belgium.

25.12.44   C-47   42-32872   314th TCG
Crashed at Chilbolton, Hants. Believed due to frost on wings.

3.3.45   C-47   4.-.....   314th TCG
Crashed at Saltby following loss of power on take-off and
instrument panel fire.

24.4.45   Stirling IV   LJ461   1665 HCU
Take-off abandoned after swing. Undercarriage collapsed.

10.5.45   Stirling IV   LK544   1665 HCU
Swung on take-off, undercarriage collapsed.

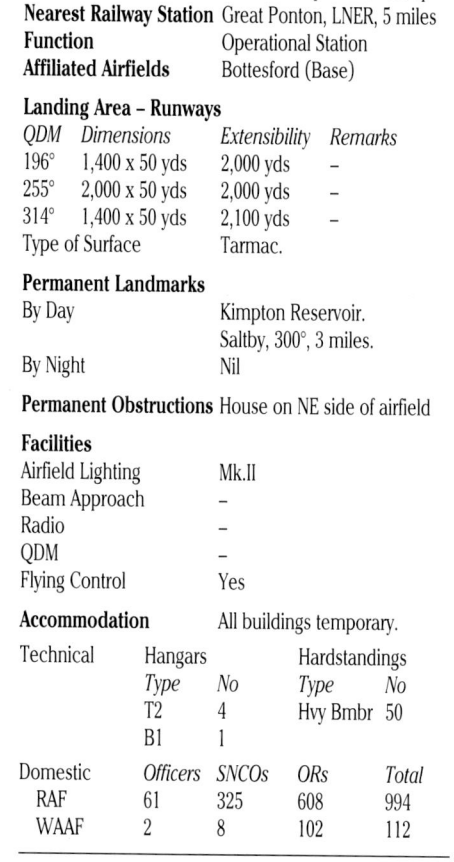

*Mr and Mrs William Bennett greet members of
the 62nd TAS on the unit's 'return' to Saltby,
1970. via W Bennett*

*Once thought to be of USAAF origin, but later
identified as depicting the Ukrainian national
emblem, this memorial is believed to have
been built by displaced persons from that
country while they occupied the former
communal site after the war. T Hickman*

29.5.45   Stirling IV   PW386   1665 HCU
Swung on take-off, undercarriage collapsed and aircraft
swerved into line of parked C-46s of 349 TCG. Two of these
were destroyed and an American serviceman, believed asleep
on one, was killed. Pilot of Stirling received serious injuries.

29.5.45   C-46 Commando   349th TCG, USAAF
44-77854 and 44-77857 destroyed – see previous entry.

27.6.45   Halifax III   NA559   1665 HCU
Major damage caused in landing accident. Tailwheel caught in
hole after landing and sheared off. Crew safe.

9.7.45   Halifax III   NA703   1665 HCU
Overshot on landing. Damaged beyond repair.

18.8.73   Terrier G-ATMS   Buckminster GC
While taking off towing a glider aircraft fouled launch cable on
runway. Wire became caught round port undercarriage causing
aircraft to nose-dive into ground from about 70ft. Aircraft
destroyed by impact and fire, two occupants killed.

Although taken at Valley in May 1946 and
therefore some time after the unit had
vacated Saltby, this view of Halifax A.VIII
PN294 'OG-B' is representative of the
equipment of 1665 HCU.
F M Taylor via A Thomas

Saltby's first control tower/watch office was a
pattern 15975/40 and 13079/41 (right).
It was kept to serve other functions when it
was replaced by one built to patterns 12779/41
and 15371/41 (below). Both were eventually
levelled after falling into dereliction.
Both Author

Chapter Twenty-Three

Woolfox Lodge

THE SECOND of Rutland's three RAF airfields to become active, Woolfox Lodge was allocated as a satellite of 14 Operational Training Unit (OTU), Cottesmore, in December 1940. (See Chapter Eight).

Although the facilities were rather basic, flying began with the introduction of night flying training on the night of the 13th. From this time the OTU's Handley Page Hampdens and Avro Ansons made frequent use of the airfield.

Contemporary records from this time lack a great deal of substance but as with most official accounts they do manage to catalogue major happenings such as the

customary crop of accidents and enemy air attacks. In the first category the very nature of night flying from a darkened airfield was not without its problems as the following episode serves to illustrate.

On the night of 22nd/23rd March 1941 a visiting Bristol Blenheim IV, Z5899 of 105 Squadron, Swanton Morley, Norfolk, experienced brake failure on landing. In order to avoid obstructions the pilot swung the aircraft off the runway, causing the undercarriage to collapse. A short time later one of 14 OTU's Hampdens, P1249, also landed. The pilot failed to observe the disabled Blenheim and crashed into it. Although both air-

Woolfox Lodge ground crew hard at work to repair the peppering of the rear fuselage inflicted by German flak to this 61 Squadron Manchester I, following the 'Channel Dash' operation on 12th February 1942. via Chaz Bowyer

craft received substantial damage both survived to fly again. This was by no means an isolated occurrence being just one of the many hazards which could be experienced by wartime aircrew under training.

As for the visits made to Woolfox by the *Luftwaffe* between 17th April and 31st July

Manchester I 'QR-D' of 61 Squadron on one of Woolfox's dispersals, 1941.

A lonely 'erk' trudges from the South Camp to the airfield, Woolfox, winter 1941-42. Both L Boot

the majority of these could almost be classified as nuisance raids in view of the minimal amount of damage most of them caused, although they did no doubt result in many hours of extra duty and lost sleep. Extracts from the Operations Record Book:

'*17th April* – 22:54 hours. During this raid the flarepath came under machine gun fire and seven high explosive bombs fell. One of these hit the runway but no serious damage was reported.

'*24th April* – 23:50 hours. Enemy aircraft again made a machine gun attack but no damage caused.

'*3rd May* – 00:25 hours. A raider circled the airfield before making an attack and subjecting an Anson, which was on the flarepath, to machine gun fire. The enemy aircraft then resumed its circling before making a diving attack from west to east across the airfield. In the process nine high explosive bombs were dropped. Two Lewis gun posts engaged the raider but no hits observed. Bomb splinters caused major damage to a Hampden and to a much lesser degree to two Ansons.

'*18th May* – 02:00 hours. While in the process of landing an Anson was machine gunned by an enemy aircraft. Return fire was made by the turret gunner in the Anson and by an airfield defence post. No damage was reported.

'*19th June*. 10 small high explosive bombs dropped on the airfield causing unspecified damage to two Ansons and a Hampden.

'*13th July*. Single enemy aircraft dropped 30 incendiary bombs most of which landed

near the centre of the airfield. Neither damage nor casualties were caused.'

None of these attacks affected the ability of Woolfox to continue to operate.

At the end of July a new airfield at Saltby (Chapter Twenty-Two) became available for 14 OTU's use whereupon the unit vacated Woolfox which then became a satellite of North Luffenham from 1st August.

In the main, during the first two months under new management, the airfield continued to be used on a training basis. It was however utilised for operational purposes by North Luffenham (Chapter Seventeen) units.

For instance, on the night of 8th/9th August, 16 Hampdens of 61 Squadron took off from Woolfox to take part in a raid on Kiel shipyards. It was not a good night for the unit, on return two aircraft were missing and a third had crashed at Fosdyke, Lincolnshire, after being hit by anti-aircraft fire from an Allied convoy off Spurn Head.

No.61 Squadron had been resident at North Luffenham since mid-July and for some of this time had endeavoured to re-equip with Avro Manchesters. These aircraft had proved extremely troublesome and the squadron continued to carry out operations with Hampdens as its main aircraft. For some time it had no Manchesters on strength at all. During October a further attempt to re-equip was made when more allocations of Manchesters began on the 4th. The squadron then took over Woolfox as its base although the station remained officially a satellite of North Luffenham.

October and November were a working up period for the unit and on 12th December it resumed operations when four Manchesters took part in an attack on the dock area of Boulogne. It was not an auspicious return to the offensive for the occasion was marred by the loss of an aircraft when L7494 failed to return. Piloting the Manchester was the commander of 'A' Flight, Squadron Leader J L Riley who, together with his crew, perished after the aircraft exploded in mid-air and crashed into the sea off Boulogne.

Thereafter there were no further operational sorties until 9th January 1942 when six aircraft were detailed for a bombing raid to Cherbourg. This time North Luffenham had to be used for take-off as a crashed aircraft had made Woolfox unserviceable. On return to base their number was again one short, but this loss could not be attributed to the enemy. While outward bound the starboard engine on R5789 had lost power and burst into flames. Underpowered, horribly overloaded with a full complement of bombs and almost a full fuel load the Manchester began to descend very rapidly. Six of the crew were ordered to bale out while the two pilots attempted to make a blind forced landing. Unfortunately luck was not on their side, the aircraft crashed into trees near Tidworth on the Wiltshire/Hampshire border and both men lost their lives.

During the rest of the month the squadron operated on eight further occasions, mostly in very small numbers. The Manchesters continued to experience trouble and there were several early returns mainly due to recurring faults in their Rolls-Royce Vulture engines. Three further aircraft were lost in the course of these operations. Two of these failed to return on the night of 31st January/1st February when the squadron managed to despatch nine aircraft, its highest number yet, against a familiar RAF target, the *Scharnhorst*, *Gneisenau* and *Prinz Eugen* in Brest Harbour.

These German naval vessels were to occupy much of 61 Squadron's time in the first 12 days of February. Such was the threat posed by the impending breakout of these capital ships that many bomber aircraft, including those at Woolfox, were kept on standby loaded and ready to go should news be received that they had eluded the watchers and were at sea.

In expectation that they would take a northerly route when heading for home ports large numbers of mines were laid along the Dutch coast in what was estimated to be their probable path. On the 6th five of Woolfox's Manchesters took part in an unescorted daylight 'Gardening' mission in support of this plan. Each aircraft was loaded with four sea mines to be laid in the area code named 'Nectarines', off the Fresian Islands. All returned safely after sowing their 'vegetables' though not without running the gauntlet of enemy flak and fighters.

Standbys followed for the next few days then on the night of 11th/12th six crews were briefed for a bombing raid on Bremen. Again it was not an auspicious occasion for the squadron. Plagued by the usual problems one Manchester landed back at base after 20 minutes while another only made it as far as the Dutch coast before having to turn back. Four Manchesters managed to reach Bremen and while three returned home safely the fourth, R5834, after a nightmare journey across the North Sea, was written off in a crash landing near Horsham St Faith, Norfolk. The crew survived the ordeal.

As luck would have it the German ships chose that night to slip away from their French haven. By the time they were first engaged it was daylight and they were travelling at high speed through the English Channel in company with many escort vessels and a protective umbrella of fighters.

Bomber Command mounted a large operation to seek and destroy the German ships and although they had operated in the early hours of the morning 61 Squadron was required to make a contribution. Five of the unit's Manchesters were sent into action including L7473 which had only landed back from Bremen at 09:15 hours.

On the whole Bomber Command's effort was a dismal failure. Beset by atrocious weather many crews found it impossible to locate the enemy and those that did failed to hamper their progress. As for the Woolfox quintet they had mixed fortunes, mostly on the debit side. Two crews returned without having found their quarry, another pair located the convoy but a combination of factors, not least being flak and fighters, prevented them from bombing. The fifth crew also found the ships and made a bombing run on a battle cruiser from 450ft but in the face of intense gunfire failed to hit the target. This latter trio returned to Woolfox liberally peppered with holes from flak bursts.

But 61 Squadron were not yet finished with these operations. That night two Manchesters sallied forth on a mining expedition. Exceptionally bad weather forced both to abandon their mission bringing to an end another sorry episode in the squadron's Manchester story.

In addition to mining operations during March, squadron aircraft made 53 bombing sorties in the course of six raids between the 3rd and 28th. Targets included the Renault works at Billancourt, the city of Lubeck, industrial centres at Cologne and Essen.

For this series of operations 61 Squadron participation was at its highest, eight Manchesters were despatched twice, nine three times and ten once. This last figure, the largest number of Manchesters the unit was to send on one operation, was achieved on the 26th, the occasion being the third trip to Essen in 18 days. It was another bad night for 61: two Manchesters were lost, both crashed after falling victim to enemy night fighters. From the two crews only two members survived the encounters.

The raids during March could be considered as the squadron's swan song as far as the Manchester was concerned. Although they continued to operate during April the numbers taking part were much reduced. For instance, on the 10th, on what proved to be the last occasion when 61 Squadron flew the Manchester operationally, only two aircraft took part. Docks at Le Havre were attacked but only one Manchester returned to Woolfox. The other, R5785, was forced to ditch in the English Channel after falling foul of the port's formidable defences. Six of the crew became prisoners of war after drifting ashore in their dinghy on the Cherbourg peninsula.

Following this, almost immediately the squadron began to re-equip with Avro Lancasters, probably much to the satisfaction of air and ground crew alike. For this purpose, 61 Conversion Flight was formed, with a unit establishment of two Manchesters and two Lancasters. The unit's remaining days at Woolfox were numbered and on 5th May a move was made to Syerston, Nottinghamshire.

Detailed and often harrowing accounts of many of 61 Squadron's operations from Woolfox can be found in the book *Avro Manchester: The Legend Behind the Lancaster*, by Robert Kirby, published by Midland Publishing in 1995.

During April, following the formation there of 29 OTU the role of North Luffenham changed. With Vickers Wellingtons as its main equipment the new unit was tasked with training tightly-knit crews ready to face operations with Bomber Command. As Woolfox was still retained as a satellite the airfield played its part in the OTUs training scheme.

In June another unit also became part of the Woolfox scene with the movement of 1429 (Czech) Operational Training Flight from East Wretham, Norfolk. Elements of the unit began to arrive on the 26th with the final movement taking place on the 29th when 85 officers and men were flown in on board the Flight's 12 Wellingtons and three Airspeed Oxfords. The tail end of the party arrived, by rail, at nearby Stamford the same day. Whether the Flight was able to do any useful training at Woolfox is open to doubt as they had not had time to become really settled before being faced with another change of station. A movement order from Bomber Command dated 17th August 1942 indicated that the flight was to transfer to

The airfield surface at Woolfox Lodge gained a terrible reputation. Digging out a Manchester, 1941. L Boot

Stirling I Fante *of 218 Squadron with F/O Allen in the foreground.* via Peter Green

Church Broughton, Derbyshire, and the move was to be completed by 1st September. This directive was carried out with all speed and by 31st August the unit had left.

Into the autumn 29 OTU continued to make use of the airfield but another change was in the offing. On 18th October 1942 Woolfox was closed to flying and handed over to civil engineering contractors. It was 1st June 1943 before the airfield reopened once more and in the interim major changes had taken place. Instead of grass, three tarmac runways were now in place, the main one (almost parallel to the A1 road) was 1,850 yards long, the other two 1,400 yards each; all were 50 yards wide. Additionally a linking perimeter track, 50 aircraft hardstandings, four hangars; three 'T2s' and a 'B1', together with other ancillary buildings were all now part of the remodelled Woolfox. At this stage the station was still under North Luffenham's jurisdiction but on the 4th this too changed and Woolfox became a parent station in its own right.

No.1665 Heavy Conversion Unit (HCU) was the first flying unit to make use of the reopened airfield when it was transferred from Waterbeach, Cambridgeshire. Equipped with Short Stirling Is and IIIs it began to move in from 4th June and by the end of the month 16 of its aircraft were on strength and conversion training was under way.

Although major facilities were in place some, including an efficient airfield lighting system, were still lacking. The new runways also gave cause for concern. In August at no time were more than two available for use; on occasion this was reduced to one and that out of wind. Months of construction work had also left the airfield in a very unprepared state and for several weeks the HCU used the United States Army Air Force (USAAF) station at Shipdham, Norfolk, for some circuit training.

While so engaged on 23rd August unit aircraft were caught up in an enemy air raid. One Stirling was forced to abort take-off; another, Mk.I BK598 while making a practice overshoot was seen to be closely followed by a Junkers Ju 88 which, in turn, was being stalked by a Bristol Beaufighter. The Junkers made no attack on the Stirling which flew blithely on, its crew apparently oblivious of their company. Three high explosive and 120 anti-personnel bombs were dropped by the raider. Shrapnel caused slight damage to Mk.I W7527, the HCU's only casualty during the incident.

Crash crews on the station had just cause to remember this period at Woolfox in view of the many occasions when they were called out. A substantial proportion of accidents were attributed to the Stirling's tendency to swing on take-off which was often followed by the collapse of the aircraft's

rather leggy undercarriage. In many cases at Woolfox when this occurred damage was further compounded by the rough state of the airfield surface.

One notable incident which started with a swing happened soon after the unit had arrived. While taking off on 5th July, Mk.I BF339 developed a swing to starboard. Out of control the Stirling careered across the airfield on to the perimeter track 90 yards away where it struck stationary transport in its path. It continued for a further 30 yards before colliding with the administration buildings. Parts of these were completely demolished; others were further damaged after the aircraft caught fire. There were no serious casualties, but BF339 was a complete write-off and the damage it had caused took over a month to repair or rebuild.

Although conditions saw a gradual improvement and the HCU made steady progress it was destined to stay at Woolfox for less than eight months. In January 1944 the powers that be decreed a move and on the 23rd it left for Tilstock, Shropshire.

Several airfields in the area had also experienced rebuilding operations and in common with these, while work was in progress Woolfox also became a storage site for assault gliders prior to their use in airborne operations. Between 14th May and 20th June 1943 32 Airspeed Horsas were delivered. Initially they were assigned to the care of 29 OTU but later 33 Heavy Glider Maintenance Section, part of 2 Heavy Glider Maintenance Unit, assumed responsibility. All were eventually transferred to the USAAF in February 1944 for use by their troop carrier units.

Following the departure of 1665 HCU, Woolfox went over to care and maintenance and an airfield unserviceable signal was displayed. Presumably this was in force to enable a Drem Mk.II airfield lighting system to be installed. However, this aid was far from complete when Woolfox became the new base for 218 Squadron from Downham Market, Cambridgeshire, on 7th March.

An operational Stirling squadron, they must have been somewhat disconcerted by the incomplete state of the airfield, especially the Drem system. Major items such as totem poles, floodlights and perimeter track lighting were not yet installed and the airfield was declared serviceable for day use only.

Although the lack of perimeter airfield lighting was a hindrance, during April the squadron was able to return to night operations after a portable system was impressed into service. Many of the sorties carried out involved mine laying, these operations were far ranging and took aircraft as far north as the Baltic and south to the Bay of

A trio of 1651 HCU Stirlings. 'S' is N3676.
via N Franklin

Biscay. In support of Bomber Command's aim to disrupt enemy rail traffic in the weeks prior to the invasion during the month the squadron was also engaged in raids on the marshalling yards at Chambly, Courtrai, Lille and Rouen.

At this time 218 was also carrying out intensive training with a new and eventually very accurate blind bombing system called Gee-H. This system which has been referred to as 'Oboe in reverse' enabled an aircraft, by sending and receiving pulse signals, to continuously measure distance and follow predetermined tracks with great precision. Early raids by the Squadron using Gee-H were on a small scale and were by nature of experiment and for the calibration of equipment.

The squadron used Gee-H on operations for the first time during an attack on Chambly marshalling yards on 20th/21st April. It would be nice to write that the event was a huge success but as with many new and untried devices there were snags. There was a minimum of opposition from the enemy and the weather was good but of the 14 crews taking part only three reported successful reception on Gee-H. Those three, the only ones to bomb the target, all secured aiming point photographs. As for the others, ten bomb loads were either brought back or jettisoned and one Stirling was lost.

Results were much better two nights later when 11 Stirlings bombed a *Luftwaffe* signals depot at Vilvorde, north of Brussels. It should have been 12 aircraft but one almost came to grief when an engine cut on take-off. Only prompt action saved the day when the pilot immediately jettisoned the full 8,000lb bomb load. Even then the Stirling was so low it brushed through trees near the airfield but it managed to stagger round the circuit and land back safely. The rest of the aircraft enjoyed success; they carried out some very accurate bombing after receiving good Gee-H signals.

On 1st/2nd May the system was again used to good effect when 16 Stirlings were again despatched to Chambly. Twelve bombed by Gee-H and achieved good results, but two received no signals and bombed using Pathfinder Force markers instead. It was a night which favoured night-fighters as the crew aboard Mk.III EF184 were to find out. Visibility was excellent, helped by a bright quarter moon and shortly after bombing four attacks were made on the Stirling by two Junkers Ju 88s. Damage caused was severe, many instruments were put out of action, large areas of mainplane and tail unit were shot away and the undercarriage would not lower. Crew casualties were also high, the flight engineer was killed and the mid-upper and rear gunners wounded. In spite of this and a steady loss of height, the pilot, Pilot Officer Scammell, managed to coax EF184 back to England where he made a successful belly-landing on the emergency runway at

Woodbridge, Suffolk. Two further Stirlings failed to return; both crashed in France.

By the end of May the Drem system on the airfield was far from finished, the perimeter track lights were as yet only 75% complete and in other respects major items had still not been installed. Some progress was made to tidy up the airfield with harrowing and seeding taking place to improve areas disturbed by construction.

For the greater part of May, 218 Squadron entered an intensive period of Gee-H training which culminated in a vital operation on the night preceding the Allied invasion of Europe, 5th/6th June 1944. On that night several squadrons flew a series of diversionary operations intended to create doubt in the enemy's mind as to the true time and place of the real Allied landings. Two of these operations concerned the simulation of convoys approaching the French coast. One, Operation 'Taxable', which has since been well publicised, was carried out by 617 Squadron. The other, lesser known to some degree, was Operation 'Glimmer' flown by 218 Squadron.

Eight Stirlings took off from Woolfox between 23:39 and 00:43 hours heading for the south coast. Six were to take part in the 'spoof' the others as reserve in case of some malfunction. On arrival at a predetermined point the six aircraft formed up and set course for Boulogne intent on producing an imaginary convoy.

By flying an intricate, very accurate series of overlapping orbits and the precise dropping of specially developed new types of 'window' aluminium foil which gave the impression of large ship echoes on enemy radars, they succeeded in simulating an invasion force approaching the coast at a steady seven knots.

German reaction to 'Glimmer' was almost instant. Searchlights came on and guns opened fire on the non-existent convoy. Night-fighters and E-boats were also diverted to the area but searched in vain. Throughout the mission, as far as 218 were concerned, everything went without a hitch and the Stirlings returned safely to Woolfox between 05:02 and 5:12 hours.

A signal was later received from the Commander-in-Chief Bomber Command, Sir Arthur T Harris, which congratulated the squadron on its success. In a later report he said that it was considered both 'Glimmer' and 'Taxable' had 'contributed very materially to tactical surprise'.

Immediately following the invasion a programme of tactical mine laying was embarked upon to hinder any efforts made by enemy U-boats and surface vessels to interfere with the transport of reinforcements and supplies. A great deal of this work was carried out during the month by 218 using Gee-H to enable precision drops to be made. Only on three occasions were the squadron called upon to carry out bombing raids to such diverse targets as the marshalling yards at Lens, a railway cutting near Montdidier and a V-1 (or 'Doddlebug') site in the Pas de Calais.

The state of the airfield lighting continued to feature in monthly reports which for July indicated that progress towards completion was still slow. The same applied to tidying up in general.

Although mine laying was still the main occupation of the squadron during July, four daylight attacks were also made on V-1 sites and storage depots. In addition to this the unit had other things to occupy its flying hours as it began to convert to Avro Lancasters towards the end of the month. This task was placed in the hands of 3 Lancaster Finishing School (LFS), Feltwell, Norfolk, and initially crews visited there for preliminary training, returning to Woolfox for circuits and bumps. Their conversion complete the crews of 'B' Flight moved out to Methwold, Norfolk, in two batches between 26th and 29th July while 'A' Flight continued with their course but at the same time remained operational on Stirlings.

At the end of July there were still ten of these aircraft on unit strength and on 2nd August six of these carried out the unit's last operation from Woolfox. Again it was a precision daylight attack on a V-1 site this time at Mont Candon and 218 were detailed to lead. From unit reports it appears to have been a copybook raid. The six Stirlings flew to March where they rendezvoused with 14

more from 149 Squadron. After making two formations with three 218 aircraft leading each they flew on to their target. Reception on Gee-H was excellent, no opposition whatsoever was met and the formations in pairs, line astern echelon to starboard, carried out some very accurate bombing with their 20 x 500lb loads. All aircraft returned to their respective bases without loss.

On 4th August, the remainder of 218 Squadron left Woolfox to join their colleagues at Methwold. For most of the remainder of the month 'C' Flight, 3 LFS continued to make use of the airfield for training other crews. They were joined by a large influx of other Lancasters in the early hours of 8th August when poor visibility was responsible for the diversion of 19 aircraft belonging to 90 Squadron, Tuddenham, Suffolk, on return from bombing German tank and troop concentrations south east of Caen. It was a brief interlude as all returned to their base during the morning.

On 28th August the 3 LFS detachment returned to Feltwell and from the 31st Woolfox was transferred to USAAF control and became their Station 478. The 9th Troop Carrier Command Substitution Unit and 62nd Station Complement Squadron occupied the station for just over six weeks and although some preparation was made no American flying units moved in.

Then, on 20th October Woolfox reverted back to RAF control once more but now within 7 Group and as a substation of 73 Base, North Luffenham. For a short time during this period of transition the Heavy Glider Conversion Unit at North Luffenham had made use of Woolfox but this association had ceased on 11th October.

After its return to the RAF the station prepared to house another new unit. This was to be 1651 HCU which was also about to convert from Stirlings to Lancasters and the process of moving from Wratting Common, Cambridgeshire, began on 30th October. Another ten days were to elapse before the main part of the unit put in an appearance but by the 14th November re-equipment and conversion were under way and at the end of the month 13 crews were considered proficient.

From arrival at Woolfox the HCU was to have roughly a further eight months of active life. Weather and other factors permitting during that time it continued to produce its quota of trained personnel for 7 Group. It experienced all the hazards of wartime flying and the trauma associated with the inevitable crashed aircraft and often resultant loss of life. This was brought home no more vividly than on the night of 3rd/4th March 1945 when two Lancasters on training exercises were shot down in flames by enemy night-fighter intruders. Only one rear gunner was to survive.

RAF Woolfox Lodge – 1st December 1944

Latitude	52° 42' 30" N
Longitude	00° 34' 30" W
Height at Sea Level	345ft
Locality	6 miles NW of Stamford
Command	Bomber (RAF)
Nearest Railway Station	Stamford, LMS, LNER, 8 miles.
Function	Operational Station
Affiliated Airfields	North Luffenham (Base)

Landing Area – Runways

QDM	Dimensions	Extensibility	Remarks
035°	1,400 x 50 yds	1,600 yds	–
086°	1,400 x 50 yds	1,400 yds	
149°	1,850 x 50 yds	1,850 yds	
Type of Surface	Tarmacadam		

Permanent Landmarks

By Day	Great North Road on western boundary.
By Night	Nil

Permanent Obstructions Ketton chimney 350ft

Facilities

Airfield Lightning	Mk.II
Beam Approach	–
Radio	–
QDM	–
Flying Control	Yes

Accommodation All buildings temporary.

Technical	Hangars		Hardstandings	
	Type	No	Type	No
	T2	4	Hvy Bmbr	50
	B1	1		

Domestic	Officers	SNCOs	ORs	Total
RAF	108	262	779	1,149
WAAF	7	6	239	252

The capitulation of the German forces in June brought welcome relief and the celebrations which followed on VE Day were as exuberant as wartime conditions allowed. At least two of the more boisterous displays within the camp made it necessary to call out the fire crews. As a precaution the aircraft were placed under guard in case anyone should be tempted to put on an impromptu flying exhibition.

The demand for bomber crews diminished almost overnight which led in turn to a rapid decline of the many units which had been responsible for their training. This soon became evident at Woolfox; flying training ceased at the end of June and on the 13th July 1651 HCU was disbanded. All that then remained was to clear the station of the impedimenta from the defunct unit. Bomber Command relinquished its hold on Woolfox and on 1st August 40 Group Maintenance Command took over the station and installed 259 Maintenance Unit (MU).

Composite vertical survey photograph of Woolfox Lodge, dated 17th January 1947. The Great North Road, the A1, is marked (A). Closer inspection of the apparently deserted airfield shows small huts on the runways and items in storage on the dispersals and elsewhere. The area occupied by the later Bloodhound sites is marked (B). DoE

One of four units which comprised 55 Wing the MU had begun to form at North Witham, Lincolnshire, in the last week of July. Although scheduled to move to Woolfox on 1st August, it was unable to do so owing to the large number of HCU personnel still awaiting posting. A fortnight elapsed before it was able to occupy Woolfox and even then a few Lancasters still waited to be flown away. After the last of these had left the main runway was kept open but this was marked for emergency use only.

The MU was classed as an Equipment Dispersal Depot (EDD) and the function of these units, which were established after the end of the war in Europe, was to receive surplus equipment from stations either closing down or changing their role. Each EDD handled a specific range of equipment and it was airborne items which were delivered to Woolfox for storage pending eventual disposal. Everything from guns and bombsights to navigator's rulers and watches were sent to the MU by road and rail.

On arrival they were first unloaded in the 'B1' hangar close to the A1. After checking and sorting into various categories, they were dispersed around the airfield. Some of the bulkier items were stored in the open on the many hardstandings, others were housed in the four 'T2' hangars, while the more valuable items were placed under lock and key in one of the many vacant brick buildings.

Some of the stored equipment was occasionally reissued to still active flying units but over several years the majority was disposed of via a series of war surplus auction sales. Eventually vacated by 259 MU in

August 1948 the airfield was then placed on a care and maintenance footing.

In the period of acute housing shortage which prevailed after the Second World War the disused hutted camps of former RAF stations provided welcome accommodation for many seeking a roof over their heads. Some of the huts on Woolfox's dispersed sites were converted into three-roomed dwellings, many were rented out to ex-service families. Others were taken over to house communities of displaced persons, many of Ukrainian origin.

Limited flying activity again began to take place at Woolfox from May 1951 when the airfield began to be used as a relief landing ground by 7 Flying Training School (FTS), Cottesmore. Until the unit was disbanded in March 1954 its aircraft could frequently be seen engaged in circuit training. The airfield was again declared inactive in April 1954.

Five years were to elapse before attention was once again focused on Woolfox. During 1959 and into 1960 a section of the airfield became the scene of construction

activities as contractors built an installation which was to give Woolfox a place in Britain's missile defence system. Between December 1958 and October 1960 eleven bases, each with a squadron of Bristol Bloodhound 1 surface-to-air missiles (SAM) became operational. One of six to be activated in 1960 was 62 Squadron at Woolfox on 1st February as part of 151 (SAM) Wing, Fighter Command with HQ and Tactical Control Centre (TCC) at North Luffenham.

The intended role of these missile units was the defence of both V-Bomber bases and Douglas Thor intermediate range ballistic missile (IRBM) sites. Like other units similarly equipped, 62 Squadron deployed 16 Bloodhounds on ready launchers with a further 16 as reloads. If called into action their targets would have been initially assigned by the TCC, then at unit level Sting Ray target illuminating radars and associated launch control post would take over.

Fortunately the missiles were not called upon to be fired in anger but for over four years 62 Squadron's white-painted Bloodhounds, aimed towards the east, were a familiar sight to the thousands of motorists who passed on the A1. The demise of the IRBM force and technical advances in control and guidance systems rendered the Bloodhound 1 obsolete. Although some of the units re-equipped with the Mk.2 version, 62 Squadron followed the path of the majority when it was one of the last pair to disband on 13th September 1964.

After another short period of care and maintenance the airfield was de-activated on 6th January 1965 and remained in limbo until September 1966 when on instructions from the Secretary of State for Defence it was sold at auction in Bourne, Lincolnshire, by Hodgkinson & Son, a firm of local auctioneers.

What of Woolfox Lodge now? Large sections of all three runways have been removed, although the main one has suffered least in this respect. The majority of hardstandings have also gone but the perimeter track can be traced, much reduced in width. Reduced to hardcore the concrete was used during alterations to the nearby A1. Although all five hangars have long since gone a small area of land around where the 'B1' stood is now the site of business premises. Part of this site is now used as a major depot for a haulage company.

Few other wartime buildings are still to be seen and most are just derelict shells fast disappearing as nature takes over; only the control tower survives structurally fairly intact. From more recent times, what was once the site of the missile complex can still be clearly defined. As for other acreage, a great deal of this is given over to arable farming and in all probability more will be reclaimed for this purpose in the future.

Woolfox Lodge-based Units and Aircraft

No.14 Operational Training Unit
From 13.12.40 to 1.8.41   Codes 'AM-', 'GL-', 'VB-'
See parent station – Cottesmore.

No.29 Operational Training Unit
N.2 HGMU / No.33 HGMS / USAAF
Airspeed Horsa I   DP540, DP602, DP655, DP705.
HG811, HG902, HG910, HG925, HG978. LF949. LG682,
LG688, HG781, HG835, HG872, HG930, HG931, HG934,
HG936, HG952, HG978, HG990. LH117, LH119, LH121,
LH967. LJ114, LJ160, LJ161, LJ162, LJ177, LJ178, LJ222.
Initially assigned to the care of 29 OTU, Woolfox Lodge, these
gliders were reassigned to 2 Heavy Glider Maintenance Unit in
August 1943. In October they became the responsibility of 33
Heavy Glider Maintenance Section before eventually being
transferred to the USAAF in February 1944. No.33 HGMS ceased
its connecton with Woolfox Lodge on 15.3.44.

No.61 Squadron
From .9.41 to 5.5.42   Code 'QR-'
Avro Manchester I   L7458, L7464, L7470, L7471, L7472,
L7473, L7475, L7477, R5784, R5785, R5786, R5787, R5789,
R5796, R5832, R5834, R5839, R5840, R5841.
Avro Manchester IA   L7494, L7495, L7496, L7497, L7516,
L7518, L7519, L7520, L7521, L7522.
Avro Lancaster I   R5511, R5517, R5543, R5561,
R5562, R5563, R5615, R5842, R5843, R5844, R5845, R5846,
R5859, L7532, L7539, L7569, L7571.

No.61 Squadron Conversion Flight
From 27.3.42 to 5.5.42   Code 'QR-'
Avro Manchester I   L7286.
Avro Lancaster I   L7532, R5488 'F.

No.29 Operational Training Unit
From 1.8.42 to 3.6.43   Codes 'NT-', 'TF-'
See parent station – North Luffenham.

Illustrations on the opposite page:

*No.62 Squadron's Bloodhound missiles
pointing eastwards at Woolfox, July 1960.
Peter Green collection*

*The control tower / watch office at
Woolfox. Listed as being of the No.
4532/3/43 type for Night-Fighter Stations,
this is unusual as night-fighters were
never based at the airfield.* R Walters

*Woolfox Lodge from the air, looking
south with the A1 very prominent (A).
While the former airfield has returned
extensively to agriculture, the perimeter
tracks and the north/south runway can
be easily discerned. The Bloodhound
hardstandings are at (B).* Author

On this page, right:

*Wing Commander T C Weir DFC, the 61
Squadron CO, and crew, walking out to
their Manchester at Woolfox Lodge. Note
the state of the airfield.* Les Boot

No.1665 Heavy Conversion Unit
From 5.6.43 to 23.1.44   Codes 'FO-', 'NY-', 'OG-'
Short Stirling I   N3670, R9143, R9198 'F', BF318,
BF339, BF341, BF349, BF412, BF434, BF444, BF446, BK597,
BK598, BK621, EF342, EF354, EF355.

No.1429 Czech Operational Training Flight
From 26.6.43 to 31.8.43
Vickers Wellington   ?

No.218 Squadron
From 7.3.44 to 4.8.44   Code 'HA-'
Short Stirling I   EF133 'A', EF181 'J', EF184 'V',
EF185 'L', EF207 'F', EF249 'H', EF259 'G', EF291 'C',
EF299 'Z', EF462, EF504 'P', EH942 'M', EJ112 'Q'.
Short Stirling III   LJ447 'F', LJ448 'A', LJ449 'E',
LJ472 'K', LJ481 'B', LJ517 'U', LJ521 'W', LJ522 'N',
LK396 'M', LK401 'I', LK568 'O'.

No.3 Lancaster Finishing School
From .5.44 to .7.44   Code 'A5-'
Avro Lancaster   ?

No.21 Heavy Glider Conversion Unit
From .9.44 to .10.44   See parent station – North Luffenham.

No.1651 Heavy Conversion Unit
From 9.11.44 to 13.7.45   Codes 'BS-', 'QQ-', 'YZ-'
Short Stirling   ?
Avro Lancaster I   L7544, L7566, L7582, R5503,
R5756, W4181, ED310, ED631, HK541, HK655, HK750, LL794,
LL967, LM236, LM287, LM340, LM594, ME319, ME325, ME590,
ME644, ME753, ME756, ME781, NG270, NG271, NG272, NG274,
NG275, NG295, PA159, PB194, PB749, PB796, PB871, PD392.
Avro Lancaster III   DV372, ED413, ED474, ED767,
JA677, JB127, JB185, JB699, ME482, ND359, ND387, ND782,
ND900, NE178.
Supermarine Spitfire V   BM129.

Station Flight   Between 11.43 and 12.44
Airspeed Oxford I   V3574, W6582, X7292.

No.7 Flying Training School
From 5.5.51 to 14.4.54   Codes 'FBA-' to 'FBE-'
See parent station – Cottesmore.

No.62 Squadron   From 1.2.60 to 30.9.64
Bristol Bloodhound I

Serious Accidents to Woolfox Lodge Aircraft

2.11.41 Manchester I L7520 61 Squadron
Crashed in forced landing, Roxton, Beds.

8.12.41 Manchester I L7494 61 Squadron
Ops Boulogne. Aircraft exploded in mid-air and crashed in sea
off Boulogne.

9.1.42 Manchester I R5789 61 Squadron
Ops Brest. Engine caught fire on outward journey. Six baled
out, two pilots killed in forced landing, Wiltshire Cross, Wilts.

16.1.42 Manchester I L7495 61 Squadron
Abandoned near Grimoldby, Lincs.

1.2.42 Manchester I R5787 'M' 61 Squadron
Ops Brest. Hit by flak over target, force-landed in France.

1.2.42 Manchester I L7396 61 Squadron
Ops Brest. Crashed in English Channel, one body recovered.

1.2.42 Manchester I L7472 61 Squadron
Ops Brest. Set on fire by flak, hit balloon cable, ditched quarter
mile off shore.

10.2.42 Manchester I R5834 61 Squadron
Ops 'Gardening'. Damaged beyond repair after forced landing
at Horsham St Faith.

16.2.42 Manchester I L7433 61 Squadron
Ops 'Gardening'. Crashed in sea near Terschelling after being
hit by flak.

13.3.42 Manchester I L7395 61 Squadron
Ops Cologne. Following engine and instrument failure on
return crew baled out, aircraft crashed at Thornhaugh,
Northants.

25.3.42 Manchester I L7518 'O' 61 Squadron
Ops Essen. Shot down by Hpt Lent, II/NJG2, crashed near
Warmenhuizen, Holland.

26.3.42 Manchester I L7497 61 Squadron
Ops Essen. Shot down by Oblt Woltersdorf NJG 1, crashed at
Werterbruch.

29.3.42 Manchester I L7454 61 Squadron
Ops 'Gardening'. Presumed crashed in sea.

8.4.42 Manchester I L7470 61 Squadron
Ops Essen. Shot down by Oblt von Bonin, II/NJG1, crashed
near St Trond, Belgium.

11.4.42   Manchester I   R5785 'M'   61 Squadron
Ops Le Havre. Hit by flak, starboard engine failed, ditched in English Channel, one of crew drowned, rest became PoWs.

1.5.42   Lancaster I   R5545   61 Squadron
Overshot landing at North Luffenham.

26.6.43   Stirling I   R9198   1665 HCU
Swung on take-off in gusting crosswind, undercarriage collapsed.

5.7.43   Stirling I   BF339   1665 HCU
Hit vehicles and buildings after swing on take-off.

24.7.43   Stirling I   BK621   1665 HCU
This aircraft still officially on strength of 1651 CU when it swung on take-off for an acceptance check by 1665 HCU. Port undercarriage leg collapsed.

25.7.43   Stirling I   EF354   1665 HCU
Hard to control when making emergency landing, another aircraft cut in, EF354 braked hard and undercarriage collapsed.

29.7.43   Stirling I   EF337   1665 HCU
Hit obstruction after swinging on landing and undercarriage collapsed.

4.8.43   Stirling I   BF446   1665 HCU
Swung on landing, undercarriage collapsed.

5.9.43   Stirling I   BF318   1665 HCU
Swung on landing in cross wind, undercarriage collapsed.

14.1.44   Oxford II   W6582   Station Flight
Crashed, no further details.

21.4.44   Stirling III   LJ448   218 Squadron
Ops Chambly Rail Depot. Failed to return, crashed Asnieres, France. Three killed, one PoW, three evaded capture.

23.4.44   Stirling III   EH942 'M'   218 Squadron
Ops Laon Railway Yards. Shot down by Oblt Dietrich Schmidt of III/NJG1 and crashed at 00.26 hours near Hautefontaine. Two killed, five evaded capture.

2.5.44   Stirling III   EF184   218 Squadron
Ops Chambly. Attacked by two Junkers Ju88s after leaving target area. Crash landed at Woodbridge, one of the crew was killed.

2.5.44   Stirling III   EF259 'G'   218 Squadron
Ops Chambly. Failed to return, crashed La Houssaye, France. Four killed, four evaded capture.

2.5.44   Stirling III   EF504 'P'   218 Squadron
Ops Chambly. Failed to return, near Poix de la Somme, France. Five killed, two evaded capture.

9.5.44   Stirling III   EF249 'H'   218 Squadron
Ops 'Gardening'. On return from mining La Gironde estuary. Port inner defective, could not lower full flap, on overshoot swung to port and undercarriage collapsed.

12.6.44   Stirling III   EF181   218 Squadron
Ops 'Gardening'. Starboard tyre burst on take-off. Aircraft swung and starboard leg broke.

13.6.44   Stirling III   EF299   218 Squadron
Ops 'Gardening'. Overshot on return from mining at Le Havre, struck ridge and undercarriage collapsed.

8.12.44   Lancaster I   PB749   1651 HCU
Crashed at Langtoft, near Market Deeping, after port elevator broke away during high speed manoeuvres. Aircraft dived, exploded and broke up in mid-air. Wreckage scattered over two mile radius.

11.12.44   Lancaster I   NG270   1651 HCU
Lost control due to icing, crashed Ailsworth, Northants.

27.1.45   Lancaster III   ED413 'BS-J'   1651 HCU
Unable to unfeather props following single engine demonstration. Crashed at Castle Farm, Barnwell, 2½ miles south of Oundle, Northants. Two seriously injured.

7.2.45   Lancaster III   ME325   1651 HCU
Crashed in field, just off Great North Road, west of airfield. Attempted to overshoot having approached Runway 33 while

27 was in use. Practice bomb had hung up and exploded in bomb bay. Cockpit filled with smoke fumes and pilot unable to see to make landing. Written off.

3.3.45   Lancaster I   ME781   1651 HCU
Reported engine trouble just prior to landing, overshot and attempted to go round again lost height and crashed. All crew except rear gunner killed.

4.3.45   Lancaster III   JB699 'BS-F'   1651 HCU
Shot down in flames by enemy intruder at 01:35 hours and crashed on Cottesmore airfield. All crew killed.

4.3.45   Lancaster III   ND387 'BS-K'   1651 HCU
Shot down in flames near Stretton, by enemy intruder. One survivor from seven crew.

24.3.45   Lancaster I   PB871   1651 HCU
Engine cut on take-off, aircraft swung and undercarriage collapsed.

2.4.45   Lancaster I   HK655   1651 HCU
Stalled on approach to Fiskerton. Hit building and crashed.

10.5.45   Lancaster I   ED631   1651 HCU
Overshot Runway 33, crossed Great North Road, crashed into quarry and burnt out.

A hut in the south camp at Woolfox Lodge during the winter of 1941/1942. L Boot

Chapter Twenty-Four

Wymeswold

Meteor F.4 VZ403 'TM-A' of 504 Squadron coming in to land at Wymeswold.
via Ian O'Neill

Buildt during the early years of the Second World War, Wymeswold was, from the outset, earmarked to serve as a training base. First by supplying night bomber crews to help meet the pressing needs of Bomber Command as it waged an all-out offensive against the Axis powers and later by training aircrew for a no less demanding role, though of an entirely different nature, for Transport Command.

The station opened in 7 Group, Bomber Command, on 16th May 1942 when the initial working party consisting of two officers, six NCOs and 26 aircraftmen arrived. They found many of the buildings on the camp were, as yet, in an unfinished state but with much hard work, plus help from the steady influx of additional personnel being posted in, the station was gradually made habitable. Following a change of title on 11th May, Wymeswold then became part of 92 Group and shortly afterwards on the 15th it became the home of an Operational Training Unit when 28 OTU was formed there.

After serving at RAF Waterbeach, Cambridgeshire, Group Captain J R Bell DFC, a former First World War pilot, arrived on 1st June to become the station's first commanding officer, a position he was destined to hold from that date until he finally relinquished it in August 1945.

Apart from improving living conditions on the camp a great deal of time was absorbed in the early weeks of occupation building up ground training facilities in readiness for the first intake of pupils. For example, various specialist sections modified or adapted buildings to serve their specific training needs; time expired airframes were acquired and converted for instructional use and one novel scheme adopted at this time was the installation of a gun turret in a disused clay-pit on a local farm as an aid for furthering the training of air gunners.

During this building-up period the airfield itself was not allowed to stand entirely idle; from 6th July it was used for a time by detachments of pupils from 16 (Polish) Service Flying Training School, from Newton, Nottinghamshire, engaged in night flying training. Also during the month use of one of the hangars was made available to Tollerton Aircraft Services to enable them to carry out urgent modifications to five Handley Page Halifax IIs. Another change of group came on 15th July when the station and the as yet unfinished satellite at Castle Donington (Chapter Seven), were moved to 93 Group, Bomber Command.

Deliveries of aircraft to equip the fledgling OTU began towards the end of July with Vickers Wellington Ics arriving. Some of these were, even at this stage, beginning to show signs of fatigue, having in the main been flown extensively by operational squadrons and in some cases by other OTUs.

Practice bombing ranges at Clifton Pastures (day) and Misson (night) were allotted to the unit and for air-to-air firing practice a range at North Fens was to be shared with 14 OTU, Cottesmore. For this latter duty two Westland Lysander IIIs were taken on strength for target-towing duties.

With the arrival on 4th August 1942 of the crews to start No.1 Course, 28 OTU were at last in business with lectures and ground training starting immediately. By the 20th 'A' Flight had been formed and completely equipped with 12 aircraft, 'B' Flight was also in the throes of being formed, but it was not until 11th September that this too was up to strength with a full complement of 12 Wellingtons.

An incident worth recording which occurred on 9th August involved the unscheduled arrival of five Boeing B-17F Flying Fortresses of the 352nd Squadron, 301st Bomb Group, USAAF. The Fortresses were flying into their new base at Chelveston, Northamptonshire, when these five landed by mistake at Wymeswold. Realising their error, maps were obtained and they took off again heading for their correct destination. Another aircraft of this squadron (41-24347) suffered damage when it landed and overshot at Church Lawford, Warwickshire, on the same day, so it would appear that their navigation was in need of a brush up.

Although the OTU had been established as a flying unit for a relatively short time it was called upon during September to provide aircraft and crews to participate in the bomber offensive against Germany. Aircraft of the unit flown by instructors and senior pupils took part in raids on three occasions during the month.

The first of these was on the night of the 10th/11th when three Wellingtons of 'A' Flight: R1011 'M' (Warrant Officer Herbert), DV948 'B' (Flight Sergeant Ross) and DV950 'A' (Flight Sergeant Taylor) were part of a force of 476 aircraft which attacked Düsseldorf, with excellent results being achieved. Three nights later, the 13th/14th, the OTU sent N2809 'H' (Flight Sergeant Gee), Z1109 'J' (Flight Sergeant Fryer) and DV948 'R' (Warrant Officer Cole) as its contributions to the raid on Bremen.

The final bombing attack by aircraft of the unit took place on the night of the 15th/16th and on this occasion only two machines, Z1109 'J' (Pilot Officer Richards) and DV948 'B' (Warrant Officer Gee) were engaged. Essen, in the Ruhr was the target but unfortunately, due to bad weather and haze, results of the raid were not good. This last bombing foray into enemy territory was the only one of the three when battle damage was sustained by unit aircraft; both Wellingtons encountered heavy flak and the navigator of Z1109, Pilot Officer Chitty, was wounded in the neck and hand.

At all wartime stations and in particular those housing training units, there were the inevitable accidents. Thankfully most were of a minor nature, but on occasions tragedy struck, resulting in loss of life. Many accidents in this category occurred during the course of one of the long cross-country flights or bombing exercises which were an essential part of the training programme but all too frequently they happened closer to home base.

The first incident of this nature to affect 28 OTU occurred on 7th October 1942, at 15:10 hours, when R1801 crashed at Woodhouse Eaves. Eyewitnesses reported that prior to the crash the engines appeared to give trouble and would-be rescuers at the scene were prevented from reaching the aircraft due to the intense heat and exploding ammunition. Warrant Officer Gee and all his crew perished; their remains were later recovered and interred at Burton on the Wolds on 11th October.

Leaflet dropping sorties, a part of every bomber OTU training itinerary, took place from Wymeswold for the first time towards the end of October. On this occasion only one aircraft took off on the night of 22nd/23rd and successfully distributed 20 packages of 'bumph' in the Lens-Bethune coal field area of France. In the ensuing months these 'Nickelling' operations over Occupied Europe multiplied and as the output of 28 OTU increased as many as 12 crews in the final phase of their training took part.

The unit inventory was boosted by further deliveries of Wellingtons during October; this enabled another flight, 'C' to be formed on the 31st. It was soon assimilated into the training programme, beginning to take an active part from 2nd November. This led to slight congestion but the situation was alleviated early in the new year with the opening of the satellite at Castle Donington on 1st January 1943, 'C' Flight leaving to take up residence there on the 2nd. They were joined there on the 7th by another flight from Finningley, Yorkshire, bringing 28 OTU up to a four flight unit. This enabled the split system of training to be adopted; conversion training was carried out at the satellite and operational training at the parent base.

'Careless talk costs lives' was the theme of many posters to be seen on service establishments during wartime. Likewise, postal censorship was another measure introduced to avoid service personnel unwittingly divulging information which might be of use to the enemy. A survey held early in 1943 illustrates that Wymeswold and satellite personnel were up to the mark as far as this aspect was concerned. Of the 824 letters examined only five contained minor breaches of security and of these none warranted disciplinary action, other than warnings and reproval.

Of the exercises so essential for adequate crew training, one staged on the night of 29th January 1943 proved to be disastrous as far as 28 OTU was concerned. Six Wellingtons took off safely but only four returned to base, the other two becoming shattered wrecks, R1583 at Longton, Stoke-on-Trent and R1011 in the Low Moors, Douston, Derbyshire area. In the first accident Sergeant Priest and Sergeant Butterley were killed and a further two crew members injured, while the crash of R1011 claimed the lives of Flying Officer Lane and two of his companions. After rescue the rest of the crew involved in this incident were taken to Ashton Hospital suffering from exposure. They had, up until this time, been the best crew in No. 7 Course.

Spring 1943 brought several interesting changes to Wymeswold. During March the long suffering Gunnery Flight received its first Miles Martinets to supplement the troublesome Lysanders; servicing problems with these had made it most difficult to maintain a schedule. On the 25th of the month the station was made responsible for the administration and control of the bombing ranges at Grandborough, Warwickshire, Mowsley, Leicestershire, a new one which was under construction for 28 OTU at Ragdale, Leicestershire, and another at Wardley, near Uppingham, Rutland, was also added to the inventory later.

From 12th to 19th April the airfield was declared unserviceable to enable the Drem system of runway and approach lighting to be installed. So that this situation interfered as little as possible with training routine, half of both 'A' and 'B' Flights of the OTU amalgamated to form a single flight, which then moved to Castle Donington and continued the programme from there. The day after they returned to Wymeswold, the new range at Ragdale was used for the first time, becoming fully operational on the 25th.

A new unit also took up residence on the base during April 1943; this was 1521 Blind Approach Training Flight (or BAT Flight) which arrived with its Airspeed Oxfords from Finningley, Yorkshire, on the 24th. The purpose of this unit was to teach pilots landing techniques using Standard Beam Approach equipment and after the Flight got down to business it often induced a weird sensation in onlookers to see one of the Oxfords loom out of the murk of a foggy day when nothing else was flying.

The need to complete the Drem System, by installing perimeter track lighting, meant that within six weeks of their return yet another movement order faced 'A' and 'B' Flights. This time they took up temporary residence at Ossington, Nottinghamshire, while work at Wymeswold was in progress. When the move took place on 1st June, to ensure the minimum loss of flying hours, an

An oft-repeated scene, aircrew posing against the background of their aircraft, in this case 28 OTU Wellington 'U-Uncle'. This was probably the only way they would be allowed a camera in the operational area to show the folks at home the 'office'. via Brandon White

Dakota IV KN380 'NU-U' of 1382 (T)CU at Wymeswold, 1947. via Dr Hugh Thomas

airlift was mounted to transport the ground support element.

This phase of the operation was carried out by 297 Squadron using their Armstrong Whitworth Whitleys and Airspeed Horsa gliders in tow; in this way sufficient maintenance personnel and a large quantity of equipment, including 150 bicycles, made the journey north in rapid time. Not only did this exercise in transport ensure speedy transit but it also provided a bonus in the form of valuable training for aircraft and glider pilots who were later destined to carry airborne troops into battle.

After a stay of almost three weeks the detachment returned home on 18th June.

By comparison with the preceding 14 months, Wymeswold then entered what might be termed a period of stability – if such a thing is possible in wartime. True, the usual accidents occurred involving the ageing Wellingtons, but no increase in frequency was noted. Monthly flying hours continued to mount, totals of 3,786 and 3,840 being logged for July and August of 1943 respectively. Life in general on the station functioned fairly smoothly, at least no major upsets are recorded.

One incident which did cause a stir happened on 23rd September when fire broke out in No.4 Hangar. The station fire crew were on the scene within three minutes and were joined by appliances of the National Fire Service from Loughborough, some 15 minutes later. Combined efforts by the two teams eventually extinguished the blaze, but not before it had destroyed Wellington Ic DV511.

During November the OTU began, at last, to dispose of its weary and battered Mk.Ics; replacements for them were still Wellingtons but of the improved Marks III and X. Transition to becoming fully equipped with these newer aircraft was a slow process and it was not until the end of April 1944 that the last Mk.Ic was finally disposed of. As 28 OTU progressively re-equipped so the unit accident rate showed a marked decline while aircraft serviceability improved considerably, monthly figures in the order of 73 to 83% being recorded over a six month period. New equipment was also added to the inventory of the Gunnery Flight when Hawker Hurricane IIcs began to replace the Martinets during May 1944.

That high standards were both set and achieved by 28 OTU is reflected in the fact that they were the first unit from any training group selected to use techniques and equipment pioneered by the Pathfinder Force. Their first demonstration in the use of these new target marking aids was held on Wardley Bombing Range on 11th June 1944, when a highly successful exercise in Target Indicator Marker dropping was carried out.

In June urgently needed runway repairs meant another station closure and the consequent movement order. On the 20th the OTU Flights flew north yet again but this time they were bound for Bircotes, Yorkshire, which was to be their base for over a month before they finally returned to Wymeswold on 31st July.

Since its opening in 1942 many aircraft had occasion to use the airfield when an emergency arose; battle damage, engine failure, enemy intruder activity and weather clamping down were just a few of the various reasons given. As operations by Bomber Command and the USAAF intensi-

fied during 1944, many aircraft returning from raids on the Continent found a temporary refuge at Wymeswold. To cope with these frequent influxes of visitors a special site was opened on the camp where they could obtain accommodation and a meal at any hour day or night. Even these facilities were stretched to the limit on 5th August when 28 Lancasters and one Halifax were diverted in. The Lancasters belonged to five different bases in Lincolnshire; by far the largest contingent of 18 aircraft came from 166 Squadron, Kirmington.

As the pattern of the war in Europe changed following the invasion, demand increased for trained crews to fly the ever-growing fleet of Transport Command aircraft engaged in the support of airborne operations, movement of freight and supplies for the liberating armies and later in maintaining communications along the many trunk routes opened up to the Middle and Far East. Wymeswold was one of the bases chosen to help meet this need.

Signals received on 1st October indicated that with effect from the 15th the station would be transferred to 44 Group, Transport Command and that 28 OTU would cease to operate. Accordingly, bomber crew training was tapered off, operations and control of the ranges at Ragdale and Wardley became the responsibility of RAF Bottesford and preparation of a new training syllabus had made significant progress by the transfer date.

On the 15th October 1944, 28 OTU was duly disbanded and in its place 108 (Transport) OTU was formed. The aircraft chosen to equip the new unit were Douglas Dakota twin-engined transports so consequently a great deal of reorganisation was necessary due to the American equipment involved. As on previous occasions at Wymeswold hard work prevailed and major problems caused by the transition had, or were, in the process of being solved by the time the first Dakota arrived on 19th October.

RAF Wymeswold – 1st December 1944

Latitude	52° 47' 38" N
Longitude	01° 07' 45" W
Height at Sea Level	272ft
Locality	3¾ miles ENE of Loughborough
Command	Transport (RAF)
Nearest Railway Station	Loughborough, LMS, LNER
Function	Operational Training Unit (Parent)
Affiliated Airfields	Castle Donington (Satellite)

Landing Area – Runways

QDM	Dimensions	Extensibility	Remarks
198°	1,250 x 50 yds	1,300 yds	Entails
254°	2,000 x 50 yds	2,000 yds	demolition in
312°	1,250 x 50 yds	1,400 yds	approaches
			of two houses and four huts.

Type of Surface – Tarmacadam.

Permanent Landmarks

By Day	Brush Electical Works, Loughborough
By Night	Town of Loughborough, 3½ miles south-west

Permanent Obstructions Woods

Facilities

Airfield Lightning	Mk.II
Beam Approach	–
Radio	–
QDM	–
Flying Control	Yes

Accommodation   All buildings temporary.

Technical	Hangars		Hardstandings	
	Type	No	Type	No
	T2	4	Hvy Bmbr	30
	B1	1		

Domestic	Officers	SNCOs	ORs	Total
RAF	190	520	1,226	1,936
WAAF	10	14	411	435

Although bomber training had ceased, the station had not seen the last of some crew members who had already passed through once. Many, now veterans of the bombing raids, reported for retraining; some after conversion to transport flying were then retrained as instructors in various categories while others were passed out for further squadron duty.

Conversion to flying Dakotas was carried out at Castle Donington after which proficient crews returned to Wymeswold to embark upon the second part of the course. This entailed long hours of day and night flying, intensive navigation practice and further ground instruction on subjects such as Staging Post procedure, stowage of freight in aircraft and the care of passengers. For this purpose part of the station was converted into a replica of one of the RAF's many Transport Command Staging Posts with crew briefing rooms, a passenger and freight section and transit mess.

It was December 1944 before 108 OTU had received a full complement of 40 Dakotas and although the 883 flying hours recorded for the month left something to be desired, an aircraft serviceability record of 82.7% illustrated that the unit was attaining some good results.

January 1945 was a bad month for the OTU in that two aircraft were lost and that they were the only two incidents involving aircrew fatalities recorded by the unit. The first accident occurred early in the month when KJ835 took off in a snowstorm, crashed and burned out near the railway line running between Barrow on Soar and Sileby; the three crew were all killed. Then on the 19th, KJ931 failed to return from a day cross-country exercise. Searches carried out located no wreckage, so, as part of the route lay over the Irish Sea it was presumed to have disappeared there leaving no trace.

Training commitments of some units eased following the end of the war in Europe. However, this did not apply at Wymeswold, trained transport crews being very much in demand in view of the continuing conflict in the Far East. To enable ground personnel to see at first hand the destruction inflicted by the RAF and USAAF daily flights over North West Germany and the Ruhr by two unit aircraft began in June. These trips or 'Ruhr Tours' as they were often called, proved extremely popular and a long waiting list was usually in evidence. Doubtless these jaunts helped in some measure to contribute to the month's total of 2,848 flying hours, a figure which no doubt found favour with Headquarters, 4 Group, Transport Command, as Wymeswold was transferred to them from 1st June.

On 10th August another change occurred when 108 (T)OTU was redesignated 1382 (Transport) Conversion Unit. Since October

1944 the OTU had been responsible for turning out over 200 crews, a weekly average of almost 600 flying hours was maintained and in the six months from February 1945 over 12,000 hours were flown without a single serious accident. As mentioned earlier August also saw the end of Group Captain Bell's tour of duty at Wymeswold and from 1st September, Group Captain E A Warfield OBE DFC, became the new Commanding Officer.

Along with over 90 other RAF establishments the station was open to the public on 15th September when open days were held to celebrate the fifth anniversary of the Battle of Britain. On this first occasion when visitors were allowed, approximately 8,000 passed through the gates to be treated to an insight into the life on an RAF camp. Displays of aircraft and ancillary equipment formed the main part of the entertainment which led to the sum of £62-16s-10d (£62.84p) being raised for the RAF Benevolent Fund. Six crews also took aircraft to Charmy Down, Halfpenny Green, Hemswell, Peterborough, South Cerney and Tilstock for the 'At Home' displays held at those stations.

In addition to the continental trips already undertaken, the (T)CU participated in other flights which enabled crews to gain practical experience of Transport Command operations. They assisted in the airlift of personnel and equipment from Dumfries, Scotland, to Aldergrove, Northern Ireland and for a time ran a shuttle service between Wymeswold and St Mawgan, Cornwall, often picking up freight from Filton en route.

On 20th October the long residence of 1521 BAT Flight came to an end when it departed to Longtown, Cumberland. Since 1st May 1944, when it was transferred to 33 Group, Flying Training Command, it had been classed only as a lodger unit on the station. Almost a year passed before the next major change occurred to affect Wymeswold; this time it was brought about by the closure of the satellite at Castle Donington in September 1946. As can be well imagined, this led to a great deal of reorganisation and progress in this direction was often hampered, mainly due to key personnel being posted, or demobllised.

Opposite page:
Seven Dakotas and a Lancaster are visible on this aerial survey photograph of Wymeswold, dated 27th August 1945. The control tower, signals square and airfield denominator 'WD' are at (A). The minor road running from Hoton to Wymeswold (B) was severed by the complex of dispersals built to the north of it (C). The minor road (D) runs from Wymeswold to Burton on the Wolds. DoE

Many changes affecting the aircraft serving with the (T)CU were also observed during the autumn of 1946. Following the end of the Lend-Lease Agreement with America, at least nine of the unit's Dakotas were flown north to 22 MU, Silloth, for eventual transfer back to the United States. Two, KG392 and KG589 were flown to Copenhagen on transfer by sale to Danish Airways and work began to remove the drab wartime finish from other aircraft. The time-spread of this latter operation was considerable in that it involved one aircraft at a time being flown to RAF Dishforth, Yorkshire. Then when it had undergone the decamouflaging process it was replaced by another unit aircraft and flown back to Wymeswold in a paint scheme more befitting peacetime operation.

Heavy snowfalls which began on 24th January heralded the start of the extremely severe winter of 1947. From that date until mid-March a flying programme was virtually non-existent. Repeated snowfalls made heavy demands on station manpower and machinery in their endeavours to keep roads and runways clear. Life within the camp became very hard. When the thaw finally came it revealed that the continual hard frosts and snow had had a detrimental effect on both runway and perimeter track surfaces; in many instances large patches had lifted and broken up. With the coming of spring, a great deal of time was spent making good the ravages of winter and although most of the urgent repairs had been completed by the end of May work continued well into the autumn with contractors carrying out complete runway resurfacing and other major operations on the airfield. Throughout this period flying continued though at times was somewhat restricted, especially when work on runways was in progress. In spite of these problems the training schedule was maintained.

On 20th September 1947 the station held its second 'At Home' day. The pattern followed was much the same as before but this time the programme was marred when a visiting de Havilland Mosquito crashed during the flying display.

The end of an era came to Wymeswold in December 1947 when, after almost six years of operation the station was closed down. No.1382 (T)CU moved out to North Luffenham (Chapter Seventeen) and the station was put on to a care and maintenance footing. While being held on this basis it was transferred on 5th January 1948, from 4 to 38 Group, Transport Command. Then nine months later, on 30th September, the airfield became a part of 64 Group, Reserve Command. This transfer brought about a change of fortune for the station and in February 1949 it was upgraded to active status once more.

From 3rd April 1949 this new lease of life became a reality and Wymeswold housed a fighter squadron for the first time when the Supermarine Spitfire F.22s of 504 Squadron, (County of Nottingham) Royal Auxiliary Air Force, flew in from Hucknall, Nottinghamshire. The Spitfires remained part of the local scene until October when 504 became the first Auxiliary squadron to be equipped with the Gloster Meteor F.4 twin-engined jet fighter. With a fighter squadron in residence it was logical that the station should be part of Fighter Command; this duly came to pass with a transfer to 12 Group on 1st April 1950.

Although the auxiliary units were often referred to, perhaps a little disparagingly, as 'weekend flyers' this expression detracts in no way from their acknowledged professionalism and in this respect 504's record was second to none. During the Second World War they led a distinguished career which resulted in no fewer than eight Battle Honours being earned by the squadron.

While at Wymeswold the unit enhanced this reputation by the results achieved in major air exercises and at annual summer camps. In July 1951, 504 Squadron was mobilised for three months continuous service, during which time they acquitted themselves creditably, proving that their training was thorough and that they could, without delay, take their place and hold their own alongside the first-line squadrons of Fighter Command. In March 1952 the squadron traded in its Meteor F.4s and received the improved F.8 version as replacements.

Illustrations of 504's Spitfire F.22s are rare. Publicity view of an example being serviced at Wymeswold.

Flight Lieutenant Whitehouse, Air Vice-Marshal Atcherley and Squadron Leader Beardsall during an AOC's inspection. One of 504 Squadron's Harvard IIs in the background.

Informal gathering around the Under Secretary of State for Air, Aiden Crawley, on his visit to Wymeswold at the time of 504 Squadron's three months mobilisation period in 1951.
All via Sid Ellis

Also at this time major alterations were carried out to the Wymeswold runway system to bring it into line with a pattern adopted at other RAF stations. Large concrete areas known as Operational Readiness Platforms (ORPs) together with taxi track extensions were added at either end of the main 08/26 runway and on the technical site, in front of No. 2 and No. 3 Hangars an even larger mass of concrete was laid to form an Aircraft Servicing Platform (ASP).

A further auxiliary unit was added to the Wymeswold inventory in July 1954; it was 1969 (AOP) Flight, equipped with Rearsby-produced Auster AOP.6s. This unit, which had been forced to move due to the closure of Desford, was one of the four flights which constituted 664 (Air Observation Post) Squadron. Although these flights were used on occasions to carry out reconnaissance and photographic sorties, their main role was to observe the effectiveness of artillery fire and for this reason the aircraft were flown by Royal Artillery officers. Maintenance was carried out by regular RAF ground staff but the remainder of the personnel were either members of the Territorial Army or Royal Auxiliary Air Force.

In 1952 a Supermarine Attacker from the Rolls-Royce test-fleet at Hucknall, Nottinghamshire, spent several weeks operating from Wymeswold, as Hucknall's grass runway was deemed to be totally unsuitable for the tail-sitter jet. Between January 1955 and February 1956, the whole R-R test fleet was evacuated to Wymeswold, while a permanent runway was constructed at Hucknall. During this period English Electric Canberras and Hawker Hunters were frequently to be seen engaged in development flying in connection with the company's Avon series of turbojet engines, as were two Avro Ashtons, modified to carry test engines beneath the fuselage. First to arrive was Mk.3 WE670 which carried out air intake icing trials on the Avon RA14; the second, Mk.2 WB491, from November 1955 was the first flying test-bed involved in the R-R Conway engine development programme. (See Chapter Two for an illustration of an Ashton.)

For varying periods of time, during 1955 and 1956, the station became home to three regular first-line RAF units. No.56 Squadron became the first of these when it arrived from Waterbeach, Cambridgeshire, early in June 1955. Urgent runway repairs were the cause of the move. At this time the unit was in the throes of re-equipping with Hawker Hunters after spending a traumatic year operating the ill-fated Supermarine Swift F.1 and F.2 jet fighters. Led by their acting Commanding Officer, Captain Gillespie, USAF, the unit brought with them 12 Hunter F.5s, four Meteor F.8s and one Meteor T.7. The Meteor F.8s were kept on strength at Wymeswold while Hunter the conversion

Meteor F.8 WH310 'J' of 504 Squadron in the Wymeswold circuit, May 1954. E Belcher

Part of the Rolls-Royce test fleet, Canberra B.2 WD959 with Avon engines and reheat units on trials work for the English Electric Lightning, while on 'detachment' at Wymeswold in 1955. Rolls-Royce via Peter Green

continued but by the end of the month they were no longer required and returned to Waterbeach. Squadron personnel found that accommodation and living standards at Wymeswold were higher than anticipated and the unit as a whole was well satisfied. This is reflected in the fact that bar profits for the period of their stay so far exceeded normal that the mess gave a party for the unit on 9th July.

The number of Hunter F.5s on squadron strength increased to 16 during the detachment and on 16th July 1955, the day of the unit's departure, eleven of these carried out a flypast of Wymeswold before returning to Waterbeach. As the remaining five aircraft subsequently became serviceable they too left to join the rest of the squadron.

Refurbishing of the runway system was again the reason why 257 and 263 Squadrons had to vacate their base at Wattisham, Suffolk and take up temporary residence at Wymeswold. They too were equipped with

Hawker Hunter F.2 and F.5s and following their arrival on 11th June 1956, flying activity in the vicinity increased considerably. To help minimise the effect of this on local residents the circuit pattern was altered to prevent aircraft flying low over the villages of Wymeswold and Hoton. In spite of these and other precautions complaints were still voiced from time to time regarding noise levels. Apart from these moments of minor discord both squadrons appear to have fitted in well with the local community and station life in general during their stay.

During the 1950s airshows in support of the RAF charities were a regular feature at Wymeswold, the main beneficiaries from these events being the RAF Benevolent Fund and the RAF Association. These displays brought many different types of aircraft, both service and civilian, to the airfield to take part and the last 'At Home' held at the station on 15th September 1956, was no exception. Over 75,000 people flocked to the event and in spite of adverse weather conditions they were treated to a ground exhibition of the highest standard and a 34 item flying programme which varied from demonstrations by individual aircraft such as the Rolls-Royce engine test-beds, the Tyne-fitted Avro Lincoln and a Hunter fitted with thrust reversers to a formation flypast by the combined Hunters and Meteors of 257, 263, 504 and 616 Squadrons.

Brand new Hunter F.5s, including WP102 – built at Bitteswell – with 56 Squadron during their detachment to Wymeswold. In the far corner of the hangar lurks VW995, a 664 Squadron Auster AOP.6. N Franklin

Wymeswold's control tower, shown here in happier times, with its complement of control staff apparently busy. A P Jarram

When the Hunter squadrons returned to Wattisham in January 1957, it was the beginning of the end for Wymeswold as an operational station, for in the same month it was announced that the Auxiliary Squadrons were to be disbanded. But one more memorable event took place at Wymeswold before this was to happen to 504 Squadron. On the afternoon of Sunday, 3rd March 1957 the airfield was the venue for the consecration and presentation of the squadron standard. The reviewing officer on this occasion was Air Chief Marshal Sir Francis J Fogarty, the Air Member for Personnel.

After the ceremonies at the airfield were over, the new standard was laid up in St Mary's Parish Church, Wymeswold, where it still remains.

RCAF Silver Star Mk.3 (a Rolls-Royce Nene-powered version of the Lockheed T-33A, built by Canadair) awaiting attention by Fields, in May 1960. D M Sargent collection

RCAF Canadair Sabre Mk.6 23639 sits on the Aircraft Servicing Platform at Wymeswold, awaiting a test flight, on 30th April 1960. The tail insignia and 'IG' code suggests its previous operator was 439 Squadron. Chris Salter

A USAF Douglas SC-54 in front of No.5 Hangar at Wymeswold (the only 'B1' type) with another C-54 poking its nose out of the doors. The tail number of the former appears to be 0-50637, in which case it would have been 45-637, an SC-54G. The official US service name for the SC-54 was Rescuemaster, but they were referred to as 'Searchmasters' by some UK enthusiasts. Brandon White

Typical of the exotic overhauls is this Ghana Airways Dakota, 9G-AAE, seen here clearing customs at Elmdon, 23rd August 1960, after an overhaul at Wymeswold. Neil Lewis

It was a sad day a week later when, after almost 30 years service, 504 Squadron was disbanded with the same fate befalling 1969 Flight, 664 (AOP) Squadron. Shortly afterwards the airfield was reduced to care and maintenance status.

From early 1958 Field Aircraft Services, a specialist organisation in the overhaul, maintenance and modification of aircraft who had previously operated a base at Tollerton, Nottinghamshire, began to use the airfield facilities in order to fulfil contracts involving large numbers of military aircraft. Canadair Sabre jet fighters, Silver Star jet trainers and Avro (Canada) CF-100 Canuck all-weather jet fighters belonging to units of the Royal Canadian Air Force serving in Europe with the North Atlantic Treaty Organisation, formed the bulk of this work but other contracts resulted in United States Air Force Douglas SC-54D Rescuemasters and United States Navy Douglas R5D-1 Skymasters being added to the programme.

Towards the end of 1962 when the military contracts began to tail off work on civilian owned aircraft increased, many of these belonged to overseas airlines, companies and governments and many aircraft wearing exotic liveries passed through Wymeswold. Although not an active RAF station throughout most of Field's tenure, the airfield was still classed as a satellite of RAF Syerston, Nottinghamshire, and as such was often used by the Percival Provosts and later Jet Provosts of 2 Flying Training School for quiet circuit training and many a first solo flight.

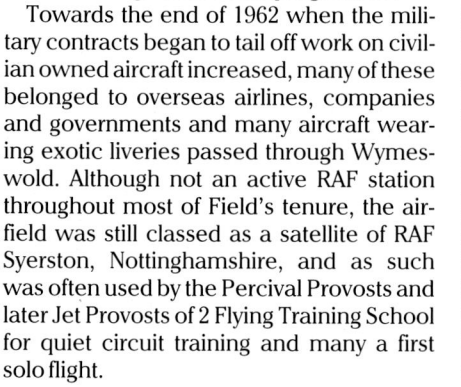

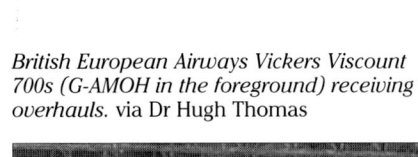

Another example of the exotica that passed through the Field hangars at Wymeswold in the early 1960s was this Canadian civilian Lockheed Hudson, CF-CRJ, in the livery of Kenting Aviation Limited. It was noted on several occasions between January 1963 and February 1964, usually in company with a Miles Marathon, CF-NUH. Chris Salter

British European Airways Vickers Viscount 700s (G-AMOH in the foreground) receiving overhauls. via Dr Hugh Thomas

The end for Wymeswold as an active airfield came with Field's decision to transfer operations to the newly-opened East Midlands Airport at Castle Donington. By April 1969 only three aircraft remained on the airfield; in due course these also left and with their departure came the end of an era.

RAF aircraft did make a brief return from 18th-20th May 1970 when six Hawker Siddeley Harrier GR.1s of 1 Squadron, Wittering, Northamptonshire, used a small section of the airfield during field mobility and deployment exercises. The Harriers were not the only new VTOL craft to grace Wymeswold in 1970. The sole Penn-Smith Gyroplane, G-AXOM, arrived for test-flying in the middle of the year, albeit with an initial restriction to a 5-mile radius of the airfield. Its Permit to Fly expired 24th February 1971 and today it is on display at Stondon Transport Museum and Garden Centre, Bedfordshire.

In the early 1970s, articles appeared in the local papers hinting that the Army was interested in the base as a possible camp and training area to replace one at Ollerton, Nottinghamshire, which was to be vacated due to lease expiry. These rumours failed to materialise so many of Wymeswold's acres continued to be used for agriculture and the buildings for light industry.

Attention was again focused on the airfield in late 1980 after planning applications were made by the Natural Environment Research Council to sink test bores on the site in order to assess whether the geological structure of the area was suitable for underground storage of nuclear waste. Not unnaturally, a storm of protest greeted these proposals and in due course Charnwood Borough Council rejected the application.

This rejection led in turn to a public inquiry during November and December 1981, the results of which were expected to be announced after some months. A surprise Government decision to scrap all test drilling studies and instead store the waste on surface sites, was announced on 17th December 1981.

The next episode to concern Wymeswold began early in 1986 when it was announced that by order of the Secretary of State for Defence, 392 acres were to be sold by auction. Much of the land on which the former technical site stood was not included. Although the sale was arranged and due to take place at the King's Head Hotel, Loughborough, on 17th February, ten days prior to the date set the auctioneers, Warner, Sheppard & Wade, gave notice that the property had been withdrawn.

The official description of Wymeswold's control tower is 'Watch Office with Meteorological Section, Type 518/40'. This photograph was taken in the early 1980s, since when it has deteriorated a great deal further. Author

A further development concerning the airfield came in October 1986 when a consortium led by Costain Homes submitted an application to Charnwood Borough Council to build a new community of 3,000 homes on 420 acres. The proposal found little favour with the residents of villages in the surrounding area and led to a great deal of opposition. Eventually a public enquiry was held into the matter and in March 1990 a ruling was given against the plans by the then Environment Secretary, Chris Patten. Shortly afterwards Costain Homes lodged an appeal only to withdraw it in October in order to submit revised plans. These are still awaited.

Since the short and noisy interlude in 1970, flying from the airfield was limited to an occasional visit by agricultural aircraft engaged in crop spraying in the area. More recently there was a slight resurgence of flying during the autumn of 1995 when East-West Aviation began to use the airfield for the maintenance of their small fleet of Ukrainian registered aircraft. The episode was short lived and by the end of the year the company, together with its Czech-built LET L-410 twin-turboprop and Polish-built (but Soviet-designed) Antonov An-2 single-engined transport biplane had departed.

Most of the airfield's arable acres are still extensively farmed. In the past the runways and perimeter track, which are still in quite good condition have been used for leisure activities such as model aircraft flying, parascending and land yachting. At present some areas are used for the tuition of various types of motor sport. All of the former RAF buildings which still stand on the consortium's land, including the control tower, have fallen into disrepair and are now derelict.

As for the Technical Site, this has now been fenced off from the airfield and has become Wymeswold Industrial Park. Here many of the original buildings survive and are currently being used for a wide variety of purposes. Unfortunately only three of the airfield's five hangars are still in use. Of the other two, No.3 a 'T2' was destroyed in a spectacular fire on 7th August 1989 and No.5, the only 'B1', met a similar fate on 5th May 1996. Both were being used for waste paper storage.

Off the airfield, on the Six Hills side, was a detached site known as 'The Cliff' which once housed the station's Training Wing. This is now occupied by the Bussman Division of Cooper (UK) Limited, an American

company. Although this site was remodelled to some extent by previous occupants many of the original buildings remain within the complex. Although some have been modified to serve purposes far removed from their original concept, most are still recognisable. They include buildings for turret instruction, gunnery and crew procedure, the AML Bombing Teacher, flight office and crew rooms and pilot's rest room, locker and drying rooms.

All the domestic sites associated with the station were situated close to and to the south of the village of Burton on the Wolds. Although most of these have now disappeared, a scattering of Stanton air raid shelters still to be seen in several fields show that they were once part of airfield life.

The former station sick quarters retains a great proportion of its buildings and is used for farming purposes. On the main communal site, purpose-built chicken houses occupy much of the land, but interesting wartime buildings still remain, including the main dining hall, post office and gymnasium.

For the present, mainly rural activity prevails in the area but only time will tell what the future holds in store for the former RAF Station, Wymeswold.

Wymeswold from the air, looking west, in September 1997. Several new buildings can be seen on the former technical site, now an industrial estate. The main runway still looks good, but this is probably deceptive. Author

Well laid out direction boards at the main entrance showing the extent of the Field Aircraft Services site in the early 1960s (left) and (right) what had become Wymeswold Industrial Park, in 1999. P Henson / Author

Once a dining hall, now a part of a chicken farm. One of several distinctive buildings on the Communal Site close to Burton on the Wolds, summer 1997. Author

Viewed from the tower, the large expanse of the Aircraft Servicing Platform (ASP) is evident from the size of the Viscount parked at the far end. A P Jarram

Wymeswold-based Units and Aircraft

No.28 Operational Training Unit
From 16.5.42 to 15.10.44   Codes 'LB-', 'QN-', 'WY-'
Vickers Wellington Ic   L7797, L7806, N2735, N2737,
N2751, N2764, N2809, N2856, N2938, R1011, R1086, R1157,
R1169, R1183, R1216, R1223, R1224, R1236, R1269, R1282,
R1324, R1458, R1514, R1521, R1532, R1538, R1605, R1645,
R1651, R1666, R1697, R1700, R1711, R1727, R1766, R1774,
R1781, R1786, R1801, R3161, R3166*, R3275, R3277, T2468,
T2544, T2579, T2808, T2896, T2920, T2922, T2994. X9603,
X9631, X9632, X9638, X9644, X9658, X9683, X9754, X9697,
X9797, X9800, X9883, X9924, X9925, X9936, X9941, Z1049,
Z1067, Z1085, Z1107, Z1109, Z1114, Z1149, Z1162, Z1169,
Z1173, DV444, DV455, DV456, DV511, DV518, DV572, DV599,
DV613, DV672, DV714, DV731, DV771, DV805, DV824, DV846,
DV866, DV871, DV895 DV940, DV948, DV950, HD981.
*R3166 was used as synthetic trainer by 28 OTU.
Vickers Wellington III   X3927, BJ794, BJ884, BJ885, BJ906,
BJ907, BK153, BK256, BK295, BK297, BK428, DF641, HF802.
Vickers Wellington X   HE417, HE198, HE234, HE284, HE417,
HE687, HE738, HF495, HZ532, HZ533, JA466, JA480, JA500,
LN169, LN608, LN610, LN617, LN636, LN690, LN698, LN738,
LN778, LN801, LN877, LN894, LN896, LN909, LN910, LN932,
LN936, LN951, LN952, LN953, LN987, LN989, LP149, LP152,
LP293, LP296, LP332, LP342, LP386, LP397, LP406, LP431,
LP520, LP613, LP849, LP863, ME881, ME951, ME976, MF200,
MF400, MF426, MF440, MF441, MF519, MF537, MF588, MF647,
MF648, MF649, MF686, MF687, MS490, NC444, NC445, NC446,
NC447, NC448, NC473, NC474, NC617, NC627.
De Havilland Moth Minor   AW151 (G-AFMZ).
Westland Lysander III   R9123, T1650, V9861.
Miles Martinet I   EM566, HP374, HP437, HP438,
HP439, JN598.
Miles Master II   DM427.
Hawker Hurricane II   LF313, LF360, LF758, PG439,
PG531, PG533, PG535.
Avro Anson I   DG830.
Avro Tutor   K3277.
Boulton Paul Defiant I   N1685.

No.1521 Blind Approach Training Flight
From 23.4.43 to 10.8.45   Code 'J6-'
Airspeed Oxford I   R6318, V4192, AT685, AT727,
AT764, AT784, AT787, AT791, DF235, DF405, DF414, DF464,
DF466, DF467, HN426, HN590, LB415, LB462, LB490, NM711.

No.108 (Transport) Operational Training Unit
From 10.10.44 to 10.8.45   No code letters.

No.1382 (Transport) Conversion Unit
From 10.8.45 to 10.12.47   Code 'NU-'
Douglas Dakota III and IV   FD789, FD864, FD904, FD939,
FL586 'B', FL596 'C', FL614, FL631, FL635, FZ628, FZ646, KG392,
KG514, KG561, KG567 'H', KG588 'E', KG589, KG594 'G', KG607,
KG611 'L', KG613 'F', KG628 'K', KG631 'S', KG636 'J', KG650,
KG655, KG663, KG667 'U', KG778, KJ806, KJ835, KJ839,
KG861, KJ863, KJ864, KJ865, KJ866, KJ872, KJ873, KJ874,
KJ875, KJ877, KJ881, KJ882, KJ907, KJ910, KJ911, KJ912,
KJ931, KJ934, KJ972, KJ973, KJ983, KK147, KK197, KN354,
KN355, KN380, KN408, KN431, KN438, KN449, KN488, KN494,
KN528, KN607, KN673, KP248, KP251, KP276, TS433, TS435.
Miles Magister I   L8359.

Station Flight   Code 'K8-'
Airspeed Oxford I   DF405 (20.06.45 to 03.08.45)
HN426 (6.45 to ?; 2.47 to ?)

No.504 Squadron
From 2.4.49 to 10.3.57   Codes 'TM-', 'RAD-'
Supermarine Spitfire F.22   PK328 'D', PK399 'C', PK435 'S',
PK495 'A', PK506 'W', PK595 'H', PK606 'G', PK621 'T',
PK671 'E'. Mk.XVI TE384 (7207M) allotted as instructional
airframe, August 1955.

Nth American Harvard T.2B   KF155, KF579, KF754, KF925 'Z',
FT457.
Gloster Meteor F.4   VT145, VT169, VT216, VT232, VT327,
VT334, VT345. VW272, VW274 'F'. VZ401, VZ403, VZ404, VZ406.
Gloster Meteor T.7   WA610 'M', WA615, WF845, WL475.
Gloster Meteor F.8   WA784 'T', WE873 'R', WF682 'C',
WF688, WH255 'E', WH257 'D', WH262 'R', WH282 'K',
WH307 'G', WH310 'J', WH318 'L', WH344 'B', WH454 'A',
WH464 'F', WH500, WH504 'U', WH511.

No.1969 Flight and No.664 (AOP) Squadron
From 15.7.54 to 10.3.57   Codes 'ROD-'
Auster AOP.6 and T.7   VW995 'O'.

Rolls-Royce Engine Trials Aircraft
Supermarine Attacker   . . . . . (1952)
Detachment from Hucknall   c. 1.55 to 2.56
Avro Ashton   WB491 Mk.2, WE670 Mk.3.
EE Canberra B.2   WD959.
Hawker Hunter F.1   WT565.
Hawker Hunter F.6   XF373.

No.56 Squadron
Detachment, from 5.6.55 to 16.7.55
Hawker Hunter F.5   WP102, WP106 'F', WP149 'H'.

No.257 Squadron
Detachment, from 10.6.56 to 15.1.57
De Havilland Vampire T.11   XE924.
Hawker Hunter F.2, F.5   WN914 'V'.

No.263 Squadron
Detachment, from 10.6.56 to 15.1.57
Hawker Hunter F.2, F.5   ?

Station Flight
Avro Anson T.21   WJ557 (15.6.56 to 21.08.56).
De Havilland Chipmunk T.10 WK642.

No.1 Squadron, RAF   From 18.5.70 to 20.5.70
Forward Operating Location evaluation exercise (6 aircraft)
Hawker Siddeley Harrier GR.1   ?

East-West Aviation   From c. 9.95 to 12.95
Let 410   UR-67519.
Antonov An-2   UR-70363.

Serious Accidents to Wymeswold-based Aircraft

13.9.42 Moth Minor AW151 (G-AFMZ) 28 OTU
Aircraft only arrived at Wymeswold 6.9.42. After crash there
taken to DH for repair but struck off charge instead.

7.10.42 Wellington R1801   28 OTU
Crashed at 15:10 hours at Woodhouse Eaves. W/O Gee and
crew all killed.

25.10.42 Wellington DV805 28 OTU
Crashed near Linton-on-Ouse while coming in to land after
engines had cut at 10,000ft. No major injuries.

28.11.42 Wellington Ic R1786 28 OTU
Undercarriage collapsed on landing at Wymeswold. Aircraft
caught fire and was burnt out. No injuries.

28.11.42 Wellington Ic X9941 28 OTU
Crashed at Hoton after hitting trees on take-off and was burnt
out. Sergeant Jamieson killed, remainder of crew injured, one
died later.

6.12.42 Wellington Ic R1223 28 OTU
Crashed and burnt out half mile outh-west of Hoton, 19:40 hrs.
Cause unknown. Sergeant Millard killed, Sergeant Loyd died
later from burns, Flight Sergeant Williams and Sergeant Page
slight injuries.

11.12.42 Wellington Ic T2896 28 OTU
23:00 hours, hit trees and crashed in bad visibility. Warrant
Officer Loughhead, 1st pilot seriously injured - extensive burns,
died later.

29.1.43 Wellington Ic R1538 28 OTU
While on 'Bullseye' exercise crashed at Cellarhead, near Stoke-
on-Trent. Two killed, one injured.

29.1.43 Wellington Ic R1011 28 OTU
Crashed on high ground in the Low Moors, Donston,
Derbyshire, area. Two killed.

15.2.43 Wellington Ic N2809 28 OTU
Flew into high ground in snowstorm and crashed at Hermitage
Farm, near Whitwick. Aircraft completely destroyed, and all
crew killed.

5.3.43 Wellington Ic Z1109 28 OTU
Ops 'Nickel'. Aircraft crashed into sea off Vlissingen after being
hit by flak. Most of crew baled out, two dead, three PoWs.

13.5.43 Wellington Ic DV714 28 OTU
Crashed and burnt out at Wymeswold.

22.5.43 Wellington Ic R1216 28 OTU
Caught fire while running up at Wymeswold.

31.5.43 Wellington Ic R1282 28 OTU
Crashed on take-off from Harwell.

3.6.43 Wellington Ic DV613 28 OTU
Developed engine trouble when returning from 'Nickel' raid on
Paris. Ditched 35 miles south-south-east, St Catherines Point.
Five of crew picked up by Air Sea Rescue Service.

12.6.43 Wellington Ic R1324 28 OTU
Failed to return after helping ASR in search for missing aircraft
in North Sea. No survivors.

17.7.43 (?) Wellington X LP406 (?) 28 OTU
Dived into ground, Ragdale bombing range.

19.7.43 Wellington Ic DV455 28 OTU
Crashed in Anglesey after crew baled out. One killed due to
falling out of parachute harness.

2.8.43 Wellington Ic Z1107 28 OTU
Abandoned while on fire, Breedon on the Hill, Leics.

7.8.43 Wellington Ic X9638 28 OTU
Crashed after take-off from Castle Donington. Five crew killed.

11.8.43 Wellington Ic DV731 28 OTU
Hit by flak while 'Nickel'-ing over France. Ditched off Shoreham,
Sussex. Two crew rescued by ASR launch, rest lost.

17.8.43 Wellington Ic X9883 28 OTU
Caught fire on ground at Castle Donington.

2.9.43 Wellington Ic Z8870 28 OTU
Crashed. No further details. Originally believed repairable, but
later struck off charge.

23.9.43 Wellington Ic DV511 28 OTU
Destroyed in hangar fire at Wymeswold.

2.9.43 Wellington Ic Z8870 28 OTU
Crashed and burnt out, Anglezarke Moor, 3 miles North of
Horwich, Lancs. Six killed..

25.11.43 Wellington Ic DV771 28 OTU
Crashed at Wymeswold on return from cross-country exercise.
Six killed, only survivor died later in Loughborough hospital.

1.1.44 Wellington Ic R1086 28 OTU
Crashed near Southwick, Hants, after engine fire.

4.1.44 Wellington Ic X9754 28 OTU
Caught fire starting up at Warmwell.

3.2.44 Wellington Ic Z1114 'T' 28 OTU
'C' Flight, Castle Donington crashed. All crew killed.

24.2.44 Wellington Ic R1269 28 OTU
Crashed on overshoot at Castle Donington.

1.3.44 Wellington 1c DV 948 28 OTU
Both engines cut, crash landed at Cranfield, Beds.

16.3.44 Wellington 1c R1183 28 OTU
Crashed on take-off from Castle Donington.

25.3.44 Wellington 1c X9644 28 OTU
Crashed on take-off, Castle Donington.

26.3.44 Wellington 1c T2922 28 OTU
Lost on this date. No further details.

26.3.44 Wellington 1c N2737 28 OTU
Caught fire on ground at Wymeswold.

1.4.44 Wellington 1c DV444 Belly-landed at Wymeswold
after engine cut.

14.4.44 Oxford I LB415 1521 BATF
Crashed after colliding with Lancaster W4103 of 5 LFS, 1½ miles
south of Syerston, Notts., at 16:30 hours. Pupil killed, pilot died
later of multiple injuries.

19.4.44 Wellington X MF200 28 OTU
Crashed Normanton on Soar, while on solo circuit and landing.
Crew of four all killed. Five crew evaded capture.

21.4.44 Wellington X LN896 28 OTU
Missing from 'Nickel' Op over Northern France. Five crew
evaded capture, but sixth died whilst doing so.

10.5.44 Wellington X HE738 28 OTU
Engine cut and forced landed 12 miles east, Ponterwyd,
Aberystwyth.

13.5.44 Wellington X HE198 28 OTU
Abandoned take-off, undercarriage raised to stop, hit hedge
and destroyed by fire, Castle Donington.

13.6.44 Wellington X LP397 28 OTU
While on a cross country exercise, aircraft dived into ground
out of cloud and crashed at Mayfield, near Ashbourne, Derbys.
Crew of six killed.

18.6.44 Wellington X MF537 28 OTU
Overshot landing at Penrhos, raised undercarriage to stop, hit
hut and destroyed by fire.

24.6.44 Wellington X LN698 28 OTU
Overshot landing at Bircotes and damaged beyond repair.

16.7.44 Wellington ? ..... 28 OTU
Aircraft from Castle Donington crashed near Ragdale bombing
range killing all crew.

18.7.44 Wellington X LP296 28 OTU
Overshot landing, swung and undercarriage collapsed,
Bircotes.

9.8.44 Hurricane IIc LF313 28 OTU
When taking off from Peterborough engine failed, aircraft belly
landed and damaged beyond repair.

13.8.44 Wellington X LN987 28 OTU
Damaged beyond repair in accident.

10.1.45 Dakota IV KJ835 108 OTU
Took off in snowstorm, crashed and burned out near railway
line between Barrow on Soar and Sileby. Crew of three killed.

28.2.45 Dakota IV KJ806 108 OTU
Overshot landing at Castle Donington.

14.8.45 Dakota III KG611 108 OTU
Overshot landing and tipped up at Castle Donington.

19.1.45 Dakota IV KJ931 108 OTU
Failed to return from cross country exercise, believed to have
flown into the Irish Sea.

17.4.46 Dakota III KG594 108 OTU
Crashed on practice single-engined overshoot two miles south-
east of Wymeswold.

21.4.50 Meteor F.4 VT345 504 Squadron
Undershot landing at Wymeswold. Undercarriage torn off.

9.8.50 Meteor F.4 VT216 504 Squadron
Ran out of fuel and ditched 18 miles east of Spurn Head.

18.3.51 Meteor F.4 VZ404 504 Squadron
Dived into ground near Desford. Pilot killed.

10.5.51 Harvard KF 925 504 Squadron
Engine cut on approach to disused airfield at Breighton while
making emergency landing following an electrical fire.

7.7.51 Meteor F.4 EE584 504 Squadron
Engine failed on approach, dived into ground and pilot killed.

7.11.52 Meteor T.7 WF823 (?) 'N' 504 Squadron
Canopy became detached in flight and jammed. Aircraft
crashed into hillside in Grimsthorpe Park, near Little Bytham
and blew up. Both occupants killed.

1.1.56 Meteor F.8 WE873 'R' 504 Squadron
Abandoned in spin and crashed at 15:40 hours three miles
north-west of Mildenhall.

*The parachute store showing 26 years of
difference. Vivid proof that there is still plenty
of use left in wartime RAF buildings.* Author

Appendix A

Blaby Wharf – No.65 Maintenance Unit

The sole surviving blister hangar, near the entrance to the site of the former 65 MU, at Blaby Wharf. Author

WITHIN the United Kingdom during the Second World War thousands of aircraft, both Allied and enemy, were damaged or destroyed, either in action or by accident. To deal with these wrecks units were established at various locations. One such unit was 65 Maintenance Unit (Salvage Sub Site), Blaby Wharf, situated on Wharf Way off the A426 Blaby to Leicester road.

When first inspected on 12th November 1940, the site housed the premises of Fred Edlin Limited, transport contractors. Its central location was considered suitable, so requisition took place and the MU was established, officially opening on 21st November and parented to 58 MU, Newark. The unit was at this time operated under contract by Aircraft Travel and Transport Limited but commanded by an RAF officer with a nucleus of staff.

By 28th November the MU was in business and salvaged aircraft began to arrive. The first two to be dealt with were Avro Anson I N9858, of 10 Flying Training School, Ternhill, which had crashed in bad visibility on Wild Boar Clough, near Macclesfield on the 14th November and Westland Lysander I L4788 of 7 Anti Aircraft Co-operation Unit,

Castle Bromwich, which came to grief in a forced landing at Seven Lanes Farm, Castle Bromwich on the 21st.

While it was in existence salvage gangs despatched from the MU travelled far and wide across the Midlands with an occasional foray further afield. Following inspection to determine the degree of damage which an aircraft had suffered it would be categorised as repairable on site, in need of more drastic attention and transported to an appropriate location or fit for salvage only. If the latter were the case then the aircraft or its remains finished up at Blaby where it was eventually stripped of all reusable components before being reduced to scrap metal.

For some time the MU made use of the existing buildings on the site, even some pigsties were cleared of their inhabitants and made use of as stores. But, by the time the unit became service manned on 21st March 1942 the process of expansion had begun. In the course of the next year many more buildings appeared. Most were of a very temporary nature and a great deal of use was made of redundant aircraft packing cases. Over 30 of these useful items

were eventually converted and impressed into use, mainly as offices and stores. There was also a considerable amount of brick construction but even much of this was classified as temporary. The largest buildings erected were two blister hangars to house salvage equipment. Staff at this time was 15 officers, 49 WAAFs and 388 airmen.

Many of the crashes with which the unit became involved often presented their own particular problems. Two incidents which occurred during 1944 serve to illustrate some of the diverse situations faced by the salvage crews. On 22nd March, a Wellington Ic, HD987 of 105 Operational Training Unit, Nuneaton, suffered engine failure and crashed in Mill Lane, Digbeth at 22:30 hours. When the team from the MU arrived to assess the situation they found the wreckage of the fuselage embedded in the roof of a garage while the wings, engines and other parts were buried by debris or lay amongst the remains of a machine shop which had been gutted by fire. The task of recovery was made doubly difficult by the precarious state of the damaged buildings and the presence of fuel remaining in some of the aircraft's tanks. To aid the process of salvage, walls had to be further demolished or shored up and a tangle of girder work removed. By painstaking and sometimes precarious work over several days, the pieces of HD987 were gradually removed and with the job complete the crew was able to report back to Blaby on the 27th.

The second incident was in an entirely different type of location and dissimilar in most other aspects. It involved the recovery of the remains of two Boeing B-17 Flying Fortresses, 42-3510, of the 337th Bomb Squadron and 42-31053, of the 338th BS, both of the 96th Bomb Group, Snetterton Heath, Norfolk. These unfortunate bombers had crashed near Blakesley, Northants, following a mid-air collision on 11th October 1944 while on a practice formation flight. Salvage of the first B-17 commenced on 15th October and after four days recovery was complete. The next aircraft presented a more complex problem as its remains were so widely scattered. In order to retrieve all the wreckage a search was made of over 150 fields and during this quest the body of the last missing crew member was found, eight days after the crash.

Increasing aerial activity during the later stages of the war meant more work coming the way of the MU. Unit records note that in the month of April 1944 its motor transport travelled 70,000 miles in the course of its duties. In August the total rose almost to 80,000 miles, a prodigious distance which was amassed while attending 124 different incidents. Also during this period the numbers of personnel at Blaby increased considerably with 26 officers, 643 airmen and 85 WAAFs on unit strength. Some of this increase was probably due to the Power Jets Unit being formed in May 1944. This comprised of RAF personnel working with Power Jets Limited. Later in December, the unit was rehoused at Bruntingthorpe.

Following the end of the war in Europe in June 1945, many of the units which had been established on a wartime basis were quickly closed down, 65 MU was one such casualty. As the amount of flying decreased so the quantity of work available for the unit grew less. The MU continued to operate for just three months longer before it was eventually disbanded on 31st August 1945.

Today the site is unrecognisable as a once busy RAF station. As many of the wartime buildings were of wooden construction these have long since disappeared while those built of slightly more durable materials have given way to units of more modern design. Armed with a site plan though certain relics of the past can still be identified. To the left of the entrance to the present day industrial estate one of the two blister hangars still survives in use as a stores, but not to house salvage equipment. Within the site, today's traffic still uses much of the road system originally laid to serve the long dead Maintenance Unit.

Key to the 65 MU site plan, below:

1 Blaby Engineering Works (not requisitioned).
2 Requisitioned buildings – MT Workshop, engine bay, repair shop, equipment store.
3 Orderly Room, CO's office, Post Office.
4 Temporary wooden buildings – offices, lecture rooms etc.
5 Various toilets and ablutions.
6 Officers' Club.
7 Equipment stores (Blister hangars).
8 Vehicle turning circle.
9 Fuel compound.
10 Cold water tank tower (1,500 gallons).
11 Air-raid shelters.

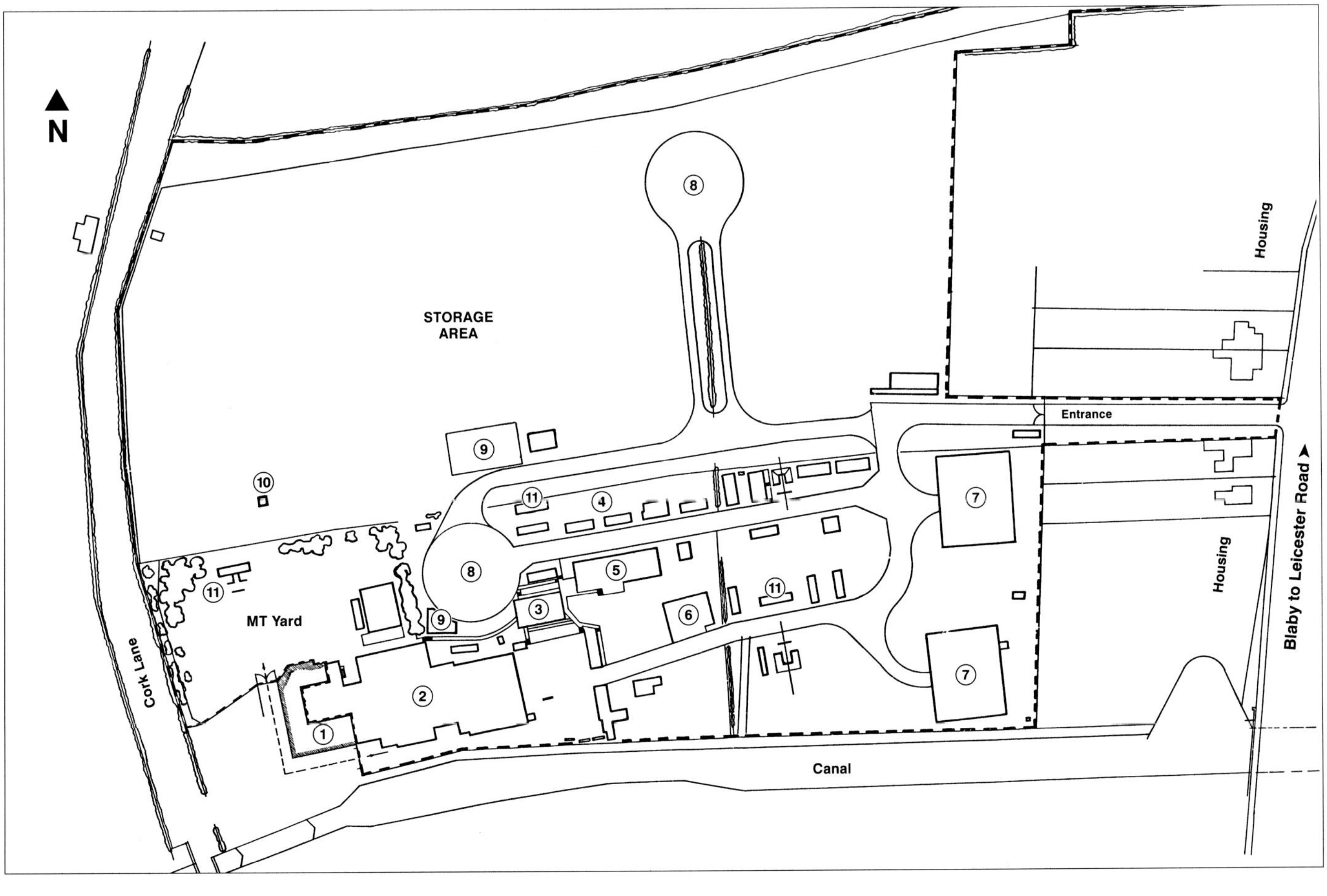

Appendix B

Airstrips and Landing Grounds

Aᴌᴌ ᴀɪʀsᴛʀɪᴘs, landing grounds and heli-pads are – by their very nature – private and it is therefore difficult and at times, improper, to chart them all. Those presented here represent a good cross section of those that have been within the two counties, but no claims are made that what follows constitutes a full listing.

Billesdon

For a short time during the early 1930s Leicestershire Gliding Club made use of an area close to this village for their activities. Contemporary reports state that the hilly site was considered by leading members of the English gliding movement to be a very suitable choice for sailplaning.

Bitteswell

On the property of Bitteswell Farm Eggs, a strip was established during the summer of 1998 with at least a resident microlight.

Brentingby

A 30 acre site located between the village and Gravel Hole Spinney was used for a short time in 1916 as a night landing ground by the Royal Flying Corps. Late in that year it was closed in favour of another site at Scalford. (See First World War Landing Grounds – page 16).

Later, in 1938, the area gained a new lease of life when a landing ground was re-established by the Automobile Association. Details of the site at this time are given as 'A level grass surface bounded on the north side by the River Eye with an available run of 480 yards southwest to northeast, 600 yards west to east and 500 yards north-north-west to south-south-east. The field was controlled on behalf of the AA by F H Brewitt, Doullens, Burton Road, Melton Mowbray'.

Desford

In the early 1980s, the rally driver Roger Clark established a landing strip close to his home at Alder Hall. He made frequent use of it when flying his Cessna 182.

Frolesworth

An airstrip on Claybrooke Lodge Farm was in use, without complaint, from 1979 until

Ferranti's Westland WS.51 Widgeon G-APVD was one of the visitors to Ratcliffe Hall on the occasion of a Helicopter Club of Great Britain Meet, Sunday 2nd April 1967. Chris Salter

June 1983 when Leicestershire Microlight Aero Club sought planning permission to use it as a permanent base. This proposal was not welcomed in the surrounding area and was vigorously opposed, the South Leicestershire Action Group being formed solely for this purpose. Feelings on both sides ran high with a great deal of coverage in the local media. The plans were not allowed to get to the debating stage as the club withdrew its application in August just before Harborough Council were due to give them consideration.

In 1984 the owner of the farm, Brian Wells, put forward further plans relating to the strip, the outcome of which was that it could continue only for his personal use. This was the start of an ongoing battle between the farmer and the authorities supported by local parish councils, pressure groups and

This scene at Claybrooke Lodge Farm, Frolesworth, includes the Helio Courier, G-ARLD, once based at Sutton Cheney. Author

A well-attended flying display in progress at Husbands Bosworth, Cote Hill, in the early 1930s. via Brandon White

One of the strips on Paddocks Farm, Kibworth Harcourt, in use for an IAPC meeting on 18th June 1988. Author

many individuals. It was a saga which was to continue for several years as Mr Wells continued to develop the site further.

Attempts to establish a light aircraft repair business met with stiff opposition and illegal use led to heavy fines. Eventually Harborough Council resorted to obtaining a High Court injunction. When this was granted in February 1992 it effectively put paid to Brian Wells' aspirations and he admitted defeat. When the farm was later put up for sale in June 1993 a private airstrip and aircraft hangar were listed amongst its amenities. There have however been no reports of the airstrips continued use.

Hallaton
A prospective farm strip here hit local headlines in June 1990 after a pilot attempting to prove its feasibility as a landing area was found guilty of dangerous flying and heavily fined.

Husbands Bosworth (1)
A grass landing ground was set up at Cote Hill Farm in 1930 by the owner of the farm C F Lees. Its initial use late that year was by members of the Rugby and District Gliding Club. In July of 1931 and 1932 flying meetings were held on the site. These were well attended by fly-in visitors and public alike. Also during July 1932 the field was the venue for one of Sir Alan Cobham's National Aviation Day displays.

When Mr Lees left the farm in March 1933 the site was closed but in 1938 it gained a new, but short lease of life when it became one of the Automobile Associations system of small landing grounds. The site was described at that time as follows: *'Situated adjacent to Cote Hill Farm, located off the short minor road connecting the A50 with the A427 approximately one mile south of Husbands Bosworth it was controlled by G T Linnell. The grass landing ground, which sloped steeply in the north and south-west corners, had landing runs of 400 yards north-south and 565 yards east-west. Lock up accommodation was available for two light aircraft with wings folded'.*

Husbands Bosworth (2)

An airstrip was established at Bosworth Hall in 1947 by the owner Major D T Constable Maxwell, a director of the brewing firm Ind Coope and Allsop. He used the site extensively for business and pleasure. The landing area consisted of one grass runway 3,000ft long by 150ft wide on a heading of 05/23.

In April 1955 a private air rally was held at the Hall which attracted visitors from across the British Isles and the continent. At an air event held here in May/June 1966, one of the visiting aircraft was a DHC Twin Otter – one of the first to be seen in the UK.

Although the strip was still extant in 1969 its use after this date is not known.

Kibworth Harcourt

Several different fields on Paddocks Farm have been used as landing strips, especially when the owner, Michael Stops has paid host to a meeting of the International Auster Pilot Club. Fields nearest the farm buildings have often been the choice though others on the eastern side of the A6 have been designated as landing areas when the occasion warranted. A small hangar not far from the main farm buildings provides a home for Michael Stops' Auster J/1N Alpha, G-AJAE.

Langham, near Oakham

A field near this village has been the home of several interesting aircraft, including examples of the Steen Skybolt, Andreasson BA-4B, Isaacs Spitfire and Piper Super Cub.

Lutterworth

The parkland surrounding Stanford Hall was the scene of some of the early flying experiments of the pioneer aviator, Percy Pilcher. Unfortunately he met with a fatal accident during one of these flights. A memorial column stands on the spot where he fell.

As air cushion vehicles can be very loosely classed as aircraft Stanford Hall qualifies to be included for this reason also. On many occasions in recent years the same parkland has echoed to the sound of racing

This rare view (sadly, slightly cropped) of Lord Furness' Lockheed 12A G-AEOI was taken at its home base of Burrough Court, Melton Mowbray. via Bob Lavender

engines when it has been the scene for International and National Hovercraft Championships. On a quieter note it has also been the venue for hot air balloon meetings of national status.

Melton Mowbray

A private airfield was built at Burrough Court in 1933 by the well known Leicestershire contractors En-Tout-Cas Co Ltd, of Syston. Established for the use of Lord Furness, a small hangar was also erected to house his aircraft which included de Havilland Dragon I G-ACIU and Lockheed 12A G-AEOI. It was at Burrough Court that His Royal Highness Edward, Prince of Wales first met the woman who was to be his future wife, Mrs Wallis Simpson. Undoubtedly his private aircraft would have used the airstrip on numerous occasions at this time. Another notable visitor during the 1930s was Rutland's distinguished aviatrix Beryl Markham who achieved fame with her solo east-west flight across the Atlantic in 1936. Although the airfield has long since reverted to farmland the derelict hangar remains as a relic of the past.

Melton Mowbray – Sandy Lane

See Chapter Sixteen.

Sutton Cheney

An airstrip was established near this village in 1965 by Peter F Hall, a local hosiery manufacturer, who lived at Shenton Hall in the nearby village of that name. After purchase, three separate fields which originally comprised the site, were combined, graded and drained. The result of these operations was to provide a grass runway approximately 1,500ft long and a small hangar-cum-store erected on the site housed a succession of

Mr Hall's aircraft. These have included the Piper Tri-Pacer G-ARZL, Super Aero 45 G-APRR and 145 G-ASWT, also the Helio Courier G-ARLD.

The field has hosted occasional visitors, included amongst these were members of the Red Devils parachute team who used the strip as a base for their BN Islander aircraft when performing at local functions. Leicestershire Microlight Aircraft Club were allowed to use the field on occasions as was Nuneaton Model Aero Club.

Whilst taking off from the strip on 12th August 1982, Piper Arrow, G-TYPE, a visitor from Essex, crashed and was written off.

Although Mr Hall died in the late 1990s, the field is still in use today, housing Taylor JT.1 Monoplane G-AWGZ, Jodel DR.1050 G-AYZK and a Clutton FRED Srs II, G-PFAF.

Thurlaston

At Knoll Farm, situated on the A47 approximately three miles west of Earl Shilton, a landing strip was in use between 1953 and 1957. The land then returned to agriculture but a small hangar which had been erected in the south-east corner of the field remained *in situ*. Today it is still there serving a more mundane purpose as a farm store.

Woodhouse Eaves

An airstrip beside Roecliffe Cottage has been used by the brothers Christopher and Nicholas Hackett. Visiting aircraft have also been noted on occasion.

Microlight Aircraft

This type of flying has become increasingly popular in recent years. Not restricted to established airfields and landing strips individual aircraft can be seen being flown from many different locations within the counties. There are more organised meetings for these enthusiasts and some of the sites where these take place are at Saddington, Swinford, near Lutterworth and Waltham Hill between Long Clawson and Eastwell.

Helipads

Because these versatile aircraft need a minimum of landing space their operations are not confined to an airfield and they are likely to be seen in almost any location. Their use in connection with business means they are often to be seen visiting industrial estates. When used to promote the armed forces and for official visits school playing fields frequently become temporary helipads. They are also seen to be a valuable asset by the emergency services for casualty evacuation and mercy flights. The farming community has also been ready to make use of their adaptability. Certain locations are however recognised as being specifically set up for helicopter use. Some of these, past and present, within the counties follow.

Rutland Water

Located on the north shore of Rutland Water, the Barnsdale Lodge Hotel maintains a helipad to the east of the complex, and is frequently visited by a variety of helicopter types.

Braunstone

For many years the Airman's Rest Inn had its own small landing pad complete with miniature windsock.

Westland Sikorsky S-55 G-ANFH of British European Airways, at the helicopter station on Saffron Lane, Leicester.

Coalville

A 250ft by 100ft grass area was/is available for patrons of the nearby Belfry Hotel.

Croft

This site, adjacent to Fosse House on the B4114 near Croft, was the home of two Bell 47 helicopters operated by Alec Wortley Ltd. At the time, visiting helicopter pilots were advised that the best approach was from the north-east over a nudist camp.

Desford

Hangar and fuel facilities set up for the use of Next Retail Limited at Desford Hall.

Donington Park

An unlicensed helipad is operated by Donington Park Racing Circuit Limited.

Great Glen

The helipad at Yew Tree Lodge Hotel was established mainly for the use of the owner David Pollard and his homebuilt Rotorway Exec 152, G-YEWS.

Husbands Bosworth

A concrete landing area has been laid and a hangar erected 500 metres south of the gliding site. It is operated by the East Midlands Air Support Unit and is normally for the use of police helicopters only.

Leicester (1)

The extensive Everard's brewery, at Fosse Park, to the north of Narborough, has a small hangar and helipad attached to it. This is used by the Everard's Robinson R-22.

Leicester (2)

Planning permission for a helipad to serve the Glenfield Hospital was granted by the Leicester City Council in 1995. Work on this much needed facility commenced in April 1997 with much of the £80,000 cost being raised by the children's charity HeartLink. Since it was opened on 2nd July 1997 it has proved to be a vital asset and sees regular use by both civil and military operators.

Leicester (3)

On the site of the present day Saffron Lane sports stadium a small helicopter station was set up in 1956 and operated by British European Airways in connection with one of its experimental passenger services.

The first proving flight over the route – Birmingham (Elmdon) to Nottingham via Leicester and return, took place on 5th April. A grand opening ceremony was held on 22nd June when two Westland Sikorsky S-55s, G-ANFH and G-AOCF, filled with civic dignitaries, were flown over the route.

Regular passenger services began on 2nd July with two return trips each weekday. But throughout the summer passenger loads were small and for the winter a revised schedule of the daily return journey was introduced. The winter schedule was to have lasted from October to March but from 10th November the service was withdrawn. Poor load factors and a shortage of fuel brought about by the Suez crisis were put forward as reasons. While it had been in operation the service had carried 1,829 passengers, a small amount of freight and had achieved 84% regularity.

The services continue to make occasional goodwill visits to the counties. The Army and their Air Corps were at Clarendon Fields in Hinckley to display Saro Skeeter AOP.12, XL765, and other wares, on 11th May 1961. In more recent years RAF Wessex and RN Sea King and Lynx helicopters have visited the Hinckley area, HMS Hermione's Lynx HAS.2 XZ720 called into Uppingham School on 31st January 1984, and an 824 Squadron RN Sea King from HMS Tiger alighted on Leicester Tigers' Welford Road Rugby Ground on 14th November 1999.
Robin Forbes

Leicester (4)
The helipad in Victoria Park is used mainly in connection with emergencies of a medical nature associated with Leicester Royal Infirmary and the General Hospital.

Market Bosworth
A large lawn on the south side of the Bosworth Hall Hotel is classified as a landing site. On 29th/30th June 1991 the hotel grounds and several of the surrounding fields were the venue for the Helicopter Club of Great Britain Championships.

North Luffenham
Although this RAF base was closed to fixed wing aircraft from 1960 a helicopter facility has remained available and was extended with the arrival of the Army – see Chapter Seventeen.

Oadby
Established by Livingston and Doughty on Oadby Industrial Estate, this helipad consisted of a 22ft concrete circle in the centre of a large lawn. It adjoined the east side of Oadby Racecourse.

Old Dalby
Until the base closed a helipad here was operated by the Army 35 Central Workshop.

Osbaston
At Field Farm is a landing area and hangar for the private use of National Lottery winner K Lee Taylor-Ryan who bases his Bell Jet Ranger G-KLEE here.

Ratcliffe
In 1966 a private landing site was laid close to Ratcliffe Hall by P A W B Everard. It consisted of a 30ft by 30ft concrete pad and a small hangar. As a founder member and also chairman of the Helicopter Club of Great Britain his guests often arrived by this mode of transport.

On 2nd April 1967 a 'Hover In' held at the Hall for members of the Helicopter Club of Great Britain attracted quite a number of helicopters. Guests who came by more conventional fixed-wing aircraft were ferried to the Hall after landing at nearby Rearsby.

From the mid-1980s, use of the facility became increasingly infrequent until it was eventually discontinued.

Thorpe Satchville
During the late 1970s Pork Farms Limited advertised that a helicopter service was available from their base here, near Melton Mowbray, using a Bell 206B JetRanger.

Twycross
During late 1998 Rare Ltd of Cliff House, Burton Road, applied for planning permission for a helicopter landing pad and maintenance facility.

Over 70 helicopters of various types landed at Bosworth Hall Hotel for the Helicopter Club of Great Britain Championships over the weekend of 29-30th June 1991. This was a typical sight, with nine Robinson R-22s and a Westland Whirlwind in view. Author

Appendix C

Major Aircraft Accidents
involving non-County-based aircraft

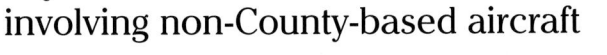

THE INCIDENTS listed are all believed to have occurred within the county boundaries and to have resulted in the aircraft in question becoming a total loss or involving loss of life or serious injury.

Agusta-Bell Sioux AH.1
4.2.72　　XT106 'R'　　3 Commando Brigade, Plymouth, Devon.
　　　　　Crashed on Beacon Hill, near Woodhouse Eaves.

Airspeed Oxford Mk.I or II
11.6.40　P1896　　15 FTS, Brize Norton, Oxfordshire.
　　　　　Crashed on take-off after a forced landing at Lutterworth.
11.1140　N6292　　14 FTS, Cranfield, Bedfordshire.
　　　　　Crashed in forced landing 1½ miles north of Ryhall, Rutland.
27.11.40　P1960　　14 FTS, Cranfield, Bedfordshire.
　　　　　Crashed in forced landing at Rearsby.
25.6.41　L9691　　11 FTS, Shawbury, Shropshire.
　　　　　Crashed in forced landing, Minden Drive, Leicester.
16.11.41　V3512　　RAFC, Cranwell, Lincolnshire.
　　　　　Flew into hill in bad visibility, Shepshed.
26.12.41　P1842　　2 FTS, Brize Norton, Oxfordshire.
　　　　　Crashed in forced landing near Stoney Stanton.
14.6.42　T1062　　12 (P)AFU, Grantham. Lincolnshire.
　　　　　Aircraft at low altitude when starboard engine failed. Spun into ground 1½ miles east of Hinckley. Crew killed.
8.4.43　　AB665　　14 (P)AFU, Ossington, Nottinghamshire.
　　　　　Collided in mid-air with Lancaster L7545 of 1645 HCU and crashed near Barton Lodge, Melton Mowbray. Two crew killed.

The crash scene at Cheney House Farm, Queniborough, where Lincoln B.II RF385 'DX-G' of 57 Squadron came to grief on 20th February 1946.
via Ian O'Neill

27.7.43　. . . . .　　288 Squadron, Digby, Lincolnshire.
　　　　　Crashed nr Whetstone at 15:10 hrs. Pilot, Sgt. Lawrence killed.
5.11.43　EB788　　16 (Polish) FTS, Hucknall, Nottinghamshire.
　　　　　Crashed while making night approach to Leicester East.
11.3.44　NM235　　20 (P)AFU, Weston on the Green, Oxfordshire.
　　　　　Stalled after taking avoiding action with another aircraft, dived into ground near Smeeton Westerby. Crew of three killed.
13.5.44　DF517　　1655 MTU, Warboys, Huntingdonshire.
　　　　　Broke up in cloud, crashed at Great Dalby. All occupants killed.
22.9.44　LX457　　6 (P)AFU, Little Rissington, Gloucestershire.
　　　　　Crashed nr Castle Donington, attempting to land in poor visibility.
7.11.44　LX638　　18 (P)AFU, Church Lawford, Warwickshire.
　　　　　Encountered rain squall, lost propeller in high speed vertical dive and crashed near Wymondham, Leics. Four killed.
6.3.45　　NM708　　16 (Polish) FTS, Hucknall, Nottinghamshire.
　　　　　Pilot lost and aircraft damaged beyond repair after overshooting night landing on unlit airfield at Cottesmore.
4.11.48　PK293　　1589 Flight*
　　　　　Damaged beyond repair after experiencing control problems and belly landing near Ibstock.
* Note that by this date 1589 Flight had disbanded. It is thought that the unit involved was 1689 (Ferry Pool Pilot Training) Flight, Aston Down, Gloucestershire, but this cannot be confirmed.

28.11.49 LX634   64 Group Comms Flight, Linton-on-Ouse, Yorks.
Undercarriage collapsed in heavy landing at Wymeswold.
Not repaired.

Armstrong Whitworth Siskin IIIA
24.6.31 J8964   3 FTS, Grantham, Lincolnshire.
Stalled on turn while low flying Ketton, Rutland.

Armstrong Whitworth Albemarle ST Mk.I srs III
28.7.44 P1605   ORTU, Hampstead Norris, Berkshire.
Crashed on approach to Cottesmore.

Armstrong Whitworth Whitley Mk.V
28.3.41 Z6477   10 Squadron, Leeming, Yorkshire.
Crashed near Blind Eye Quarry, Pickworth Great Wood, four
miles north of Casterton, Rutland after crew baled out following
engine failure due to shortage of fuel.

Auster AOP.9
3.9.64 XP246   6 Flight, Army Air Corps
Precautionary landing in bad weather at Lowesby. Hit fence.

Avro 504K
24.9.17 F4443
Developed engine trouble while over Leicester. The pilot, a
local man, attempted to land on Victoria Park but saw children
playing there, altered course towards Knighton Fields, but lost
height too quickly and crashed at the rear of 31 Cecilia Road.

Avro 621 Trainer (Mongoose Tutor)
13.7.31 K1788   3 FTS, Grantham, Lincolnshire.
Made practice forced landing two miles west of Ashwell, Rutland.
Undercarriage torn off after hitting water tank on take-off.

Avro Anson Mk.I
4.12.39 L7067   12 FTS, Grantham, Lincolnshire.
Damaged beyond repair four miles north east of Nuneaton,
when aircraft hit hedge and farm machinery during a forced
landing in bad weather.
14.10.40 N5118   4 AONS, Watchfield, Berkshire.
Stalled at low altitude and hit tree near North Kilworth.
Three crew received serious injuries.
30.3.41 N4910   12 FTS, Grantham, Lincolnshire.
Hit tree while low flying one mile north of Ram Jam Inn,
Stretton, Rutland.

Avro Lancaster
22.2.42 L7549 'KM-Q'   44 Squadron, Conversion Flt., Waddington, Lincs.
Mk.I. Crash-landed in field nr Ashwell, Rutland, after engine cut.
23.10.42 W4278 'OF-'   97 Squadron, Woodhall Spa, Lincolnshire.
This Mk.1 overshot landing at North Luffenham.
18.2.43 W4270 'QR-'   61 Squadron, Syerston, Lincolnshire. Mk.1.
Crashed at Bottesford after engine caught fire while in circuit.
8.4.43 L7545   1654 CU, Swinderby, Lincolnshire.
This Mk.I collided in mid-air with Oxford AB665 and crashed
near Burton Lazars, Melton Mowbray. All crew killed.
8.9.43 JB153   103 Squadron, Elsham Wolds, Lincolnshire.
Crashed within three minutes of take-off from Wymeswold.
Crew of six and three ATC cadets in this Mk.III, all killed.
7.6.44 ME579 'WS-A'   9 Squadron, Bardney, Lincolnshire.
After returning from attacking railway communications at
Argenta, this Mk.I was descending through cloud when it hit
trees and crashed near Belvoir Castle. One survivor.
11.7.44 LL675 'EQ-T'   408 Squadron, Linton-on-Ouse, Yorkshire.
Caught fire in the air and crashed near Eaton, seven miles
north-east of Melton Mowbray. Six crew of this Mk.II killed.
27.11.44 PB745 'CA-Q'   189 Squadron, Fulbeck, Lincolnshire.
This Mk.III took off at 23:53 hours to take part in an attack on
Munich but crashed between Croxton and Saltby. Three of the
crew killed and four injured, one of whom died later.
6.3.45 NG410 'DX-G'   57 Squadron, East Kirkby, Lincolnshire.
This Mk.I was lost and short of fuel after returning from ops on
Germany. Pilot attempted forced landing at RAF Nuneaton but
undercarriage collapsed and aircraft crashed at runways end.
Pilot and Flight Engineer received slight injuries.
10.4.45 ND949 'LE-Z'   630 Squadron, East Kirkby, Lincolnshire. Mk.III.
Returning from an attack on an oil refinery at Lutzkendorf, it
was diverted, due to poor weather. Crashed at Foxton, nr Mkt
Harborough at 03:10 hours. Aircraft burnt out, no survivors.

1.2.46 NE140 'PH-D'   12 Squadron, Binbrook, Lincolnshire.
This Mk.III crashed at Beeby, all crew killed.
4.2.46 PA269 'BH-U'   300 Squadron, Faldingworth, Lincolnshire.
This Mk.I aircraft came out of cumulo nimbus cloud in a steep
diving turn to starboard, hitting the ground at Wigston Magna
and exploding on impact. Crew of six, all Polish, were killed.
Over 100 houses in the Aylestone Lane area of Wigston were
damaged.

Avro Lincoln B.2
20.2.46 RF385 'DX-G'   57 Squadron, Scampton, Lincolnshire.
Crashed at 18:45 hours at Cheney House Farm, Queniborough.
All crew killed.

Avro Manchester Mk.I
1.3.41 L7278 'EM-A'   207 Squadron, Waddington, Lincolnshire.
Crashed near Wymondham, while trying to make emergency
landing due to engine failure.

Avro Tutor
22.6.38 K3199   RAFC, Cranwell, Lincolnshire
Lost, stalled in forced landing and crashed nr Castle Donington.

Avro York C.1
1.8.48 MW259 'TB-W'   242 Squadron, Abingdon, Berkshire.
While on air test engine overspeeded. Made belly landing on
Desford aerodrome, hit bump and broke back.

Blackburn Shark II
28.11.38 K8490 'O' or 'D'   'D' Flight, Ford, Sussex.
Crashed in forced landing at Hathern near Loughborough. One
of five aircraft of this type which made forced landings in this
locality on this date, due to adverse weather while on ferry
flight. Others were K5635, K8468, K8486 and K8519.

Boeing B-17 Flying Fortress
10.10.43 42-29557 'SO-S', 547thBS, 384th BG, Grafton Underwood, Northants.
At 17:30 hours, this B-17F, named *Yankee Gal*, lost and short of
fuel, overshot landing at Desford and hit Bellman hangar on
south side of airfield. Two of the ten crew were injured.
13.02.44 . . -. . . . . ?   *Serial and unit details not known.*
Crashed in trees at East Norton. Three occupants unhurt.
11.9.44 42-102957 'SC-F', 612th BS, 401st BG Deenethorpe, Northants.
On return from ops against synthetic oil plant this battle-
damaged B-17G, named *Fearless Fosdick*, crashed at King's
Norton after crew had bailed out.
28.9.44 43-37776   490th Bomb Group, Eye, Suffolk
This B-17G crashed at 20:45 hours at Belcher's Bar, Nailstone,
while on night training mission. Aircraft exploded on impact and
all 12 occupants killed.
20.1.45 42-97251 'BK-O', 546 BS, 384th BG, Grafton Underwood, N'hants.
Nine crew baled out from this B-17G after returning from ops
and two were injured. Aircraft crashed near Tur Langton.
22.1.45 43-38125 'IY-D', 615th BS, 401st BG, Deenethorpe, Northants.
Two engines failed during assembly pattern and this B-17G
crashed in the Buckminster/Saltby area. Three crew injured.
4.3.45 44-6464 'IW-H', 614th BS, 401st BG, Deenethorpe, Northants.
Crew baled out after No.1 engine caught fire and could not be
extinguished. This B-17G crashed near Bitteswell airfield at
07:20 hours and blew up. All crew safe.
25.3.45 42-97395 'IW-F', 614th BS, 401st BG, Deenethorpe, Northants.
This B-17G was abandoned by its crew over Saltby airfield.

Boulton Paul Defiant I
28.8.40 L7003   1 FPP, White Waltham, Berkshire.
Force-landed at Market Bosworth following engine failure.
23.2.41 N3388   151 Squadron, Wittering, Northamptonshire.
Ran out of fuel and abandoned. Crashed near Walton, Leics.
4.3.41 N1794   151 Squadron, Wittering, Northamptonshire.
Aircraft broke up in mid-air and crashed at Ketton, Rutland.
Two occupants killed.
2.7.43 . . . . .   10 AGS, Barrow in Furness, Lancashire.
Crashed at Braunstone at 17:15 hours. No casualties.
17.7.43 N3509   26 OTU, Wing, Buckinghamshire.
On delivery flight. Overshot on landing at Desford in poor
weather, hit Tiger Moth N6741, 7EFTS.
5.9.43 N3505   10 AGS, Barrow in Furness, Lancashire.
Crashed on Desford aerodrome. No casualties.

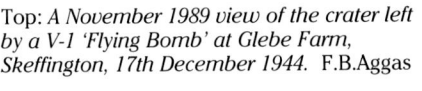

Top: *A November 1989 view of the crater left by a V-1 'Flying Bomb' at Glebe Farm, Skeffington, 17th December 1944.* F.B.Aggas

Above: *Blackburn Shark II, K8490, force-landed near Loughborough, 28th November 1938.* Author' collection

Left: *Bristol Blenheim V, AZ890, that flew into the ground at night, near Wymondham, on 19th August 1944.* Bill Taylor

Bristol F.2b Fighter
11.1.29 C763   5 FTS, Sealand, Cheshire.
        Lost, forced landed and crashed, Hinckley.

Bristol Beaufighter VIf
7.9.42 X8198   409 Squadron, Coleby Grange, Lincolnshire.
        Attempted forced landing at Wymeswold after engine failure at 10,000ft. Crashed on approach runway downwind and turned over. No injuries.
5.8.43 V8702   141 Squadron, Wittering, Northamptonshire.
        After breaking cloud, aircraft dived into the ground, one mile south of Braunston, Rutland.

Bristol Beaufort T.Mk.II
25.4.45 ML714   12 (P)AFU, Hixon, Staffordshire.
        Engine lost power, damaged beyond repair in belly landing four miles south of Desford.

Bristol Blenheim
3.12.37 K7110   114 Squadron, Wyton, Huntingdonshire
        After running into snowstorm, this Mk.I came out of cloud layer inverted and out of control. Pilot baled out, other two crew members stayed with aircraft but were able to walk away from the wreck after it had crashed near Brick Kiln Hill, Hinckley.
22.12.40 L4896   17 OTU, Upwood, Huntingdonshire.
        This Mk.IV aircraft hit high tension cable and crashed two miles north-east of Market Harborough.
13.3.42 R3607   13 OTU, Bicester, Oxfordshire.
        This Mk.IV crashed in forced landing at Ratby.
2.5.42 L9206   13 OTU Bicester, Oxfordshire.
        Dived into ground 3 miles east of Billesdon. Three killed. Mk.IV.
6.5.43 K7159   12 (P)AFU, Spitalgate, Lincolnshire.
        This Mk.I crashed near Croxton Kerrial.
26.12.43 AZ922   12 (P)AFU, Spitalgate, Lincolnshire.
        This Mk.V crashed in forced landing at Bottesford.

5.5.44 L1224   12 (P)AFU, Spitalgate, Lincolnshire.
        This aircraft, a Mk.I, crashed at Houghton on the Hill.
19.8.44 AZ890   12 (P)AFU, Spitalgate, Lincolnshire.
        Flew into ground at night near Wymondham. Pilot on solo training in this Mk.V was killed.

Bristol Bulldog IIa
113.1.36 K2962   3 FTS, Grantham, Lincolnshire.
        Lost in bad weather, made forced landing, overshot and hit wall, ½ mile south-east of Thistleton, Rutland.

Canadair DC-4M1
8.5.54 17522, 4 (Transport) OTU, RCAF
        During a trans-Atlantic training flight, to Paris and return, the aircraft made a precautionary landing at North Luffenham but touched down 75ft short of the runway. It struck a mound of clay and concrete and the landing gear was driven up into the wing. The aircraft remained intact but was written off. There were no injuries among the 17 crew, instructors and students on board.

Canadair Sabre 2
11.10.52 19370   416 Squadron RCAF, Grostenquin, France.
        Damaged beyond repair after flame out was followed by wheels-up landing at North Luffenham.

De Havilland DH.9A
2.9.28 J8107   605 Squadron, Castle Bromwich, Warwickshire.
        On cross country flight Henlow-Waddington-Castle Bromwich but crashed at Great Glen. Aircraft burst into flames on impact. One killed.

De Havilland Mosquito
14.10.43 HJ817 'AT- ' 60 OTU, High Ercall, Shropshire.
        This FB Mk.VI crashed at Elliston Farm, Coalville. Pilot was descending to check position in bad visibility when aircraft hit ground. Instrumention possibly faulty. Two killed.

4.5.44 HJ783 2 GSU, Swanton Morley, Norfolk
After flying low over Market Harborough airfield with engine trouble, this FB Mk.VI crashed at 11:04 hours near Foxton. Crew received slight injuries.

1.10.45 RV352 3 FP, Hawarden, Clwyd.
This B Mk.XVI belly landed on Wymeswold airfield after undercarriage jammed up while on a delivery flight, Ayr to Henlow. Pilot, First Officer Frisby, ATA, unhurt.

20.9.47 .....? ?
Visiting aircraft crashed at Lings Farm, Rempstone, during display commemorating Battle of Britain at Wymeswold. Wreck collected by 58 MU 29.9.47. (The actual crash site may possibly be 'over the border' in Nottinghamshire.)

De Havilland Puss Moth
3.11.40 X9405 3 FPP, Hawarden, Clwyd.
Crashed on take-off at Ashby de la Zouch.

De Havilland Tiger Moth II (or I)
15.3.37 K4278 24 Squadron, Hendon, Middlesex.
This Mk.I ran out of fuel and crashed in forced landing near Melton Mowbray.

30.7.41 T7225 25 (P)EFTS, Hucknall, Nottinghamshire.
Crashed force-landing eight miles north of Nuneaton, Warks.

17.9.41 T8239 2 EFTS, Staverton, Gloucestershire.
Crashed in forced landing at Nunnery Farm, Leicester.

14.11.42 K4261 14 EFTS, Elmdon, Warwickshire.
This Mk.I spun in near Botcheston, Desford, after mid-air collision with Mk.II T6288 of 7 EFTS. Both occupants killed.

8.6.43 R4853 14 EFTS, Elmdon, Warwickshire.
Collided with R4967 of 7 EFTS and crashed near Market Bosworth.

2.7.43 DE300 18 EFTS, Fairoaks, Surrey.
Engine cut and aircraft crashed in forced landing three miles north of Oakham.

17.11.50 T6243 50 Squadron, Waddington, Lincolnshire
Crashed and overturned in forced landing when lost. Two different sources give conflicting locations for this incident – near Tilton and Rathy (Ratby?).

De Havilland Vampire FB.5
12.5.58 VZ178 8 FTS, Swinderby, Lincolnshire.
Crashed ½ mile south-east of Beeby.

Dornier Do 17Z-3
14.11.40 2892 '5K+BP' 6/KG3
Aircraft had been attacking Coventry when it was hit by AA fire and an engine put out of action. Crashed at Prestwold Hall, Burton on the Wolds. The crew of four were all killed.

Douglas Boston
8.1.43 ..... ?, ATA
Crashed on take-off from Cottesmore airfield. No casualties.

19.2.44 BZ217 88 Squadron, Hartford Bridge, Hampshire.
This Mk.IIIa crashed at Dishley after take-off from Loughborough.

Douglas C-47 Skytrain
8.7.44 42-108873 309th TCS, 315th TCG, Spanhoe, Northants.
43-15341 309th TCS, 315th TCG, Spanhoe, Northants.
Collided in mid-air and crashed near Tinwell, Rutland, while on practice para-drop exercise carrying troops of the Polish 1st Independent Airborne Brigade. 34 men lost their lives.

English Electric Lightning F.2
25.3.64 XN723 Rolls-Royce, Hucknall, Nottinghamshire.
While on test flight, engine test instrumentation failed, aircraft caught fire and was abandoned by R-R test pilot Denis Whitham. Aircraft crashed near Keyham

Fairey Battle I
3.8.40 L5433 103 Squadron, Newton, Nottinghamshire.
Crashed at 23:45 hours near Market Overton, Rutland, and burnt out. Pilot killed, two other crew injured one later died.

21.12.40 P6636 12 FTS, Grantham, Lincolnshire.
Pilot lost and making a forced landing when engine lost power and aircraft hit trees, Cossington.

11.6.41 P6686 12 FTS, Grantham, Lincolnshire.
Hit high ground while low flying 2 miles N of Melton Mowbray.

Fieseler Fi103, FZG-76, V-1 Flying-bomb
18.12.44 At 04:40 hours the first and only one of these vengeance weapons to land in the county fell at Glebe Farm, Skeffington. Believed to have been air launched it left a crater ten feet deep and ten yards across. Damage caused to farm cottage and outbuildings 150 yards away. One occupant slightly injured.

Gloster Gauntlet II
2.1.39 K7890 151 Squadron, North Weald, Essex.
While making forced landing near Great Dalby in bad weather overshot and hit ditch.

Gloster Meteor
22.7.52 VT264 215 AFS, Finningley, Yorkshire.
This F.4 variant ran out of fuel and hit tree on approach to land on the then disused airfield at Castle Donington. Pilot killed.

8.6.54 WK906 211 FTS, Worksop, Nottinghamshire.
This F.8 aircraft flew into ground five miles west of Cottesmore while on night navigation exercise.

Handley Page Halifax
20.5.42 W1099 102 Squadron, Dalton, Yorkshire.
This Mk.II crashed in forced landing at Cottesmore.

24.5.43 JB792 51 Squadron, Snaith, Yorkshire.
Mk.II overshot landing at Woolfox Lodge due hydraulic failure.

18.8.43 DK269 76 Squadron, Holme-on-Spalding Moor, Yorkshire.
This Mk.V swung and struck obstruction at Wymeswold.

21.8.43 DT697 1658 HCU, Riccall, Yorkshire.
Crashed and caught fire at approximately 01:00 hours near Bruntingthorpe after experiencing engine failure. Five of the crew of this Mk.II were killed and one seriously injured.

4.11.43 HR921 10 Squadron, Melbourne, Yorkshire.
Overshot and crashed at Woolfox Lodge. Three casualties on board this Mk.II aircraft were the result of an engagement with an enemy night fighter.

2.9.44 LW344 1656 HCU, Lindholme, Yorkshire.
This Mk.II broke up in mid-air due to icing and crashed at Little Casterton, Rutland. Eight occupants killed.

5.11.44 DT519 1669 HCU, Langar, Nottinghamshire.
Control of this Mk.II was lost, it struck trees and a hut, during three-engined approach to Bottesford.

24.2.45 PN366 1663 HCU, Rufforth, Yorkshire.
Returning from a 'Sweepstake' operation when at around 22:00 hours this Mk.III crashed near Edmonthorpe. It hit the ground in a steeply banked turn and disintegrated on impact, wreckage scattered over a wide area. The seven crew, all members of the Free French Air Force, were killed. Accident inspectors found that the port inner engine had caught fire but the port outer propeller had been feathered by mistake.

4.7.46 NP884 4 FP, Hawarden
This Mk.VI overshot landing at Loughborough when on delivery to College for use as instructional airframe. Main undercarriage torn off in Blackbrook, aircraft belly landed in field beyond. Removed by RAF salvage crew.

Handley Page Hampden I
1.5.40 L4119 61 Squadron, Hemswell
Aircraft returning from ops when it flew into ground in poor visibility at Croxton Kerrial. Four killed, aircraft written off.

21.11.40 X3053 83 Squadron, Scampton
Forced landed 17:40 hours at Lutterworth. Was on collection flight from Burtonwood when became lost in poor visibility.

10.4.41 AD830 50 Squadron, Lindholme, Yorkshire.
Pilot was low flying and carrying out unauthorised aerobatics over the home of a lady friend when aircraft struck houses in Evington, Leics. at 15:30 hours. Two killed in aircraft, one civilian killed and one injured.

25.10.41 AE184 50 Squadron, Swinderby
Overshot Ratcliffe at 18:30 hours and swung to avoid the Watch Office.

23.1.42 AT142 50 Squadron, Skellingthorpe
Returning from Munster when aircraft crashed at Exton, Rutland, at 22:00 hours. Cause unknown, four killed.

25.1.42 AD782 408 Squadron, Balderton
Climbed too steeply after take-off from Balderton for operations, stalled from 1,000ft and crashed on the Lyndon to Wing road near North Luffenham at 17:37 hours. Four crew killed.

Hawker Audax I
23.9.37   K5217   11 FTS Wittering, Northamptonshire.
Crashed due to engine trouble on farm belonging to Captain J H Porter at Hathern, near Loughborough. Crew unhurt.
7.10.39   K7334   9 FTS, Hullavington, Wiltshire.
On Nav-Ex, during bad weather flew into high ground near Uppingham, Rutland. Pilot killed. Aircraft destroyed by fire.
17.11.39 K7550   12 FTS, Grantham, Lincolnshire.
Forced landed in bad weather, hit hedge at Coalville Grammar School.

Hawker Demon I
7.8.38   K8185   64 Squadron, Church Fenton, Yorkshire.
Ran out of fuel and abandoned while lost in fog. Crashed near Leicester.

Hawker Hart (Special)
8.10.40   K4368   7 FTS, Peterborough, Huntingdonshire.
Flew into ground near Tilton on the Hill while instrument flying. One killed.

Hawker Hart Trainer
17.11.39 K4978   12 FTS, Grantham, Lincolnshire.
Hit tree while force-landing in bad weather near Loughborough. Destroyed by fire.
4.1.40   K4994 '19'   7 FTS, Peterborough, Huntingdonshire.
Undershot forced landing in bad weather and hit fence near Lutterworth.
29.3.40   K5798   3 FTS, South Cerney, Gloucestershire.
Landing to repair K5046 which had force-landed. Applied brakes and overturned in field near Theddingworth.

Hawker Hind
15.7.37   K6630   218 Squadron, Upper Heyford, Oxfordshire.
Lost formation in poor visibility, made forced landing at Kirby Bellars but hit tree. Wreck taken to 3 FTS.
17.1.40   K6725   12 FTS, Grantham, Lincolnshire.
Overshot and tipped up while attempting to land beside an aircraft which had force-landed at Barsby.

Hawker Hurricane
29.9.40   R4095 'M'   302 Squadron, Leconfield, Yorkshire.
This aircraft, a Mk.I, force-landed at Rugby Co-op Farm, Misterton near Lutterworth.
19.10.42 V6606   288 Squadron, Digby, Lincolnshire.
This Mk.I caught fire in the air and abandoned near Bottesford.

7.9.44   PG494   51 0TU, Cranfield, Bedfordshire.
Mk.IIe stalled while on approach to Saltby in bad weather.
12.12.44 LF393   1669 HCU, Langar, Nottinghamshire.
Mk.IIc crashed on landing in thick mist at Saltby.

Hawker Hunter FGA.9
17.6.74   XG130 '61'   45 Squadron, Wittering, Northamptonshire.
Pilot (from 58 Squadron) became disorientated in cloud and abandoned the aircraft which then crashed near a railway tunnel entrance at Grimston, near Melton Mowbray, Leics.

Hawker Typhoon Ia
24.4.42   R7654   266 Squadron, Duxford, Cambridgeshire.
Flew out of cloud and dived in ground, Great Casterton, Rutland.
15.8.43   R8652   59 OTU, Milfield, Northumberland.
Crashed on landing at Rearsby.

Heinkel He 111
9.4.41   2962 'GI+DL', 3/KG55, Dreux, France
Shot down by night fighter over Kirby Muxloe. Two baled out and were later captured near Rothley by members of the Home Guard. The pilot and one other stayed with the aircraft which crashed at Roe's Rest Farm near Desford. Aircraft broke up and caught fire in the front garden of the farm. The two crew were found alive in the wreckage.

Hunting Jet Provost
17.6.60   XM382 '28'   2 FTS, Syerston, Nottinghamshire.
This aircraft, a T Mk.3, spun in 3¼ miles north-north-east of Melton Mowbray, during aerobatics.
19.4.63   XP623 '44'   2 FTS, Syerston, Nottinghamshire.
Pilot of this T Mk.4 baled out and aircraft crashed near Thrussington.
29.7.63   XM380   2 FTS, Syerston, Nottinghamshire.
Engine of this T Mk.3 cut and aircraft abandoned after fire warning one mile south of Seagrave.
20.9.63   XP622   2 FTS, Syerston, Nottinghamshire.
Engine of this T Mk.4 cut on take-off, undercarriage collapsed when heavy landing made on grass. Wymeswold.
28.6.67   XN597   2 FTS, Syerston, Nottinghamshire.
Nosewheel of this T Mk.3 collapsed in heavy landing at Wymeswold. Nose section became instructional airframe 7984M.

Below: *The Heinkel He 111 that crashed at Roe's Rest Farm, Desford, on 9th April 1941. via Author*

Right: *The 11 FTS Hawker Audax, K5217, that crashed near Hathern on 23rd September 1937. Author's collection*

Below right: *The mortal remains of Miles Magister L6902, from 9 ERFTS at Ansty, Warwickshire, at Hathern, 9th February 1938, within yards of where Hawker Audax K5217 had crashed, the year before. via Author*

Junkers Ju 88C-2
9.4.41   0776 'R4+CM'   4/NJG 2
   Shot down in the vicinity of Oakham, Rutland, by Beaufighter R2122, 25 Squadron, RAF Wittering. Ju 88 crashed in field bordering the Burley to Langham road. Pilot found dead in wreckage, other two crew members baled out. One broke leg on landing other walked into Oakham and surrendered to ARP personnel.

Miles Magister I
9.2.38   L6902   9 ERFTS, Ansty, Warwickshire.
   Crashed in forced landing at Hathern near Loughborough. Site was within a few yards of Audax K5217 crash of previous year.
30.3.43   T9837   ATA
   Blown over in gale after landing at Ratcliffe.
1.9.44   T9747   ATA
   Crashed taking off at Desford due to engine failure.

Miles Master I
22.11.41   T8390   9 FTS, Hullavington, Wiltshire.
   Crashed in forced landing at Illston on the Hill due to engine trouble. Pilot F/O Key uninjured.
28.8.42   N7889   7 AACU, Castle Bromwich, Warwickshire.
   Hit tree while in circuit at Husbands Bosworth.
23.2.43   T8840   7 (P)AFU, Peterborough, Huntingdonshire.
   Belly landed on approach to Woolfox Lodge.
6.11.43   T8628   53 OTU, Kirton in Lindsey, Lincolnshire.
   Crashed in forced landing at Ashwell, Rutland.
20.3.44   DL844   7 (P)AFU, Peterborough, Huntingdonshire.
   This Mk.II crashed on approach to land at Braunstone and was a complete write-off. Pilot taken to Leicester Royal Infirmary.

Miles Martinet I
17.9.45   EM641 '2'   2 ATS, Sutton Bridge, Lincolnshire.
   Engine cut, aircraft belly landed crashing through drystone wall at Brickhill Farm, Woodhouse Eaves. Pilot W/O J Howell was unhurt.

Miles Mentor I
21.3.40   L4395   24 Squadron, Hendon, Middlesex.
   Crashed at Burbage Wood, near Hinckley.

Noorduyn UC-64 Norseman
7.9.44   . . - . . . . .   USAAF
   Crashed near Desford Railway Station, both occupants killed.

North American Harvard
15.4.40   N7054   10 FTS, Ternhill, Shropshire.
   This Mk.I abandoned in spin, crashed near Walton on the Wolds.
6.4.53   FS746   RAFC, Cranwell, Lincolnshire.
   This aircraft, a Mk.IIb, ran short of fuel and hit ground during forced landing at Packington.

North American Mustang Mk.X
12.44   AM203   12 Group Comms Flt, Hucknall, Nottinghamshire.
   Written off in forced landing at Ratcliffe.

Republic P-47C Thunderbolt
1.2.43   41-6213   8th Air Service Ferry Unit, USAAF
   41-6348   8th Air Service Ferry Unit, USAAF
   Mid-air collision, approx 13:30 hours. Pilots of both aircraft killed: 2nd Lt Alfred Esposite (A10320) crashed Park Farm near Desford; 2nd Lt Samuel Rey (A10397) crashed nr Kirby Muxloe.
15.9.44   41-6178   495th FTG, USAAF, Atcham, Shropshire.
   Pilot thought cloud base was 3,000ft when it was actually 800ft and when aircraft broke cloud in steep dive he was unable to pull out and crashed in Dovedale Road, Leicester. Pilot, 2nd Lt Herbert C Belford and one civilian killed.
28.10.44   . . - . . . .   USAAF, Atcham, Shropshire.
   Crashed near Shepshed, pilot killed.

Short Stirling III
7.6.44   LK594   1654 HCU, Wigsley, Nottinghamshire.
   Control believed to have been lost while descending through cloud. Dived into the ground at Saltby.
14.1.45   LK618   11 FU, Talbenny, Pembrokeshire.
   Overshot after abandoning take off, hit bank and undercarriage collapsed, near Melton Mowbray.

Vickers Wellington
20.5.41   W5712   37 MU, Burtonwood, Lancashire.
   Aircraft (a Mk.Ic) dived into ground near Market Harborough.
28.5.41   R1044 'JN-Y'   150 Squadron, Newton, Nottinghamshire.
   Returning from Boulogne, this Mk.Ic emerged from cloud to check position and flew into Colborough Hill, Halstead, 10 miles east of Leicester. Five killed, one injured.
23.10.41   R1138   18 OTU, Bramcote, Warwickshire.
   This aircraft, a Mk.Ic, dived into ground at Ullesthorpe.
8.11.42   Z1325   18 OTU, Bramcote, Warwickshire.
   This Mk.IV stalled at low altitude, crashed and burned near Hinckley.
11.12.42   BJ620   25 OTU, Finningley, Yorkshire.
   A Mk.III, hit trees on approach to Wymeswold.
10.1.43   X9953   18 OTU, Bramcote, Warwickshire.
   This Mk.Ic aircraft was abandoned after icing up, and crashed near Burbage, Leics.
25.1.43   . . . . . 'C'   12 OTU, Chipping Warden, Northamptonshire.
   Crashed landed on uncompleted airfield at Melton Mowbray after returning from 'Nickel' raid on Fontainebleu. Crew uninjured.
7.2.43   N2761   11 OTU, Westcott, Buckinghamshire.
   This Mk.Ic was abandoned after engine failure near Market Harborough.
17.8.43   Z1694   23 OTU, Pershore, Worcestershire.
   A Mk.III on special exercise was 22 miles off course when it crashed 2½ miles north-west of Wymeswold. It dived from a great height and broke up before striking the ground. Pieces were found up to 1½ miles from the main impact point. All the crew were killed.
26.9.43   . . . . . ?   11 OTU, Westcott, Buckinghamshire.
   Crashed on approach three miles north of Woolfox Lodge.
3.2.44   N2764   22 OTU, Wellesbourne Mountford, Warwickshire.
   This Mk.Ic crashed at Hoton after take off from Wymeswold.
11.2.44   HZ372   27 OTU, Lichfield, Staffordshire.
   This aircraft, a Mk.X, crash-landed at Orton on the Hill following engine failure, due to fuel starvation.
14.1.45   X3465   27 OTU, Lichfield, Staffordshire.
   This Mk.III crashed in the circuit at Wymeswold. One killed.
14.1.45   MF116   26 OTU Wing, Oxfordshire.
   The engine of this Mk.X cut and the aircraft crashed in a forced landing at Sketchley (?), Leics.
13.7.45   LN844   11 OTU, Westcott, Buckinghamshire.
   Engine cut and second failed on approach to Bottesford. The aircraft, a Mk.X, caught fire but controlled by station crash crew. Four occupants injured.
2.8.45   MF229   11 FU, Talbenny, Pembrokeshire.
   This Mk.XIII was written off in belly landing, Melton Mowbray, after undercarriage failed to lock down.
5.6.47   NC474   201 AFS, Swinderby, Lincolnshire.
   Dived into ground six miles east of Cottesmore. Control of this Mk.X believed lost in cloud.

Vickers-Supermarine Seafire F.47
13.3.53   VP433 '160-BR'   1833 Squadron RNVR, Bramcote, Warwicks.
   Crashed in forced landing at Gilmorton. Pilot killed.

Vickers-Supermarine Spitfire
30.3.42   . . . . . ?   1 PRU, Benson, Oxfordshire.
   Crashed on Desford Aerodrome, no casualties.
24.12.42*EN114   Rolls-Royce, Hucknall, Nottinghamshire.
   This Mk.IX damaged beyond repair in accident at Rearsby. (*possibly 29th)
25.7.43   BL389   349 Squadron, Kingscliffe, Northamptonshire.
   This Mk.Vb went out of control in dive, pilot thrown out and parachute opened. Location given as MR414208, Rutland.
3.10.43   P7986 and R6801   61 OTU, Rednal, Shropshire.
   Mid-air collision of two Mk.Vs; both aircraft crashed near Wymeswold, one pilot killed, other seriously injured.
7.8.44   MJ413   1 FPP, White Waltham, Berkshire.
   Stalled making a steep turn after take-off and dived into ground, Ratcliffe. Pilot of this Mk.IX, Captain F A White, was killed.
11.10.44   RR237   MAP, Castle Bromwich, Warwickshire.
   This Mk.IX aircraft was on initial test from Castle Bromwich when it dived into Nuneaton airfield at high speed, killing the pilot.

RAF Westland Whirlwind HAR.10 XP396 was damaged beyond repair after tail rotor failure led to a forced-landing at Saddington on 7th June 1969. A Wessex hovers above the wreck. F B Aggas

20.1.45 NH523 5 (T)FP, ATA, Thame, Oxfordshire.
Pilot of this Mk.IX Spitfire, Third Officer A A Lock, baled out and aircraft crashed near Stonton Wyville at 14:45 hours. Control had been lost after aircraft entered cumulo nimbus cloud.

Westland Lysander
23.7.41 L4806 12 Group AAC Flight, Digby, Lincolnshire.
The pilot of this MK.II was attempting a forced landing and hit trees near Leicester.
19.8.42 V9776 340th FS, USAAF, Polebrook, Northamptonshire.
This Mk.IIIa crashed on landing at Cottesmore airfield; one of the crew killed, other seriously injured.

Westland Whirlwind HAR.10
7.6.69 XP396 'S' 230 Squadron, Wittering
Crashed at Saddington, following tail rotor failure.

Westland Lynx AH.7
18.5.99 XZ199 9 Regt, Army Air Corps, Dishforth, Yorkshire.
Crashed near Tilton-on-the-Hill following suspected engine problems. Three killed, one badly injured.

Civilian Aircraft

Aeronca 100
11.7.50 G-AEVT Hit by line squall on take-off from Loughborough and crashed in nearby field. Pilot, Paul Simpson, a student at the College of Aeronautical Engineering, seriously injured but eventually made a good recovery.

Agusta-Bell AB206B JetRanger
13.3.89 G-TPTR Alan Mann Ltd., Chobham, Surrey.
While filming vehicle on test track at MIRA near Nuneaton (once RAF Nuneaton) rotor blade touched ground and helicopter crashed. Minor injuries, aircraft broken up for spares.

Auster J/5B Autocar
18.9.50 G-AJYK Aireviews Ltd., Barton, Lancs.
Crashed 4 miles north of Leicester.

Avro 748 Srs 1
26.6.81 G-ASPL This Dan-Air aircraft was on a mail run between Gatwick and Castle Donington. Rear baggage door blew open in flight, was torn off its hinges, struck starboard tailplane causing loss of control and aircraft crashed at approx 19:10 hours near Nailstone. All three crew killed.

BA Eagle II
2.10.37 G-AEER Reported crashed at Breedon (on the Hill ?).

Beech King Air 90
25.1.88 G-BNAT This National Airways aircraft on a mail delivery flight, stalled, crashed and burst into flames at East Midlands. Pilot, Captain Ron Stirman, killed. Aircraft destroyed.

Bell 206B JetRanger
17.9.94 G-REVS Clipped tree and crashed when attempting to land at Hambleton Hall, Rutland. Minor injuries to four occupants.

Brantly B.2B
10.4.76 G-ATFH Exploded in flight and crashed at Highfield Farm, Empingham, Rutland.

Cassutt Speed One
6.9.98 G-AXDZ 'No.66, White Lightning' After competing in and winning the Formula One Air Racing Association British Grand Prix at Leicester Airport, the aircraft crashed on the airfield at high speed. The pilot, Andrew Chadwick, suffered serious injuries but made a full recovery.

Cessna 152
6.5.88 G-BOGE Forced landed in field at Smockington Hollow, near Sharnford due to engine failure, *en route* Bristol to East Midlands. Pilot underestimated duration of flight, ran out of fuel.

Cessna 340A
7.9.93 G-XGBE Forced landed in field at Sheepy Magna due to both engines failing in flight.

Cessna FA.150K
17.1.80 G-AXUW This Coventry Air Training School aircraft was damaged beyond repair at Leicester East.

De Havilland Tiger Moth
22.8.64 G-APKE Crashed and burned at Rearsby.

De Havilland Tiger Moth
2.10.65 G-ANHI Crashed in field near Shawell, following engine failure. One occupant killed, other died later from injuries sustained.

Enstrom F.28A
26.6.92 G-BAWI Crashed following loss of power on take-off from Bosworth Hall Hotel, Market Bosworth.

Enstrom F.280 Shark
18.2.83 G-TOYS Crashed in blinding snowstorm at Noseley off B6047 road between Market Harborough and Melton Mowbray. Of the two occupants only one received minor injuries.

Hughes 369E
31.7.89 G-OABG Crashed in field near St Peters Primary School, Market Bosworth after tail rotor sheared. Possibly repaired later.

Jodel DR.1050
2.6.89 G-AYMT While attempting emergency landing in rainstorm aircraft struck 11,000 volt power cable and crashed on disused runway at Melton Mowbray airfield. Four occupants injured.

Jodel DR.1050M
10.10.98 G-JODL Overshot landing at Wharf Farm, Mkt Bosworth.

Partenavia P.68B
20.10.90 G-BMCB Crashed in field near A453 shortly after take off from East Midlands. Pilot killed, aircraft written off.

Piper PA-28 Cherokee D
8.11.81 G-BAHR Crashed at Kirby Bellars near Melton Mowbray.

Piper PA-28 Cherokee F
28.5.82 G-BBSO Crashed on take-off from Leicester East.

Piper PA-28-161 Warrior II
18.9.97 G-BOHA Badly damaged in a landing near Bottesford.

Piper PA-28R Cherokee Arrow
12.8.82 G-TYPE Crashed taking off from private strip near Shenton.

Robinson R-22B Beta
31.8.94 G-KAYT This Euro Executive machine force-landed and overturned in a field near Keyham while on a flight from France to East Midlands Airport.

Royal Aircraft Factory BE.2e
4.20 G-EAJA Squadron Leader A H Curtis forced landed at Aylestone. The aircraft was later torn from its pickets during a gale, blown into a hedge and wrecked.

Scheibe SF-25E Super Falke
28.12.79 G-BDGX   Crashed at Husbands Bosworth.
Short 360
31.1.86 EI-BEM   Aer Lingus
         Believed due to icing almost all control lost at 1,000ft while on
         approach to East Midlands. Hit power cables and crashed two
         miles short of runway. Aircraft written off, no serious injuries.
Simmonds Spartan
6.9.30   G-AAGN   Captain A R P Kirby RN.
         Engine failed on take-off from Ratcliffe after attending the
         opening display. Aircraft crashed, the pilot was flung clear and
         escaped with minor injuries, his wife, his passenger, suffered a
         broken leg, fractured arm and facial injuries. Aircraft written off.
Slingsby T.67A
23.7.97 G-BIZN   Badly damaged on take-off from Leicester.
Westland Gazelle Srs.1
5.7.97   G-BDGX   Badly damaged in a crash at Springfield Farm,
         Melton Mowbray.
Westland Scout AH.1
15.7.98 (G-BXRL)   XT630 'X'   While coming in to land at
         Hambleton Hall, Rutland, the tail rotor struck trees and it crashed.
         No fatal injuries. Restored to the civil register until it fell into the
         Tarmac Quarry, Hartshill, Nuneaton, on 16th October 1999.

*The morning after . . . Cessna 152 G-BOGE looking decidedly crestfallen
following its unscheduled arrival in a field adjacent to Smockington
Hollow, near Sharnford, on 6th May 1988.* Neville Martin
*. . . the disaster that befell British Midland's Boeing 737 G-OBME on the
M1 near Kegworth on 8th January 1989.* Dr Hugh Thomas collection

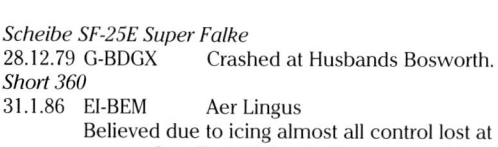

*Visiting Piper Cherokee Arrow, G-TYPE, crashed and was written off
near Sutton Cheney after taking off from the nearby private strip, on
12th August 1982.* Dave Peel

*Aer Lingus Shorts 360, EI-BEM, got into difficulties during the evening of
31st January 1986, landed well short of the East Midlands Airport
runway, and ended up near a wood.* Ken Ellis collection

Appendix D

Aviation Memorials

AT VARIOUS locations throughout the two counties there are examples, in many varied forms, of memorials and mementoes with aeronautical associations. Some of these are recorded here.

Monuments erected to the dead of the two World Wars which contain the names of those who made the ultimate sacrifice abound, while a headstone in a local cemetery or churchyard marks the final resting place of many an airman.

To attempt to include all these locations is beyond the scope of this appendix. Only a volume devoted to the subject would do it justice.

Bottesford
A commemorative plaque dedicated to the memory of fallen comrades was placed in the control tower here by members of 467, 463 and 207 Squadron Associations in April 1993 and in 1995 a eucalyptus tree was planted in the former signals square by returning Australians to become another symbol of remembrance. In the village church of St Mary the Virgin a Roll of Honour dedicated to 207 Squadron members can also be found.

Broughton Astley
On a memorial plaque in St Mary's Church an observer's brevet surmounts the following inscription:

'*In loving memory of Sgt Alfred James Baum, RAF. Killed in action over Westphalia August 12th 1940 aged 28 years.*'

Handley Page Hampden L4036 'EA-R' of 49 Squadron took off from Scampton on the night of 11th/12th August 1940 with Sergeant Baum and three other crew members on a bombing mission to Dortmund. Sadly the aircraft was brought down by flak. There were no survivors and all are buried in the Reichwald Forest War Cemetery.

Cottesmore
Mounted on a plinth in front of the Station Headquarters is a bronze plaque presented by the Troop Carrier units based at the station during the Second World War. It bears the words '*May the memory of the comradeship sown in the skies of Europe forever be as green as the fields of Cottesmore.*'

In the churchyard of St James, Birstall, lie the remains of RAF Flight Sergeant John Hannah, who was awarded the Victoria Cross, the nation's highest award for bravery. F B Aggas

Within the village church of St Nicholas is a beautiful memorial chapel in remembrance of all who gave their lives whilst serving at RAF Cottesmore. First dedicated on 8th September 1949, it was re-dedicated on 25th January 1987 following extensive refurbishment. The two stained glass windows that overlook the altar have the RAF crest and Cottesmore's station badge as their central motifs. In the chapel itself a Book of Remembrance is displayed, also the ensigns of the RAF and several Commonwealth air forces, which together with the flag of the United States of America provide a colourful addition to the walls. Also to be seen is the standard of 98 Squadron

which was laid up in the chapel on 27th February 1976, following disbandment of the unit. A model of a de Havilland Mosquito, in the markings of 16 OTU, hangs from the roof, whilst the latest addition to the chapel, a panel depicting the striking badge of the TTTE, is to be seen in one of the windows. Close by, on the approach road to the RAF station, the local cemetery is the last resting place of many of the fallen, each grave marked by a distinctive Commonwealth War Graves Commission headstone.

Eyebrook Reservoir
On the dam at the southern end of the reservoir, south of Uppingham, can be found two plaques (with a duplicate in the fishing lodge) which serve as a reminder of the role played by the reservoir during training sorties by the Lancasters of 617 Squadron – 'The Dambusters' – who trained for the historic raid on the Möhne, Eder and Sorpe Dams in Germany on 16th/17th May 1943. The Eyebrook dam wall was mocked up with canvas towers and was also used beyond the Dams raid for other training with the 'Upkeep' weapon.

Hoby
A family memorial tablet inside All Saints Church holds the name of Flight Lieutenant H R A Beresford who was killed during the Battle of Britain. Reported missing on 7th September 1940 in Hawker Hurricane I P3049 of 257 Squadron, his whereabouts were unknown until 1979 when his remains were discovered after wreckage of his aircraft was excavated. They are now interred in Brookwood Military Cemetery, Surrey.

Husbands Bosworth Aerodrome
At the gliding site, in the clubhouse, a framed Roll of Honour records the names of the airmen who lost their lives when the aerodrome was an RAF Station.

Kegworth
There are two memorials from the crash of the BMA Boeing 737 G-OBME on the night of 8th January 1989. This aircraft was experiencing engine problems when it crashed on the M1 motorway whilst attempting to land at nearby East Midlands Airport.

Top left, then clockwise:

The commemorative plaque and unit badges in the Bottesford control tower; the plaque to Sgt A J Baum in St Mary's Church, Broughton Astley; the Beresford family memorial tablet in All Saints Church, Hoby; the memorials at Kegworth to the victims of the 1989 Boeing 737 crash, the plaque on the M1 motorway bridge and the memorial garden within the village cemetery on Whatton Road the bronze plaque on the grandstand at Oadby Racecourse, a former US Army base (Deryk Wills); and the plaque at Eyebrook Reservoir with 'Dambuster' connections (Ken Ellis).

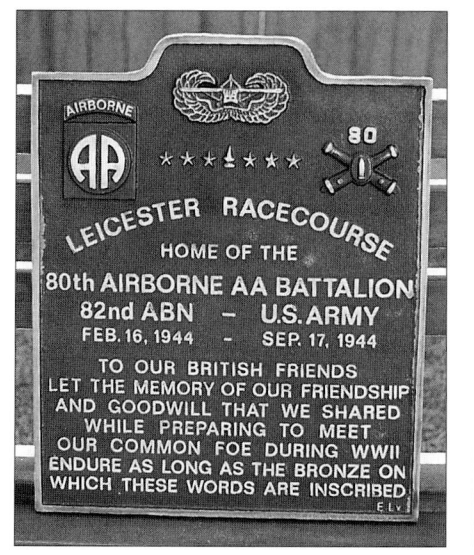

From the top, then clockwise:

Sir Frank Whittle alongside his bust, at the Church Street Memorial Gardens, Lutterworth; the Roberton memorial tablet, dating from the First World War, at Stoke Golding (Author); *the memorial in Tinwell village church to the American and Polish men who died when two Dakotas collided* (A Goodrum); *the 504 Squadron standard at Wymeswold Church; the Lancaster memorial plaque at Scraptoft* (Author) *and the 82nd Airborne Memorial in Victoria Park, Leicester* (W Woodward).

One, just outside the village, in the form of a plaque, is placed on a bridge which spans the motorway and overlooks the site of the tragedy. The other in the village cemetery on Whatton Road, is a memorial garden dedicated to the 47 people who lost their lives. A striking centrepiece of this garden is a massive granite boulder upon which all the victims' names are recorded.

Leicester Airport
Until recently, within the Leicestershire Aero Club clubhouse (the control tower) could be found a plaque in memory of the ten members of the Leicester Aircraft Preservation Group who perished when their Vickers Varsity T.1 WJ897 (G-BDFT) crashed near Marchington, Staffordshire, *en route* to an airshow at Liverpool, 19th August 1984.

Leicester Cathedral
Following the disbandment of 207 Squadron, considered to be 'Leicester's Own', the squadron standard was laid up in the cathedral in October 1984. A memorial book dedicated to the unit is also to be found here.

Leicester, Victoria Park
Near the main entrance a granite boulder stands as a memorial to the men of the 82nd Airborne Division. Unveiled on 10th May 1986 by the division's wartime Commanding Officer, Major General Matthew B Ridgway, it bears a plaque with the inscription *'In tribute and memory of those men of the United States (All American) 82nd Airborne Division who served in Leicester and county prior to the 'D' Day Invasion of Europe. They came in freedom. They fought with gallantry. Many never to return to their Homeland'.*

Leicester, Welford Road Cemetery
A memorial here marks the last resting place of a young woman who died as the result of a bizarre aerial accident.

In September 1926, a Captain A F Muir of the Surrey Flying Club offering 'a spectacular aerial experience' advertised for volunteers to parachute from his aircraft. Four people responded, one of whom was 25 year old Mrs Dorothy Cain, daughter of the landlord of the Empire Hotel.

Four days previously, one young lady, a Miss B Bruntlett, had made a successful drop, but Mrs Cain's attempt on 9th September was to end in tragedy. After taking off from 'Blackbird Road flying ground', Mrs Cain baled out at around 1,000ft but before leaving the aircraft she is believed to have accidentally disconnected herself from the parachute, which was stowed beneath the aircraft. Watched by a huge crowd estimated at around 40,000, she fell to her death.

Following a service at St Augustine's Church over 8,000 mourners, mainly women, are said to have attended her interment.

Lutterworth
On 15th June 1987, Dr G B R Fielden CBE unveiled a plaque, mounted on the north wall of the Town Hall. It commemorates the 50th anniversary of the first test run of a British gas turbine on 12th April 1937 at the BTH Works in Rugby and the development which followed at the Ladywood Works in Lutterworth.

On the same day, in the nearby Church Street Memorial Gardens, a bust of the jet engine pioneer, Sir Frank Whittle, was also unveiled, with the great man himself in attendance. Sadly, in February 1997, this £4,000 monument, the work of Leicestershire sculptor Kenneth Ford, was badly damaged by vandals . Undeterred by this wanton act the town council has had the decapitated bust repaired and replaced in its original location.

A further tribute to Sir Frank Whittle was granted final approval by Leicestershire County Council on 12th August 1999. This is to take the form of a full-size replica of a Gloster E28/39, the first aircraft to be fitted with a Whittle-designed engine. This ambitious monument is due to be erected on the traffic island at the junction of Rugby Road and the Lutterworth eastern by-pass, close to the outskirts of the town, in May 2001.

Oadby, Leicester Racecourse
On 11th September 1997 a bronze plaque was unveiled by the Lord Lieutenant of Leicestershire, Mr Tim Brooks. Mounted in the new grandstand, it records the sentiments felt towards the people of Leicestershire by the men of the 80th Airborne Anti-Aircraft Battalion, 82nd Airborne Division, US Army, who were based on the racecourse during 1944. Many of the unit's veterans were present for the ceremony, and for some it was their first visit to Europe since those momentous days.

Saltby
At the edge of one of the former domestic sites bordering the Wyville road are the remains of a concrete relic once thought to have had an aviation connection. The device depicted has, however, been identified as the Ukranian national emblem, so in all probability it was constructed by displaced persons housed in the camp after 1945. Some time ago thought was given to its restoration but this did not take place and it is now badly overgrown and disintegrating.

Hanging within St Peter's church are two plaques acting as mementoes of visits made in June 1984 by members of the 314th Troop Carrier group and a successor unit, the 62nd Tactical Airlift Squadron. In 1992 the church acquired a fine peal of ten bells. The three original bells had become unringable but thanks largely to the generosity shown by the US servicemen based at Saltby Airfield during the Second World War, the new installation was made possible.

Somerby
Within the beautiful All Saints' Church are many memorials dedicated to the British Airborne Forces. Mounted on a wall near the entrance is a fine tablet in memory of the officers and men of the 10th Battalion, Parachute Regiment who gave their lives at Arnhem in September 1944. Close by is a pair of stained glass windows (see below) dedicated to all airborne forces, wherein a panel reads: *'Remember O God for good, all ranks of the Airborne Forces who gave their lives for their country'*. Many oak-framed kneelers line the pews, each a memorial to a deceased member of the Parachute Regiment Association in Leicester.

Scraptoft
Set into the brickwork of the parapet of a bridge spanning a small stream that runs under Drumcliff Road is a memorial plaque. This records details of a tragic accident that occurred on the afternoon of Sunday, 8th April 1945. While engaged in a fighter affiliation exercise, Avro Lancaster ND647 of 1653 Heavy Conversion Unit from North Luffenham, crashed close to this spot with the loss of all on board.

Sproxton
After residing for a time in the village hall and also the Crown Inn, an inscribed plaque presented by the members of the 62nd Tactical Airlift Squadron on 3rd August 1970 is now in safe keeping at 3 Coston Road, the home of Ray Bennett, one time publican at the Crown. These words are written on it: *'In deep appreciation to the people of Leicestershire for their hospitality and friendship to the United States Troop Carrier Forces station at Saltby Aerodrome, February 1944 to February 1945. May the bonds of friendship founded in war continue in peace ad infinitum. Presented by the Officers and Men of the 62nd Tactical Airlift Squadron'.*

Stoke Golding
Within St Margaret's Church is a memorial tablet that perpetuates the memory of James Leslie Roberton. This young man, a 2nd Lieutenant in the Yorkshire Regiment and of the Royal Flying Corps, died near Lens, France, on 6th September 1916, during the course of an aerial fight.

Tinwell
Mounted on a wall in the village church is a memorial to the 34 men who died when two C-47s of the 315th Troop Carrier Group, Spanhoe, Northants, collided and crashed nearby on 8th July 1944. The tragic accident occurred as the aircraft were forming up to take part in a practice parachute drop.

Wigston Magna
When preparations were being made to build All Saints School in Long Street, contractors unearthed some wreckage of Avro Lancaster I, PA269, of 300 Squadron, Faldingworth, Lincolnshire, which crashed on the site now occupied by the school, on 4th February 1946, after the pilot lost control in a violent thunderstorm raging over Wigston at the time. The six members of the all-Polish crew died. Their memory is perpetuated by a plaque mounted within the school.

Wymeswold
The nearby airfield was the last home of 504 (County of Nottingham) Squadron, Royal Auxiliary Air Force. After the unit disbanded there on 10th March 1957, its standard was laid up in St Mary's Parish Church.

Appendix E

Royal Observer Corps

Members of the Royal Observer Corps' No.5 Group 'George 2' Post at Stoke Golding pose for the camera in 1945. On the front row, Observer Lieutenant R S (Ron) Palmer is flanked by Head Observer E (Ted) Beeby and Leading Observer A P (Phil) Palmer. In the background is St Margaret's Church, which features in Chapter Eighteen. via Ron Bass

ALTHOUGH its origins can be traced back to the First World War it was not until 1928 that the Observer Corps became firmly established under the auspices of the Air Ministry. Ten years later, a period of expansion, saw the formation of the Midland Area of the Corps. Posts to observe and report aerial activity and provide air intelligence were set up throughout the region. By the outbreak of the Second World War a comprehensive system of posts existed. The full-time and volunteer Observers who manned these installations came from all walks of life; they carried out their duties exposed to fair weather and foul and throughout the war made a sterling contribution to the defensive system of the country.

The Corps, which had been granted the prefix 'Royal' in 1941, stood down on 12th May 1945, only to be re-activated once more on 1st January 1947, although it took 12 months or so for all the posts to be reconnected to the telephone network. The posts then continued much as before with their primary role of aircraft reporting, but on 1st November 1953 there was a nationwide re-organisation and from 1956 onwards the Corps became increasingly involved in the system for reporting on the bearing and strength of any bomb bursts and the plotting of any fallout following a nuclear attack.

To enable them to carry out this task, posts were redesigned and rebuilt underground and new equipment installed. The practice of aircraft reporting diminished, the overground posts eventually disappeared and the sole function of the Corps became its radio-active fallout reporting role. Following adverse defence estimates in 1968 the Corps suffered swingeing cuts and many posts were closed.

Although much reduced, the organisation continued to train and practice for events it was thankfully never called upon to report, but the changing political climate eventually brought an end to the Royal Observer Corps. All groups and their allied posts were stood down on 30th September 1991, only to be followed by the remaining elements, the Corps Headquarters and Nuclear Reporting Cells, in March 1996.

ROC Posts within Leicestershire and Rutland

Location	Open	Map ref	Gp/Post	U/G	Closed
Billesdon	1948	K717023	5-A1		
	11.53	K717023	7-K1		
resited	1.59	K716022	7-K1	7.59	10.68
Birstall	12.37	K599097	5-A1		
	7.40	K599097	5-H1		
resited	7.43	K585084	5-H1		
	11.53	K585084	8-L4		
resited	11.63	K590107	8-L4	12.64	
	10.68	K590107	8-G3		9.91
Bottesford	5.43	K813396	5-J1		
	11.53	K813396	15-F3	2.60	10.68
Buckminster	11.49	K873224	5-K2		
	11.53	K873224	15-G1	5.61	
	10.68	K873224	15-K2	5.61	10.68
Coleorton	7.54	K387164	8-M4	4.59	10.68
Fleckney	12.37	P641937	5-A2		
resited	3.43	P638932	5-A2		
	11.53	P638932	8-L3	10.60	
	10.68	P638932	8-J2		9.91
Langham	1947	K833122	5-K1		
resited	12.52	K842137	5-K1	renamed as –	
Wissendine	11.53	K842137	15-G3		
resited	5.54	K806097	15-G3	renamed as –	
Cold	4.56	K806097	15-G3	4.59	
Overton	10.68	K806097	7-A1		9.91
Lutterworth	12.37	P535848	5-B1		
	11.53	P535848	8-P2		
resited	8.62	P520855	8-P2	8.63	
	10.68	P520855	3-B1		9.91
Markfield	12.37	K485097	5-H2		
resited	1.40	K487103	5-H2		
	11.53	K487103	8-M3		
resited	3.61	K500092	8-M3	10.66	10.68
Melton	5.48	K750206	5-K3		
Mowbray	11.53	K750206	15-G4		
resited	9.54	K742214	15-G4	5.59	10.68
Rearsby	11.40	K663138	5-H4		
	11.53	K663138	8-L2	7.61	
	10.68	K663138	8-G2		9.91
Shepshed	12.37	K437194	5-H3		
	11.53	K437194	8-M2		
resited and renamed as –					
Hathern	1.54	K495218	8-M2	11.60	
	10.68	K495218	8-C1		9.91
Stoke	12.37	P398968	5-G2		
Golding	11.53	P398968	8-P4	5.60	
	10.68	P398968	8-J1		9.91
Thurlaston	12.37	P489990	5-A3		
	5.39	P489990	5-G3	renamed as –	
Croft	11.53	P489990	8-P1	7.59	10.68
Twycross	12.37	K329061	5-G1		
	11.53	K329061	8-N2	6.60	10.68
Wymeswold	12.37	K616236	5-H1		
	5.39	K616236	5-J3		
	11.53	K616236	8-L1	11.61	10.68

Top: Leading Observer Ron Bass (manning the plotting instrument) and Observer Sid Spencer on exercise in the mid-1950s. Ron Bass

Above: *The original Stoke Golding ROC post was built by the Head Observer, Ted Beeby, for around £90. The two-storey post had lost its windscreens by the late 1960s and was demolished in the 1980s. Martin Cooke*

Above: *Here, No.8 Group's underground ROC post at Stoke Golding is 'open'; the radio aerial is erected, the generator and nuclear bomb-burst and radiation detection instruments – (Ground Zero Indicator, Fixed Survey Meter probe and Bomb Power Indicator baffle) are all at the ready. By 1990, Stoke Golding was reporting as '55 Post', having been '50 Post' and before that 'Juliet 1'. via Martin Cooke*

By 1961, the ROC post at Stoke Golding was known as 'Papa 4 (Fow-er)' and although the new undergound post was available, use was made of the wartime surface post for occasional aircraft reporting exercises. From left to right are Observer Michael L Wood, Woman Observer Kathleen M Cooke, Observer Officer Ron Smith and Observer Mark Swain. via Martin Cooke

Appendix F

USAAF Stations
in Leicestershire and Rutland

For security reasons and also to avoid any direct reference to specific geographical locations, most USAAF units assigned to the UK during the Second World War were allocated an AAF or 'station' number. Those known to have existed within the two counties are listed as follows:

477   **North Luffenham**
Intended for 9th Air Force use.
Airfield not used by the USAAF.

478   **Woolfox Lodge**
IX Troop Carrier Command.
Brief occupation, ground echelon only.

481   **Bottesford**
436th and 440th Troop Carrier Groups.

489   **Cottesmore**
316th Troop Carrier Group,
317th Service Group

520   **Melton Mowbray**
1720th Ordnance Munition Company
1961st Ordnance Depot Company
1962nd Ordnance Depot Company
(VIII Air Force Service Command)
BADA 7.43 - 1.44, to USSTAF.
Combat Support Wing Transport
  (trucks).

527   **Leicester**
Detachment of the 892nd Signal
  Depot Company.
(VIII Air Force Service Command)
BADA (Base Air Depot Area) 1943
  to USSTAF Quartermaster Stores.

538   **Saltby**
314th Troop Carrier Group,
317th Service Group.

565   **Preston, Rutland**
Air Service Command
(believed to be Preston Hall, a rest and recuperation centre).

566   **Tugby, Keythorpe Hall**
Detachment 'K', 93rd SCSRD (Sp).
8th Air Force rest home opened
26.7.44. Up to 30 enlisted men
allowed to recuperate from battle
fatigue or after taking part in many
missions.

Appendix G

The Duke of Rutland

Although not a 'county' aircraft by any means, it is hoped the inclusion of this view of Wellington I L4340 *Duke of Rutland* may redress the balance of the plethora of Leicestershire 'named' aircraft given in Chapter One!

L4340 was converted into a so-called C.Ia transport by removal of the nose and rear turrets and fairing them over for use by 24 Squadron at Hendon in the summer of 1943. Coded 'NQ-A', it was named Duke of Rutland *and flown extensively until it was struck off charge on 19th November 1944. Ken Ellis collection.*

Select Bibliography

Books

abc Military Aircraft Markings 2000: Peter R March; Ian Allan Publishing, UK, 2000.

Airborne Operations in World War Two — European Theatre: USAF Historic Studies No.97, J C Warren; MA/AH Publications, USA, 1956.

Aircraft of the Royal Air Force since 1918, 7th edition: Owen Thetford; Putnam, UK, 1979.

Airfields of the 9th, Then and Now: Roger Freeman; After the Battle, UK, 1991.

Air War Against Germany and Italy, 1939-43: J Herington; Australian War Memorial, Australia, 1962.

Attack Warning Red, Royal Observer Corps, 1925-1975: D Wood; Macdonald, UK, 1976.

The Avro Lancaster: Francis K Mason; Aston, UK, 1989.

Bomber Squadrons of the Royal Air Force and their Aircraft: Philip J R Moyes, Macdonald, UK, 1984.

Birth of a Spitfire: G Beckles; Collins, UK, 1941.

Brief Glory - The Story of the ATA: E C Cheesman; Harborough, UK, 1946.

Britain's Military Airfields 1939-45: David J Smith; Patrick Stephens, UK, 1989.

British Aviation Memorials and Mementoes: David J Smith; Patrick Stephens, UK, 1992.

British Civil Aircraft Registers since 1919: Dave Peel; Midland Counties Publications; UK, 1985 and supplement 1987.

British Civil Aircraft since 1919: A J Jackson, in three volumes; Putnam, UK, 1973-74.

British Gliders and Sailplanes: Norman Ellison; A & C Black, UK, 1971.

British Midland Airways: B G Cramp; Airline Publications, UK, 1979.

British Military Aircraft Serials 1878-1987: Bruce Robertson; Midland Counties Publications, UK, 1987.

British Military Aircraft Serials and Markings: M H Pettit, D J Allen, M I Draper, D A Rough, T E Stone; Barg/Nostalgair/Aviation Hobby Shop, UK, 1983.

Canadair Sabre: Larry Milberry, Canav, Canada, 1986.

The Forgotten Pilot:, Lettice Curtis; Nelson & Saunders, UK, 1985.

The Green Fields and the Sky: Norman Roberson and Jack Talliss; GMS Enterprises, UK, 1991.

Intruders over England: Simon W Parry; Air Research, UK, 1987.

Jet: Sir Frank Whittle, Muller, UK, 1953.

Mighty Eighth – A History of the US 8th Army Air Force, The : Roger A Freeman; Macdonald, UK, 1970.

Mighty Eighth War Diary, The: Roger A Freeman; Janes, UK, 1981.

Military Airfield Architecture: Paul Francis; Patrick Stephens, UK, 1996.

Military Airfields: Steve Willis and Barry Hollis; Enthusiasts Press, UK, 1990.

On the Wings of the Morning: Vince Holyoak; privately published, 1995.

RAF 1939-1945: D Richards and H St G Saunders, in three volumes; HMSO, UK, 1953-1954.

RAF Squadrons: Wing Commander C G Jefford MBE; Airlife, UK, 1988.

Royal Air Force Bomber Command Losses of the Second World War: Volumes 1 to 6: W R Chorley; Midland Counties Publications, UK, 1992-1997.

Royal Air Force Flying Training and Support Units: Ray Sturtivant, John Hamlin and James J Halley; Air-Britain, UK, 1997.

Source Book of the RAF: Ken Delve; Airlife, UK, 1994.

Squadrons of the Royal Air Force and Commonwealth 1918-1988: James J Halley; Air-Britain, UK, 1988.

Squadron Codes 1937-1956: M J F Bowyer and J D R Rawlings; Patrick Stephens, UK, 1979.

The Thousand Plan: Ralph Barker; Chatto, UK, 1965.

The Tiger Moth Story: Alan Bramson and Neville Birch; Airlife, UK, 1982.

U.S. Military Aircraft Designations and Serials 1909-1979: John M Andrade; Midland Counties Publications, UK, re'prtd 1997.

Whittle – The True Story: J Golley; Airlife, UK, 1982.

Wings over Rutland: John Rennison, Spiegl Press, UK, 1990.

Wrecks & Relics – various editions: Ken Ellis; Midland Publishing, UK.

Additionally, wide reference was made to the *Royal Air Force Aircraft* series published by Air-Britain, chronicling serial batches, eg *Royal Air Force Aircraft W1000 to Z9999*: by James J Halley; 1998.

Also the Air-Britain *Aircraft File* series, detailing in depth various types, for example the Anson, Defiant, Hampden, Harvard, Lancaster and Stirling.

Periodicals

The Aeroplane, Aeroplane Monthly, Aeromilitaria (Air-Britain), *Air Enthusiast, Air International, Air Pictorial, Aircraft Illustrated, Aviation News, British Aviation Review, Flight, FlyPast, Vintage Aircraft.*

Newspapers

Leicester Mercury, Leicester Evening Mail, Leicester Illustrated Chronical, Loughborough Echo, Stamford and Rutland Mercury plus many local publications.

Principal Manuscript Sources

Air Historical Branch, Ministry of Defence, London: Air Record and Accident Cards.

Albert F Simpson Historical Research Centre, Maxwell Air Force Base, Alabama, USA: USAAF Group and Squadron Records.

County Record Office, Wigston and Bishop Street Reference Library.

Public Record Office, Kew, London: Air Ministry documents mainly Classes AIR 27, 28, 29 and Avia 2, 27.

Air Ministry: *Air Pilot Great Britain and Ireland.*

Index

To keep this index within reasonable proportions, 'umbrella' terms such as RAF, RFC, USAAF, Bomber Command etc are not itemised. Likewise, material given within tables and in the Appendices is not included – being overwhelmingly self-indexed.

Abingdon 81, 273
Acton, Cllr F 305
Advanced Flying Schools, (RAF):
  202 AFS 152
  204 AFS 151
  206 AFS 271
  215 AFS 129
Adwest 307
Aero Club de France 305
Aeronca 100 225
Aeroplane & Armament Experimental Establishment 185
Aerospacelines Super Guppy 201, 121
Ahlhorn 152
Air Ambulance Training School 215, 216
Air Base Group/Squadron, (USAF):
  3912th ABS 114
  7542nd ABS 114
Airborne Divisions:
  1st (UK) 147, 334, 337
  6th (UK) 148
  82nd (US) 95, 146, 147, 148, 149, 204, 205, 212, 213, 215, 334, 335
Air Bridge Carriers 131
Airbus
  A300 / Beluga 121
  A320/321 127
  A330 131
Air Courier 200
Air Division, (USAF):
  7th AD 114
Aircrew Holding Unit, (RAF):
  11 AHU 112
  26 AHU 206, 245
Air Despatch 105
Airfield Construction Wing, No.5352 334
Air League of the British Empire 305
Airlines of Great Britain – see British Midland Airways
'Airmans Rest, The' 108
Air National Guard / Air Force Reserve 116
Air Observer and Navigator School, (RAF):
  3 AONS 178, 193
Air Refuelling Squadron, (USAF):
  420th ARS 116
Air Service Training 39, 184
Airspeed Envoy 102
  Horsa 91, 145, 149, 213, 214, 216, 245, 266, 268, 270, 353
  Oxford 91, 95, 142, 143, 150, 206, 213, 214, 216, 242, 256, 268, 270, 291, 306, 334, 343, 352
Air Observation Post Flight, (RAF):
  1969 AOP Flt 190, 357, 359
Air Training Corps 20, 110, 182, 190, 225, 278, 296
Air Transport Auxiliary 20, 87, 291, 296, 297, 298
Airways and Air Communications Service Flight, (USAF) 114
Airwork General Trading Ltd 223, 224, 227
Alconbury 114, 115, 117
Aldergrove 354
Alexander, Wing Commander N 212
Alidair 135
All Weather Operational Conversion Unit 274

Allen, Leading Aircraftman 106
Alsthom Automation 32
Ambrose, Squadron Leader B S 89
Ancaster, Earl of 151
Andover 297
Ansty 298
Antonov An-2 361
Appleby, S V 251
Armstrong Siddeley Motors 39-56, 112, 113
  Adder 42
  ASX 39 42
  Mamba/Double Mamba 39, 42, 43
  Python 42, 43
  Sapphire 42, 47, 49, 154
  Screamer 42
  Snarler 42
  Viper 42
Armstrong Whitworth Aircraft Ltd, Sir W G 36-56, 57-82, 117, 199
Armstrong Whitworth
  Albemarle 145, 235, 266, 268, 291, 297, 306, 334
  Apollo 40
  Argosy 48, 49, 52, 57, 58, 59, 77-80, 81, 132, 133, 157, 158, 159
  Atlas 222
  AW.52 39, 40, 41, 42, 44
  AW.681 48, 49, 59
  Siskin 172, 293
  Whitley 39, 59, 145, 266, 268, 297, 334, 353
Arnold, Douglas 52, 54
Ashbourne 215
Ashby Folville 251
Ashton Down 257
Aston Down 257
Auster Aircraft Ltd 33, 298, 313-332
  Auster, all high wing types 190, 218, 300, 306, 308, 311, 312, 313-332, 357, 358
  B3 target drone 324, 325
  B8 Agricola 325, 327
Auster Pilot Club – see International Auster Club
Auster Flying Club 39, 306
Austin Motors 59
Aviation Medicine Training Centre 277
Avro 504 18, 231, 232, 233, 234, 292, 293
  Anson 37, 38, 141, 142, 143, 144, 178, 181, 188, 190, 242, 256, 266, 291, 296, 306, 341
  Ashton 51, 357
  Avian 173, 174
  Cadet 102
  Five 174
  Lancaster/Lancastrian 28, 35, 36, 46, 54, 58, 59, 85, 81, 87, 88, 89, 90, 91, 92, 93, 95, 96, 97, 112, 113, 148, 150, 151, 182, 205, 206, 225, 238, 257, 269, 288, 333, 346, 353, 355
  Lincoln 40, 42, 54, 59, 357
  Manchester 83, 84, 85, 86, 87, 263, 265, 341, 342, 343, 344, 348
  Shackleton 49, 50, 76, 77, 78, 81
  Tutor 103, 180
  Vulcan 49, 51, 54, 59, 76, 81, 118, 120, 121, 122, 132, 152, 153, 154
  York 188, 257
Avro (Canada) CF-100 Canuck 359

BA Drone – see Kronfeld
BAC TSR.2 326
BAC/SNIAS Concorde 131, 137
Baginton 35, 40, 41, 48, 49, 58, 59, 60, 70, 199, 208
Balderton 93, 95, 264

Banff 298
Barkston Heath 97, 145, 148, 337
Barnes, Flight Sergeant 204
Barratt, Group Captain J F T 263
Barton 105, 174
Basic Flying Training school, (RAF):
  5 BFTS 190
Bassingbourn 157, 165
Bastard, Group Captain L G A 157
Bates, F 305
Baxter, J T L 171, 173, 174, 293
Beagle Aircraft Ltd 33, 306, 313-332
Beagle types (for 'Auster' developments, Terrier etc, see under Auster)
  206 and Basset 132, 329
  Airedale 307, 329, 330, 331, 332
  Pup 330, 331
Beamish, Air Commodore G R 254
Beamont, Roland P 159
Beaumaris 296, 297
'Beaumont', see Conneau
Beaumont, Wing Commander J 182
Beetham, Air Chief Marshal Sir Michael 160
Belgian Air Force 60, 70
Bell
  JetRanger/Long Ranger 246
  P-39 Airacobra 184
Bell, Group Captain J R 351, 354
Belton 158
Benson 141
Berger, Lieutenant Colonel H 147
'Big Thunder' / 'Rolling Thunder' 120, 121
Billett, Flight Lieutenant 288
Binbrook 158
Bircotes 353
Birmingham 174
Bishop, Sir Michael 130
Bitteswell 20, 30, 32, 33, 35-56, 57-82,109, 111, 117, 120, 206, 284, 286, 358
Black, C T 14
Blackburn Baffin 222
  Beverley 80
  Bluebird 174
  Botha 298
  HST.10 221, 228
  YB-1 35
Blakehill Farm 256, 268
Blaston, landing ground 16
Blériot monoplane 11, 12, 13
Blind Approach Training Flights, (RAF):
  1521 BATF 352, 354
  1524 BATF 93, 95
Blomfield, L 35, 284
Boeing
  B-17 Flying Fortress 52, 55, 121, 218, 254, 352
  B-47 Stratojet 114, 115
  B-50 Superfortress 114, 115
  C-97 Stratofreighter 114
  KC-135 Stratotanker 163
  707 52, 131
  737 134, 136
  747 121, 131
  757 131
  777 131, 132
Bomb Group, (USAF):
  301st BG 352
Bomb Squadron, (USAF):
  352nd BS 352

Bomb Wing, (USAF):
  96th BW 114, 115
  100th BW 114
  308th BW 114
Bomber Command Instructors School 111
Bomber Command WAAF Senior NCO School 205
Bomber Defence Training Flights, (RAF):
  1321 BDTF 96
  1683 BDTF 109, 111, 242
Boreham 148
Boscombe Down 39, 70, 165, 185
Bottesford 20, 30, 83-100, 145, 147, 150, 354
Boulton Paul
  Balliol 152, 274, 275, 276
  Defiant 144
  Overstrand 103
Boulton & Paul Ltd 222
Bovingdon 114
Bower, Charles 198
Bowhill, Air Chief Marshal Sir Frederick W 213
Boyd, Air Vice-Marshal 213
Boyle, Sir Dermot 153, 159
Bramcote 35, 39, 111, 206, 284, 286, 298
Brancker, Sir Sefton 17, 173, 293
Braunstone 17, 20, 101-108, 174, 175, 180, 294, 304
Brawdy 81
Breguet biplane 11
Brentingby, landing ground 16, 249
Brew, Flight Lieutenant J R 287
Britannia Airways 136
Bristol Aero Engines 48
Bristol biplane 11
  Beaufighter 96, 150, 253, 255, 256, 268, 344
  Beaufort 253
  Blenheim 139, 253, 341
  Bloodhound (missile) 33, 277, 278, 279, 348
  Brigand 274, 275, 276, 282
  Bullpup 221, 222
British Aerospace 120, 227
  EAP 227, 230
  Harrier (and Sea Harrier) 33, 55, 80, 81, 118, 164, 219, 360
  Jetstream 131, 134
British Aircraft Eagle 102
  Swallow 102
British Aviation Heritage 118, 119
British European Airways 78, 80
British Midland Airways / bmi british midland (from Feb 2001) 130, 132, 134, 135, 136
British Regional Airlines – see British Midland Airways
British Thomson Houston 31
Brize Norton 114, 159, 245, 267
Broadhurst, Air Chief Marshal Sir Harry 153
Brookes, E H G 106
Broome, Squadron Leader (later Air Vice-Marshal Sir) I G 152, 159
Brown, Winifred 174
Browne, Claude 172
Bruntingthorpe 20, 31, 32, 37, 39, 109-126, 205, 216, 242, 267, 299, 307
Bruntingthorpe Aviation Collection 119
Bruntingthorpe Base Flight 116
Brush Electrical Engineering Co 15, 221, 225, 231-240
Brussels (B.19) 215
Buchanan, Flying Officer G M 243
Buckminster Gliding Club 34, 307, 338
Buckminster, landing ground 16, 17
Bullmore, Squadron Leader A G 199

Burnaston 130
Burton on the Wolds, landing ground 16
Burtonwood 114
Burrows, David 21
Butcher, Flight Sergeant 205

Canadair – see Douglas and North American
Cantello, R W 223
Capitol Airlines 78
Cascelloid Ltd 26, 29
Cassidy, Squadron Leader J R 103
Cassutt IIIM 219
Castle Bromwich 14, 15, 28, 29, 104, 171, 193, 249, 287, 296
Castle Donington (and East Midlands Airport) 20, 30, 34, 118, 127-138, 351, 352, 354, 360
Castle Donington, landing ground 16
Caterpillar (UK) Ltd 191
Central Landing Establishment 296
Cessna 150/152 163, 216, 219
Chadwick, Andrew 219
Chamier, Air Commodore J A 305
Charmy Down 354
Charnwood Museum 308
Chedburgh 212, 268
Chelveston 115, 352
Cheshire, Group Captain W G 83
Chilton DW.1 299
Chipping Ongar 148
Chipping Warden 242
Chrysler (UK) Ltd 118
Church Broughton 344
Church Lawford 39, 113, 352
Civil Air Guard 105, 305, 314
Civil Aviation Authority 121
Civilian Air Navigation School, (RAF):
   3 CANS 177, 178
Civilian Repair Organisation 178, 184, 191, 224, 306
Classic Aircraft Projects 120
Clifford, Peter 223, 225
Clifton Pastures 352
Coalville 17, 26, 29, 198, 201
Cobham, Sir Alan 17, 101, 174, 175
Cochrane, Air Vice-Marshal Hon Ralph A 90
Cody, S F 11
Cody Biplane 11
Colerne 257, 274
Collins, Bernard 251
Combat Support Group, (USAF), 3912th 114
Communications Analysis Training School 277
Comper Swift 19, 174
Coningsby 152, 263
Conneau, Lt de V (aka 'Beaumont') 11, 12
Connolly, Squadron Leader J B 211
Consolidated
   B-24 (and C-109) Liberator 148, 150, 257, 333, 337
   PBY Catalina 163, 296, 297
Controller Research and Development 112
Conversion Flight, (RAF):
   61 CF 343
   207 CF 85, 86, 87
Conversion Units, (RAF):
   21 Heavy Glider CU 267, 269, 270, 346
   1332 Heavy Transport CU 111
   1333 Transport Support CU 216, 245
   1381 Transport CU 286, 288
   1382 Transport CU 128, 129, 270, 298, 300, 354, 355, 356
   1651 Heavy CU 345, 346
   1653 Heavy CU 268, 269
   1661 Heavy CU 242
   1665 HCU 337, 340, 344
   1668 Heavy CU 92, 95, 96, 97, 150
   1669 Heavy CU 96
Cooke, Geoff 297
Co-operative Wholesale Society 211, 219
Cosford 180, 199, 235, 296
Cottesmore 19, 30, 33, 86, 93, 95, 97, 113, 139-170, 241, 266, 333, 341, 347, 352
Countesthorpe 20
County Flying Club 18, 250, 253, 291, 294, 295, 298, 303, 304, 307, 308, 314
Coventry 57, 112
Coventry Gliding Club 34, 208, 307

Coxwell, Henry Tracey 9
Cranwell 32, 50, 54, 85, 114, 161, 163
Crilly Airways 102, 104, 108
Croft 20
Crosby-on-Eden 35, 287, 288
Cross, Air Vice-Marshal K B B 153
Cunliffe-Lister, Sir Phillip 103
Curtin, Pilot Officer 144
Curtiss
   C-46 Commando 336, 337
   Tomahawk 109, 242

Daily Mail Circuit of Britain 11, 249
Davies, Alfred Ltd 26, 29
de Havilland
   Comet 80, 121, 122
   DH.9A 172
   DH.86 235
   Dove/Devon 270
   Dragon 102, 104, 294, 307
   Dragon Rapide (and Dominie) 46, 176, 188, 225, 227, 235-240, 291
   Fox Moth 174
   Giant Moth 17, 18
   Heron 153, 216
   Hornet Moth 102, 306
   Leopard Moth 104
   Mosquito 119, 121, 150, 151, 235, 256, 268, 291, 298, 355
   Moth (and Gipsy Moth) 103, 172, 173, 293, 294
   Puss Moth 102, 173, 174
   Sea Vixen 158, 280
   Tiger Moth 106, 143, 151, 175, 176, 178, 179, 182, 183, 185, 188, 195, 227, 261, 299, 300, 305, 306
   Vampire 114, 200, 270, 271, 297
   Venom (and Sea Venom) 276
de Havilland Canada Chipmunk 190, 191, 209
de Havilland, Geoffrey 297
de Montalent, Olivier 11
Derby Aviation – see British Midland Airways
Derby Locomotive Works 235
Desborough 109, 111, 242, 288
Desford 20, 30, 33, 101, 105, 171-202, 293, 299
Desford (town) 17, 19
DFS Grunau Baby 208
Dimond, Flying Officer 288
Dishforth 271, 355
Dishley Engineering Ltd 227
Dixon, Pilot Officer F W 90
Dixon Primary 306
Donair Flying Club 132
Doree, V H 252, 303
Dornier Do 217 144
Douglas
   B-66 Destroyer 114, 115, 117
   Boston/Havoc (inc Turbinlite) 223, 224, 225, 227, 253, 255, 256
   C-54/R5D Skymaster (and North Star, Rescuemaster) 114, 282, 359
   C-118 Liftmaster 114
   C-124 Globemaster II 115, 116, 277
   C-133 Cargomaster 115, 277
   Dakota/C-47 Skytrain/C-53 Skytrooper/DC-3 37, 38, 46, 95, 114, 115, 128, 129, 144, 145, 148, 149, 150, 204, 213, 214, 215, 216, 245, 255, 256, 266, 268, 269, 270, 271, 286, 288, 291, 298, 300, 334, 335, 336, 337, 354, 355, 359
   DC-10 135
   Thor IRBM 249, 258, 277, 348
Douglas Boston-Havoc Preservation Trust 289
Down Ampney 254
Downham Market 344
Drew, Wing Commander H V 139
Driffield 151
Druine Turbulent 307
Duke, Neville 70
Duke of Edinburgh, Prince Philip 130, 216
Duke of Gloucester 173, 174
Dumfries 354
Dunholme Lodge 257
Dunsfold 41, 70, 71, 80, 81
Duxford 77, 289
Dyer, Eric C 130
Dyess AFB 114

East Kirkby 288
East Langton 70
East Midlands Aero Park 132
East Midlands Airport – see Castle Donington
East Midlands Airport Volunteers Association 134
East Midlands Air Support Unit 208, 209
East Midlands Flying Club 132
East Midlands Gliding Club 307
East Wretham 343
Edith Weston 264, 270
Edwards, Geoffrey 306
Eisenhower, General Dwight D 212, 215
Elementary [& Reserve] Flying Training Schools (RAF):
   7 E&RFTS 19, 106, 175, 177, 178, 179, 180, 182, 183, 188, 198, 261, 305
   58 E&RFTS 105
Elmdon 359
Elsham Wolds 269
EMBRAER / Short Tucano 131
Empingham 266
Empire Central Flying School 185, 255, 268
En-Tout-Cas Ltd 17, 18, 101, 176, 303
Enemy Aircraft Flight, No.1426 85
English Electric
   Canberra 35, 43, 49, 114, 120, 153, 155, 156, 157, 158, 159, 164, 357
   Lightning 119, 120, 121, 122
Entertainments National Service Association 90
Essendine 20
Essex Aero Club 102
Eurocopter AS.355N 208, 209
   EC.135T 208
Eurofighter EF2000 Typhoon 227
Evanton 140
Everard, Captain Anthony 299, 300
Everard, Sir W Lindsay 17, 18, 172, 173, 174, 176, 216, 251, 252, 253, 291, 292, 294, 295, 296, 298, 299, 303, 307
Excalibur Airways 136
Exeter 95
Explosive Ordnance Disposal Squadron 278, 279
Exton Hall 147

Fairchild
   A-10 Thunderbolt II 52
   Argus 291, 296, 297, 299
Faire, Sir Samuel 17
Fairey
   Barracuda 291
   Battle 139, 140
   Firefly 113, 291
   Gannet 35, 43, 51
   S9/30 221
Falconer, Squadron Leader 143
Faldingworth 97
Farman types
   Astral 232, 233, 234
   F.193 305
   S.7 'Longhorn' 231, 232
Farnborough 39, 42, 50, 71, 86, 153, 195, 199
Fayer, Leutnant U 163
Feltwell 95
Ferry Crew Pool, (RAF):
   1 FCP 253, 254
Ferry Pilot Pool, (ATA):
   6 FPP 296, 297, 299
Ferry Unit, (RAF):
   1 FU 254
   4 FU 227
   12 FU 256, 257
Ferry Training Unit, (RAF):
   301 FTU 253, 254
   303 FTU 253
   304 FTU 253, 254, 255
   307 FTU 253
   311 FTU 253
Field Artillery Battalions, (US Army):
   250th 286
   319th (Glider) 205
   320th (Glider) 205
   376th (Parachute) 205
   456th (Parachute) 205
Field Aviation Services / Field Aircraft Services 116, 131, 359, 360

Field Signals Unit, (RAF):
   5 FSU 256
   6 FSU 256
   7 FSU 256
Fieseler Fi156 Storch 306, 311
Film Aviation Services 200
Filton 256
Finmere 253
Finningley 111, 127, 129, 141, 284, 352
Fleet, Lieutenant Colonel B R 147
Flight Refuelling Ltd 66
Flude & Co 26, 29
Flying Flea – see Mignet
Flying Refresher School, (RAF):
   102 FRS 270, 271
Flying Training Schools, (RAF):
   2 FTS 50, 359
   3 FTS 141, 172
   7 FTS 151, 152, 347
   11 FTS 141
   12 FTS 141, 142
Folkingham 145, 277
Fokker F.XII 104
Folland Gnat 49, 50, 51, 80, 81, 120
Fontes, Luis 103
Formula Air Racing Association 219
Forward Repair Unit, No.511 185
Fouga CM-170 Magister 158
Foxton 12
Foxton Lodge 20
Frankenburg, K 14
Franklin, Eric 39, 60, 199
Freeman, Flight Sergeant 87
Freeman Hardy & Willis 26, 30
French, C F 199
French Air Force 60
Frost, Tom 43
Fuerza Aerea Venezolana 152
Fulbeck 93, 145, 216

Gauntlett, Victor 201
Gartree Prison 245, 246
Gaydon 116
General Aircraft
   Hamilcar 267
   Monospar 102, 104
Glider Pick-Up Training Flight 215
Gliding Schools, (RAF):
   M42 GS 306
   M44 GS 113, 190, 306
Gloster
   AS.31 Survey 228
   E28/39 32
   Gauntlet 103
   Javelin 43, 47, 48, 49, 59, 60, 75, 76, 81, 117, 153
   Meteor 35, 39, 41, 42, 43, 44, 48, 59, 60, 61, 62, 63, 64, 65, 75, 81, 113, 129, 199, 202, 206, 269, 271, 274, 276, 279, 280, 297, 351, 356
Gomez, Wing Commander P S 255
Gomm, Wing Commander C L 87, 88, 89
Goodwood 165
Grace, Group Captain C F H 254, 255
Grace, Nick 118, 119, 120, 200
Graham, Wing Commander 144
Grandborough 109, 352
Grange, Baron De La 305
Grantham 93, 95, 141, 145, 172
Green, Mr 10
Green, Wing Commander D A 152
Greenham Common 165
Grenfell, Wing Commander E B 140
Grierson, John 304
Griffiths, 'Eddie' 43
Grimsthorpe Park 143
Grosvenor Cup Air Race 103
Ground Radio Servicing Unit/Centre 277
Group Communications Flights, (RAF):
   7 GCF 96
Groups, RAF:
   1 Group 155, 157, 160
   2 Group 139, 141
   3 Group 87, 152, 164, 204, 212, 277
   4 Group 37, 129, 288, 354, 356
   5 Group 83, 88, 90, 95, 141, 145, 203, 261, 266, 334

Groups, RAF (continued):
6 Group 141
7 Group 96, 264, 266, 268, 351
11 Group 110
12 Group 356
21 Group 151, 206, 245
22 Group 257
23 Group 113, 151, 266, 268, 269
25 Group 271
33 Group 354
38 Group 212, 213, 257, 337, 356
40 Group 216, 346
44 Group 111, 128, 253, 254, 255, 257, 284, 354
46 Group 213, 256
51 Group 261
54 Group 206, 245
64 Group 188, 356
90 Group 157
91 Group 245, 269
92 Group 37, 203, 109, 204, 241, 266, 334, 351
92 Group Defence School 37
93 Group 37, 211, 213, 253, 284, 351
93 Group (Screened) Pilots' School 213
216 Group 257
Grumman
Hellcat 256, 291
Martlet (Wildcat) 224, 226, 227, 229

Halfpenny Green 354
Hamble 39, 174
Hamel, Gustav 11, 12, 13
Handley Page
Halifax 113, 143, 205, 206, 227, 253, 257, 266, 268, 269, 270, 291, 297, 337, 340, 351, 353
Hampden/Hereford 140, 141, 143, 144, 235, 225, 237, 261, 262, 263, 264, 266, 333, 341, 342
Harrow (and Sparrow) 306
Hastings 48
Herald 130, 131
HP.42 294, 295
Jetstream 163
Victor 50, 80, 81, 116, 118, 120, 121, 152, 153, 154, 155
W.10 173
Hanworth 174
Harlaxton 142
Harrier (BAe/HS) – see British Aerospace
Harrier Maintenance Flight 164
Harrington 277
Harris, Air Chief Marshal Sir Arthur T 16, 266, 346
Harrison, Wing Commander 213
Harrogate 245
Hart, J A 199
Hatfield, 235
Hawker
Audax 141, 177, 180, 306
Fury 103
Hart (and Hart Special, Hart Trainer) 104, 177, 229
Hector 180
Hind 176, 177
Hurricane 111, 205, 206, 224, 225, 227, 229, 242, 244, 256, 268, 269, 284, 291, 306, 310, 353
Hunter 41, 43, 47, 48, 49, 50, 59, 70-74, 81, 227, 229, 276, 357, 358
P.1072 42, 46
Sea Hawk 41, 42, 43, 48, 59, 65-69, 70, 81
Tempest 291
Tomtit 195
Typhoon 306, 310
Hawker Siddeley
Andover/HS.748 80, 131, 134, 161
Buccaneer 49, 50, 59, 80, 81, 121
Harrier – see British Aerospace
Hawk 50, 51, 59, 81, 82, 160, 191
HS.125/Dominie 50
Nimrod 80
Trident 50, 80
Heavy Conversion Unit – see Conversion Unit
Heavy Freighter Flights, (RAF):
1588 HFF 257
1589 HFF 257
Heavy Glider Maintenance Section, (RAF):
30 HGMS 90
32 HGMS 334

33 HGMS 344
34 HGMS 145
Heavy Glider Maintenance Unit, (RAF):
2 HGMU 90, 145, 334, 344
Hedon 174
Hemswell 111, 261, 263, 354
Henderson & Sons 26, 30
Hendy 302 103
Henri Farman – see Farman
Henshaw, Alex 193, 182, 195, 297, 305
Heston 251, 294
Heston JC.6 323
Hewes, Vic 300
High Ercall 296
Hinckley 12, 13, 18, 26, 29
Hindercks, Flying Officer 205
Hindustan Aeronautics 50
HMS Illustrious 164
Hodges, Air Chief Marshal Sir Lewis 159
Holbeach 143
Holme-on-Spalding Moor 51
Honiley 47
Honington 152
Hooton Park 174
Hopton and Sons 15
Horsham St Faith 48, 143, 343
Howie, Wing Commander G R 213
Hucclecote 32
Hucks, Benjamin C 11, 12
Hucknall 39, 139, 356, 357
Hue-Williams, Flying Officer I V 103
Hullavington 185
Hunter AFB 114
Hunting Firecracker 131
Jet Provost 43, 49, 50, 54, 131, 227, 229, 326, 359
Hunting Aviation Aircraft Engineering 131
Hunting Cargo Airlines 131, 135
Huntsman, Leading Aircraftwoman E 244
Hurn 213, 254
Husbands Bosworth 20, 34, 109, 118, 145, 203-210, 241, 334

Ibing, Leutnant Kurt 37
Ibstock 19
Imperial Air Fleet Committee 14
Imperial Airways 173
Indian Navy 48, 66, 68
Institute of Aviation Medicine 199
International Auster Club 307, 313
Iraqi Air Force 70

Jet Heritage Ltd 227
Johnson, Squadron Leader H F 257
Johnson, Group Captain J E 152, 153
Junkers Ju 52 270
Ju 88 22, 142, 204, 344, 345
Ju 188 96
Junior 174

Kastner, Leutnant P 162
Kemble 52, 75, 80
Kemps Aerial Services 200
Kent, Duchess of 153
Ketton 274
Kibworth Beauchamp 303
Kilby 20
King George V 174
King George VI 244
King Hussein of Jordan 153
King's Cup 174, 217, 218, 219
Kingston 41, 59, 70
Kingstown 178
Kinloss 80
Kirby, A R P 293
Kirby Cadet (see also Slingsby) 112, 306
Kirkbride 60, 185
Kirkby Mallory 179, 288
Kirkbymoorside 132
Kirkington 353
Kirton in Lindsey 151
Klemm L.27a 294
Kronfeld Drone (inc BA) and Ground Trainer 18, 251, 252, 253, 295, 299, 303, 304
Kronfeld, Robert 251, 295

Ladywood Works, Loughborough 31
Lancaster, J O 40
Lancaster Finishing School, (RAF):
3 LFS 346
5 LFS 333
Langar 76, 87, 93, 95, 96
Lasham 122
Laughlin AFB 114
Leadenham 16
Lee, Wing Commander D H 212
Leeming 274
Leicester Airport – see Leicester East
Leicester and County Spitfire Fund 21
Leicester, Blitz 28
Leicester Bus Garage 28, 29
Leicester, city area
Belgrave Gate 9
Bell Hotel 11
Blackbird Road 27
County Cricket ground 13
Frog Island 250
generally 15
London Road 278
Victoria Park 9
Western Boulevard 27, 29
Western Park 14
Weymouth Street 26
Leicester Corporation Bus and tram Depot 28
Leicester East (and Leicester Airport) 20, 30, 33, 211-220, 245, 308
Leicestershire Aircraft Preservation Group 97
Leicestershire Air Sports Club 102, 175
Leicestershire [and Rutland] Aero Club 11, 12, 17, 19, 33, 101, 102, 103, 105, 106, 108, 171, 173, 174, 175, 195, 216-220, 251, 291, 293, 298, 307
Leicestershire Flying Pou Club 17, 250, 251, 252, 295, 303
Leicestershire Gliding Club 298, 299, 306, 307
Leicestershire International Air Display 216
Leicestershire Model Aero Club 175
Leicestershire Museums 198, 201, 202, 218, 308, 314, 319
Leicestershire War Agricultural Committee 106
LET L-410 361
Leuchars 245
LeVier Cosmic Wind 307
Lewis, Wing Commander K P 83
Lichfield 296
Lightning Preservation Group 119, 122
Lilienthal, Otto 10
Lincolnshire Aviation Society 227
Lindholme 97, 151, 269
Lindley – see Nuneaton
Linton on Ouse 205, 206
Little Horwood 111
Little Staughton 211
Lockheed
C-130 Hercules 338
F-104 Starfighter 34
Hudson 253, 291, 297, 350
T-33 (and Silver Star) 115, 116, 359
TriStar 131, 132
Ventura 297
Loganair – see British Midland Airways
Long Kesh 253
Long Range Ferry Unit, No.1 273
Longtown 354
Lord Cromwell 216
Lossiemouth 66
Loughborough 20, 33, 221-230, 231-240, 308, 353
Loughborough and Leicestershire Aircraft Museum 118, 119, 132
Loughborough College, Department of Aeronautical Engineering 222, 223, 225, 227
Loughborough Meadows, landing ground 16, 221, 231, 232
Loughborough, town 12, 13, 14, 15, 17, 18
Lovett, Terry 130
Lowdell, G E 182, 195
Lowe, A 15
Lubenham – see Market Harborough
Luton 106
Luton Minor 251, 252, 304
Lutterworth 31, 32, 37, 47, 50, 55

Lyndon 264
Lyneham 215, 253

Mackay, Flight Lieutenant 215
Mackenzie, Squadron Leader D C 89
Mackenzie, Wing Commander G 152
MacMillan, Harold 153
Maintenance Units, (RAF):
6 MU 245
8 MU 204
9 MU 180
12 MU 185
15 MU 199
22 MU 355
23 MU 204
47 MU 184
48 MU 204
92 MU 97
93 MU 97
216 MU 206, 216, 337
255 MU 216, 337
256 MU 97, 337
259 MU 346, 347
266 MU 39
273 MU 245
Manx Airlines – see British Midland Airways
Marham 159, 163, 213
Market Harborough 20, 203, 206, 109, 111, 145, 216, 241-248, 334
Market Harborough, town 13, 15, 17, 32
Marshall's Flying Club 102
Marston Moor 337
Martin, Neville 120, 132
Martin RB-57 114
Masefield, Sir Peter 326
Mathy, Heinrich 14
Maurice Farman S.7 'Longhorn' – see Farman
MBB Bö 105 136
McDonnell F-101 Voodoo 116
McDonnell Douglas Phantom 51
McDowell, Wing Commander 206
McEvoy, A A Ltd 105
McGavin, Flight Sergeant 87
Meir 251
Melton Mowbray 14, 15, 20, 30, 215, 249-260, 277, 294, 303, 337
Melton Mowbray and District Spitfire Fund 22
Melton Mowbray, town 11, 17
Membury 95
Merrett, Flight Sergeant 110
Merryfield 95
Messerschmitt Bf 109 21, 22, 90, 264
Methwold 346
Metropolitan-Vickers 59
Middle Wallop 165
Middleton St George 205
Midland Aircraft Company 305
Midland Ultralights 52, 54, 59
Firefly 52
Sirocco 52
Mignet, Henri 18, 250
Mignet HM.14 Pou du Ciel (Flying Flea) 18, 250, 251, 252, 303, 304
Mildenhall 339
Miles Falcon 102
Hawk 251
Hawk Speed Six 103
M.18 299
Magister 188, 268
Master 242
Martinet (and Queen Martinet) 109, 206, 242, 245, 352, 353
Master 85, 206
Monarch 302
Monitor 245
Ministry of Aircraft Production 223
Misson 352
Mobile Repair and Reclamation Squadron, 33rd (USAAF) 95
Mollison, Amy (née Johnson) 19
Montague, F 172
Morane-Borel monoplane 11
Morcott 263
Moreton-in-Marsh 36

Moreton Valence 60, 75
Motor Industry Research Association 288, 289
Mowlem, J R & Co 241
Mowsley 203, 205, 206, 352

Napier, C S 103
Napier, D & Son 105, 106
National Aviation Day Displays 17, 104, 174
National Gas Turbine Establishment 32, 39, 42, 44, 46, 113
Naylor, Joan 298
Neal, Ron 220
Netheravon 271
Newark Air Museum 158, 308, 319
Newberry, Flight Lieutenant 106
Newcastle 174
Newton 351
Nieuport monoplane 11
Night Bomber Tactical School 111
Nipper Flying School / Nipper Aircraft Ltd 132
Normanton 86
North American
    B-25 Mitchell 184, 291
    B-45 Tornado 114, 116
    F-86 Sabre (and Canadair) 271, 272, 273, 274, 282, 359
    F-100 Super Sabre 114, 116
    P-51 Mustang 52, 54, 121, 187, 256, 288, 291, 311
    Harvard 39, 119, 151, 152, 256, 271, 356
North Atlantic Treaty Organisation 33, 115, 116
North Coates 279
North Eastern Airways 105
North Kilworth 52
North Luffenham 20, 37, 109, 144, 258, 261-282, 342, 343, 346, 348, 356
North Weald 165, 276
North Witham 147
Northolt 173, 174
Norton Disney 84
Numan, Gary 119
Nuneaton 20, 30, 37, 38, 283-289
Nutt, Richard J 289
Nutts Corner 111, 286
IXth Troop Carrier Command, USAAF 30, 93
IXth Troop Carrier Command Pathfinder School, USAAF 95, 147

Oadby 213
Oakes, Sir Harry 21
Oakham 110, 161
Oakington 271
Oakley, Wing Commander B A 253, 284
Odiham 152, 185, 271, 274
Offensive Support Squadron 164
Old Warden 195
Olley Air Services 188, 227
Oliver, Sergeant G W 90
Operational Conversion Units (RAF):
    231 OCU 155, 156, 157, 158, 159
    232 OCU 116, 154
    233 OCU 55
    238 OCU 274, 275, 276
    240 OCU 270, 271
Operational Training Flight, No.1429 343
Operational Training Units (RAF):
    12 OTU 141, 204, 242
    14 OTU 32, 141, 142, 143, 144, 145, 203, 204, 206, 241, 242, 244, 245, 333, 334, 341, 352
    16 OTU 150, 151, 204
    17 OTU 204
    18 (Polish) OTU 35, 36, 284
    25 (MB) OTU 212
    26 OTU 204
    28 OTU 20, 127, 351, 353, 354
    29 OTU 37, 109, 110, 111, 204, 242, 266, 267, 343, 344
    82 OTU 213
    84 OTU 111, 204, 242
    85 OTU 204, 205, 206
    105 (T)OTU 37, 38, 111, 284, 287, 288
    107 OTU 213, 215, 216, 255, 256
    108 (T)OTU 128, 354
Orion Airways 136
Ossington 213, 352

Overseas Aircraft Preparation Unit, (RAF);
    4 OAPU 253, 254, 255, 256
Owen, Wing Commander C B 152
Oxley, Commander G 158

Palmer, Peter 307
Panavia Tornado 33, 51, 120, 159, 160, 161, 162
'Paraslasher' 178, 179
Partridge, Lieutenant Colonel L J 115
Pathfinder Force 88, 90, 203
Paynes Garage 29
Pease AFB 114
Peberdy, Bettina 252
Peckleton (and landing ground) 16, 171, 178, 184
Pegg, Mr 9
Penn-Smith Gyroplane 360
Percival Gull Six 104
    Mew Gull 19
    Prentice 151, 152, 188, 190, 299
    Proctor 188, 227, 256, 299
    Provost 359
Percival, Edgar 104
Pershore 254
Personnel Reception Centre, (RAF):
    7 PRC 206, 245
Peterborough 141, 261, 354
Peugeot-Talbot Ltd 118
Phillips, Lieutenant Commander C W 103
Phoenix Aviation, and Museum 119, 120
Phoenix Dynamo Manufacturing Co 232
Pickering, Jim 185
Pickworth 9
Pilcher Bat 10
    Hawk 10, 11
Pilcher, Percy Sinclair 10
Piper L-4 Grasshopper 204, 286
Pitts Special 217, 219
Pixton, Howard 11
Pizey, Collyns 11
Pooley, Les 244
Polebrook 245, 277
Popular Flying Association 211, 216
Port Ellen 253
Power Jets Ltd 30, 32, 39, 112, 113
Presentation aircraft (by name):
    Barwell 22, 23
    Brenda 21, 23
    Burbage 22, 23
    City of Leicester Flight, I II and III 21, 23, 25
    Crispin of Leicester 21, 23, 24
    Dirty Girty of Vancouver 22
    Earl Shilton 22, 24
    George Parbury, The 21, 24
    Harry Livingston, The 21, 24
    Hinckley - HHMA 22, 24
    Hosiery Flight Leicester 21, 24
    Leicester 15
    Leicester-Canada 15
    Loughborough 22, 25
    Melton Mowbray & District 22, 24
    NFHMA - Leicester I 21, 24
    NFHMA - Leicester Section 21, 25
    Pastures, The 22, 25
    St George 21, 25
    Tangerine of Loughborough 22
    Wendy Leigh of Hungerton 22
Pressed Steel Company 326
Preston 264
Prince Bira of Siam 306, 311
Prince of Wales 174
Princess Anne 132
Princess Margaret 153
Probyn, Group Captain 306
Provincial Airways 102
Pyestock 32

Queen Elizabeth II 151, 161, 216
Queen's Flight 153, 161
Queniborough, and landing ground 16, 306

Radar Approach Training Flight, (RAF):
    1513 RATF 38
Radio Introduction Unit 277
Ragdale 20, 352, 354

Raphael, Squadron Leader A S 90
Ratcliffe 17, 18, 20, 33, 103, 106, 291-302, 303, 305, 307, 314
Rawlings, Lieutenant Colonel G D 116
Rawnsley, A H 250, 253
Rayner, Harry 43
Rearsby 18, 20, 33, 39, 113, 225, 251, 252, 253, 295, 296, 298, 303-312
Rearsby Automotive Ltd 307
Recruits Centre, (RAF);
    14 RC 257, 258
'Red Arrows' 80, 81, 82
Reeves, Dr Q R 43
Reid, Squadron Leader George 176, 190
Reid & Sigrist 17, 19, 105, 106, 175, 176, 178, 180, 184, 188, 191, 195-202
    RS.1 Trainer (or 'Snargasher') 178, 180, 195-198
    RS.2 197, 198
    RS.3 Desford 60, 188, 198-200, 202
    RS.4 Bobsleigh 199-202
    RS.5 (?) 202
Rendcombe 15
Republic P-47 Thunderbolt 54
Reserve Flying School, (RAF):
    7 RFS 188, 190, 299
Resettlement Unit, (RAF):
    9 RU 257, 258
Riccall 287
Riddle Airlines 57, 78
Ridgewell 87
Ridgway, General M 215
Roberts, Sir William J D 200
Roberts, Gp Capt W J H 157
Robinson R-22 300
Robey & Co 232
Rochester 296, 297
Rolls-Royce 32, 39, 132
Rose, John 97
Rosenbauer, Lieutenant 288
Rover Motor Company 32
Royal Aero Club 217, 291
Royal Aircraft Establishment 42, 71, 86, 195, 199
Royal Aircraft Factory types
    BE.2 15, 127, 171
    BE.12 9, 14, 15, 127, 171
    FE.2 14, 127
Royal Air Force Museum 199
Royal Australian Air Force 87
Royal Canadian Air Force 33, 271, 273
    Squadrons, post-war:
        410 271, 273, 274
        421 271
        439 271, 273, 274, 359
        441 271, 272, 274
Royal Danish Air Force 60
Royal Flying Corps landing grounds 16, 17
Royal Netherlands Air Force 70
Royal Netherlands Navy 48, 66
Royal Observer Corps 96, 287
Royal Saudi Air Force 71, 160
Rugby 31
Rutland 163

Sadler, Mr 9
Saltby 20, 30, 34, 96, 143, 144, 145, 241, 333-340, 342
Sancean, Squadron Leader R J 253
Sandtoft 279
Saunders-Roe 296
    Cutty Sark 174
Sayer, P E G 32
Scalford, landing ground 16, 17, 249
Scheibe SF-27A Zugvogel 209
School of Gas Turbine Technology 32
Scott, C W A 104
Scottish Aircraft Collection Trust 201
Sculthorpe 116
Sealand 184
Searles Ltd 27, 29
Semelab 43
SEPECAT Jaguar 227, 230
Sequoia F8L Falco 217
Service Flying Training School, RAF:
    7 STFS 151
    12 SFTS 84

16 SFTS 351
20 SFTS 39
Shawbury 80, 141, 296
Shepherds Grove 334, 337
Sherburn 174
Shipdham 344
Short 184 233, 235
    330 135
    827 233
    Skyvan 133
    Stirling 87, 212, 242, 255, 256, 257, 268, 297, 334, 337, 344, 345, 346
    Sunderland 296, 297
Shuttleworth Trust 195, 227
Siam, King of 104
Sibbertoft 203, 206, 207, 208
Silloth 355
Simmons Spartan 293
Simpson, Group Captain J H T 150
Skeffington 115
Slack, R B 12
Slingsby Aircraft 132
Slingsby glider types (see also Kirby)
    50, 190, 306, 307, 311
Snailwell 91, 145, 334
Snaith 216
Snargasher – see Reid & Sigrist
Snibston Discovery Park 198, 201, 308
Sopwith Snipe 15
South Cerney 354
South Luffenham 264
Spanhoe Lodge 335
Special Air Service 119
Special Duties Flight, (RAF):
    1341 SDF 257
Spilsby 206
Spitalgate 84, 96, 152
Spooner, John 130
Spooner, Winifred 294
Sproxton 14
Squadrons (RFC, RAF, RAuxAF, FAA and Empire):
    1 Sqn 118, 164, 360
    3 Sqn 164
    4 Sqn 164
    7 Sqn 19
    9 Sqn 155
    10 Sqn 154
    15 Sqn 152, 153, 154, 163
    19 Sqn 103
    20 Sqn 164
    24 Sqn 176
    25 Sqn 117
    35 Sqn 139, 155
    38 Sqn 14, 16, 127, 171, 249
    39 Sqn 156
    43 Sqn 293
    44 Sqn 77, 152, 158, 206
    45 Sqn 163
    50 Sqn 77
    55 Sqn 120, 152
    56 Sqn 357, 358
    61 Sqn 261, 262, 341, 342, 343
    62 Sqn 277, 348
    78 Sqn 143
    90 Sqn 16, 17, 87, 346
    97 Sqn 263
    98 Sqn 139, 155, 157, 159
    100 Sqn 118
    101 Sqn 77, 103, 158
    106 Sqn 140, 141
    111 Sqn 276, 277
    115 Sqn 155, 157, 158, 159
    130 Sqn 277
    139 Sqn 118, 154
    144 Sqn 261, 262, 263, 264, 266, 277
    149 Sqn 152
    166 Sqn 353
    185 Sqn 140
    187 Sqn 190
    190 Sqn 212, 213
    196 Sqn 212, 334
    207 Sqn 83, 84, 85, 86, 139, 140, 141, 263
    218 Sqn 277, 343, 345, 346

223 Sqn 277
233 Sqn 268
242 Sqn 188
248 Sqn 298
254 Sqn 258, 277
257 Sqn 277, 357
263 Sqn 357
266 Sqn 84
295 Sqn 257
297 Sqn 353
328 Sqn 298
360 Sqn 155, 156, 157, 158, 159, 164
408 Sqn 264
426 Sqn 206
428 Sqn 205
467 Sqn 87, 88, 89, 90, 91, 92
504 Sqn 164, 293, 299, 351, 356, 357, 358, 359
570 Sqn 257
605 Sqn 104, 292, 298
616 Sqn 357
617 Sqn 77, 345
620 Sqn 213
664 Sqn 190, 357, 358, 359
800 Sqn 164
801 Sqn 164
899 Sqn 164
1833 Sqn 299
Squire, Group Captain P 161
Squires, J S 251, 304
Squires Gate 70
St Athan 121, 164
St Mawgan 158, 257, 354
Stabbert, Franz 14
Stamford 16
Stanford Hall 10
Steward's Cup 217
Stinson Reliant 291
Stoke Golding 283, 284, 287, 288
Storer, W W 303
Strategic Air Command 113
Strategic Reconnaissance Wing, (USAF):
  4080th SRW 114
Strathallan 200, 201
Strodl, Toni 311
Sub Storage Site (SSS), (RAF)
  113 SSS 245
Sukhoi Su-27 *Flanker* 121
Sullivan, Flight Lieutenant J McD 89
Supermarine (and Vickers-Supermarine)
  Attacker 357
  Seafire 217, 299
  Sea Otter 291
  Spitfire 23-27, 28, 29, 30, 52, 54, 84, 85, 96, 119,
    121, 132, 135, 178, 191, 193-195, 225, 227, 229,
    230, 253, 256, 268, 269, 270, 271, 283, 287, 291,
    297, 299, 306, 356
  Swift 156, 357
  Walrus 110
Surrey Flying Services 174
Sutton, Wing Commander D H 257
Sutton Bridge 215, 266
Sutton Coldfield 206, 216
Swain, Wing Commander 84
Swanton Morley 341

Sydenham 48
Syerston 50, 87, 216, 343, 359
Symington, Phillip 174
Syston 101, 303
Tactical Airlift Squadron, (USAF):
  62nd TAS 339
Tactical Bomb Wing, (USAF):
  47th TBW 114
Tactical Fighter Wing, (USAF):
  20th TFW 114
  49th TFW 115
  81st TFW 52
Tactical Reconnaissance Wing, (USAF):
  10th TRW 115, 116
  66th TRW 116
Tactical Reconnaissance Squadron, (USAF):
  1st TRS 115, 116, 117
  19th TRS 115, 116
  30th TRS 115, 116
  42nd TRS 115, 116
Talbenny 254
Tangmere 293
Tarrant Rushton 66, 212
Taylorcraft Aeroplanes (England) Ltd
  18, 33, 295, 303, 313-332
Taylorcraft (all types) 295, 303, 305, 306, 308, 313-332
Tedder, Air Vice-Marshal 31, 271
Ternhill 271, 296
Thistleton 14
Thornaby 140
Thorold, Air Vice-Marshal H K 205
Thurmaston 12, 13, 18, 295, 305
Tiger Club 307
Tilstock 337, 344, 354
Tipsy Nipper 132, 134
Tizard, Sir Henry 31
Tollerton 235, 359
Tollerton Aircraft Services 235
Topen, Sandy 120
Toul-Rosières 115, 116
Tornado Operational Conversion Unit 160
Tornado Weapons Conversion Unit 163
Towl, Squadron Leader J 162
Training Depot Stations:
  45 TDS 15
(Transport) Operational Training Unit –
  see Operational Training Units
Tranum, John 172, 173
Trent Aero 132
Tri-National Tornado Training Establishment
  160, 161, 162, 163
Troop Carrier Groups, (USAAF):
  61st TCG 145
  313rd TCG 145
  314th TCG 37, 145, 333, 334, 335, 337
  315th TCG 335
  316th TCG 145, 147, 148, 150, 163
  349th TCG 148, 337
  434th TCG 93, 145
  435th TCG 93
  436th TCG 93, 95
  437th TCG 93
  439th TCG 95
  440th TCG 95

441st TCG 95
442nd TCG 95
Troop Carrier Squadrons, (USAAF):
  32nd TCS 333, 334, 335
  36th TCS 146, 147, 149
  37th TCS 146, 147, 150
  44th TCS 147, 149
  45th TCS 146, 147
  50th TCS 334
  61st TCS 334, 336
  62nd TCS 334, 335, 336, 338
Troop Carrier Wings, (USAAF):
  50th TCW 93, 95, 145, 147
  52nd TCW 95, 145, 147, 148, 334
  53rd TCW 95, 147
Tuddenham 346
Tupolev Tu-16 *Badger* 154
Turbinlite – see Douglas Boston/Havoc

Ullesthorpe 36
Uppingham 13
Upward Bound Trust 50
Upwood 262, 277
United States Air Force 33
United States Army Air Force 91, 93
University Air Squadrons, (RAF):
  Nottingham 227
Upottery 95
Upper Heyford 150

Valentine, Wing Commander G E 263
Valley 152, 287
Vedrine, Jules 11, 12
Vickers
  Merchantman (Vanguard) 135
  Valetta 48, 269, 270
  Valiant 116, 152, 153
  Varsity 50, 97, 155, 217
  Virginia 19
  Viscount 40, 129, 133, 135, 360
  Warwick 291
  Wellesley 139, 140
  Wellington 35, 37, 38, 48, 83, 109, 110, 111, 113,
    127, 128, 144, 145, 168, 169203, 204, 205, 213,
    225, 226, 227, 241, 242, 244, 253, 254, 256, 266,
    284, 286, 287, 288, 291, 333, 343, 351, 352, 353
Vickers-Armstrong 59
Victor Training Flight 154
Victory Aircraft 59
Vintage Aircraft Team 120
Vought Corsair 256
Vulcan Operating Company 122
Vulcan Restoration Trust 77, 122
Vultee Vengeance 256

Waco CG-4A Hadrian/Haig 37, 146, 148, 215, 268, 334
Waddington 83, 84, 92, 93
Wadkin & Co 14, 15
Walker Brothers 304
Walton, C, C Walton Ltd, and Aviation Division
  118, 120, 208
Walton, P Martin R 43, 70
Wanstell, Wing Commander B N 160
Warbirds of Great Britain 54

Warboys 277
Wardley 109, 352, 353, 354
Warfield, Group Captain E A 354
Warton 120, 159, 216
Waterbeach 117, 344, 351, 357
Wattisham 357, 358
Watton 157
Watts, Flight Lieutenant J 163
Weather Reconnaissance Squadron, (USAF):
  53rd WRS 114
Welford 203
Welham, landing ground 17
West Freugh 81
West German Navy 48, 66, 69
Westland
  Lysander 143, 144
  Wallace 293
  Wapiti 174
  Wyvern 35, 43
Weston Zoyland 95
Wethersfield 114, 148
Weymann, C F 11
Whetstone 32, 112
Whitchurch 174
White, Group Captain H McC 150
White Waltham 297
Whitley 36, 58
Whitley, Air Marshal Sir John 159
Whittle, Sir Frank 31, 55, 113
Whittlesey 143
Whitwick 27, 29
Wickenby 97
Wig Bay 297
Wilder, Sergeant 110
Wilford, W E 103, 106
Williams, A R 105
Willowbrook Coachworks 15, 235
Wilson Estates 120, 258
Wilson, Warrant Officer W L 90
Winthorpe 242
Witchford 212
Wittering 55, 118, 154, 163, 164, 219, 278, 279
Woodford 50, 76, 80, 81, 174
Woodley 245
Woolfox Lodge 20, 33, 109, 142, 148, 152, 262, 263,
  266, 268, 277, 341-350
Worksop 60
Wratting Common 346
Wroughton 60, 199
Wykes, A L 18, 295, 305, 306, 314
Wykes, P 305
Wymeswold 20, 30, 32, 127, 128, 129, 131, 213, 270,
  298, 299, 300, 337, 351-364
Wyton 156, 159

Yates, A S Ltd 27, 29
Yeovilton 33, 164
Yorkshire Airways 105

Zantop Air Transport 78
Zeals 215
Zeppelins 14, 15, 171, 233

We hope that you have enjoyed this book . .

Midland Publishing book titles are carefully edited and designed by an experienced and enthusiastic team of specialists. A catalogue detailing our aviation publishing programme is available upon request from the address on page four.

Our associate company, Midland Counties Publications, offers an exceptionally wide range of aviation, railway, spaceflight, naval, military, astronomy and transport books and videos, for purchase by mail-order and delivery around the world.

To order further copies of this book, or to request a copy of the appropriate mail-order catalogue, write, telephone or fax to:
Midland Counties Publications
4 Watling Drive, Hinckley, Leics. LE10 3EY
Tel: 01455 254 450 Fax: 01455 233 737